TORTS

CAROLINA ACADEMIC PRESS
Context and Practice Series
Michael Hunter Schwartz
Series Editor

Administrative Law
Richard Henry Seamon

Civil Procedure for All States
Benjamin V. Madison, III

Constitutional Law
David Schwartz and Lori Ringhand

Contracts
Michael Hunter Schwartz and Denise Riebe

Current Issues in Constitutional Litigation
Sarah E. Ricks, with contributions by Evelyn M. Tenenbaum

Employment Discrimination
SECOND EDITION
Susan Grover, Sandra F. Sperino, and Jarod S. Gonzalez

Evidence
Pavel Wonsowicz

International Business Transactions
Amy Deen Westbrook

International Women's Rights, Equality, and Justice
Christine M. Venter

The Lawyer's Practice
Kris Franklin

Professional Responsibility
Barbara Glesner Fines

Sales
Edith R. Warkentine

Torts
Paula J. Manning

Workers' Compensation Law
Michael C. Duff

TORTS

A Context and Practice Casebook

Paula J. Manning

CAROLINA ACADEMIC PRESS

Durham, North Carolina

ISBN 978-1-59460-768-4
LCCN 2012950549

Carolina Academic Press
700 Kent Street
Durham, North Carolina 27701
Telephone (919) 489-7486
Fax (919) 493-5668
www.cap-press.com

Printed in the United States of America

To my husband, Mike and my son, Ben,
who make three a magic number.

Contents

Table of Cases   xiii
Series Editor's Preface   xv
Acknowledgments   xvii
Introduction   xix

Chapter One · Evaluating the Claim: Immunity, Intentional
                 Torts to the Person, and Privileges   3
Objectives   3
 Skill Focus: Develop a Professional Vocabulary   4
A. Evaluating a Claim   5
 1. Are There Any Barriers to Filing the Claim?   8
  a. Governmental Immunity: The Federal Tort Claims Act   8
   Skill Focus: Rule Deconstruction   9
   Exercise 1-1 Reflective Learning   13
  b. Governmental Immunity: State Statutes   13
   Exercise 1-2 Rule Deconstruction   13
   Exercise 1-3 Law Practice   15
 2. Can Plaintiff "Prove Up" the Prima Facie Case?   15
  a. An Introduction to Intentional Torts   15
  b. Proving the Prima Facie Case for Battery   16
   Skill Focus: Case Reading   17
    Wagner v. Utah   19
    White v. Muniz   24
   Skill Focus: Case Briefing   28
   Exercise 1-4 Case Briefing   29
   Exercise 1-5 Law Practice   29
    Nelson v. Carroll   30
   Exercise 1-6 Evaluating Legal Arguments   34
   Exercise 1-7 Zealous Advocacy or Unprofessional Behavior?   45
   Exercise 1-8 Fact Investigation and Analysis   47
   Exercise 1-9 Using a Court's Reasoning to Apply a Rule to
    New Situations   49
   Exercise 1-10 Organizing Analysis of a Battery Claim   49
   Skill Focus: Organizing Your Thoughts before You Write   49
 3. Are There Any Defenses?   50
  a. Consent   50
   Murphy v. Implicito   51
   Exercise 1-11 Using a List of Factors to Organize Your Answer 54
B. Other Claims Based on Intentional Conduct   54
 1. Assault   54
   Exercise 1-12 Synthesizing Material   55

2. Intentional Infliction of Emotional Distress 55
    Shumate v. Twin Tier Hospitality, LLC 56
    Chehade Refai v. Lazaro 63
    Turner v. Wong 68
    Sawyer v. Southwest Airlines Co. 71
3. False Imprisonment 77
    <u>Skill Focus</u>: Applying and Distinguishing Precedent 77
    Exercise 1-13 Applying and Distinguishing Cases to Resolve
      a Dispute 78
    Exercise 1-14 Using Cases to Support Your Reasoning 80
    Randall's Food Markets, Inc. v. Johnson 80
    Cuellar v. Walgreens Co. 82
    Exercise 1-15 Evaluating Judicial Opinions 85
    Oramulu v. Washington Mut. Bank 85
    <u>Skill Focus</u>: Applying and Distinguishing Precedent Part Two
      —The Lawyer's Perspective 87
    Exercise 1-16 Applying and Distinguishing Revisited 89
    Exercise 1-17 The Burden of Proof 89
C. Affirmative Defenses: Self-Defense and Defense of Others 90
    Exercise 1-18 Law School Skills Applied to Law Practice 91
    Arizona v. Grannis 108
    Arizona v. Buggs 111
    Arizona v. Reid 114
    Exercise 1-19 Zealous Advocacy or Unprofessional Behavior 2.0 116
    Exercise 1-20 Law Practice 116

Chapter Two · Investigating the Claim and Developing
      a Theory of the Case—Negligence 117
Objectives 117
Introduction 118
    Exercise 2-1 Assessing Risk 119
    Exercise 2-2 Applying the Hand Formula 121
    Exercise 2-3 Questioning Values 122
A. The Negligence Cause of Action 123
   1. Establishing Duty and Breach 123
     a. Proving the Existence and Extent of Duty 124
      (1) Establishing That a Duty is Owed to the Plaintiff 125
    Exercise 2-4 Establishing the Existence of a Duty 126
    Satterfield v. Breeding Insulation Company 126
    In re Certified Question from the Fourteenth District
      Court of Appeals of Texas v. Ford Motor Company 137
      (2) Establishing the Scope of the Duty Owed to the Plaintiff 144
       a. The Duty of Ordinary Care—Evaluating the Facts 144
    Exercise 2-5 Evaluating the Existence and Extent of Duty 144
       b. Duty Established by Professional Standards—Developing
        Subject Matter Expertise 146
    Exercise 2-6 Developing an Initial Theory of the Duty Owed
      by a Professional 163
    Exercise 2-7 Evaluating Conflicting Theories and Expert
      Witness Testimony 163

Exercise 2-8 Establishing the Standard of Care—Review
and Practice 178
   c. Duty Defined by Law—Understanding and Applying Cases
and Statutes 179
     (i) Premesis Liability—Duty Defined by Common Law 179
Exercise 2-9 Evaluating Duty Based on the Land Entrant's Status 180
Exercise 2-10 Understanding Variations of a Rule of Law 181
   Stitt v. Holland Abundant Life Fellowship 181
Exercise 2-11 Using Policy to Support Legal Arguments 193
   Rowland v. Christian 194
Exercise 2-12 Law Practice 198
Skill Focus: Synthesizing Materials 198
Exercise 2-13 Synthesizing Materials to Determine the Existence
and Extent of the Duty Owed 199
   Isaacs v. Huntington Memorial Hospital 200
   Yu Fang Tan v. Arnel Management Company 206
Exercise 2-14 To Foresee or Not to Foresee 213
   A.W. v. Lancaster County School District 214
Exercise 2-15 Law Practice 220
     (ii) Negligence Per Se—Duty Imposed by Statute 220
Exercise 2-16 Using Statutes to Establish Duty and Breach 221
     (iii) Rescuers—Duty Curtailed by Statute 221
Exercise 2-17 Understanding Statutory Language 222
(3) Using Circumstantial Evidence—res ipsa loquitur 222
Exercise 2-18 A Matter of Law 226
2. Damages 241
Skill Focus: Organizing Material 242
Exercise 2-19 Evaluating Damages 244
Exercise 2-20 Calculating the "Value" of Injuries 251
Exercise 2-21 Recovery for Emotional Injuries 251
Exercise 2-22 Law Practice 253
   Burgess v. Superior Court 254
Exercise 2-23 Emotional Distress Claims and Noneconomic
Damage Caps 259
3. Causation 260
   a. Factual Cause—The "but for" Test 260
Exercise 2-24 Proving Factual Cause 261
Exercise 2-25 Law Practice 261
   b. Factual Cause—The Substantial Factor Test 261
Exercise 2-26 Selecting and Applying the Appropriate Test to
Determine Factual Cause 263
   c. Proximate Cause 264
Exercise 2-27 Evaluating Proximate Cause 266
Exercise 2-28 Understanding Historical Context 266
Exercise 2-29 Analyzing Causation and Evaluating Expert Opinions 272
4. Defenses 298
   a. Contributory Negligence and Comparative Fault 298
Exercise 2-30 Identifying the Applicable Standard 299
   b. Assumption of Risk 300
Exercise 2-31 Identifying Risks 302

c. Statute of Limitations 303
Exercise 2-32 Statutory Deconstruction—Determining the
Limitations Period 303
Skill Focus: Creating Issues Checklists 307
Exercise 2-33 Preparing for Essay Examinations—Spotting
the Issues 309
Skill Focus: Law School Essay Examinations 310
Exercise 2-34 Preparing for Essay Examinations—Drafting an
Answer Using IRAC 313

Chapter Three · Advocating for Extension, Modification or
Imposition of a Rule—Strict Liability 315
Objectives 315
Introduction 316
A. Strict Liability for Animals 317
Exercise 3-1 Strict Liability for Dog Bites 318
Exercise 3-2 Obtaining Evidentiary Support 319
Exercise 3-3 Imposing Strict Liability 319
Tracey v. Solesky 321
Exercise 3-4 Born to Be Wild? 339
B. Abnormally Dangerous Activities 342
Exercise 3-5 Extending, Modifying and Rejecting Strict Liability 344
Skill Focus: Applying and Distinguishing Cases Part Three 345
Turner v. Big Lake Oil Co. 345
Cities Service Co. v. State 347
Exercise 3-6 Applying Factors 350
Klein v. Pyrodyne Corp. 351
Cadena v. Chicago Fireworks Mfg. Co. 354
Exercise 3-7 Improving the "A" in IRAC—Explaining
Your Reasoning 356
C. Causation 357
Exercise 3-8 Evaluating Causation 358

Chapter Four · The "Burden" of Proof: Marshalling the
Evidence—Strict Products Liability 359
Objectives 359
Introduction 360
1. Is the Item That Caused the Injury a Product? 362
Way v. Boy Scouts of America 363
Aetna Cas. & Sur. Co. v. Jeppesen & Co. 365
Exercise 4-1 Synthesizing and Applying Material 367
Exercise 4-2 Classifying Products 367
2. Was the Defendant a Commercial Seller or Distributor of the Product
That Injured Plaintiff? 367
a. Was the Defendant Engaged in the Business of Selling or Otherwise
Distributing the Product that Injured Plaintiff? 368
Exercise 4-3 Identifying Commercial Sellers and Distributors 368
Exercise 4-4 Proof that Defendant is a Seller, Distributor or
Manufacturer of the Product 369

Vandermark v. Ford Motor Company 371
   b. Will the Defendant Have Immunity? 373
     Exercise 4-5 Statutory Immunity 374
     Exercise 4-6 Naming Responsible Parties as Defendants 375
     Exercise 4-7 Law Practice 376
   c. Did Defendant Sell, Distribute or Manufacture the Specific
     Product that Caused Plaintiff's Injury? 376
     Healey v. Firestone Tire & Rubber Company 376
     Exercise 4-8 Identifying the Manufacturer 379
  3. Can Plaintiff Prove the Product was Defective at the Time it Left the
  Defendant's Control? 379
     Exercise 4-9 Circumstantial Evidence 381
     Exercise 4-10 Identifying Evidentiary Support 381
     <u>Skill Focus</u>: The Value and Purpose of Expert Testimony 382
     Dico Tire, Inc. v. Cisneros 383
     Exercise 4-11 Legally Sufficient Evidence 387
     Exercise 4-12 Thinking Like a Jury 396
     Jurls v. Ford Motor Co. 396
     Woodin v. J.C. Penney Co., Inc. 402
     McCabe v. American Honda Motor Co. 404
     Exercise 4-13 Elements of Proof 409
     Rawlings Sporting Goods Co., Inc. v. Daniels 410
     Pavlides v. Galveston Yacht Basin 412
     Exercise 4-14 Adequacy of Warning Label 418
     Exercise 4-15 Obtaining Evidence — Drafting Interrogatories 419
  4. Causation and Injury 425
   a. Presumption plaintiff would "read and heed" an adequate warning 425
   b. Anticipating foreseeable misuse 425
     Exercise 4-16 Anticipating Misuse 426
     Exercise 4-17 Essay Exam Practice 426

Chapter Five · Putting It All Together — Representing the
             Defendant in a Defamation Action 427
Objectives 427
Introduction 428
     Exercise 5-1 Using Practice Guides to Develop Knowledge
       and Understanding 448
     Exercise 5-2 Summarizing and Organizing Materials 463
     Exercise 5-3 Using Information from a Practice Guide to Identify
       Issues and Direct Research 463
     Exercise 5-4 Using Cases to Enhance Existing Knowledge 464
     Dobson v. Harris 464
     Kroh v. Kroh 467
     Tallent v. Blake 470
     Towne v. Cope 473
     Troxler v. Charter Mandala Center, Inc. 476
     Kwan-Sa You v. Roe 479
     White v. Town of Chapel Hill 481
     Losing v. Food Lion, L.L.C. 484

Exercise 5-5 Integrating Information   487
Exercise 5-6 Evaluating the Evidence — Creating a Discovery Plan   487
Exercise 5-7 Identifying Weaknesses — Preparing for Your
    Client's Deposition   487
Exercise 5-8 Adapting Learning to Evaluate New Claims   491
Exercise 5-9 Reflection and Revision   493
Exercise 5-10 Developing a Better Understanding of
    Constitutional Concerns   495
Exercise 5-11 Law Practice   496

Chapter Six · Putting It All Together — Representing the Plaintiff   497
  Objectives   497
  Introduction   497

Index   519

Table of Cases

A.W. v. Lancaster County School District, 214

Aetna Cas. & Sur. Co. v. Jeppesen & Co., 365

Arizona v. Buggs, 111

Arizona v. Grannis, 108

Arizona v. Reid, 114

Burgess v. Superior Court, 254

Cadena v. Chicago Fireworks Mfg. Co., 354

Chehade Refai v. Lazaro, 63

Cities Service Co. v. State, 347

Cuellar v. Walgreens Co., 82

Dico Tire, Inc. v. Cisneros, 383

Dobson v. Harris, 464

Healey v. Firestone Tire & Rubber Company, 376

In re Certified Question from the Fourteenth District Court of Appeals of Texas v. Ford Motor Company, 137

Isaacs v. Huntington Memorial Hospital, 200

Jurls v. Ford Motor Co., 396

Klein v. Pyrodyne Corp., 351

Kroh v. Kroh, 467

Kwan-Sa You v. Roe, 479

Losing v. Food Lion, L.L.C., 484

McCabe v. American Honda Motor Co., 404

Murphy v. Implicito, 51

Nelson v. Carroll, 30

Oramulu v. Washington Mut. Bank, 85

Palsgraf v. Long Island Railroad, 266

Pavlides v. Galveston Yacht Basin, 412

Randall's Food Markets, Inc. v. Johnson, 80

Rawlings Sporting Goods Co., Inc. v. Daniels, 410

Re: Strickland v. Wong, 431

Rowland v. Christian, 194

Satterfield v. Breeding Insulation Company, 126

Sawyer v. Southwest Airlines Co., 71

Shumate v. Twin Tier Hospitality, LLC, 56

Stitt v. Holland Abundant Life Fellowship, 181

Tallent v. Blake, 470

Towne v. Cope, 473

Tracey v. Solesky, 321

Troxler v. Charter Mandala Center, Inc., 476

Turner v. Big Lake Oil Co., 345

Turner v. Wong, 68

Vandermark v. Ford Motor Company, 371

Wagner v. Utah, 19

Way v. Boy Scouts of America, 363

White v. Muniz, 24

White v. Town of Chapel Hill, 481

Woodin v. J.C. Penney Co., Inc., 402

Yu Fang Tan v. Arnel Management Company, 206

Series Editor's Preface

Welcome to a new type of casebook. Designed by leading experts in law school teaching and learning, Context and Practice casebooks assist law professors and their students to work together to learn, minimize stress, and prepare for the rigors and joys of practicing law. Student learning and preparation for law practice are the guiding ethics of these books.

Why would we depart from the tried and true? Why have we abandoned the legal education model by which we were trained? Because legal education can and must improve.

In Spring 2007, the Carnegie Foundation published *Educating Lawyers: Preparation for the Practice of Law* and the Clinical Legal Education Association published *Best Practices for Legal Education*. Both works reflect in-depth efforts to assess the effectiveness of modern legal education, and both conclude that legal education, as presently practiced, falls quite short of what it can and should be. Both works criticize law professors' rigid adherence to a single teaching technique, the inadequacies of law school assessment mechanisms, and the dearth of law school instruction aimed at teaching law practice skills and inculcating professional values. Finally, the authors of both books express concern that legal education may be harming law students. Recent studies show that law students, in comparison to all other graduate students, have the highest levels of depression, anxiety and substance abuse.

The problems with traditional law school instruction begin with the textbooks law teachers use. Law professors cannot implement *Educating Lawyers* and *Best Practices* using texts designed for the traditional model of legal education. Moreover, even though our understanding of how people learn has grown exponentially in the past 100 years, no law school text to date even purports to have been designed with educational research in mind.

The Context and Practice Series is an effort to offer a genuine alternative. Grounded in learning theory and instructional design and written with *Educating Lawyers* and *Best Practices* in mind, Context and Practice casebooks make it easy for law professors to change.

I welcome reactions, criticisms, and suggestions; my e-mail address is michael.schwartz@washburn.edu. Knowing the author(s) of these books, I know they, too, would appreciate your input; we share a common commitment to student learning. In fact, students, if your professor cares enough about your learning to have adopted this book, I bet s/he would welcome your input, too!

Professor Michael Hunter Schwartz, Series Designer and Editor
Co-Director, Institute for Law Teaching and Learning
Associate Dean for Faculty and Academic Development

Acknowledgments

I am grateful to Michael Hunter Schwartz for a great number of things, including his vision in conceiving this series; for convincing me that this book was needed; and for the support, guidance and encouragement he has unwaveringly provided throughout this process. Without him, this book would not exist, and without his vision and encouragement my students would still be receiving inadequate and inactive instruction. He has been an invaluable mentor and friend.

I am also lucky to have been given the opportunity to teach so many remarkable people—and I would like to thank my students, who have contributed to this book in countless ways—from their willingness to work with very rough drafts of these chapters, to their thoughtful suggestions for improving its content. I would like to specifically thank those students who served as research assistants on this project: Kurtis Urien, Jaqueline Salazar, Stephen Strobel, Jeff Loposer, Camille Boudreau, Taylor Dudley, Sam Solodar and Matthew Greife.

Much of the skills instruction throughout this text was developed and refined while working with many of my gifted colleagues from around the country, including Ruth McKinney, Corie Rosen, Rebecca Flannagan, Larry Kreiger and Jeremiah Ho. Special thanks to Lisa Blasser for her thoughtful suggestions and observations, as well as her constant willingness to discuss skills instruction and how to better serve our students. I also want to thank my colleagues at Western State, whose dedication to teaching serves as both example and inspiration, and whose commitment to our students and to academic support in general, makes my work both possible and enjoyable.

I also want to thank Carolina Academic Press, and specifically Linda and Keith, for their vision in creating and supporting this series, and for allowing me to be a part of it. Also, thanks to Chris Harrow for his unending patience, for making my drawings into beautiful graphics and for helping me to achieve my vision for this book.

Finally, I am so very thankful to my husband Mike, the practicing lawyer in our family, for his insights about the practical aspects of practicing tort law; for his wisdom and advice about the mentoring of new lawyers; and for patiently reviewing so many of the exercises in this text—his contributions make this a much better, richer book. Even more than that I am grateful to him for being my partner in caring for our son, which provided me with much needed time and space to write this book; thanks also to my son Ben, who was equally patient and supportive, without you both little of what I do would be worthwhile.

Introduction

Learning from This Book

Many students believe that they are coming to law school in order to "learn the law." While this is true to some extent, what most students at the start of law school do not yet realize is that learning the law is only one, relatively small, aspect of law school. Law students really come to law school to learn how to learn and apply the law. In fact, you may have heard that the goal of law school is to teach students to "think like a lawyer." This involves several things, including: learning how judges reason their way to a conclusion; learning about what kinds of legal arguments are legitimate, and will help your client prevail; learning how to marshal the evidence to prove your client's case; and learning how to identify and use the facts of a case. This last point is particularly important in torts, because tort cases are usually very fact intensive and fact driven. For this reason, this book focuses on teaching you to solve problems that, like real tort cases, are factually complex. This focus on problem solving, and working with client facts, is one of the unique features of this book.

For the most part law schools, and law school textbooks, have utilized a very narrow range of methods for teaching students how to "think like a lawyer." Essentially, students read appellate court decisions (cases) to learn (1) how judges reason (in hopes that students will later model such reasoning), and (2) how to derive the rules and policy from reading cases. These are important skills, and they are included in this book. However, this book moves beyond that method and that skill set, in order to provide you with a broader range of skills and experiences, in hopes that you will be better equipped for the practice of law. This book utilizes a problem solving approach — setting the materials and cases in the context of client problems. This simulates the practice of law because lawyers read material (including cases) with their client's facts in mind (rather than in a vacuum).

Each chapter of this book contains materials and exercises designed to help you acquire (1) learning and study skills; (2) law practice skills; and (3) knowledge and understanding of the basic substantive law of torts in the identified area. Each chapter begins by identifying the specific chapter objectives for each of these three areas.

It is important to understand at the outset that this book is not designed to teach you every area of tort law, or to make you an expert on the topic of torts. In fact, tort law, for the most part, is state specific, meaning each state has established its own rules, which you will have to learn in order to practice in that jurisdiction. Rather than focus on all of the potential tort causes of action, this book focuses on teaching you how to learn and understand the law and apply it to solve client problems. It provides you with the tools and guidance to accomplish this task so that in the future you will be able to learn and apply the law in any area or context.

This book is designed to provide multiple opportunities to learn and practice law school skills—like reading, briefing, and exam writing—and to see how these skills connect to skills lawyers use in practice.

This book is also designed to provide you with an opportunity to learn and practice critical lawyering skills. You will review, use, and draft the types of documents lawyers use—including complaints, answers, motions, and discovery devices. The exercises will guide you through real lawyering tasks, including how to: evaluate claims; develop a theory of a case; make legal arguments to support your position on the law; develop factual subject matter knowledge; obtain and use evidence; grapple with complex factual issues; select and use expert witnesses; and many other practical skills.

Each section provides the background material needed to understand the law, followed by exercises designed to help you learn and organize the material, and then apply it, to resolve a client problem. The exercises are designed to help you see how a lawyer would apply the concept in practice.

Throughout the book you will find skill specific instruction; each time the book introduces a new skill it will be accompanied by a description of that skill, and how the skill is employed.

This book encourages you to think about and develop a professional identity, by asking you to think about the kind of lawyer you would like to be—the values you hold, and would like to maintain, when you enter practice.

This book also encourages you to think about your client's perspective, to remember that clients are real people with a range of human emotions, and to understand the types of emotions your client may experience, and how those emotions may impact the client's case.

The book culminates in a capstone experience which allows you to use the combined knowledge, skills and values you have gained from the materials in the book, to represent a client, and practice what you have learned.

This book ultimately seeks to help you bridge the gap between law school and law practice.

Introduction to the Study of Torts

A tort is a civil wrong, other than a breach of contract, for which the law provides a remedy. Tort litigation occurs in the context of the civil system. Therefore, it is helpful to have working knowledge of how a lawsuit moves through the civil system. The following chart depicts key aspects of the litigation process you will encounter in your reading in this book.

Plaintiff files a complaint
A complaint states the basic information about the suit, including the causes of action (the basis for liability)

↓

Plaintiff serves the defendant with the complaint

↓

Defendant responds by filing	
An answer	A motion to dismiss
A response to the complaint, admitting or denying the plaintiff's allegations and stating the defendant's affirmative defenses	The defendant's allegation that the lawsuit should be dismissed immediately because the plaintiff has not stated a valid cause of action, followed specific procedural requirements, or another reason

↓

The parties engage in pre-trial litigation			
The parties engage in discovery: the process by which each side learns information about the other side's case	Parties file pre-trial motions: many lawsuits are resolved without a trial, based on motions (such as a motion for summary judgement)	Where a motion is granted and resolves a case, the losing party may appeal	The parties engage in settlement discussions (this may happen at any stage of the litigation including prefiling or post judgement)

↓

The case is tried

↓

A party may file a motion for non-suit

↓

A verdict or judgement is rendered

↓

The losing party may appeal

Generally speaking torts are divided into three categories—intentional acts, negligent acts and actions for which there is strict liability. You will learn about examples of each of these categories in this book. Tort law covers a wide array of conduct for which an actor can be held liable, and you may be familiar with many examples; for instance, each of the following is an example of a case involving one or more torts:

- A toy distributor sends toy stores shipments of toys painted with a lead-based paint; children ingest the paint and develop brain injuries
- One waiter locks another waiter in a walk-in refrigerator
- A landowner does not install railing in a swimming pool and her tenant slips and falls while climbing into pool
- A restaurant patron eats lobster at a local restaurant and is hospitalized for food poisoning
- A child is attacked by a neighbor's dog and suffers physical injury
- A doctor implants the wrong embryos into a patient, who delivers twins that are not biologically her children
- A newspaper publishes false reports that a school teacher is a convicted pedophile
- A company dumps toxic waste into a town's water supply causing injury to the residents
- A teenager is talking on her cell phone in violation of a new state law, and causes an automobile accident
- A security guard wrongly suspects a customer of shoplifting and detains him in a back room for two hours

In the chapters that follow, you will learn that each tort cause of action has a series of elements that a plaintiff must prove, in order to establish a prima facie case (and liability). A defendant may prevail by showing that plaintiff did not prove her case, or by proving that defendant has a valid affirmative defense. With this in mind, we turn to the first task—evaluating the claim.

TORTS

Chapter One

Evaluating the Claim: Immunity, Intentional Torts to the Person, and Privileges

The main goal of this book is to equip you with tools that will help you succeed in your professional career as a lawyer. Each chapter of this book contains materials and exercises designed to help you simultaneously acquire (1) learning and study skills, (2) law practice skills, and (3) knowledge and understanding of the basic substantive law of Torts in the identified area. Each chapter begins by identifying the specific chapter objectives for each of these three areas. It is a good idea to keep the objectives in mind as you go through the materials in each chapter and then to revisit the objectives as a final review of the materials—to evaluate whether you have acquired the skills and knowledge that are the goals of each chapter.

Objectives

Learning and Study Skills

This text is designed to help you develop some of the learning and study skills you will need for learning and understanding any area of law. Successful law students (and lawyers) are life-long learners—whether it is a new area of law, medical terminology and procedures for a medical malpractice case, the products and practices of a business client in an intellectual property case, and any number of other examples, lawyers frequently must devote themselves to learning and understanding new concepts and then applying what they have learned to help resolve their clients' cases. To develop your life-long learning skills, you will find that in addition to learning the substantive law of Torts, this text will also help you develop some of the learning and study skills that law students and lawyers should possess. For example, the skills objectives for this section are:

Become part of the legal discourse community by developing a vocabulary of legal terms

Develop expert legal reading skills

Develop case briefing skills

Develop reflective learning skills

Law Practice Skills

Another goal of this text is to help you to learn and develop some of the practical skills new lawyers should possess. If you plan to practice in an area of tort law you will likely need to possess some or all of the practical skills covered in this text, and you will need to be able to understand and apply substantive law. In this chapter you will have the opportunity to learn about and practice the following skills:

Deconstructing rules

Applying and distinguishing legal authority (cases)

Evaluating potential and existing claims and defenses, more specifically:

> Understanding what immunity is and how it may prevent a plaintiff from recovering from a potential defendant

> Evaluating whether a set of facts provides a sufficient basis upon which to allege and/or establish a claim for battery, assault, false imprisonment, and intentional infliction of emotional distress

> Evaluating whether a set of facts provides a sufficient basis upon which to allege and/or establish a defense of consent, self-defense, and defense of others

Reviewing and evaluating legal documents and arguments drafted by other lawyers

Counseling a client

Advising a client as to potential liability

Substantive Legal Knowledge

Finally, in each chapter the materials are designed to help you learn the substantive law (so that you may then understand and apply it). By the time you have finished this chapter you should:

Be able to define what immunity is and the effect it may have on a claim

Be able to identify the elements required to establish a prima facie claim for battery, assault, false imprisonment and intentional infliction of emotional distress

Be able to identify the elements required to establish a defense of consent, self-defense and defense of others

---

Skill Focus: Develop a Professional Vocabulary

Part of becoming a lawyer means becoming part of the legal discourse community—by learning key terms that are part of lawyers' everyday language. As you develop this vocabulary it will improve your reading comprehension and speed, as well as make class discussion and preparation more manageable. In addition, you will be better equipped to communicate in the manner that characterizes legal thinking and writing. It is good practice to look up terms in a legal dictionary, since many terms, even familiar ones, may have unexpected meaning when used in legal contexts. For the next section **some** of the key terms are:

tort, tortious, tortfeasor, immune, immunity, liability, defenses, statute, statutory, plaintiff, defendant, cause of action, claim, defense, costs, cause of action, prima facie case, complaint, answer, and motion to dismiss

Note that developing a professional vocabulary does not mean that your everyday language and writing should be filled with legalese (legal terms that are unfamiliar to lay persons), but rather that you should understand such terms when you hear and read them so that you do not have to stop and think about what they mean in order to understand the materials you will read and work with in your everyday practice. When you speak or write, however, you will want to make your written work as clear as possible and that may mean communicating your ideas without using unnecessary legal terminology. Good legal writing is usually written in plain English.

A. Evaluating a Claim

As part of evaluating any claim, a tort lawyer's job is to consider whether the plaintiff can prove the elements of her claim (the prima facie case), whether there are issues that may preclude a plaintiff from bringing the action at all (because it would be dismissed outright by the court) and whether there are defenses that may limit or preclude recovery. In this chapter we will evaluate a claim for battery, one of the seven intentional torts, in the manner that a tort lawyer might examine a claim, by (1) considering whether there are any barriers to filing the claim (which would be raised by defendant in a motion to dismiss the action); (2) examining whether the elements of the prima facie case can be established (which must be plead by the plaintiff in the complaint); and (3) evaluating whether there are any defenses to the action (which must be plead by defendant in the answer).

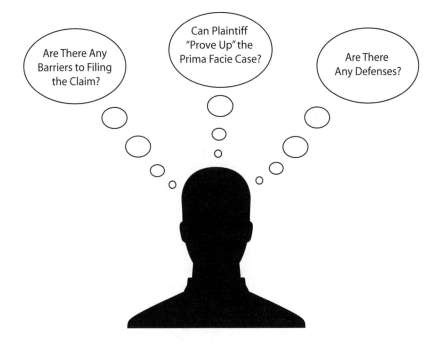

While it might seem strange to start a unit on intentional torts with something other than an intentional tort, in practice, a lawyer's decision making is impacted by more than just consideration of whether the prima facie case can be established. A lawyer may be able to prove up all of the elements of a client's claim and establish that her client was injured as the result of someone's tortious conduct, but nonetheless be unable to obtain relief for her client for any number of reasons. For example, before a plaintiff lawyer files an action, and even before she begins to incur costs by investigating the client's claim, she should determine the appropriate statute of limitations for the claim, to determine the amount of time she has to investigate and file the claim, and to be certain that the statute has not yet run. Similarly, a lawyer for a defendant must evaluate not only whether the client engaged in conduct that is tortious and whether there are defenses to that conduct, but must also think about whether even if the client's conduct is tortious, there are bars or limits on the client's liability — such as an immunity statute that prohibits suits against the client for the causes of action pleaded in the plaintiff's complaint. A defense lawyer should determine whether the claim can be dismissed on such grounds, which may eliminate the need for the defense to spend time and resources challenging the substantive merits of the claim. Conversely, a plaintiff lawyer who files an action without considering such issues may waste resources investigating and developing a case only to find themselves facing a motion to dismiss the action, followed by a motion to recover costs from the client if the action is dismissed.

Note that in this section we will examine only one potential barrier — immunity; one potential cause of action (claim) — battery; and one potential defense — consent. In any action there may be several potential threshold questions to resolve besides questions of immunity and the statute of limitations, and there will likely be several potential claims and defenses to consider. However, an objective of this first section is to expose you to the process of evaluating a claim, and to help you learn to consider the three critical questions set out above, which can be demonstrated using a single topic for each question.

Chapter Problem

In order to simulate the experience of a tort lawyer, you will consider material in the context of a client problem. As you learn the substantive law from the materials in the next section, use what you learn to evaluate the following hypothetical case:

Ryan Watson is a 170-pound starting left guard and defensive tackle on the West City High School varsity football team. Bud Rajcic is an assistant coach for the same team. West City High School is located in the Central County Unified School District.

Watson injured his ankle in a Friday-night football game. He continued to play for some time after being injured. After the game, the team trainer examined the ankle which he thought was a mild sprain. Watson wrapped it in an ace bandage and iced it over the weekend. He had no trouble walking when he attended school on Monday and did not feel any pain.

After school on Monday, the head coach wrapped the ankle and told Watson to practice. Watson put on his pads and practice uniform and ran some warm-up drills. For example, he participated in a drill which involved several linemen hitting and driving back tackling dummies attached to a large steel sled (a "sled drill"). He also participated in a drill which involved one player ramming a large, cushion-like blocking shield held by another player and pushing the holding player and the shield back several yards (a "fit and drive" drill). For the "fit and drive" drill, Watson held a shield while the team's 265-pound center, James Taylor, rammed into it and drove forward with his legs.

According to Watson, after several drills he told Taylor to take it easy because his ankle hurt, so the two teammates merely went through the motions. Rajcic yelled at Watson and Taylor for their half-hearted efforts. Rajcic proceeded to demonstrate the proper technique by driving his own body into the shield, driving Watson back; Rajcic is a 230-pound ex-lineman. Watson says that following Rajcic's first blow, he felt a sharp pain go to his ankle. Rajcic grew angrier and told Watson to "hold the damned bag" (meaning the blocking shield). Watson held the bag again; he stated that when Rajcic hit the bag the second time, he took another step back, felt his ankle "pop" and told Rajcic that he could not do the drill anymore. Rajcic, in a fit of rage, ordered Watson off the field. Watson walked ten yards to the edge of the field, but he continued to exchange heated words with Rajcic about Rajcic's expectations and Watson's lack of effort and heart.

Watson described the incident as follows:

> I told him, like, "Well, you know, I want to do the drills, but I can't. What more do you expect out of me?" And he goes, "Just get off—just get off my damn field," or something like that. "Get off the damn field." I started walking off the field and he came up behind me calling me a baby, telling me that, you know, I'm just—I'm just being a baby and that. It's not that I can't do it, it's that I don't want to—and swearing at me and calling me all kinds of names. And so I got off to the sideline and I'm like, "What am I supposed to do now?" And he's like, "Hold the bag." And I'm like, "I can't hold the bag." And he's walking towards me still and I'm on the sideline. I unstrapped my helmet and I had it pushed up to where, you know, my—the face mask was up and I was taking a drink of water. I told him, "I'm done." And he came up and just grabbed the bag, and he put his hands on the little handles and came up to me and just slammed it in my face and the face mask went up and sent my head backwards. I stepped back from the blow it gave me and when I stepped back, I felt my ankle just snap, and when it snapped, it—I just—I just went and like I just put my hand down on the ground and it just—it was just the most painful thing that I've ever had happen to me in my life. And I got up and I could barely walk.

Watson was not on the field's practice area when Rajcic pushed the blocking shield (the bag) into him, causing the injury. Watson had removed his chin strap and had his helmet pushed back on top of his head. According to Watson he was unprepared for and not expecting Rajcic's action because he had essentially stopped practicing, was drinking water when struck, was not participating in the actual blocking drills, and had informed Rajcic that he could not do the drills because he was hurting. Watson also claims Rajcic was irate and frenzied when striking Watson with the blocking shield (the bag).

Several players have also been interviewed. The team's players generally acknowledge their fondness for Rajcic, but many portray him as being "a little crazy." Some players indicated they believe Rajcic was out of control at the time of the incident. Player Connor Dinco indicated that Rajcic actually threw the blocking shield at Watson after Watson moments earlier had asked Rajcic, "What more do you expect from me?" He also says he is certain that Rajcic's act of throwing the blocking shield at Watson was not part of a drill; it was "outside of the drill." Dinco indicated that Watson's chin strap was off, that his helmet was up, and that his face mask was off his face. He also says that it caught Watson off guard and Watson took a step back. Player Hunter Tedesco described the incident as follows:

Ryan told coach that he could not do the blocking drills, and, in response, Coach went crazy. Ryan was pretty much fed up and Coach said, "Get the hell off my field." Ryan starts walking away. Right as Ryan gets off the field—we're in our own little corner down there and Ryan gets off the field and turns around and says, "What the hell do you want me to do?" or something like that. Coach came walking up with the bag and says, "What I want you to do is hold the goddamn bag," and he shoved Ryan with the bag. And when Ryan was walking off he had taken the straps off his head, so the helmet was sitting there free. When Coach went to give him the bag he hit the face mask and it drove into Ryan's face or face mask.

According to the school district's incident report:

Rajcic, after seeing Watson and Taylor's half-hearted effort and sloppy technique, immediately chastised them. Rajcic became angry when Watson walked off the field, and he acknowledged that he struck Watson with the blocking shield. According to Rajcic, his action was controlled and calculated and meant merely to stun and arouse Watson's emotions, but it was not intended to injure him. The report concludes that Rajcic was attempting to motivate Watson and the team, by encouraging the team to play tougher despite discomfort or weakness, and he did not intend to do anything that might harm a starting lineman such as Watson.

Except for the pushed-back helmet, Watson was wearing all of his football pads at the time of the incident. A blocking shield (the bag used by Rajcic) is designed to cushion heavy blows. Torn ligaments on Watson's ankle required him to have orthopedic surgery.

---

1. Are There Any Barriers to Filing the Claim?

A client may be the victim of an intentional tort, but nonetheless be barred from bringing an action against a party for any number of reasons. Some of these reasons are grounds for dismissing an action at the very outset of a case. For example, a case may be dismissed on the grounds that the status of the defendant entitles defendant to immunity from liability for the tort. There are several types of immunity, including charitable immunity, spousal immunity, parental immunity, and the one we will cover in this section: governmental immunity.

Since immunity is a threshold issue that must be considered by lawyers involved in representing parties in intentional tort cases, and since many intentional tort cases, including those you will read in this chapter, are situated in the context of a dispute over whether an immunity statute applies, it is useful to begin the study of intentional torts with a basic understanding of immunity statutes before proceeding to consideration of the intentional torts themselves. Also, since one of the first skills law students should possess is an understanding of how to deconstruct rules of law, immunity, which is frequently set out in state or federal statutes, and is thus a more "pure" rule of law than those you will encounter in cases, is a great place to begin.

a. Governmental Immunity: The Federal Tort Claims Act

Under the common law, tort suits against the government were prohibited. Modernly many states and the federal government have enacted statutes that modify this absolute immunity. For example, the Federal Tort Claims Act (FTCA), waives sovereign immunity for some torts, while retaining immunity for others. Below are selected sections of the FTCA, including sections pertaining to intentional torts.

28 U.S.C. Section 1346:

(b)(1) ... the district courts ... shall have exclusive jurisdiction of civil actions on claims against the United States, for money damages, accruing on and after January 1, 1945, for injury or loss of property, or personal injury or death caused by the negligent or wrongful act or omission of any employee of the Government while acting within the scope of his office or employment, under circumstances where the United States, if a private person, would be liable to the claimant in accordance with the law of the place where the act or omission occurred.

28 U.S.C. Section 2680

The provisions of ... section 1346(b) of this title shall not apply to—

(a) Any claim based upon an act or omission of an employee of the Government, exercising due care, in the execution of a statute or regulation, whether or not such statute or regulation be valid, or based upon the exercise or performance or the failure to exercise or perform a discretionary function or duty on the part of a federal agency or an employee of the Government, whether or not the discretion involved be abused.

...

(h) Any claim arising out of assault, battery, false imprisonment, false arrest, malicious prosecution, abuse of process, libel, slander, misrepresentation, deceit, or interference with contract rights: Provided, that, with regard to acts or omissions of investigative or law enforcement officers of the United States Government, the provisions of this chapter and section 1346(b) of this title shall apply to any claim arising, on or after the date of the enactment of this proviso, out of assault, battery, false imprisonment, false arrest, abuse of process, or malicious prosecution. For the purpose of this subsection, "investigative or law enforcement officer" means any officer of the United States who is empowered by law to execute searches, to seize evidence, or to make arrests for violations of Federal law.

To better understand this rule we should deconstruct it by creating an outline, flow chart or other organized version of the rule which sets out each of the elements that should be considered, and which shows the elements' relationship to one another.

Skill Focus: Rule Deconstruction

In addition to learning the substantive law of torts, a lawyer must possess certain critical skills which will also be covered in this text. The first skill we will cover, as part of this section on immunity, is rule deconstruction. Deconstructing a rule is the process of separating the rule into its component parts and understanding which of the parts must be proven in order to satisfy the rule. To deconstruct a rule you must first identify each part and subpart of the rule and then examine the language of the rule to determine the significance of that part or subpart. It is important to be able to identify, for example, whether that part or subpart is a required element that must be proven in order to succeed, or whether it is a factor that may be given consideration by the court, or whether it is an alternative to proving another element.

Lawyers need this skill for a variety of reasons. For example, when evaluating whether a client has a valid claim or defense, a lawyer might isolate each of the "parts" of that claim or defense, evaluating whether the facts presented by the client will be enough to allow the lawyer to prove each element, whether she needs additional facts to make that determination, or whether the client simply does not have a claim or defense. Lawyers also deconstruct rules as part of the process of drafting some legal documents. For example, rule deconstruction is used in the drafting of complaints, the document filed by the plaintiff to initiate a lawsuit. In many states the complaint must identify the elements of each cause of action alleged by the plaintiff and the key facts supporting such allegations—which requires that the lawyer identify each of the elements (i.e., the required "parts" and subparts"). Finally, this process of deconstructing a rule and applying it to the facts to evaluate each element of a rule (or cause of action) is also similar to what you will do on a law school examination to evaluate and answer hypothetical problems posed by your professor. As you can see, rule deconstruction is a very valuable skill.

Deconstructing a rule requires that you (1) identify all of the components of the rule; (2) understand which of the components must (as opposed to may) be proven in order to succeed; and (3) understand how the components are related to one another. In order to deconstruct rules of law it helps to know some of the most common rule components. Rules will typically be made up of one or more of these components:

A list of *factors* the court *may* consider in making its decision

A list of *mandatory elements* that *must* be proven in order to establish the rule is met

A *balancing test* requiring the court to *weigh* competing interests

An *either/or test* allowing proof of one or more *alternatives* to satisfy the rule

An *exception* to the general rule

You will probably begin to deconstruct rules automatically by the time you become a lawyer, but initially it will take some practice. This section contains rule deconstruction exercises in order to provide you with some initial practice, and you will likely want to deconstruct each of the rules you encounter, even if it is not assigned in one of the exercises.

It may help you to identify and understand the components of the rule if, as you begin to develop this skill, you ask yourself the following questions:

Are there any key words (and, or, either, factor, must, shall) to guide me in understanding the type of rule component and what must be proven?

What are all the things I would have to prove in order for my client to prevail?

What are all of the issues a trier of fact (judge, jury, etc.) would need to consider?

Have any cases isolated one of the parts of the rule—and further defined it?

A deconstructed version of 28 U.S.C. sections 1346(b)(1) and 2680(a) might look like this:

The federal government is not immune from liability where:

– an Employee (of the federal government)

– acting within the scope of his:

    office or

    employment,

– commits a:

    Negligent act, or

    Negligent omission, or

    Wrongful act, or

    Wrongful omission

– which causes

– money damages

    that accrue on or after January 1, 1945, and

    are for:

        Injury, or

        loss of property, or

        personal injury, or

        death

– if in accordance with the law of the place where the act or omission occurred,

– a private person in the same circumstances would be liable to the claimant

– unless, the employee

    was exercising due care,

    in the execution of a

        valid or invalid statute or

        valid or invalid regulation

– unless, the claim is based on

    the employee

        exercising or

        performing, or

        failing to exercise, or

        failing to perform, or

        abusing

    a discretionary

        function, or

        duty

    on the part of

        a federal agency or

        an employee of the Government

Notice that this deconstructed version of the rule allows you to "see" all of the pieces of the rule. To understand exactly what must be proven to satisfy the rule and to understand how the pieces of the rule are related to one another we will next want to identify the type of rule component (mandatory element, alternative test, etc.). Once you are finished, the deconstructed version of the rule should help you to identify each of the issues you must consider and help you evaluate whether you can prove all of the necessary "parts." For example, the deconstructed immunity rule could be used to help a lawyer analyze whether the federal government is immune by considering each piece of the statute and evaluating the client's facts by asking this series of questions:

> **Is the federal government immune from liability? (broad issue which requires consideration of each of the following issues)**
>
>> Is the potential defendant an employee of the federal government? (mandatory element)
>>
>> Was he acting within the scope of his office? Or his employment? (alternatives)
>>
>> Did he commit any of the following:
>>
>>> Negligent act, or
>>>
>>> Negligent omission, or
>>>
>>> Wrongful act, or
>>>
>>> Wrongful omission? (alternatives)
>>
>> Was his act or omission the cause of plaintiff's damages? (mandatory element)
>>
>> Is the suit for money damages? (mandatory element)
>>
>> Did the damages accrue on or after January 1, 1945? (mandatory element)
>>
>> Are the damages for one of the following:
>>
>>> Injury, or
>>>
>>> loss of property, or
>>>
>>> personal injury, or
>>>
>>> death? (alternatives)
>>
>> Where did the act or omission occur? (a necessary step to evaluate what law will apply)
>>
>> What is the law of the place where the act or omission occurred? (it is the law that applies to the next section)
>>
>> Would a private person in the same circumstances be liable to the claimant under that law? (this will require deconstructing the law from the prior question and applying it the same way we've just deconstructed the FTCA)

These are the questions a lawyer would ask in order to determine whether immunity existed. These are also the questions you would ask (and be required to answer) on an examination testing this immunity issue. These questions can also be turned into affirmative statements that could help a lawyer organize a motion related to this topic. For example:

I.   This action should be dismissed because the federal government is immune from liability for [state cause of action]

    A.   Defendant is an employee of the federal government

    B.   Defendant was acting within the scope of his office

There are multiple ways to organize this (and most other) statute(s). For example, for the statutes in this exercise you could start by asking whether the suit is for money damages. The key to rule deconstruction is to be certain you've identified each element so that you do not miss issues or skip analytical steps. Note that sometimes a deconstructed rule will follow the same order as the original rule and sometimes, if it makes it easier to understand the rule, it will be in a different order. So long as the deconstructed version does not alter or change the meaning of the rule, and includes all of the parts and subparts of the rule that are necessary to resolve the issue presented, it is acceptable to order the pieces of the rule differently.

For practice with this critical skill continue to draft questions (or statements) for the remaining deconstructed sections; you may also want to deconstruct 28 U.S.C. section 2680(h).

Exercise 1-1 Reflective Learning

A crucial skill for law students and lawyers is reflective learning. This means taking time to think about whether a selected strategy is working and how you might change what you are doing in order to do a better job in the future. For example, after reviewing the deconstructed rule set out above, you should think about the following:

1. Does the deconstructed version help you to understand the rule? Why or why not?

2. Are there changes you can make that would help you better understand the rule? (Note: be sure that changes you make do not alter the original meaning of the statute)

3. Is the federal government immune from suit for the intentional torts of its employees?

---

b. Governmental Immunity: State Statutes

Many states have enacted statutes retaining governmental immunity and thus limiting liability for state government entities. Many of these immunity statutes, like the Federal Tort Claims Act, apply to intentional conduct, including the intentional torts you will study in this chapter. Below is an example of one such immunity statute. For the next exercise you will deconstruct the statutes so that you understand each of the elements you should consider in evaluating whether a claim may be barred by the statute. You will then use your deconstructed statutes to evaluate whether any of the defendants from the chapter problem are potentially immune.

Exercise 1-2 Rule Deconstruction

Deconstruct the following immunity statutes. Remember that the purpose of deconstructing a statute is to determine which elements you would need to consider and prove to demonstrate to a court that either a plaintiff's claim is not covered by an immunity statute, if you represent the plaintiff, or, if you represent the defendant, to prove that it is. Also, remember that it is important not only to break the rule into each of its parts but also to think about how each of the parts are related to one another. Use your deconstructed statutes to evaluate whether any of the defendants from the chapter problem are potentially immune.

§ 50-21-22. Definitions

As used in this article, the term:

(1) "Claim" means any demand against the State for money only on account of loss caused by the tort of any state officer or employee committed while acting within the scope of his or her official duties or employment.

(2) "Discretionary function or duty" means a function or duty requiring a state officer or employee to exercise his or her policy judgment in choosing among alternate courses of action based upon a consideration of social, political, or economic factors.

(3) "Loss" means personal injury; disease; death; damage to tangible property, including lost wages and economic loss to the person who suffered the injury, disease, or death; pain and suffering; mental anguish; and any other element of actual damages recoverable in actions for negligence.

(4) "Occurrence" means an accident, including continuous or repeated exposure to substantially the same general harmful conditions.

(5) "State" means the State and any of its offices, agencies, authorities, departments, commissions, boards, divisions, instrumentalities, and institutions, but does not include counties, municipalities, school districts, other units of local government, hospital authorities, or housing and other local authorities.

(6) "State officer or employee" means an officer or employee of the state, elected or appointed officials, law enforcement officers, and persons acting on behalf or in service of the state in any official capacity, whether with or without compensation, but the term does not include an independent contractor doing business with the state. The term state officer or employee also includes any natural person who is a member of a board, commission, committee, task force, or similar body established to perform specific tasks or advisory functions, with or without compensation, for the state or a state government entity, and any natural person who is a volunteer participating as a volunteer, with or without compensation, in a structured volunteer program organized, controlled, and directed by a state government entity for the purposes of carrying out the functions of the state entity. Except as otherwise provided for in this paragraph, the term shall not include a corporation whether for profit or not for profit, or any private firm, business proprietorship, company, trust, partnership, association, or other such private entity.

§ 50-21-23. Limited waiver of sovereign immunity

(a) The state waives its sovereign immunity for the torts of state officers and employees while acting within the scope of their official duties or employment and shall be liable for such torts in the same manner as a private individual or entity would be liable under like circumstances; provided, however, that the state's sovereign immunity is waived subject to all exceptions and limitations set forth in this article. The state shall have no liability for losses resulting from conduct on the part of state officers or employees which was not within the scope of their official duties or employment.

§ 50-21-24. Exceptions and limitations

The state shall have no liability for losses resulting from:

(1) An act or omission by a state officer or employee exercising due care in the execution of a statute, regulation, rule, or ordinance, whether or not such statute, regulation, rule, or ordinance is valid;

(2) The exercise or performance of or the failure to exercise or perform a discretionary function or duty on the part of a state officer or employee, whether or not the discretion involved is abused.

Exercise 1-3 Law Practice

Find an immunity statute in the jurisdiction where you intend to practice. Imagine you represent a client whose claim is barred by the statute. How would you explain to a client that has suffered an injury that the law may not allow them to pursue their claim, and that they may not be compensated? Before you advise the client, it might be helpful to consider these questions (and your own reaction to the reading in this section): Did it surprise you to learn that some parties may be immune from liability for their tortious conduct or for the conduct of their employees? How would you feel if your claim was barred?

---

2. Can Plaintiff "Prove Up" the Prima Facie Case?

If the claim is not barred by governmental or other immunity (and, in actual practice, if there are no other bars to filing the suit) the next step to consider is whether the plaintiff can prove the prima facie case. The plaintiff has the burden of establishing the elements of the prima facie case, usually by a preponderance of the evidence. If the plaintiff fails to meet this burden, or if the defendant can negate one of these elements, there will be no liability. The plaintiff pleads these elements in the complaint she files to initiate the action. If the defendant believes the plaintiff has failed to sufficiently allege a cause of action, the defendant may file a motion to dismiss the claim, arguing to the court that the facts in plaintiff's complaint do not demonstrate that plaintiff will be able to prove up each of the required elements. It is therefore important to know and understand what is required to prove each element of the cause of action, also known as the prima facie case.

a. An Introduction to Intentional Torts

The seven intentional torts—battery, assault, intentional infliction of emotional distress, false imprisonment, trespass to land, trespass to chattel and conversion—each have a series of elements that must be proven in order to establish a cause of action for that tort. While the elements are different for each intentional tort, what they have in common is that each intentional tort requires an act, intent and a resulting consequence.

The act refers to the actual physical process by the tortfeasor that affects the injured person. To constitute an act for intentional torts purposes, the tortfeasor's conduct must be volitional, meaning that it involves a voluntary muscular contraction or movement, as opposed to a movement that results from a reflex or from a condition, such as sleep, during which the actor has no conscious control. In practice the act is usually not the difficult part to determine or prove. Rather, the more complicated and thus more challenging and more frequently litigated issue is whether the required intent was present.

In this chapter we will come to understand that in the context of intentional torts, intent means either (1) a desire or purpose that a given consequence will occur or (2) knowledge to a substantial certainty that a given consequence will occur. The required consequence is different for each of the intentional torts. For example, for false imprisonment, one of the intentional torts covered in this chapter, the required consequence is: confinement. Using the intent definition from above, this means that the intent element of false imprisonment requires that the tortfeasor either (1) desire or have the purpose to bring about (intend) the confinement (the consequence) or (2) know with substantial certainty (intend) that confinement (the consequence) will result.

Since the meaning of intent is inextricably linked to the consequence, it is important to understand the required consequence for the intentional tort before analyzing whether the tortfeasor has the requisite intent for that tort. As you study each of the intentional torts ask yourself the following questions:

1. What is the required consequence?

2. Did the tortfeasor have the desire to bring about that consequence? Or know with substantial certainty that the consequence would occur?

b. Proving the Prima Facie Case for Battery

Battery is the first of the seven intentional torts we will study. While there is some variation, liability for battery usually requires proof of (1) intent; (2) a contact that is harmful or offensive; and (3) that the contact be with the person of another.

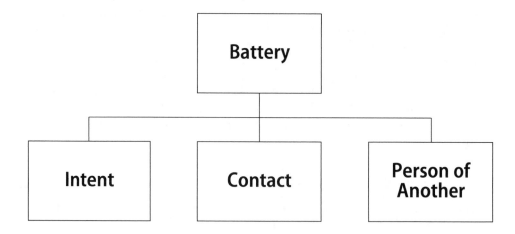

These elements, which we will explore in detail, make up the prima facie case for battery. As you develop your understanding of the law in the next section, remember to evaluate whether Ryan Watson (from our chapter problem) will be able to prove up the elements of the prima facie case.

(1) Intent: What Consequences Must the Actor Intend?

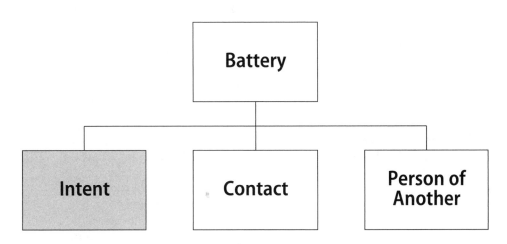

In this section you will learn about the law of intent through reading case opinions. Lawyers use cases for a number of reasons, including to learn about the law, to analyze and predict what the court will do in their cases and to argue to the court on behalf of their clients. For this reason, it is important to become proficient at reading cases and extracting the details and information a lawyer would need, which is why we will focus on several critical case related skills in this chapter: case reading, case briefing, and applying and distinguishing case law.

Skill Focus: Case Reading[1]

During the three to four years you spend in law school you will spend a good deal of your time reading, and that reading will include large quantities of complex material. This reading will be different from other academic reading you have done in the past. You will read not only to develop knowledge and understanding of the substantive rules of law and the subject area you are studying, but also to develop a new professional vocabulary and an understanding of how the legal system works. You will also read to develop your ability to think in the way that characterizes legal decision-making.

Your goal should be to become an expert at reading legal materials, including cases. As you develop expertise, you'll read more efficiently, and you'll be better able to participate in class discussions, to prepare for exams, and to keep your life balanced. You can begin to develop expert reading skills by understanding what expert readers do. Below are some important characteristics of expert readers.

---

1. This section is based on: Ruth McKinney, *Reading Like a Lawyer* (Carolina Academic Press), an excellent text for any student interested in improving legal reading skills.

- **Expert readers read for a clearly identified purpose.** Before you read a case in this text, read and think about the introductory materials, chapter problems and questions that precede the case. These materials, problems and questions are designed to help you understand the purpose for including the case in this text, as well as to provide you context and purpose for reading the materials.

- **Expert readers pay attention to words that have special meaning in the context of the reading.** As a novice legal reader you will encounter terminology that you have not seen before, as well as terminology that is familiar, but seems to have special meaning in the context of legal reading. You should look up these terms in a legal dictionary and continue to look up new terms throughout your legal career, whenever a term is unfamiliar or appears to have special meaning.

- **Expert readers read for the main idea, while understanding that they may need to attend to many small concepts in order to grasp the main idea.** When you read a case, pay attention to the headings in the text to understand why the case is included—i.e., the main point the author hopes you will learn and understand. In addition, pay attention to the facts and details the court relied on in reaching the decision, including the reasons articulated by the court and any examples or other cases the court compares with the facts of the dispute presently before the court. Also, any questions at the beginning or end of the reading are intended to help you evaluate whether you understood the material, including the main idea and key details.

- **Expert readers look for large themes and important principles as they read.** Each of the cases you read is intended to apply not only to the dispute in the case but to future disputes. Cases establish precedent to be followed by courts in deciding future cases. Understanding the general principles and rules in each case, as well as how the court applied the rules, and why the court reached its decision, will help you predict the outcome of future disputes the court will hear (including those involving your clients). If you develop an understanding of the overarching principles in each case you will be able to apply those principles to future hypotheticals (e.g., class discussion and law school exams) and it may help you understand how the cases in the text are related to one another. You will also use this skill in practice when you apply the reasoning from the cases you read to the disputes your clients face, to predict what the court will do, or to persuade the court to rule for your client.

- **Expert readers understand that they need to interact with the text, and they engage in a dialogue with the text rather than simply "taking in" the information.** As you read the text, and cases, visualize the "action" in the cases and take note of your own ideas. You may not be encouraged to voice your personal feelings in class, but ignoring or dismissing your personal reactions can slow down your reading process, so you should continue to acknowledge personal reactions even if they do not have an outlet in the classroom. If you visualize what is going on, rather than merely moving from word to word, and allow yourself to have personal reactions to what you read, your reading skills will improve.

In addition to reading for all of these purposes, you should also understand that the assigned reading is just one part of an interrelated experience. The reading you are assigned before class begins is related to the discussion that follows in class. Your class session will not usually be a review of what you have read, but a discussion of how the reading applies in new and different contexts.

(a) Proving Intent: A Difference of (Judicial) Opinion

The first two cases in this chapter are written by two different courts confronting the same issue: intent in the context of battery. The dilemma in both cases is whether, for purposes of establishing liability for battery, the tortfeasor must intend that the contact be harmful or offensive or whether the tortfeasor must simply desire to make a contact and that such contact end up being a harmful or offensive one. The courts reach different conclusions. As you read the cases evaluate the reasoning each court employs and think about which decision you agree with (and the reasons you agree). You may want to consider the following:

1. What accounts for the differing results in these cases?

2. Did the courts apply the same legal rules? In the same way? If not, why not?

3. In writing legal opinions, courts purport to engage in doctrinal analysis; in other words, the courts apply legal rules to the facts of the case in order to reach a result. Sometimes, indeed perhaps often, a court's decision does not rest solely on doctrinal concerns. Rather, courts consider or are influenced by policy considerations both in their adoption of a given legal rule, and in their application of existing rules. "Policy" refers to any social, economic, political, moral or other principle, goal or value reflected in a legal rule. Can you identify any policies that might have prompted these courts to rule the way they did?

Wagner v. Utah

122 P.3d 599 (Utah 2005)[2]

Tracy and Robert Wagner seek review of the court of appeals' ruling that the trial court properly granted a motion dismissing their suit [for failure to state a claim] against the State. The Wagners' suit, which sought recovery for injuries Mrs. Wagner sustained when a mentally handicapped man attacked her while he was in the custody of state employees, was dismissed at the trial court, and affirmed at the court of appeals, on the ground that

---

2. Much of the litigation involving intentional torts is actually about disputes over whether the defendant is immune from liability. For this reason many of the cases you will read, including cases in this section, are set in the context of whether an immunity statute applies. In such cases, students beginning the study of intentional torts may feel a little confused. You might expect the plaintiff, the party who is injured, to be arguing that the defendant committed an intentional tort so that she might establish a basis for holding the defendant liable for her injuries. However, if the immunity statute will prevent the plaintiff from recovering against the defendant for intentionally tortious conduct, the plaintiff may instead be trying to establish the defendant's conduct was not intentional and thus not covered by the immunity statute. On the other hand, the defendant in such cases is likely arguing the tortious conduct was intentional, so that the conduct is covered by the immunity statute, which will prevent the court from holding defendant liable. Essentially, the parties expected roles are reversed.

the attack constituted a battery, a tort for which the State has retained immunity from suit. The Wagners then petitioned this court for certiorari, which we granted. We now affirm.

BACKGROUND

Tracy Wagner was standing in a customer service line at a K-Mart store in American Fork, Utah, when she was suddenly and inexplicably attacked from behind. The Wagners' alleged that Sam Giese, a mentally disabled patient of the Utah State Development Center ("USDC"), "became violent, took [Mrs. Wagner] by the head and hair, threw her to the ground, and otherwise acted in such a way as to cause serious bodily injury to her."

USDC employees had accompanied Mr. Giese to K-Mart as part of his treatment program and had remained in K-Mart to supervise him. While this particular episode of violence was sudden, it was not altogether unpredictable. Mr. Giese had a history of violent conduct and presented a potential danger to the public if not properly supervised.

Mrs. Wagner and her husband subsequently filed a complaint against USDC for failing to "properly supervise the activity of" Mr. Giese while he was in its care. [D]efendants . . . moved to dismiss the complaint . . . for failure to state a claim, arguing that Mrs. Wagner's injuries arose out of a battery, a tort for which the government is immune from suit. The district court agreed with the government and dismissed the Wagners' complaint, holding that because Giese initiated a contact with "deliberate" intent, his attack constituted a battery and the government was immune under the statute.

The Wagners appealed the decision to the court of appeals, arguing that the intentional tort of battery requires proof of both an intent to make a contact and an intent to cause harm thereby, and because Mr. Giese was mentally incompetent to formulate the intent to cause harm, his attack could not constitute a battery as a matter of law. The defendants, on the other hand, maintained that a person need only intend to make a harmful or offensive contact in order for that contact to constitute a battery upon another. A person need not intend to cause harm or appreciate that his contact will cause harm so long as he intends to make a contact, and that contact is harmful.

* * *

The court of appeals . . . declin[ed] to incorporate a requirement that the perpetrator have a certain mental state at the moment of the attack in order for that attack to constitute a battery. The Wagners appealed to this court. . . .

* * *

ANALYSIS

The Wagners argue that Mr. Giese's attack could not legally constitute a battery because that intentional tort requires the actor to intend harm or offense through his deliberate contact, an intent Mr. Giese was mentally incompetent to form. The State, on the other hand, argues that the only intent required under the statute is simply the intent to make a contact. The contact must be harmful or offensive by law, but the actor need not intend harm so long as he intended contact.

The outcome of this case, then, turns upon which interpretation of the definition of battery is correct. Accordingly, we turn our attention now to the law of battery as defined in the Restatement.

THE RESTATEMENT DEFINITION OF BATTERY

While there is some variation among the definitions of the tort of battery, [citations omitted], Utah has adopted the Second Restatement of Torts to define the elements of this intentional tort, including the element of intent. *Tiede v. State,* 915 P.2d 500, 503 n. 3. The Restatement reads:

> An actor is subject to liability to another for battery if:
>
> (a) he acts intending to cause a harmful or offensive contact with the person of the other or a third person, or an imminent apprehension of such a contact, and
>
> (b) a harmful contact with the person of the other directly or indirectly results.

Restatement (Second) of Torts § 13 (1965).

The only point of dispute in this case is whether the language of the Restatement requires Mr. Giese to have intended not only to make physical contact with Mrs. Wagner, which the Wagners concede he did, but also to have intended the contact to be harmful or offensive. In other words, is a battery committed only when the actor intends for his contact to harm or offend, or is it sufficient that the actor deliberately make physical contact, which contact is harmful or offensive by law? Determining the answer requires a careful dissection of the elements of battery and the meaning of intent.

* * *

We hold that the actor need not intend that his contact be harmful or offensive in order to commit a battery so long as he deliberately made the contact and so long as that contact satisfies our legal test for what is harmful or offensive.

* * *

We begin our analysis with the language in the Restatement itself. The Restatement defines a battery as having occurred where "[an actor] acts intending to cause a harmful or offensive contact." Restatement (Second) of Torts § 13. The comments to the definition of battery refer the reader to the definition of intent in section 8A. *Id.* § 13 cmt. c. Section 8A reads: The word "intent" is used throughout the Restatement of this Subject to denote that the actor desires to cause *the consequences of his act,* or that he believes that the consequences are substantially certain to result from it. *Id.* § 8A (emphasis added).

Although this language might not immediately seem to further inform our analysis, the comments to this section do illustrate the difference between an intentional act and an unintentional one: the existence of intent as to the contact that results from the act. Because much of the confusion surrounding the intent element required in an intentional tort arises from erroneously conflating the act with the consequence intended, we must clarify these basic terms as they are used in our law before we analyze the legal significance of intent as to an act versus intent as to the consequences of that act.

Section 2 of the Restatement (Second) of Torts defines the term "act" as "an external manifestation of the actor's will and does not include any of its results, even the most direct, immediate, and intended." *Id.* § 2. To illustrate this point, the comments clarify that when an actor points a pistol at another person and pulls the trigger, the act is the pulling of the trigger. *Id.* at cmt. c. The consequence of that act is the "impingement of the bullet upon the other's person." *Id.* It would be improper to describe the act as "the shooting," since the shooting is actually the conflation of the act with the consequence. For another example, the act that has taken place when one intentionally strikes another with his fist "is only the movement of the actor's hand and not the contact with the others body immediately established." *Id.* Thus, presuming that the movement was voluntary rather than spastic, whether an actor has committed an intentional or negligent contact with another, and thus a tort sounding in battery or negligence, depends not upon whether he intended to move his hand, but upon whether he intended to make contact thereby.

The example the Restatement sets forth to illustrate this point is that of an actor firing a gun into the Mojave Desert. Restatement (Second of Torts) § 8A cmt. a. In both accidental and intentional shootings, the actor intended to pull the trigger. *Id.* Battery liability, rather than liability sounding in negligence, will attach only when the actor pulled the trigger in order to shoot another person, or knowing that it was substantially likely that pulling the trigger would lead to that result. *Id.* § 8A cmts. a & b. An actor who intentionally fires a bullet, but who does not realize that the bullet would make contact with another person, as when "the bullet hits a person who is present in the desert without the actor's knowledge," is not liable for an intentional tort. *Id.*

A hunter, for example, may intentionally fire his gun in an attempt to shoot a bird, but may accidentally shoot a person whom he had no reason to know was in the vicinity. He intended his act, pulling the trigger, but not the contact between his bullet and the body of another that resulted from that act. Thus, he intended the act but not the consequence. It is the consequential contact with the other person that the actor must either intend or be substantially certain would result, not the act — pulling the trigger — itself. He is therefore not liable for an intentional tort because his intentional act resulted in an unintended contact. On the other hand, the actor is liable for an intentional tort if he pulled the trigger intending that the bullet released thereby would strike someone, or knowing that it was substantially likely to strike someone as a result of his act. *Id.* at cmts. a & b.

Can an actor who acknowledges that he intentionally pulled the trigger, and did so with the intent that the bullet make contact with the person of another, defeat a battery charge if he can show that he did so only as a joke, or did not intend that the contact between the bullet and the body of the person would cause harm or offense to that person? The Wagners argue that such a showing would provide a full defense to a battery charge because the actor lacked the necessary intent to harm.

We agree with the Wagners that not all intentional contacts are actionable as batteries, and that the contact must be harmful or offensive in order to be actionable. We do not agree, however, that, under our civil law, the actor must appreciate that his act is harmful or offensive in order for his contact to constitute a battery.

* * *

The linchpin to liability for battery is not a guilty mind, but rather an intent to make a contact the law forbids. The actor need not appreciate that his contact is forbidden; he need only intend the contact, and the contact must, in fact, be forbidden.

The Restatement comments illustrate this principle using two examples. In the first, an actor playing a good-natured practical joke, under the mistaken belief that he has his victim's consent to make the contact, has committed a battery. *Id.* In the second example, the healing contact of a physician, acting with helpful intent but against the patient's wishes, constituted a battery. *Id.* The fact that the procedure preserved the patient's life does not change the result. *Id.* (citations omitted).

If a physician who has performed a life-saving act of assistance upon an unconsenting patient with the hope of making that patient whole is liable for battery under the express terms of the Restatement, and a practical joker who makes a contact which he thinks will be taken as a joke or to which he thinks his victim has actually given consent is likewise liable, we cannot then say that other actors must intend harm through their deliberate contact in order to perfect a battery. It is beyond argument that the Restatement itself requires neither a "desire to injure" nor a realization that the contact is injurious or offensive. Restatement (Second) of Torts § 13. Instead, the actor need only intend the contact itself, and that contact must fit the legal definition of harmful or offensive.

* * *

Otherwise, the law would err on the side of protecting actors who voluntarily make physical contacts with other people, producing injury or offense, from liability for their deliberate action. The result would be that the victims who were subjected to a harmful or offensive physical contact are at the mercy of those who deliberately come into contact with them, and must bear the costs of the injuries inflicted thereby. The practical consequences of such an interpretation would turn the law of our civil liability on its head.

For example, a man who decides to flatter a woman he spots in a crowd with an un-petitioned-for kiss, ... would find no objection under the Wagners' proposed rule so long as his intentional contact was initiated with no intent to injure or offend. He would be held civilly liable for his conduct only if he intended to harm or offend her through his kiss. A woman in such circumstances would not enjoy the presumption of the law in favor of preserving her bodily integrity; instead, her right to be free from physical contact with strangers would depend upon whether she could prove that the stranger hoped to harm or offend her through his contact. So long as he could show that he meant only flattery and the communication of positive feelings towards her in stroking her, kissing her, or hugging her, she must be subjected to it and will find no protection for her bodily integrity in our civil law.

The law would serve to insulate perpetrators of deliberate contact from the consequences their contact inflicts upon their victims. Bodily integrity would be secondary to protecting a perpetrator's right to deliberately touch another person's body without being accountable for the consequences that contact occasioned. The "harmful or offensive" element would, in essence, be viewed from the perspective of the actor, not the objective eye of the law. Under this rule, so long as the actor does not deem his deliberate contact to be harmful or offensive, he may touch others however he wishes without liability under our law of battery. It is clear that the purpose of our civil law on battery was designed to create the opposite incentive. See, e.g., Restatement (Second) of Torts § 283B cmts. b & c.

The objection can be raised that such a theory of liability as we posit today expands liability beyond all reasonable bounds. Perhaps a handshake or other similar gesture will now expose a person to a lawsuit for battery if he happens to unknowingly shake the hand of an unwilling individual. The Restatement, however, ... yields this objection wholly without basis.

We must bear in mind that not all physical contacts deliberately initiated constitute batteries, only harmful or offensive ones. Though it is true that the actor need not appreciate that his contact is, nor need he intend it to be, harmful or offensive in order for it to be so and for him to be accountable for the injuries he inflicted by his intentional contact, the contact must in fact be harmful or offensive in order to constitute a battery.

* * *

[I]f we were to adopt the rule urged by the Wagners, we would be contorting the law in order to provide recovery in this isolated instance. Yet, in doing so, we would be contracting the recoveries of all other plaintiffs victimized by insane or mentally handicapped individuals who are suing a non-State entity, and, in the process, limiting the protection of the bodily integrity of everyone.

The policy behind the Restatement definition of battery is to allow plaintiffs to recover from individuals who have caused them legal harm or injury, and to lay at the feet of the perpetrators the expense of their own conduct.

We recognize that, in this instance, the retained immunity doctrine bars the caretakers of such a handicapped person from taking responsibility for the conduct of their charge.

It is unfortunate, and perhaps it is improvident of the State to retain immunity in this area. But it is not our role as a judiciary to override the legislature in this matter; it is for us only to interpret and apply the law as it is. We will not limit the recoveries of all other plaintiffs similarly injured by defining the tort of battery in such a way as to make it far more burdensome for plaintiffs to satisfy its elements and recover, nor will we distort the plain language of the Restatement so as to elevate an actor's "right" to deliberately touch others at will over an individual's right to the preservation of her bodily integrity.

CONCLUSION

Applying the rule we have laid out today to the facts of this case, it is clear that Mr. Giese's attack constituted a battery upon Mrs. Wagner. The fact that the Wagners allege that Mr. Giese could not have intended to harm her, or understood that his attack would inflict injury or offense, is not relevant to the analysis of whether a battery occurred. So long as he intended to make that contact, and so long as that contact was one to which Mrs. Wagner had not given her consent, either expressly or by implication, he committed a battery. Because battery is a tort for which the State has retained immunity, we affirm the court of appeals' decision to dismiss the case for failure to state a claim.

White v. Muniz
999 P.2d 814 (Colo. 2000)

Petitioner, Barbara White, as personal representative of the estate of Helen Everly, appeals the decision of the court of appeals in *Muniz v. White*, 979 P.2d 23, 25 (Colo.App.1998), which determined that a mentally incapacitated adult should be held liable for her intentional tort even if she was unable to appreciate the wrongfulness of her actions. We disagree with the court of appeals. Rather, we conclude that under the facts present in this case, in order to recover on a theory of intentional tort, the plaintiff, Sherry Lynn Muniz, was required to prove that Everly intended to commit an act and that Everly intended the act to result in a harmful or offensive contact. Accordingly, we reverse the court of appeals, and remand for reinstatement of the jury verdict in favor of the defendant.

In October of 1993, Barbara White placed her eighty-three year-old grandmother, Helen Everly, in an assisted living facility, the Beatrice Hover Personal Care Center. Within a few days of admission, Everly started exhibiting erratic behavior. She became agitated easily, and occasionally acted aggressively toward others.

On November 21, 1993, the caregiver in charge of Everly's wing asked Sherry Lynn Muniz, a shift supervisor at Hover, to change Everly's adult diaper. The caregiver informed Muniz that Everly was not cooperating in that effort. This did not surprise Muniz because she knew that Everly sometimes acted obstinately. Indeed, initially Everly refused to allow Muniz to change her diaper, but eventually Muniz thought that Everly relented. However, as Muniz reached toward the diaper, Everly struck Muniz on the jaw and ordered her out of the room.

The next day, Dr. Haven Howell, M.D. examined Everly at Longmont United Hospital. She diagnosed Everly with "[p]rimary degenerative dementia of the Alzheimer type, senile onset, with depression."

In November of 1994, Muniz filed suit alleging assault and battery against Everly.... While arguing outside the presence of the jury for specific jury instructions, the parties took differing positions on the mental state required to commit the alleged intentional torts. Muniz requested the following instruction: "A person who has been found incompetent may intend to do an act even if he or she lacked control of reason and acted unreasonably." White tendered a different instruction:

A person intends to make a contact with another person if he or she does an act for the purpose of bringing about such a contact, whether or not he or she also intends that the contact be harmful or offensive. The intent must include some awareness of the natural consequences of intentional acts, and the person must appreciate the consequences of intentional acts, and the person must appreciate the offensiveness or wrongfulness of her acts.

The trial court settled on a slightly modified version of White's instruction. It read:

A person intends to make a contact with another person if she does an act for the purpose of bringing about such a contact, whether or not she also intends that the contact be harmful or offensive.

The fact that a person may suffer from Dementia, Alzheimer type, does not prevent a finding that she acted intentionally. You may find that she acted intentionally if she intended to do what she did, even though her reasons and motives were entirely irrational. *However, she must have appreciated the offensiveness of her conduct.* (Emphasis added.)

In selecting the instruction on intent, the trial court determined that Everly's condition rendered her mental state comparable to that of a child.

Muniz's counsel objected to the last sentence of the instruction, claiming that it misstated the law. He argued that the instruction improperly broadened the holding in *Horton v. Reaves,* 186 Colo. 149, 526 P.2d 304 (1974), where the supreme court held that an infant must appreciate the offensiveness or wrongfulness of her conduct to be liable for an intentional tort. The jury rendered verdicts in favor of Everly and White.

The court of appeals reversed the decision of the trial court and remanded the case for a new trial. The court of appeals reasoned that most states continue to hold mentally deficient plaintiffs liable for their intentional acts regardless of their ability to understand the offensiveness of their actions. "[W]here one of two innocent persons must suffer a loss, it should be borne by the one who occasioned it." *Muniz v. White,* 979 P.2d 23, 25 (Colo.App.1998). The court of appeals ... concluded that the trial court erred in "instructing the jury that Everly must have appreciated the offensiveness of her conduct." *Id.* at 26.

II.

The question we here address is whether an intentional tort requires some proof that the tortfeasor not only intended to contact another person, but also intended that the contact be harmful or offensive to the other person.

A.

State courts and legal commentators generally agree that an intentional tort requires some proof that the tortfeasor intended harm or offense. *See* W. Page Keeton et al., *Prosser and Keeton on the Law of Torts* § 8 (5th ed.1984); Dan B. Dobbs, *The Law of Torts* § 30 (2000). According to the Restatement (Second) of Torts,

(1) An actor is subject to liability to another for battery if

(a) he acts *intending to cause a harmful or offensive contact* with the person of the other or a third person, or an imminent apprehension of such a contact, and

(b) an offensive [or harmful] contact with the person of the other directly or indirectly results.

(2) An act which is not done with the intention stated in Subsection (1, a) does not make the actor liable to the other for a mere offensive contact with the other's person although the act involves an unreasonable risk of inflicting it and, therefore, would be negligent or reckless if the risk threatened bodily harm.

Restatement (Second) of Torts § 18 (1965) (emphasis added).

Historically, the intentional tort of battery required a subjective desire on the part of the tortfeasor to inflict a harmful or offensive contact on another. *See* Restatement, *supra*, § 8A; Keeton, *supra*, § 8; 6 Am.Jur.2d *Assault and Battery* § 8 (1999). Thus, it was not enough that a person intentionally contacted another *resulting* in a harmful or offensive contact. *See* Restatement, *supra*, § 18 cmt. e; Keeton § 8. Instead, the actor had to understand that his contact would be harmful or offensive. *See* Keeton, *supra*, § 8; Dobbs, *supra*, § 29. The actor need not have intended, however, the harm that actually resulted from his action. *See* Restatement, *supra*, § 16(1). Thus, if a slight punch to the victim resulted in traumatic injuries, the actor would be liable for all the damages resulting from the battery even if he only intended to knock the wind out of the victim. *See id.*

Juries may find it difficult to determine the mental state of an actor, but they may rely on circumstantial evidence in reaching their conclusion. No person can pinpoint the thoughts in the mind of another, but a jury can examine the facts to conclude what another must have been thinking. *See* Keeton, *supra*, § 8. For example, a person of reasonable intelligence knows with substantial certainty that a stone thrown into a crowd will strike someone and result in an offensive or harmful contact to that person. *See id.* Hence, if an actor of average intelligence performs such an act, the jury can determine that the actor had the requisite intent to cause a harmful or offensive contact, even though the actor denies having such thoughts. *See id.*

B.

More recently, some courts around the nation have abandoned this dual intent requirement in an intentional tort setting, that being an intent to contact and an intent that the contact be harmful or offensive, and have required only that the tortfeasor intend a contact with another that *results* in a harmful or offensive touching. *See Brzoska v. Olson,* 668 A.2d 1355, 1360 (Del.1995) (citations omitted). Under this view, a victim need only prove that a voluntary movement by the tortfeasor resulted in a contact which a reasonable person would find offensive or to which the victim did not consent. *See University of Idaho,* 118 Idaho 400, 797 P.2d at 111. These courts would find intent in contact to the back of a friend that results in a severe, unexpected injury even though the actor did not intend the contact to be harmful or offensive. *See id.* 118 Idaho 400, 797 P.2d at 109. The actor thus could be held liable for battery because a reasonable person would find an injury offensive or harmful, irrespective of the intent of the actor to harm or offend.

Courts occasionally have intertwined these two distinct understandings of the requisite intent. In most instances when the defendant is a mentally alert adult, this commingling of definitions prejudices neither the plaintiff nor the defendant. However, when evaluating the culpability of particular classes of defendants, such as the very young and the mentally disabled, the intent required by a jurisdiction becomes critical.

In *Horton v. Reaves,* 186 Colo. 149, 526 P.2d 304 (1974), we examined the jury instructions used to determine if a four-year-old boy and a three-year-old boy intentionally battered an infant when they dropped a baby who suffered skull injuries as a result. We held that although a child need not intend the resulting harm, the child must understand that the contact may be harmful in order to be held liable. *See Horton,* 186 Colo. at

155–56, 526 P.2d at 307–08. Our conclusion comported with the Restatement's definition of intent; it did not state a new special rule for children, but applied the general rule to the context of an intentional tort of battery committed by a child. Because a child made the contact, the jury had to examine the objective evidence to determine if the child actors intended their actions to be offensive or harmful. This result complied with both the Colorado jury instruction at the time, and the definition of battery in the Restatement. *See id.*

C.

In this case, we have the opportunity to examine intent in the context of an injury inflicted by a mentally deficient, Alzheimer's patient. White seeks an extension of *Horton* to the mentally ill, and Muniz argues that a mere voluntary movement by Everly can constitute the requisite intent. We find that the law of Colorado requires the jury to conclude that the defendant both intended the contact and intended it to be harmful or offensive.

III.

Because Colorado law requires a dual intent, we apply here the Restatement's definition of the term. As a result, we reject the arguments of Muniz and find that the trial court delivered an adequate instruction to the jury.

Operating in accordance with this instruction, the jury had to find that Everly appreciated the offensiveness of her conduct in order to be liable for the intentional tort of battery. It necessarily had to consider her mental capabilities in making such a finding, including her age, infirmity, education, skill, or any other characteristic as to which the jury had evidence. We presume that the jury "looked into the mind of Everly," and reasoned that Everly did not possess the necessary intent to commit ... a battery. *See Hall v. Walter,* 969 P.2d 224, 238 (Colo.1998) (stating that the court presumes the jury followed instructions in reaching its verdict).

A jury can, of course, find a mentally deficient person liable for an intentional tort, but in order to do so, the jury must find that the actor intended offensive or harmful consequences. As a result, insanity is not a defense to an intentional tort according to the ordinary use of that term, but is a characteristic, like infancy, that may make it more difficult to prove the intent element of battery. Our decision today does not create a special rule for the elderly, but applies Colorado's intent requirement in the context of a woman suffering the effects of Alzheimer's.

Contrary to Muniz's arguments, policy reasons do not compel a different result. Injured parties consistently have argued that even if the tortfeasor intended no harm or offense, "where one of two innocent persons must suffer a loss, it should be borne by the one who occasioned it." Keeton, *supra,* § 135. Our decision may appear to erode that principle. Yet, our decision does not bar future injured persons from seeking compensation. Victims may still bring intentional tort actions against mentally disabled adults, but to prevail, they must prove all the elements of the alleged tort.

IV.

With regard to the intent element of ... battery, we hold that regardless of the characteristics of the alleged tortfeasor, a plaintiff must prove that the actor desired to cause offensive or harmful consequences by his act. The plaintiff need not prove, however, that the actor intended the harm that actually results. Accordingly, we reverse the decision of the court of appeals, and remand the case to that court for reinstatement of the jury verdict in favor of White and consideration of any remaining issues.

Questions for *Wagner* and *White*

1. According to *Wagner*, what is the consequence that the tortfeasor must intend in order to have sufficient intent for battery?

2. According to *White*, what is the consequence that the tortfeasor must intend in order to have sufficient intent for battery?

3. Does the standard adopted by the *White* court make intent for battery more or less difficult to prove? Why?

4. The courts both cite to the Restatement. What is the Restatement? Are courts required to follow the Restatement? How does the Restatement differ from state statutes?

Skill Focus: Case Briefing

Now that you have finished reading these first two cases, you will want to take notes so that you are able to remember information about the cases and be able to discuss and apply the concepts you have learned during class discussion. As a lawyer you will likely have to remember and discuss cases you have read with clients, other attorneys in your practice, and judges. When you discuss concepts and cases in class and in practice you may or may not be asked about the traditional parts of a case brief. However, most legally trained readers (which includes your professor) will probably be thinking in terms of the specific types of information that are included in traditional case briefs. Even if you do not write out a traditional brief for each case, it is important that you have identified and thought about each of these pieces so that you are prepared to participate in class discussion and so that you practice thinking about cases the way a legally trained reader will. Below is a list and description of the parts of a traditional case brief.

- **The Heading or Citation.** This tells you where you can find the case.

- **The Parties.** These are the people or entities involved in the conflict described in the case.

- **The Procedural History.** This is what happened to the case before it got to the court writing the opinion you are reading.

- **The Legally Significant Facts.** These are the facts that created the conflict and that the court considers when resolving the conflict. Sometimes this will include procedural facts.

- **The Issue or Question Presented.** This is the legal question the court is answering or resolving. There may be more than one issue or question presented. As you try to identify the issue or question presented, consider the sub-topic heading of your casebook.

- **The Holding.**[3] This is the court's decision—the answer to the issue or question presented. It resolves the conflict.

---

3. Sometimes the term holding is used to indicate the rule and reasoning the court uses to answer the question presented. In this text the term holding will be used to include the answer to the question presented, as well as the rule and reasoning used by the court.

- **The Rule.** This is the legal principle applied by the court to answer or resolve the issue or question presented. A rule can be carried forward to resolve similar conflicts in the future.

- **The Reasoning.** This is the court's train of thought as it reaches the answer to the issue presented. Sometimes this section includes an analysis of policy issues that influenced the court. This section can be carried forward to determine whether and how the case should be applied to future conflicts

In addition to the traditional parts of a case brief, you may also find it helpful to include other sections. For example, it may be helpful to include a section about your own ideas — the thoughts and questions that you have as you read the case. Keeping notes of the thoughts that emerge as you read a case helps you focus, keeps you invested in what you read, clarifies your thinking, and encourages you to find patterns. It also helps you to remember what you have read, so that you can apply it later — in class discussion and on examinations.

It may also help to think about what "category" each party can fall into. This will help you to develop skills you will need as a lawyer. In practice, you will usually read cases in an effort to determine how a court might rule in your client's case or to find a case that helps you persuade the court to rule for your client. You will rarely find a case that is exactly like yours, and instead will have to look to similar cases to predict the outcome in your case. It helps to learn to think about cases in terms of broad categories, rather than as limited to the exact facts in the case you are reading, and to think about how the case will apply to new and different contexts.

You should also try to develop a working hypothesis about the point of the case and how it fits into the course as a whole. This will help you to understand how the cases that you read are related to one another, to other topics and to the course as a whole, rather than to view each case in isolation.

Exercise 1-4 Case Briefing

Complete a brief for *White* and *Wagner*, using the guidelines above, and any instructions from your professor.

Exercise 1-5 Law Practice

The *Wagner* court follows the majority rule. Find the battery rule in the jurisdiction in which you intend to practice; does the jurisdiction follow *Wagner* or *White* or something else entirely?

(b) Proving Intent: Establishing Defendant's State of Mind

When a plaintiff files a claim for battery it is rare that the defendant will admit to possessing the required intent. Instead, intent must be inferred from the facts and circumstances (proven by circumstantial evidence). It may help to imagine the dispute as similar to a common school yard dispute, where one child reports to the teacher: "She hit me!" and the accused child responds: "I didn't mean to!" or "It was an accident." The teacher cannot see into the mind of the accused child so the teacher must determine the accused child's intent from the facts and circumstances, much the same way the jury (or court) must infer the accused tortfeasor's intent from the facts and circumstances surrounding the battery claim. The *White* court describes the process this way:

> Juries may find it difficult to determine the mental state of an actor, but they may rely on circumstantial evidence in reaching their conclusion. No person can pinpoint the thoughts in the mind of another, but a jury can examine the facts to conclude what another must have been thinking. *See Keeton, supra,* §8. For example, a person of reasonable intelligence knows with substantial certainty that a stone thrown into a crowd will strike someone and result in an offensive or harmful contact to that person. *See id.* Hence, if an actor of average intelligence performs such an act, the jury can determine that the actor had the requisite intent to cause a harmful or offensive contact, even though the actor denies having such thoughts. *See id.*

If you were the teacher attempting to determine whether the child really "didn't mean to," what facts and circumstances might help you assess the accused child's intent? How can you infer intent from the facts and circumstances?

As you read the next case, consider how the court draws inferences from the facts and circumstances to determine that the defendant had the required intent for battery even though the defendant claimed that the contact was accidental.

Nelson v. Carroll

355 Md. 593, 735 A.2d 1096 (Md. Ct. App 1999)

This case requires that we determine the extent to which a claim of accident may provide a defense to a civil action for battery arising out of a gunshot wound. Charles A. Nelson, the plaintiff in this case and the petitioner here, asserts that the trial court should have held Albert Carroll, the defendant and respondent, liable for the tort of battery as a matter of law, sending to the jury only the issue of damages. We agree with Nelson that a claim of "accident" provides no defense to a battery claim where the evidence is undisputed that Nelson was shot by Carroll as Carroll threatened and struck him on the side of his head with the handgun.

Carroll shot Nelson in the stomach in the course of an altercation over a debt owed to Carroll by Nelson. The shooting occurred on the evening of July 25, 1992, in a private nightclub in Baltimore City that Nelson was patronizing. Carroll, who was described as being a "little tipsy," entered the club and demanded repayment by Nelson of the $3,800 balance of an $8,000 loan that Carroll had made to Nelson. Nelson immediately offered to make a payment on account but that was unsatisfactory to Carroll. At some point Carroll produced a handgun from his jacket.

Carroll did not testify. There were only two witnesses who described how the shooting came about, Nelson and Prestley Dukes (Dukes), a witness called by Carroll. Dukes testified that when Nelson did not give Carroll his money Carroll hit Nelson on the side of the head with the handgun and that, when Nelson did not "respond," Carroll "went to hit him again, and when [Carroll] drew back, the gun went off." Nelson, in substance, testified that he tendered $2,300 to Carroll, that Carroll pulled out his pistol and said that he wanted all of his money, and that the next thing that Nelson knew, he heard a shot and saw that he was bleeding.

Carroll never testified. Because Prestley Dukes' testimony was the only evidence supporting Carroll's argument that his shooting of Nelson was an accident, we quote the relevant parts:

"[Carroll's attorney]: [T]ell me what happened [when Carroll entered the nightclub]?

[Dukes]: Well, when [Carroll] came in, he walked up and told [Nelson], asked him to give him his money. He didn't give it to him, so he hit him.

* * *

[Carroll's attorney]: Okay. Now, did [Carroll] have the gun out when he came into the club?

[Dukes]: Yes.

[Carroll's attorney]: Okay. And you say he hit him on the side of the head?

[Dukes]: Yeah.

[Carroll's attorney]: All right, and said, give me my money?

[Dukes]: Yeah.

[Carroll's attorney]: All right. And what happened then?

[Dukes]: Well. He didn't respond to that.

* * *

[Carroll's attorney]: Okay. [Nelson] didn't respond to it at all?

[Dukes]: No. He said, 'didn't you hear me; give me my money.'

[Carroll's attorney]: Okay.

[Dukes]: And went to hit him again, and when he drawed back, the gun went off."

On cross-examination, Dukes further testified:

"[Nelson's attorney]: How much had Mr. Carroll had to drink that evening?

[Dukes]: He had a little.

[Nelson's attorney]: He was drunk at that time, wasn't he?

[Dukes]: He was a little tipsy.

[Nelson's attorney]: And he was angry, too, wasn't he?

[Dukes]: I imagine he was. He hit him aside the head with that gun.

[Nelson's attorney]: All right. He was angry from the time he saw him, wasn't he? Is that correct?

[Dukes]: Yes.

* * *

[Nelson's attorney]: Okay. And when he walked over to Mr. Nelson … and asked him for his money, did he have the gun out at that point?

[Dukes]: Yes.

[Nelson's attorney]: Had the gun out right from the beginning?

[Dukes]: Yes.

* * *

[Nelson's attorney]: Okay. And was there anybody else around him?

* * *

[Dukes]: It's a crowd in there.

* * *

[Nelson's attorney]: And what hand did Mr. Carroll have the gun in?

* * *

Had it in his left hand; hit him on the left side?

[Dukes]: Yeah.

[Nelson's attorney]: Okay. And then the gun went off?

[Dukes]: Not then. No.

[Nelson's attorney]: Then he pulled back, and squeezed the trigger and the gun went off?

[Dukes]: Then he asked him, said, give me my money again, and he went to hit him again, and then it went off.

[Nelson's attorney]: All right...."

Nelson testified to undergoing extensive medical treatment resulting from his gunshot wound. Immediately after being shot, Nelson lost consciousness as a result of blood loss and did not fully regain consciousness for three or four months, until November 1992. He continued to spend months in various hospitals and rehabilitation facilities, undergoing multiple operations. He testified to the nearly complete loss of his eyesight.

Nelson's sole contention before this Court is that he was entitled to a motion for judgment on the issue of liability for battery. He contends that the evidence that Carroll committed a battery is uncontested.

Our task is to determine whether, considering the essential elements of a tort claim for battery, there is any dispute over material facts from which a jury could conclude that Carroll had not committed a battery when he shot Nelson. Since the only disputed fact relates to whether Carroll shot Nelson accidentally as he was striking him, we need only address the narrow question of whether, under the facts of this case, the defense that the shot was fired accidentally is capable of exonerating Carroll of liability.

A battery occurs when one intends a harmful or offensive contact with another without that person's consent. *See* RESTATEMENT (SECOND) OF TORTS § 13 & cmt. d (1965). "The act in question must be some positive or affirmative action on the part of the defendant." *Saba v. Darling*, 320 Md. 45, 49, 575 A.2d 1240, 1242 (1990). A battery may occur through a defendant's direct or indirect contact with the plaintiff. In this case, Carroll unquestionably committed a battery when he struck Nelson on the side of his head with his handgun. *See Saba*, 320 Md. at 49, 575 A.2d at 1242. Likewise, an indirect contact, such as occurs when a bullet strikes a victim, may constitute a battery. "[I]t is enough that the defendant sets a force in motion which ultimately produces the result." PROSSER & KEETON, THE LAW OF TORTS § 9, at 40 (5th ed.1984). Thus, if we assume the element of intent was present, Carroll also committed a battery when he discharged his handgun, striking Nelson with a bullet.

Nelson's action in the instant case focuses on the indirect contact of the bullet and not the battery that occurred when Carroll struck him on the head. It is the bullet that allegedly caused the harm for which Nelson seeks damages. As the analysis that follows suggests, however, the circumstances surrounding the gunshot are relevant in determining whether a battery occurred.

Carroll's defense that he accidentally discharged the handgun requires us to examine the "intent" requirement for the tort of battery. It is universally understood that some form of intent is required for battery. It is also clear, however, that the intent required is not a specific intent to cause the type of harm that occurred. "The defendant's liability for the resulting harm extends, as in most other cases of intentional torts, to consequences which the defendant did not intend, and could not reasonably have foreseen, upon the obvious basis that it is better for unexpected losses to fall upon the intentional wrongdoer than upon the innocent victim." (Footnote omitted). PROSSER & KEETON, THE LAW OF TORTS § 9, at 40 (5th ed.1984). *See also* PROSSER & KEETON, THE LAW OF TORTS § 8, at 36 (5th ed. 1984) ("The intent with which tort liability is concerned is not necessarily a hostile intent, or a desire to do any harm. Rather it is an intent to bring about a result which will invade the interests of another in a way that the law forbids." (Footnote omitted)).

On the other hand, a purely accidental touching, or one caused by mere inadvertence, is not enough to establish the intent requirement for battery. *See, e.g., Steinman v. Laundry Co.,* 109 Md. 62, 66, 71 A. 517, 518 (1908). The intent element of battery requires not a specific desire to bring about a certain result, but rather a general intent to unlawfully invade another's physical well-being through a harmful or offensive contact.... All that is necessary is (a) that the actor engage in volitional activity and (b) that he intend to violate the legally protected interest of another in his person. * * * Since it is the invasion of another's interest that is intended, the actor takes the risk of the existence of a legal privilege to make it; it is no defense that the mistake is reasonable and due to no fault ... on the part of the actor. As in other cases of mistake, the actor must bear the losses incident thereto." HARPER, JAMES & GRAY, THE LAW OF TORTS § 3.3, at 3:13–14 (3d ed.1996). Thus, innocent conduct that accidentally or inadvertently results in a harmful or offensive contact with another will not give rise to liability, but one will be liable for such contact if it comes about as a result of the actor's volitional conduct where there is an intent to invade the other person's legally protected interests.

Even though intent is a subjective element usually left for the jury's determination, there are circumstances under which the law will imply the intent element of an intentional tort or a crime. One such example in a battery case is found in *Norman v. Insurance Co. of North America,* 218 Va. 718, 239 S.E.2d 902 (1978). Under facts less favorable to the plaintiff than those of the instant case, the Virginia Supreme Court addressed a trial court's ruling that an assault and battery occurred as a matter of law, despite the defendant's contention that the shooting was an accident. Clark S. Norman, Jr., the owner of an apartment building, was removing the property of a tenant when he got into an argument with the tenant and her brother, Ronald Wilson. During the course of the argument, Norman shot Wilson. At the subsequent civil trial for assault and battery brought by Wilson, Norman alleged that the shooting was accidental. He contended that, believing he was going to be attacked, he "fired his pistol at the floor without removing it from his pocket and without aiming it at anyone; and that the bullet, however, ricocheted from the floor and hit Ronald Wilson." *Norman,* 239 S.E.2d at 903 (internal quotations omitted). The trial court instructed only as to self-defense, directing the jury that the owner's "inflict[ion of] a gunshot wound upon the plaintiff ... constitutes a ... battery upon him." *Norman,* 239 S.E.2d at 904. In subsequent litigation between Norman and his insurer, the Virginia Supreme Court rejected Norman's complaint that the jury was not given the opportunity to find that "his wounding of Wilson was unexpected and accidental and that 'the jury never considered whether [Norman] intended or expected to injure Wilson....' " *Id.* That court said: "The intentional ... battery of Wilson by Norman cannot be converted into an accident by a mere statement from the person making the [battery] that he did not intend the act or its consequences. [Norman] will not be permitted to say that an intentional and malicious firing of a pistol at another, resulting in an injury, was neither expected nor intended." *Norman,* 239 S.E.2d at 905.

In order to decide this case, our holding need not reach as far as the Virginia Supreme Court's ruling in *Norman.* In *Norman,* the defendant claimed to have never removed the gun from his pocket, and he never struck a blow at the plaintiff; in the instant case, the unchallenged evidence shows that Carroll entered the bar openly carrying the gun, which he then used to strike Nelson, and then the shot occurred as he went to strike him again. If the law infers the necessary intent for battery in *Norman, a fortiori* the intent should be inferred in the instant case.

The only reasonable inference that can be drawn from the circumstances of this shooting, which in essence are uncontested, is that Carroll's actions evidenced an intent to commit a battery. Carroll presented no evidence disputing the fact that he carried a loaded handgun and that he struck Nelson on the head with the gun. The merely speculative evidence upon which Carroll claims the shot was an accident was Dukes' testimony that when Carroll "went to hit him again … the gun went off." In contrast, the evidence is undisputed that Carroll possessed a handgun which he openly carried into the nightclub, that Carroll struck Nelson with the handgun, and that the handgun discharged simultaneously as Carroll went to strike Nelson again. Indeed, taking every possible inference in favor of Carroll, the gunshot occurred as he attempted to strike Nelson with the gun. Under such circumstances, no reasonable inference can be drawn that Carroll lacked the required intent to commit the battery.

The law imposes upon Carroll the responsibility for losses associated with his wrongful actions. It is of no import that he may not have intended to actually shoot Nelson since the uncontested facts demonstrate that he did intend to invade Nelson's legally protected interests in not being physically harmed.… He violated those interests by committing an assault and battery when he threatened Nelson with the handgun and struck Nelson on the head. Even assuming as we must that Carroll did not intend to inflict the particular damages arising from the gunshot wound, it is more appropriate that those losses fall to Carroll as the wrongdoer than to Nelson as the innocent victim. Therefore, the motion for judgment as to liability should have been granted, with the only question remaining for the jury being the damages resulting from the discharge of the gun.

JUDGMENT OF THE COURT OF SPECIAL APPEALS REVERSED. CASE REMANDED TO THAT COURT WITH DIRECTIONS TO REVERSE THE JUDGEMENT OF THE CIRCUIT COURT FOR BALTIMORE CITY AND TO REMAND THE CASE TO THE CIRCUIT COURT FOR BALTIMORE CITY FOR FURTHER PROCEEDINGS CONSISTENT WITH THIS OPINION.

Questions for *Nelson*

1. Does the court apply the *Wagner* or *White* standard?
2. Is intent a subjective or objective standard?
3. What facts and circumstances does the court use to infer Carroll's intent?
4. Why did the plaintiff need to establish battery with the bullet when the court acknowledged that there was already battery when Carroll hit plaintiff in the head with the gun?

Exercise 1-6 Evaluating Legal Arguments

This exercise contains actual pleadings from *Wynn v. MJ Harbor Hotel*, Case No. N 24-C-08-001376 OT, which was filed in the Circuit Court of Maryland on Feb. 26, 2008. You will be evaluating the legal arguments made by the parties in that case and making a decision as to whether the plaintiff's claim for battery should be dismissed.

In addition to helping you understand the law of intent, another goal of this exercise is for you to understand how the procedural posture of a case affects a court's decision. Most of the cases you read are written by appellate court judges, who are reviewing what happened in a lower court. When an appellate court reviews a case it must evaluate the case based on the applicable standard of review. Similarly, trial courts are also bound by certain standards when they rule on parties' motions, including a motion to dismiss.

It might help for you to think about the standard of review as a lens that the court must look through to view the case. Imagine that you were looking at the world through the fish eye lens of a camera. Think about the way that it would change your view. In the same way, when a court looks at a case through a certain standard of review, it alters the court's "view" of the case—it colors or limits what the court is allowed to "see" and review.

The standard the court uses to review a case changes depending on what the court is asked to evaluate. For example, an appeals courts must be very deferential to a trial court when reviewing factual issues, because the trial court is in the best position to weigh things the appellate court cannot see, like witness demeanor and credibility. For factual issues an appellate court will usually have to find a clear error by the lower court to change the decision. On the other hand, the appeals court may review the law and application of the law without giving any deference to the trial court, and may conclude that the trial court applied a rule incorrectly, or did not choose the correct rule to apply. This is called de novo review, which means "anew," and that is what the appellate court is allowed to do—take a new look at the case without deferring to the lower court.

Appellate courts will sometimes apply the same standards of review used by the trial court, but substitute their own judgment. For example, both the trial court and the appellate court will review a motion for summary judgment to determine whether there are any issues of law and fact that must be decided by a jury or whether a judgment can be entered for one of the parties without the need for a trial because even after looking at the evidence in the best light possible for the party opposing the motion, there is no way a jury could find in that party's favor.

The trial court likewise must view the case using the applicable standard. When deciding whether to grant a motion to dismiss for failure to state a claim, the trial court reviewing the motion to dismiss must determine whether the complaint includes facts that show a claim is possible under the facts and circumstances as they are alleged.

In this exercise you will be examining the case from the position of the trial judge ruling on defendant's motion to dismiss the plaintiff's claim for battery. You will be reviewing excerpts from three different documents from the case:

1. Plaintiffs' Third Amended Complaint

2. Memorandum of Points and Authorities in Support of Defendants' Motion to Dismiss Count V, Battery, in Plaintiffs' Third Amended Complaint; and

3. Plaintiffs' Opposition to Defendants' Motion to Dismiss Count V (Battery) of Plaintiffs' Third Amended Complaint.

For purposes of this exercise, assume that in ruling on the motion to dismiss for failure to state a claim upon which relief can be granted, a court (in this case, you) must assume the truth of the facts and allegations in the complaint, as well as all inferences that can reasonably be drawn from these alleged facts. However, the court is not bound by the plaintiff's legal conclusions.

A court (again, you) may dismiss a cause of action if the alleged facts in the complaint and permissible inferences, even if later proven to be true, would fail to provide a basis for the court to award relief to the plaintiff based on the cause of action alleged by the plaintiff. In this case that means you must assume the facts alleged in the complaint and all reasonable inferences that can be drawn from those facts are true and decide whether based on those facts the plaintiff has stated a cause of action for battery.

Based upon your reading thus far and the pleadings set out below, how would you rule on Defendants' motion to dismiss the battery cause of action alleged in Plaintiff's complaint? Be sure to explain the basis of your ruling.

The relevant portion of **Plaintiff's Complaint** alleged as follows:

1	**CIRCUIT COURT OF MARYLAND**
2	**BALTIMORE CITY**
3	
4	Adrienne WYNN, et al., No. N 24-C-08-001376 OT.
5	Plaintiff, PLAINTIFF'S COMPLAINT
6	v.
7	MJ HARBOR HOTEL
8	d/b/a Pier V Hotel, et al.,
9	Defendants.
10	

11 ¶ 29 While working in the Ruth's Chris Steak House, Plaintiffs were exposed to car-
12 bon monoxide released from defective equipment owned and maintained by Defen-
13 dants in their Pier 5 hotel premises located at 711 Eastern Avenue, Baltimore,
14 Maryland.

15 ¶ 37 The source of the carbon monoxide was the mechanical room located on the
16 Pier 5 property where Defendants maintained and operated two gas fired boilers.

17 ¶ 41 There are four boilers in the mechanical room. Two service Defendant MJ's
18 Pier 5 Hotel, and the other two boilers service the two restaurants in the premises, the
19 Ruth's Chris Steak House and a McCormick and Schmick restaurant.

1 | ¶ 86. Without the Plaintiffs' consent, the Defendants, inter alia: (a) intentionally
2 | chose to operate a venting system that did not develop a positive air flow adequate to
3 | remove flue or vent gasses from the boilers to the outside atmosphere; (b) intentionally
4 | chose to install or maintain a draft system which did not prevent leakage of flue or vent
5 | gases into the maintenance room and the Ruth's Chris Steak House located in the Pier
6 | 5 building; (c) intentionally chose to install or maintain a mechanical draft system
7 | which utilized the electric fan on the roof of the Pier 5 building without providing for
8 | the prevention of gas flow to the boilers when the draft system is not performing; (d)
9 | intentionally chose to install or maintain an electric fan mechanical draft system that
10 | was not installed or maintained in accordance with the terms of the manufacturer's in-
11 | structions; (e) after installation of the electric fan mechanical draft system, Defendants
12 | intentionally chose to disable the safety lock system that would have prevented the boil-
13 | ers from operating if the fan became inoperable; (f) intentionally chose to damage,
14 | alter, breach and penetrate the common wall between the mechanical room and the
15 | Ruth's Chris Steak House by drilling or cutting openings in the common wall; (g) in-
16 | tentionally chose not to properly repair, replace, or restore the common wall between
17 | the mechanical room and Ruth's Chris Steak House where the common wall was dam-
18 | aged, altered, breached, and penetrated by openings; (h) intentionally chose not to
19 | provide for an interlock system to prevent the flow of gas to the boilers when the me-
20 | chanical draft system was not performing; (i) intentionally chose not to maintain the
21 | mechanical venting system according to the terms of the boiler manufacturer's instruc-
22 | tions with respect to a safety interlock system; (j) intentionally chose not to properly
23 | inspect or maintain the boilers in the mechanical room so that they would burn with-
24 | out producing excessive amounts of carbon monoxide; (k) intentionally chose to dis-
25 | able the safety interlock system and thereafter used boilers with disabled relay switches;
26 | (l) intentionally chose to use a flue end cap with detached draft sensing probes; (m) in-
27 | tentionally chose to use an improperly fitted and improperly fastened flue end cap; (n)
28 | intentionally chose not to inspect, maintain and/or repair the vent ducts and fan; (o)
29 | intentionally chose not to comply with local, state, and/or federal laws requiring the
30 | boilers to be interlocked with the fan so that the boilers cannot operate without proven
31 | airflow and which require that all damage, alteration, breach, or penetration of the
32 | common wall be properly repaired, replaced, or restored; (p) intentionally chose to
33 | disable many of the safety devices that had been previously installed to prevent unsafe

1 operation of the boilers; and, (q) intentionally chose not to install carbon monoxide
2 detectors on the Pier 5 property including the mechanical room and the Ruth's Chris
3 Steak House, notwithstanding the Defendant MJ's preexisting corporate policy requir-
4 ing installation of carbon monoxide detectors.

5   ¶ 87. Without the Pier 5 Plaintiffs' consent, the Defendants' actions resulted in ex-
6 posing the Pier 5 Plaintiffs to deadly levels of carbon monoxide.

7   ¶ 88. The Defendants' intentional conduct was substantially certain to result in ex-
8 posing the Pier 5 Plaintiffs to deadly levels of carbon monoxide.

9   ¶ 89. Unpermitted exposure to deadly levels of carbon monoxide is harmful and
10 offensive.

The relevant portion of the **Memorandum of Points and Authorities in Support of Defendants' Motion to Dismiss Count V, Battery, in Plaintiffs' Third Amended Complaint** is reprinted below:

1	**CIRCUIT COURT OF MARYLAND**	
2	**BALTIMORE CITY**	
3		
4	Adrienne WYNN, et al.,	No. N 24-C-08-001376 OT.
5	Plaintiff,	MEMORANDUM OF POINTS
6	v.	AND AUTHORITIES IN SUPPORT OF DEFENDANT'S
7	MJ HARBOR HOTEL	MOTION TO DISMISS
8	d/b/a Pier V Hotel, et al.,	COUNT V, BATTERY, IN PLAINTIFFS' THIRD
9	Defendants.	AMENDED COMPLAINT
10		
11		
12		
13	B. Plaintiffs Cannot Recover for Battery	
14	*Plaintiffs' Complaint Fails to Adequately Allege the Elements of Battery*	

15 Plaintiffs' claim fails because they have not adequately stated the cause of action it-
16 self. A battery occurs "when one intends a harmful or offensive contact with another
17 without that person's consent." *Nelson v. Carroll*, 355 Md. 593, 600, 735 A.2d 1096,
18 1099 (1999). "The intent element of battery requires not a specific desire to bring
19 about a certain result, but rather a general intent to unlawfully invade another's physi-
20 cal well-being through a harmful or offensive contact or an apprehension of such a
21 contact." *Id*. at 602–603. "An indirect contact, such as when a bullet strikes a victim,
22 may constitute a battery. It is enough that the defendant sets a force in motion which
23 ultimately produces the result." *Id*. at 601. "Thus innocent conduct that accidentally or
24 inadvertently results in a harmful or offensive contact with another will not give rise to
25 liability." *Id*. at 603.

26 Under this legal standard, Plaintiffs' battery claim fails as a matter of law, on the
27 face of the pleading, because Plaintiffs do not allege that Defendants intended to in-
28 vade Plaintiffs' physical well being. Of the seventeen aforementioned intentional acts
29 (a–q), only three can be considered intentional acts, rather than omissions. Subsec-
30 tions (e) and (p) allege that Defendants disabled safety devices, and subsection (f) al-

1 | leges that Defendants intentionally damaged the common wall by drilling holes in it.
2 | Although Plaintiffs allege that the corporate entity acted intentionally when allegedly
3 | disabling alleged safety devices, there is no allegation that Defendants' *intent* was to *in-*
4 | *vade Plaintiffs' physical well being.* In fact, Plaintiffs allege that the Defendants drilled
5 | holes in the wall to "allow various service pipes to pass through the common wall,"
6 | (Third Amended Complaint at 47), not to invade Plaintiffs' person through exposure
7 | to carbon monoxide gas. Plaintiffs do not specify any particular intent on the part of
8 | Defendants with regard to the alleged disabling of safety devices.

9 | Moreover, from the face of the pleading, there is no indication of when Defendants
10 | allegedly immobilized the safety mechanisms or drilled holes in the wall, the specific
11 | acts that "set a force in motion" which ultimately [allegedly] harmed the Plaintiffs. Al-
12 | though courts hold that a battery may occur through a defendants' indirect contact with
13 | the plaintiff after an event is set in motion, the indirect contact must be linked to the in-
14 | tended act. *See generally Nelson v. Carroll*, 335 Md. at 603–604; *Northfield Insurance. Co.*
15 | *v. Boxley*, 215 F. Supp. 2d 656, 662 (D. Md. 2002); *Norman v. Insurance Co. of N. Amer-*
16 | *ica*, 218 Va. 718, 239 S.E.2d 902, 903 (Va. 1978). For example, in *Nelson*, the court held
17 | that a shooter was liable to his gun shot victim for battery after his gun went off when
18 | he used his gun to strike plaintiff on the head. *Nelson*, 355 Md. at 604–605. Likewise,
19 | in *Franklin v. Montgomery County, Md*, 2006 U.S. Dist. Lexis 68476 (D. Md. September
20 | 13, 2006), the court found defendant liable for battery when he indirectly touched
21 | plaintiff in a harmful and offensive manner by unlawfully deploying his tazer. In con-
22 | trast to established case law, in the instant case, not only do the Defendant entities lack
23 | any intent to commit offensive contact, their alleged intentional acts were not aimed at
24 | setting an event in motion that would ultimately harm the Plaintiffs. Further, Defen-
25 | dants' alleged acts are not remotely linked to Plaintiffs' alleged harm.

26 | Plaintiffs list seventeen events that Defendants either allegedly failed to carry out or
27 | changed, yet they fail to allege an act that caused the injury. Carbon monoxide was re-
28 | leased due to an alleged malfunction of one of the boilers, not the disabling of a safety
29 | device or drilling holes in the wall. What allows carbon monoxide to enter an area, *i.e.*
30 | [allegedly] through holes in the common wall, is separate and distinct from the alleged
31 | malfunction of a boiler. Allegedly disabling a safety device or drilling holes in a wall
32 | years before an injury is completely unlike actively firing a tazer at a person or firing a
33 |

1 gun, which immediately injures the plaintiff. At best, the release of carbon monoxide

2 was an accident, which as a matter of law is not a battery. *Nelson*, 355 Md. at 603.

3   Count V of Plaintiffs Third Amended Complaint fails to state a claim upon which

4 relief can be granted because Plaintiffs fail to establish that Defendants intended to in-

5 vade Plaintiffs' physical well being through their acts. Accordingly, Count V of Plain-

6 tiffs Third Amended Complaint should be dismissed.

7   WHEREFORE, Defendants hereby request that this Court grant their Motion to

8 Dismiss Count V of Plaintiffs Third Amended Complaint.

9

10

11

12

13

14

15

16

17

18

19

20

21

22

23

24

25

26

27

28

29

30

31

32

33

Plaintiff opposed Defendant's Motion. The relevant portion of **Plaintiffs' Opposition to Defendants' Motion to Dismiss Count V (Battery) of Plaintiffs' Third Amended Complaint** is reprinted below:

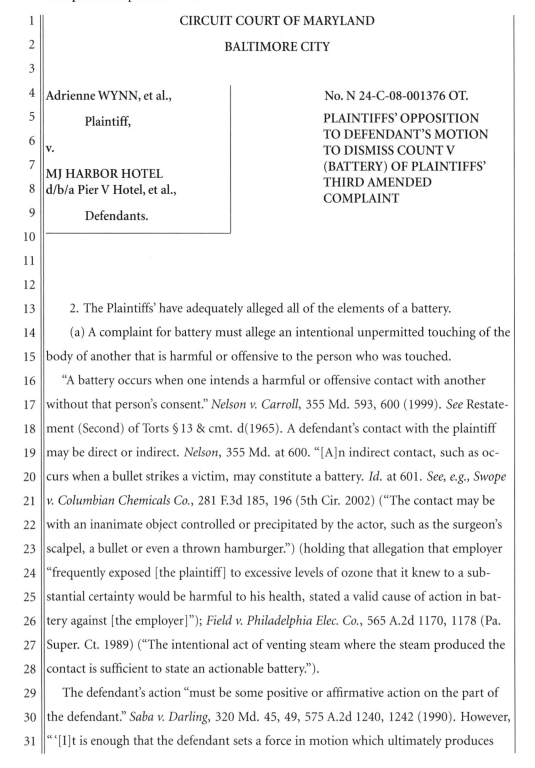

1	CIRCUIT COURT OF MARYLAND
2	BALTIMORE CITY
3	
4	Adrienne WYNN, et al., No. N 24-C-08-001376 OT.
5	Plaintiff, PLAINTIFFS' OPPOSITION
6	v. TO DEFENDANT'S MOTION TO DISMISS COUNT V
7	MJ HARBOR HOTEL (BATTERY) OF PLAINTIFFS'
8	d/b/a Pier V Hotel, et al., THIRD AMENDED COMPLAINT
9	Defendants.

10

11

12

13   2. The Plaintiffs' have adequately alleged all of the elements of a battery.

14   (a) A complaint for battery must allege an intentional unpermitted touching of the

15   body of another that is harmful or offensive to the person who was touched.

16   "A battery occurs when one intends a harmful or offensive contact with another

17   without that person's consent." *Nelson v. Carroll*, 355 Md. 593, 600 (1999). *See* Restate-

18   ment (Second) of Torts § 13 & cmt. d(1965). A defendant's contact with the plaintiff

19   may be direct or indirect. *Nelson*, 355 Md. at 600. "[A]n indirect contact, such as oc-

20   curs when a bullet strikes a victim, may constitute a battery. *Id.* at 601. *See, e.g., Swope*

21   *v. Columbian Chemicals Co.*, 281 F.3d 185, 196 (5th Cir. 2002) ("The contact may be

22   with an inanimate object controlled or precipitated by the actor, such as the surgeon's

23   scalpel, a bullet or even a thrown hamburger.") (holding that allegation that employer

24   "frequently exposed [the plaintiff] to excessive levels of ozone that it knew to a sub-

25   stantial certainty would be harmful to his health, stated a valid cause of action in bat-

26   tery against [the employer]"); *Field v. Philadelphia Elec. Co.*, 565 A.2d 1170, 1178 (Pa.

27   Super. Ct. 1989) ("The intentional act of venting steam where the steam produced the

28   contact is sufficient to state an actionable battery.").

29   The defendant's action "must be some positive or affirmative action on the part of

30   the defendant." *Saba v. Darling*, 320 Md. 45, 49, 575 A.2d 1240, 1242 (1990). However,

31   "'[I]t is enough that the defendant sets a force in motion which ultimately produces

1   the result....'" *Nelson*, 355 Md. at 601 (quoting Prosser & Keeton, The Law of Torts

2   §9, at 40 (5th ed.1984)).

3   (b) The Defendants misstate the requisite intent for a battery.

4   The Defendants argue that the battery count is defective because the Plaintiffs' fail to

5   allege that the "Defendants intended to invade Plaintiffs' physical well being." The De-

6   fendants' argument, like their previous arguments, is plainly wrong. It is based on a

7   narrow and misplaced understanding of the intent needed for a battery.

8   The Restatement (Second) of Torts defines intent to mean that "the actor desires to

9   cause consequences of his act, *or that he believes that the consequences are substantially*

10 *certain to result from it.*" Restatement (Second) of Torts §8A (1965). The Court of Spe-

11 cial Appeals has similarly held: "The word 'intent' for purposes of tort law ... denotes

12 that the actor desires to cause the consequences of his act *or believes that consequences*

13 *are substantially certain to result from it.* In order for an act to be intentional, its conse-

14 quences must be substantially certain to result as opposed to the feature of wanton acts

15 that the consequences be only probably certain to result...."*Allstate Insurance Co. v.*

16 *Sparks*, 63 Md. App. 738, 744 (1985) (emphasis added).

17   "[I]ntent to do harm is not essential to a battery. As the probability of injury to an-

18 other, apparent from the facts within his knowledge, becomes greater, his conduct takes

19 on more of the attributes of intent, until it reaches that substantial certainty of harm

20 which juries, and sometimes courts, may find inseparable from intent itself." *Ghassemieh*

21 *v. Schafer*, 52 Md. App. 31, 41 (1982). *See Frey v. Kouf*, 484 N.W.2d 864, 867–68 (S.D.

22 1992) ("By way of example, an actor who fires a bullet into a crowded room may desire

23 that no one be hit, but if he knows it is substantially certain someone will be hit, the actor

24 intends that consequence.")

25   Comporting with the aforementioned authorities, the Plaintiffs' pled that the Defen-

26 dants knew their actions were substantially certain to result in exposing the Plaintiffs to

27 deadly levels of carbon monoxide. *See* the Third Amended Complaint at ¶88. Indeed,

28 there can be no doubt that a reasonable person would have known, for instance, that

29 disabling the boiler safety mechanisms was substantially certain to result in exposing

30 the hotel's occupants to deadly levels of carbon monoxide.[2]

---

2. Even though the Plaintiffs pled the "consequences are substantially certain" prong for intent, the jury may very well find that the "desired to cause the consequences" prong is satisfied based on the fact that the safety mechanisms were deliberately removed by the Defendants who were conscious of both the functions and importance of the mechanisms.

1 Further, even if there is a factual dispute about whether the conduct was substan-
2 tially certain to result in carbon monoxide exposure, the dispute cannot be resolved
3 on a motion to dismiss. "Intent is a subjective element usually left for the jury's deter-
4 mination." *Nelson*, 355 Md. at 603. Accordingly, the Defendants' argument concern-
5 ing intent should be rejected.

6 Assuming the truth of the pleaded facts, allegations, and inferences in complaint,
7 the Defendants cannot demonstrate that the battery count is deficient as a matter of
8 law. The Plaintiffs have properly alleged that the Defendants' actions resulted in a bat-
9 tery via carbon monoxide poisoning. For all of the foregoing reasons, the Defendants'
10 Motion should be DENIED.
11
12
13
14
15
16
17
18
19
20
21
22
23
24
25
26
27
28
29
30
31
32
33

Exercise 1-7 Zealous Advocacy or Unprofessional Behavior?

If you were defense counsel would you have filed a motion to dismiss the battery claim? In other words, do you believe that based on the alleged facts and permissible inferences, there was no basis on which the court could find that Defendants were liable for battery?

If you were the Plaintiffs' lawyer would you amend the complaint to address the concerns raised by Defendants' motion (because you believe defendants' motion was correct) or would you have opposed the motion (because you believe the pleadings stated a valid cause of action)?

In plaintiff's motion they state: "The Defendants' argument, *like their previous arguments*, is plainly wrong." (emphasis added). Was the information in italics really necessary? Was it professional? Would you write such a statement in a motion to the court?

Did the parties' motions characterize *Nelson* accurately? Why or why not?

(c) Transferred Intent

In addition to proving intent by proving the defendant desired or was substantially certain a contact would occur, intent for battery may also be proven by establishing a defendant desired to place the plaintiff (or was substantially certain the plaintiff would be placed) in apprehension of a harmful or offensive contact. Later in this chapter you will learn that placing someone in apprehension of a contact is the consequence required for proving intent for assault; for now, you should know that if a defendant intends an assault, and it results in a battery, the defendant has committed a battery. The intent to commit an assault transfers to the resulting battery. Below is an excerpt from *Nelson* that explains this concept:

The rule is widely recognized that when one commits an assault, and in the course of committing the assault that person comes into contact with the person assaulted, the intent element of battery may be supplied by the intent element of the assault.

. . .

Because the defendant has committed an assault, the intent element of assault is subsumed into the battery claim even though the defendant contends that the actual harm was accidental or otherwise unintentional.... Therefore, one who intends to frighten another by assaulting him or her, and touches this person in a harmful or offensive manner and claims the touching was inadvertent or accidental, is liable for battery, notwithstanding the contention that the actual touching was never intended. *See, e.g., Alteiri v. Colasso,* 168 Conn. 329, 362 A.2d 798, 801 (1975) (affirming liability for battery when minor plaintiff was injured by defendant's throwing of an object into the yard where minor was playing, even though defendant had only attempted to scare the minor).... Thus, the risk is mitigated that a wrongdoer will be found free from liability while the innocent victim suffers the consequences of the wrongful conduct.

Historically, a writ of trespass (a single action) encompassed five of the intentional torts—assault, battery, false imprisonment, trespass to land and trespass to chattel—

and so intent to commit any one of these five intentional torts would transfer to any other of these five torts, meaning a defendant could intend any one of the five torts and if any other of the five torts resulted, the defendant would be liable (assuming the other elements existed). The Restatement only recognizes this concept of transferred intent (from tort to tort) between assault and battery.

Transferred intent applies in other contexts as well. For example, where a person intends a harmful contact with Person A and instead a harmful contact with Person B results, the intent to contact Person A transfers to the resulting battery to Person B, so that Person B can recover for battery (assuming the other elements exist). In other words the tortfeasor's intent transfers from an intended victim to an actual one. In sum, intent may transfer from both person to person and tort to tort.

(2) Did Defendant's Act Result in a Harmful or Offensive Contact?

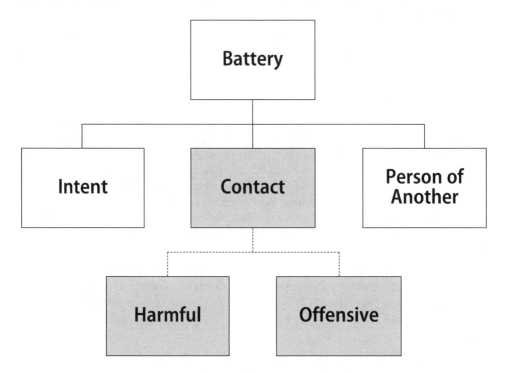

In addition to establishing intent, in order to establish a prima facie case for battery, the plaintiff must show that the defendant's intentional act resulted in a harmful *or* offensive contact.

A contact is harmful where there is any physical impairment of the plaintiff's body, physical pain or illness, no matter how slight. Establishing that a contact was harmful is fairly easy, because any harm will do. However, the plaintiff's damage award is based on the extent of her harm, and so where the plaintiff suffers very little harm, she is entitled to only nominal damages.

A contact is offensive if a reasonable person in the same circumstances as the plaintiff would find the contact offensive. Thus, a socially acceptable contact, like a tap on the shoulder to get someone's attention, will not result in a battery; a particularly hypersensitive party may be subjectively offended by such contact, but a reasonable person would not be. Since the contact is evaluated in the context of the circumstances in which the contact occurred, consideration of the prior types of contacts between the parties involved in the dispute may be important. Where, for example, the parties have a history of practical jokes, or horseplay, the parties should probably expect such contact from each other, and such contact would not be objectively offensive in that context, even if a stranger would find such contact offensive.

Exercise 1-8 Fact Investigation and Analysis

As you might imagine, determining whether contact is offensive requires careful consideration of the facts in the dispute. Examine the facts below and for each situation answer the following questions: Would a reasonable person find any of the following contacts offensive? Why or why not? Are there additional facts you would like to know before making a decision? What are they?

a.   A paralegal attempted to enter his Supervising Attorney's office without knocking on the door. Another attorney, who was talking to the paralegal's supervisor, pushed the door closed, which pushed the paralegal back into the hall.

b.   An antismoking advocate was in a radio broadcast studio to discuss with a talk-show host the harmful effects of smoking and breathing secondary smoke. While they were on the air, another talk-show host lit a cigar and repeatedly blew smoke in the advocate's face.

c.   An automobile repair-shop customer, who believed she was "ripped-off" by an automobile mechanic, attempted to take a photograph of the mechanic for use on a local television news consumer-advocacy program exposing fraudulent repair shops. Enraged, the mechanic grabbed the camera from her hand.

d.   An Airline employee was the victim of a practical joke in which her coworkers arranged to have her "arrested" by city police officers. The "officers" were courteous and professional while they placed her arms in position to be handcuffed and handcuffed her.

e.   A Rabbi who officiated at a wedding ceremony ate nonkosher food— such as shrimp, octopus, and eel—from a caterer hired by the wedding parties to provide kosher food for the wedding reception.

f.   Participants in a flash mob in City's downtown area were arrested. The officer who transported the participants drove the police van to the jail in an intentionally jerky manner. Participants arrived at the jail unharmed.

g.   During a security screening at City International Airport, a Transportation Safety Administration (TSA) employee placed her fingers under Traveler's brassiere, grazing her breasts.

(3) Was the Contact with the Person of Another?

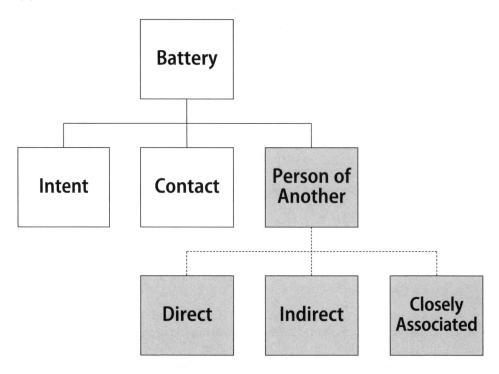

The requirement that the defendant make contact with the plaintiff's person may seem straight forward, but two issues commonly arise that require consideration. The first is that contact may be established not only where there was direct contact—e.g., the defendant's fist with the plaintiff's nose, but also where there is indirect contact with the plaintiff's person—e.g., the defendant ties a string across a sidewalk in order to trip the plaintiff, who falls and hits the ground. The second issue is that contact with the plaintiff's person may be established where defendant made contact with something closely or intimately associated with the plaintiff's person.

In *Fisher v. Carousel Motor Hotel*, 424 S.W.2d 627 (Tex. 1967), a well-known torts case, the court held that when a manager of the Defendant hotel's dining club intentionally snatched a patron's dinner plate from him while speaking to him in a loud and offensive manner, it was sufficient to constitute a battery. In so holding the court reasoned:

> The intentional snatching of an object from one's hand is as clearly an offensive invasion of his person as would be an actual contact with the body.... The rationale for holding an offensive contact with such an object to be a battery is explained in 1 Restatement of Torts 2d section 18 (Comment p. 31) as follows: "Since the essence of the plaintiff's grievance consists in the offense to the dignity involved in the unpermitted and intentional invasion of the inviolability of his person and not in any physical harm done to his body, it is not necessary that the plaintiff's actual body be disturbed. Unpermitted and intentional contacts with anything so connected with the body as to be customarily regarded as part of the other's person and therefore as partaking of its inviolability is actionable as an offensive contact with his person. There are some things such as clothing or a cane or, indeed, anything directly grasped by the hand which are so intimately connected with one's body as to be universally regarded as part of the person."

Exercise 1-9 Using a Court's Reasoning to Apply a Rule to New Situations

Apply the reasoning from *Fisher* (and the Restatement) to determine which of the following would be considered a contact for purposes of battery (be sure you are able to explain why or why not):

Grabbing a plate from the table while a person is still eating from, but not touching, the plate

Grabbing a coat from the back of a person's chair while the person is sitting in the chair

Hitting a bicycle with a baseball bat while a person is riding the bicycle

Hitting a vehicle with a baseball bat while a person is sitting in the vehicle

Exercise 1-10 Organizing Analysis of a Battery Claim

Now that you have reviewed the elements of the prima facie case for battery, use the graphic organizers preceding each topic to help you organize what you have learned. Create a chart or outline that organizes the material in the order you expect to encounter and address issues when confronted with a fact pattern that presents a battery issue. Add the information you have learned about each of the elements from the reading and materials in the chapter. This will help you create an organizational tool for the materials on battery and will serve as an example for each of the torts you learn about from this text. Use the chart or outline you create to construct an outline of a written answer to the chapter problem evaluating whether Ryan Watson will be able to establish the prima facie case for battery.

Skill Focus: Organizing Your Thoughts before You Write

Imagine that you were asked to give a speech. Most likely you would think about what you were going to say—maybe even making some notes to organize your thoughts. You would probably do this because you would want your speech to sound coherent and polished. Unfortunately, this is not the process adopted by many students when they write essay exams during law school, and the result is that the written product sounds much like an unprepared speech.

You can choose to "sound" just as polished in your essay exam writing as you would in a prepared speech—and thereby impress your reader, the professor who is grading your paper. In this age of computer written exams, you might think that by cutting and pasting material it will have the same effect, but that is rarely true. Instead, minor issues and major issues are given equal time, issues are not presented in the best order, students do not have time to finish exams, and key facts go unused. You can avoid all of these pitfalls by organizing before you write— like you would for the prepared speech. The organizational tool (flow chart, outline, etc.) that you create will help you create structure for your essay exam. You can use it to organize your thoughts before you write. Here is one example of how to outline an essay answer before writing it:

- As you read a fact pattern and begin to spot issues, write those issues on one side of a sheet of scratch paper
- Once you identify an issue, write the rule elements from your organizational tool next to each of the issues you spot (be sure to use shorthand or abbreviations for this process)
- As you read through the fact pattern, write the key facts next to the rule elements
- Once you have completed this process (you have spotted the issues, and utilized the facts), review the outline/grid you have created and determine which issues are major and minor
- Finally, try to see the big picture: Solve the problems you were asked to solve. Think about the order you will use to address issues, using your organizational tool as a guide. Visualize your answer with emphasis on major issues. (i.e., think about how your "speech" will sound)

Each time you finish organizing a practice exam, evaluate whether your outline helped you accomplish the task of writing an organized answer, and reflect on how it might be improved for future use.

---

3. Are There Any Defenses?

If plaintiff establishes the prima facie elements of her claim, defendant may take the position that there is additional evidence (e.g., facts) that justifies or privileges defendant's conduct and enables defendant to avoid liability. This additional evidence is part of proving what is usually called an affirmative defense. Defendants bear the burden of proving an affirmative defense exists. Defenses are typically plead in the defendant's answer, the document defendant files in response to plaintiff's complaint (assuming defendant decides not to raise procedural or other issues—like immunity—which would be raised in the form of a motion to dismiss the action).

a. Consent

A defendant is not liable for battery where the plaintiff consents to the contact. In many torts texts and supplements, consent is referred to as a privilege or defense, for which defendant bears the burden of proof; in many jurisdictions, however, lack of consent is actually an element of the prima facie case for some torts, including battery, and in such cases plaintiff will bear the burden of proving she did not consent. Where plaintiff bears the burden she must plead facts establishing lack of consent in her complaint. Where defendant bears the burden she must plead consent as an affirmative defense in her answer. While this is a critical issue when you are litigating a claim (because you must ascertain who has the burden of proof and what must be included at the pleading stage), it is not essential to your initial understanding of the meaning of consent. For the purposes of evaluating the chapter problem, assume that consent is not one of the elements of the prima facie claim and that any potential defendants bear the burden of proving Ryan Watson did not consent to the conduct.

Consent may be expressly given or implied by the plaintiff's conduct (words or actions), by custom or by law. Plaintiff's consent may be implied by plaintiff's conduct where plaintiff's words or actions would be understood by a reasonable person as indicating consent. The following illustrations, from Restatement (Second) Torts section 50, comment a, are examples of implied consent:

> As passengers are leaving a ship they are informed that they must be vaccinated to enter the United States. A, a passenger, is unwilling to be vaccinated, but stands in line, passes before B, the ship's surgeon, and holds up her arm. B vaccinates A.
>
> A, a young man, is alone with B, a girl, in the moonlight. A proposes to kiss B. Although inwardly objecting, B neither resists nor protests by word or gesture. A kisses B.
>
> A suffers an injury in an accident, as a result of which he is unable to move his right arm without great pain. B, a surgeon, tells A that he proposes to operate on him "on top of the shoulder," and taps A's shoulder near the neck to indicate where the operation will be performed. A says to B, "Don't go too much up in the neck," but offers no other comment or objection. B performs an operation which remedies a fracture of the sixth cervical vertebra, making the incision over the neck.

Consent may be invalidated for a number of reasons, for example, consent is invalid if obtained by fraud or duress; where it is based on mistake; where the plaintiff does not have the capacity to consent; or where defendant exceeds the scope of the consent given.

Consent is an issue frequently litigated in the context of medical malpractice cases. Typically physicians require patients to sign a document consenting to treatment. For battery claims against physicians, the issue in such cases is whether the patient consented to the actual contacts that occurred (meaning the physician is not liable for battery), or whether Defendant's contacts were outside those covered by plaintiff's consent. As you read the next case, try to identify all of the ways plaintiff's consent may be vitiated.

Murphy v. Implicito

245, 920 A.2d 678 (N.J.Super. 2007)

In September 1996, plaintiff injured his back while lifting a pallet at work, causing him "horrific" pain, and leaving him unable to sleep, sit in a chair, or lie down. His treating physician referred him to defendant Dr. Dante Implicito, an orthopedic surgeon. After conservative treatment was unsuccessful, Dr. Implicito proposed surgery to remove pieces of bone from plaintiff's spine and replace them with bone grafts. Plaintiff alleges he consented to the surgery only on the condition that the doctor not place cadaver bone in his spine, and the doctor agreed to use plaintiff's own bone material ("autograft" bone). The doctor testified that he did not recall this discussion.

At the request of plaintiff's workers compensation carrier, he received a second opinion from another orthopedic surgeon, defendant Dr. George Jacobs, who agreed that plaintiff needed surgery. Plaintiff testified that he also informed Dr. Jacobs, who was to act as a co-surgeon with Dr. Implicito, that he did not want cadaver bone used in the surgery, and that the doctor agreed not to use it. Dr. Jacobs denied this conversation.

On the day of the surgery, July 22, 1997, plaintiff signed a consent-to-surgery form, which was also to be signed by a doctor. The form described the surgery as a "lumbar diskectomy and fusion with iliac crest bone graft + 'steffe plates.'" Though someone had signed the form on the line where a doctor was to sign, both doctors denied signing it.

During the surgery, the doctors removed bone fragments and grafted plaintiff's own bone to his spine. They also used cadaver bone as dowels for the bone graft. Defendants do not dispute that they used cadaver bone in the surgery.

The grafted bone did not fuse, and consequently, because plaintiff remained in pain and continued to be totally disabled, his workers compensation carrier referred him to another orthopedist, Dr. Steven Reich. After reviewing an x-ray of plaintiff's spine, Dr. Reich informed him that cadaver bone had been used in the surgery. Plaintiff asserts that upon learning that defendants used cadaver bone in the surgery, he became so upset that he bent a chair in the doctor's office. During his deposition, Dr. Reich, who did not testify at trial, could not remember plaintiff having that reaction to the information.

Dr. Reich subsequently performed a second surgery, without using cadaver bone. He removed all the material from the first surgery, including the cadaver bone. After the second surgery, plaintiff continued to experience pain and remained totally disabled.

* * *

[T]he question is whether the doctors' breach of the condition plaintiff placed on his consent to the surgery constituted a failure by the doctors to perform the operative procedure that plaintiff had authorized. A failure to conduct the procedure authorized is the equivalent of operating with no consent, which constitutes a battery. *Whitley-Woodford v. Jones*, 253 N.J.Super. 7, 11, 600 A.2d 946 (App.Div.1992). ***

A battery is an unauthorized touching or invasion of the patient's body. *Matthies v. Mastromonaco*, 160 N.J. 26, 36, 733 A.2d 456 (1999). It is an intentional tort that may occur, for example, "when a doctor does not obtain the consent of his patient to perform a particular operative procedure." *Whitley-Woodford, supra*, 253 N.J.Super. at 11, 600 A.2d 946. "Any non-consensual touching is a battery. Even more private than the decision who may touch one's body is the decision who may cut it open and invade it with hands and instruments." *Perna, supra*, 92 N.J. at 461, 457 A.2d 431 (internal citations omitted).

A claim against a doctor based on principles of battery is often restricted to cases in which a physician has not obtained any consent or has exceeded the scope of consent. *Matthies, supra*, 160 N.J. at 35, 733 A.2d 456. Where the consent granted by the patient is subsequently vitiated, the surgery is rendered a battery. *Howard*, 172 N.J. at 550, 800 A.2d 73; see also *Hogan v. Tavzel*, 660 So.2d 350, 352–53 (Fla.Dist.Ct.App.1995) (cause of action in battery will lie, and consent will be ineffective, if consenting person was mistaken about the nature and quality of the invasion intended), review denied, 660 So.2d 901 (Fla.1996). As we have noted, an action for battery also lies where the patient consents to one type of surgery, but the physician performs a substantially different surgery from that for which the consent was obtained. *Howard, supra*, 172 N.J. at 550, 800 A.2d 73. A battery action is also proper where a patient consents to the surgery being performed by one doctor, but the surgery is performed by another. See id. at 551–52, 800 A.2d 73 (commonly referred to as "ghost surgery"). "It is immaterial to the issue of battery that ... the operation was not negligently performed." *Pugsley v. Privette*, 220 Va. 892, 263 S.E.2d 69, 75 (1980); *Perna, supra*, 92 N.J. at 463, 457 A.2d 431 (nonconsensual operation is battery even if skillfully performed).

When a patient gives limited or conditional consent, a doctor has committed a battery if the evidence shows that the doctor acted with disregard of the consent given and thus exceeded its scope. *Duncan v. Scottsdale Med. Imaging, Ltd.*, 205 Ariz. 306, 70 P.3d 435, 440 (2003); *Murphy, supra*, A-3172-03 (slip op. at 15). Consent is vitiated wherever the "nature and quality," *Hogan, supra*, 660 So.2d at 353, of the surgery performed is "substantially different," *Howard, supra*, 172 N.J. at 550, 800 A.2d 73, from the one to which the patient consented. Simply put, if the condition a patient places on his consent to a surgical procedure is material, and that condition is not fulfilled, the surgery is rendered a battery, just as if the doctors had not obtained the patient's consent in the first instance.

Thus, here, if plaintiff can prove that the non-use of cadaver bone was a material condition of his consent to the surgery, that defendants agreed not to use cadaver bone, and that they violated the condition, the surgery became a battery.

The chapter problem presents a similar issue: was the nature and quality of the contact that occurred substantially different than what plaintiff may have consented to (expressly or impliedly) by participating in the sport? Voluntary participants in sports activities are generally held to have consented, by virtue of their participation, to injury-causing events which are known, apparent, or reasonably foreseeable consequences of their participation. The Restatement (Second) section 50 comment b explains: "Taking part in a game manifests a willingness to submit to such bodily contacts or restrictions of liberty as are permitted by its rules or usages. Participating in such a game does not manifest consent to contacts which are prohibited by rules or usages of the game if such rules or usages are designed to protect the participants and not merely to secure the better playing of the game as a test of skill. This is true although the player knows that those with or against whom he is playing are habitual violators of such rules." The following examples illustrate this point:

> A, a member of a football team, tackles B, a player on the opposing side. A's conduct is within the rules of the game. A is not liable to B.

> A, a member of a football team, tackles B, an opposing player, while he, A, is "offside." The tackle is made with no greater violence than would be permissible by the rules and usages of football were he "onside." A has not subjected B to a violence greater than, or different from, that permitted by the rules, although he is guilty of a breach of a rule. A is not liable to B.

> A, while tackling B, deliberately injures him. A is subject to liability to B, whether the tackle was or was not otherwise within the rules and usages of football.

As you can see from the examples, consent in the context of voluntary sports participation does not typically include acts where another player had a specific intent to cause physical injury separate and apart from the game. The challenge is to determine whether there was a deliberate attempt to injure and what acts are separate and apart from the game. Consider the following excerpt from *McKichan v. St. Louis Hockey Club*, 967 S.W.2d 209 (Mo.App. E.D. 1998), where a professional hockey goaltender sued for injuries resulting from a severe body check administered by an opposing player after the referee's whistle had blown and play had stopped for several seconds. In finding defendants were not liable, the court reasoned:

> In practice, ... consent must be analyzed on a case-by-case basis. Whether one player's conduct causing injury to another is actionable hinges upon the facts of an individual case. *Ross*, 637 S.W.2d at 14. Relevant factors include the specific game involved, the ages and physical attributes of the participants, their respective skills at the game and their knowledge of its rules and customs, their status as amateurs or professionals, the type of risks which inhere to the game and those which are outside the realm of reasonable anticipation, the presence or absence of protective uniforms or equipment, the degree of zest with which the game is being played, and other factors. *Id.*

> We apply these concepts and factors to the case before us. The specific game was a professional hockey game, not an amateur game. It was not a pickup, school, or college game.

> Rough play is commonplace in professional hockey. Anyone who has attended a professional hockey game or seen one on television recognizes the violent nature

of the sport. In order to gain possession of the puck or to slow down the progress of opponents, players frequently hit each other with body checks. They trip opposing players, slash at them with their hockey sticks, and fight on a regular basis, often long after the referee blows the whistle. Players regularly commit contact beyond that which is permitted by the rules, and, we are confident, do it intentionally. They wear pads, helmets and other protective equipment because of the rough nature of the sport.

Professional hockey is played at a high skill level with well conditioned athletes, who are financially compensated for their participation. They are professional players with knowledge of its rules and customs, including the violence of the sport. In part, the game is played with great intensity because its players can reap substantial financial rewards. We also recognize that the professional leagues have internal mechanisms for penalizing players and teams for violating league rules and for compensating persons who are injured.

In summary, we find that the specific conduct at issue in this case, a severe body check, is a part of professional hockey. This body check, even several seconds after the whistle and in violation of several rules of the game, was not outside the realm of reasonable anticipation. For better or for worse, it is "part of the game" of professional hockey. As such, we hold as a matter of law that the specific conduct which occurred here is not actionable.

Exercise 1-11 Using a List of Factors to Organize Your Answer

Using what you have learned in this section, identify all of the factors to consider in evaluating consent. Use your list to evaluate whether Ryan Watson, from the chapter problem, consented to contact. Be sure to explain the basis for your decision by using the rules, cases and materials from this section.

B. Other Claims Based on Intentional Conduct

The remainder of this chapter focuses on three more intentional torts — Assault, False Imprisonment, and Intentional Infliction of Emotional Distress — all of which involve injury to the person. The remaining intentional torts not covered in this chapter — Conversion, Trespass to Land, and Trespass to Chattel — involve injury to real and personal property; in Chapters Three and Six we will cover some of these and other causes of action used to recover for damage to real property.

1. Assault

Assault, the second intentional tort we will cover, occurs when defendant intentionally causes plaintiff's reasonable apprehension of a harmful or offensive contact. As a reminder, although the text will not specifically instruct you to do so for every new tort, when you encounter a new rule it is a good idea to deconstruct it and use that deconstructed rule to help you organize the information you learn about the rule. Also, for each of the intentional torts, remember to think about the following questions:

What consequence must the defendant intend?

What elements make up the prima facie case?

Exercise 1-12 Synthesizing Material

As you have seen from your reading thus far, judicial opinions (cases) aid in your understanding of how rules are applied. As a lawyer, in addition to case reading skills, you will also need to possess case and rule synthesis skills—the ability to take several cases, statutes, etc., and understand how they fit together to produce a complete rule. Below are several summaries of case outcomes establishing key principles about the law of assault. As you review each summary try to develop a statement of the rule that explains the outcome. Keep track of each of the concepts that you learn from the summaries and the rules you create and then draft a statement of the rule for assault that synthesizes what you have learned. This will help you develop your understanding of assault as well as begin to develop your ability to put several concepts together to draft a synthesized, complete rule for a topic.

1) While Pam was sleeping Michelle tried to hit her with a bat. Held: No Assault.

2) George threw a rock at Edgar, who did not see it coming, but felt it graze his arm. Held: No Assault.

3) Teri pointed an unloaded gun at Benjamin and told him she would shoot him, which Benjamin believed. Held: Assault.

4) On Halloween night, Serina came to Bouton's door, dressed in military fatigues and carrying a plastic, but realistic looking machine gun. Bouton believed Serina was an assailant. Held: No Assault.

5) Ed, a hit man, visited Michael in prison. During their visit Ed, who was speaking to Michael through a plexi-glass wall, told Michael he was going to kill him. Held: No Assault.

6) Duffy, in the course of a robbery, told Pesty, "Give me your wallet or I'll shoot." Held: Assault.

7) Jacob, who was very angry with his friend Tessa, told Tessa, "Leave or I'll break your neck." Held: No Assault.

8) While pointing to the loaded gun tucked into her waist band, Gami told Armin that she would kill him if the police officer on the corner weren't standing there. Held: No Assault.

---

2. Intentional Infliction of Emotional Distress

Intentional Infliction of Emotional Distress (IIED) is a relatively new intentional tort, which did not gain general recognition until the second half of the twentieth century.

The elements are easy enough to state: (1) extreme and outrageous conduct; (2) intentionally or recklessly (3) causing (4) severe emotional distress. The elements, however, are not always easy to prove or clearly define, as the cases below illustrate. After you evaluate the cases below, try constructing a synthesized statement of the rule that explains what is required to prove each of these elements. Consider the following questions:

1. Are the elements viewed from a subjective or objective perspective?

2. Is the relationship between the plaintiff and defendant important in assessing whether defendant's conduct is extreme and outrageous? What about defendant's knowledge of plaintiff's hypersensitivity or susceptibility?

3. Is social and/or historical context an important factor? Why?

4. What is the severity of emotional distress that is required?

5. Should plaintiffs be required to prove they suffered physical manifestations of the emotional distress (stomach problems, heart conditions, etc.)? Why?

Shumate v. Twin Tier Hospitality, LLC
655 F.Supp.2d 521 (M.D.Pa. 2009)

The instant action arises from an incident that occurred on or about Wednesday, July 12, 2006, at the Clarion Hotel on Meadow Avenue in Scranton, Pennsylvania. (Plaintiffs' Amended Complaint (Doc. 10) (hereinafter "Amend. Comp.") at ¶ 24). Plaintiffs Eric Davis, his fiancé Natasha Shumate, and their minor child Naera Shumate were in the Scranton area visiting family and looking at property. (*Id.* at ¶ 25). Each plaintiff is African-American. (*Id.* at ¶ 24).

Seeking overnight accommodations, plaintiffs went to the Clarion Hotel. (*Id.*) When they arrived, Eric Davis "went inside the Clarion Hotel and inquired about room availability for himself, his fiancé, and his minor child. [Natasha] Shumate stayed outside in the car with [their] daughter." (*Id.* at ¶ 27). Davis spoke with the front desk clerk, Defendant Lisa Pierce, who told him that there were no rooms available and directed him to the nearby Comfort Suites on Montage Mountain Road in Moosic, Pennsylvania. (*Id.* at ¶ 28). Plaintiffs took Pierce's suggestion and proceeded to the Comfort Suites. (*Id.* at ¶ 29). There were no rooms available at the Comfort Suites, but the clerk there told Davis she knew the Clarion Hotel had rooms available and suggested plaintiffs seek accommodations there. (*Id.*) Davis asked her to call to confirm that information since plaintiffs had just come from the Clarion. (*Id.*) The clerk called and confirmed that there were fifty-two rooms available at the Clarion Hotel. (*Id.* at ¶ 30).

Plaintiffs returned to the Clarion Hotel, again seeking overnight accommodations. (*Id.* at ¶ 31). Plaintiffs' amended complaint (Doc. 10) and affidavits later submitted with the plaintiffs' answer (Doc. 27) to defendants' statement of facts supporting summary judgment (Doc. 26) provide slightly different chronological accounts of the events following plaintiffs' return to the Clarion Hotel. *Compare* (Amend. Comp. at ¶¶ 31–34), *with* (Affidavit of Eric Davis (Doc. 27, Attachment A) (hereinafter "Davis Affidavit") at ¶¶ 14–16), *and* (Affidavit of Natasha Shumate (Doc. 27, Attachment B) (hereinafter "Shumate Affidavit") at ¶¶ 12–14).

According to plaintiffs' amended complaint, Davis entered the Clarion Hotel first. (*Id.* at ¶¶ 31–33). When he entered, a new clerk, Ms. Demarese "Dee" Dinardo, was at the front desk. (*Id.* at ¶ 32). Davis asked to speak with the clerk who had been at the desk previously but was told she — Pierce — was no longer there. (*Id.* at ¶ 32). Davis then told Dinardo that he would like to rent a room and she acknowledged that rooms were available. (*Id.*) After Dinardo confirmed that rooms were in fact available, Pierce — who was still at the hotel — appeared from a back room and "[a]t this same time, [Natasha] Shumate and the couple's minor daughter, Naera Shumate entered the Clarion Hotel[.]" (*Id.* at ¶¶ 32–33). Plaintiffs assert that "[d]uring this same time frame," three white males entered the Clarion Hotel, asked to rent a room, and were provided one without hesitation by the staff. (*Id.* at ¶ 34).

While the amended complaint asserts that Davis entered the Clarion first, the affidavits submitted by Eric Davis and Natasha Shumate each state that all three plaintiffs entered the Clarion Hotel together and that Natasha and Naera Shumate were present for the dialogue between Davis and Dinardo and that Natasha and Naera witnessed the three white males enter, request a room, and receive one without hesitation. (Davis Affidavit at ¶¶ 14–16); (Shumate Affidavit at ¶¶ 12–14).

Following both Dinardo's confirmation of the fact that there were rooms available at the Clarion and Natasha and Naera Shumate's entry into the Clarion Hotel, a confrontation occurred between Pierce and Davis, which Natasha and Naera Shumate witnessed. (Amend. Comp. at ¶¶ 33–36); (Davis Affidavit at ¶ 18); (Shumate Affidavit at ¶¶ 15–16). According to plaintiffs' complaint:

[U]pon seeing Defendant Lisa Pierce appear, Mr. Davis stated, he had just called and was back to obtain a hotel room. Mr. Davis stated to Lisa Pierce, "Why did you tell me there was no room?", to which Lisa Pierce replied, "There was a cancellation." Mr. Davis replied, "You had [fifty-two] cancellations?" to which Lisa Pierce replied, "I don't have to explain anything to you. Get out of my hotel." Mr. Davis then asked, "Did you say there were suddenly no rooms available because I was black?", to which Lisa Pierce replied, "Yes." (Amend. Comp. at ¶ 35).

The account of the verbal exchange between Davis and Pierce provided in the complaint is consistent with the account given by Davis and Shumate in their affidavits. *See* (Davis Affidavit at ¶ 17); (Shumate Affidavit at ¶ 15). The affidavits also state explicitly that all three plaintiffs were present for and heard the confrontation between Davis and Pierce. *See* (Davis Affidavit at ¶ 17) ("This entire exchange was done in the presence of, and was seen, heard, witnesse[d], and experienced by myself, my fiancé Natasha Shumate, and my minor daughter Naera Shumate.")

Defendants argue that all three IIED claims fail because the challenged conduct was not "extreme and outrageous" and plaintiffs, therefore, cannot establish the necessary elements of the tort. *See* (Def's. MTD Brf. at 14–16); (Def's. MSJ Brf. at 13–15); (Def's. MTD Reply Brf. at 5); (Def's. MSJ Reply Brf. at 5). Third, defendants argue that even if defendants' conduct was extreme and outrageous, Natasha and Naera Shumate's IIED claims fail because neither experienced any such conduct by defendants. *See* (Def's. MTD Brf. at 16–17); (Def's. MSJ Brf. at 15–16); (Def's. MTD Reply Brf. at 5); (Def's. MSJ Reply Brf. at 5).

III. STANDARD OF REVIEW

A. Motion to Dismiss

When a defendant files a motion to dismiss pursuant to FED. R. CIV. P. 12(b)(6), this court must "accept all factual allegations as true, construe the complaint in the light most favorable to the plaintiff, and determine whether, under any reasonable reading of the complaint, the plaintiff may be entitled to relief." *McTernan v. City of York,* 564 F.3d 636,

646 (3d Cir.2009) (citing *Phillips v. County of Allegheny,* 515 F.3d 224, 233 (3d Cir.2008)) (quoting *Pinker v. Roche Holdings Ltd.,* 292 F.3d 361, 374 n. 7 (3d Cir.2002)).

B. Motion for Summary Judgment

Granting summary judgment is proper if the pleadings, depositions, answers to interrogatories, and admissions on file, together with the affidavits, if any, show that there is no genuine issue as to any material fact and that the moving party is entitled to judgment as a matter of law. *See Knabe v. Boury,* 114 F.3d 407, 410 n. 4 (3d Cir.1997) (citing FED. R. CIV. P. 56(c)). "[T]his standard provides that the mere existence of *some* alleged factual dispute between the parties will not defeat an otherwise properly supported motion for summary judgment; the requirement is that there be no *genuine* issue of *material* fact." *Anderson v. Liberty Lobby, Inc.,* 477 U.S. 242, 247–48, 106 S.Ct. 2505, 91 L.Ed.2d 202 (1986) (emphasis in original).

In considering a motion for summary judgment, the court must examine the facts in the light most favorable to the party opposing the motion. *Int'l Raw Materials, Ltd. v. Stauffer Chemical Co.,* 898 F.2d 946, 949 (3d Cir.1990). The burden is on the moving party to demonstrate that the evidence is such that a reasonable jury could not return a verdict for the non-moving party. *Anderson,* 477 U.S. at 248, 106 S.Ct. 2505 (1986). A fact is material when it might affect the outcome of the suit under the governing law. *Id.* Where the non-moving party will bear the burden of proof at trial, the party moving for summary judgment may meet its burden by showing that the evidentiary materials of record, if reduced to admissible evidence, would be insufficient to carry the non-movant's burden of proof at trial. *Celotex v. Catrett,* 477 U.S. 317, 322, 106 S.Ct. 2548, 91 L.Ed.2d 265 (1986). Once the moving party satisfies its burden, the burden shifts to the nonmoving party, who must go beyond its pleadings, and designate specific facts by the use of affidavits, depositions, admissions, or answers to interrogatories showing that there is a genuine issue for trial. *Id.* at 324, 106 S.Ct. 2548.

IV. DISCUSSION

. . .

C. Plaintiffs' Claims for Intentional Infliction of Emotional Distress

Plaintiffs assert claims of IIED against the defendants. (Amend. Comp. at 11). Defendants Twin Tier, Scranton Hospitality, and Lisa Pierce filed a motion to dismiss (Doc. 15) and Defendant Choice Hotels filed a motion for summary judgment (Doc. 24) for plaintiffs' IIED claims. Although asserted under the respective procedural rules and standards of decision for each motion, defendants' arguments in support of the motion to dismiss and the motion for summary judgment before the court are the same.

Defendants argue, ... that their conduct did not rise to the level of extremity and outrageousness required to state or sustain a claim of IIED, and ... even if their conduct was extreme and outrageous, Natasha and Naera Shumate did not actually experience the defendant's conduct and therefore cannot state or sustain a claim for IIED. *See* (Def's. MTD Brf. at 13–17); (Def's. MSJ Brf. at 12–16).

. . .

[D]efendants contend that, as a matter of law, their alleged conduct was not "extreme and outrageous." (Def's. MTD Brf. at 15); (Def's. MSJ Brf. at 14). Defendants maintain that plaintiffs IIED claims are based on the refusal to rent a hotel room to Eric Davis on account of his race and assert that the "[p]laintiffs have alleged no additional facts in the Complaint which possibly be found to constitute 'extreme and outrageous conduct.'" (Def's. MTD Brf. at 15); (Def's. MSJ Brf. at 15).

Although the Supreme Court of Pennsylvania has not expressly recognized the tort of IIED and its definition in the Restatement (Second) of Torts § 46 (1965), it has recognized the requirements of Section 46 as establishing the minimum requirements of the tort. (*See Taylor v. Albert Einstein Med. Ctr.*, 562 Pa. 176, 754 A.2d 650, 652 (2000)). Section 46 provides that [o]ne who by extreme and outrageous conduct intentionally or recklessly causes severe emotional distress to another is subject to liability for such emotional distress, and if bodily harm to the other results from it, for such bodily harm. *Id.*

To state and sustain a claim for IIED, plaintiff must allege and show that defendants' conduct was (1) extreme and outrageous (2) intentional or reckless, and (3) caused severe emotional distress. *Livingston v. Borough of Edgewood*, No. Civ. A. 08-812, 2008 WL 5101478 at *6 (W.D.Pa.2008) (citing *Hargraves v. City of Philadelphia*, 2007 WL 1276937 (E.D.Pa. April 26, 2007))

Pennsylvania courts have defined "extreme and outrageous conduct" as conduct "so outrageous in character, and so extreme in degree, as to go beyond all possible bounds of decency, and to be regarded as atrocious, and utterly intolerable in a civilized society." *Hoy v. Angelone*, 554 Pa. 134, 720 A.2d 745, 754 (1998) (citing *Buczek v. First Nat'l Bank of Mifflintown*, 366 Pa.Super. 551, 531 A.2d 1122, 1125 (Pa.Super.Ct.1987)). Liability for IIED is "reserved by the courts for only the most clearly desperate and ultra extreme conduct." *Id.* The challenged conduct is sufficiently extreme and outrageous when "recitation of the facts to an average member of the community would arouse his resentment against the actor, and lead him to exclaim, 'Outrageous!'" (*Kazatsky v. King David Mem'l Park*, 515 Pa. 183, 527 A.2d 988, 994 (1987)).

... In *Chestnut Hill Hosp.*, the court found that the hospital's allegedly discriminatory hiring practices were not sufficiently extreme or outrageous as a matter of law and plaintiffs' IIED claim failed as a result. 874 F.Supp. at 96. In particular, the court noted that

> it is extremely rare to find conduct in the employment context that will rise to the level of outrageousness necessary to provide a basis for recovery for the tort of intentional infliction of emotional distress." *Cox v. Keystone Carbon Co.*, 861 F.2d 390, 395 (3d Cir.1988) ... As this court has noted, "[r]acial discrimination alone ... does not state a claim for intentional infliction of emotional distress." *Nichols v. Acme Markets, Inc.*, 712 F.Supp. 488 (E.D.Pa.1989), aff'd, 902 F.2d 1561 (3d Cir.1990).

Chestnut Hill Hosp., 874 F.Supp. at 96.

The case law relied upon by defendants to argue that racial discrimination cannot be "extreme and outrageous" as a matter of law is factually distinguishable from the present case. Moreover, the case law arguably does not go as far as to support the categorical proposition that racial discrimination may never constitute extreme and outrageous behavior for the purposes of an IIED claim. *Hargraves v. City of Phila.*, No. Civ. A. 05-4759, 2007 WL 1276937 at *3 (E.D.Pa. Apr. 26, 2007), collects a number of cases, including *Chestnut Hill Hospital*, to support the conclusion that if the plaintiff's cryptic and confusing filings asserted a claim of IIED, that claim should be dismissed because racial discrimination is not extreme and outrageous as a matter of law. Although the court in *Hargraves* states that "Courts in [the Eastern District of Pennsylvania] have found that racial discrimination alone does not meet the 'extreme and outrageous conduct' standard necessary to state a claim for [IIED]," the question of what additional factors or circumstances could be combined with racial discrimination to support a valid claim for IIED is not addressed. *Id.* (citing *Harry v. City of Phila.*, No. Civ. A. 03-661, 2004 WL 1387319 at *15 (E.D.Pa. June 18, 2004)).

While it would be incorrect to assert that racial discrimination is per se extreme and outrageous, it is equally incorrect to suggest that racial discrimination cannot constitute extreme and outrageous behavior for the purposes of an IIED claim. Cases where racial discrimination did not amount to extreme and outrageous conduct was less overt and flagrant than the alleged discrimination in the instant case. *See, e.g., Garcia v. Matthews,* No. Civ. A. 01-1514, Memorandum, Doc. 28 at 9–10 (M.D.Pa. Feb. 4, 2002) *aff'd on other grounds,* 66 Fed.Appx. 339 (3d Cir.2003) (allegedly discriminatory deprivation of procedural safeguards prior to termination of employment was not extreme and outrageous as a matter of law); *Farrell v. Ashcombe Dover Homeowner's Ass'n,* 2009 WL 811714, at *7 (M.D.Pa. Mar. 26, 2009) (allegedly discriminatory enforcement of homeowner's association policies was not extreme and outrageous as a matter of law); *Harry v. City of Phila.,* No. Civ. A. 03-661, 2004 WL 1387319, 14–15 (E.D.Pa. June 18, 2004) (allegedly discriminatory evaluation, promotion and hiring practices were not extreme and outrageous as a matter of law); *Barbosa v. Tribune Co.,* No. Civ. A. 01-1262, 2003 WL 22238984, at *6 (E.D.Pa. Sept. 25, 2003) ("broad and non-specific allegations of harassment [in the form of racial slurs by co-workers] and discrimination [in training, evaluation and promotion decisions by supervisors] do not meet the standard" for extreme and outrageous conduct). While these cases represent instances where IIED claims arising out of alleged racial discrimination did not survive motions for dismissal or summary judgment, they do not involve the type of overt discrimination alleged by the plaintiff in this case. In none of those cases did an employee's supervisor state directly and in the presence of others that the employee was denied a promotion or was being fired because he was black.[1]

It is true that the "'extreme and outrageous' standard is not easily satisfied" and "mere insults, indignities, threats, annoyances, petty oppressions, and other trivialities" do not constitute the type of conduct necessary to sustain a claim of IIED. *Bowersox v. P.H. Glatfelter Co.,* 677 F.Supp. 307, 310 (M.D.Pa.1988) (quoting Restatement (Second) of Torts § 46, cmt. d). However, Section 46 of the Restatement (Second), which establishes the minimum requirements for extreme and outrageous conduct per *Taylor,* states in part:

Generally, the case is one in which the recitation of the facts to an average member of the community would arouse his resentment against the actor, and lead him to exclaim, "Outrageous!"

The liability clearly does not extend to mere insults, indignities, threats, annoyances, petty oppressions, or other trivialities. The rough edges of our society are still in need of a good deal of filing down, and in the meantime plaintiffs must necessarily be expected and required to be hardened to a certain amount of rough language, and to occasional acts that are definitely inconsiderate and unkind. There is no occasion for the law to intervene in every case where some one's feelings are hurt. There must still be freedom to express an unflattering opinion, and some safety valve must be left through which

---

1. Plaintiffs' amended complaint and the affidavits from Eric Davis and Natasha Shumate allege that not only did Lisa Pierce refuse to rent a room to the family, but that Pierce openly admitted to lying about availability and sent Davis to another hotel because of the color of his skin. Pierce also told Davis she did not have to explain herself to him and ordered him to leave the hotel. This confrontation took place in the presence of Natasha and Naera Shumate and others in the hotel lobby. Moreover, while this altercation was occurring, three white men entered the hotel, asked for a room and received one without hesitation from the staff. Not only were plaintiffs openly denied a room because of their race, they witnessed firsthand the hotel grant the privileges they were denied to three non-minority patrons. A reasonable jury could certainly find that openly admitting to racial discrimination in a such a public manner while openly providing the same services to white patrons is extreme and outrageous.

irascible tempers may blow off relatively harmless steam. Restatement (Second) of Torts § 46, cmt. d.

This court cannot conclude that the challenged conduct — most notably Pierce's comments upon the plaintiffs' return to the Clarion Hotel — were "mere insults … annoyances … petty oppressions … [or] trivialities." *See Id.* Plaintiffs' amended complaint asserts that Pierce told Davis there were no rooms available at the Clarion Hotel and sent the plaintiffs to another hotel to seek accommodations. (Amend. Comp. at ¶¶ 24–29). When Davis inquired with the Comfort Suites about rooms, he was told none were available, but was directed to try the Clarion Hotel by the clerk who claimed to know that the Clarion Hotel had rooms available. (*Id.* at ¶ 29). After the clerk at the Comfort Suites confirmed that there were fifty-two rooms available at the Clarion Hotel, the plaintiffs returned to there to seek accommodations a second time. (*Id.* at ¶ 31). Davis reentered the Clarion Hotel and spoke to a different clerk, Dinardo. (*Id.* at ¶ 32). He asked Dinardo for the clerk who was working earlier — Pierce — and was told she was no longer there. (*Id.*). Dinardo confirmed there were rooms available. (*Id.*). While Davis and Dinardo were speaking, Pierce — who was in fact still at the hotel — "appeared from a back room." (*Id.* at ¶ 32–33). "At this same time, [Natasha] Shumate and the couple's young daughter, Naera [Shumate] entered the Clarion Hotel[.]" (*Id.* at ¶ 33). The complaint goes on to assert that

> [u]pon seeing Defendant Lisa Pierce appear, Mr. Davis stated, he had just called and was back to obtain a hotel room. Mr. Davis stated to Lisa Pierce, "Why did you tell me there was no room?", to which Lisa Pierce replied, "I don't have to explain anything to you. Get out of my hotel." Mr. Davis then asked, "Did you say there were suddenly no rooms available because I was black?", to which Lisa Pierce replied, "Yes".

(*Id.* at ¶ 35).

The conduct alleged here was intentional, wanton, and assertedly discriminatory. Such conduct could easily cause a reasonable member of our society to exclaim, "Outrageous!," upon hearing of it. Regarding defendants' motion to dismiss, the facts included in the plaintiffs' amended complaint and discussed above, taken as true and with all fair and reasonable inferences drawn in favor of the plaintiff, state a valid claim of IIED for which relief may be granted. Therefore, the defendants' motion to dismiss on the grounds that defendants' conduct was not extreme and outrageous will be denied.

Defendants also moved for summary judgment on the grounds that "[t]here are no additional facts of record or allegations in the Complaint which could possibly found to constitute 'extreme or outrageous conduct'" and therefore, they are entitled to judgment in their favor as a matter of law and summary judgment should be granted. (Def's. MSJ Brf. at 15). In addition to the facts plead in the amended complaint and discussed above, Eric Davis and Natasha Shumate attached affidavits to their answer to the defendant's brief statement of material facts supporting their motion for summary judgment. (Answer to Statement of Facts (Doc. 26) at 2). The affidavits substantially recount the facts included in the amended complaint and provide clarification of some ambiguity the complaint contains. *See* (Davis Affidavit ¶¶ 17–18); (Shumate Affidavit ¶¶ 13–19). Davis specifically states that the entire exchange between he and Pierce upon the plaintiffs' return to the Clarion Hotel was "witnessed, heard and experienced" by both Natasha and Naera Shumate. (Davis Affidavit at ¶¶ 17–18). Natasha Shumate substantially corroborates those assertions in her affidavit. (Shumate Affidavit at ¶¶ 13–19). Specifically, she asserts that she and Naera were with Davis from the time that Dinardo confirmed that rooms were available at the Clarion Hotel. (Shumate Affidavit at ¶ 13). Furthermore, she and Naera witnessed the white individuals enter, ask for, and receive a room without any hesitation by the Clarion staff, as well as the entire altercation between Davis and Pierce during which Pierce ordered Davis to leave the hotel and acknowledged that she refused him a room because of his race. (*Id.* at ¶¶ 13–19).

Although the " 'courts may have no particular wisdom with respect to what is socially intolerable[,]' … '[i]t is the duty of the court to determine, in the first instance, whether the defendants' conduct could reasonably be regarded as so extreme and outrageous as to permit recovery' " for IIED. *Bowersox v. P.H. Glatfelter Co.*, 677 F.Supp. 307, 311 (M.D.Pa.1988) (internal citations omitted). Defendants have not demonstrated that a reasonable jury could not find their conduct extreme and outrageous. Moreover, the body of case law cited by the defendants is factually distinguishable from the present case and does not support the categorical proposition that racial discrimination is not extreme and outrageous conduct under any factual circumstances and therefore not extreme and outrageous as a matter of law. As such, the defendants' motion for summary judgment will be denied on this point.

Third, defendants also argue that even if plaintiffs' IIED claims are not statutorily excluded and defendants' conduct is extreme and outrageous, "Natasha and Naera Shumate cannot maintain such a claim because there is no evidence that Natasha or Naera experienced any such conduct by any Defendant." (Def's. MTD Brf. at 16). Plaintiff's amended complaint states that Natasha and Naera Shumate entered the Clarion Hotel while Davis was speaking with Dinardo and witnessed Davis' confrontation with Pierce. (Amend. Comp. at ¶¶ 32–35) ("At this same time, Plaintiff [Natasha] Shumate and the couple's minor daughter, Naera, entered the Clarion Hotel[.]"). Furthermore, ¶ 37 of the amended complaint lists the "discriminatory treatment" that the "plaintiffs" — plural — were subjected to by the defendants. (*Id.* at ¶ 37). Taking the facts included in the complaint as true, it can be inferred that Plaintiffs Natasha and Naera were present for and did in fact experience the challenged conduct by the defendants. As such, defendants' motion to dismiss will be denied on this point.

Defendants restate this argument in support of their motion for summary judgment and assert that "the Complaint alleges only that Natasha and Naera at some point 'entered' the hotel, but there is no averment or evidence that either Natasha or Naera saw, heard, or experienced any conduct by the defendants, much less any 'extreme' or 'outrageous' conduct." (Def's. MSJ Brf. at 15–16). Defendants' statement of material facts filed with their motion for summary judgment states the race of both Natasha and Naera Shumate and states expressly that both remained in the car while Plaintiff Davis entered the Clarion Hotel for the first time. (Def. MSJ SOF at ¶¶ 2–3, 6). However, defendants' statement of material facts makes no mention of either Natasha or Naera's location upon their return to the Clarion Hotel when the second interaction with Defendant Pierce occurred. (Def. MSJ SOF at ¶ 9–10) ("Plaintiffs returned to the Clarion Hotel. Mr. Davis entered the hotel [.]"). Defendants' brief in support of summary judgment correctly acknowledges that plaintiffs' amended complaint alleges that Natasha and Naera Shumate entered the Clarion Hotel while Davis was speaking with Dinardo and before the second interaction with Pierce. (Amend. Comp. at ¶¶ 32–35). Furthermore, both Natasha Shumate and Eric Davis provided affidavits in opposition to defendant's motion for summary judgment which state specifically that Natasha and Naera Shumate were inside the hotel and did see and experience the hotel staff rent a room to several white individuals without hesitation as well as the verbal confrontation between Davis and Pierce. (Davis Affidavit at ¶¶ 16–17); (Shumate Affidavit at ¶¶ 12–15). Examining the facts in the light most favorable to the plaintiffs, this court concludes that a reasonable jury could find that Plaintiffs Natasha and Naera Shumate were present for and did experience conduct by the defendants. Given this dispute over a genuine issue of material fact, summary judgement will be denied on this point.

Finally, defendants assert that "as a minor, Naera [Shumate] may have been so young as to make it impossible for her to have understood any conduct, even if she had witnessed it. The complaint contains no averments to the contrary." (Def's. MTD Brf. at 16). The defendants offer no support for the implied proposition that the plaintiffs were required specifically to include in their pleadings either Naera Shumate's age or an assertion that, although a minor, she is capable of comprehending the defendants' challenged conduct. Plaintiffs' complaint is sufficient to create a reasonable expectation that discovery will reveal evidence of Naera Shumate's experience with defendants and her level of comprehension of any such experience. As such, defendants' motion to dismiss will be denied on this point.

Defendants recycle this argument to support summary judgment, stating "there is no evidence that, as a minor, Naera was mature enough to have understood any conduct, even if she had witnessed it." (Def's. MSJ Brf. at 16). Although none of filings related to the motions for dismissal or summary judgment reveal Naera Shumate's actual age, whether she was capable of comprehending conduct by any defendant that she may have witnessed is a question of fact. Defendants assert "there is no evidence … Naera was mature enough" to understand any conduct she might have witnessed. (*Id.*). The defendants have offered nothing more than this assertion to demonstrate that Naera Shumate was not sufficiently mature to comprehend any such conduct. Furthermore, the affidavit filed by the Plaintiff Davis supports the assertion that Naera was mature enough to and did in fact comprehend the conduct she allegedly witnessed. (Davis Affidavit at ¶ 21) ("My daughter, Naera Shumate, was visibly upset and shaken by the incident and events unfolding around her because of the actions and behavior of Clarion Hotel employee Lisa Pierce"). Because a genuine issue of fact remains as to whether Naera Shumate was mature enough to comprehend or be affected by the defendants' alleged conduct, summary judgment will be denied on this point.

V. CONCLUSION

For the reasons discussed above, defendants' motion to dismiss (Doc. 15) and motion for summary judgment (Doc. 24) will be denied. An appropriate order follows.

Chehade Refai v. Lazaro

614 F.Supp.2d 1103 (D. Nev. 2009)

As alleged in the First Amended Complaint ("FAC"), Plaintiff Mohamed Majed Chehade Refai ("Chehade") is a sixty-three-year-old German citizen and resident. (First Am. Compl. ("FAC") ¶¶ 12, 26.) Chehade married a United States citizen, Joanne Mulligan ("Mulligan"), in 1976. (*Id.* ¶ 12.) The two have three children, all of whom are United States citizens. (*Id.*) Chehade has visited the United States almost every year since 1978 and has owned a home in Massachusetts for approximately thirty years. (*Id.*)

On December 28, 2006, Chehade arrived at McCarran International Airport in Las Vegas on a flight from Frankfurt, Germany. (*Id.* ¶ 21.) Chehade was entering the United States to visit his daughter, a California resident. (*Id.*) At the immigration counter, Customs and Border Patrol Officer William Jones ("Jones") spoke with Chehade and checked information on a computer. (*Id.* ¶ 22.) Jones then escorted Chehade to a room where Jones announced without explanation that Chehade was being denied entry into the United States. (*Id.*) Jones proceeded to question Chehade about his nationality, ancestry, and personal information, recording the answers on a Department of Justice "Record of Sworn Statement in Administrative Proceedings" and forcing Chehade to sign the document. (*Id.*) Jones thereafter told Chehade he either could voluntarily return to Germany on the 4:55 p.m. flight that day or await further investigation while in detention. (*Id.* ¶ 23.) Chehade opted to return to Germany. (*Id.*)

Defendant Peter Lazaro ("Lazaro"), a Department of Homeland Security ("DHS") Senior Special Agent of Investigation, then arrived to interrogate Chehade. (*Id.* ¶¶ 14, 24.) Some of Lazaro's questions "bordered on the bizarre," such as whether Chehade knew who killed former Lebanese Prime Minister Rafiq Al Hariri. (*Id.* ¶ 24.) Chehade answered the questions fully and truthfully but was not permitted to catch the 4:55 flight. (*Id.*) Thereafter, DHS agents transferred Chehade to the North Las Vegas Detention Center ("NLVDC"). (*Id.* ¶ 26.) En route, DHS agents handcuffed Chehade behind his back, causing him shoulder pain. (*Id.*) DHS agents also placed Chehade in the backseat of a car without buckling his seatbelt, thereby causing him to hit his head on the front seat at every stop. (*Id.*)

Upon arrival at NLVDC, jail officials placed Chehade in a cell overnight with twenty-five other inmates, including those charged with violent offenses. (*Id.* ¶ 27.) The cell had no heat, bed, or blankets, and Chehade passed the night on the floor without a jacket. (*Id.*) Chehade feared the humiliation of using the toilet in front of the other inmates and thus did not eat until his transfer to another cell the next day. (*Id.*)

On December 29, Chehade was taken back to the airport for further questioning. (*Id.* ¶ 28.) He waited four to five hours but nobody came to question him. (*Id.*) At one point a female officer came into the room and shouted something similar to "You, Syrian, come here!" (*Id.*) Chehade was then returned to NLVDC, where he was placed in a four-man cell with at least one other inmate. (*Id.* ¶¶ 28, 36.)

After he arrived back at NLVDC, officers took Chehade and another inmate to a room where the officers told them to strip. (*Id.* ¶ 36.) The officers then told them to kneel down and cough, while the officers visually examined their anuses and genitals from the backside. (*Id.*) The officers asked Chehade to repeat the procedure, purportedly because Chehade did not expose himself to the officers' satisfaction the first time. (*Id.*)

On December 30, Lazaro and an unidentified woman questioned Chehade at NLVDC. (*Id.* ¶ 29.) They told Chehade they were the only ones who could help him but he had to cooperate. (*Id.*) They demanded that upon returning to Germany, he provide them with information on people with anti-American sentiments. (*Id.*) They informed him if he did not cooperate he would not be able to return to the United States. (*Id.*) Lazaro allegedly gave him a card with contact information and instructed Chehade to email him upon arrival in Germany. (*Id.*) Chehade understood these comments as demanding he spy for the United States if he wanted to return to see his daughter and grandchild. (*Id.*)

During his detention, DHS and NLVDC officials allegedly denied Chehade his heart medication for approximately thirty-six hours. (*Id.* ¶ 33.) Prior to Chehade's transport to NLVDC, Lazaro had been informed that Chehade suffered a massive heart attack two years prior, underwent multiple bypass surgeries, and took medication to prevent future problems. (*Id.*) However, upon arrival at NLVDC, jail officials took Chehade's heart medication along with his other possessions, refusing Chehade's request to keep the medication and claiming they would dispense their own medication to him. (*Id.*) On December 29, Chehade requested his medication but was refused. (*Id.* ¶ 34.) At around lunchtime that day, medics took Chehade's blood pressure, expressing concern over a dangerously high systolic pressure. (*Id.*) Chehade explained his heart conditions but did not receive any medication. (*Id.*) Chehade also experienced nosebleeds and an arrhythmic heartbeat. (*Id.*) Although a doctor allegedly was on call, Chehade was not aware of the doctor's presence nor permitted to see him or her. (*Id.* ¶ 35.) At approximately 9:30 a.m. on December 30, Chehade was given medication. (*Id.* ¶ 34.)

On December 31, DHS and NLVDC officials released Chehade from custody and returned him to the airport, without allowing him to change clothes or shave, and forcing him to appear in public in handcuffs. (*Id.* ¶ 30.) He was allowed to change clothes at the terminal before his flight back to Germany. (*Id.*) Shortly thereafter, a U.S. Customs and Border Protection spokesperson, Roxanne Hercules, told the press Chehade had been detained and excluded because of a criminal record or terrorism issue. (*Id.* ¶ 31.) No criminal charges were filed against Chehade concerning this incident and he has never been connected to terrorism. (*Id.*)

Subsequently, in the summer of 2007, two members of the Federal Bureau of Investigation's ("FBI") Joint Task Force in Boston, Special Agent John Crane and Massachusetts State Trooper Thomas Sarrouf ("Sarrouf"), approached Chehade's wife, Mulligan, at Boston's Logan International Airport and informed her the detention and exclusion of Chehade from the United States had been a mistake. (*Id.* ¶ 32.) They offered to assist in obtaining another U.S. visa for Chehade and gave her their business cards. (*Id.*) In early 2008, Sarrouf told Mulligan over the telephone that Chehade had been placed on a watch list incorrectly but his name had been removed after his detention. (*Id.*)

II. LEGAL STANDARD

When ruling on a motion to dismiss, the Court "must construe the complaint in the light most favorable to the plaintiff and must accept all well-pleaded factual allegations as true." *Siaperas v. Mont. State Comp. Ins. Fund,* 480 F.3d 1001, 1003 (9th Cir.2007) (quotation omitted). Although a plaintiff's factual allegations need not be detailed, a plaintiff must allege "more than labels and conclusions, and a formulaic recitation of the elements of a cause of action will not do." *Bell Atl. Corp. v. Twombly,* 550 U.S. 544, 555, 127 S.Ct. 1955, 167 L.Ed.2d 929 (2007). Dismissal is proper only if no cognizable legal theory exists or the plaintiff has alleged insufficient facts to support a cognizable legal theory. *Siaperas,* 480 F.3d at 1003. " 'The issue is not whether a plaintiff will ultimately prevail but whether the claimant is entitled to offer evidence to support the claims.' " *Hydrick v. Hunter,* 500 F.3d 978, 985 (9th Cir.2007) (quoting *Scheuer v. Rhodes,* 416 U.S. 232, 236, 94 S.Ct. 1683, 40 L.Ed.2d 90 (1974)).

III. LAZARO'S MOTION TO DISMISS

...

The United States argues the FAC does not allege extreme and outrageous conduct because federal officials did not engage in any extreme abuse of their authority as their statements to Chehade about spying were aimed at achieving a legitimate law enforcement objective of enlisting Chehade in gathering foreign intelligence. The United States argues it could deny Chehade entry under the Visa Waiver Program ("VWP") and thus the "suggestion" that Chehade would not be allowed to return to the United States was not contrary to the United States' authority to decide which aliens to admit. The United States also contends that if the federal officials' spying statements qualify as extreme and outrageous, then many questioning techniques would subject law enforcement officers to IIED claims. Finally, the United States notes the FAC does not allege that federal officials intended to cause Chehade emotional distress.

Chehade responds that the United States' employees' conduct was extreme and outrageous because they abused their authority by denying Chehade entry for no reason and attempting to coerce him into spying at a time when he was particularly susceptible to emotional distress, after a strip search and denial of medication. Chehade also argues the United States' conduct was unlawful and thus outrageous because immigration inspectors could refuse Chehade entry to the United States under the VWP only for specified reasons, none of which applied to Chehade. Further, Chehade notes the United States does not argue other actions, such as strip searches, deprivation of medication, and rough treatment en route to NLVDC, do not constitute extreme and outrageous conduct. Finally, Chehade notes the FAC alleges Defendants acted with the requisite intent.

The United States replies that the FAC indicates the IIED claim against the United States relates only to the request to spy. Nevertheless, the United States argues an IIED claim based on the decision to house Chehade at NLVDC fails because federal officials did not decide to strip search or deny medication to Chehade, and they did not intend to cause Chehade emotional distress. The United States also argues the car ride from the airport to NLVDC cannot constitute an IIED claim because that is not alleged as an IIED claim in the FAC and the allegations are not extreme and outrageous.

Under Nevada law, IIED requires three elements: "(1) extreme and outrageous conduct with either the intention of, or reckless disregard for, causing emotional distress, (2) the plaintiff's having suffered severe or extreme emotional distress and (3) actual or proximate causation." *Dillard Dep't Stores, Inc. v. Beckwith*, 115 Nev. 372, 989 P.2d 882, 886 (1999) (en banc). The Court determines whether the defendant's conduct may be regarded as extreme and outrageous so as to permit recovery, but, where reasonable people may differ, the jury determines whether the conduct was extreme and outrageous enough to result in liability. *Norman v. Gen. Motors Corp.*, 628 F.Supp. 702, 704–05 (D.Nev.1986) (considering "totality of the circumstances" in determining whether conduct is extreme and outrageous); Restatement (Second) of Torts § 46 cmt. h. "[E]xtreme and outrageous conduct is that which is outside all possible bounds of decency and is regarded as utterly intolerable in a civilized community." *Maduike v. Agency Rent-A-Car*, 114 Nev. 1, 953 P.2d 24, 26 (1998) (per curiam) (quotation omitted). However, "persons must necessarily be expected and required to be hardened to occasional acts that are definitely inconsiderate and unkind." *Id.* (omission and quotation omitted); *see also* Restatement (Second) of Torts § 46 cmt. d ("The liability clearly does not extend to mere insults, indignities, threats, annoyances, petty oppressions, or other trivialities.").

The Nevada Supreme Court has referred to the Restatement (Second) of Torts § 46 as relevant authority for IIED claims under Nevada law. *See, e.g., Olivero v. Lowe*, 116 Nev. 395, 995 P.2d 1023, 1027 (2000); *Selsnick v. Horton*, 96 Nev. 944, 620 P.2d 1256, 1257 (1980). The Restatement states that extreme and outrageous conduct may arise "from the actor's knowledge that the other is peculiarly susceptible to emotional distress, by reason of some physical or mental condition or peculiarity." Restatement (Second) of Torts § 46 cmt. f. "[H]owever, … major outrage is essential to the tort; and the mere fact that the actor knows that the other will regard the conduct as insulting, or will have his feelings hurt, is not enough." *Id.* Extreme and outrageous conduct also "may arise from an abuse by the actor of a position, or a relation with the other, which gives him actual or apparent authority over the other, or power to affect his interests."[6] *Id.* cmt. e (stating police officers have been held liable for "extreme abuse of their position").

---

6. The parties dispute whether Nevada law, like Nebraska law, requires a showing of an improper purpose in an IIED claim based on a threat by a law enforcement officer. *See Cole v. United States*, 874 F.Supp. 1011, 1045 (D.Neb.1995) ("[F]or a police officer's improper threat to be actionable, the action must normally involve some plainly improper motive, such as extortion."). Although an

Nevada has not addressed an analogous factual scenario to the present case. However, in a case factually similar to this one, the District of Connecticut found that the plaintiff alleged an IIED claim under Connecticut law. *El Badrawi v. Dep't of Homeland Sec.*, 579 F.Supp.2d 249, 279 (D.Conn.2008). In *El Badrawi*, ICE agents arrested El Badrawi on suspected immigration violations, even though he allegedly was lawfully in the United States, and transported him to a state correctional facility, where he was strip searched and placed into the general population. *Id.* at 252, 254. Although ICE agents took El Badrawi's Crohn's disease medicine from his residence, the medicine was not transported to the correctional facility nor was it given to him for seven days. *Id.* at 254. El Badrawi agreed to leave the United States after he was subjected to confinement, but he remained at the detention facility for another forty-two days. *Id.* at 254–55. The court held El Badrawi alleged extreme and outrageous conduct as to his initial arrest and detention because ICE agents "arrested El Badrawi and took him into custody alongside a general prison population, even though they knew or should have known that he had committed no immigration violation." *Id.* at 279. The court also held El Badrawi stated an IIED claim based on the post-voluntary-departure detention as this conduct could be found to shock the conscience. *Id.*[7]

Here, the FAC alleges that "[b]y asking Mr. Chehade to spy for the United States government, and suggesting that his ability to obtain an entry visa was conditioned upon his cooperation, the United States engaged in extreme and outrageous conduct." (FAC ¶ 52.) The request to have Chehade spy, although perhaps odd or even offensive, is not outside all possible bounds of decency during an interrogation at the border. However, Lazaro and the unidentified woman also told Chehade if he did not cooperate he would never be able to return to the United States where his daughter and grandchild live. Further, the FAC alleges that Lazaro and the woman stated they were the "only ones who could help [Chehade]" but first he needed to cooperate. (*Id.* ¶ 29.) Lazaro and the unidentified woman had authority over Chehade with the power to affect Chehade's ability to return to Germany. Given their control over Chehade's movements, their alleged knowledge of his heart condition, and that he would be subjected to a strip search, a reasonable jury could find the federal officials knew Chehade was peculiarly susceptible to emotional distress.

---

improper motive would add additional support to this conduct being extreme and outrageous, the Court cannot conclude that the Nevada Supreme Court, which has tended to rely on the Restatement, necessarily would require an improper motive.

7. *See also Ramirez v. City of Reno,* 925 F.Supp. 681, 687, 690 (D.Nev.1996) (concluding defendants were not entitled to summary judgment on IIED claim where defendant police officers pushed plaintiff's face first into a puddle, effectively drowning him, dragged him face down through loose gravel, and knew at the time he was not involved in knife attack and was physically and mentally disabled); *Reindl v. City of Leavenworth, Kan.,* 443 F.Supp.2d 1222, 1227, 1233–34 (D.Kan.2006) (granting summary judgment on plaintiff's mother's IIED claim in favor of police officer for officer's rude comments to plaintiff at hospital and in mother's presence that plaintiff was "going to jail" but denying summary judgment for plaintiff's IIED claim for officer's actions in beating plaintiff's leg with a baton during arrest and later comments at hospital). *But see Rondelli v. Pima County,* 120 Ariz. 483, 586 P.2d 1295, 1302 (Ariz.Ct.App.1978) (affirming summary judgment in favor of defendant police officers because stereotyping plaintiff as "Mafiosi," detaining him for an hour without explanation, searching and handcuffing him in public, treating him as a dangerous criminal for failing to file a tax return, and falsely arresting him was not extreme and outrageous conduct); *Keates v. City of Vancouver,* 73 Wash.App. 257, 869 P.2d 88, 92 (1994) (affirming summary judgment for investigator because conduct was not outside all possible bounds of decency where police officer was lawfully engaged in murder investigation of which plaintiff was suspect, officer was not aware plaintiff was particularly susceptible to emotional distress, plaintiff knew he could terminate the interview at any time, no physical contact took place, and, although officer yelled at plaintiff, it did not rise to the level of outrage).

Nevada has not considered similar circumstances in the context of an IIED claim, but at least one other federal district court has found a potentially viable IIED claim under similar facts. The Court concludes reasonable minds could differ over whether the federal officials' conduct under the totality of the circumstances in this case was extreme and outrageous and therefore the question is one for the fact finder.[8] Count four therefore states a claim upon which relief may be granted.[9]

Turner v. Wong

832 A.2d 340 (N.J. Super. 2003)

Plaintiff Delois Turner appeals from the Law Division's summary judgment dismissal of her complaint against defendants Nancy Wong and The Donut Connection Cooperative Corporation for malicious prosecution, intentional infliction of emotional distress, and denial of the benefits of a public accommodation based on race in violation of the New Jersey Law Against Discrimination (LAD), *N.J.S.A.* 10:5-1 to -49, and 42 *U.S.C.A.* § 1981.

On review of this summary judgment determination, we view the facts in a light most favorable to plaintiff. *Brill v. Guardian Life Ins. Co. of Am.,* 142 *N.J.* 520, 540, 666 *A.*2d 146 (1995). They may be briefly stated. On March 4, 2000, plaintiff, a fifty-seven-year old African-American who resides in New York State, entered defendant's store in Cape May Court House, New Jersey, to buy a cup of coffee and a donut. She was waited on by defendant Wong (defendant), the owner and operator of the store, who served plaintiff the donut first. While defendant turned to get the cup of coffee, plaintiff tasted the donut and complained that it was stale. Defendant replied that her donuts were baked fresh daily. Plaintiff responded that, while she did not doubt this, her donut was nevertheless stale. She requested a new one.

Defendant refused, insisting that plaintiff had to pay first. Plaintiff, having no intention of paying for the stale donut, instead demanded that she be given a new donut first. Defendant then called plaintiff a "black nigger from Philadelphia," repeating that phrase three or four times in front of other customers in the shop, who were all white. According to plaintiff, defendant railed, "you black niggers come in here, give me a hard time. White people don't give me a hard time. White people nice people." Although she threatened to call the police, defendant never did. Instead her son Kevin intervened, voided the charge for the donut from the cash register, and told plaintiff to pay for just the coffee, which she did.

When plaintiff asked defendant where there was a phone, defendant pointed to the door and told plaintiff to "get out of my store." Unable to obtain another donut and having been subjected to these racial insults, plaintiff left the store and filed a complaint with the Middle Township police who charged defendant with an indictable bias crime, *N.J.S.A.* 2C:33-4(d). On the same day, while at the police station being processed, defendant filed a complaint against plaintiff who, as a result, was charged with theft of a donut in violation of *N.J.S.A.*

---

8. The parties also dispute intent. The FAC alleges Defendants "engaged in the above acts and/or omissions with either the intention of, or reckless disregard for, causing Mr. Chehade physical injury and severe or extreme emotional distress." (FAC ¶ 53.) As such, the FAC alleges the requisite intent.

9. The parties dispute whether the FAC also alleges IIED against the United States based on strip searches, deprivation of medication, and rough treatment en route to NLVDC. Although a fair reading of the FAC suggests it asserts an IIED claim against the United States only with respect to the request to spy, viewing the FAC in the light most favorable to Chehade, a jury may consider the totality of the circumstances to determine whether the United States' conduct is extreme and outrageous enough to warrant liability.

2C:20-3(a). That charge was administratively dismissed by the Cape May County Prosecutor's Office on May 17, 2000, pursuant to *R.* 3:25-1. On the same date, the prosecutor downgraded the bias charge against defendant to the petty disorderly persons offense of harassment, *N.J.S.A.* 2C:33-4(a), for which she was tried in municipal court, convicted, and fined $250. The municipal judge found that defendant had used the word "nigger" several times in a loud voice and had accused black people of giving her a hard time, that defendant's son even tried to quiet her down, and that the words were uttered intentionally to cause plaintiff alarm.

As a result of the March 4, 2000, incident, plaintiff was embarrassed, shocked, mortified, hurt, angry and humiliated, although she never sought medical, therapeutic or psychiatric treatment. She claimed that since the incident, her self-esteem had deteriorated and that she viewed herself differently. Consequently, she filed this lawsuit against defendants, alleging ... intentional ... infliction of emotional distress....

After completion of discovery, defendants moved for summary judgment. The trial court granted the motion, dismissing all of plaintiff's claims. Specifically, the court found that plaintiff failed to demonstrate ... "severe" emotional distress to sustain the intentional tort alleged....

Plaintiff appeals from the summary judgment dismissal of her complaint. For reasons that follow, we affirm the dismissal of the claim of intentional infliction of emotional distress, finding no proof that plaintiff suffered severe emotional distress....

On this appeal, we accept plaintiff's version of defendant's conduct as true and give plaintiff the benefit of all reasonable inferences from the facts. *Baliko v. Stecker,* 275 *N.J.Super.* 182, 186, 645 *A.2d* 1218 (App.Div.1994). If there is no genuine issue of material fact, we decide whether the trial court's ruling on the law was correct. *Prudential Prop. Ins. v. Boylan,* 307 *N.J.Super.* 162, 167, 704 *A.2d* 597 (App.Div.1998). However, "[a] trial court's interpretation of the law and the legal consequences that flow from established facts are not entitled to any special deference." *Manalapan Realty L.P. v. Township of Manalapan,* 140 *N.J.* 366, 378, 658 *A.2d* 1230 (1995).

I

Plaintiff claims that proof of humiliation, embarrassment and disbelief, caused by racial slurs, was sufficient to establish a prima facie case of intentional infliction of emotional distress. We disagree.

To establish a claim for intentional infliction of emotional distress, a plaintiff must show that: the defendant acted intentionally or recklessly, both in doing the act and producing emotional distress; the conduct was so outrageous in character and extreme in degree as to go beyond all bounds of decency; the defendant's actions were the proximate cause of the emotional distress; and the distress suffered was so severe that no reasonable person could be expected to endure it. *Buckley v. Trenton Sav. Fund Soc'y,* 111 *N.J.* 355, 366, 544 *A.2d* 857 (1988). Here, the court dismissed plaintiff's claim solely on the ground that she did not prove this last element of severe emotional distress.

We, therefore, need not decide whether a single racial slur occurring outside of the employment context is sufficient to constitute extreme and outrageous conduct. Although our Supreme Court has held that a single event may be extreme and outrageous under the right circumstances, *Taylor v. Metzger,* 152 *N.J.* 490, 512, 706 *A.* 2d 685 (1998), that case involved a single racial slur uttered by a county sheriff who was not only the plaintiff's superior but also the chief executive and second highest-ranking law enforcement official in the county. *Ibid.* The Court expressly did not hold that a single racial slur spoken by a stranger on the street would amount to extreme and outrageous conduct. *Id.* at 511,

706 A. 2d 685. Rather, the "power dynamics" of the workplace may contribute to the extremity and outrageousness of a defendant's conduct. *Ibid.*

Severe emotional distress is a severe and disabling emotional or mental condition which may be generally recognized and diagnosed by trained professionals. *Taylor v. Metzger,* 152 *N.J.* 490, 515, 706 A. 2d 685 (1998). The emotional distress must be sufficiently substantial to result in either physical illness or serious psychological sequelae. *Aly v. Garcia,* 333 *N.J.Super.* 195, 204, 754 A.2d 1232 (App.Div.2000), *certif. denied,* 167 *N.J.* 87, 769 A.2d 1050 (2001). The standard is an objective one. The defendant's conduct must be "sufficiently severe to 'cause genuine and substantial emotional distress or mental harm to average persons.'" *Taylor, supra,* 152 *N.J.* at 516, 706 A. 2d 685 (quoting *Decker v. Princeton Packet, Inc.,* 116 *N.J.* 418, 430, 561 A.2d 1122 (1989)). The average person, of course, must be one similarly situated to the plaintiff. *Ibid.* "Whenever an intentional infliction of emotional distress claim arises out of conduct that also constitutes invidious discrimination on the basis of 'race' ..., the average person standard must be adapted to reflect those characteristics of the plaintiff that are the focus of the alleged discrimination." *Id.* at 516–17, 706 A. 2d 685.

Mere allegations of "aggravation, embarrassment, an unspecified number of headaches, and loss of sleep," are insufficient as a matter of law to support a finding of severe mental distress that no reasonable person could be expected to endure. *Buckley, supra,* 111 *N.J.* at 368, 544 A.2d 857. In *Aly, supra,* 333 *N.J.Super* at 204–05, 754 A.2d 1232, we held that it is not enough for the plaintiff to allege that he or she was "acutely upset" by the incident in question, especially where no medical assistance or counseling is sought. And in *Griffin v. Tops Appliance City, Inc.,* 337 *N.J.Super.* 15, 26, 766 A.2d 292 (App.Div.2001), we found no cause of action where the plaintiff claimed merely that he felt terrible, that he was devastated, and that his whole personality changed as a result of the incident in question. He did not suffer from any headaches, he had no difficulty sleeping, he was not unable to perform his daily routine, and he did not seek medical assistance or present an expert medical opinion. *Ibid.*

Similarly, in *Lascurain v. City of Newark,* 349 *N.J.Super.* 251, 280, 793 A.2d 731 (App.Div.2002), the plaintiff did not establish severe emotional distress where she claimed that she became nauseous and upset, was depressed, had nightmares, and no longer enjoyed her daily activities. The court found that, although the plaintiff's personal physician corroborated her depression, there had been no dramatic impact on her everyday activities or her ability to function and she had not sought regular psychiatric counseling. *Ibid.; see Harris v. Middlesex Cty. College,* 353 *N.J.Super.* 31, 47, 801 A.2d 397 (App.Div.2002) (no evidence of severe emotional distress where no allegation of interference with daily activities, no expert to support claims of emotional devastation or loss of self-esteem, and no evidence of counseling or treatment).

To be sure, the invocation of racial slurs may conceivably be sufficient to cause severe emotional distress to the average African-American. *Taylor, supra,* 152 *N.J.* at 518, 706 A. 2d 685. In *Taylor,* the plaintiff demonstrated that she had regularly undergone psychotherapy, resorted to wearing a bullet-proof vest because of fear, had been treated for anxiety, had suffered mood changes, insomnia, nightmares, and flashbacks, and had been diagnosed as suffering from post-traumatic stress disorder. *Id.* at 514, 706 A. 2d 685. The Court determined, based on these injuries, that a rational factfinder may find that the defendant's conduct would have caused severe emotional distress in the average African-American. *Id.* at 518, 706 A. 2d 685.

Of course, the inquiry here is not whether racial insults *could* inflict severe emotional distress, but rather whether the racial epithets uttered in this case actually did cause plaintiff severe emotional distress. In marked contrast to *Taylor*, plaintiff here never sought medical, psychological or other professional treatment as a result of the March 4, 2000, incident. Nor did she offer any medical or expert proof to corroborate her feelings of lost self-esteem or anger. Moreover, plaintiff's claimed distress never manifested itself physically or objectively by way of headaches, loss of sleep, inability to perform her daily functions, or any condition that was professionally diagnosed. Instead, plaintiff merely claimed that she felt humiliated and mortified because of the racial insults. Yet we cannot infer severe emotional distress simply from proof of racial slurs alone without further evidence of resultant physical illness or serious psychological sequela, *see Taylor, supra,* 152 *N.J.* at 515, 706 *A.* 2d 685, none of which has been proffered by plaintiff.

Nothing in our recent decision in *Tarr v. Bob Ciasulli's Mack Auto Mall, Inc.,* 360 *N.J.Super.* 265, 822 *A.*2d 647 (App.Div.2003), is to the contrary. In holding that a plaintiff alleging discrimination in a workplace environment does not have to meet the severe and substantial standard in order to create a jury question, *Tarr, supra,* 360 *N.J.Super.* at 271, 822 *A.*2d 647, we expressly distinguished that claim from those, as alleged here, based on the intentional tort of outrage. Emotional distress suffered by reason of proscribed discrimination is a "category distinct and separate from claims of negligent or intentional infliction of emotional distress in other contexts." *Ibid.* As to the latter, the injury is compensable "only if it is severe and substantial, ... not merely transitory but rather has a discernible effect on the plaintiff's ability to function normally, either physically or psychologically, on a daily basis." *Id.* at 271, 822 *A.*2d 647 (citing *Buckley, supra,* 111 *N.J.* at 369, 544 *A.*2d 857; *Lascurain, supra,* 349 *N.J.Super.* at 280–82, 793 *A.*2d 731).

While plaintiff's proofs of humiliation and indignity may very well be sufficient to withstand a motion to dismiss her LAD claim (see *infra*), they fall far short of sustaining a cause of action for the intentional tort. Without corroborating medical proof or evidence of physical or psychological symptoms, there exists no genuine issue of material fact as to the severity or substantiality of plaintiff's emotional distress. Accordingly, we conclude that the trial court properly dismissed this cause of action.

Sawyer v. Southwest Airlines Co.

243 F.Supp.2d 1257 (D. Kansas 2003)

Louise Sawyer and Grace Fuller bring suit against Southwest Airlines Co. ("Southwest"), alleging that it violated their rights under 42 U.S.C. § 1981 and intentionally inflicted emotional distress under Kansas law ....

Plaintiffs are African-American. On February 12, 2001, plaintiffs—who are sisters— flew from Kansas City, Missouri to Las Vegas, Nevada on Southwest Airlines.... [Plaintiffs were late checking in for their scheduled return flight. Because they had checked in late, the gate agent] placed them on the "priority standby" list at no additional cost, for the next available Southwest flight to Kansas City [flight 524].... After it boarded all non-standby passengers on Flight 524, Southwest allowed plaintiffs to board. When plaintiffs first boarded, they could not find open seats. As plaintiffs stood in the aisle, searching for seats, Southwest flight attendant Jennifer Cundiff said over the intercom, "eenie, meenie, minie, moe, pick a seat, we gotta go." Plaintiffs recognized the comment as a reference to a racist nursery rhyme which began: "eenie, meenie, minie, moe; catch a nigger by his toe ..." Plaintiffs were the only passengers standing in the aisle and in response to Cundiff's comment, many passengers snickered and directed their attention to plaintiffs. After the comment, Sawyer sat down in a seat near the front of the airplane. Because no other seats were open, Fuller remained standing until another Southwest employee instructed a different flight attendant, who was an unticketed passenger on the flight, to give up her seat for Fuller.

Defendant's conduct humiliated, angered and alienated plaintiffs. Fuller did not feel that she had received the same treatment as other passengers on the flight. Plaintiffs worried that the comment would cause Fuller to have a seizure on the plane. After Cundiff's comment, a male flight attendant gave Fuller special attention by offering her drinks and peanuts and trying to make her comfortable. As Fuller sat on the airplane, she became more angry and embarrassed at the way she was treated. During the flight, her hands were shaking. She took epilepsy medication and tried to calm down. When the airplane landed, Fuller's hands were still shaking. Fuller has significant and unexplained memory gaps about Flight 524 and her drive home from the airport.[4] Fuller rested when she got home because she was drained and upset. Fuller had a grand mal seizure on the evening of February 15, 2001, and was bedridden for three days, but she was uninsured and she therefore did not seek medical attention.[5]

After February 15, plaintiffs wrote letters of complaint to Southwest. Southwest instigated an investigation and asked Cundiff to write a report. In her report, Cundiff wrote "the statement I made on Flight 524 was not racist or discriminating, and I am offended that because I have white skin suddenly I am a racist. Maybe those that run around pointing fingers yelling racist should stop and turn that finger around." *Cundiff Deposition*, Exhibit 6 in *Plaintiffs' Response To Defendant's Motion For Summary Judgment* (Doc. # 87) filed December 30, 2002. Southwest did not believe the phrase was racist and did not reprimand Cundiff for using it or instruct her to stop using it. Cundiff no longer uses it, however, because of the ordeal it has put her and Southwest through.

...

Cundiff has worked as a Southwest flight attendant since 2000. On several prior flights, Cundiff had said "eenie meenie, minie, moe, pick a seat, we gotta go" over the intercom to get passengers to sit down and inject humor on board the aircraft. She first heard the phrase from other flight attendants. *Cundiff Deposition* at 9–10. Cundiff used it only when the aircraft was completely full and running late and passengers were in the aisle. When Cundiff made the remark on Flight 524, Southwest was running about ten minutes late, passengers had been on the plane for "quite a while," and some people were getting up and standing in the aisle. Cundiff testified that she directed the remark to all passengers, that she did not believe it was racist, and that she did not intend to be discriminatory or racist. She intended only to make the flight enjoyable.

Cundiff, who was born on April 11, 1978, and grew up in Argyle, Texas, was 22 years old on February 15, 2001. When she was growing up, she never heard the word "nigger" or the phrase "eenie, minie, minie, moe, catch a nigger by the toe." She had heard the nursery rhyme, "eenie, meenie, minie, moe, catch a tiger by its toe. If he hollers, let him go, my mother told me ..." and "eenie, meenie, minie, moe, here comes a piggy to grab your toe."

Since October 5, 1998, Ivan Osorio, M.D., has treated Fuller for seizures which probably result from epilepsy. According to Dr. Osorio, Fuller can suffer a seizure virtually any time,

---

4. Fuller does not know whether she had a petit mal seizure on the flight. She does not remember whether she talked to other passengers or slept during the flight. During and immediately after the flight she was very upset at what had happened.

5. Fuller testified that she does not always seek medical treatment after a seizure because she does not receive specific treatment for seizures and, after the fact, a doctor cannot do anything about a seizure.

any place, without any apparent cause other than the fact that she may suffer from epilepsy. Before February 15, 2001, Fuller had seizures and complained to Dr. Osorio about shaking hands. According to Fuller, stress is a trigger for her seizures. Dr. Osorio could not pinpoint any particular seizure that Fuller had suffered on account of stressful activity, however, and he testified that shaking hands may be a side effect of her medication.

Fuller did not seek professional counseling after the events of February 15, 2001, but she called Dr. Osorio's office on February 21 about her grand mal seizure on February 15. During the call, Fuller told Dr. Osorio's nurse that she had a loss of appetite and difficulty sleeping, but that she did not have insurance at the time and could not seek medical care.

Dr. Osorio cannot express an opinion about the cause of the symptoms that Fuller experienced on February 15, 2001.

Sawyer did not become physically ill or seek treatment from a psychologist or psychiatrist as a result of the events on February 15, 2001. She did not miss work and except for the fact that a lawsuit is on file, her life has not been altered in any way.

Southwest seeks summary judgment on all claims.... On plaintiffs' claim for intentional infliction of emotional distress, Southwest maintains that plaintiffs cannot prove that it intentionally and recklessly subjected them to extreme and outrageous conduct which caused extreme mental distress....

Analysis

Plaintiffs offer Dr. Winn's testimony to provide non-scientific factual and opinion testimony to educate the jury about the historical genesis of "eenie, meenie, minie, moe".... Dr. Winn, who holds a Doctorate of Philosophy, has been a college professor of history, political science, American foreign policy and labor studies from 1972 to the present. She has engaged in extensive lecturing, teaching, reading and study in the areas of Black History and racial and ethnic stereotypes in American society. She proposes to testify that:

(1) The phrase "eenie, meenie, minie, moe ..." is the first line to a racist nursery rhyme that incorporates the word "nigger."

(2) There are many derivations of the racist nursery rhyme, but almost all versions begin with "Eenie meenie minie moe/Catch a nigger by the toe...."

(3) The "eenie, meenie, minie, moe" nursery rhyme was common in pre-Civil War America when slavery was legal, and blacks were considered property and less than human.

(4) The use of the word "nigger" in the nursery rhyme and the imagery of a "nigger" being something a white person could "catch" had the intended effect of dehumanizing blacks and teaching white children that blacks were inferior.

...

(7) "White" society continued to use the "eenie, meenie, minie, moe" nursery rhyme after the Civil War and throughout the Jim Crow era.

(8) During the Jim Crow era and throughout the 1960s the "eenie, meenie, minie, moe" nursery rhyme [was] used to depict blacks as inferior to whites, to dehumanize blacks, and to teach racism and separatism to white children.

(10) In the year 2002, virtually all adult African Americans would understand the phrase "eenie, meenie, minie, moe" to be the opening line to the racist nursery rhyme containing the word "nigger"....

(11) African Americans born prior to 1960 would be particularly sensitive to and outraged by the racist message and purpose of the phrase "eenie, meenie, minie, moe."

(12) The "eenie, meenie, minie, moe" nursery rhyme is still in use today, but the word "nigger" is generally removed and replaced with the word "tiger."

...

The parties dispute how "eenie, meenie, minie, moe" is reasonably interpreted in the year 2001.... Even Southwest is apparently of two minds on the question, variously arguing that (1) it is "common knowledge" that "eenie, meenie, minie, moe" is the first line of a racist nursery rhyme that originally ended "catch a nigger by the toe," and (2) that the phrase is totally benign and could not reasonably be interpreted as a racial slur.

Intentional Infliction Of Emotional Distress

Kansas recognizes the tort of intentional infliction of emotional distress. *Moore v. State Bank of Burden*, 240 Kan. 382, 388, 729 P.2d 1205 (1986). Liability arises when a person engages in extreme and outrageous conduct and thereby intentionally or recklessly causes severe emotional distress to plaintiffs. *Id.*

Plaintiffs allege that Southwest's conduct was extreme and outrageous and amounted to intentional infliction of emotional distress. *Pretrial Order* (Doc. # 77) at 9. To prevail on a claim for intentional infliction of emotional distress, plaintiffs must prove that (1) the conduct of Southwest was intentional or in reckless disregard of plaintiffs; (2) the conduct was extreme and outrageous; (3) a causal connection existed between Southwest's conduct and plaintiffs' mental distress; and (4) plaintiffs' mental distress was extreme and severe. *Id.* (citing *Hoard v. Shawnee Mission Med. Ctr.*, 233 Kan. 267, Syl. ¶ 3, 662 P.2d 1214 (1983)). Southwest argues that it is entitled summary judgment because its conduct was not "extreme and outrageous" and, even if it was, plaintiffs did not suffer emotional distress which was so severe that no reasonable person should be expected to endure it.

In evaluating Southwest's argument, the Court must first ascertain whether its conduct may reasonably be regarded as so extreme and outrageous as to permit recovery. *See Roberts v. Saylor*, 230 Kan. 289, 292, 637 P.2d 1175, 1179 (1981). To be regarded as "extreme and outrageous," defendant's conduct must satisfy the following test:

> Liability may be found only in those cases where the conduct has been so outrageous in character, and so extreme in degree, as to go beyond the bounds of decency, and to be regarded as atrocious and utterly intolerable in a civilized society.... [F]urther ... liability may be found to exist generally in a case when the recitation of facts to an average citizen would arouse resentment against the actor, and lead that citizen to spontaneously exclaim, "Outrageous!" It should be understood that liability does not arise from mere insults, indignities, threats, annoyances, petty expression, or other trivialities. Members of the public are necessarily expected and required to be hardened to a certain amount of criticism, rough language and to occasional acts and words that are definitely inconsiderate and unkind. The law should not intervene where someone's feelings merely are hurt.... Conduct to be a sufficient basis for an action to recover for emotional distress must be outrageous to the point that it goes beyond the bounds of decency and is utterly intolerable in a civilized society.

Id. at 293, 637 P.2d at 1179.[12] If defendant's conduct rises to this level, the Court must determine whether the emotional distress suffered by plaintiffs is so severe that no reasonable person should be expected to endure it. If plaintiffs' claim fails either of these threshold requirements, the claim cannot survive. If the Court determines that "reasonable fact finders might differ as to whether defendant's conduct was sufficiently extreme and outrageous as to subject him to liability for emotional distress," and that "plaintiff's emotional distress was such that reasonable fact finders might differ as to whether plaintiff's emotional distress was genuine and so severe and extreme as to result in liability, then and only then, it must be left to the jury to determine liability based on the evidence at trial." *Taiwo v. Vu,* 249 Kan. 585, 590, 822 P.2d 1024, 1027–28 (1991).

In seeking to recover for intentional infliction of emotional distress, plaintiffs rely solely on one remark which plaintiffs heard one time. While the Court does not doubt the power of language, it is satisfied that as a matter of law, Cundiff's language is not actionable under the tort of outrage.[13] The few Kansas cases which have survived summary judgment have involved repeated physical threats and racially or sexually abusive language. *See White v. Midwest Office Tech., Inc.,* 5 F.Supp.2d 936, 953 (D.Kan.1998); *Oliphant v. Perkins Rests. Operating Co.,* 885 F.Supp. 1486, 1489–90 (D.Kan.1995) (claim survived summary judgment when supervisor repeatedly cursed at and threw objects at employee for a year and berated her at home with daily phone calls when she was pregnant and on medical leave); *Miller v. Bircham, Inc.,* 874 F.Supp. 337, 341 (D.Kan.1995) (claim survived summary judgment when supervisor took no action in face of knowledge that employee was subjected to offensive touching by co-employee on numerous occasions).

The Court recognizes that the phrase "eenie, meenie, minie, moe" is burdened by racial connotations and that a person of any race, familiar with its history, could take reasonable offense at hearing it broadcast over the intercom of an airplane. In this case, as noted above, a reasonable jury could find that (1) Cundiff's statement was objectively offensive, regardless of her intent, and (2) depending on plaintiffs' testimony at trial, that plaintiffs themselves took offense. Nonetheless, plaintiffs have not shown that Cundiff's remark was so extreme and outrageous as to be "utterly intolerable in a civilized society." It bears repeating that Cundiff's remark was not expressly racist in nature. Its ability to offend lay exclusively in its history, of which—according to Dr. Winn—recent generations are increasingly unaware. Therefore, while plaintiffs may have been insulted, annoyed and humiliated, and Cundiff's language may have been deliberately unkind, impolitic and insensitive, no reasonable jury

---

12. "The extreme and outrageous character of the conduct complained of may arise from the actor's knowledge that the other is particularly susceptible to emotional distress, by reason of some physical or mental condition or peculiarity." *Wiehe v. Kukal,* 225 Kan. 478, 481–82, 592 P.2d 860, 863 (1979) (quotations omitted). Here, however, the record contains no evidence that Cundiff knew that Fuller was unusually susceptible to stress or unusually likely to suffer epileptic seizures as a result of stress.

13. The following cases demonstrate the types of conduct that may constitute outrageous behavior under Kansas law: *Perry v. Saint Francis Hosp. & Med. Ctr.,* 886 F.Supp. 1551, 1560–62 (D.Kan.1995) (nurse exploited position of trust and intentionally misled grieving family to complete consent forms to donate tissue from dead body of loved one in violation of family's express wishes); *Bernard v. Doskocil Cos., Inc.,* 861 F.Supp. 1006, 1015 (D.Kan.1994) (racial slurs, pranks and threat to throw flammable rag around plaintiff's neck while he was welding); *Laughinghouse v. Risser,* 754 F.Supp. 836, 843 (D.Kan.1990) (continuous harassment for two years, including screaming and cursing, unwanted touchings and sexual comments and fits of rage because plaintiff would not sleep with defendant); *Taiwo,* 249 Kan. at 593, 822 P.2d 1024 (assault, battery, false imprisonment, false accusations, inducing employee to falsely accuse, and filing of false police reports against plaintiff); and *Gomez v. Hug,* 7 Kan.App.2d 603, 604–05, 645 P.2d 916 (1982) (verbal attack with vulgar racial slurs, grossly offensive insults and repeated threats of physical violence).

would agree that in these circumstances her language was so outrageous in character and so extreme in degree as to be regarded as atrocious and utterly intolerable in a civilized society.

Even if plaintiffs met the threshold requirement of showing "extreme and outrageous" conduct, they have not established that they suffered emotional distress which was so severe that no reasonable person should be expected to endure it. The Kansas Supreme Court has adopted Restatement (Second) of Torts § 46(1) (1963), and comments j and k to that section are instructive on this issue:

> The law intervenes only where the distress inflicted is so severe that no reasonable man could be expected to endure it. The intensity and the duration of the distress are factors to be considered in determining its severity. Severe distress must be proved; but in many cases the extreme and outrageous character of the defendant's conduct is in itself important evidence that the distress has existed. * * *

> The distress must be reasonable and justified under the circumstances, and there is no liability where the plaintiff has suffered exaggerated and unreasonable emotional distress, unless it results from a peculiar susceptibility to such distress of which the actor has knowledge. * * *

> It is for the court to determine whether on the evidence severe emotional distress can be found; it is for the jury to determine whether, on the evidence, it has in fact existed. * * *

> Normally, severe emotional distress is accompanied or followed by shock, illness, or other bodily harm, which in itself affords evidence that the distress is genuine and severe. The rule stated is not, however, limited to cases where there has been bodily harm; and if the conduct is sufficiently extreme and outrageous there may be liability for the emotional distress alone, without such harm. In such cases the court may perhaps tend to look for more in the way of outrage as a guarantee that the claim is genuine; but if the enormity of the outrage carries conviction that there has in fact been severe emotional distress, bodily harm is not required.

Taiwo, 249 Kan. at 594–95, 822 P.2d at 1030–31. Kansas does not permit recovery for emotional distress in tort actions unless that emotional distress is accompanied by physical injury. *See Maddy v. Vulcan Materials Co.,* 737 F.Supp. 1528 (D.Kan.1990) (citing *Anderson v. Scheffler,* 242 Kan. 857, 752 P.2d 667 (1988)).

Sawyer and Fuller claim that as a direct result of Cundiff's comment, they suffered humiliation, stress and extreme and severe mental and emotional distress. The record evidence, however, is that Sawyer did not have any physically symptoms; except for the fact that a lawsuit is on file, her life has not been altered in any way. Fuller did provide evidence of emotional distress — she was humiliated, upset, her hands began to shake and she suffered seizures as a result of her stress — but she has provided no evidence that it was "so severe that no reasonable person should be expected to endure it." *Lindemuth v. Goodyear Tire & Rubber Co.,* 19 Kan.App.2d 95, 100, 864 P.2d 744, 749 (1993) (citations omitted). The record also contains no evidence that Cundiff knew that Fuller was unusually susceptible to stress or unusually likely to suffer epileptic seizures as a result of stress. A reasonable jury would not hold Southwest liable for Fuller's atypical response to the events of February 15, 2001, which Cundiff had no reason to anticipate.

The Court sustains Southwest's summary judgment motion as to plaintiffs' claim for intentional infliction of emotional distress.

IT IS THEREFORE ORDERED that ... *Defendant Southwest Airlines Co.'s Motion For Summary Judgment* (Doc. # 79) filed November 15, 2002, be and hereby is SUSTAINED in part. Southwest is entitled to summary judgment on plaintiffs' claims for intentional infliction of emotional distress....

3. False Imprisonment

False Imprisonment, the final of the four intentional torts to the person covered in this chapter, occurs when the defendant intentionally confines plaintiff. The confinement may be by means of physical barriers, force or threat of force, or duress. The confinement must be within a boundary that is real and not just imagined by the plaintiff, and there must be no reasonable means of escape. There is disagreement as to whether the plaintiff must be aware of the confinement; some jurisdictions allow plaintiff to satisfy this element with proof of either actual awareness by the plaintiff or proof that the plaintiff was harmed as a result of the confinement.

Skill Focus: Applying and Distinguishing Precedent

As you have probably discovered, judicial opinions (cases) are drafted not just for the parties involved in the dispute for which the opinion is drafted, but also as precedent for future disputes. Lawyers use judicial opinions to argue to the court — orally or in writing when drafting motions, briefs and other documents — that a dispute should be resolved in the client's favor. When a lawyer wants the same outcome established by a precedent case, the lawyer will argue that the precedent case is sufficiently similar to the client's case to warrant that outcome — i.e. that the rule and reasoning **apply** to the present client's case, warranting the same result. When a lawyer wants a different outcome than the one established by a precedent case, the lawyer will argue that the precedent case is sufficiently different from the client's case to warrant a different outcome — i.e. that the rule and reasoning can be **distinguished** from the present client's case, warranting a different result. This process of applying and distinguishing cases is one of the most critical skills in the lawyer's arsenal — because it is often the skill required to persuade a court to rule in the client's favor. You will also see courts utilizing this skill in the opinions they draft.

In order to apply or distinguish a precedent case from your client's case you must both (1) identify the similarities or differences; and (2) establish that those similarities or differences were significant to the court's reasoning. When a court applies or distinguishes a precedent case it will usually engage in the first step — identification, but not always the second step — establishing significance. The court has the luxury of presuming that the similarities and differences they point out are the significant ones; you, however, must convince the court (and your professor) that the similarities and differences you identify are the significant ones, and so you cannot skip this step.

Read the excerpt from *Lyshak v. City of Detroit*, 88 N.W. 2d 596 (Mich. 1958) below. Does the court apply or distinguish the precedent? Does the court both (1) identify the similarities or differences; and (2) establish that those similarities or differences were significant to the court's reasoning?

Here we consider the case of a small boy whose eye was put out when he was struck by a golf ball as he played, with other boys, on the Redford golf course. He was 7 years old at the time, in the second-grade at school. He ... is the plaintiff.... The City of Detroit was one of the defendants and is the sole appellee.

If a defendant baits his traps with stinking meat and thus lures a trespassing dog to destruction, the defendant has been held liable (*Townsend v. Wathen*, 9 East 277, 103 Eng.Rep. 578). There seems to be here a valid (and perplexing) analogy. The theory is that one is liable if he lures something to its destruction. In the case before us, a great city maintained, in a densely populated residential section, a park-like area, a golf course, with ample lawn, trees, and 'a little creek.' Upon this area, in the summer, children entered daily. They were drawn to it for purposes of play as naturally as the dog to the bait. The City of Detroit knew this, knowing it the only way a 'city' can know anything, through the knowledge of its employees, servants, and agents. However, knowing of the daily entrance of children onto the course, for purposes of childish play, the city, it is asserted, nevertheless continued to conduct thereon an enterprise of such character as to subject these children to risk of grave bodily injury, resulting in ... plaintiff's loss of one eye.

[The] plaintiff, like the dog, was a trespasser. The dog's owner, nevertheless, recovered for his loss. The boy, according to the trial court, is to get nothing. What kind of law is this? Is there a real difference in the cases? In the trespassing dog case Lord Ellenborough, C. J., said that the defendant (who had baited the trap) must be considered as having contemplated the probable consequences of his act, that he had influenced 'the instinct of those animals' and had, in effect, drawn them 'irresistibly to their destruction.' In fact, said the Chief Justice, the dog 'might scent the bait, without committing any trespass,' so near was it placed to where the dog had a right to be without committing any trespass whatsoever. It takes great legal skill to distinguish the trespassing boy, having viewed the allurements of the park-like area across the crowded city street, where he had the right to be, from the trespassing dog that followed his instincts to his destruction, denying recovery to the trespassing boy, but granting it to the owner of the trespassing dog. We are not sure we possess the skill required. [Judgment of lower court reversed.]

Exercise 1-13 Applying and Distinguishing Cases to Resolve a Dispute

The following facts are from *Oramulu v. Washington Mutual Bank*, 699 F.Supp.2d 898 (S.D.Tex. 2009):

Plaintiff Ifeanyi Oramulu is from Nigeria where he attended college in the mid-1990s before moving to the United States in 1997; he became a permanent resident of the United States in 2002. In July 2002, he was hired by Washington Mutual Bank in Houston, Texas, as a Personal Financial Representative ("PFR"). He was promoted to Senior PFR and, in 2004, he was transferred to the Company Financial Center (the Fondren branch) at the invitation of Erica Wade, the branch manager. In his role as Senior PFR, Plaintiff helped customers open new accounts, serviced those accounts, and helped with customer complaints. Wade considered Plaintiff a good worker who was very intelligent and had excellent customer service skills. Plaintiff received awards for high sales numbers, and, on the day of his termination, was awarded a television for his exemplary sales record.

Debbie K. Smith, a regional manager for Defendant who oversaw several branches in the Houston, Texas area, learned that computers logged on to Plaintiff's User ID had been used repeatedly to process transactions that were found to be fraudulent. Defendant Washington Mutual Bank began a fraud investigation.

On January 25, 2006, after the workday had begun, Wade asked Plaintiff to follow her to a partially glassed-in room at the Fondren branch where representatives from Washington Mutual Financial often sit. Patrick Jude Griggs, at that time a senior fraud investigator and physical security specialist working for Defendant, was in the room when Plaintiff arrived. Griggs is 5'11" and weighs between 175–85 pounds. According to Plaintiff, Griggs informed him that he was going straight from the room to detention and that he had to "be here" that day. Griggs allegedly told Plaintiff that he was going to suffer in prison and described how men are raped there. Defendant calls this period an investigation or interview; Plaintiff calls it an interrogation. Plaintiff contends that the interrogation lasted 8 hours.

Plaintiff admits that Griggs never used physical force to detain him and never threatened to use physical force. Instead, Griggs said that the police were coming, accused him of theft, and told Plaintiff he could not leave the branch. Plaintiff was never handcuffed and no one guarded the door. Plaintiff never asked to leave the room or to use the bathroom. Several times, during the course of the interrogation with Defendant and the police, Plaintiff was instructed to leave the room, but to remain where the interrogators could see him. People walked in and out of the interview room throughout the course of the day.

Teresa Moreau, another Defendant employee who was acting as a witness to Griggs' interrogation of Plaintiff, told Plaintiff that he could not use his phone to cancel an appointment he had with a client that day. Moreau is approximately 5'5" and weighs 165–70 pounds. Griggs would not let Plaintiff go back to his desk. Subsequently, the police arrived, questioned Plaintiff, and then left without arresting him. After the police left, Griggs escorted Plaintiff outside and searched his car.

Griggs presents a slightly different account of the investigation/interrogation. He contends that he did not call the police, although someone must have because members of the police did arrive. Griggs believes the police were called because of documents found in Plaintiff's desk, including a list of account numbers. Griggs did not have a weapon during the interview, and the room where Griggs interviewed Plaintiff had no lock. Griggs insists that he did not threaten Plaintiff and did not prevent him from eating lunch or going to the bathroom, and he contends that he did not accuse Plaintiff of stealing or theft. Griggs denies detaining Plaintiff in the confines of the Fondren branch, telling him that he was under custody for theft, or informing Plaintiff that he was not allowed to leave the Fondren branch. Griggs contends that the entire period from the beginning of the interview until Plaintiff was escorted out of the building was less than four hours.

Exercise 1-14 Using Cases to Support Your Reasoning

As you read the next two cases, think about how the cases are similar to and different from the facts you've just read. Based on these cases, evaluate whether Plaintiff Ifeanyi Oramulu was falsely imprisoned. Use the cases to draft an opinion explaining your reasoning.

Randall's Food Markets, Inc. v. Johnson

891 S.W.2d 640, 645 (Tex.1995)

SPECTOR, Justice, delivered the opinion of the Court, in which PHILLIPS, Chief Justice, and GONZALEZ, HIGHTOWER, HECHT, CORNYN, GAMMAGE, and ENOCH, Justices, join.

Mary Lynn Johnson, a manager of a Randall's store, purchased several items from the store, but did not pay for a large Christmas wreath that she was holding. Vernon Davis, the check-out clerk, did not charge Johnson for the twenty-five dollar wreath because, after ringing up her other items, he asked her if there was anything else, and she replied that there was nothing else. Davis reported Johnson's failure to pay him for the wreath to management. The store's security guard was then requested to investigate the incident. The guard contacted Lewis Simmons (director of the store), and Simmons reported the incident to Mike Seals (the district manager for that store).

When Johnson returned to work two days later, Simmons escorted her to an office in the back of the store and questioned her about the wreath. Johnson admitted that she left the store without paying for the wreath, explaining that she had a lot on her mind at the time. With Johnson in the room, Simmons then called Seals and reported the results of this interview to him. Because Seals wanted to meet with Johnson later that day, Simmons asked her to stay at the store. Simmons told Johnson that he did not think it would be a good idea for her to be on the store's floor; he suggested that she either remain in the office or work on a volunteer project painting a booth for a parade. Johnson chose to wait for Seals in the office. While she waited, Johnson left the office twice, once to use the restroom and the second time to visit a friend in the floral department and to pay for the wreath.

When Seals arrived at the store, he and Simmons questioned Johnson further. They asked how she could forget to pay for an item when she was checking out with several other items at the same time. This questioning caused Johnson to cry. At the end of this interview, Seals suspended Johnson for thirty days without pay and informed her that at the conclusion of the thirty days she would be transferred to another, nearby store. Johnson never reported to work at the other store. She subsequently sued Randall's, Seals, Simmons, and Davis (collectively, "Randall's"), alleging various claims, including … false imprisonment.…

The trial court granted Randall's motion for summary judgment on all of Johnson's claims. The court of appeals affirmed in part and reversed in part, reversing the judgment of the trial court on the claims of intentional infliction of emotional distress, false imprisonment, and defamation.

To prevail on a motion for summary judgment, a movant must establish that there is no genuine issue as to any material fact and that he or she is entitled to judgment as a matter of law. TEX.R.CIV.P. 166a(c). A defendant who conclusively negates at least one of the essential elements of a cause of action is entitled to summary judgment as to that cause of action. *Wornick Co. v. Casas*, 856 S.W.2d 732, 733 (Tex.1993); *Gibbs v. General Motors Corp.*, 450 S.W.2d 827, 828 (Tex.1970). Likewise, a defendant who conclusively establishes each element of an affirmative defense is entitled to summary judgment. In reviewing a summary judgment, we must accept as true evidence in favor of the non-movant, indulging every reasonable inference and resolving all doubts in his or her favor. *El Chico Corp. v. Poole*, 732 S.W.2d 306, 315 (Tex.1987).

*   *   *

The essential elements of false imprisonment are: (1) willful detention; (2) without consent; and (3) without authority of law. *Sears, Roebuck & Co. v. Castillo*, 693 S.W.2d 374, 375 (Tex.1985). A detention may be accomplished by violence, by threats, or by any other means that restrains a person from moving from one place to another. *Martinez v. Goodyear Tire & Rubber Co.*, 651 S.W.2d 18, 20 (Tex.App. — San Antonio 1983, no writ). Where it is alleged that a detention is effected by a threat, the plaintiff must demonstrate that the threat was such as would inspire in the threatened person a just fear of injury to her person, reputation, or property. *Id.* at 20–21; *Black v. Kroger Co.*, 527 S.W.2d 794, 796 (Tex.Civ.App. — Houston [1st Dist.] 1975, writ dism'd). We hold that, as a matter of law, Randall's did not willfully detain Johnson.

Johnson bases her false imprisonment claim on her alleged confinement in a back office for several hours while awaiting the arrival of Seals. According to Johnson's testimony, Simmons told Johnson that, while waiting for Seals, she could either paint a booth for a volunteer project or remain in the office, but he did not think it would be a good idea for her to be on the floor of the store. Johnson testified that she believed that Simmons would physically prevent her from leaving the back room had she wanted to leave. She based this belief on Simmons' "sternness, his tone of voice, [and] his insistence that I stay put."

Johnson does not contend that her detention was effected by actual physical force; rather, she alleges that Simmons detained her by sternly insisting that she stay put, which caused her to fear that he would physically prevent her from leaving had she attempted to leave. In effect, Johnson alleges that Simmons impliedly threatened her person. This allegation is conclusively negated by the fact that Johnson left the area that she was allegedly confined to twice, and no one tried to stop her from doing so. Neither Simmons nor anyone else guarded Johnson. Simmons never stated that he would physically restrain Johnson if she attempted to enter the floor of the store. Simmons did not even attempt to confine Johnson to a particular place; he merely suggested that she avoid one area of the store. In short, no threat was made to detain Johnson.

Simmons' request that Johnson not work in one area of the workplace does not constitute false imprisonment. When an employer supervises its employees, it necessarily temporarily restricts the employees' freedom to move from place to place or in the direction that they wish to go. Without more, however, such a restriction is not a "willful detention."[4] An

---

4. This type of restriction could constitute a willful detention where the employer also uses physical force or threatens the employee's person, reputation, or property. *See, e.g., Black*, 527 S.W.2d at 801 (holding that the jury could reasonably conclude that threats of being taken to jail and of not seeing her daughter for a long time could have intimidated the plaintiff to the extent that she was unable to exercise her free will to leave the interview room); *Kroger Co. v. Warren*, 420 S.W.2d 218, 220–22 (Tex.Civ.App. — Houston [1st Dist.] 1967, no writ) (upholding trial court's finding of false imprisonment where the plaintiff was told that she could not leave the room until she signed a statement and was physically restrained when she attempted to leave).

employer has the right, subject to certain limited exceptions, to instruct its employees regarding the tasks that they are to perform during work hours. Johnson was compensated for the time that she spent waiting for Seals, and Simmons gave her the choice of passing this time working on a volunteer project or sitting and waiting in the office. In order to effectively manage its business, an employer must be able to suggest, and even insist, that its employees perform certain tasks in certain locations at certain times. As a matter of law, Randall's did not falsely imprison Johnson.

* * *

We accordingly reverse the judgment of the court of appeals and render judgment that Johnson take nothing.

Cuellar v. Walgreens Co.

2002 WL 471317 (Tex.App. 2002)

Appellant, Dulcinea Cuellar, appeals from a summary judgment granted in favor of appellees, Walgreen Company and its loss prevention specialist, Jim Lindsey. Cuellar contends generally that the trial court erred in granting summary judgment on her claim … for … false imprisonment. We affirm.

Background

The summary judgment evidence, viewed in the light most favorable to Cuellar, shows that Cuellar began her employment with Walgreen's on February 13, 1999. According to Cuellar, cashiers routinely rang up items priced as "two for" a particular amount by entering the first item at the listed price and the second item at one cent. In late April, Cuellar purchased some items at the store. In accordance with the recommended practice, the purchases were entered by another Walgreen's cashier. The price entered for a purchase of photographs was one cent. On June 2, 1999, in response to a request from the store manager, Lindsey arrived at the store to investigate the incident. Lindsey escorted Cuellar to the "tape room," a room at the rear of the store used by employees to review training tapes, and interviewed her for approximately an hour and fifteen minutes. Cuellar contends Lindsey threatened that she would be charged with theft and taken away in handcuffs by the police unless she confessed to stealing store merchandise. According to Cuellar, she was not specifically informed of the nature of the allegations against her, nor was she given an opportunity to explain. Lindsey accused her of "grazing," a term used to describe a store employee's taking of a product from the store and consuming it without paying for it. Cuellar admitted she had eaten two candy bars without paying for them. Although Cuellar denies that she ever stole any items from the store, at the end of the two-hour interview, she was so distraught that she signed a statement confessing to "passing" $350 in store merchandise, plus four dollars for the two candy bars.

Cuellar filed suit against Walgreen's and Lindsey on June 23, 1999. On July 11, 2000, the trial court granted a "take nothing" summary judgment in favor of appellees. This appeal followed.

Standard of Review

In a traditional summary judgment proceeding, the standard of review on appeal is whether the successful movant at the trial level carried the burden of showing that there is no genuine issue of material fact and that judgment should be granted as a matter of law. *M.D. Anderson v. Willrich,* 28 S.W.3d 22, 23 (Tex.2000); *Am. Tobacco Co., Inc. v. Grinnell,* 951 S.W.2d 420, 425 (Tex.1997); *Nixon v. Mr. Prop. Mgmt. Co., Inc.,* 690 S.W.2d 546, 548 (Tex.1985). In resolving the issue of whether the movant has carried this burden, all evidence favorable to the non-movant must be taken as true and all reasonable inferences, including any doubts, must be resolved in the non-movant's favor. *Willrich,* 28 S.W.3d at 23–24; *Nixon,* 690 S.W.2d at 548–49; *Noriega v. Mireles,* 925 S.W.2d 261, 266 (Tex.App.-Corpus Christi 1996, writ denied). When the defendant is the movant and submits summary judgment evidence disproving at least one essential element of each of the plaintiff's causes of action, then summary judgment should be granted. *Grinnell,* 951 S.W.2d at 425; *Science Spectrum, Inc. v. Martinez,* 941 S.W.2d 910, 911 (Tex.1997). If the movant has established his or her right to summary judgment, the burden shifts to the non-movant to present evidence that would raise a genuine issue of material fact. *Fojtik v. Charter Med. Corp.,* 985 S.W.2d 625, 629 (Tex.App.-Corpus Christi 1999, pet. denied). If a summary judgment is granted generally, without specifying the reason, it will be upheld if any ground in the motion for summary judgment can be sustained. *Bradley v. State ex rel. White,* 990 S.W.2d 245, 247 (Tex.1999) (*citing Star Telegram, Inc. v. Doe,* 915 S.W.2d 471, 473 (Tex.1995)); *Weakly v. East,* 900 S.W.2d 755, 758 (Tex.App.-Corpus Christi 1995, writ denied).

Cuellar contends the trial court erred in granting summary judgment because there are material fact issues regarding: (1) whether holding her against her will for two hours constitutes false imprisonment....

False Imprisonment

The elements of false imprisonment are: (1) a willful detention; (2) performed without consent; and (3) without the authority of law. *Randall's Food Markets, Inc. v. Johnson,* 891 S.W.2d 640, 644 (Tex.1995); *Wal-Mart Stores, Inc. v. Cockrell,* 61 S.W.3d 774, 777 (Tex.App.-Corpus Christi 2001, no pet.). A willful detention may be accomplished by violence, by threats, or by any other means restraining a person from moving from one place to another. *Randall's,* 891 S.W.2d at 644–45. In a false-imprisonment case, if the alleged detention was performed with the authority of law, then no false imprisonment occurred. *Cockrell,* 61 S.W.3d at 777 (*citing Wal-Mart Stores, Inc. v. Resendez,* 962 S.W.2d 539, 540 (Tex.1998)). The plaintiff must prove the absence of authority in order to establish the third element of a false-imprisonment cause of action. *Id.* An employer has a common-law privilege to investigate reasonably credible allegations of the dishonesty of its employees. *Randall's,* 891 S.W.2d at 644.

Where, as here, it is alleged that a detention is effected by a threat, the plaintiff must demonstrate that the threat was such as would inspire in the threatened person a just fear of injury to his person, reputation, or property. *Fojtik,* 985 S.W.2d at 629 (*citing Randall's,* 891 S.W.2d at 645). Threats to call the police are not ordinarily sufficient in themselves to effect an unlawful imprisonment. *Id.* In determining whether such threats are sufficient to overcome the plaintiff's free will, factors such as the relative size, age, experience, sex, and physical demeanor of the participants may be considered. *Id.* (*citing Black v. Kroger Co.,* 527 S.W.2d 794, 800 (Tex.App.-Houston [1st Dist.] 1975, writ dism'd)).

Even when we consider the evidence in the light most favorable to Cuellar, we find she has not raised a fact issue as to whether she was willfully detained without her consent and without authority of law. Appellees contend Cuellar's false imprisonment claim fails because: (1) she consented to the interview by never attempting to leave the room; and (2) they were privileged to investigate the suspected theft. As summary judgment proof, Cuellar "incorporate[d] by reference all of the depositions, documents, and exhibits attached to [appellees'] Motion for Summary Judgment." In particular, Cuellar pointed to her deposition testimony, in which she testified that she signed the statement saying she had "passed" $350 in merchandise because she was "scared to death." Cuellar testified that what "scared [her] the most" was Lindsey's statement that she had a choice between riding home in her own car or in a "cop car." She noted that as a twenty-two-year-old, she had "never had to do this before."

Cuellar points to *Kroger,* 527 S.W.2d at 800–01, and *Skillern & Sons v. Stewart,* 379 S.W.2d 687, 689–90 (Tex.App.-Fort Worth 1975, writ ref'd n.r.e.), as "factually similar" to the instant case. To support her argument that she is like the plaintiff in *Kroger,* Cuellar notes that she is a twenty-two-year old woman, living at home with her parents, and that she is five feet three inches in height, whereas Lindsey is six feet five inches. Although we agree that factors such as the relative size, age, experience, sex, and physical demeanor of the participants may be considered, *see Kroger,* 527 S.W.2d at 800, we find that the instant case is factually distinguishable from the circumstances in *Kroger.* In *Kroger,* the plaintiff was an eighteen-year-old woman with a tenth-grade education and a two-year-old daughter. *See Kroger,* 527 S.W.2d at 796. She had very little business experience, having worked as a clerk at Kroger since she was sixteen. *See id.* The plaintiff in *Kroger* testified that the security investigators accusing her of theft spoke to her in a loud voice and threatened her that if she did not confess, she would go to jail and not see her daughter for a long time. *See id.* at 800–01. After the plaintiff confessed, the Kroger investigators accompanied her to the bank, where they forced her to withdraw money from her checking account to pay for the allegedly stolen merchandise. *See id.* at 798. They also told the plaintiff's sister that if she did not bring additional money in cash within thirty minutes, they would take the plaintiff to jail. *See id.*

The facts in *Skillern* are similarly distinguishable. In *Skillern,* the plaintiff, who was accused of theft, was taken by the arm and led to a room for questioning. *See Skillern,* 379 S.W.2d at 689. At one point, she left the room to call her son, but was physically escorted back to the room. *See id.* She denied the accusations and asked to see a lawyer, but was not allowed to do so. *See id.* When she tried to get up, one of the men put his hands on her shoulders and prevented her from leaving. *See id.* at 689–90.

We have reviewed Cuellar's deposition testimony in its entirety and conclude she has failed to raise a fact issue regarding whether she was willfully detained without her consent. According to Cuellar, when Robert Pena, the assistant store manager, told her Lindsey needed to speak with her, she went into the tape room. She testified Lindsey never physically touched her, physically threatened her, or restrained her from leaving the room. Cuellar did not ask if she could call her parents. Although Cuellar described Lindsey's manner as "rude," "abrupt," and "short," he remained "calm," and did not touch her, yell at her, call her a thief, call her bad names, or curse at her. Although he did not tell her she could leave, he never told her she could not leave. Lindsey was not in the room when Cuellar wrote her statement confessing to the "passing" of merchandise and "grazing."

Cuellar testified she is a journalism major, with two-and-a-half years of college at Del Mar College and Texas A & M University-Corpus Christi. Prior to her employment at Walgreen's, she worked as a reporter at a television station and at two newspapers. At the time of her deposition, she was employed as a newspaper reporter. As a journalism major, Cuellar testified that she enjoys writing and believes she has strong grammar and vocabulary skills. When Lindsey asked her about "grazing," she asked him to define it. She stated she "asked him to define a lot of things that evening." We conclude that viewing the evidence in the light most favorable to Cuellar, she has failed to raise a fact issue as to whether she was unreasonably detained without her consent. We hold the trial court properly granted summary judgment as to Cuellar's claim of false imprisonment.

* * *

We AFFIRM the trial court's judgment.

Exercise 1-15 Evaluating Judicial Opinions

After drafting your opinion, read the following section to see how the court of appeals resolved *Oramulu v. Washington Mut. Bank*, 699 F.Supp.2d 898 (S.D.Tex. 2009). Compare the opinion you've drafted with the one set out below.

1. Do you agree or disagree with the court's conclusion? Why or why not?

2. Did the court characterize the cases the same way you did?

Oramulu v. Washington Mut. Bank

699 F.Supp.2d 898 (S.D.Tex. 2009)

*** VI. FALSE IMPRISONMENT

Defendant argues that Plaintiff was not detained without his consent because Plaintiff was never physically restrained nor verbally threatened. In the alternative, Defendant contends that it was legally justified in detaining Plaintiff because he was suspected of perpetrating fraud on bank customers. Plaintiff responds that he was detained without his consent because Griggs threatened him with federal prison and told him to sit until the police arrived, and these threats overcame Plaintiff's free will to leave. In addition, Plaintiff contends that the interview, which he alleges lasted over eight hours, was unreasonably long. Lastly, Plaintiff insists that Defendant was aware, or reasonably should have been aware that a manager could have assumed Plaintiff's identity and performed the acts of which Plaintiff was accused.

"The essential elements of false imprisonment are: (1) willful detention; (2) without consent; and (3) without authority of law." *Wal-Mart Stores, Inc. v. Rodriguez*, 92 S.W.3d 502, 506 (Tex.2002) (internal citations omitted). The first element is satisfied by conduct that is "intended to cause one to be detained and in fact causes the detention, even when the actor does not participate in the detention." *Id.* at 507. The detention may be accomplished by violence, by threats, or by any other means that restrain a person from moving from one place to another. *Randall's Food Markets, Inc. v. Johnson*, 891 S.W.2d 640, 645 (Tex.1995) (citing *Martinez v. Goodyear Tire & Rubber Co.*, 651 S.W.2d 18, 20 (Tex.App.-San Antonio 1983, no writ)).

1. *Detention Without Consent*

In the case of an alleged detention by threat, "the plaintiff must demonstrate that the threat was such as would inspire in the threatened person a just fear of injury to her person, reputation, or property." *Johnson*, 891 S.W.2d at 645 (internal citations omitted). Threats to call the police and other threats of future action are not ordinarily sufficient, without more, to effect an unlawful imprisonment without contemporaneous events such as extended interrogation and intimidation. *Fojtik v. Charter Medical Corp.*, 985 S.W.2d 625, 629

(Tex.App.-Corpus Christi 1999, pet. denied) (internal citations omitted); *Morales v. Lee*, 668 S.W.2d 867, 869 (Tex.App.-San Antonio 1984, no writ). A court may examine the relative age, size, sex, and physical demeanor of the participants to determine whether such threats are sufficient to overcome the plaintiff's free will. *Charter Medical Corp.*, 985 S.W.2d at 629; *Black v. Kroger Co.*, 527 S.W.2d 794, 800 (Tex.App.-Houston [1st Dist.] 1975, writ dism'd).

In other false imprisonment cases, courts have examined the timing of the interview, whether the plaintiff was prevented from leaving the area, whether the plaintiff was prevented from leaving when he made such a request, and whether he was told to remain in the interview area. *Compare, e.g. Safeway Stores, Inc. v. Amburn*, 388 S.W.2d 443, 446 (Tex.App.-Fort Worth 1965, no writ.) (holding that a 30 to 40 minute interview in a partially blocked hallway during which the plaintiff did not ask to leave nor was he told to remain did not constitute false imprisonment even though the interviewer intimidated plaintiff into signing a false confession), *Randall's Food Markets, Inc. v. Johnson*, 891 S.W.2d 640, 645 (Tex.1995) (holding that, even though the plaintiff believed that the interviewer, because of his sternness and his insistence that the plaintiff stay put, would physically prevent her from leaving, the plaintiff had no false imprisonment claim because she left the area twice, no one guarded her, and the interviewer never said that he would physically restrain her); *with Black v. Kroger Co.*, 527 S.W.2d at 801 (upholding the jury's verdict of false imprisonment when the plaintiff was intimidated because she had a "healthy respect for the authority" of the interviewer, the interviewer spoke in a loud voice, and the plaintiff was threatened with a long incarceration if she did not confess).

Here, Plaintiff was never handcuffed or told that he could not leave or eat his lunch. Plaintiff was not touched or threatened with a weapon. Griggs and Moreau do not have extremely large and imposing builds. Griggs left the interview room during the interview/interrogation, and Plaintiff was required to sit outside the interview room for portions of the day. This case is factually similar to an unpublished decision issuing from an appeals court in Corpus Christi. There, the court granted the defendant's motion for summary judgment after concluding that the person interviewing her for regarding her alleged theft: never physically touched her, physically threatened her, or restrained her from leaving the room. [The plaintiff] did not ask if she could call her parents. Although [the plaintiff] described [the interviewer's] manner as "rude," "abrupt," and "short," he remained "calm," and did not touch her, yell at her, call her a thief, call her bad names, or curse at her. Although he did not tell her she could leave, he never told her she could not leave. Lindsey was not in the room when Cuellar wrote her statement confessing to the "passing" of merchandise and "grazing."

Cuellar v. Walgreens Co., 2002 WL 471317, at *3–4 (Tex.App.-Corpus Christi 2002 no pet.) (unpublished). On the other hand, Plaintiff contends that he was held for 8 hours, and that Griggs threatened that he would go to prison for a long time, someone working for Defendant did call the police, Griggs accused him of theft, and Griggs would not allow him to leave the bank branch.

The Court also notes that the instant facts bear some resemblance to *Johnson* because Plaintiff left the area and his interviewer was allegedly stern. The Court, however, ultimately finds *Johnson* and *Cuellar* distinguishable because Plaintiff avers that he was confined to the bank branch for eight hours, that he was told to stay put because the police were actually coming, and that he was threatened with prison rape. *See Johnson*, 891 S.W.2d at 645 n. 4 (explaining that temporarily restricting an employee's movement may constitute willful detention if the employer uses physical force or threatens the employee's person, reputation or property, citing *Black*). The Court finds that, viewing the facts in the light most favorable to Plaintiff, he has testified to circumstances that create a material fact issue over whether he was detained without his consent.

2. *Authority of Law*

In order to make out a claim for false imprisonment, the plaintiff must provide facts to prove that the detention was without the authority of law. In Texas, "[a] person who reasonably believes that another has stolen or is attempting to steal property is privileged to detain that person in a reasonable manner and for a reasonable time to investigate ownership of the property." Tex. Civ. Prac. & Rem.Code § 124.001. "Reasonable cause for an investigative detention is something less than probable cause." *Wal-Mart Stores, Inc. v. Odem*, 929 S.W.2d 513, 520 (Tex. App-San Antonio 1996, no writ). Reasonableness is examined based on the employee's actions under the circumstances and not on the actual guilt or innocence of the examined party. *Id.* at 520. Reasonableness is typically a jury question.

Although the shopkeeper's privilege does not always apply to employer-employee situations, in this case, Defendant was questioning Plaintiff about a fraud through which a bank employee had taken funds that belonged to a bank customer. The inquiry becomes, then, whether Defendant was reasonable in its belief and whether it detained plaintiff in a reasonable manner and for a reasonable time. Again, the Court finds that fact questions remain because of the length of the questioning and the manner in which the questioning was conducted. Defendant's Motion as to this claim will be denied.

VII. CONCLUSION

… Defendant's Motion for Summary Judgment (Doc. No. 16) is DENIED as to [the] false imprisonment claim.

IT IS SO ORDERED.

Skill Focus: Applying and Distinguishing Precedent Part Two — The Lawyer's Perspective

You have just experienced how a judge might apply and distinguish authority in order to render a decision. The next step is to understand how lawyers utilize that same skill.

One of a lawyer's goals is to persuade the court to rule favorably for her client. One of the ways that a lawyer might persuade the court is by demonstrating that there is authority that requires the court to rule in the client's favor — this is called binding authority. One source of such binding authority is case law from a higher court in the jurisdiction where the client's claim is filed.

When the claim is filed in a jurisdiction that has not yet decided an issue, the lawyer has two goals (1) to persuade the court to adopt authority from other jurisdictions, and (2) to persuade the court that the authority to be adopted results in a favorable decision to the lawyer's client. In this chapter, we will focus on this second part (which mirrors what a client must do when she has the benefit of binding authority). As a result of this goal, lawyers read cases with several objectives, including predicting what a court might do in their client's case; finding cases they might use to persuade the court to rule in their client's favor; and finding cases that might be used by an opponent so that they are prepared to respond to, and hopefully defeat, counter arguments. In other words, when lawyers review cases they read with their client's case in mind—looking for cases that may help or hurt their client's case.

In an effort to obtain a decision that is favorable to the client, lawyers must demonstrate that favorable cases apply to the client's case and that unfavorable cases can be distinguished. Rarely will a lawyer find binding cases that are identical to her client's case. This is why lawyers must be able to explain to the court how the case is similar to or different from their client's case—the skill we call applying and distinguishing.

One of the ways to apply and distinguish cases is to find similarities and/or differences between the facts of a client's case and the facts the court considered in making their decision in the precedent case. Another way is to use the social policy reasons the court utilized as the basis for the opinion and to show that the social policy applies to the current case, such that the same outcome should result (or to show that a different social policy applies, such that a different result is warranted).

To persuade a court to follow or reject precedent, a lawyer must demonstrate not just that the similarities or differences exist, but also that they were important to the court's decision. For example, if similar facts exist, and the court relied on those facts to reach the decision in the precedent case, the court will be bound to make the same decision in the client's case; conversely, if the court relied on facts in the precedent case that are missing or different from the client's case, the court is not bound to make the same decision.

To apply a case a lawyer would identify the similarities (facts, policy, or reasoning) with the precedent case and the client's case and convince the court that those similarities were the basis for the court's decision, so the result should be the same in the client's case. To distinguish a case a lawyer would identify differences (facts, policy, or reasoning) between the precedent case and the client's case and convince the court that those differences mean that the result should be different in the client's case. Here are the steps you might take to demonstrate that precedent applies:

1. Establish that the precedent case stands for proposition that: when a fact or set of facts, policy or other reason exists (as set out in the precedent case), the result must be the outcome in the precedent case.

2. Establish that the same or very similar facts, policies or other reasons also exist in the current client's case, so the result must also be the same as the outcome in the precedent case.

Here are the steps you might take to demonstrate that precedent does not apply (i.e. the precedent is distinguishable):

1. Establish that the precedent case stands for the proposition that when a fact or set of facts, policy or other reason exists (as set out in the precedent case), the result must be the outcome in the precedent case.

2. Establish that either

   a. the same fact or set of facts, policies or other reasons do not exist in the current client's case, or

   b. the fact or set of facts, policies or other reasons are sufficiently different from the client's case so that

the result should not be the same as the outcome in the precedent case.

As you practice this skill, it may help to ask yourself the following questions:

What is the outcome you want?

Did that happen in the precedent case?

> If yes, you will want the case to apply. Consider:
>
>> What was the basis for the court deciding that outcome? What facts, policy or other reasons did the court rely on?
>>
>> Are those facts, policies or other reasons or similar facts, policies or other reasons, present in your case?
>
> If no, you will want to distinguish the case. Consider:
>
>> What was the basis for the court deciding that outcome? What facts, policies or other reasons did the court rely on?
>>
>> Are there any significant differences between those facts, policies or other reasons and the facts, policies or other circumstances in your case?

In other words, as you are reading a case, think about what was important to the court's decision and whether those facts, set of facts, policies or other reasons are similar or different from your client's. Also, look for places where the court applies or distinguishes other cases—because such cases may end up being helpful to your client's argument. For example, if the court reaches an outcome you wish to avoid, by distinguishing another case, you might be able to show your case is closer to the case the court distinguished—warranting the result in that distinguished case, rather than the case you are reading.

This skill will also be helpful for law school examinations where you are given fact patterns that are a variation of one or more of the cases you have read in class. If you identify the facts, set of facts, policies or other reasons, the court relied on in making the decision in each case you read in this text, then when you are given a fact pattern on an examination, you can identify the similarities or differences between the cases you have read and the examination, and discuss how those similarities or differences were important to the court, and thus require a specific outcome for the parties in the exam fact pattern.

Exercise 1-16 Applying and Distinguishing Revisited

Review the opinion you drafted in exercise 1-14. In that exercise you were able to decide the law, and then set out your reasons (because you were the judge). How would you change the opinion if your task was to convince the court to adopt the decision you have written (as you will do when you are a lawyer)? In other words, redraft the opinion so that it conveys to the court the reasons the court should reach the outcome your client desires.

Exercise 1-17 The Burden of Proof

The *Oramulu* court mentions the shopkeeper's privilege—which allows a "shopkeeper" (store manager, owner, etc.) to detain a suspected thief. The rule for false imprisonment articulated in *Oramulu*, requires the plaintiff to show defendant detained plaintiff without authority of law, placing the burden of proof for this privilege on plaintiff rather than defendant. Compare Restatement (Second) Torts § 35, which does not:

> False Imprisonment
>
> (1) An actor is subject to liability to another for false imprisonment if (a) he acts intending to confine the other or a third person within boundaries fixed by the actor, and (b) his act directly or indirectly results in such a confinement of the other, and (c) the other is conscious of the confinement or is harmed by it.

Now look at Texas rule for false imprisonment found in *Oramulu*, which places the burden of proof on plaintiff. Which side do you think should bear the burden of proof on this issue? Why? Consider the following statements:

> "[A]ffirmative defenses are those in which the defendant admits doing the act but seeks to justify, excuse, or mitigate his conduct." *Carlson v. State*, 240 Ga.App. 589, 524 S.E.2d 283, 286 (1999).

> It would be "manifestly unsound and impractical to require a plaintiff to negative at the outset all possible excuses or justifications"; thus, defendant must "plead and prove" such justifications. *Prosser and Keeton on the Law of Torts* § 16 (5th ed.1984).

C. Affirmative Defenses: Self-Defense and Defense of Others

Defendants may raise affirmative defenses of self-defense and defense of others to claims of assault, battery and false imprisonment. Remember that the defendant has the burden to prove an affirmative defense. For each of these defenses, the defendant must establish (1) she used reasonable force; (2) she actually believed force was necessary; (3) it was reasonable to believe force was necessary; and (4) she used force to prevent unlawful and immediate harm.

Generally, reasonable force is force that is not intended or likely to cause death or serious bodily harm. The force used must be force that is objectively reasonable under the circumstances and no more force than is necessary to prevent or avert the threat of immediate harm. The reasonableness of the amount of force used is to be determined in the light of all the facts and circumstances of the case, which may include: the relative age, size, and strength of the parties, their reputations for violence, who was the aggressor, the degree of physical harm reasonably feared, and the presence or absence of weapons. In order to justify the use of deadly force, a person must be in imminent danger of death or serious bodily harm, or reasonably and actually believe she is in imminent danger of death or serious bodily harm.

In addition to establishing that she used reasonable force, defendant must also prove that she subjectively (actually and honestly) believed that force was necessary. It must also be reasonable for her to have believed such force was necessary—which is measured objectively, but from her subjective standpoint. In other words, it is possible to prove self-defense if a reasonable person in the same circumstances would have believed force was necessary even if it later turns out such force was not necessary. For example, where defendant reasonably believes she is being attacked by a criminal, who later turns out to be a plain clothes police officer making an arrest, she would be justified in using reasonable force to defend herself against the police officer if she actually believed it was necessary and if a reasonable person in her position would also believe it was necessary—i.e., it was reasonable to believe she was being attacked by a criminal (and not a police officer) and the attack was without justification or privilege.

Finally, defendant must prove she used force to stop or avert an immediate threatened harm. Force may not be used for revenge, retaliation or as a preemptive strike.

In the majority of jurisdictions, there is no duty to retreat before using force, even if the defendant can safely retreat without using force. In a minority of jurisdictions, a defendant must retreat before using deadly force, where it is safe to do so. In every jurisdiction a defendant is not required to retreat in her own home before using any force, even deadly force.

Another issue related to self-defense is the right of a person who is the initial aggressor to use force to defend themselves. As a general rule a person cannot start a fight and then rely on a claim of self-defense when they are struck by the victim. However, if the initial aggressor withdraws from the fight, abandoning the attack, and sufficiently communicates this withdrawal to the victim such that the victim should no longer reasonably believe she is under threat of harm, the initial aggressor may then be privileged to use force to defend herself from the initial victim.

Exercise 1-18 Law School Skills Applied to Law Practice

Reprinted below are: Plaintiff's Motion for Partial Summary Judgment and Defendant's Opposition to Plaintiff's Motion from *Eyster v. Colon*, No. CV 2005-052870, an action filed in Arizona Superior Court. These motions are both an illustration of the skills covered in this chapter as well as an exercise in understanding the law of self defense.

1. Review the pleadings to identify where the lawyers use the following skills:

    a. Rule deconstruction

    b. Rule synthesis

    c. Applying and Distinguishing Cases

2. Identify the rules related to self-defense. Are there any differences between the rules articulated in the introduction to this chapter, and if so, what are they?

3. Draft a summary of what you learn about self-defense from reading these motions.

4. Determine whether plaintiff's motion should be granted or denied and on what grounds. For this portion you may find it helpful to read the relevant portions of the key cases cited by the parties, which are printed after the parties' motions.

1 | FRANKLIN & ASSOCIATES, P.A.

2 | Scottsdale, AZ 85259

3

4 | Attorney for Plaintiffs

5

6

7 | SUPERIOR COURT OF ARIZONA

8 | MARICOPA COUNTY

9

10 | Daniel EYSTER, a single man,   No. CV 2005-052870.

11 | Plaintiff,   PLAINTIFFS' MOTION FOR
                                               PARTIAL SUMMARY
12 | v.   JUDGEMENT RE LIABILITY

13 | Aaron C. COLON and Jane Doe
     Colon, husband and wife; John
14 | Does I–V, Jane Does I–V, Black
15 | Corporations I–V, White
     Partnerships I–V,
16
              Defendants.
17

18

19

20 | Plaintiff DANIEL EYSTER, by and through counsel undersigned, hereby submit this

21 | Motion for Partial Summary Judgment regarding liability in this matter. This motion is

22 | supported by a separate "Statement of Facts in Support of Plaintiffs Motion for Sum-

23 | mary Judgment," which is hereby incorporated by this reference. In addition, this mo-

24 | tion is supported by the following Memorandum of Points and Authorities.

25

26

27

28

29

30

31

32

MEMORANDUM OF POINTS & AUTHORITIES

I.

FACTUAL BACKGROUND

Plaintiff hereby states that the set of facts set forth below constitute Defendant's version of what happened. They should not be viewed as being Plaintiff's version of the incident in question. Instead, Plaintiff has put forth Defendant's version of the facts in an effort to show that even when taken at his word, Defendant cannot justify his shooting of Plaintiff on the morning of June 12, 2005.

Prior to the incident that is the subject of this litigation, Plaintiff and Defendant were neighbors, and enjoyed an amicable and friendly relationship. SOF ¶¶ 1, 2. On the afternoon of June 11, 2005, Plaintiff went to Defendant's house to visit. SOF ¶ 3. When he arrived, Plaintiff found Defendant working in his garage with a cooler of beer. SOF ¶ 3. Plaintiff asked Defendant if he could have a beer, and the two then spent time visiting in Defendant's garage. SOF ¶¶ 4, 5. At some point during Plaintiff's visit, Defendant told Plaintiff that he was going to leave the residence and get something to eat. SOF ¶ 5. Knowing that Defendant was leaving the residence, Plaintiff asked Defendant if he would give him a ride to a local Circle K. SOF ¶ 6. After leaving Defendant's home, Plaintiff and Defendant wound up going to a restaurant/bar called Shillelagh's. SOF ¶ 7.

While Plaintiff and Defendant were at Shillelagh's, they consumed beer and watched as other patrons performed Karaoke. SOF ¶ 8. At some point while the two were at Shillelagh's, Plaintiff became involved in a verbal altercation with the person running the bar's Karaoke. SOF ¶ 9. Due to his dispute with the person running Karaoke, Plaintiff was asked by management to leave the bar. SOF ¶ 10. After initially resisting the request that he leave the bar, Plaintiff did in fact leave Shillelagh's. SOF ¶ 1. He was given a ride back to his residence by deputies from the Maricopa County Sheriffs Office (hereinafter "MCSO"). SOF ¶ 12.

Once he was returned to his home, Plaintiff was upset that Defendant had not given him a ride home. SOF ¶ 13. When Defendant arrived back at his residence it was sometime after midnight. SOF ¶ 15. As he pulled into his driveway, Defendant found his driveway blocked by items that had previously been stored on the side of his house. SOF ¶ 17. Upon finding his path blocked, Defendant got out of his truck and began to

move the items causing the blockage. SOF ¶ 18. While Defendant was moving the
items, Plaintiff appeared and said "you let the cops take me home mother fucker." SOF
19. As Plaintiff made the aforementioned statement, he struck Defendant. SOF ¶ 20.
Defendant responded by taking defensive measures and saying "what are you doing?"
SOF ¶ 21. Despite the defensive measures, Defendant was knocked to the ground during the altercation. SOF ¶ 23. Once Defendant was on the ground, Plaintiff ceased his
attack and disappeared. SOF ¶ 23. During this part of the altercation Defendant suffered a split lip and bruises to his facial area. SOF ¶ 24. In addition, Defendant admits
that he never saw Plaintiff with a weapon during this altercation. SOF ¶ 25.

Once Plaintiff had disappeared, Defendant retrieved his .357 revolver from the glove
box of his truck SOF ¶ 26. Now armed, Defendant began walking towards his home.
SOF ¶ 27. As he approached the front door, Defendant saw Plaintiff walking approximately 40 to 50 feet away. SOF ¶ 28. Defendant then heard Plaintiff say "I'm going to
kill you." SOF ¶ 29. At this point, Defendant could see Plaintiff's outline, and thought
that he was approaching him. SOF ¶ 30. Defendant did not see any weapons on Plaintiff's person. SOF ¶ 31. Defendant then responded to Plaintiff's verbal threat by telling
Plaintiff to "get lost," and by firing a warning shot from his revolver. SOF ¶ 32. Plaintiff
responded to the warning shot by stating that Defendant didn't have the "balls" to
shoot him. SOF ¶ 34. As Plaintiff continued to walk towards Defendant, Defendant
shot Plaintiff in the abdomen. SOF ¶ 35.

After Plaintiff was shot, he said "I can't believe you just shot me." SOF ¶ 36. Plaintiff
then ran off towards his own residence. SOF ¶ 37. After Plaintiff fled the area, Defendant called the police. SOF ¶ 38. Officers from MCSO responded to the scene, and Detective Scudella interviewed Defendant. SOF ¶ 39. In his deposition, Defendant
confirmed the accuracy of Detective Scudella's investigation report. SOF ¶ 39. According to Detective Scudella, he asked Defendant why he felt threatened prior to the
shooting. SOF ¶ 40. Defendant responded that he had felt threatened because Plaintiff
had said "I'm going to kill you." SOF ¶ 40. Detective Scudella then asked Defendant if
Plaintiff had been holding anything or had anything on him. SOF ¶ 41. Defendant responded that he had not seen anything. SOF ¶ 41.

At some point after his interview with Detective Scudella, Defendant found a 3/8
inch ratchet driver on the ground, that he thought Plaintiff might have used as a
weapon during the altercation. SOF ¶ 41. However, Defendant admits that he never

1 | saw Plaintiff in possession of anything that could be construed as a weapon prior to the

2 | shooting. SOF ¶ 43. Lastly, it should be noted that Plaintiff was intoxicated during the

3 | aforementioned events. SOF ¶ 44.

4 | **II.**

5 | **LAW & ARGUMENTS**

6 | Plaintiff respectfully requests that this Court grant partial summary judgment on

7 | the issue of liability. In his complaint, Plaintiff alleged that Defendant negligently exer-

8 | cised his right to self defense when he shot him on the morning of June 12, 2005.

9 | Plaintiff now asks for summary judgment on the issue of whether Defendant negli-

10 | gently exercised his right to self defense. Plaintiff makes this motion due to the fact

11 | that no reasonable juror could find that Defendant's shooting of Plaintiff was justified

12 | under any of Arizona's justification statutes.

13 | **A. Legal Standard for Granting Summary Judgment:**

14 | To grant a motion for summary judgment, the trial court must find that no genuine

15 | issue of material fact exists in the record (including the pleadings, depositions, answers

16 | to interrogatories, admissions, and affidavits) and that the moving party is entitled to

17 | judgment on the merits as a matter of law. *Mercy Healthcare Arizona, Inc. v. Arizona*

18 | *Health Care Cost Containment System,* 180 Ariz. Adv. Rep. 12 (App. 1994); Rule

19 | 56(c)(1), Arizona Rules of Civil Procedure.

20 | The Arizona Rules of Civil Procedure permit summary judgment only "if the plead-

21 | ings, deposition, answers to interrogatories, and admissions on file, together with the

22 | affidavits, if any, show that there is no genuine issue as to any material fact and that the

23 | moving party is entitled to a judgment *as a matter of law.*" Rule 56, Arizona Rules of

24 | Civil Procedure (emphasis added).

25 | The burden of showing no genuine dispute of a material fact rests on the party

26 | moving for summary judgment. *Molever v. Roush,* 152 Ariz. 367, 732 P.2d 1105 (App.

27 | 1986). In considering a motion for summary judgment, all facts shown by the record,

28 | and all reasonable inferences which may be drawn from the evidence, must be consid-

29 | ered in a light most favorable to the party against whom judgment is sought; if there is

30 | the slightest doubt or uncertainty in respect to any issue of material fact, the request

31 | for summary judgment should be denied. *Overson v. Cowley,* 136 Ariz. 60, 664 P.2d 210

32 | (App. 1982).

33 |

1 In the present case, the only issue is whether Defendant's exercise of his right to use

2 deadly force was justified under the circumstances. This motion for summary judg-

3 ment should be granted, as Defendant's use of deadly force was not justified under any

4 relevant statute, even when the facts are viewed in the light most favorable to him.

B. Justification Defenses Available to Defendant

6 The law in Arizona only allows the use of deadly force under certain circumstances.

7 One can use deadly force in self defense, in defense of another, and to prevent the

8 commission of certain crimes. See A.R.S. §§ 13-405, 406, and 411. In the present case,

9 even when the facts are viewed in the light most favorable to Defendant, Defendant's

10 shooting of Plaintiff cannot be justified under any of the justification statutes. Accord-

11 ingly, the Court should grant this Motion for Partial Summary Judgment on the issue

12 of liability.

1. Defendant's Use of Deadly Force is Not Justified Under A.R.S. § 13405:

14 Defendant's use of deadly physical force was not justified under A.R.S. § 13-405 (self

15 defense). According to AR.S. § 13-405, "[a] person is justified in threatening or using

16 deadly physical force against another (1) if such person would be justified in threatening

17 or using physical force against the other under section 13-404; and (2) when and to the

18 degree a reasonable person would believe that deadly physical force is immediately neces-

19 sary to protect himself against the other's use or attempted use of unlawful deadly physi-

20 cal force."

21 For purposes of this motion only, Plaintiff agrees that the circumstances gave De-

22 fendant the right to use physical force against Plaintiff under AR.S. § 13-404. However,

23 no reasonable jury could find that Defendant's use of deadly physical force was justified

24 under A.R.S. § 13-405.

25 In ruling on this motion, the Court must examine A.RS. § 13-405 and resolve the fol-

26 lowing issues: (1) was Defendant's use of deadly force immediately necessary, and (2) was

27 Defendant's use of deadly force reasonably calculated to stop Plaintiff from using deadly

28 force upon him. If the Court finds against Defendant on any of these issues, then Defen-

29 dant's shooting of Plaintiff was not legally justifiable as an act of self defense. See A.R.S.

30 §§ 13-404 and 13-405.

31

32

33

a. Defendant's Use of Deadly Force was Not Immediately Necessary at the Time of the Shooting:

In analyzing whether Defendant's use of deadly force was immediately necessary the Court must look at several factors, including: (1) whether Plaintiff being unarmed, had the *ability* to cause Defendant death or serious physical injury at the time of the shooting; (2) whether Plaintiff being unarmed, had the *opportunity* to wreak death or serious physical injury upon Defendant at the time of the shooting; and (3) whether Plaintiff took action that placed Defendant in immediate danger of death or serious physical injury at the time of the shooting.

It is undisputed that Defendant never saw Plaintiff with a weapon at any point during the altercation. SOF ¶ 25. It is also undisputed that Defendant did not see Plaintiff with a weapon at the time he shot him. SOF ¶ 39. Accordingly, the only way that Plaintiff would have had the opportunity to kill or cause serious physical injury to Defendant, would be if he was within arms reach and had the training necessary to do Defendant serious harm in hand to hand combat.

An attacker's ability to cause death or serious bodily harm is most often demonstrated through the use of a weapon. However, an attacker's fists or feet can cause death or serious physical injury where he has superior strength or size, or specialized training or ability (example: a professional heavyweight boxer attacking an elderly man could cause death or serious physical injury). That said, judicial notice can be taken that in the vast majority of cases where someone gets punched in anger, the most serious injury is a bruise. A bruise does not count as a serious physical injury under A.R.S. § 13-105. Accordingly, absent some special skill or strength, punching someone does not place them in mortal fear such that deadly force is immediately necessary.

In the present case, Plaintiff was still some distance from Defendant when Defendant made the decision to shoot. SOF ¶ 44. In addition, Plaintiff and Defendant are roughly the same size, and neither of them have any specialized training or abilities. Accordingly, due to the aforementioned facts, Plaintiff did not have the ability or the opportunity to use deadly force on Defendant at the time he was shot.

The last factor in a complete "self defense" analysis is whether Plaintiff took any action immediately prior to the shooting that could be construed as placing Defendant in immediate jeopardy. Typically, an action that would place someone in immediate jeopardy would be the drawing of a weapon, or some other act that makes deadly force im-

1 mediately necessary for self defense. In this case, Defendant claims that Plaintiff was

2 walking towards him, and that he didn't see Plaintiff with a weapon. Accordingly,

3 Plaintiff did nothing immediately prior to the shooting that could be reasonably con-

4 strued as placing Defendant in immediate jeopardy, such that the use of deadly force

5 was immediately necessary under A.R.S. § 13405.

6   Due to the fact that Plaintiff did not have the ability or opportunity to use deadly

7 force on Defendant at the time he was shot, Defendant's shooting of Plaintiff was not

8 immediately necessary to prevent Plaintiff's use of deadly force upon him. For this

9 reason, Defendant's shooting of Plaintiff cannot be justified as a lawful act of self de-

10 fense under A.R.S. § 13-405.[1]

11 b. Defendant's Use of Deadly Force was Not Reasonably Calculated to Prevent Plaintiff

12 From Using Deadly Force Upon Him:

13   As discussed above, Plaintiff did not have the ability or opportunity to deal death or

14 serious physical injury upon Defendant at the time he was shot. In Arizona, "apparent

15 deadly force can be met with deadly force, so long as the person's belief as to apparent

16 deadly force is a reasonable one." *State v. Grannis,* 183 Ariz. 52, 60(1995). Furthermore,

17 in the criminal context, "a self defense instruction will be given only if the defendant

18 can demonstrate the following three elements: (1) he reasonably believed he was in im-

19 mediate physical danger; (2) he acted solely because of this belief, and (3) he used no

20 more force than appeared reasonably necessary under the circumstance." *State v. Gran-*

21 *nis,183 at 60.*

22   Although not binding for purposes of a motion for summary judgment, the above

23 statement from *Grannis* is an appropriate reference regarding the reasonableness of De-

24 fendant's conduct. Given that Plaintiff did not have the ability or opportunity to use

---

1. See *State v. Reid,* 155 Ariz. 399 (1987). In that case, the defendant shot her father while he was sleeping, The defendant then testified at trial that her father had sexually and physically abused her throughout her lifetime. She also testified that she could tell from experience when her father's violent episodes were approaching, and was in fear of imminent death or serious bodily harm at the time of the shooting. On appeal, the Arizona Supreme Court held that because her father did not have the ability or opportunity to immediately inflict death or serious bodily harm at the time of the shooting, the defendant was not entitled to a self defense instruction at trial.

See also *State v. Buggs,* 167 Ariz. 333 (App. 1990). In that case, the Court discussed at length the immediacy requirement of the self defense statutes. They noted that "as a general matter, the requirement that the attack reasonably appear imminent is a sensible one. If the threatened violence is scheduled to arrive in the more distant future, there may be avenues open to the defendant to prevent it other than to kill or injure the prospective attacker; but this is not so where the attack is imminent" The Court also notes that the "proper inquiry is not the immediacy of the threat but the immediacy of the response necessary in defense (i.e., is it immediately necessary to prevent deadly forced from being used by the attacker).

1 deadly physical force on Defendant immediately prior to the shooting, no reasonable

2 jury could find that he reasonably believed that he was in mortal danger. Similarly, the

3 evidence seems to suggest that Defendant shot Plaintiff not because he was in fear for

4 his life, but because he was angry at him for beating him up. Lastly, Defendant's shoot-

5 ing of Plaintiff was excessive force under the circumstances, given that Plaintiff had

6 neither the ability nor opportunity to use deadly force on Defendant at the time (be-

7 cause he was unarmed).

8   * * *

9   ### III.

10   ### CONCLUSION

11   Defendant shot an unarmed man who had demonstrated no ability to do major

12 damage in hand to hand combat. Accordingly, even when taking the facts in the light

13 most favorable to Defendant, no reasonable jury could possibly find that his shooting

14 of Plaintiff was justified under the law. For this reason, Plaintiff respectfully requests

15 that this Honorable Court grant this Motion for Partial Summary Judgment regarding

16 the issue of liability (i.e., that Defendant negligently exercised the right to use deadly

17 force in self defense).

18   RESPECTFULLY SUBMITTED this 13 day of February, 2008.

19   FRANKLIN & ASSOCIATES, P.A.

20

21

22

23

24

25

26

27

28

29

30

31

32

33

1 | THE CAVANAGH LAW FIRM,

2 | A PROFESSIONAL ASSOCIATION

3 | Phoenix, AZ 85004

4 |

5 | Attorneys for Defendant

6 |

7 | SUPERIOR COURT OF ARIZONA

8 | MARICOPA COUNTY

9 |

10 | Daniel EYSTER, a single man,   No. CV 2005-052870.

11 | Plaintiff,   DEFENDANT'S RESPONSE
                                                  TO PLAINTIFF'S MOTION
12 | v.   FOR PARTIAL SUMMARY
                                                  JUDGEMENT
13 | Aaron C. COLON and Jane Doe
     Colon, husband and wife; John
14 | Does I–V, Jane Does I–V, Black
15 | Corporations I–V, White
     Partnerships I–V,
16 |
17 | Defendants.

18 |

19 |

20 | Assigned to the Honorable <u>Robert C. Houser</u>.

21 | (Oral Argument Requested)

22 | Defendant, Aaron Colon, responds to Plaintiffs Motion for Partial Summary Judg-

23 | ment and requests that the Court deny the Motion for the reasons that it mischaracter-

24 | izes the facts, misapplies the law and then improperly asks the Court to determine, as a

25 | matter of law, the reasonableness of Defendant's conduct in defending himself.

26 | <u>I.</u>

27 | <u>INTRODUCTION</u>

28 | This case arises out of a shooting that occurred at Defendant Aaron Colon's residence

29 | on June 12, 2005, in the early morning hours, after he and Plaintiff, Daniel Eyster, re-

30 | turned home separately from a local karaoke bar. Prior to Mr. Colon returning home

31 | from the bar, Plaintiff trespassed onto Defendant's property and barricaded Defendant's

32 | driveway so that Defendant could not get to his garage and home. After forcing Mr.

33 | Colon to get out of his vehicle (in order to remove the barricade), Plaintiff then repeat-

1 edly beat Mr. Colon, eventually knocking him to the ground. After this initial serious

2 assault, Plaintiff left and then returned to. Mr. Colon's property and confronted him

3 again, *this time threatening to kill him!* The altercation ended with Defendant firing two

4 shots from his handgun, which he had retrieved from his truck-first, a warning shot that

5 Plaintiff ignored, and then another that hit Plaintiff in the abdomen. The question is

6 whether Defendant had a right to defend himself against this lunatic Plaintiff under the

7 circumstances. The answer is most assuredly yes. In any event, Plaintiffs request for

8 summary judgment on these facts is entirely inappropriate.

9   **II.**

10   **SUMMARY OF MATERIAL FACTS**

11   Plaintiff has testified that on the night of the incident, Defendant and Plaintiff went

12 together to a local karaoke bar, Shillelagh's, in Defendant's truck. DSOF ¶ 1. Plaintiff

13 further testified that while at the bar, he drank half a pitcher of beer. DSOF ¶ 2. Also

14 while at the bar, Plaintiff became involved in a fight with the female bartender because

15 she apparently was "skipping" Defendant when it came time for him to sing karaoke.

16 Plaintiff thought the bartender was being rude; so he called her a "fat bitch." DSOF ¶ 3.

17 Plaintiff was kicked out of the bar after his remark. DSOF ¶ 4.

18   Plaintiff also testified that after he left the bar, he waited outside the bar for Defen-

19 dant to come out and take him home, but Defendant did not leave the bar at that time.

20 DSOF ¶ 5. Instead, the police drove Plaintiff home and dropped him off in front of his

21 sister's house, which is located next to the Defendant's property. DSOF ¶ 6. Plaintiff

22 indicates that he was upset with Defendant and walked over to Defendant's house and

23 waited for him to come home. DSOF ¶ 7. While he was waiting, Plaintiff trespassed

24 onto Defendant's property and then moved "all of the stuff on the side of [Defendant's]

25 house ... into [Defendant's] driveway." Plaintiff intentionally placed the items in such a

26 way as to block the driveway, thereby forcing the Defendant out of his vehicle when he

27 got home. DSOF ¶ 8.

28   Plaintiffs and Defendant's versions concerning what occurred after Defendant ar-

29 rived home that night are slightly different. Plaintiffs Statement of Facts sets forth a

30 "watered down" version of Defendant's testimony and omits important facts. Defen-

31 dant's testimony is more accurately summarized as follows:

32   Defendant testified that when he arrived home, he was forced to get out of his truck

33 to move the items blocking his driveway and that Plaintiff then came out of nowhere

and said, "You let the cops take me home, mother fucker." DSOF ¶ 9. Defendant testified that as he was asking "What the hell's going on here?," Plaintiff "pummeled" him. DSOF ¶ 10. Defendant testified that Plaintiff hit him "repeatedly," and that *Defendant could not tell with what he was being hit.* DSOF ¶ 11. He estimated that he was struck "half a dozen times or more" before he fell to the ground. DSOF ¶ 11. Defendant does not know if he was rendered unconscious by Plaintiff's blows. DSOF ¶ 12.

After Defendant fell to the ground, Plaintiff disappeared, and Defendant thought the assault was over. DSOF ¶ 13. Defendant then went to his truck to get his keys and his handgun. DSOF ¶ 14. Defendant had planned to go inside his house at that point, when he saw Plaintiff returning from somewhere behind Defendant. DSOF ¶ 15. When Defendant first saw Plaintiff, he was about 40 to 50 feet away; DSOF ¶ 16. Plaintiff then threatened Defendant by stating *"I'm going to kill you."* DSOF ¶ 17. Though Defendant testified that he did not see anything in Plaintiffs hand at the time, he also said that his house was not well lit. DSOF ¶ 18. He therefore could not tell if Plaintiff was holding a weapon.

Defendant could hear Plaintiff and could see his "figure" but could not exactly tell from which direction he was coming. Plaintiff was advancing quickly on Defendant. DSOF ¶ 19, 20. When Defendant heard Plaintiff's death threat and saw him walking quickly towards, him, he told the Plaintiff to "get lost" and then fired a warning shot in Plaintiffs direction. DSOF ¶ 20. Plaintiff laughed at Defendant and said "You don't have the balls to shoot me." DSOF ¶ 21. Plaintiff continued to quickly advance on Defendant after the warning shot, and Defendant, in fear for his life, fired a second shot that hit Plaintiff. DSOF ¶ 22. *Defendant testified that the reason he was in fear for his life is because Plaintiff had already brutally attacked him and then threatened to kill him!* DSOF ¶ 23.

III.

LEGAL ARGUMENT

A. The Reasonableness of Defendant's Conduct is an Issue for the Jury.

Plaintiff correctly points out in his Motion that the relevant issue is whether Defendant's conduct was "justified under the circumstances." (Plaintiffs Motion at pg. 5.) He also accurately states that *"apparent* deadly force can be met with deadly force, so long as the person's belief as to apparent deadly force is a *reasonable* one." (Emphasis added). (Plaintiffs Motion at pg. 8.) While correctly setting forth the standard to be applied,

1 Plaintiff ignores Arizona law holding that whether a defendant acted "reasonably"
2 under the circumstances is a question of fact for the trier of fact. *See Tierra Ranchos*
3 *Homeowners Ass'n v. Kitchuko,* 216 Ariz. 195, 165 P.3d 173, 180 (App. 2007) (the issue
4 of reasonableness usually is a question of fact) *See also In re Estate of Jung,* 210 Ariz.
5 202. 207. 1 28. 109 P.3d 97.102 (App.2005) ([I]ssues of reasonableness are generally
6 questions of fact."); *Trustmark Ins. Co. v. Bank One, Arizona, NA,* 216 Ariz. 195, ___,
7 165 P.3d 173, 180 (App. 2007) (noting that "determinations of reasonableness are usu-
8 ally questions of fact").

9   In this case, whether Defendant was justified in using a firearm to defend himself
10 after this drunk, belligerent and angry maniac of a Plaintiff trespassed onto Defen-
11 dant's property, blockaded his driveway (forcing Defendant out of his truck), brutally
12 attacked Defendant, left and then returned to do so again, this time threatening to kill
13 him, is most certainly a question of fact for the jury. As part of this inquiry the jury
14 will also consider the fact that Defendant asked Plaintiff to leave the premises and even
15 fired a warning shot to get him to do so, which was met by Plaintiff's continued ag-
16 gressive advance on Defendant in the dark. To suggest that no reasonable jury could
17 find on these facts that Defendant's use of a weapon to protect himself was reasonable
18 and justified is ludicrous.

19   Moreover, even under the cases upon which Plaintiff relies in support of his Mo-
20 tion, the rule is that "[w]here there is the slightest evidence of self-defense," the issue
21 must be submitted to the jury. *State v. Johnson,* 108 Ariz. 42, 43, 492 P.2d 703,
22 704(1972). *See also State v. Buggs, infra* at 335, 806 P.2d at 1383 (a defendant is entitled
23 to an instruction on self-defense if there is the slightest evidence of justification for his
24 act ... The 'slightest evidence' is that evidence which tends to prove a hostile demon-
25 stration which might be reasonably regarded as placing the accused in imminent dan-
26 ger of losing his life or sustaining great bodily harm.") Under this broad standard
27 advocated by Plaintiff, Defendant is most certainly entitled to have the jury determine
28 the reasonableness of his actions.

29   In *State v. Johnson, supra,* the Arizona Supreme Court considered whether the defen-
30 dant in an assault trial was entitled to assert a justification defense. In that case defen-
31 dant Johnson and the victim, Woods, were shooting dice at Woods' house. At some
32 point, Johnson noticed that his money was missing and saw that Woods had Johnson's
33 wallet. Johnson confronted Woods who denied having the money but said that he

1   could get it. After that, Johnson was warned by two men that Woods carried a gun

2   with him at all times and that Woods was going to kill him. Johnson testified that he

3   then armed himself with his shotgun before going to a barbecue stand. Woods appar-

4   ently drove up shortly after Johnson arrived at the stand. Johnson testified that Woods

5   was leaning to one side of his truck and that he did not know if Woods was trying to

6   get his gun. Johnson then shot his gun, explaining that "... I picked up the gun and it

7   shot before I even knew it was going to shoot." There was no evidence that Johnson

8   ever saw a gun. *Id.* at 43, 492 P.2d at 704.

9   In holding that a self-defense instruction should go to the jury, the Court explained

10 that Johnson's testimony was sufficient to establish an inference that he saw Woods lean

11 over in his truck and that Johnson raised his gun in self-defense. The Court reasoned

12 that the jury could have concluded that the defendant was justified in arming himself

13 with a gun and it further could have concluded that the force used was "commensurate

14 with the circumstances of the case." *Id.*

15   In our case the evidence establishes that Plaintiff brutally attacked Defendant and

16 then left. He then returned and this time threatened to kill Defendant. He then ignored

17 Defendant's warning shot and request to leave his property, and instead continued to

18 aggressively advance on Defendant in the dark, leaving Defendant uncertain as to

19 whether Plaintiff had a weapon. As stated in *Johnson*, a jury could certainly conclude

20 that Defendant was "justified in arming himself" and further could certainly conclude

21 that the force Defendant used was "commensurate with the circumstances of the case."

22 As such, the issue of whether Defendant was justified in using his weapon must go to

23 the jury.

24   **B. Actual Deadly Force is Not Required Before Deadly Force**

25   **May be Used in Self-Defense.**

26   Plaintiff has argued that Defendant is not entitled to a self-defense instruction be-

27 cause "Plaintiff did not have the ability or opportunity to use deadly force on Defen-

28 dant at the time that he was shot." (Plaintiffs Motion at pg. 7). This is an incorrect

29 statement of the law as well as a gross mischaracterization of the facts.

30   First, Plaintiff himself relies on *State v. Grannis,* 83 Ariz. 52, 60, 900 P.2d 1, 9

31 (1995), in his Motion, which rejects a requirement that a defendant be in "actual dan-

32 ger" at the time he uses deadly force. In *Grannis,* the Arizona Supreme Court found

33 that the trial court erred by including a self-defense jury instruction that" '[a] defen-

dant may only use deadly physical force … to protect himself from another's use or at-tempted use of deadly force' because the instruction *incorrectly suggested that only actual deadly force could justify defendant's deadly force.*" (Emphasis added.) The Court explained that:

> Under A.R.S. §§ 13-404 and 405 apparent deadly force can be met with deadly
> force, so long as defendant's belief as to apparent deadly force is a reasonable one.
> *An instruction on self-defense is required when a defendant acts under a reasonable*
> *belief: actual danger is not required.* (Emphasis added.)

See also State v. Barraza, 209 Ariz. 441, 445 104 P.3d 172, 176 (App. 2005) (discussing *State v. Grannis;* noting that the Arizona Supreme Court found that the instruction misstated the law because it may have led the jury to believe that deadly force could be used only to protect against "actual deadly force" even though *§§ 13-404 and -405 also allow deadly force to protect against "reasonably apparent deadly force."* (Emphasis added.)

In arguing that Defendant is not entitled to assert self-defense, Plaintiff admitted in his Motion but then ignored the following critical facts in analyzing the law:

• After being returned home from the bar by police, *Plaintiff trespassed onto* Defendant's property and blockaded *Defendant's driveway* with items stored at the side of his house, thereby forcing Defendant out of the safety of his truck to unblock his driveway. *See* PSOF ¶¶ 11, 1217 and 18.

• While Defendant was clearing his driveway, Plaintiff appeared and said "you let the cops take me home you mother fucker." *See* PSOF ¶ 19.

• At the same time he was yelling at Defendant, *Plaintiff repeatedly struck Defendant and knocked him to the ground. See* PSOF ¶ 20.

• After Plaintiff apparently left momentarily, he then returned, this time threatening: "I'm *going to kill you." See* PSOF ¶¶ 26 and 29.

• Defendant could see Plaintiffs outline in the dark, and he appeared to be approaching Defendant again. *See* PSOF ¶ 30.

• *Defendant told Plaintiff to leave his property and fired a warning shot. See* PSOF ¶ 32.

• *Plaintiff ignored the warning shot and responded that Defendant did not have the* "balls" *to shoot him. See* PSOF ¶ 34.

• *Plaintiff continued* to advance *on Defendant in an aggressive manner,* despite his requests that he leave. *See* PSOF ¶ 35.

1   Plaintiff left out of his Statement of Facts, the following additional testimony from
2   Defendant:

3   • Defendant estimates he was *struck at least half a dozen times* by Plaintiff before
4   being knocked to the ground. *See* DSOF ¶ 12.

5   • Defendant was *not certain with what he was being hit. See* DSOF ¶ 11.

6   • Defendant *does not know if he was knocked unconscious* during the attack. *See*
7   DSOF ¶ 13.

8   • Defendant was *scared for his life* at the time he shot Plaintiff. *See* DSOF ¶ 24.

9   Defendant was entitled to use deadly force to protect against "reasonably apparent
10 deadly force." Whether Plaintiff's conduct could be construed as such and whether De-
11 fendant was in reasonable fear of the imminent loss of his life or great bodily harm,
12 justifying the use of his handgun, are simply not questions for the Court to resolve as a
13 matter of law.

14 **C. Plaintiffs Own Cases Support the Giving of a Self-Defense Instruction.**

15 Plaintiff relies on *State v. Buggs,* 167 Ariz. 333, 806 P.2d 1381 (App. 1990), a case
16 where the availability of a self-defense instruction was discussed. In that case, the de-
17 fendant was involved in a fight that had moved from a neighborhood pool hall into the
18 parking lot. During the initial altercation, the defendant had been kicked and then
19 stabbed in the back with a knife. The fight ended. The defendant then left the area of
20 the fight, obtained a gun from a friend and went back and shot into a crowd. The de-
21 fendant testified that he believed that some of the men were dangerous gang members
22 of whom he was afraid. He missed the men but shot the woman who had stabbed him
23 in the leg. The court held that a self-defense instruction was not appropriate because
24 the group "w[as] not advancing upon or physically menacing him in any way." *Id.* at
25 336, 806 P.2d at 1384.

26 Importantly, however, the court explained that:

27   The proper inquiry is not the immediacy of the threat but the immediacy of
28   the response necessary in defense. *If a threatened harm is such that it cannot be*
29   *avoided if the intended victim waits until the last moment, the principle of self-*
30   *defense must permit him to act earlier—as early as is required to defend himself*
31   *effectively.*

32   *Id.* at 336, 806 P.2d at 1384.

33

1   *State v. Buggs* is factually distinguishable from this case for the simple reason that

2   Plaintiff was "advancing upon" Defendant and was "physically menacing" at the time of

3   the shooting. Further, applying the reasoning of *Buggs* to our case, it may be said that

4   the threatened harm to Defendant was such that it could not be avoided if Defendant

5   waited until the last moment, and thus, "the principle of self-defense must permit him

6   to act earlier—as early as [was] required to defend himself effectively." In other words,

7   while Plaintiff was "advancing" on Defendant for a second time, after Plaintiffs first

8   brutal attack and subsequent death threat, Defendant was not required to wait until

9   Plaintiff was in arm's reach before Defendant used his weapon to defend himself.

10 Plaintiff also inexplicably relies on *State v. Reid,* 155 Ariz. 399, (1987), a case where

11 *the victim was asleep in his bed* at the time of the shooting, to argue that Defendant is

12 not entitled to a self-defense instruction here. In *Reid, the* Court refused to allow a

13 criminal defendant to assert self-defense because the victim did not have the ability to

14 immediately inflict death or seriously bodily harm at the time of the shooting, *because*

15 *he was sleeping during the attack!* The facts of *Reid* are so far removed from those of this

16 case, where the *Plaintiff was awake, aggressive, advancing and making a death* threat at

17 the time of the shooting, that it has no precedential value whatsoever.

18   * * *

19   **IV.**

20   **CONCLUSION**

21 For the foregoing reasons, Defendants respectfully request that this Court deny

22 Plaintiff's Motion for Partial Summary Judgment and properly allow the jury to decide

23 the reasonableness of Defendant's actions in this matter.

24 DATED this 14th day of March, 2008.

25 THE CAVANAGH LAW FIRM, P.A.

26

27

28

29

30

31

32

33

The following are the key cases discussed in the parties' motions. Note that the cases are criminal cases; in the jurisdiction where the parties litigated the matter the law relating to self-defense (at least on this issue) is the same for both torts and criminal law. This is not true for every jurisdiction.

Arizona v. Grannis

183 Ariz. 52, 900 P.2d 1 (1995)

Defendants David Wayne Grannis and Daniel Ethan Webster were jointly tried in Pima County Superior Court. On May 28, 1992, the jury convicted them both of pre-meditated first degree murder, two counts of theft, and trafficking in stolen property. After holding an aggravation/mitigation hearing, the trial court sentenced Grannis and Webster to death. Their convictions and death sentences are automatically appealed to this court. ***

FACTS AND PROCEDURAL HISTORY

I. *Facts*

Webster and Grannis first met in Phoenix in May 1989. Grannis, who was 31 years old at the time of the murder, had no criminal record and had completed two semesters of college. The 20-year-old Webster was a high school dropout with a history of substance abuse. When Webster lost his job, he moved in with Grannis who testified that he became Webster's "caretaker." Although Grannis admits to having had a homosexual experience and having possessed homosexual pornography, he claimed that his relationship with Webster was not sexual.

In June 1989, Webster and Grannis went to Las Cruces, New Mexico, where they stayed first with Grannis's mother for a few weeks and then with a friend. In August 1989, the two began hitchhiking to Los Angeles to see Webster's family. Outside of Tucson on the evening of August 24, 1989, the victim, Richard, picked up Grannis and Webster in his BMW automobile. According to Grannis, Richard invited them to spend the night at his house and offered to give them a ride back to the freeway in the morning. Grannis and Webster accepted the invitation, and they rode back to Richard's house, stopping on the way to buy beer and food.

Neighbors called the police in the early morning hours of August 25 to report screaming coming from Richard's house. When the sheriff's department arrived at Richard's house around 1:30 a.m., they found Richard's dead body in the hallway off the living room. Richard had sustained approximately 13 sharp force injuries and numerous blunt force injuries. During their investigation, the police discovered that Richard's BMW was missing from his house. In tracking down the missing car, the police conducted interviews that led them to suspect Grannis and Webster of Richard's murder.

At trial, the state produced fingerprint evidence that placed Grannis and Webster at the scene of Richard's murder. The state argued to the jury that Webster and Grannis had killed Richard in the course of robbing him or burglarizing his home. Webster did not testify at the trial.

Grannis testified on his own behalf and gave the following account of what took place at Richard's house during the late evening and early morning hours of August 24 and 25. Upon arriving at Richard's house, the three men talked and drank beer on the back patio.

After about two hours, Webster showered and went to bed. Richard then sexually propositioned Grannis, who refused the offer, explaining that Webster did not approve of homosexual activity. After Richard persisted, Grannis reluctantly consented to having sex, and they headed toward the master bedroom. At the bedroom door, Richard became sexually aggressive, at which point Grannis changed his mind and tried to resist Richard's advances. Richard grabbed Grannis's wrists to push him into the bedroom, and Grannis began to scream. His screams awakened Webster, who came into the room and punched Richard in the face. Richard still would not loosen his grip on Grannis, so Webster kept trying to pull them apart.

When Grannis finally broke loose from Richard's grasp, he began to run away intending to leave the house. Grannis saw Webster and Richard struggling with each other on the floor, and he heard Webster yelling to get their things together. Grannis replied, "Let's just get out of here." Grannis grabbed Richard's keys from the kitchen and went to get their belongings from his car. Several minutes later Webster ran out of the house yelling, "Let's get out of here," and Grannis, thinking that Richard was chasing them, started Richard's car. They drove away. Grannis testified that he and Webster never again discussed what had happened at Richard's that night. Grannis alleged that he did not know Richard was dead until the police arrested him for murder.

II. *Procedural History*

* * *

The trial began on May 14, 1991. Webster claimed self-defense, and Grannis alleged that he was not present when the murder occurred and lacked any culpability for the murder. The jury found both Grannis and Webster guilty of premeditated first degree murder, two counts of theft, and trafficking in stolen property. ***

DISCUSSION

* * *

III. *Jury Instruction on Use of Deadly Force*

Webster argues that the trial court gave improper instructions regarding the use of deadly force, thereby depriving him of his right to due process and a fair trial, in violation of the Fifth, Sixth, and Fourteenth Amendments to the United States Constitution and art. 2, §§ 4, 24 of the Arizona Constitution.

Arizona permits the use of deadly force as follows:

A person is justified in threatening or using deadly physical force against another:

1. If such person would be justified in threatening or using physical force against the other under § 13-404, and

2. When and to the degree a reasonable person would believe that deadly physical force is immediately necessary to protect himself against the other's use or attempted use of unlawful deadly physical force. A.R.S. § 13-405.

Under A.R.S. § 13-404, a person is justified in threatening or using physical force against another when and to the extent a reasonable person would believe that physical force is immediately necessary to protect himself against the other's use or attempted use of unlawful physical force.

Deadly force may also be used to protect a third person pursuant to A.R.S. § 13-406:

A person is justified in threatening or using physical force or deadly physical force against another to protect a third person if:

1. Under the circumstances as a reasonable person would believe them to be, such person would be justified under § 13-404 or 13-405 in threatening or using physical force or deadly physical force to protect himself against the unlawful physical force or deadly physical force a reasonable person would believe is threatening the third person he seeks to protect; and

2. A reasonable person would believe that such person's intervention is immediately necessary to protect the third person.

Under A.R.S. §§ 13-404 and -405, *apparent* deadly force can be met with deadly force, so long as defendant's belief as to apparent deadly force is a reasonable one. An instruction on self-defense is required when a defendant acts under a reasonable belief; actual danger is not required.

In Arizona, a self-defense instruction will be given only if the defendant can demonstrate the following three elements: (1) he *reasonably believed* he was in immediate physical danger; (2) he acted solely because of this belief; and (3) he used no more force than *appeared reasonably necessary* under the circumstance.

State v. Dumaine, 162 Ariz. 392, 404, 783 P.2d 1184, 1196 (1989) (emphasis added). "Even the slightest evidence of self-defense mandates an instruction on the issue." *Dumaine,* 162 Ariz. at 404, 783 P.2d at 1196.

Webster objected to the instruction given to the jury regarding deadly force, arguing that he was entitled to an instruction on self-defense and that the instruction given misstated Arizona law. The trial court gave the following instruction:

A defendant is justified in threatening or using physical force in self-defense if the following two conditions exist:

1. A reasonable person in the defendant's situation would have believed that physical force was immediately necessary to protect against another's use or attempted use of physical force; and

2. The defendant threatened or used no more physical force than would have appeared necessary to a reasonable person in the defendant's situation.

Actual danger is not necessary to justify the threat or use of physical force in self-defense. It is enough if a reasonable person in the defendant's situation would have believed that he was in immediate physical danger.

. . . .

A defendant may only use deadly physical force in self-defense to protect himself from another's use or attempted use of deadly physical force.

(Emphasis added.)

Webster argues that the instruction incorrectly led the jury to believe that actual deadly force rather than reasonably apparent deadly force was necessary to justify deadly force in response. We agree that the jury could easily have interpreted the trial court's instruction that way.

Although the initial description of when self-defense is justified correctly reflected the statutory language of A.R.S. § 13-404(A), the later description regarding deadly force was incorrect. It could plausibly be interpreted as a limitation on the entire instruction. By concluding with the statement that "[a] defendant may *only* use deadly physical force . . . to protect himself from another's use or attempted use of deadly force" (emphasis added), the instruction suggested that reasonably apparent physical force could justify non-deadly physical force by the defendant, but that only actual deadly force could justify defendant's deadly force. Accordingly, we hold that the trial court's instruction regarding justification for deadly force constitutes error.

Webster did not claim in his defense that the victim was actually armed or attempting to use deadly force against Webster or Grannis; instead, Webster claimed that he reasonably believed, even if incorrectly, that deadly force was necessary based on the victim's actions. Webster was entitled to have the jury properly consider whether his use of deadly force was justified under A.R.S. § 13-405. The jury could not adequately consider this question without being properly instructed as to the correct standard set forth in § 13-405. *See, e.g., Everett v. State,* 88 Ariz. 293, 299, 356 P.2d 394, 398 (1960) (reversing conviction for assault with deadly weapon where trial court failed to instruct jury on self-defense). On retrial the trial court should correctly instruct the jury on self-defense. ***

DISPOSITION

For the foregoing reasons, we reverse the convictions and death sentences of Grannis and Webster and remand their cases for further proceedings consistent with this opinion.

Arizona v. Buggs
167 Ariz. 333, 806 P.2d 1381 (1991)

The defendant, Johnny Frank Buggs, was convicted upon a trial by jury of aggravated assault. He was sentenced to a maximum term of imprisonment of twenty years. Although the trial court gave an improper instruction on self-defense, we affirm because in our opinion the evidence does not justify the giving of a self-defense instruction at all.

The defendant's version of the facts is as follows. The defendant became involved in a fight with two women, Shirley Hall and V.B., in a pool hall in a neighborhood notorious for the prevalence of illegal drugs. The fight spilled outside to the parking lot, and the defendant tripped over a cement curb. When the defendant fell down, three men with whom he had had a prior "incident" began kicking him. While this was going on, one of the women the defendant had been fighting stabbed him in the back. A friend of the defendant's grabbed him and picked him up.

The defendant went to the side of the building, and his friend put a pistol in his hand and told him to take care of himself. The defendant went back to the area in front of the pool hall where there were a number of people standing around. Two of the men who had assaulted the defendant were present. The defendant believed they were members of the Crips gang and assumed, because of their reputations, that they had firearms. The defendant also saw one of the women he had been fighting, V.B., and she had a knife in her hand, although she did not then threaten him with it. The defendant was afraid of the men, and he fired his pistol at them. He missed the men but hit V.B. in the leg.

At various points in his testimony, the defendant elaborated on his fear of the Crips. When asked why he felt he was in danger when he returned to the parking lot, he said: "Because I know the Crips, I know what they do. You have to get them before they get you." He explained that when he was on the side of the building and his friend handed him the pistol, he returned to the front of the building because he was afraid that if he left the area by another route, he would be ambushed. He explained: "Well, see, I've been on the streets a long time, I have seen how the Crips act, I know what they do, and they get you in a position where you don't know no protection, they will wipe you."

When asked why he fired at the two men he said:

> I guess if you haven't—well, you wouldn't understand it but once you get into it with one of them they going to retaliate on you, I don't know where you are at, they all pack, they all holding a gun. So, you want to stay alive the best thing to do is get them when you see them.

The defendant went on to explain that, because they had set upon him just shortly before, he believed that the two men were about to kill him.

The trial judge gave an instruction on self-defense which the state concedes was improper under the rulings in *State v. Hunter,* 142 Ariz. 88, 688 P.2d 980 (1984) and *State v. Garcia,* 152 Ariz. 245, 731 P.2d 610 (App.1986). The instruction failed to inform the jury that the state had the burden of proving beyond a reasonable doubt that the defendant did not act in self-defense.

The state argues that the error was harmless. It points out that in closing argument, defense counsel adequately informed the jury of the state's burden concerning self-defense, but it cites no authority for the proposition that this will cure fundamental error.

As far as we can discern from the record made available to us, the state never objected to the giving of a self-defense instruction and, indeed, does not suggest on appeal that the evidence was insufficient to justify a self-defense instruction. We nonetheless consider that question relevant to whether giving the wrong instruction was harmless error.

Under A.R.S. section 13-404(A), self-defense constitutes justification for conduct if: (1) a reasonable person would believe (2) that physical force is *immediately* necessary (3) to protect oneself against another's use or attempted use of unlawful physical force.

A defendant is entitled to an instruction on self-defense if there is the slightest evidence of justification for his act. *State v. Lujan,* 136 Ariz. 102, 104, 664 P.2d 646, 648 (1983); *State v. Martinez,* 122 Ariz. 596, 598, 596 P.2d 734, 736 (App.1979). The "slightest evidence" is that evidence which tends to prove a hostile demonstration which might be reasonably regarded as placing the accused in imminent danger of losing his life or sustaining great bodily harm. *State v. Walters,* 155 Ariz. 548, 553–54, 748 P.2d 777, 782–83 (App.1987); *State v. Wallace,* 83 Ariz. 220, 223, 319 P.2d 529, 531 (1957). Other Arizona cases have said that the defendant's burden with respect to self-defense extends no further than to raise a reasonable doubt in the minds of the jury as to whether his act was justifiable. *E.g., State v. Garcia,* 114 Ariz. 317, 320, 560 P.2d 1224, 1227 (1977).

The aspect of this case which gives us concern is that, at the time the defendant shot in the direction of the Crips, they were not advancing upon or physically menacing him in any way. Characterized most strongly for the defendant, all that the evidence showed was that the defendant thought the men he shot at were highly dangerous individuals who meant to do him harm, and who he decided had to be eradicated right away to prevent them from gaining an advantage over him and injuring him at some later time. The question is, does this kind of threat justify the defendant's action? We believe it does not. The defendant's action was not immediately necessary to prevent the harm he feared.

The Arizona case most closely on point is *State v. Reid,* 155 Ariz. 399, 747 P.2d 560 (1987). There, the defendant shot and killed her father while he was asleep. The defendant testified that she feared her father because he had a long history of having abused her sexually and physically. She also said that she could detect a change in personality when one of the victim's fits of violence was approaching and, by inference, apparently believed that such a fit was imminent.

The defendant was convicted of murder and appealed. The state cross-appealed, claiming that the trial court erred in instructing the jury on self-defense. The supreme court agreed with the state, but indicated that in some circumstances knowledge of the victim's violent reputation *may* warrant a less restrictive definition of what is "immediately necessary" for self-defense than is usually applied. It noted the following language from a Kansas case, *State v. Hundley*, 236 Kan. 461, 467–68, 693 P.2d 475, 479 (1985):

> '[I]mmediate,' in the instruction on self-defense places undue emphasis on the immediate action of the deceased, and obliterates the nature of the buildup of terror and fear which had been systematically created over a long period of time.

The Arizona Supreme Court then went on to say that even *if* it were to hold that a history of violence could be a factor in supporting a self-defense instruction, the facts in the case before it did not rise to that level.

Arizona is one of several states whose statutes relating to self-defense are couched in terms of the immediate need to use force. Most statutes speak in terms of allowing the use of force against the threat of imminent attack by another. W.R. LaFave & A.W. Scott, Jr., Substantive Criminal Law, § 5.7(d) (1986). This difference in terms and the structure of the statutes does not seem to result in any practical distinction in the application of the law. LaFave and Scott bring the problem into sharp focus with the following discussion:

> As a general matter, the requirement that the attack reasonably appear to be im- minent is a sensible one. If the threatened violence is scheduled to arrive in the more distant future, there may be avenues open to the defendant to prevent it other than to kill or injure the prospective attacker; but this is not so where the attack is imminent. But the application of this requirement in some contexts has been questioned. 'Suppose A kidnaps and confines D with the announced intention of killing him one week later. D has an opportunity to kill A and escape each morning as A brings him his daily ration. Taken literally, the *imminent* requirement would prevent D from using deadly force in self-defense until A is standing over him with a knife, but that outcome seems inappropriate. * * * The proper inquiry is not the immediacy of the threat but the immediacy of the response necessary in defense. If a threatened harm is such that it cannot be avoided if the intended victim waits until the last moment, the principle of self-defense must permit him to act earlier — as early as is required to defend himself effectively.'

Id. at 656 (quoting 2 P. Robinson, Criminal Law Defenses § 131(c)(1) (1984)).

The authors go on to acknowledge that a debate exists, usually discussed in the context of the battered wife, between those who urge that the "imminency" requirement be abolished or loosely construed and those who argue that it remain in place. At least one other commentator has recognized the same problem and has called for the courts to address it squarely. LaFond, *The Case for Liberalizing the Use of Deadly Force in Self-Defense*, 6 U. Puget Sound L.Rev. 237 (1983).

We have not found any case that would allow a claim of self-defense under the circumstances presented here. While we agree that a victim's past acts and reputation for violence will often be relevant on the question of the reasonableness of a defendant's use of force in self-defense, it would be inappropriate in a case such as this to dispense with or dilute the requirement that one may resort to deadly force only if it is necessary to prevent immediate harm. The defendant's "self-defense" in this case was nothing other than a "pre-emptive strike" against the men he feared. While there may be some circumstances imaginable that would allow for a defense based on that concept, this case does not present them. This case, for instance, does not present the same dire need as does the example used by LaFave and Scott of the kidnapper who plans to kill his victim in a week. Here, when the defendant returned to the area of the confrontation and fired his pistol at the men who had kicked him, he was not under their domination and control, and they gave no signal that they intended to renew their attack. Our conclusion is in line with settled authority to the effect that after a fight has broken off, one cannot pursue and kill merely because he once feared for his life. *See State v. Powers,* 117 Ariz. 220, 227, 571 P.2d 1016, 1023 (1977).

Since the defendant was not entitled to an instruction on self-defense, the flawed instruction was harmless beyond a reasonable doubt. *See State v. Rhymes,* 129 Ariz. 56, 59–60, 628 P.2d 939, 942–43 (1981). While it is conceivable that an erroneous instruction not otherwise supported by the evidence could, in some circumstances, so skew the presentation of a case as to call for a reversal, this is not that case. ***

It is ordered affirming the conviction and sentence imposed.

Arizona v. Reid

155 Ariz. 399, 747 P.2d 560 (1991)

*** Around 2:00 a.m. on 16 October 1985, Somerton police officers were called to a house trailer owned by Lewis Trimble. Trimble was found in his bed with a fatal gunshot wound to the head. He was holding a hand gun. Defendant, Trimble's daughter, lived in the same trailer with Trimble and her fiancé James Warnes,[1] a co-defendant in the case. Warnes' sister, Betty, was also staying at the trailer that night.

Defendant, Warnes, and Betty all told the police that Trimble's death was a suicide. Further investigation revealed that there were two gunshot wounds to Trimble's head, which ruled out suicide. As a result of police interrogation, Betty made a statement inculpating defendant in Trimble's murder. Defendant was indicted for the crimes of first-degree murder, A.R.S. § 13-1105(A)(1), and hindering prosecution, A.R.S. § 13-2512.

At trial, evidence indicated that defendant killed Trimble while he was asleep. Defendant's main defense centered around fear of the victim accentuated by a long history of physical and sexual abuse and violent and psychotic acts by the victim towards the defendant and others. Additionally, defendant also testified that she could detect a change in personality when one of the victim's fits of violence was approaching. This evidence was contradicted by other family members.

Defendant also indicated that at the time of the killing, she was under the influence of drugs and alcohol. Defendant testified that she had been drinking at a local bar and at the victim's trailer. Additionally, throughout the day, defendant had ingested a central nervous system stimulant "Ritalin," and "Parnate," an anti-depressant, in excess of the prescribed dosage. Betty also testified that the defendant had been drinking throughout the day. Defendant, according to her own testimony, however, remembered: (1) every detail of the night she shot her father; (2) feelings of hysteria she felt after shooting the victim; and (3) details of the police arrival and discovery of the body. Defendant also

---

1. Warnes was acquitted of first-degree murder. The jury convicted him of two counts of hindering prosecution.

testified that she stayed awake for two and a half hours after her father had gone to bed (and had fallen asleep) before making a search of the victim's bedroom for the gun with which she used to kill him.

After submission of the case to the jury, the foreman reported that one of the jurors was ill and could not continue. The court determined that the juror would not be able to return and, upon stipulation of counsel, allowed the jury to deliberate with eleven jurors. The jury found defendant guilty of first-degree murder. Defendant appeals.

* * *

VII. SELF-DEFENSE

*** By statute a person is: ... justified in threatening or using physical force against another when and to the extent a reasonable person would believe that physical force is *immediately* necessary to protect himself against the other's use or attempted use of unlawful physical force. A.R.S. § 13-404(A) (emphasis added). Thus, to determine whether a self-defense instruction was required, we look to evidence of threats of future harm, even if the evidence is in conflict on this issue, and to any other evidence that might support a claim of self-defense. *State v. Noriega*, 142 Ariz. 474, 482, 690 P.2d 775, 783 (1984). As this court has stated, the slightest evidence will mandate an instruction on this issue. *Id*. An instruction on self-defense must be given if an accused shows that:

> 1) the defendant reasonably believed that he or she was in *immediate* physical danger; 2) the defendant acted solely because of this belief; and 3) the defendant used no more force than appeared reasonably necessary under the circumstances.

Id. at 482, 690 P.2d at 783 (emphasis added).

The state maintains that since the victim was asleep, the *immediacy* of physical danger did not exist. The defendant maintains, however, that she reasonably believed she was in immediate physical danger. We consider the use of the word "immediate" as addressed by the Kansas Supreme Court, in which it stated in a battered wife case:

> ... "immediate", in the instruction on self defense places undue emphasis on the immediate action of the deceased, and obliterates the nature of the buildup of terror and fear which had been systematically created over a long period of time.

State v. Hundley, 236 Kan. 461, 467–68, 693 P.2d 475, 479 (1985). However, even considering the events of the evening, we do not find sufficient evidence to show defendant was in immediate danger. In a Washington case, the court held the instruction given by the trial court which narrowed the focus of the inquiry to the time immediately before the shooting was impermissible since it restricted the jury's inquiry into the surrounding circumstances. *State v. Wanrow*, 88 Wash.2d 221, 236, 559 P.2d 548, 556 (1977). Hence, knowledge of the victim's violent reputation in some circumstances may warrant a deviation from the normal use of the self-defense instruction. Even if we were to hold that a history of battering and brutalizing could be a factor in supporting the instruction of self-defense, *see generally*, *Jahnke v. State*, 682 P.2d 991 (Wyo.1984), the facts in the instant case do not rise to that level. Even though the victim may have been capable of violence towards the defendant, we do not find that the facts indicate a reasonable fear in the mind of defendant to warrant an instruction on self-defense. The trial court improperly instructed the jury on self-defense.

VIII. HOLDING

We have searched the record for fundamental error according to the mandate of A.R.S. § 13-4035 and *Anders v. California*, 386 U.S. 738, 87 S.Ct. 1396, 18 L.Ed.2d 493 (1967), and have found none. Defendant's conviction for first-degree murder is affirmed.

Exercise 1-19 Zealous Advocacy or Unprofessional Behavior 2.0

Did the parties' motions characterize *Grannis, Buggs,* and *Reid* accurately? Why or why not? Did either party cross the line between advocacy and misrepresentation? Did either party display a lack of professionalism?

Exercise 1-20 Law Practice

Find the rules for self-defense (for torts) in the jurisdiction where you intend to practice. Does the jurisdiction follow the minority or majority position with regard to retreat? Does the jurisdiction apply the same rules for evaluating self-defense in both civil (tort) and criminal cases?

Chapter Two

Investigating the Claim and Developing a Theory of the Case — Negligence

Objectives

Learning and Study Skills

Continue to develop:

  Case reading and briefing skills

  Reflective learning skills

Create an issues checklist

Learn to write and organize answers to law school essay examination questions using IRAC format

Law Practice Skills

Practice and develop:

  Rule deconstruction skills

  Applying and distinguishing legal authority (Cases)

Develop ability to find and utilize resources related to understanding non-legal concepts related to a claim

Acquire and develop knowledge in areas other than the applicable law — including subject matter and factual knowledge

Review and evaluate legal documents and arguments drafted by other lawyers

Evaluate the facts of a client's case to determine:

  Which facts are significant for purposes of proving or disproving liability

  Whether additional factual information is needed

Evaluate expert opinions and testimony

Develop preliminary theories based on the facts and law

Evaluate a set of circumstances to determine:

> Whether any legal duty is owed by any party;
>
> The extent of any duty owed; and
>
> Whether the duty has been breached

Be able to identify the type of damages suffered by a plaintiff, and estimate the value of such damages for purposes of engaging in settlement discussions

Acknowledge client emotions and feelings and understand how they impact a case

Assess whether a damage award may be limited by statute

Evaluate whether circumstances and events may break the causal link between the defendant's conduct and the plaintiff's harm, thereby absolving defendant of liability

Evaluate whether a plaintiff's claim is barred or limited because of a defense

Determine the applicable statute of limitations period, when the limitations period begins to run, and whether the limitations period may be tolled

Substantive Legal Knowledge

State the elements required to establish a cause of action for negligence

Know what is required to prove each of the elements of negligence, including:

> How duty is established
>
> How the standard of care is established
>
> The common law classification for land entrants and the duty owed to such entrants by the land owner or possesor
>
> The requirements for establishing, and the effect of proving, res ipsa loquitur
>
> The requirements for establishing, and the effect of proving, Negligence Per Se

Know the difference between contributory negligence and comparative fault, and the potential impact of each on a plaintiff's claim(s)

Know the requirements for proving a plaintiff assumed the risk of injury

Introduction

Negligence is a term used to describe conduct that falls below the legal standard of care and which subjects others to an unreasonable risk of harm. It is also the name of a specific cause of action a plaintiff may file against a defendant in order to attempt to recover for harm caused by the defendant. A negligence cause of action may be alleged for an extremely wide array of situations—automobile collisions, improper or inadequate medical treatment, environmental pollution, construction defects, airplane crashes, failure to supervise employees, failure to adequately maintain property, and many others. Some courts (and even some authors of torts texts and supplements) also use the term to mean the first two elements of the negligence cause of action—duty and breach. For this reason, when you encounter the term, it is important to pay close attention to the context and to how the term is used, so as not to be confused.

As you begin your study of this topic, it might help to think about negligence as a system of liability that seeks to assess risk and then assign responsibility to those that take unreasonable risks (which cause injury). Because the concepts of negligence, and duty, are rooted in the notion that one should not subject others to an *unreasonable* risk of harm, it is helpful to first have an understanding of how risk is evaluated, because such understanding may help you determine whether the risk taken in any given situation was a reasonable or unreasonable one.

Exercise 2-1 Assessing Risk

Under a negligence system, there are some injuries that are not eligible for compensation, meaning sometimes a party is injured and there is no basis for liability. The goal of a negligence system is not to eliminate all injury or even all risk of injury, but rather to reduce or eliminate injuries that occur in situations where the harm could be reasonably avoided. The law of negligence only provides a remedy for injuries that result from unreasonable conduct on the part of a defendant.

Generally speaking, an unreasonable risk is one that is greater than what society is willing to accept in light of the benefits derived from the activity. Consider whether the following risks are reasonable or unreasonable.

a. CarCo. produces and sells automobiles, including an economy line, a moderately expensive sedan series, and a luxury line. CarCo. could equip each of the cars it sells and manufactures with an anti-lock brake system for approximately 7% of the cost of each automobile. This cost increase would significantly decrease sales of the economy line by pricing the car above others on the market. The cost would have relatively little impact on sales in the luxury line. Cars without anti-lock brakes are 25 times more likely to be involved in a collision than cars with anti-lock brakes. Although collisions are more likely, there is no greater risk of injury from a collision resulting from a car without anti-lock brakes. Approximately 1 in every 250,000 automobile accidents results in a fatality. CarCo does not equip its cars with anti-lock brake systems.

b. Store-Mart is a large retail store that stocks a wide array of items including groceries, sporting goods, electronics, kitchen supplies, toys, cleaning products and health and beauty aids. Store-Mart is located in a high-crime area. Several thefts and theft related assaults have occurred in Store-Mart's parking lot. Store-Mart has security cameras installed in the parking lot, but does not hire Security Guards to protect patrons from criminal acts.

c. Amusement Park operates a roller coaster that is known to cause severe neck and back injuries, especially to persons under 48 inches tall. Amusement park posts a warning disclosing the risks, but does not have a height requirement limiting riders to those over 48 inches tall.

d. The Federal Food and Drug Administration allows candy bar manufacturers to have 60 insect fragments per 100 grams of chocolate (approximately 2½ chocolate bars).

e.   Homeowner invited Friends and their Children over for a backyard bar-
     beque and to swim in Homeowner's pool. Homeowner did not hire a
     lifeguard.

f.   City does not employ a lifeguard for the pool it keeps open to the public.

g.   1 in every 3.5 million infants is born with a genetic predisposition to
     develop a deadly disease. 50% of the infants born with the
     predisposition will die as a result of the disease. A genetic screening
     test can be performed to determine whether a child is predisposed to
     develop the disease. With this early detection at least half of the deaths
     could be prevented. The screening test costs $2,500 to administer. State
     does not include the test in the mandated screening tests and immu-
     nizations required for all children as a precursor for attending State's
     schools.

h.   Railroad Company does not have gates (arms that lower when a train
     approaches) at approximately two-thirds of the 220,000 train crossings
     it owns and operates. Approximately one person per day dies at a railroad
     crossing. Gates are approximately 85% more effective at stopping railroad
     crossing deaths than passive measures (signs).

As you assessed risk in the previous exercise you probably relied on your own experiences and maybe even your sense of fairness to guide your assessment. You may also have engaged in a cost-benefit analysis—balancing concerns about the costs of doing business and providing products and services against the costs of making products and services safe. These types of fairness and efficiency considerations are also the concerns courts consider when assessing whether conduct is reasonable. In perhaps the most well-known attempt to formulate an approach for measuring reasonableness, Judge Learned Hand, in *United States v. Carroll Towing Co.*, 159 F.2d 169, reduced this type of assessment to an algebraic formula, describing it as follows: "liability depends upon whether B [the burden of adequate precautions] is less than L [the gravity of the resulting injury, i.e., the loss] multiplied by P [the probability injury will result if adequate precautions are not taken]; i.e., whether $B < PL$." If the algebraic formula intimidates you (perhaps you are math phobic) you can represent the formula graphically. For example:

Defendant is negligent if:

Defendant is not negligent if:

Exercise 2-2 Applying the Hand Formula

Review the hypotheticals from exercise 2.1. This time, use the Hand formula to evaluate each one. Consider the following:

    1.   Did your assessment change?

2.   Does using the formula make it easier to articulate the reasons for your assessment?

3.   Do you believe this is a helpful or useful formula for evaluating reasonableness?

It is important to understand that the Hand formula will not usually be applied explicitly by a court or jury, and you will not likely be called upon to set out the formula and apply it on an examination. Rather, it is a means of conceptualizing and thus evaluating the evidence, so it can be a helpful tool for law students and lawyers constructing legal arguments relating to risk.

Exercise 2-3 Questioning Values

It is worth knowing that the Hand formula has been criticized on a number of fronts. For example, it is criticized for valuing economics over other important values — including social relationships. It is also criticized for being dehumanizing, by focusing on the monetary costs of injury, rather than focusing on responsibility for the well-being of others and their protection from harm, and by taking the focus off of the human suffering involved in circumstances. Before deciding whether you share these concerns, consider the following:

During the 1970s the Ford Motor Company was embroiled in a controversy surrounding their newly released subcompact car — the Ford Pinto. Ford was allegedly aware that during the Pinto's design phase crash testing revealed that in a rear collision at speeds of 31 miles per hour or above, the Pinto's gas tank could rupture, and cause the Pinto to catch fire. Ford had developed the technology to make improvements to the design of the Pinto that would have decreased the chance of the gas tank rupturing after a rear-end collision, but Ford decided not to make any changes to the design.

A document emerged from the Pinto litigation, sometimes referred to as "the Ford Memo." This memo has been described (depending on the party's perspective) as either evidence of the callousness of Ford's corporate culture because Ford compared the cost of $11 repairs against the cost of deaths and injuries, or as a letter to the National Highway Traffic Safety Administration to urge them to reconsider proposed safety regulations unrelated to the rear end collision issues. From either perspective it is clear the memo was not an evaluation of Ford's tort liability, nor did it pertain exclusively to the Pinto. In any event, whatever the reason for the memo, which is not critical for purposes of this exercise, it contained a cost benefit analysis, and included human fatalities and injuries as one of the "costs."

In the memo, Ford estimated the cost of making a design change that would reduce certain fuel tank fires. According to Ford the design change would cost $11 per vehicle, for a total cost of $137 million. Ford also estimated that making the design change would result in a total of 180 fewer burn deaths, 180 fewer serious burn injuries, and 2,100 fewer burned vehicles. Ford multiplied theses numbers by the National Highway Traffic Safety Administration "societal costs" estimates of: $200,000 per death, $67,000 per injury, and $700 per vehicle, for a total of $49.5 million. Here is the comparison:

Benefits

Savings: 180 burn deaths, 180 serious burn injuries, 2,100 burned vehicles

Unit Cost: $200,000 per death, $67,000 per injury, $700 per vehicle

Total Benefit: 180 x ($200,000) + 180 x ($67,000) + 2,100 x ($700) = $49.5 Million

Costs

Sales: 11 million cars, 1.5 million light trucks

Unit Cost: $11 per car, $11 per truck

Total Cost: 11,000,000 x ($11) + 1,500,000 x ($ 11) = $137 Million

Whether Ford's Pinto related design decisions were based on a cost/benefit analysis like the one in the memo has never been established. What is clear from the memo is that the benefit of $49.5 million (as estimated by Ford) was much less than the $137 million cost to make the design change. In other words, this risk/ benefit analysis indicated the cost for 180 people to die and 180 additional people to burn would be less than the cost of $11 per vehicle to prevent such deaths and injuries.

Under the Hand formula would Ford be justified if, based on this analysis, they did not make the $11 design change? Why or why not? Should they be? Why or why not?

A. The Negligence Cause of Action

Now that you have some understanding of the general principles involved in assessing risk, it is time to move to considering each of the elements required for establishing a cause of action for negligence. In order to succeed in proving negligence a plaintiff must establish (1) that the defendant owed her a duty, (2) that the defendant breached that duty, (3) that plaintiff was injured (damaged) and (4) that the defendant's breach was the actual and proximate cause of the plaintiff's damages.

1. Establishing Duty and Breach

Duty is the legal standard that a person must adhere to, and breach is the failure to do so. The first step in proving defendant owed plaintiff a duty is to establish the existence of a legal standard governing the defendant's conduct. Generally speaking, each of us owes one another the duty to use ordinary care, also sometimes known as due care, which means we should do what a reasonably prudent person would do, and refrain from doing what a reasonably prudent person would refrain from doing. In addition to this general duty, there are special standards that may be used to evaluate conduct for certain categories of persons — including lawyers, doctors, landowners, school employees and common carriers — and for certain circumstances — such as emergency or rescue situations. As you might suspect, given these examples and the exercises you've already completed, the existence and extent of the duty owed is dependent on the time, place and surrounding circumstances.

In practice, when a plaintiff's lawyer evaluates the defendant's conduct to determine whether that conduct is a breach of any legal duty owed to the plaintiff, the plaintiff's lawyer will already know (at least generally) what conduct occurred. Thus, the lawyer's initial focus will be on determining whether any standard exists that proscribes the conduct that has already occurred. By finding such a standard the plaintiff's lawyer essentially evaluates both duty and breach — because if the plaintiff's lawyer can demonstrate that there was such a legal standard, she establishes a duty, and the fact that defendant failed to adhere to that standard is a breach. In other words, by not following or adhering to the legal standard, the defendant breached the duty that was owed. Because these two concepts are so intertwined at this initial evaluation stage, and because one of the goals of this text is to simulate the practice of law — these two concepts are covered together in this section. However, it is important to understand that duty and breach are separate elements — and require consideration of separate questions. For example, once the plaintiff's lawyer is satisfied that there is a legal standard that will be applied (a duty was owed) and the standard was breached, she must then turn her attention to proving both of these elements — and the evidence required to prove the duty element will be different from the evidence required to prove the breach element.

Proving duty requires establishing the existence of a standard that applies to the defendant's conduct. Proving breach requires proving the defendant's conduct did not adhere to the standard. In other words, the evidence proving a duty was owed will be evidence of the existence of a standard governing the defendant's conduct — e.g., a case, a statute, an expert opinion, or argument that due care was necessary. The evidence proving breach will be evidence of the "facts" plaintiff related to her lawyer or that were "discovered" during the course of litigating the case — e.g., witness testimony and documents establishing the defendant did not adhere to the required standard. For example, if the plaintiff was injured when her brakes failed, and she had just taken the car to a mechanic for an inspection, the plaintiff's lawyer would initially focus on determining whether there was any obligation for the mechanic to have inspected the brakes. If there was, the plaintiff's lawyer establishes there is a standard governing the conduct — this is the defendant's duty. The plaintiff's lawyer would then also need to establish through admissible evidence (witnesses, documents, etc.) that the mechanic did not inspect the brakes. The fact that defendant did not adhere to this standard — by not checking the plaintiff's brakes — would be the breach of duty. The plaintiff will also have to show that the mechanic's breach caused her injury — but for now that is not our concern. If the plaintiff is not owed a duty it will not matter that the defendant's actions caused the injury; the defendant's lawyer will succeed in having the action dismissed by the court at the outset of the litigation. Thus, establishing duty is the first step in proving negligence.

a. Proving the Existence and Extent of Duty

The plaintiff's lawyer must prove both that a duty exists (that there is a standard that applies to this defendant, situation and plaintiff) and that the duty covers the breach alleged in the case. Simply stated, in examining duty there are really two questions to evaluate: (1) whether a duty is owed, and (2) if so, what is the extent (or scope) of that duty.

(1) Establishing That a Duty Is Owed to the Plaintiff

Whether a duty exists is a matter of law; this means it is up to the court to determine whether a duty is owed in any given situation. The court will make this determination based on a number of factors which may include: the foreseeability and extent of the likely harm resulting from the defendant's conduct; the burden that creating a duty will place on the defendant; the benefits to society of imposing a duty on defendant; whether defendant is uniquely positioned to prevent the harm, or whether others might be better situated to avert the risk; and whether there are alternative ways of protecting the plaintiff's interest.

If a court decides society will be better off if certain categories of persons are required to exercise due care, it will create a duty. If the court concludes that public policy dictates that a category of persons should not be legally bound, it will refuse to create a duty. This might make it seem as if there is no way for a law student to evaluate duty; if it is simply up to the court to decide, you might think your only option is to wait for a decision addressing your issue. However, a lawyer in a negligence action, where the existence of duty is in issue, must formulate arguments for or against imposing a duty, so it is important for you to learn about and understand how to apply the factors courts will consider in making the determination so you are able to make such arguments. Also, although lawyers may not guarantee results, and are not required to foresee the future, in order to advise clients, lawyers must be able to review the client's case and existing law and make reasoned predictions (or educated guesses) about the conclusions the court will draw—and learning to evaluate whether a duty exists will help you develop this skill. In some cases, this evaluation will be rather easy. There are a number of frequently recurring situations for which courts have defined duty—both whether it exists and its' scope. However, even in these situations it is important to remember that because duty is a policy judgment by the court, such duties may be reconsidered as societal concerns and attitudes change; in fact, you will see the evolution of certain duties in this chapter.

In determining whether a duty exists courts frequently make distinctions between failures to act and choices to take action. Courts do not usually impose a duty to affirmatively act for the benefit of another person. In other words, a court does not usually impose liability for a failure to act—i.e., for doing nothing (subject, of course, to a number of exceptions). The most frequent example of this principle is the unwillingness of courts to impose a duty to rescue. For example, if a really great swimmer is standing on the shore and sees a person is drowning, in most jurisdictions the great swimmer is not obligated to rescue the drowning person (meaning they are not liable if the person drowns), even if they could have saved the person without any risk to themselves. This might seem like an immoral or unreasonable rule to you, and in fact it does to many scholars and commentators, but proponents defend the rule on the basis that a person should not be held liable when his or her conduct is not what created the risk of harm, and also because it would be an infringement on personal liberty to coerce unwilling bystanders into serving others. There are exceptions to the no duty to act (and no duty to rescue) rule. For example, even in rescue situations courts require action (impose a duty to take an affirmative act) when there is a special relationship between the parties that would justify imposition of such a duty.

Courts will usually impose liability once action is voluntarily undertaken. For example, once a person chooses to rescue another, they must exercise ordinary care in performing the rescue, and they may not leave the person in a worse position than he or she was in before the rescue began. This means that if the swimmer in our earlier example decides to save the drowning person and in so doing negligently causes injury, the swimmer is liable for that injury. You may find it ironic that a person who chooses to do nothing and watches someone drown has no liability, yet one who makes the choice to attempt to rescue assumes a duty of care and can be found liable. Some states have resolved this issue by enacting "Good Samaritan" statutes, limiting or eliminating liability for negligence for those who choose to undertake a rescue.

Since most litigation results from actions by defendants which create risks of harm, rather than failures to act, this aspect of duty is not litigated all that frequently, especially when compared to the other elements of negligence. Nonetheless, in some cases it is a critical issue, especially where new categories of cases seek to establish the scope of negligence liability, which is the subject of in the next two cases in this chapter. Since you may be called upon to make such arguments, it is important to understand how to determine whether there is a duty, before proceeding to the second question—the extent or scope of the duty.

Exercise 2-4 Establishing the Existence of a Duty

In the following cases, two different courts, considering nearly identical issues, reach opposite conclusions about duty. As you read these two opinions, focus on the factors considered and the rationales used by the courts for imposing and not imposing a duty. As you read, consider:

1. What factor (or factors) does the court consider?

2. What social polic(ies) does the court cite as the basis for its decision?

3. What facts does the court emphasize in its analysis?

4. What is the court's reasoning?

5. Do you agree or disagree with the court's decision? Why?

Satterfield v. Breeding Insulation Company

266 S.W.3d 347 (Tenn. 2008)

This appeal involves the efforts of the estate of a twenty-five-year-old woman who contracted mesothelioma to recover damages for her death. While she was alive, the woman filed a negligence action against her father's employer, alleging that the employer had negligently permitted her father to wear his asbestos-contaminated work clothes home from work, thereby regularly and repeatedly exposing her to asbestos fibers over an extended period of time. After the woman died, the Circuit Court for Blount County permitted her father to be substituted as the personal representative of her estate. The employer moved for a judgment on the pleadings on the narrow ground that it owed no duty to its employee's daughter. The trial court granted the motion. The deceased woman's father appealed the dismissal of his daughter's wrongful death claim. The Tennessee Court of Appeals reversed the trial court. We granted ... permission to appeal to determine whether the deceased woman's complaint can withstand a motion for judgment on the pleadings. We have determined that it does because, under the facts alleged in the complaint, the employer owed a duty to those who regularly and for extended periods of time came into close contact with the asbestos-contaminated work clothes of its employees to prevent them from being exposed to a foreseeable and unreasonable risk of harm.

The only issue on this appeal is whether the complaint of a woman who succumbed to mesothelioma should have been dismissed solely because the defendant did not have a duty to act reasonably to prevent her from being exposed repeatedly and regularly over an extended period of time to the asbestos fibers on her father's work clothes. The purpose of this appeal is not to determine whether, in fact, the defendant was negligent or whether its conduct caused the woman's death....

I.

Alcoa, Inc. is an international manufacturer of aluminum and aluminum products. It owns and operates facilities in various locations throughout the United States, including a facility in Alcoa, Tennessee. Alcoa uses materials containing asbestos in many of its manufacturing operations. Since the 1930s, Alcoa has been aware that asbestos is a highly dangerous substance, and it has closely monitored the research into the dangers posed by asbestos.

Beginning in the 1940s, Alcoa opened its own internal hygiene department which provided directives to Alcoa's local facilities regarding the handling of materials containing asbestos. Because of the frequent use of materials containing asbestos in its manufacturing processes, Alcoa was aware that the air in its factories contained high levels of asbestos fibers and that its employees were being exposed to these fibers on a daily basis.

Alcoa became aware in the 1960s that the dangers posed by asbestos fibers extended beyond its employees who were in constant direct contact with the materials containing asbestos or the asbestos fibers in the air. It learned that even intermittent exposure to low levels of asbestos fibers resulted in an increased risk of disease. At approximately the same time, Alcoa also learned that persons living near facilities that made extensive use of materials containing asbestos were experiencing higher disease rates, as were the family members of its employees who were being exposed regularly and repeatedly to the asbestos fibers on the employees' work clothes.

In 1972, the Occupational Safety and Health Administration ("OSHA") promulgated regulations prohibiting employees who had been exposed to asbestos from taking their work clothes home to be laundered. Tests that Alcoa conducted at a number of its facilities, including those in Tennessee, revealed that the levels of asbestos fibers on the workers' clothes were extremely high.

In 1973, Doug Satterfield began working at Alcoa's facility in Alcoa, Tennessee. He worked there for two years until he entered the United States Army in 1975. After three years of military service, Mr. Satterfield resumed working at the Alcoa plant in 1978. He continued to work for Alcoa until at least 1984. His job assignments resulted in his exposure to high levels of asbestos dust and fibers on a daily basis.

Contrary to the OSHA regulations, Alcoa failed to educate Mr. Satterfield and its other employees regarding the risk of asbestos or how to handle materials containing asbestos. Even though Alcoa's employees worked extensively with materials containing asbestos, these materials did not contain warning labels or notices stating that they contained asbestos. Despite the fact that Alcoa was aware of the dangers posed by asbestos before Mr. Satterfield became an employee, it failed to apprise him or its other employees of the dangers of asbestos or specifically of the danger associated with wearing home their asbestos-contaminated work clothes. In addition, Alcoa failed to provide protective coveralls for its employees, discouraged the use of its on-site bathhouse facilities, and did not offer to launder its employees' work clothes at its facility. Accordingly, Alcoa's employees, including Mr. Satterfield, left the plant each day unaware of the dangers posed by the asbestos fibers on their contaminated work clothes and without Alcoa making an effort to prevent others from being exposed to the asbestos fibers on its employees' clothes.

On September 7, 1979, Amanda Nicole Satterfield was born to Mr. Satterfield and Donna Satterfield. Because her birth was premature, she was required to spend the first three months of her life at the University of Tennessee Hospital in Knoxville, Tennessee. Mr. Satterfield visited his infant daughter every day she was hospitalized. He came to the hospital immediately after work wearing his asbestos-contaminated work clothes and stayed with his daughter until late into the evening. Thus, from the day of her birth, Ms. Satterfield was exposed to the asbestos fibers on her father's work clothes.

Ms. Satterfield was eventually diagnosed with mesothelioma. On December 8, 2003, she filed suit against … Alcoa in the Circuit Court for Knox County. She alleged that mesothelioma is a highly lethal form of cancer that is almost exclusively caused by exposure to asbestos and that she contracted mesothelioma as a direct result of the negligent acts and omissions of … Alcoa…. Ms. Satterfield died from mesothelioma on January 1, 2005.

* * *

Because strikingly similar issues related to "take-home" or "transmission" asbestos exposure cases have sharply divided courts throughout the country and because this case implicates core principles of Tennessee's tort law, we granted Alcoa's application for permission to appeal. We have determined that the trial court erred by dismissing Ms. Satterfield's complaint and that the Court of Appeals properly reversed the trial court's dismissal of the complaint. Based on the facts alleged in the complaint, Alcoa owed a duty of reasonable care to Ms. Satterfield.

II.

In its most succinct form, the pivotal question in this case is whether, under the facts alleged in Ms. Satterfield's complaint, Alcoa owed a duty of reasonable care to Ms. Satterfield. Alcoa asserts that it did not owe a duty to Ms. Satterfield. It contends that imposing such a duty on it would improperly create an affirmative obligation to act despite the absence of any special relationship between Alcoa and either Ms. Satterfield or her father. On the other hand, Mr. Satterfield insists that his daughter's complaint is premised on the assumption that Alcoa owed Ms. Satterfield a duty of reasonable care because it created an unreasonable and foreseeable risk of harm to her.

A.

The underlying dispute in this case is fundamentally one of characterization and classification. Has Alcoa engaged in an affirmative act that created an unreasonable and foreseeable risk of harm to Ms. Satterfield? If Alcoa did create such a risk of harm, are there countervailing legal principles or policy considerations that warrant determining that Alcoa nevertheless owed no duty Ms. Satterfield? Or, alternatively, does this case involve an omission by Alcoa in failing to control the actions of Mr. Satterfield, its employee? If so, then does Alcoa have the sort of special relationship with either Mr. Satterfield or Ms. Satterfield that gives rise to a duty to restrain Mr. Satterfield or to protect Ms. Satterfield? The answers to these questions emerge from considerations of precedent and public policy, as well as the basic foundations of Tennessee's tort law.

***[D]uty has become an essential element of all negligence claims, as well as a question of law to be determined by courts. *West v. E. Tenn. Pioneer Oil Co.*, 172 S.W.3d 545, 550

(Tenn.2005); *Bradshaw v. Daniel,* 854 S.W.2d 865, 869 (Tenn.1993). Thus, if Alcoa does not owe a duty to Ms. Satterfield, her claim must fail.

B.

Duty is a legal obligation to conform to a reasonable person standard of care in order to protect others against unreasonable risks of harm. *Burroughs v. Magee,* 118 S.W.3d 323, 328–29 (Tenn.2003); *Staples v. CBL & Assocs.,* 15 S.W.3d 83, 89 (Tenn.2000). As a general rule, persons have a duty to others to refrain from engaging in affirmative acts that a reasonable person "should recognize as involving an unreasonable risk of causing an invasion of an interest of another" or acts "which involve[ ] an unreasonable risk of harm to another." Restatement (Second) of Torts §§ 284, 302, at 19, 82 (1965). Thus, if an individual "acts at all, [he or she] must exercise reasonable care to make his [or her] acts safe for others." Restatement (Second) of Torts § 4 cmt. b, at 8. The core of negligence is the violation of this requirement by engaging in "behavior which should be recognized as involving unreasonable danger to others." W. Page Keeton, *Prosser and Keeton on the Law of Torts* § 31, at 169 (5th ed.1984) [hereinafter "*Prosser and Keeton*"].

These rules do not, however, require that persons always act reasonably to secure the safety of others. Rather, they serve a more limited role as restraints upon a person's actions that create unreasonable and foreseeable risks of harm to others. Expounding upon this point more than a century ago, Professor Francis H. Bohlen asserted that "[t]here is no distinction more deeply rooted in the common law and more fundamental than that between misfeasance and non-feasance, between active misconduct working positive injury to others and passive inaction, a failure to take positive steps to benefit others, or to protect them from harm not created by any wrongful act of the defendant." While the primacy of this distinction is certainly subject to debate, that it has played a significant role in the formation of the law of negligence is beyond reasonable dispute.

Professor Bohlen is not the only scholar to offer an eloquent and enlightening articulation of the distinction between misfeasance and nonfeasance. Dean Keeton and Dean Prosser explained the distinction as follows:

> In the determination of the existence of a duty, there runs through much of the law a distinction between action and inaction.... [T]here arose very early a difference, still deeply rooted in the law of negligence, between "misfeasance" and "nonfeasance"—that is to say, between active misconduct working positive injury to others and passive inaction or a failure to take steps to protect them from harm. The reason for the distinction may be said to lie in the fact that by 'misfeasance' the defendant has created a new risk of harm to the plaintiff, while by 'nonfeasance' he has at least made his situation no worse, and has merely failed to benefit him by interfering in his affairs.

* * *

The distinction between misfeasance and nonfeasance can be easily misunderstood. One can be led astray by thinking that a defendant's negligent act must be characterized "as an affirmative act for a duty to exist, rather than appreciating that it is the defendant's entire course of conduct that must constitute an affirmative act creating a risk of harm and that negligence may consist of an act or omission creating an unreasonable risk." A classic illustration of this point is the example of a driver who fails to apply his or her brakes to avoid hitting a pedestrian walking in a crosswalk. Even though the driver's negligent act—failing to apply the brakes—is an omission, the "driver's careless failure to apply the brakes is negligent driving, not negligent failure to rescue." Accordingly, distinguishing between misfeasance and nonfeasance can best be accomplished, not by focusing on whether an individual's "specific failure to exercise reasonable care is an error of commission or omission," but rather by focusing on whether the individual's entire course of conduct created a risk of harm. Thus, even though the specific negligent act may constitute an omission, the entirety of the conduct may still be misfeasance that created a risk of harm.

The distinction between misfeasance and nonfeasance is far from academic. It has practical significance, and Tennessee's courts regularly employ it when called upon to decide whether a duty exists. *See, e.g., Bradshaw v. Daniel,* 854 S.W.2d at 870; *Newton v. Tinsley,* 970 S.W.2d at 492. With regard to misfeasance, this Court has held that "all persons have a duty to use reasonable care to refrain from conduct that will foreseeably cause injury to others." *Burroughs v. Magee,* 118 S.W.3d at 328; *Bradshaw v. Daniel,* 854 S.W.2d at 870. As for nonfeasance, Tennessee's courts generally have declined to impose a duty to act or to rescue. *Bradshaw v. Daniel,* 854 S.W.2d at 870; *Newton v. Tinsley,* 970 S.W.2d at 492. Simply stated, persons do not ordinarily have a duty to act to protect others from dangers or risks except for those that they themselves have created. *Biscan v. Brown,* 160 S.W.3d 462, 478–79 (Tenn.2005); *Nichols v. Atnip,* 844 S.W.2d 655, 661 (Tenn.Ct.App.1992).

*** Accordingly, Tennessee law provides that while "an actor is always bound to prevent his acts from creating an unreasonable risk to others, he is under the affirmative duty to act to prevent another from sustaining harm only when certain socially recognized relations exist which constitute the basis for such legal duty." ***

III.

Courts across the country have disagreed as to how these broad principles of tort law should be used to determine whether an employer owes a duty to persons who develop asbestos-related illnesses after exposure to asbestos fibers on its employees' clothing. Although the courts have reached inconsistent conclusions, a pattern has begun to emerge. The courts that ultimately recognize the existence of a duty when faced with facts similar to this case have focused on the foreseeability of harm resulting from the employer's failure to warn of or to take precautions to prevent the exposure. On the other hand, the courts finding that no duty exists have focused on the relationship—or lack of a relationship—between the employer and the injured party. *See In re Asbestos Litig.,* C.A. No. 04C-07-099-ASB, 2007 WL 4571196, at *3 (Del.Super.Ct. Dec.21, 2007).

* * *

While the courts, like the Michigan Supreme Court, that have found, as a matter of law, that employers have no duty in take-home asbestos exposure cases, rely upon the absence of a special relationship, this argument is misplaced under Tennessee tort law as it has developed over the years. This Court has recognized that a duty of reasonable care arises whenever a defendant's conduct poses an unreasonable and foreseeable risk of harm to persons or property. *McCall v. Wilder,* 913 S.W.2d 150, 153 (Tenn.1995). Thus, like the drafters of the new Restatement (Third) of Torts containing the principles applicable to liability for physical harm, we are of the view that

> [e]ven when the actor and victim are complete strangers and have no relationship, the basis for the ordinary duty of reasonable care ... is conduct that creates a risk to another. Thus, a relationship ordinarily is not what defines the line between duty and no-duty; conduct creating risk to another is.

Restatement (Third) of Torts § 37, Reporter's Note, cmt. c, at 721. Because the requirement of privity no longer plays a role in negligence claims, "[w]hen a defendant causes physical harm through misfeasance—affirmative acts of negligence—rather than nonfeasance, he [or she] is liable to the foreseeably injured person for the harm." 2 Dan B. Dobbs, *The Law of Torts* § 321, at 870 (2001).

Whether a case involves a simple automobile accident or a complicated toxic tort, Tennessee law currently provides that one owes a duty to refrain from engaging in conduct that creates an unreasonable and foreseeable risk of harm to others. *Draper v. Westerfield,* 181 S.W.3d at 291; *Biscan v. Brown,* 160 S.W.3d at 478; *Burroughs v. Magee,* 118 S.W.3d at 328–29; *McCall v. Wilder,* 913 S.W.2d at 153.

According to Ms. Satterfield's complaint, Alcoa's employees worked with materials containing asbestos on a daily basis. Employees, including Mr. Satterfield, worked under improper and unsafe conditions which violated internal safety requirements and OSHA standards. As a result, the employees' clothes collected significant amounts of asbestos fibers. Even though Alcoa was aware of the dangerous amounts of asbestos on its employees' clothes, Alcoa did not inform its employees that the materials that they were handling contained asbestos or of the risks posed by asbestos fibers to the employees or to others. The danger was compounded even further because Alcoa dissuaded its employees from using on-site bathhouse facilities, and it failed to provide coveralls or to wash its employees' work clothes at the factory. Under the facts alleged in Ms. Satterfield's complaint, Alcoa's alleged misfeasance created a significant risk of harm to Ms. Satterfield.

Despite Alcoa's protestations to the contrary, this is not a failure to act case wherein a defendant "declined to interfere, ... was in no way responsible for the perilous situation, ... did not increase the peril, ... took away nothing from the person in jeopardy, [but instead] ... simply failed to confer a benefit." The rules establishing no duty to protect, to rescue, or to control the conduct of third parties, the underlying basis of Alcoa's argument, are all subsets of the same no affirmative duty to act absent a special relationship rule. That rule, however, is inapplicable to this case. Instead, this case involves a risk created through misfeasance. *Rochon v. Saberhagen Holdings, Inc.,* 140 Wash.App. 1008, 2007 WL 2325214, at *3 & n. 23; *see also In re Certified Question from Fourteenth Dist. Ct.App. of Tex.,* 740 N.W.2d at 225 (Cavanagh, J., dissenting). Thus, as in *Rochon v. Saberhagen Holdings, Inc.,* the outcome of this case does not turn on a failure to act or on the act of a third party, but instead, it turns on the employer's own misfeasance—its injurious affirmative act of operating its facility in such an unsafe manner that dangerous asbestos fibers were transmitted outside the facility to others who came in regular and extended close contact with the asbestos-contaminated work clothes of its employees. *Rochon v. Saberhagen Holdings, Inc.,* No. 58579-7-I, 2007 WL 2325214, at *3;32 *see also In re Certified Question from Fourteenth Dist. Ct.App. of Tex.,* 740 N.W.2d at 225 (Cavanagh, J., dissenting).

As illustrated by *West v. East Tennessee Pioneer Oil Co.,* liability for misfeasance is not cabined within the confines of boxes created by particular relationships. To the contrary, "[l]iability for 'misfeasance'... may extend to any person to whom harm may reasonably be anticipated as a result of the defendant's conduct ...; while for 'nonfeasance' it is necessary to find some definite relation between the parties, of such a character that social policy justifies the imposition of a duty to act." *Prosser and Keeton* § 56, at 374. Alcoa engaged in misfeasance that set in motion a risk of harm to Ms. Satterfield. Because Ms. Satterfield's complaint rests on the basic tort claim of misfeasance, it is not necessary to analyze in detail whether Alcoa also had duties arising from special relationships with third parties.

IV.

Concluding that Ms. Satterfield's complaint alleges that Alcoa's misfeasance caused her to contract mesothelioma does not end the inquiry into whether Tennessee recognizes that Alcoa owed a duty to Ms. Satterfield based on the factual allegations in her complaint. Determinations regarding the existence and scope of a particular legal duty also reflect "society's contemporary policies and social requirements concerning the right of individuals and the general public to be protected from another's act or conduct." *Bradshaw v. Daniel*, 854 S.W.2d at 870. After all, the concept of duty is largely an expression of policy considerations. Accordingly, our consideration of the existence and scope of Alcoa's duty must also include an analysis of the relevant public policy considerations. *Burroughs v. Magee*, 118 S.W.3d at 329.

It would be erroneous, however, to assume that the concept of duty is a freefloating application of public policy, drifting on the prevailing winds like the seeds of a dandelion. Like the courts in our sister states, Tennessee's courts have not become so intoxicated on the liquor of public policy analysis that we have lost our appreciation for the moderating and sobering influences of the well-tested principles regarding the imposition of duty.

A.

In most cases today, prior court decisions and statutes have already established the doctrines and rules governing a defendant's conduct. Generally, the presence or absence of a duty is a given rather than a matter of reasoned debate, discussion, or contention. The common law, however, must and does grow to accommodate new societal realities and values—or simply better reasoning—as it moves toward refinement and modification with the aim of improving while maintaining a sufficient stability so as to seek, and one hopes, to find, prudent reformation as opposed to anarchic revolution.

When the existence of a particular duty is not a given or when the rules of the established precedents are not readily applicable, courts will turn to public policy for guidance. Doing so necessarily favors imposing a duty of reasonable care where a "defendant's conduct poses an unreasonable and foreseeable risk of harm to persons or property." *McCall v. Wilder*, 913 S.W.2d at 153. When conducting this analysis, the courts have considered, among other factors: (1) the foreseeable probability of the harm or injury occurring; (2) the possible magnitude of the potential harm or injury; (3) the importance or social value of the activity engaged in by the defendant; (4) the usefulness of the conduct to the defendant; (5) the feasibility of alternative conduct that is safer; (6) the relative costs and burdens associated with that safer conduct; (7) the relative usefulness of the safer conduct; and (8) the relative safety of alternative conduct. *Burroughs v. Magee*, 118 S.W.3d at 329; *McCall v. Wilder*, 913 S.W.2d at 153.

With these factors firmly in mind, Tennessee's courts use a balancing approach to determine whether the particular risk should give rise to a duty of reasonable care. *West v. E. Tenn. Pioneer Oil Co.*, 172 S.W.3d at 551; *Burroughs v. Magee*, 118 S.W.3d at 329. A duty arises when the degree of foreseeability of the risk and the gravity of the harm outweigh the burden that would be imposed if the defendant were required to engage in an alternative course of conduct that would have prevented the harm. *West v. E. Tenn. Pioneer Oil Co.*, 172 S.W.3d at 551; *Burroughs v. Magee*, 118 S.W.3d at 329; *McCall v. Wilder*, 913 S.W.2d at 153. The foreseeability and gravity of the harm are linked insofar as the degree of foreseeability needed to establish a duty is inversely proportional to the magnitude of the foreseeable harm. *Turner v. Jordan*, 957 S.W.2d at 818. The greater the risk of harm, the less degree of foreseeability is required. *Pittman v. Upjohn Co.*, 890 S.W.2d 425, 433 (Tenn.1994). During the balancing process, it is permissible for the courts to consider the contemporary values of Tennessee's citizens.

While every balancing factor is significant, the foreseeability factor has taken on paramount importance in Tennessee. *Hale v. Ostrow*, 166 S.W.3d 713, 716–17 (Tenn.2005);

Biscan v. Brown, 160 S.W.3d at 480. This factor is so important that if an injury could not have been reasonably foreseen, a duty does not arise.... *Doe v. Linder Constr. Co.,* 845 S.W.2d 173, 178 (Tenn.1992). Conversely, foreseeability alone is insufficient to create a duty. *McClung v. Delta Square Ltd. P'ship,* 937 S.W.2d 891, 904 (Tenn.1996). Thus, to prevail on a negligence claim, a plaintiff must show that the risk was foreseeable, but that showing is not, in and of itself, sufficient to create a duty. Instead, if a risk is foreseeable, courts then undertake the balancing analysis. *** For the purpose of determining whether a duty exists, the courts' consideration of foreseeability is limited to assessing whether there is some probability or likelihood of harm that is serious enough to induce a reasonable person to take precautions to avoid it. In this context, the courts are not concerned with the ultimate reasonableness, or lack of reasonableness, of the defendant's conduct. Rather, the courts are simply ascertaining "whether [the] defendant was obligated to be vigilant of a certain sort of harm to the plaintiff."

B.

Viewing the allegations in Ms. Satterfield's complaint in the light most favorable to her, it is not difficult to conclude that Ms. Satterfield falls within a class of persons that could, with reasonable foreseeability, be harmed by exposure to asbestos. That class includes persons who regularly and for extended periods of time came into close contact with the asbestos-contaminated work clothes of Alcoa's employees.

Under the facts alleged in Ms. Satterfield's complaint, Alcoa was aware of the presence of significant quantities of asbestos fibers on its employees' work clothes. It was also aware of the dangers posed by even small quantities of asbestos and that asbestos fibers were being transmitted by its employees to others. Nevertheless, despite its extensive and superior knowledge of the dangers of asbestos, Alcoa allegedly (1) failed to inform its employees that they were working with materials containing asbestos; (2) failed to provide its employees with or to require them to wear protective covering on their clothes; (3) actively discouraged its employees' use of on-site bathhouse facilities for changing or cleaning; and (4) failed to inform its employees of the dangers posed by the asbestos fibers on their work clothes. Under these circumstances, it was foreseeable that Ms. Satterfield would come into close contact with Mr. Satterfield's work clothes on an extended and repeated basis.

C.

Because the risk of Ms. Satterfield being exposed to the asbestos fibers on her father's work clothes was foreseeable, the analysis shifts to considering the balancing factors: (1) the foreseeable probability of the harm or injury occurring; (2) the possible magnitude of the potential harm or injury; (3) the importance or social value of the activity engaged in by the defendant; (4) the usefulness of the conduct to the defendant; (5) the feasibility of alternative conduct that is safer; (6) the relative costs and burdens associated with the safer conduct; (7) the relative usefulness of the safer conduct; and (8) the relative safety of alternative conduct. *Burroughs v. Magee,* 118 S.W.3d at 329; *McCall v. Wilder,* 913 S.W.2d at 153.

When considering these factors, courts should take care not to invade the province of the jury. A court's function is more limited than a jury's. As a practical matter, a court serves as a gate-keeper and may exclude a claim only if it finds, as a matter of law, that the defendant does not owe a duty to the plaintiff. For claims that should not be excluded as a matter of law, it is ultimately the jury's function to determine whether the defendant actually breached its duty of reasonable care.

While the facts alleged in Ms. Satterfield's complaint may not permit a precise assessment of the full extent of the risk to Ms. Satterfield, they certainly support a conclusion that the risk to her was real and substantial. In light of the debilitating and fatal illnesses that can be caused by exposure to asbestos fibers, the magnitude of the potential harm to Ms. Satterfield was great.

Alcoa argues that its manufacturing operations create jobs and provide useful products and that recognizing that it owes a duty to persons like Ms. Satterfield will have an adverse impact on its ability to provide jobs and to produce useful products. This assertion warrants serious consideration. However, at least at this stage of the proceeding, Alcoa has not articulated a connection between its allegedly negligent acts and its ability to provide employment or to produce useful products. For example, it has not demonstrated that the sort of exposure to asbestos that is involved in this case is a largely unavoidable part of its manufacturing operations.

Ms. Satterfield's complaint, on the other hand, asserts that Alcoa could have greatly reduced the risk of asbestos exposure. It asserts that her risk of being exposed to the asbestos on her father's work clothes could have been greatly reduced had Alcoa (1) provided basic warnings to its employees about the dangers of asbestos, (2) required safer handling of the materials containing asbestos, (3) provided coveralls to its employees, (4) required employees to change their clothes before leaving the workplace, (5) laundered its employees' work clothes on site, or (6) encouraged its employees to use the on-site bathhouse facilities before leaving work.

Based on the present record, many of the measures described in Ms. Satterfield's complaint to protect workers and their families from exposure to asbestos appear to be feasible and efficacious without imposing prohibitive costs or burdens on Alcoa. For its part, however, Alcoa has offered no explanation why any or all of these precautions were not feasible or how they would have had a deleterious effect on its ability to provide jobs or to produce useful products.

Based on the facts alleged in Ms. Satterfield's complaint, Alcoa was a knowledgeable and sophisticated company that was fully aware (1) that it used materials containing asbestos in its manufacturing operations, (2) that high volumes of asbestos fibers were being deposited on its employees' work clothes, and (3) that exposure to asbestos fibers created a substantial health risk. In light of this knowledge, Alcoa had a duty to use reasonable care to prevent exposure to asbestos fibers not only to its employees but also to those who came into close regular contact with its employees' contaminated work clothes over an extended period of time.

V.

Alcoa articulates additional reasons for declining to hold that it has a duty to persons like Ms. Satterfield. First, it argues that the current asbestos litigation crisis in the United States will be worsened if employers that have utilized asbestos in manufacturing are exposed to additional costly litigation. Second, Alcoa asserts that manufacturers could face bankruptcy and a substantial loss of jobs could result if they are exposed to the burden of additional liability. Third, Alcoa claims that finding that it has a duty to persons like Ms. Satterfield will expose premises owners to a host of similar claims by other plaintiffs.

A.

There can be little doubt that there is an asbestos products liability litigation crisis in the United States. The United States Supreme Court has noted that the "elephantine mass of asbestos cases ... defies customary judicial administration and calls for national legislation." *Ortiz v. Fibreboard Corp.,* 527 U.S. 815, 821, 119 S.Ct. 2295, 144 L.Ed.2d 715 (1999). While calls for legislative action have produced much debate and have resulted in various remedial proposals, this sound and fury has not resulted in any significant national legislation.

Unimpaired claimants stand at the center of the asbestos exposure litigation crisis. Estimates compiled in surveys funded by asbestos defendants suggest that between sixty-six and ninety percent of claimants are unimpaired. These claimants are persons who have been exposed to asbestos and who usually have some marker of exposure, but who are not impaired by an asbestos-related disease and likely never will be. The enormous number of claims that have been filed by unimpaired or mildly impaired persons was unexpected. As a result of these claims, the funds available to compensate persons gravely affected by exposure to asbestos has been depleted, and the persons with more serious illnesses caused by exposure to asbestos have been "lost in the shuffle."

Alcoa's argument that liability should be foreclosed as a matter of law because of the current asbestos litigation crisis might have resonance with regard to recognizing a duty to unimpaired claimants where the magnitude of the harm is significantly less. However, it rings hollow with regard to a claimant, like Ms. Satterfield, who has died of mesothelioma.

The various efforts to reform asbestos litigation have been directed toward stemming the tide of lawsuits in large part to ensure that seriously ill claimants are able to recover and are not drowned out by unimpaired claimants. Victims of mesothelioma are regularly identified as precisely the type of claimants whose claims should be protected. It is not surprising that individuals with mesothelioma are put in such a category because mesothelioma is a serious and fatal illness that rarely occurs in the general population and that is closely associated with exposure to asbestos. Ms. Satterfield is precisely the type of claimant whose claims should be permitted rather than inhibited.

B.

Alcoa also contends that it does not manufacture asbestos and that the manufacturers who use materials containing asbestos in their manufacturing process will face enormous financial burdens if they are exposed to liability for illnesses caused by exposure to asbestos fibers in their manufacturing processes. We find this argument unpersuasive. If the financial burden of compensating these injuries is lifted from the employers' shoulders, it does not vanish into the ether. Rather, the burden will fall on persons like Ms. Satterfield. We see no particular public policy reason to favor imposing these costs upon the persons who have been harmed by exposure to asbestos rather than upon the manufacturers who used asbestos in their manufacturing processes. Furthermore, based on the facts alleged in Ms. Satterfield's complaint, Alcoa is far from an uninformed manufacturer who had the misfortune of using materials containing asbestos in its manufacturing process.

C.

Alcoa also asserts that if it is found to be liable to persons like Ms. Satterfield, all premises owners, including schools and home owners, will be exposed to liability for asbestos exposure to persons who were never on their premises. This concern is misplaced for two reasons. First, this opinion is not addressed to premises liability law but rather to the law applicable in a general negligence misfeasance case. *See Rochon v. Saberhagen Holdings, Inc.,* 140 Wash.App. 1008, 2007 WL 2325214, at *2–5. Second, viewing the facts in the light most favorable to Ms. Satterfield, Alcoa is a sophisticated manufacturer that was aware of, or should have been aware of, the risk to others that could result from exposure to asbestos fibers. Under the facts alleged in the complaint, Alcoa knew its employees' work clothes contained significant quantities of asbestos fibers, and it understood the danger of transmitting these asbestos fibers to others. It is not readily apparent, though the facts of a future case may warrant a contrary finding, that such a transmission injury would be reasonably foreseeable by school officials or home owners.

* * *

VI.

Both Alcoa and Mr. Satterfield address the proper scope of the class of persons to whom a duty is owed in cases of this sort. The Court of Appeals limited Alcoa's duty "to members of employees' households who routinely come into close contact with employees' contaminated clothing over an extended period of time." In addition, it expressly excluded "individuals who might possibly come into contact with the employees' clothing, but whose contacts are sporadic or unpredictable."

Even though the cases that have recognized the duty we recognize today have involved claims by an employee's family members, they have not necessarily rejected claims by other plaintiffs. In support of its argument against recognizing any duty in cases like this one, Alcoa asserts that no principled basis exists to limit the duty to the members of the employee's immediate family living in the employees house and thus that recognizing a duty to these family members will eventually result in the recognition of a duty with regard to babysitters, housekeepers, home repair contractors, and next-door neighbors. Alcoa makes a valid point with regard to restricting the duty to family members.

There is no magic talisman that protects persons from the harmful effects of exposure to asbestos simply because they do not live under the same roof or are not a member of the employee's family by blood or marriage. It is foreseeable that the adverse effects of repeated, regular, and extended exposure to asbestos on an employee's work clothes could injure these persons. Public policy does not warrant finding that there is no duty owed to such persons. Accordingly, the duty we recognize today extends to those who regularly and repeatedly come into close contact with an employee's contaminated work clothes over an extended period of time, regardless of whether they live in the employee's home or are a family member.

We note that the Michigan Supreme Court has cautioned that allowing liability in cases like this one could result in "mass tort actions brought by remotely exposed persons such as extended family members, renters, house guests, carpool members, bus drivers, and workers at commercial enterprises visited by the worker when he or she was wearing dirty work clothes." *In re Certified Question from Fourteenth Dist. Ct.App. of Tex.*, 740 N.W.2d at 219. However, in light of the magnitude of the potential harm from exposure to asbestos and the means available to prevent or reduce this harm, we see no reason to prevent carpool members, babysitters, or the domestic help from pursuing negligence claims against an employer should they develop mesothelioma after being repeatedly and regularly in close contact with an employee's asbestos-contaminated work clothes over an extended period of time.

We also note the Delaware Superior Court's concern regarding the potentially limitless liability that could arise from requiring employers to undertake to warn or otherwise protect every potentially foreseeable victim of off-premises exposure to asbestos. *In re Asbestos Litig.*, 2007 WL 4571196, at *12. We agree that a duty to warn all foreseeable persons who might be exposed to asbestos fibers on an employee's work clothes would be too great a burden. However, the imposition of a duty of reasonable care with regard to safe handling of asbestos fibers on employees' work clothes to prevent transmission to others is not such a burden.

Recognizing the existence of a duty to exercise reasonable care to avoid the risk of harm to another involves considerations of fairness and public policy. Under Tennessee law, Alcoa has a duty to prevent foreseeable injury from an unreasonable risk of harm that it had itself created. Under the facts alleged in Ms. Satterfield's complaint, Alcoa failed to inform its employees, including Mr. Satterfield, of the risks associated with asbestos and failed to provide them with meaningful alternatives to wearing home their contaminated work clothes. Based on these allegations, Alcoa created a risk that persons who came into close and regular contact over an extended period of time with its employees' work clothes would be exposed to the asbestos fibers on the clothes. The fair and proportional duty we recognize today is neither limitless nor impractical.

VII.

We have determined that Ms. Satterfield's complaint states a claim upon which relief can be granted. Accordingly, the trial court erred by granting Alcoa a judgment on the pleadings, and the Court of Appeals correctly reversed that order. Based on the facts in Ms. Satterfield's complaint, we cannot conclude, as a matter of law, that Alcoa did not owe a duty to Ms. Satterfield. Our ruling does not foreclose the possibility that Ms. Satterfield's estate will not be able to present sufficient evidence to support her claim. Thus, Alcoa is certainly free to challenge any element of Ms. Satterfield's claim via a motion for summary judgment or motion for directed verdict. Accordingly, we affirm the Court of Appeals and remand the case to the trial court for further proceedings consistent with this opinion.

In re Certified Question from the Fourteenth District Court of Appeals of Texas v. Ford Motor Company

479 Mich. 498 (2007)

Plaintiffs allege that the decedent, Carolyn Miller, died from mesothelioma, an incurable and fatal form of lung cancer, that she contracted from washing the work clothes of her stepfather, Cleveland "John" Roland. From 1954 through 1965, Roland worked for independent contractors who were hired on various occasions by defendant to reline the interiors of blast furnaces used to melt iron ore at the Ford Rouge plant in Dearborn, Michigan. Plaintiffs allege that the materials used to reline the interiors of the blast furnaces contained asbestos. There is no dispute that Miller was never on or near defendant's premises. Miller was diagnosed with mesothelioma in 1999 and died in 2000. After the Texas trial court denied defendant's motion for a directed verdict, a Texas jury awarded plaintiffs $9.5 million for Carolyn Miller's death on the basis of a theory of negligence. After the trial court denied defendant's motion for judgment notwithstanding the verdict, defendant filed an appeal in the Fourteenth District Court of Appeals of Texas. At defendant's request and over plaintiffs' objections, the Fourteenth District Court of Appeals of Texas certified the above-quoted question to this Court. We granted the request to answer the question and heard oral argument.

*** A. LEGAL DUTY IN GENERAL

There is no dispute among the parties that the substantive law of Michigan governs plaintiffs' claims. In Michigan, "the question whether the defendant owes an actionable legal duty to the plaintiff is one of law which the court decides after assessing the competing policy considerations for and against recognizing the asserted duty." *Friedman v. Dozorc,* 412 Mich. 1, 22, 312 N.W.2d 585 (1981). That is, " '[d]uty' is not sacrosanct in itself, but is only an expression of the sum total of those considerations of policy which lead the law to say that the plaintiff is entitled to protection.'" *Buczkowski v. McKay,* 441 Mich. 96, 100–101, 490 N.W.2d 330 (1992), quoting *Friedman, supra* at 22 n. 9, 312 N.W.2d 585, quoting Prosser, Torts (4th ed.), § 53, pp. 325–326. Thus, the ultimate inquiry in determining whether a legal duty should be imposed is whether the social benefits of imposing a duty outweigh the social costs of imposing a duty. The inquiry involves considering, among any other relevant considerations, "'the relationship of the parties, the foreseeability of the harm, the burden on the defendant, and the nature of the risk presented.'" *Dyer, supra* at 49, 679 N.W.2d 311, quoting *Murdock v. Higgins,* 454 Mich. 46, 53, 559 N.W.2d 639 (1997), citing *Buczkowski, supra* at 100, 490 N.W.2d 330.

The most important factor to be considered is the relationship of the parties. "[A] duty arises out of the existence of a relationship 'between the parties of such a character that social policy justifies' its imposition." *Dyer, supra* at 49, 679 N.W.2d 311, quoting Prosser & Keeton, Torts (5th ed.), § 56, p. 374. "'The determination of whether a legal duty exists is a question of whether the relationship between the actor and the plaintiff gives rise to any legal obligation on the actor's part to act for the benefit of the subsequently injured person.'" *Buczkowski, supra* at 101 n. 5, 490 N.W.2d 330, quoting *Rodriguez v. Sportsmen's Congress,* 159 Mich.App. 265, 270, 406 N.W.2d 207 (1987). "The duty to protect others against harm from third persons is based on a relationship between the parties." *Buczkowski, supra* at 103, 490 N.W.2d 330, citing Prosser & Keeton, Torts (5th ed.), § 56, p. 385. "Only if the law recognizes a duty to act with due care arising from the relationship of the parties does it subject the defendant to liability for negligent conduct." *Friedman, supra* at 22, 312 N.W.2d 585. "Duty ... 'concerns' 'the problem of the relation between individuals which imposes upon one a legal obligation for the benefit of the other.'" *Buczkowski, supra* at 100, 490 N.W.2d 330, quoting *Friedman, supra* at 22, 312 N.W.2d 585, quoting Prosser, Torts (4th ed.), § 53, p. 324. See also *Buczkowski, supra* at 100, 490 N.W.2d 330 (referring to "duty" as "the relational obligation between the plaintiff and the defendant").

In *Buczkowski,* this Court ... focused exclusively on the relationship between the parties to determine whether the defendant owed the plaintiff a legal duty. We concluded that because there was no relationship between the parties, no duty could be imposed on the defendant. More specifically, this Court concluded that because there was no relationship between the retailer who sold the shotgun ammunition to the intoxicated customer and the bystander who was injured by the use of the ammunition, the retailer owed no duty to the bystander. We explained, "Our ultimate decision turns on whether a sufficient relationship exists between a retailer and a third party to impose a duty under these circumstances." *Buczkowski, supra* at 103, 490 N.W.2d 330. Because we found that no relationship existed, we again did not even address the other factors. This was unnecessary because when there is no relationship between the parties, no duty can be imposed.

On the other hand, even when there is a relationship between the parties, a legal duty does not necessarily exist. In order to determine whether a duty exists, the other enumerated factors must also be considered. The foreseeability of the harm is one of these. Just as the existence of a relationship between the parties is not dispositive, that the harm was foreseeable is also not dispositive. A defendant does not have a duty to protect everybody from all foreseeable harms. Although foreseeability is a factor to be considered, "other considerations may be, and usually are, more important." *Id.* at 101, 490 N.W.2d 330.

> "[T]he mere fact that an event may be foreseeable does not impose a duty upon the defendant to take some kind of action accordingly. The event which he perceives might occur must pose some sort of risk of injury to another person or his property before the actor may be required to act. Also, to require the actor

to act, some sort of relationship must exist between the actor and the other party which the law or society views as sufficiently strong to require more than mere observation of the events which unfold on the part of the defendant. It is the fact of existence of this relationship which the law usually refers to as a duty on the part of the actor." [*Id.*, 490 N.W.2d 330, quoting *Samson v. Saginaw Professional Bldg., Inc.*, 393 Mich. 393, 406, 224 N.W.2d 843 (1975).]

When the harm is not foreseeable, no duty can be imposed on the defendant. But when the harm is foreseeable, a duty still does not necessarily exist.

To summarize, in determining whether a defendant owes a duty to a plaintiff, competing policy factors must be considered. Such considerations include the relationship of the parties, the foreseeability of the harm, the burden that would be imposed on the defendant, and the nature of the risk presented. Where there is no relationship between the parties, no duty can be imposed, but where there is a relationship, the other factors must be considered to determine whether a duty should be imposed. Likewise, where the harm is not foreseeable, no duty can be imposed, but where the harm is foreseeable, other factors must be considered to determine whether a duty should be imposed. Before a duty can be imposed, there must be a relationship between the parties and the harm must have been foreseeable. Once it is determined that there is a relationship and that the harm was foreseeable, the burden that would be imposed on the defendant and the nature of the risk presented must be assessed to determine whether a duty should be imposed.

B. DUTY WITH REGARD TO ASBESTOS LIABILITY

Because this Court has never addressed whether property owners owe a duty to protect people who have never been on or near their property from exposure to asbestos carried home on a household member's clothing, it is helpful to review the decisions of other courts that have addressed this issue.

In *CSX Transportation, Inc. v. Williams,* 278 Ga. 888, 891, 608 S.E.2d 208 (2005), the Supreme Court of Georgia, answering a certified question from the United States Court of Appeals for the Eleventh Circuit, held that "an employer does not owe a duty of care to a third-party, non-employee, who comes into contact with its employee's asbestos-tainted work clothing at locations away from the workplace." That court explained:

> " '[I]n fixing the bounds of duty, not only logic and science, but policy play an important role.' However, it must also be recognized that there is a responsibility to consider the larger social consequences of the notion of duty and to correspondingly tailor that notion so that the illegal consequences of wrongs are limited to a controllable degree. The recognition of a common-law cause of action under the circumstances of this case would, in our opinion, expand traditional tort concepts beyond manageable bounds and create an almost infinite universe of potential plaintiffs. Accordingly, we decline to promulgate a policy which would extend the common law so as to bring the ... plaintiff[s] within a class of people whose interests are entitled to protection from the defendant's conduct." [*Id.* at 890, 608 S.E.2d 208, quoting *Widera v. Ettco Wire & Cable Corp.,* 204 A.D.2d 306, 307–308, 611 N.Y.S.2d 569 (1994) (other citations omitted).]

In *In re New York City Asbestos Litigation,* 5 N.Y.3d 486, 840 N.E.2d 115, 806 N.Y.S.2d 146 (2005), New York's highest court held that the defendant owed no duty to the defendant's employee's wife, who was allegedly injured from exposure to asbestos the employee introduced into the family home on soiled work clothes that the plaintiff wife laundered. That court explained:

> "[I]n determining whether a duty exists, courts must be mindful of the precedential, and consequential, future effects of their rulings, and limit the legal consequences of wrongs to a controllable degree".... "Foreseeability, alone, does not define duty...." A specific duty is required because otherwise, a defendant would be subjected "to limitless liability to an indeterminate class of persons conceivably injured" by its negligent acts.... "Moreover, any extension of the scope of duty must be tailored to reflect accurately the extent that its social benefits outweigh its costs." [*Id.* at 493, 806 N.Y.S.2d 146, 840 N.E.2d 115, quoting *Hamilton v. Beretta USA Corp.*, 96 N.Y.2d 222, 232, 750 N.E.2d 1055, 727 N.Y.S.2d 7 (2001) (other citations and internal quotation marks omitted).]

The court was concerned about "limitless liability" and questioned why, if a duty was owed to an employee's spouse, a duty would not also be owed to the employee's babysitter or an employee of a neighborhood laundry. *In re New York City Asbestos Litigation, supra* at 498, 806 N.Y.S.2d 146, 840 N.E.2d 115.

> [W]e must consider the likely consequences of adopting the expanded duty urged by plaintiffs. While logic might suggest (and plaintiffs maintain) that the incidence of asbestos-related disease allegedly caused by the kind of secondhand exposure at issue in this case is rather low, experience counsels that the number of new plaintiffs' claims would not necessarily reflect that reality. [*Id.*]

The court explained, "[T]he 'specter of limitless liability' is banished only when 'the class of potential plaintiffs to whom the duty is owed is circumscribed by the relationship.' Here, there is no relationship between the [defendant] and [the defendant's employee's wife]." *Id.*, quoting *Hamilton, supra* at 233, 727 N.Y.S.2d 7, 750 N.E.2d 1055. The court held that because there was no relationship between the defendant and the defendant's employee's wife, no duty could be imposed.

In *Adams v. Owens-Illinois, Inc.,* 119 Md.App. 395, 705 A.2d 58 (1998), the Maryland Court of Special Appeals held that the defendant did not owe a duty to the defendant's employee's wife who was allegedly exposed to asbestos from her husband's clothes. The court explained:

> If liability for exposure to asbestos could be premised on Mary Wild's handling of her husband's clothing, presumably Bethlehem would owe a duty to others who came in close contact with Edwin Wild, including other family members, automobile passengers, and co-workers. Bethlehem owed no duty to strangers based upon providing a safe workplace for employees. [*Id.* at 411, 705 A.2d 58.]

In *Zimko v. American Cyanamid,* 905 So.2d 465, 482 (La.App., 2005), the Louisiana Court of Appeals, "recogniz[ing] the novelty of the duty," held that the defendant owed a duty to the defendant's employee's son who was allegedly exposed to asbestos from his father's work clothes that he brought home.... However, "Louisiana relies more heavily upon foreseeability in its duty/risk analysis...." *Id.* at 182. Unlike Louisiana, Michigan relies more on the relationship between the parties than foreseeability in determining whether a duty exists.

In addition, in Louisiana, unlike in Michigan, "a 'no duty' defense in a negligence case is seldom appropriate," *Zimko, supra* at 482; "resolution of a negligence case based on a finding that a defendant has 'no duty' should be reserved for the exceptional situation," *id.* at 482–483, such as "cases involving 'failure to act, injuries to unborn victims, negligently inflicted mental anguish or purely economic harm unaccompanied by physical trauma to the claimant or his property,'" *id.* at 482 n. 19 (citation and emphasis omitted). In Michigan, however, "[o]nly if the law recognizes a duty to act with due care arising from the relationship of the parties does it subject the defendant to liability for negligent conduct." *Friedman, supra* at 22, 312 N.W.2d 585. See also *Murdock, supra* at 53, 559 N.W.2d 639 ("Only after finding that a duty exists may the factfinder determine whether, in light of the particular facts of the case, there was a breach of the duty.")....

In *Olivo v. Owens-Illinois, Inc.*, 186 N.J. 394, 895 A.2d 1143 (2006), the New Jersey Supreme Court held that if the defendant owed a duty to the worker, the defendant owed a duty to the wife of the worker who was exposed to asbestos when she washed the clothes of her husband, who was hired by an independent contractor to perform work at the defendant's premises. However, as explained by the New York Court of Appeals, "*Olivo* is distinguishable legally in that New Jersey, unlike New York, relies heavily on foreseeability in its duty analysis." *In re New York City Asbestos Litigation, supra* at 497, 806 N.Y.S.2d 146, 840 N.E.2d 115. In *Olivo, supra* at 402, 895 A.2d 1143, the New Jersey Supreme Court described "foreseeability of harm" as "a crucial element in determining whether imposition of a duty on an alleged tortfeasor is appropriate." (Citations omitted.) It further explained, "in respect of a landowner's liability, whether a duty of care can be owed to one who is injured from a dangerous condition on the premises, to which the victim is exposed off-premises, devolves to a question of foreseeability of the risk of harm to that individual or identifiable class of individuals." *Id.* at 403, 895 A.2d 1143. However, as explained above, Michigan, like New York, relies more on the relationship between the parties than foreseeability of harm when determining whether a duty exists. For this reason, we do not find *Olivo* persuasive.

C. APPLICATION TO THIS CASE

As explained above, under Michigan law, the ultimate inquiry in determining whether a legal duty should be imposed is whether the social benefits of imposing that duty outweigh the social costs of imposing a duty. The inquiry involves considering, among any other relevant considerations: "'the relationship of the parties, the foreseeability of the harm, the burden on the defendant, and the nature of the risk presented.'" *Dyer, supra* at 49, 679 N.W.2d 311 (citations omitted).

In the instant case, the relationship between Miller and defendant was highly tenuous-defendant hired an independent contractor who hired Roland who lived in a house with Miller, his stepdaughter, who sometimes washed his clothes. Miller had never been on or near defendant's property and had no further relationship with defendant. Therefore, the "relationship between the parties" prong of the duty test, which is the most important prong in this state, strongly suggests that no duty should be imposed.

The "burden [that would be imposed] on the defendant" prong also suggests that no duty should be imposed because protecting every person with whom a business's employees and the employees of its independent contractors come into contact, or even with whom their clothes come into contact, would impose an extraordinarily onerous and unworkable burden.

Given what we know about asbestos today, i.e., that there is a causal relationship between exposure to asbestos and mesothelioma, and assuming that defendant directed the independent contractor to work with asbestos-containing materials, the "nature of the risk" was serious. Therefore, the "nature of the risk" prong suggests that a duty should be imposed.

* * *

Because the ultimate inquiry in determining whether a duty should be imposed involves balancing the social benefits of imposing a duty with the social costs of imposing a duty, we cannot decide whether a duty should be imposed without "assessing the competing policy considerations...." *Friedman, supra* at 22, 312 N.W.2d 585. We must be "concerned with whether it is appropriate public policy to impose liability...." *Smith, supra* at 716 n. 24, 303 N.W.2d 702. "[I]n fixing the bounds of duty, not only logic and science, but policy play an important role." *CSX Transportation, supra* at 890, 608 S.E.2d 208, quoting *Widera, supra* at 307, 611 N.Y.S.2d 569 (other citations omitted). "'[T]here is a responsibility to consider the larger social consequences of the notion of duty and to correspondingly tailor that notion so that the illegal consequences of wrongs are limited to a controllable degree.'" *CSX Transportation, supra* at 890, 608 S.E.2d 208, quoting *Widera, supra* at 307, 611 N.Y.S.2d 569. "'[I]n determining whether a duty exists, courts must be mindful of the precedential ... effects of their rulings, and limit the legal consequences of wrongs to a controllable degree.'" *In re New York City Asbestos Litigation, supra* at 493, 806 N.Y.S.2d 146, 840 N.E.2d 115, quoting *Hamilton, supra* at 232, 727 N.Y.S.2d 7, 750 N.E.2d 1055 (other citations and internal quotation marks omitted). "'Moreover, any extension of the scope of duty must be tailored to reflect accurately the extent that its social benefits outweigh its costs.'" *Id.*

As the United States Supreme Court has recognized, this country is experiencing an "asbestos-litigation crisis" as a result of the "'elephantine mass of asbestos cases' lodged in state and federal courts...." *Norfolk & W. R. Co. v. Ayers,* 538 U.S. 135, 166, 123 S.Ct. 1210, 155 L.Ed.2d 261 (2003) (citation omitted). Asbestos claims have given rise to one of the most costly products-liability crises ever within our nation's legal system. "Asbestos claims continue to pour in at an extraordinary rate [and] scores of employers have been forced into bankruptcy." Behrens & Cruz-Alvarez, *A potential new frontier in asbestos litigation: Premises owner liability for "take home" exposure claims,* 21 Mealey's Litig Rep. Abs. 1, 4 (2006). Some commentators have said that "[b]efore it ends, the litigation may cost up to $195 billion— on top of the $70 billion spent through 2002." *Id.* These same commentators have explained:

> Premises owner liability for "take home" exposure injuries represents the latest frontier in asbestos litigation. These actions clearly involve highly sympathetic plaintiffs. Yet, as several leading courts have appreciated, the law should not be driven by emotion or mere foreseeability. Broader public policy impacts must be considered, including the very real possibility that imposition of an expansive new duty on premises owners for off-site exposures would exacerbate the current "asbestos-litigation crisis." Plaintiffs' attorneys could begin naming countless employers directly in asbestos and other mass tort actions brought by remotely exposed persons such as extended family members, renters, house guests, carpool members, bus drivers, and workers at commercial enterprises visited by the worker when he or she was wearing dirty work clothes....
>
> Furthermore, adoption of a new duty rule for employers could bring about a perverse result: nonemployees with secondary exposures could have greater rights to sue and potentially reap far greater recoveries than employees. Namely, secondarily exposed nonemployees could obtain noneconomic damages, such as pain and suffering, and possibly even punitive damages; these awards are not generally available to injured employees under workers' compensation. [*Id.* at 5.]

In *Henry v. Dow Chemical Co.,* 473 Mich. 63, 701 N.W.2d 684 (2005), this Court held that mere exposure to a negligently released dioxin, a synthetic chemical that is potentially hazardous to human health, does not give rise to a negligence action. We explained:

> [W]e have on occasion allowed for the development of the common law as circumstances and considerations of public policy have required. But as Justice

Young has recently observed, our common-law jurisprudence has been guided by a number of prudential principles. See Young, *A judicial traditionalist confronts the common law,* 8 Texas Rev. L. & Pol. 299, 305–310 (2004). Among them has been our attempt to "avoid capricious departures from bedrock legal rules as such tectonic shifts might produce unforeseen and undesirable consequences," *id.* at 307, a principle that is quite applicable to the present case.

Plaintiffs have asked us to recognize a cause of action that departs drastically from our traditional notions of a valid negligence claim. Beyond this enormous shift in our tort jurisprudence, judicial recognition of plaintiffs' claim may also have undesirable effects that neither we nor the parties can satisfactorily predict. For example, recognizing a cause of action based solely on exposure-one without a requirement of a present injury-would create a potentially limitless pool of plaintiffs. [*Id.* at 83, 701 N.W.2d 684 (citations and emphasis omitted).]

Just as recognizing a cause of action based solely on exposure would create a potentially limitless pool of plaintiffs, so too would imposing a duty on a landowner to anybody who comes into contact with somebody who has been on the landowner's property. "We would be unwise, to say the least, to alter the common law in the manner requested by plaintiffs when it is unclear what the consequences of such a decision may be and when we have strong suspicions ... that they may well be disastrous." *Id.* at 88, 701 N.W.2d 684 (citation omitted). "The recognition of a common-law cause of action under the circumstances of this case would, in our opinion, expand traditional tort concepts beyond manageable bounds and create an almost infinite universe of potential plaintiffs. Accordingly, we decline to promulgate a policy which would extend the common law so as to bring the ... plaintiff[s] within a class of people whose interests are entitled to protection from the defendant's conduct." *CSX Transportation, supra* at 890, 608 S.E.2d 208 (citation omitted).

*** CONCLUSION

In Michigan, "the question whether the defendant owes an actionable legal duty to the plaintiff is one of law which the court decides after assessing the competing policy considerations for and against recognizing the asserted duty." *Friedman, supra* at 22, 312 N.W.2d 585. The social benefits of imposing a duty must outweigh the social costs of doing so. The inquiry involves considering, among any other relevant considerations: "'the relationship of the parties, the foreseeability of the harm, the burden on the defendant, and the nature of the risk presented.'" *Dyer, supra* at 49, 679 N.W.2d 311, quoting *Murdock, supra* at 53, 559 N.W.2d 639, citing *Buczkowski, supra* at 100, 490 N.W.2d 330. However, the most important factor pertains to the relationship between the parties. Because any relationship between Miller and defendant was highly tenuous, the harm was, in all likelihood, not foreseeable, the burden on defendant would be onerous and unworkable, and the imposition of a duty, under these circumstances, would "'expand traditional tort concepts beyond manageable bounds and create an almost infinite universe of potential plaintiffs,'" *CSX Transportation, supra* at 890, 608 S.E.2d 208 (citation omitted), we conclude that a legal duty should not be imposed. For these reasons, we answer the certified question in the negative. That is, we hold that, under Michigan law, defendant, as owner of the property on which asbestos-containing products were located, did not owe to the deceased, who was never on or near that property, a legal duty to protect her from exposure to any asbestos fibers carried home on the clothing of a member of her household who was working on that property as the employee of independent contractors, where there was no further relationship between defendant and the deceased. Having answered the certified question, we now return the matter to the Fourteenth District Court of Appeals of Texas for such further proceedings as that court deems appropriate.

(2) Establishing the Scope of the Duty Owed to the Plaintiff

Once it has been established that a duty is owed to the plaintiff, the next issue to consider is: what is the scope of the duty that is owed? In other words, we have to define exactly what it was that defendant was obligated to do or refrain from doing. This second question—the scope or extent of the duty owed—is sometimes referred to as the standard of care.

a. The Duty of Ordinary Care—Evaluating the Facts

Remember that the general standard is to act as a reasonably prudent person—i.e., to use ordinary care, or to act reasonably under the circumstances. Typically this determination (whether defendant's conduct was reasonable under the circumstances) is left to the jury. These determinations are heavily fact dependent, because they involve consideration of all of the external circumstances surrounding the event—e.g., whether there was an emergency, what the weather was like, the location, etc., as well as the defendant's external physical attributes—e.g., blindness, height, limited mobility, etc.; however, they do not involve consideration of the internal circumstances related to the specific person committing the act, such as whether the person was intoxicated, inexperienced, or had reduced mental or intellectual abilities; of course, there are exceptions to this rule as well—defendants with superior knowledge, skill, or intelligence are expected to use those abilities.

Exercise 2-5 Evaluating the Existence and Extent of Duty

Consider each of the following scenarios and the questions that follow. Evaluate whether there was a duty owed and if so, what the duty of ordinary care requires (what the defendant is obligated to do or refrain from doing under the circumstances).

a.   One evening Bittena was leaving a local pub. She saw two people engaged in a fight. While she was watching them fight, she saw one of the fighters fall to the ground, obviously injured. The fighter who remained standing continued to hit and kick the fallen fighter. Did Bettina have a duty to stop the fight? To report it to authorities? To ask them to stop fighting? To help the injured fighter? What if Bittena was the owner of the bar and the fighters were patrons of that bar? What if Bittena is a police officer?

b.   A 13-year-old girl falsely stated that she was 18, and joined an online social networking site, in violation of the site's terms and conditions. She used the system to meet a 19-year-old boy. The pair exchanged contact information, spoke several times by phone, and met in person, at which point the girl was sexually assaulted by the boy. Did the site have a duty to verify her age? To protect her from sexual assault? Do they have a duty to prevent future assaults to others? What if many underage girls have been assaulted as a result of similar circumstances and the site is aware that this happens somewhat frequently?

c. Maxfore complained repeatedly to his Teacher that he had stomach pains. Teacher believed Maxfore was attempting to get out of doing his school work and did not send Maxfore to the school nurse. Maxfore's appendix ruptured and he was taken to the hospital for emergency surgery. Did Teacher have a duty to send Maxfore to the school nurse? To ensure he received medical attention? What if Maxfore had been sent to the nurse on several prior occasions and it was determined he did not have any medical issues?

d. Teen, a 15-year-old, learning to drive, failed to brake in time to avoid a collision with Driver. Did Teen have the same duty of care that an adult would have had under the circumstances? Does Teen's inexperience change Teen's duty? Do Teen's parents have a duty to supervise Teen's driving? To keep Teen from driving?

e. Two employees, in an effort to avoid working, hit the "STOP" button in the elevator, in hopes that they could claim the elevator was "stuck." Unfortunately for the employees, this caused the elevator to shut down, trapping employees inside. As soon as she discovered the elevator was out of order, Supervisor reviewed the security camera footage from the elevator and learned what employees had done. She decided that because employees were trapped due to their own poor choices, she did not have to "rescue" them right away. She decided to leave employees in the elevator until she returned from lunch later that afternoon. Does Supervisor have a duty to restore the elevator service and let employees out? Does she have a duty to do it before she goes to lunch?

f. Mitch visited his neighbor Ben several times each week. During these visits they would sit together on Ben's outdoor deck. Mitch was aware that one of the boards on Ben's deck was loose. One evening, Mitch stepped on the board, lost his footing and was injured. Did Ben have a duty to warn Mitch that the board was loose? To repair the board? To make sure Mitch was not injured? Does he have a duty to warn others that might sit on his deck?

g. Poddar, a student at University, told his Therapist, a University employed psychologist, that he was going to kill his ex-girlfriend, Tatiana. Therapist reported the threat to University's campus police department. The University police briefly detained Poddar, but released him when he appeared rational. No one warned Tatiana of the threat. Poddar killed Tatiana. Did therapist have a duty to warn Tatiana? Did the police? Did University? Does it matter whether Tatiana is a student at University? Why or why not?

As you can see from the scenarios in exercise 2.5, some negligence actions involve situations where the standard governing the conduct would likely be part of the common experience or knowledge of ordinary persons. In these situations, jurors (presumably ordinary people) evaluate claims of duty and breach and make these determinations themselves—without the need for expert testimony. Sometimes, however, a different approach is required, because the standard (and required conduct) is beyond the understanding of the ordinary person, such as situations involving the negligence of professionals—our next subject.

b. Duty Established by Professional Standards — Developing Subject Matter Expertise

When the standard governing the defendant's conduct (the duty owed) is outside the experience and expertise of the ordinary person — you will probably not be able to rely on your own experiences to evaluate the duty owed under the circumstances. For example, in a case involving the negligence of a professional (e.g. doctor, lawyer, accountant, etc.), the general standard is to do what a reasonable professional in these circumstances should have done. Unless you are one of these professionals, with expertise in the area involved in the case, you will likely need to consult the literature on the topic, other professionals, or an expert, in order to understand and establish the applicable standard. Your research will most likely include materials different from what you would typically use to conduct legal research. For example, in determining whether a surgeon's actions during a surgery did not conform to the applicable standard required, you might first need to consult a medical text to read about the procedure. Although your first instinct might be to contact an expert who has knowledge of such things, and while that might be a very prudent decision in some cases (and in many cases an expert witness might be required to establish the standard), you will want to be able to discuss the critical facts with the expert once you do make contact, which will require you to first understand the basic procedures and medical terminology. It is also a good idea to think about and find ways to learn about a topic before approaching or consulting with an expert so that you can make good use of the expert's time (and your client's resources, since the client will likely be paying for the time you spend with the expert, and for the expert's time). For example, if you understand foundational material, such as the basic procedures typically used in such surgeries, and the medical terminology typically used to describe the injuries and procedures involved, you can use the expert's time to ask pointed questions about your case. You will also be better equipped to provide the expert with necessary facts and documents, and to discuss the significance of those facts and documents, rather than relying exclusively on the expert to sift through documents to determine what may or may not be useful. Another reason you should develop knowledge in the area is that you may have to depose or cross examine the opposing side's expert, who may testify differently than your expert — which requires an understanding of the facts, the terminology, and the basis for the expert's knowledge. These are some of the reasons this chapter will focus on the skills of acquiring and developing subject matter knowledge in areas other than the applicable law, and the skill of developing an understanding of the meaning of the facts of a client's case when those facts are outside your area of knowledge.

Chapter Problem

In Chapter One, the facts for the chapter problem were set out in the same format you would expect to find on a law school exam. While some of the facts for this problem are presented in the same way, others are set out in some of the formats that lawyers might expect to see them; for example, some of the facts in this problem are contained in the Plaintiffs' complaint and in a summary of medical records — which you may be lucky enough to receive in some cases; however, know that in many cases facts will come in the form of boxes of documents that you will have to sift through in order to derive such a summary (and, when you are a new lawyer, to produce such a summary for other attorneys).

Another difference between the problem in Chapter One and the problem in this chapter is that for this problem you will use non-legal sources of information to evaluate the case. In practice, to understand the significance of the facts in your clients' cases, and to develop your understanding of the legal issues, you may need to consult sources other than cases, statutes and other legal research. This chapter problem contains such non-legal sources, in the form of relevant excerpts from medical literature. It is also very likely that you will need to use a medical dictionary to evaluate this problem, in order to help you understand the terminology used in this problem. This is not unusual; lawyers often need to consult outside sources when cases involve unfamiliar terminology. Several reliable sources are available on-line, including: http://www.nlm.nih.gov/medlineplus/mplusdictionary.html and www.webmd.com.

When you use such sources (literature, dictionaries, internet searches) to develop an initial understanding of the existence and extent of a defendant's duty (one of the first issues you will evaluate), be aware that the relevant standards that will apply to your case are those that existed at the time of the injury—and not those that exist at the time of your research, which may occur many years later, when new information and developments impact what is reasonable under the circumstances (the applicable standard).

Your Assignment

You represent Henry Ford Health System, defendants in a medical malpractice suit. Your client has been sued by Latrice McCoy, on her own behalf, and on behalf of her son, Marcus Ricks. Plaintiffs allege your client was negligent. You and the plaintiffs' counsel agreed to dismiss each of the individual doctors named as defendants and to allow plaintiffs to proceed solely against Henry Ford Health Systems, who will accept responsibility for any negligence committed by the individual doctors and nurses. (Therefore, when evaluating the negligence of your client, you must also evaluate the potential negligence of the individual doctors and nurses.)

Your client was served with the complaint that begins on the next page.

CIRCUIT COURT OF MICHIGAN	
WAYNE COUNTY[1]	

Latrice MCCOY, Individually and as Next Friend of Marcus, Ricks a Minor,	No. 06634717NH.
Plaintiffs,	FIRST AMENDED COMPLAINT AND JURY DEMAND
v.	
HENRY FORD HEALTH SYSTEM d/b/a Henry Ford Hospital; Womack Stokes, M.D; Nicholai Hinds, M.D.; Lisa Mcintosh, M.D.; Deborah Skannal, M.D.; jointly and severally,	Date: February 6, 2007.
Defendants.	

NOW COMES the Plaintiff, LATRICE McCOY, Individually and as Next Friend of MARCUS RICKS, a Minor, by and through her attorneys … and for her First Amended Complaint against the above-named Defendants, states unto this Honorable Court as follows:

1. The Plaintiffs, Latrice McCoy and Marcus Ricks, are residents of Wayne County, State of Michigan.

2. Defendant Womak Stokes, M.D. (hereinafter "Stokes") is a physician licensed to practice medicine in the State of Michigan, who conducted business in the County of Wayne, State of Michigan.

3. Defendant Nicholai Hinds, M.D. (hereinafter "Hinds") is a physician licensed to practice medicine in the State of Michigan, who conducted business in the County of Wayne, State of Michigan.

4. Defendant Lisa McIntosh, M.D. (hereinafter "McIntosh") is a physician licensed to practice medicine in the State of Michigan, who conducted business in the County of Wayne, State of Michigan.

---

1. The pleadings are edited versions of the actual pleadings from *McCoy v. Henry Ford Health System*, No. 06634717NH. The depositions used throughout the chapter for this problem are a compilation of edited materials and testimony from this and other cases addressing similar issues. The materials have been altered to suit the parameters of this problem.

1   5. Defendant Deborah Skannal, M.D. (hereinafter "Skannal") is a physician licensed
2   to practice medicine in the State of Michigan, who conducted business in the County
3   of Wayne, State of Michigan.

4   6. Defendant Henry Ford Health System, d/b/a Henry Ford Hospital (hereinafter
5   "Henry Ford") is a Michigan Corporation authorized to do business in the State of
6   Michigan.

7   7. That at all times relevant hereto, Defendant Henry Ford employed doctors,
8   nurses, and other health care professionals.

9   8. That at all times relevant hereto, a special and unidentified relationship existed
10 between Defendants Stokes, Hinds, McIntosh, Skannal and Defendant Henry Ford.

11 9. That at all times relevant hereto, Defendant Henry Ford did hold itself out to the
12 public in general and to the Plaintiffs, in particular, as being a safe place for business, an
13 institution of healing, and that its agents, servants, independent contractors and/or em-
14 ployees, including Defendants Stokes, Hinds, McIntosh, and Skannal, would perform
15 necessary and proper medical care in accordance with the applicable standards of care in
16 the community.

17 10. That at all times relevant hereto, Defendants Stokes, Hinds, McIntosh, and
18 Skannal were the actual or apparent/ostensible agents or servants of Defendant Henry
19 Ford, or in the alternative, Defendant Henry Ford was the employer of Defendants
20 Stokes, Hinds, McIntosh, and Skannal.

21 11. That Defendant Henry Ford, its owner, operator, and governing body are re-
22 sponsible for the operation of its hospital, the selection of its medical staff, and the
23 quality of care rendered by its physicians (MCLA 333.21513).

24 12. That all Defendants are agents, servants, and employees of each other, that De-
25 fendant hospital is the agent, servant, employee of the Defendant doctors; that the De-
26 fendant doctors are agents, servants, and employees of the Defendant hospital; and
27 finally, all agents, servants, and employees of the Defendant hospital are agents, ser-
28 vants, and employees of the Defendant doctors.

29 13. That the amount in controversy exceeds Twenty-five Thousand Dollars
30 ($25,000), exclusive of costs, interest and attorneys fees.

31 14. This cause of action is for medical malpractice committed upon Latrice McCoy
32 and Marcus Ricks during the labor and delivery of Marcus Ricks.

33

15. Latrice McCoy was pregnant, with an estimated date of confinement of October 22, 1999.

16. On October 4, 1999, Latrice McCoy treated with Dr. Skannal for an outpatient obstetrical appointment.

17. The doctor did an ultrasound examination which showed "a cord around the neck indenting the soft tissues of the neck."

18. A non-stress test was done which was reactive on that day.

19. On that visit, the fundal height was 37 centimeters and fetal heart tones were 150.

20. Latrice McCoy was being treated at this clinic due to a diagnosis of gestational diabetes.

21. Ms. McCoy had delivered on one previous occasion, and during that earlier pregnancy she also was diagnosed with gestational diabetes.

22. On October 12, 1999, Latrice again reported to the Henry Ford Clinic.

23. She was noted to be on the ADA diet and that her blood sugars were meeting goals.

24. Ms. McCoy again had a non-stress test performed which was reactive.

25. On October 21, 1999, Latrice was admitted to Henry Ford Hospital for induction of labor.

26. Latrice was 39-6/7 weeks pregnant at the time of induction.

27. The induction of labor was scheduled because Latrice was near term and because she had gestational diabetes.

28. No note was made of Dr. Skannal's observation that the cord was around the baby's neck.

29. Throughout the laboring process, Ms. McCoy was being monitored with a fetal heart monitor strip.

30. As early as 1800 hours on October 21, 1999, the fetal heart monitor strip showed late decelerations.

31. By 0200 hours in the morning of October 22, 1999, there were clearly late decelerations with hyperstimulation present on the fetal monitor strip.

32. No action was taken by any physician in response to these findings.

33. On October 22, 1999, Dr. Hinds reviewed the fetal heart monitor strip at approximately 1045 hours and noted there were decelerations to the 60s.

34. He questioned whether these were late decelerations.

35. At 1220 hours, Dr. Hinds was again called and he again noted that there were decelerations to the 70s and questioned whether these were late decelerations

36. At 1225 hours, Dr. MacIntosh also reviewed the fetal monitor strip.

37. Despite the fact that the fetal heart monitor tracing was becoming more and more ominous, their instructions were to observe the patient.

38. At 1500 hours, the doctors again note that there are late decelerations.

39. At this time, a scalp pH was taken and was 7.28.

40. No further notes were written until 1740 hours.

41. At 1740 hours, the doctors again noted repetitive decelerations and questioned whether these were late in nature.

42. A repeat scalp pH was performed at 1740 hours and found to be 7.04.

43. At 1806 hours, the scalp pH was performed again and had decreased to 7.02.

44. Finally, an emergency C-section was called and Marcus Ricks was delivered at 1816 hours.

45. Upon delivery, it was noted that the nuchal cord was tightly wrapped around the baby's neck.

46. In the immediate neonatal time period, Marcus suffered from severe hypo-glycemia for several hours before receiving treatment.

47. It was noted that Marcus had seizure-like activity in the neonatal time period which was noted by the nurses but not recognized and was not treated by the physicians.

48. As a result of the asphyxia and distress Marcus Ricks suffered during labor and delivery, compounded by the severe, untreated hypoglycemia he endured following his birth, he suffers from numerous injuries, including mental retardation and cere-bral palsy.

<u>COUNT I</u>

<u>NEGLIGENCE ... OF DEFENDANT HENRY FORD HEALTH SYSTEM</u>

<u>d/b/a HENRY FORD HOSPITAL</u>

49. Plaintiff hereby repeats and realleges paragraphs 1 through 48 of Plaintiff's Complaint as though more fully stated herein.

50. Defendant Henry Ford is liable for acts of medical malpractice relating to Plain-tiff's care and treatment.

51. In treating Plaintiffs, Defendant Henry Ford was required to exercise reasonable and ordinary care, skill and ability ordinarily exercised by physicians, surgeons nurses,

etc., in the same or somewhat similar circumstances and exercised by other hospitals clinics, physicians, surgeons, nurses and other medical personnel, etc., to assure that the proper diagnoses and treatments were performed upon Plaintiffs by Defendant Henry Ford, its employees actual and/or apparent and/or ostensible agents, independent contractors and/or servants.

52. Defendant Henry Ford, its owner, operator, and governing body are responsible for the operation of its hospital, the selection of its medical staff, and the quality of care rendered by its physicians, pursuant to MCLA 333.21513.

53. Defendant Henry Ford failed to exercise reasonable and/or ordinary care, skill and ability, and was therefore negligent, grossly negligent, and/or is liable for wanton and willful misconduct, including, but not limited to the following:

a. Upon diagnosing a cord around the neck, failing to advise the labor and delivery unit of this, so appropriate treatment can be rendered;

b. Failing to properly assess and treat a woman in labor who has a finding of nuchal cord wrapped around the soft tissues of the neck;

c. Failing to properly assess and evaluate a woman in labor, including proper interpretation of the fetal monitor strip;

d. Failing to properly monitor a woman in labor and note signs of intrauterine fetal distress, including recognition of late decelerations;

e. Failing to properly and timely treat a woman in labor, including performing a Caesarean section to deliver a child before he suffered from birth asphyxia, acidosis, and hypoxia;

f. Failing to appropriately monitor a patient when the physician requests "close observation";

g. Failing to properly and timely inform the attending physicians of signs of intrauterine fetal distress, including repositioning the laboring woman, administering oxygen to her, and administering fluid boluses;

h. Failing to properly and timely test for hypoglycemia following labor and delivery;

i. Failing to properly and timely treat hypoglycemia following labor and delivery.

54. As a direct and proximate result of the Defendant Henry Ford's acts and/or omissions, the Plaintiff, Marcus Ricks, suffered serious injuries and complications, including, but not limited to:

a. Birth asphyxia and severe hypoglycemia;

1   b. Numerous and multiple medical complications;

2   c. Global developmental delay;

3   d. Severe hypotonia;

4   e. Physical pain and suffering;

5   f. Mental anguish;

6   g. Fright and shock;

7   h. Denial of social pleasure and enjoyments;

8   i. Embarrassment, humiliation or mortification;

9   j. Reasonable expenses of necessary medical care, treatment and services;

10 k. Wage loss and loss of earning capacity; and

11 l. Any and all other damages deemed to be reasonable and just.

12 WHEREFORE, Plaintiff, LATRICE McCOY, Individually and as Next Friend of

13 MARCUS RICKS, a Minor, respectfully requests that this Honorable Court enter Judg-

14 ment in their favor and against Defendants and award costs, interest and attorney fees

15 wrongfully incurred.

16 **<u>DEMAND FOR TRIAL BY JURY</u>**

17 NOW COME the Plaintiffs, LATRICE MCCOY, Individually and as Next Friend of

18 MARCUS, RICKS a Minor, by and through their attorneys, FIEGER, FIEGER, KEN-

19 NEY & JOHNSON, P.C., and hereby demand a trial by jury in the above-captioned

20 matter.

21 Respectfully submitted,

22 Attorneys for Plaintiff

23

24

25

26

27

28

29

30

31

32

33

In Michigan, the state where this action occurs, plaintiffs in medical malpractice cases are required to file an affidavit of merit, signed by a qualifying expert. Below are the affidavits plaintiffs filed with the complaint.

1

2

3

4   Latrice MCCOY, Individually and   No. 06634717NH.
5   as Next Friend of Marcus,
     Ricks a Minor,
6
          Plaintiffs,   AFFIDAVIT OF MERIT OF
7   MICHELLE PETERSON, M.D.
     v.
8
     HENRY FORD HEALTH
9   SYSTEM d/b/a Henry Ford   Date: February 6, 2007.
     Hospital; Womack Stokes, M.D;
10   Nicholai Hinds, M.D.; Lisa
11   Mcintosh, M.D.; Deborah
     Skannal, M.D.; jointly and
12   severally,
13
          Defendants.
14

15

16   Michelle Peterson, M.D., being duly sworn, deposes and states as follows:

17   1. I have received the relevant medical records regarding the care and treatment of

18   Latrice McCoy and Marcus Ricks.

19   2. I am a board certified Neonatologist and spend more than 50 percent of my pro-

20   fessional time practicing in the field of neonatology.

21   3. It is my professional opinion that the Defendant neonatologists deviated from the

22   standard of care in their treatment of Plaintiff Marcus Ricks.

23   4. To comply with the required standard of care, Defendant neonatologists should

24   have done the following:

25   a. Properly and timely test for hypoglycemia following labor and delivery;

26   b. Properly and timely treat hypoglycemia following labor and delivery; and,

27   c. Any other breaches of the standard of care which may be revealed over the course

28   of discovery.

29

5. As a proximate result of the negligent acts and/or omissions of Defendants as set forth above, Plaintiff suffered unnecessary brain injuries which have led to permanent disabilities. Specifically, Marcus Ricks was the infant of a diabetic mother (IDM), a condition that bathes the fetus in higher-than-normal glucose levels, producing a state of hyperinsulinism. Separation of the placenta at birth suddenly interrupts glucose infusion into the neonate without a proportional effect on the hyperinsulinism, and hypoglycemia develops during the first hour after birth.

Birth trauma of the hypoxic-ischemic encephalopathy (HIE) type was a second and independent cause of MR's hypoglycemia. The two causes (IDM and HIE) compounded each other, depleting the brain's glucose stores. Since the brain utilizes glucose for energy, Marcus Ricks's hypoglycemia starved his brain. Further, Marcus was hypotensive, which causes decreased oxygenated blood to reach the brain, causing ischemia. Coupled with HIE, the oxygen was depleted (hypoxia) and the blood flow was also compromised (ischemia). The outcome of combined cerebral hypoglycemia, hypoxia, and ischemia, starved many of Marcus Ricks's brain cells, causing irreversible injury.

6. This affidavit is filed in accordance with the mandates of M.C.L. 600.2912(d).

1 | CIRCUIT COURT OF MICHIGAN

2 | WAYNE COUNTY

3

4 | Latrice MCCOY, Individually and   No. 06634717NH.
5 | as Next Friend of Marcus,
    | Ricks a Minor,

6 | Plaintiffs,   AFFIDAVIT OF MERIT OF
7 | v.   SLOAN RODRIGUEZ, M.D.

8 | HENRY FORD HEALTH
9 | SYSTEM d/b/a Henry Ford   Date: February 6, 2007.
   | Hospital; Womack Stokes, M.D;
10 | Nicholai Hinds, M.D.; Lisa
11 | Mcintosh, M.D.; Deborah
   | Skannal, M.D.; jointly and
12 | severally,

13 | Defendants.

14

15

16   Sloan Rodriguez, M.D., being duly sworn, deposes and states as follows:

17   1. I have received the relevant medical records regarding the care and treatment of

18 Latrice McCoy and Marcus Ricks.

19   2. I am board certified in Obstetrics and Gynecology.

20   3. It is my professional opinion that the Defendants deviated from the standard of

21 care in their treatment of Plaintiffs, Latrice McCoy and Marcus Ricks.

22   4. To comply with the required standard of care, Defendants should have done the

23 following:

24   a. Upon diagnosing a cord around the neck, advise the labor and delivery unit of this.

25   b. Properly assess and evaluate a woman in labor.

26   c. Properly assess and treat a woman in labor who has, on ultrasound, a finding of

27 nuchal cord wrapped around the soft tissues of the neck.

28   d. Properly monitor a woman in labor and note signs of intrauterine fetal distress.

29   e. Properly and timely perform a cesarean section to deliver a child before he suffers

30 from hypoxic ischemic encephalopathy.

31   f. Any other breaches of the standard of care which may be revealed over the course

32 of discovery should the litigation be pursued.

33

5. As a proximate result of negligent acts and/or omissions of Defendants as set forth above, Plaintiff suffered unnecessary pain, surgery and brain damage.

6. This affidavit is filed in accordance with the mandates of MCL 600.2912(d) MSA 27A.2912(4).

Upon receipt of the plaintiff's complaint, one of the attorneys in your law firm obtained and reviewed the medical records relating to Plaintiff Latrice McCoy's labor and delivery of Plaintiff Marcus Ricks. Here is a summary of those records:

> On October 21, 1999, Latrice McCoy was admitted to Henry Ford Hospital for induction of labor, which was scheduled because she was near term and had gestational diabetes. About two weeks earlier on October 4, 1999, at her outpatient obstetrical appointment, an ultrasound showed "a cord around the neck indenting the soft tissues of the neck." This information does not appear to be recorded in any charts or notes relating to the labor and delivery. During labor there was hyperstimulation and titanic contractions. Plaintiff McCoy was polysystole or tachysystole with contractions occurring more frequently than every 2–3 minutes at several points during her labor.
>
> McCoy was monitored with a fetal heart monitor strip. According to the chart, on October 22, 1999, Dr. Hinds reviewed the fetal heart monitor strip at approximately 1045 hours and noted there were decelerations to the 60s. At 1220 hours, Dr. Hinds noted there were decelerations to the 70s. At 1225 hours, Dr. MacIntosh reviewed the fetal monitor strip. At 1500 hours, the doctors noted late decelerations. At 1740 hours, the doctors again noted repetitive decelerations.
>
> At 1600 hours the infant scalp pH was 7.28; at 1800 hours, the scalp pH was 7.04; at 1806 hours, the scalp pH was 7.02, and an emergency C-section was called. Plaintiff Ricks was delivered at 1816 hours.
>
> Upon delivery, it was noted that the nuchal cord was tightly wrapped around Ricks' neck. Following delivery, cord blood gases showed a pH of 7.12, a bicarb of 24.2, and base excess of minus 7. Ricks was awarded Apgar scores of 7 at one minute and 8 at five minutes. The narrative notes at delivery describe "marked reduction in tone and reflexes, acrocyanosis, and shallow breathing" as well as "indications of hypoxia and mild respiratory acidosis." Ricks was given oxygen and taken to the newborn transition nursery; he arrived in the nursery at 1833 hours.
>
> At 1845 hours, it was noted on the nursing flow sheet that he had desaturations to 75–86 percent. At 1850 hours Ricks had an apneic episode, and stopped breathing for approximately 20 seconds. According to the nursing flow sheet, His glycemic level at 1839 hours was 50; normal range for Henry Ford is 50–140. At 1930 hours his glycemic level was 23 and Ricks was given a bolus of 7ccs glucose. The nurse ordered a laboratory blood glucose level, which came back as 14. At 2015 hours it was 32, and at 2045 hours it was 60. At 2130 hours, the chemstrip was 40, and the IV of dextrose was continued. At 2220 hours, the chemstrip was 70, and after that the levels were never below 40.
>
> According to the nursing flow sheets, on October 23, 1999, Ricks had occasional tremors and was lethargic and jittery.

You performed a search of the literature related to the medical conditions and procedures that are the basis of the action. Some of the relevant literature you discovered is set out below.

To: Attorney

From: Associate

Re: *McCoy v. Henry Ford*, Case No. No. 06634717NH

As you requested, I searched NIH, medline, healthline, ACOG and AAFP for information relating to the conditions and symptoms listed in the plaintiffs' affidavits of merit and complaint. Below is a summary.

Fetal Scalp Testing

Fetal scalp pH testing is a procedure to determine if the fetus is getting enough oxygen. The test is performed when a woman is in active labor. Usually this test is performed to obtain information about fetal acid-base balance (blood pH), and is useful when fetal heart monitoring is not providing enough information about the well-being of a fetus. In these cases, the scalp pH can indicate whether the fetus is getting enough oxygen during labor. This helps determine whether the fetus is healthy enough to continue labor, or if a forceps delivery or cesarean section might be the best route of delivery.

In general, low pH suggests that the fetus does not have enough oxygen, which could mean that the fetus is not tolerating labor very well. A scalp pH less than 7.25 but greater than 7.20 is considered suspicious or borderline. Results in this range must also be interpreted in light of the fetal heart rate pattern and the progress of labor, and generally should be repeated after 15 to 30 minutes. A scalp pH of less than 7.20 is considered abnormal and generally is an indication for intervention, immediate delivery, or both.

Fetuses with a normal pH (greater than 7.25), respond with an acceleration of the fetal heart rate following fetal scalp stimulation. Fetal scalp sampling for pH is recommended if there is no acceleration with scalp stimulation. A pH less than 7.20 should also be assumed where there is no acceleration following fetal scalp stimulation, and fetal scalp pH sampling is not available

The results of a fetal scalp pH sample need to be interpreted in the context of each individual labor. Fetal scalp pH testing may need to be repeated a few times during a complicated labor to continue to check on the fetus.

Risks include continued bleeding from the puncture site (more likely if the fetus has a pH imbalance), infection, and bruising of the fetus' scalp.

Fetal Heart Rate Monitoring

Fetal Heart Rate (FHR) assessment may be equal or superior to fetal blood pH to predict both good and bad fetal outcomes. Electronic FHR monitoring is commonly used to assess fetal well-being during labor. One benefit of FHR monitoring is to detect early fetal distress resulting from fetal hypoxia and metabolic acidosis, which, in the United States, is associated with an estimated 700 infant deaths per year. Another benefit of FHR includes closer assessment of high-risk mothers; high-risk indications for continuous monitoring of FHR include: maternal medical illness, gestational diabetes, hypertension, obstetric complications, post-date gestation, intrauterine growth restriction, premature rupture of the membranes, oxytocin induction/augmentation of labor, preeclampsia, tobacco use and drug abuse.

Since variable and inconsistent interpretation of fetal heart rate tracings may affect management of labor and delivery, a systematic approach to interpreting the patterns is important. Fetal heart rate patterns are classified as reassuring, nonreassuring or ominous. Nonreassuring patterns require intervention to rule out fetal acidosis. Ominous patterns require emergency intrauterine fetal resuscitation and immediate delivery. Accurate interpretation requires differentiating between a reassuring and nonreassuring fetal heart rate pattern, which is essential to making appropriate triage decisions.

- Nonreassuring patterns include: fetal tachycardia; fetal bradycardia; saltatory variability; variable decelerations associated with a nonreassuring pattern; and late decelerations with preserved beat-to-beat variability.

- Ominous patterns include: persistent late decelerations with loss of beat-to-beat variability; nonreassuring variable decelerations associated with loss of beat-to-beat variability; prolonged severe bradycardia; sinusoidal pattern; and confirmed loss of beat-to-beat variability not associated with fetal quiescence, medications or severe prematurity.

Accelerations are short-term rises in the heart rate of at least 15 beats per minute, which last at least 15 seconds. The presence of fetal heart rate accelerations is one of the most important signs of well-being during labor. Viewing the accelerations assures the doctor that the fetus is not lacking oxygen or accumulating acid, which results from lack of oxygen. Most fetuses have spontaneous accelerations at various points throughout the labor and delivery process. Where there is concern about the well-being of a fetus and there are no accelerations, a physician may attempt to induce accelerations by gently rocking the mother's abdomen, pressing on the fetus' scalp through the cervix with a finger, or administering a short burst of sound (vibro acoustic stimulation) to provide reassurance of the fetus' well-being.

Decelerations are temporary drops in the fetal heart rate. There are three basic types of decelerations: early decelerations, late decelerations, and variable decelerations.

Early decelerations begin to dip early during the uterine contraction or even before the contraction is visible, and are seen when the fetus' head is compressed. They frequently occur during the later stages of labor as the fetus descends through the birth canal. Early decelerations may also occur during early labor if the fetus is premature or in breech position, causing its head to be squeezed by the uterus during contractions. Early decelerations have no clinical significance.

Late decelerations do not begin until the peak of a contraction or thereafter. They are smooth, shallow dips in heart rate that mirror the shape of the contraction. Late decelerations are among the most ominous form of heart rate patterns because they usually signify a reduced oxygen supply to the fetus. If delivery is near and there are other reassuring features of the heart rate tracing (such as accelerations), it is often permissible to observe a fetus carefully and not intervene with a cesarean section. However, a rapid intervention and delivery might be called for if there are other troubling indications, such as fast heart rate (tachycardia), reduced variability, and an absence of accelerations—since prolonged exposure to the type of contractions causing late decelerations may be harmful to the fetus.

Variable decelerations are generally irregular, often jagged dips in the fetal heart rate that look more dramatic than late decelerations. Variable decelerations are caused when the umbilical cord is temporarily compressed. Multiple variable decelerations can be found during the course of nearly all labors, and as a rule, are not worrisome. However, variable decelerations that are prolonged or repetitive can signify a reduction of blood flow, which is harmful to the fetus. Variable decelerations are judged primarily in terms of the fetal heart rate tracing, and proximity to delivery. Severe variable decelerations with no variability in early labor is an indication for immediate delivery. Severe variable decelerations with good variability and accelerations close to delivery would not indicate the need for immediate delivery.

Infants of Diabetic Mothers

Infants born to Diabetic Mothers (IDM) are at an increased risk of morbidity and mortality related to respiratory distress, growth abnormalities (large for gestational age and small for gestational age); hypoglycemia; congenital malformations; hypomagnesemia, and iron abnormalities.

According to the literature, a policy to screen infants of diabetic mothers (IDMs) for hypoglycemia should be in place in every hospital. An infant with IDM should undergo blood glucose measurements: (1) as soon as possible after birth, (2) within 2–3 hours after birth and before feeding, and (3) at any time abnormal clinical signs are observed.

Hypoglycemia

A screening policy during the hours after birth is necessary to detect hypoglycemia. Neonatal hypoglycemia occurs when the newborn's glucose level is below the level considered safe for the baby's age. A healthy, term infant experiences a brief, self-limited period of relatively low blood glucose during the first two hours of life. Since this drop is physiologic, routine glucose screening of all infants is not recommended. Screening should be directed towards those infants at risk for pathologic hypoglycemia.

Infants at increased risk for pathological hypoglycemia include infants who are born to diabetic mothers; large for their gestational age (LGA); small for their gestational age (SGA); and premature, as well as infants with low Apgar scores (<5 at one minute, <6 at five minutes); or who experience respiratory distress, have a serious infection, or required oxygen right after delivery. Screening is recommended for such infants.

Glucose screening is also recommended for infants with clinical signs consistent with hypoglycemia including: jitteriness; irritability; bluish-colored or pale skin; breathing problems, such as apnea, rapid breathing, or a grunting sound; listlessness; loose or floppy muscles; tremors; apathy; poor feeding; high-pitched or weak cry; Hypothermia; temperature instability; or seizure activity.

Some research suggests determination of plasma or whole blood glucose should be made as soon as possible after birth; at any time abnormal clinical signs are observed; and should repeated at 30 minutes, 1 hour, 2 hours, 4 hours, 8 hours, and 12 hours after birth

Serum or whole blood glucose levels of less than 20–40 mg/dL within the first 24 hours after birth are generally agreed to be abnormal and to require intervention, but the precise level remains controversial. The following guidelines have been adopted by the American Academy of Pediatrics.

Within the first 4 hours of life:

Any glucose level less than 40 mg/dL in a baby with symptoms requires immediate IV fluid therapy.

In an asymptomatic baby, an initial glucose level (within the first 4 hours of life) of less than 25 mg/dL should prompt an immediate feeding with another glucose check in an hour. If the subsequent test is still <25 mg/dL, immediate IV fluid therapy is indicated. If the subsequent test is >25 but <40 mg/dL, the infant should again be fed and retested, although IV fluid therapy may be indicated for some patients in this group.

Between 4–24 hours of life:

Any glucose level less than 40 mg/dL in a baby with symptoms requires immediate IV fluid therapy.

In an asymptomatic baby, a glucose level of less than 35 mg/dL should prompt an immediate feeding with another glucose check in an hour. If the subsequent test is still <35 mg/dL, immediate IV fluid therapy is indicated. If the subsequent test is >35 but <45 mg/dL, the infant should again be fed and retested, although IV fluid therapy may be indicated for some patients in this group.

Sustained or repetitive hypoglycemia in infants may severely impact normal brain development and function. Evidence suggests that hypoxemia and ischemia potentiate hypoglycemia, causing brain damage that may permanently impair neurologic development. Seizures, coma, and long-term brain damage may occur if neonatal hypoglycemia is unrecognized and untreated.

Although hypoglycemia can be associated with adverse neurologic outcomes, in many cases infants also have other risk factors or pathology. Scientific evidence has not established a connection between isolated low glucose levels in asymptomatic infants and neurologic injury.

Hypoxic Ischemic Encephalopathy (HIE)

HIE is a condition in which the brain, as a whole, does not receive enough oxygen. The term most often refers to injury sustained by newborns, but HIE can be used to describe any injury from oxygen deprivation.

A fetus gets its oxygen from the mother. The placenta, which is embedded into the wall of the mother's uterus, serves the same function a fetus' lungs will serve after birth. The placenta consists of a pool of the mother's blood vessels. Oxygen in the mother's blood stream flows across the placenta and into the umbilical cord, which carries oxygenated blood from mother to fetus, and carries carbon dioxide and waste products away from the fetus by the mother's circulation. The mother's oxygenated blood supplies all the fetal organs.

Oxygen and nutrients, especially glucose, are essential for the proper growth, development and function of all the organs, including the brain. If the supply of oxygen is reduced or shut off brain damage occurs. Neurons die and the cell bodies break down. As that happens the contents of the neurons are released into the fetus' brain and it swells. The swelling can compress blood vessels in the brain, which causes reduced blood flow in the brain, which further reduces the oxygen supply.

When the uterus contracts, flow in or out of the placenta slows or stops. For the placenta to work properly there must be sufficient time between contractions for the placenta to recharge with a fresh supply of oxygen. Excessive frequency of contractions is called hyperstimulation of the uterus, or tachysystole.

Compression of the umbilical cord can also lead to reduced oxygenation. Some compression of the umbilical cord is normal as the uterus contracts. However, if a loop of umbilical cord comes out of the cervix in front of the baby's head, it is called a cord prolapse. When the baby descends or contractions occur the cord is compressed significantly more than if the cord were normally placed. The cord must be elevated until the fetus is delivered via immediate emergency cesarean section. An occult cord prolapse is one where the cord lies low and is compressed during delivery but no one can feel or see the cord. This condition is diagnosed by seeing the signs of serious cord compression on the fetal heart monitor strips. The treatment for an occult umbilical cord prolapse is also an emergency caesarean section.

Lack of oxygen frequently damages not only the brain, but other organs as well. The disease can cause long-term damage, including intellectual disability, delayed development, seizures, cerebral palsy, abnormal blood pressures or heart rhythms, liver damage with elevated liver enzymes, kidney damage with low urine output and abnormal kidney function, gastrointestinal problems with abnormal feeding, low or high tone with floppy or stiff muscles and/or impaired control of breathing often requiring ventilation.

Exercise 2-6   Developing an Initial Theory of the Duty Owed by a Professional

For this exercise your assignment is to review the facts and literature from the chapter problem and make a preliminary determination of the scope of the duty owed in this case — which is referred to in medical malpractice (and other negligence cases) as the standard of care. You are making this determination for several reasons: (1) to evaluate and assess your client's potential liability; (2) to enable you to understand the terminology sufficiently to be able to discuss the case with your expert witnesses and to depose plaintiff's expert witnesses; and (3) to make a preliminary assessment of whether any of the alleged conduct falls below the relevant standard of care (i.e., is a breach).

Exercise 2-7   Evaluating Conflicting Theories and Expert Witness Testimony

As required by Michigan state law, plaintiffs filed Affidavits of Merit, which contain general information about the standard of care (from the plaintiffs' perspective), and alleged breaches of the standard of care. As part of your firm's representation of defendant Henry Ford Systems in the action by Ms. McCoy, an attorney in your firm deposed these expert witnesses, in part to ascertain further information about each of plaintiffs' expert's view of the standard of care. The portions of the depositions related to the standard of care are also set out below.

Based on your reading of the facts, the literature from the previous exercise, and what you know about standard of care, (1) identify the standard of care articulated by plaintiffs' expert witness, and then (2) determine whether you agree with plaintiffs' experts, or whether you believe the standard of care is different from the standard set out by plaintiffs' experts; and (3) identify all of the potential breaches of the standard of care.

Transcript Excerpt from Deposition of Plaintiffs' Obstetrics Expert

1 Q. What are the pertinent facts that support your opin-
2 ion in this case?
3 A. I believe the most important facts are the fetal
4 monitoring strips. The strips, as labor progressed became
5 very, very ominous.
6 The increased baseline, decreased variability which
7 began at 1230 on 10-22, also late decelerations began
8 about 12 o'clock on 10-22. At approximately one o'clock
9 in the morning on 10-22 there was a start of hyperstimu-
10 lation, and my conclusion was that a C section should
11 have been performed by approximately 3:30 on 10-22, 1530.
12 Also a scalp ph should have been performed every 30
13 minutes starting at two o'clock, and Pitocin should not
14 have been started at 1630.
15 On 10-22, some times between 1400 to 1700 there was a
16 dramatic rise in baseline, dramatic fall in variability,
17 and there were repetitive late decelerations.
18 The fetus was under obvious duress or stress, and it
19 was mandated that the obstetricians take action and de-
20 liver this child sooner than they did.
21 Q. I guess—so I understand, the primary basis of your
22 opinion is on interpretation of the fetal monitor tracing?
23 A. Yes.
24 Q. I think you gave me a time that you would have
25 called the section at 1530?
26 A. Yes.

1   Q. Doctor, how would you define the standard of care?

2   A. It's the quality of care that's expected in a given

3 community or in this case national standards since ob-

4 stetrics has national standards, not just local standard.

5   Q. Where do we find it?

6   A. There are teaching programs. There are residency

7 training programs all throughout the country which basi-

8 cally teach the same standard to all residency students.

9   There are continuing medical education courses which

10 reinforce different issues in obstetrics and gynecology.

11 There are technical bulletins, ACOG puts out bulletins

12 and opinions which are not necessarily authoritative but

13 certainly excellent references, and just from general ex-

14 perience in practicing obstetrics.

15   Q. Okay. Would you agree that even with the standard of

16 care you could have one or two doctors doing different

17 things, but they could all be within the standard of care?

18   A. Yes, yes.

19   Q. Is the nuchal cord significant at all, in your opin-

20 ion?

21   A. It's certainly significant—I think it's something

22 that the doctor should have been cognizant of, but I

23 don't think that should have changed necessarily the

24 course of events.

25   Q. I guess my question is: Nuchal cord, if you had

26 knowledge of that, does that change labor management?

27   A. I think it makes you a little more aware and tuned in

28 to be monitoring things a little more closely, but in and

29 of itself nuchal cord wasn't a reason to do a C section.

30   Q. If you had a fore knowledge there was nuchal cord,

31 do you have a standard of care, duty, or obligation to

32 somehow communicate that to the labor and delivery unit?

33   A. Oh, of course.

1   Q. How would you do that?

2   A. Either it should be written on the chart after the
3 ultrasound was performed and it was recognized, or when
4 you arrive on the labor suite, you have to share all in-
5 formation with everyone taking care of this patient.

6   Q. So in your opinion, writing that information on the
7 chart is sufficient?

8   A. I would think if it was written in a manner everyone
9 else could appreciate.

10   Q. I want to start off with the strip. Just for brevity
11 sake, I think your criticisms began on the 22nd?

12   A. Yes.

13   Q Okay. What do you find significant about that tracing?

14   A There is hyperstimulation. There's obviously fetal
15 reaction. There are a series of late decelerations.

16   Q. What makes it ominous?

17   A. The contraction pattern appears to be hyperstimula-
18 tory. The uterus does not seem to be relaxing. Then you
19 have late decelerations occurring with heart rates down
20 to 60 or 70 range. With minimal variability. Good vari-
21 ability means the central nervous system is still reac-
22 tive and getting some oxygen to allow it to function, but
23 as this proceeds it becomes non-reactive. Late decelera-
24 tions will occur up until a point where the baby's re-
25 serve runs out.

26   The fetal heart rate not only is going down to 60 or 70
27 but it's staying there for a good minute and a half.

28   This is certainly something that should be alerting the
29 physicians and nurses that something might be wrong.

30   Q. Okay. Go ahead.

31   A. The baby is not getting enough oxygen and obviously
32 becoming hypoxic, and at this stage is not really toler-
33 ating the hypoxia as well as before. The reserve is run-

1 ning out, and the reflex decelerations are slowly turning

2 in non-reflex, which means the baby is almost crying out

3 for something to be done.

4   It can affect the child becoming more and more hypoxic

5 as a result of the child not getting enough oxygen. If

6 you see a child having late decelerations, you have to do

7 something to correct the situation.

8   In this situation, it's probably being caused by hyper-

9 stimulation and nothing is being done to correct that.

10   Q. Did you notice about 12:05 the care provider went

11 ahead and put mom on her lateral side.

12   A. Yes.

13   Q. And they gave her oxygen, yes?

14   A. Yes.

15   Q. I think they gave her IVs, yes?

16   A. Okay.

17   Q. They responded appropriately to the tracing?

18   A. They're doing the measures sort of putting a Band-

19 Aid on the wound. They're not addressing the real problem

20 which is whether the baby is getting severely hypoxic to

21 the point where its irreversible.

22   Certainly at this point I would say the tracing is omi-

23 nous enough so they should have started doing scalp pHs

24 and not waited until 2:30 in the afternoon.

25   And once you start scalp pH, if the tracing does not

26 get dramatically better, which this one certainly didn't,

27 it's your obligation to continue the scalp pH every 30

28 minutes to keep reassuring that even though the tracing

29 Is ominous, the baby is being oxygenated. They only did

30 one at 2:45.

31   Q. You're only aware of one scalp pH in this case?

32   A. Let me back up. They did one at about 2:30, which

33 was reassuring, 7.28. Rather than doing one every half

1 hour after that, they didn't do another one until 1800
2 hours, just before the C section.
3   They waited for two or three hours in between. They
4 should have been doing five or six scalp pHs during that
5 time instead of waiting for a scalp pH of 7.04.
6   If they had seen a trend from 7.28, they certainly
7 should have realized this baby was getting into more and
8 more trouble and called a C section much earlier.
9   Q. If it's your patient, would you try to do other
10 measures before you sought C section? Would you try to
11 reassure yourself?
12   A. As I said, if I was undertaking scalp pHs, I would
13 have been doing them every half hour for the last two
14 hours.
15   Q. Okay.
16   A. I'm quite sure the trend would have been a downward
17 one, and that would mean the baby is getting hypoxic.
18   Q. You would describe labor as a hypoxic event,
19 wouldn't you?
20   A. Everything is relevant.
21   Q. So the baby has mechanisms to tolerate the hypoxia?
22   A. Yes, up to a certain point.
23   Q. Do you know—do we know what the point is?
24   A. I don't like to be in the position questioning the
25 point If I'm concerned enough about a strip, If there's a
26 deep increasing baseline, dramatically increased variabil-
27 ity, late deceleration occurring with almost every con-
28 traction for several hours, I don't want to be at a point
29 where I'm too late.
30   There reaches a point where the damage is irreversible.
31   Q. Have you had great strips and a depressed baby?
32   A I don't recall that.
33   Q. Have you had horrible strip and a great baby?

1   A. A great baby, no, a salvageable baby where hypoxia

2 was reversed. The point when you're doing this, you owe

3 it to the mother and child not to deliver a hypoxic baby.

4   It's not your goal to say: I was right, the fetal strip

5 is terrible and I delivered a terrible baby.

6   You're supposed to react prior to coming to a non-

7 reversible situation.

8   That's why I'm saying at 12:30 this strip was ominous

9 enough I would have wanted reassurance with scalp pHs.

10   If someone for whatever reason doesn't entertain doing

11 scalp pHs, then a C section should have been performed

12 much earlier.

13   In this situation, they chose to do a scalp pH. They

14 only did one, and they were reassured that one scalp pH

15 would take them through another two and a half hours,

16 even though the strip was looking worse and worse.

17   Q. When was the first scalp pH done?

18   A. I believe it was about 2:45, if I'm correct.

19   Q. And what was the scalp pH?

20   A. 7.28.

21   Q. Is that reassuring?

22   A. Yes.

23   Q. What are you looking for?

24   A. Anything over 7.2.

25   Q. And given that's reassuring, what does that tell you?

26   A. It tells you that so far the baby is not—is in a

27 reversible situation, although the fetal heart tracing

28 looks terrible and ominous, this baby has enough reserve

29 to tolerate what's going on.

30   It doesn't tell you the baby will continue to tolerate

31 this insult over the next three hours. It tells you every

32 30 minutes you have to check on the baby, unless this

33

1 tracing automatically and magically becomes reassuring,

2 which it never does.

3   Q. By having the scalp pH at 7.28, that tells us at

4 least before this time the baby is not acidotic?

5   A. Right.

6   Q. Okay. Go ahead.

7   A. But despite the pH, the decelerations continue. This

8 is a very non-reassuring strip, and you have to be leery

9 and not be too complacent with that 7.2 pH. Within 20

10 minutes, 30 at the most this scalp pH should have been

11 repeated or, as I said, this is the time I would have

12 said let's do a C section. I'm very worried about this

13 child, and I want a healthy baby.

14   Q. You said there was second scalp pH?

15   A. Yes, I believe that was done just about 1800. I

16 don't know if it's marked on this page.

17   Q. How long does it take from getting a sample to get-

18 ting the report?

19   A. Within five minutes.

20   Q. Ok. Just one more. I believe you said in your affi-

21 davit that that we did not properly and timely perform a

22 cesarean section to deliver a child before he suffers hy-

23 poxic ischemic encephalopathy.

24   A. Yes.

25   Q. You went over when we called the section, it was

26 timely done. What are your criticisms?

27   A. This baby should have been delivered hours before.

28 The tracing should have been recognized as being very,

29 very ominous as far as the baby situation.

30   The baby was not getting enough oxygen. It was demon-

31 strating it as clearly as it could. These were not sub-

32 tle changes that you had to be a magician to see. These

33 are very obvious.

1 Q. Do you have any other things that we haven't cov-
2 ered today?

3 A. I don't believe so.

4 Q. Okay. [To Plaintiff's Attorney]: Do you have anything?

5 [Plaintiff's Attorney]: Q. You were asked a number of
6 questions about this nuchal cord.

7 If the written note was not available to any of the
8 doctors or nurses who were actually on the labor and de-
9 livery unit, say the note was written in an outpatient
10 office, not available in the hospital where they were ac-
11 tually caring for the patient, is that sufficient?

12 A. I assumed that the note was part of her chart that
13 they had access to at the hospital.

14 If the note wasn't available for whatever reason, then,
15 of course, that's a deviation from the standard of care.

16 [Plaintiff's Attorney]: Okay.

17

18

19

20

21

22

23

24

25

26

27

28

29

30

31

32

33

Transcript Excerpt from Deposition of Plaintiffs' Neonatology Expert

1   Q. So let's talk about standard of care here. So he's
2 born at 18:16, he's taken to the nursery, and somewhere
3 around 18:39 they do a chem strip or a glucometer and
4 they get a 50, correct?
5   A. What did you say, 18:39?
6   Q. The time noted is 18:39. So we don't know exactly
7 when she did it. But that is when the note is.
8   A. Uh-huh.
9   Q. Is that within the standard of care that she would
10 have done that at that time?
11   A. Yes.
12   Q. So at that point at 18:39, she's got a 50. Does the
13 standard of care require at that time she then do a ran-
14 dom blood sugar after that?
15   A. No. The standard of care would require her to check
16 the blood sugar again in probably half an hour.
17   Q. Okay. So at 18:45—
18   A. Because, and here's the because, this is why you
19 can't always use a cookbook to determine these things.
20 This baby is having desats when he's on two liters of oxy-
21 gen at 100 percent.
22   He's having desats right about that time down to 75 to
23 86 percent. And he's having apnea. So he's having symp-
24 toms of hypoglycemia. So you're going to want to check
25 and see what the glucose is in half an hour. 50 is—it's
26 okay but it's not 80, it's not 90. So you don't have a
27 big margin there.
28   Q. Let me ask you, though, wouldn't you expect that a
29 baby that's just been born might have some temporary
30 breathing incident like some apnea?

1   A. No, no, that is not normal.

2   Q. What about a baby of a diabetic, don't you expect

3 that a baby of a diabetic is going to have more likely a

4 little bit of respiratory problems after birth?

5   A. No.

6   Q. Okay. So—

7   A. When I see this apnea and desats, I'm concerned

8 about this baby's central nervous system. I'm concerned

9 about why is he having desats if he's on 100 percent?

10 Well, he was having shallow breathing and then he was

11 having actually apnea which was lasted 20 seconds which

12 is pretty significant apnea and they had to stimulate him.

13   Q. So—

14   A. So he's symptomatic. So you want to check that blood

15 sugar quickly.

16   Q. So the fact that she took the blood sugar at 19:30,

17 which is about 50 minutes after the first one, then are

18 you saying that is a violation of the standard of care?

19   A. I think that once you have the apnea, you want to

20 take it as soon as possible. Because apnea is often a

21 symptom of hypoglycemia.

22   Q. Aren't the symptoms of hypoglycemia very nonspecific?

23 Can't they be symptoms of many things in a baby—sepsis,

24 various things?

25   A. Sure. You know, they can be fairly nonspecific. But

26 here's a baby who is a—who is a setup for hypoglycemia.

27 This baby is at super high risk. He is not just an infant

28 of a gestational diabetic. He is a big baby. He is a baby

29 that's had asphyxia. So he's got lots of reasons to first

30 of all use up his sugar quickly because of hyperinsulin-

31 ism. Which I'm sure he had but they didn't test for it.

32 A, because he's an infant of a diabetic. And B, he's big.

33 And insulin is the main growth hormone of the fetus. If

1 you have a lot of insulin, you grow big. So he's got a

2 lot of insulin around. He's only starting out with a chem

3 strip of 50, he's had hypoxia and ischemia so he's

4 shifted into anaerobic metabolism. He's probably used up

5 glucose stores and glycogen stores during labor. This

6 baby was at such high risk of hypoglycemia he should have

7 had an IV started immediately.

8   Q. Even with a 50 blood sugar?

9   A. Yes.

10   Q. That is not the standard of care, though, is it?

11   A. For this baby? This baby was at extremely high risk

12 for hypoglycemia.

13   Q. Isn't it true that it is much better to feed a baby

14 if the baby can eat, that they are going to get more glu-

15 cose that way than through an IV?

16   A. Well—no, they will get it quicker if it is by IV.

17 And in fact when they are symptomatic, you don't just

18 feed them, you start an IV. When they are hypoglycemic,

19 we start an IV and give them a bolus of glucose. We don't

20 just feed them. Okay, feed him at maybe 19:00. He didn't

21 get fed until 19:30.

22   Q. Assuming hypothetically this child was not hypoxic

23 at birth, or encephalopathic in any way, you would still

24 say that this baby with the 50 chem strip would need to

25 have an IV right away?

26   A. Yes, I would. Because he's at super high risk. He is

27 an infant of a diabetic. He's big so he's got extra in-

28 sulin on board. And that is going to chew up his blood

29 sugar very quickly. Plus he's already—he's probably de-

30 pleted reserves because of the prolonged fetal distress

31 that he went through.

32   Q. The mom had an IV, right, a glucose IV?

33

1   A. Well, so that's going to send glucose to him. He's
2 going to try to deal with that by producing more insulin
3 to keep his blood sugar normal.
4   Q. But he may have—if he has the 50 glucose at birth,
5 then he probably was not hypoglycemic in the womb.
6   A. Oh, I don't think he was. But he was hypoglycemic
7 shortly after the 50.
8   Q. Wouldn't you agree that even children who are not
9 children of gestational diabetics are going to have a low
10 glucose level at one to two hours after birth?
11   A. They may have a dip, but this baby had deranged me-
12 tabolism because of being an infant of a diabetic and
13 having gone through the prolonged fetal distress.
14   Q. Would you expect that if a child—this child was en-
15 cephalopathic at birth from hypoxia and distressed and
16 then hypoglycemic, would you expect that he would be able
17 to eat as much as he ate in that first several hours
18 after birth?
19   A. 20 cc's is not that much. It is not even an ounce.
20   Q. So the child had 20 cc's and then the nurse did his
21 chem stick and got a 23. She testified that she sent—took
22 some more blood and sent it to the lab. But before that,
23 they gave him a bolus, seven cc's D10 at 20:30. In your
24 opinion, that isn't—
25   A. No, the lab—the lab was done shortly after 19:30.
26   Q. Well, it was done—yeah, well, probably right. You
27 are right. Before he finished eating or after he finished?
28   A. I think he finished at 8 o'clock. The chem strip was
29 23. I think what she did was feed him and then checked a
30 lab and the lab was 14. So she checked the chem strip
31 again at 20:15 after he had fed, and it was still low at
32 32. At that point, 15 minutes later is when he got an IV
33

1 bolus. And then they didn't give him continuous IV. They

2 didn't even start the IV until 21:30.

3   Q. Well, she got—according to the lab note, she got the

4 notification of the 14 at 20:30. And that's when she did

5 the bolus, seven cc's?

6   A. She had to start an IV.

7   Q. And I believe she testified that she started that IV

8 very quickly. So then after that bolus was started, she

9 got a 60 at 20:45 which is normal, correct?

10   A. Uh-huh.

11   Q. And then she did another one at must have been prior

12 to 21:35 because she got—21:30, she got a 40 which went

13 down, and that is when she started the IV, correct?

14   A. But she should have started the IV way back.

15   Q. Well, it is your opinion that the IV should have

16 been started at birth?

17   A. Yes.

18   Q. How can you have hypoglycemia if you have a blood

19 glucose of 68? The symptoms must be of something else.

20   A. No, that is a fallacy. Once the damage has been

21 done to the neurons, even if you have a normal glucose,

22 the neurons are damaged. And you will continue to have

23 symptoms.

24   Q. Well, you know, if we look at the neonatal intensive

25 care flow sheet from 10-23, and we look at the blood glu-

26 coses after the IV was started, you have 71 at 24:00, 47

27 at 3 o'clock, 55 at 6 o'clock, 55 at 9 o'clock, 57 at

28 noon. 53, 63, 52. Those are all normal, correct?

29   A. Yes. Those are all normal.

30   Q. And then if you look at 10-24, again the glucose was

31 down and we've got 46, 64, 49, 50, 62, 56, 49. All normal

32 again, correct?

33

1   A. 46 I would challenge a bit. It is right there on

2 the border. But you have other things going on on the

3 23rd, too. Now you have a baby who is hypotensive. So

4 you have got problems with perfusion. So your brain is

5 being insulted by not getting enough oxygen, not getting

6 enough blood flow. And the baby's blood pressure initially

7 for an almost four kilo baby was low, and he didn't get

8 a bolus, he didn't get an IV. So there were other rea-

9 sons to have an IV and to get fluids other than just to

10 prevent hypoglycemia.

11   Q. Do you have a criticism of the amount for the ini-

12 tial IV?

13   A. The amount seems very low to me. Because this was a

14 big—this was quite a big baby. And even if you figure—you

15 should be giving at least a hundred cc's per kilo when

16 you have hypoglycemia.

17   Q. Okay.

18   A. 100 to 110 cc's per kilo. And he was three point—let

19 me see if I can find his weight in kilos. He was 3.9, al-

20 most four kilos. So just for convenience sake, I'll say

21 he was four kilos, so four times—just go 100, that's 400

22 divided by 24. He probably should have been on, like, 15,

23 16 cc's an hour. 11 was too low, the rate was too low.

24   Q. And I'm assuming that you are also critical then of

25 the fact that they had started to lower that IV very soon

26 after they started it?

27   A. Yes. That didn't make any sense to me. Although he

28 was getting some PO feeds, you know, so that would be a

29 reason to adjust—that you could adjust the IV fluids

30 downward.

31

32

33

Exercise 2-8 Establishing the Standard of Care —
Review and Practice

Now that you have had a chance to work through exercises designed to help you identify and define the standard of care (duty owed) in a professional negligence (medical malpractice) case, it is time to apply that knowledge to other types of cases. Below are several scenarios where understanding and establishing the specific standard (the duty owed) would likely require developing some subject matter expertise. As you consider each scenario think about the following:

1. What knowledge could you develop that would help you prove the existence and extent of a duty?

2. How would you acquire such knowledge? What resources besides expert witnesses are available to you?

a. You have been contacted by investors who lost their money in fictitious investments created by a now deceased investment Broker. The investors would like to file suit against the brokerage Firm who employed Broker, for failing to monitor or investigate the outside activities of its brokers. Did Firm have a duty to monitor or investigate?

b. Buyer leased property from Seller. The lease contained an option to purchase the property. Buyer asked Seller to have the property appraised. Buyer also asked Seller to have the appraisers determine whether the dwelling on the property was a "mobile home" that had been placed on a permanent foundation. At Seller's request, appraisers performed separate appraisals of the property. They issued written reports valuing the property at $336,000 and $410,000, respectively. Their reports each stated that the dwelling had been a "modular" home, but was now attached to a permanent foundation. One report added that some modular homes were used as comparisons in the appraisal process. Both reports stated that the dwelling "was never a mobile home." Upon receiving these appraisals, Buyer spent substantial money and time toward purchasing the property. She then obtained a third appraisal from another source, which stated that the dwelling had been "brought in as a mobile home," and that the property was actually worth less than $252,500 at the time of the earlier appraisals. Buyer is now suing Seller for the money expended. Seller has contacted you to find out whether he can sue the appraisers he hired. Did the appraisers breach any duty?

c. You have been contacted by County to evaluate whether Firm breached any duty owed to County. County hired Engineering Firm to design a water-bearing pipeline. Firm's design specifications for the project called for the pipe to be manufactured in conformity with a national standard adopted by the American Water Works Association (AWWA). Concrete Pipe Inc (CPI), a pipe manufacturer, submitted a bid and proposal to County and Engineer. In its proposal, CPI indicated its intent to use "class IV wire" to manufacture pipe segments for the project. As part of its overall duties under its contract with the County, Firm prepared the project plans and specifications; reviewed bids and proposals submitted by pipe manufacturers; recommended a pipe manufacturer (CPI); and reviewed/approved CPI's shop drawings on the pipe materials and design, including the use of class IV wire. Based on Firm's recommendation, County ultimately contracted with CPI to manufacture the concrete pipe segments. One year after the pipeline was completed, one segment of pipeline broke, and County commenced an investigation. An engineer hired by County performed a pressure test and another explosion occurred. The pipeline ruptured two additional times over the next three years. All of these ruptures occurred at a level of pressure much less than the 210 pounds of pressure per square inch which the pipeline was designed by Firm to bear.

c. Duty Defined by Law — Understanding and Applying Cases and Statutes

In some situations, the existence and extent of the duty owed in a particular set of circumstances is proscribed specifically by law — either by judicial decision, statute, or other regulation. It is important at the outset of the case to determine whether such a decision, statute, or other regulation exists — and then to be able to ascertain from those cases and statutes what specifically that standard is — which will require those skills covered in Chapter One, including reading and synthesizing the law from cases and statutes, applying and distinguishing cases, and deconstructing the rules found in statutes and cases. You may want to return to Chapter One to review the instruction relating to these skills before completing the reading and exercises in this section. Also note that in the first chapter, the text identified the required skills for you; in this chapter you must decide which of the skills are required for each exercise (and then apply the skill).

(i) Premises Liability — Duty Defined by Common Law

Although some jurisdictions have codified the standard of care particular landowners or possessors owe to the persons that enter their real estate, in many jurisdictions the standards governing such situations are set out in the common law. This area of law is known as premises liability — because it governs the liability to a person who enters the premises and is injured because of the condition of the premises. Premises liability covers a fairly wide array of situations, because real estate includes land and structures of all types, such as vacant land, farm land, parking lots, athletic fields, suburban homes and yards, apartment complexes, shopping malls, grocery stores, office buildings, houses of worship, subway stations, and hospitals. Defendants in premises liability actions may include land owners and possessors. For example, where a tenant in a shopping plaza or mall possesses the space for the retail store, but does not own the land for that space, they might be liable to a person injured in the retail store. The same is true for a renter in an apartment complex and those that lease office space.

The traditional common law approach to defining duty in premises liability cases has been to define the scope of the duty to the person entering the land (the entrant) based on the entrant's legal status at the time the injury occurred. Historically, many jurisdictions recognized three different common law categories of persons who enter the premises of another; those categories are: trespassers, licensees, and invitees.

Trespassers — those who enter land without permission — are further divided into two different categories: known trespassers and undiscovered trespassers. Known trespassers are, as the name suggests, those trespassers the possessor is actually aware of and also those that she suspects or should know are coming on the land. Conversely, undiscovered trespassers are those that are not known to the possessor and that the possessor has no reason to suspect will be there.

Undiscovered trespassers are owed no duty at all in many jurisdictions; in others, the possessor owes a duty to refrain from willful, wanton or reckless conduct. Under either standard the undiscovered trespasser would lose an action for ordinary negligence because willful, wanton or reckless conduct involves conduct beyond the duty to act reasonably under the circumstances, covering truly extreme situations — like shooting the trespasser (which would likely result in an action for battery, not negligence).

A possessor owes known trespassers a duty to carry on all *activities* with reasonable care. With regard to *conditions* on the land, the law is further divided into two categories, artificial and natural conditions. A possessor owes a known trespasser no duty with regard to natural conditions. With regard to artificial conditions — if those conditions involve a risk of serious bodily harm or death, and if the trespasser was unlikely to discover the danger on his own — the possessor has a duty to warn the known trespasser of the dangerous condition.

Licensees — those who enter the land with permission, but who are not there to conduct business and are not a member of the general public — essentially take the premises in the same condition as the possessor. The possessor's only duty is to warn the licensee of concealed dangers on the property, meaning those dangers that are known to the possessor but would not be readily apparent to others. The possessor does not have a duty to inspect the premises to discover dangers or to make the premises safe for the licensee. The possessor also has a duty to use ordinary care with respect to the activities carried out on the property.

Invitees — those who enter land with permission and who are on the land either for the financial benefit of the owner or because the land is open to the public — are owed a duty of reasonable care with regard to activities carried out on the premises. Possessors must also use reasonable care in maintaining the premises, which means possessors have a duty to inspect the premises and to discover dangers on the property. Where a possessor knows or should know of any dangers on the property, the possessor must either eliminate the danger, when it is reasonable to do so, or warn the invitee of the danger.

Not surprisingly, because the duty owed is dependent on the status of the entrant, many disputes in premises liability cases focus on the classification of the entrant. For example, plaintiffs may argue they were invitees, rather than licensees, because the possessor's duty is to inspect for danger and then, depending on the circumstances, eliminate the danger or warn the invitee — a higher duty than that owed to a licensee, which means a greater chance of finding liability.

Exercise 2-9 Evaluating Duty Based on the Land Entrant's Status

Determine the status of the entrant in each of the scenarios below, and the duty owed by the possessor. You may find it helpful to first create an outline or flow chart representing the information contained in the introductory section, and the tests that you should apply.

a. An unpaid babysitter who slipped on ice at the defendant's home

b. A former mother-in-law who fell on former daughter-in-law's driveway while returning children from a visit with the daughter-in-law's former husband (mother-in-law's son)

c. A trick-or-treater (a.k.a. a child wearing a Halloween costume who goes door to door in hopes of receiving free candy) who tripped on the steps of the defendant's front porch in an effort to get to the open front door where the homeowner was passing out candy to other trick-or-treaters (on Halloween)

d. A homeless person who sought shelter from sudden rain under the awning of a retail store and was crushed by the awning when it collapsed from the weight of the rain

e. A postman who was bitten by a tenant's dog while delivering the mail

f. A firefighter who was injured while putting out a kitchen fire in owner's home

g. A group of children who regularly use a vacant lot to play baseball

h. A visitor, who was having a romantic relationship with homeowner, had been a guest at homeowner's residence on about 20 prior occasions, and who fell down the stairs at homeowner's residence

Exercise 2-10 Understanding Variations of a Rule of Law

In law school (and while studying for the bar exam) you will often learn generally applicable rules, or rules followed by a majority of jurisdictions. For example, the Restatements often represent an effort to summarize generally applicable principles from many jurisdictions; however, a Restatement is not binding in any jurisdiction until and unless the section at issue is specifically adopted. In practice, your job will be to identify and apply the specific rules for the jurisdiction where your case is filed. You will need to be able to determine whether (and how) that rule varies from the one you learned in law school — a skill you will practice in this exercise.

Many jurisdictions have adopted a different approach to the common law classifications described above. As you read the majority and dissenting opinions in the next case consider:

1. How would this court determine whether a person is an invitee?

2. Would applying the test adopted by the majority change your answer to any of the scenarios in the previous exercise? What about the test advanced by the dissent?

3. Do these tests differ from the common law approach described in the introduction to this chapter? If so, how do they differ?

4. Which test would you adopt? Why?

Stitt v. Holland Abundant Life Fellowship

614 N.W.2d 88 (Mich. 2000)

In this premises liability case the plaintiff, Violet Moeller, was injured when she tripped over a concrete tire stop in defendant church's parking lot.[2] Plaintiff was visiting the church

---

2. Violet Moeller is now deceased. Jill Stitt, decedent's personal representative has been substituted as the named plaintiff. For purposes of this opinion, Ms. Moeller will be referred to as the plaintiff.

to attend bible study. Plaintiff sued the church, alleging that the defendant negligently placed the tire stops and failed to provide adequate lighting in the parking lot.

At trial, the jury was instructed on the obligations property owners owe to licensees. The jury returned a verdict in favor of the church. The Court of Appeals reversed and remanded the case for a new trial after determining that the trial court erred by instructing the jury on the obligations owed to licensees rather than "public invitees" as defined in *Restatement Torts, 2d*, § 332.[3]

We granted leave in this case to determine the proper standard of care owed to individuals on church property for noncommercial purposes. We hold that the trial court correctly instructed the jury that such individuals are licensees and not invitees. Accordingly, we reverse the Court of Appeals decision and reinstate the trial court judgment in favor of the church.

I. Factual and Procedural Background

On the evening of November 22, 1989, Violet Moeller accompanied her friend Pat Drake to defendant's church to attend bible study. Ms. Moeller was not a member of the church. Ms. Drake parked her car in the church parking lot. As she exited Ms. Drake's car, plaintiff tripped and fell over a tire stop, fracturing her left arm. Plaintiff subsequently sued the defendant church, asserting that defendant negligently placed the concrete tire stops and failed to provide adequate lighting in the parking lot.

Before trial, the church twice filed motions for summary disposition. The trial court denied both motions, but determined that Ms. Moeller was a licensee and not an invitee at the time of the accident. The case proceeded to trial, at which time the judge instructed the jury on the duties owed to licensees.[4] At the close of trial, the jury returned a verdict in favor of the defendant. The court subsequently entered a judgment of no cause on the verdict.

Plaintiff appealed, contending that the trial court erred in determining that she was a licensee at the time of her accident. The Court of Appeals held that the plaintiff was a "public invitee" as defined in 2 Restatement Torts, 2d, § 332, and not a licensee. The Court of Appeals acknowledged that this Court has never explicitly adopted the Restatement provision. However, on the basis of its reading of *Preston v. Sleziak*, 383 Mich. 442, 175 N.W.2d 759 (1970), the Court of Appeals concluded that this provision applies in Michigan and that the trial court improperly instructed the jury. Accordingly, the Court of Appeals reversed the trial court judgment and remanded the case for a new trial. We granted defendant's application for leave to appeal. 461 Mich. 861, 602 N.W.2d 577 (1999).

* * *

---

3. Section 332 of the Restatement provides:
   (1) An invitee is either a public invitee or a business visitor.
   (2) A public invitee is a person who is invited to enter or remain on land as a member of the public for a purpose for which the land is held open to the public.
   (3) A business visitor is a person who is invited to enter or remain on land for a purpose directly or indirectly connected with business dealings with the possessor of the land.
   4. The trial court gave the following instructions: The possessor of land or premises is liable for physical harm caused to the licensee by a condition on the premises if, but only if, (A) the possessor knew or should've known of the condition, and should have realized that it involved an unreasonable risk of harm to the licensee, and should have expected that she would not discover or realize the danger and (B) the possessor failed to exercise reasonable care to make the conditions safe or to warn the licensee of the condition and the risk involved, and (C) the licensee did not know or have reason to know of the condition and risk involved.

III. Analysis

A. The Common-Law Classifications

Historically, Michigan has recognized three common-law categories for persons who enter upon the land or premises of another: (1) trespasser, (2) licensee, or (3) invitee. *Wymer v. Holmes*, 429 Mich. 66, 71, n. 1, 412 N.W.2d 213 (1987). Michigan has not abandoned these common-law classifications. *Reetz v. Tipit, Inc.*, 151 Mich.App. 150, 153, 390 N.W.2d 653 (1986). Each of these categories corresponds to a different standard of care that is owed to those injured on the owner's premises. Thus, a landowner's duty to a visitor depends on that visitor's status. *Wymer, supra* at 71, n. 1, 412 N.W.2d 213.

A "trespasser" is a person who enters upon another's land, without the landowner's consent. The landowner owes no duty to the trespasser except to refrain from injuring him by "wilful and wanton" misconduct. *Id.*

A "licensee" is a person who is privileged to enter the land of another by virtue of the possessor's consent. *Id.* A landowner owes a licensee a duty only to warn the licensee of any hidden dangers the owner knows or has reason to know of, if the licensee does not know or have reason to know of the dangers involved. The landowner owes no duty of inspection or affirmative care to make the premises safe for the licensee's visit. *Id.* Typically, social guests are licensees who assume the ordinary risks associated with their visit. *Preston, supra* at 451, 175 N.W.2d 759.

The final category is invitees. An "invitee" is "a person who enters upon the land of another upon an invitation which carries with it an implied representation, assurance, or understanding that reasonable care has been used to prepare the premises, and make [it] safe for [the invitee's] reception." *Wymer, supra* at 71, n. 1, 412 N.W.2d 213. The landowner has a duty of care, not only to warn the invitee of any known dangers, but the additional obligation to also make the premises safe, which requires the landowner to inspect the premises and, depending upon the circumstances, make any necessary repairs or warn of any discovered hazards. *Id.* Thus, an invitee is entitled to the highest level of protection under premises liability law. *Quinlivan v. Great Atlantic & Pacific Tea Co., Inc.*, 395 Mich. 244, 256, 235 N.W.2d 732 (1975).

A possessor of land is subject to liability for physical harm caused to his invitees by a condition on the land if the owner: (a) knows of, or by the exercise of reasonable care would discover, the condition and should realize that the condition involves an unreasonable risk of harm to such invitees; (b) should expect that invitees will not discover or realize the danger, or will fail to protect themselves against it; and (c) fails to exercise reasonable care to protect invitees against the danger. *Id.* at 258, 235 N.W.2d 732, citing Restatement, § 343.

The Court of Appeals correctly recognized that invitee status is commonly afforded to persons entering upon the property of another for business purposes. See, e.g., *Nezworski, supra*; *Pelton v. Schmidt*, 104 Mich. 345, 62 N.W. 552 (1895). In this case, we are called upon to determine whether invitee status should extend to individuals entering upon church property for *non* commercial purposes. Because invitee status necessarily turns on the existence of an "invitation," we must examine our common law in order to ascertain the meaning of that term.

B. The Meaning of Invitation in Michigan's Common Law

Unfortunately, our prior decisions have proven to be less than clear in defining the precise circumstances under which a sufficient invitation has been extended to a visitor to confer "invitee" status. On the one hand, several of our decisions appear to support the requirement that the landowner's premises be held open for a commercial business purpose. See, e.g., *Perl v. Cohodas, Peterson, Paoli, Nast Co.,* 295 Mich. 325, 294 N.W. 697 (1940); *Diefenbach v. Great Atlantic & Pacific Tea Co.,* 280 Mich. 507, 273 N.W. 783 (1937); *Sink v. Grand Trunk Western R. Co.,* 227 Mich. 21, 198 N.W. 238 (1924). For example, in *Diefenbach,* the plaintiff was injured when he entered the defendant's store. He alleged he entered the store for the purpose of purchasing groceries and denied defendant's contentions that he entered the store to participate in a rat hunt that was going on at the time. The Court noted that, although plaintiff actually bought no groceries, if he came to the store for a business purpose he would undoubtedly be an invitee.

Indeed, several panels of our Court of Appeals have interpreted our decisions as supporting the requirement of a business purpose. See, e.g., *Butler v. Ramco-Gershenson, Inc.,* 214 Mich.App. 521, 542 N.W.2d 912 (1995); *Bradford v. Feeback,* 149 Mich.App. 67, 385 N.W.2d 729 (1986); *Leep v. McComber,* 118 Mich.App. 653, 325 N.W.2d 531 (1982). In *Butler,* the Court of Appeals defined invitees as persons who enter the premises at the owner's express or implied invitation to conduct business concerning the owner. Correlatively, in *Bradford,* the Court of Appeals defined licensee as a person who, other than for a business purpose, enters another's land with the express or implied permission of the owner or person in control of the property.

The "commercial purpose" distinction is sufficiently recognized in Michigan case law that there are even secondary authorities that include Michigan among those jurisdictions conferring invitee status only on business visitors. See, e.g., 95 A.L.R.2d 992, § 4, p. 1014.

In contrast with the line of cases supporting a commercial purpose requirement, some of our earlier decisions are replete with broad language suggestive of the Restatement's "public invitee" definition, although the precise contours of the definition are difficult to discern. See, e.g., *Polston v. S.S. Kresge Co.,* 324 Mich. 575, 37 N.W.2d 638 (1949); *Sheldon v. Flint & P.M. R. Co.,* 59 Mich. 172, 26 N.W. 507 (1886); *Hargreaves v. Deacon,* 25 Mich. 1 (1872). In *Polston,* this Court held that members of the public who use a sidewalk with the defendant's knowledge, permission, and acquiescence were not trespassers but licensees. The *Polston* Court provided that the rule for licensees is different when the licensee is using a path that has been openly and notoriously held out to the public for use. In such cases, the Court held that the defendant owed a greater duty of ordinary care. We note that *Polston* and other cases decided about that time seem to impose a special heightened duty for persons injured on sidewalks, bridges, and roadways held open to the public. Hence, where such persons would ordinarily be considered licensees, they were nonetheless entitled to a duty of ordinary care. See, e.g., *Brown v. Michigan R. Co.,* 202 Mich. 280, 168 N.W. 419 (1918); *Morrison v. Carpenter,* 179 Mich. 207, 146 N.W. 106 (1914).

In *Hargreaves,* this Court stated that a landowner owes a duty of care when an injured party has been induced to come by personal invitation or employment or by resorting there as a place of business or "of general resort held open" to customers or others whose lawful occasion may lead them to come visit. *Id.* at 5. Interestingly, *Hargreaves* is cited in 95 A.L.R.2d 992, § 4, p. 1014 as supporting a commercial purpose requirement.

Finally, there is *Preston, supra* which is internally inconsistent on this point. *Preston* was interpreted by the Court of Appeals as having implicitly adopted the Restatement definition of "public invitee." At the same time, *Preston, supra* at 448, 175 N.W.2d 759, quoting Cooley on Torts, appears to recognize the commercial purpose requirement associated with invitee status:

> An invitation may be inferred when there is a common interest or mutual advantage, a license when the object is the mere pleasure or benefit of the person using it. "*To come under an implied invitation, as distinguished from a mere license, the visitor*

must come for a purpose connected with the business with which the occupant of the premises is engaged, or which he permits to be carried on there. There must be some mutuality of interest in the subject to which the visitor's business relates, although the particular business which is the object of the visit may not be for the benefit of the occupant. The distinction between a visitor who is a mere licensee and one who is on the premises by invitation turns largely on the nature of the business that brings him there, rather than on the words or acts of the owner which precede his coming." [3 Cooley, Torts (4th ed.), §440, pp. 193–194 (emphasis added).]

Given that *Preston* is purported to have adopted the Restatement *"public invitee"* definition, which does not require a business purpose, we find it difficult to reconcile *Preston's* citation to Cooley, which expressly requires a business purpose, as an accurate statement of Michigan law. *Id.* at 448, 450, 175 N.W.2d 759.

Cooley's acknowledgment that an invitee's status is dependent upon a visit associated with a "commercial purpose" and "mutuality of interest" concerning the reason for the visit demonstrate the extent to which Michigan has historically, if not uniformly, recognized a commercial business purpose as a precondition for establishing invitee status.

Despite the divergence of our cases concerning the elements necessary to confer invitee status, one thing *has* been consistent: to our knowledge, this Court has never squarely addressed the question whether a mere "public invitee" such as a churchgoer is entitled to invitee status. While plaintiff suggests that our cases have already recognized invitee liability for churches, a careful review of these cases shows that this is a less than accurate analysis. To the contrary, Michigan cases that have conferred invitee status upon an individual injured on church premises reveals that each has involved a plaintiff who was on the church premises for a *commercial* business purpose. For example, in *Bruce v. Central Methodist Episcopal Church*, 147 Mich. 230, 110 N.W. 951 (1907), the plaintiff was allowed to recover from the defendant church for injuries he sustained while painting the church building. The plaintiff was working for a contractor, painting the ceiling of the church when the scaffolding on which he was standing broke.

Almost fifty years later, a defendant church was held liable in *Manning v. Bishop of Marquette*, 345 Mich. 130, 76 N.W.2d 75 (1956). In *Manning*, the plaintiff fell and was injured on church property as she was leaving a bingo game.... The Court ... held that the plaintiff was an invitee.

Later, in *Kendzorek v. Guardian Angel Catholic Parish*, 178 Mich.App. 562, 444 N.W.2d 213 (1989), overruled on other grounds in *Orel v. Uni-Rak Sales Co.*, 454 Mich. 564, 563 N.W.2d 241 (1997), a child was injured on a swing at a carnival held on the church grounds. The carnival was a church fund-raiser. The child's mother brought suit against the church. The Court of Appeals held that, at the time the child was injured, she was an invitee.

As these cases illustrate, invitee status has traditionally been conferred in our cases only on persons injured on church premises who were there for a commercial purpose.

C. The Restatement

We begin by noting that a large number of jurisdictions have adopted §332 of the Restatement.... Subsection (2) of §332 of the Restatement creates an invitee status that does not depend on a commercial purpose. In this case, the Court of Appeals interpreted *Preston*, *supra*, as having implicitly adopted the Restatement definition of "public invitee." We certainly agree that *Preston* relied on §332 of the Restatement. However, the issue whether to adopt the Restatement definition of "public invitee" was not before this Court in *Preston*.

In *Preston,* the plaintiffs were social guests who had been invited to the defendant's cottage for the weekend. In order to access the cottage, the plaintiffs entered a lift. The lift consisted of a car that was controlled by cable and an electric winch. After the plaintiffs entered the lift, a shaft broke and the car crashed, injuring the plaintiffs. *Id.* at 445, 175 N.W.2d 759. The plaintiffs filed suit against the defendants. The jury returned a verdict in favor of the defendants. The Court of Appeals erroneously determined that the plaintiffs were invitees merely because they had been "invited" onto the premises. That Court reversed and remanded the case for a new trial. *Id.* This Court held that the Court of Appeals committed error requiring reversal because the trial judge properly instructed the jury on the duty owed by a host to his social guests, licensees. *Id.* at 454, 175 N.W.2d 759. As stated by the trial judge, a host has no duty to reconstruct his premises or make his home more convenient or more safe for those accepting his hospitality. The guest assumes the ordinary risks that come with the premises. *Id.* at 446, 175 N.W.2d 759.

There was no contention in *Preston* that the plaintiffs were "public invitees," because that case involved only the duty owed to social guests. Thus, the issue whether to adopt the Restatement definition of "public invitee" was not before this Court in *Preston* and there is room for doubt regarding whether *Preston* can properly be regarded as binding precedent on this point. However, to the extent *Preston* purported to adopt the Restatement definition, and this could be properly considered a binding holding, we overrule *Preston.* Moreover, as explained below, we decline to adopt § 332 of the Restatement here.

D. Business Purpose As a Precondition of Invitee Status

Given the divergence of our cases on what circumstances create invitee status, we must provide some form of reconciliation in this case. In harmonizing our cases, we conclude that the imposition of additional expense and effort by the landowner, requiring the landowner to inspect the premises and make them safe for visitors, must be directly tied to the owner's commercial business interests. It is the owner's desire to foster a commercial advantage by inviting persons to visit the premises that justifies imposition of a higher duty. In short, we conclude that the prospect of pecuniary gain is a sort of quid pro quo for the higher duty of care owed to invitees. Thus, we hold that the owner's reason for inviting persons onto the premises is the primary consideration when determining the visitor's status: In order to establish invitee status, a plaintiff must show that the premises were held open for a *commercial* purpose.

With regard to church visitors, we agree with the court in *McNulty v. Hurley,* 97 So.2d 185 (Fla., 1957), that such persons are licensees. In *McNulty,* a churchgoer was injured when, as she was leaving the church, she was pushed to the ground by a crowd of people. The lower court granted the defendant church's motion to dismiss on grounds that the plaintiff failed to state a cause of action. The defendant contended that one entering church premises for the purpose of attending religious services is a mere licensee. Thus, the only duty of the church was to refrain from wanton negligence or wilful misconduct and to refrain from intentionally exposing her to danger. *Id.* at 187. The plaintiff, on the other hand, argued that she was on the church premises by invitation and that most religions urge members and others to enter their churches and hold their doors open as a standing invitation. *Id.* The Florida Supreme Court disagreed, stating:

> [A]n invitation to enter and worship, whether it be either express or implied, does not constitute one who accepts the invitation an invitee in the legal sense. In order for such relationship to arise the person entering onto the premises, i.e., the invitee, must have done so for purposes which would have benefited the owner

or occupant of the premises, i.e., the invitor, or have been of mutual benefit to the invitee and the invitor. And as we view it this benefit must be of a material or commercial rather than of a spiritual, religious, or social nature. [*Id.* at 188.]

Thus, as we do, the *McNulty* court considered a business purpose or a business or commercial benefit to the landowner as a necessary requirement in order for a visitor to be deemed an invitee. The *McNulty* court rejected the argument that church members confer a benefit to the church by supporting the church, stating:

It cannot be successfully or logically argued that a person enters a place of worship, call it by any name, and participates in worship and prayer to the God or Supreme Being of his choice for the benefit of the body or organization which owns the church, the religious or lay readers who conduct the services, or the God or Supreme Being whom he worships and asks for guidance, help or forgiveness. One of the concepts of all religious beliefs known to us is that participation in religious activities is for the benefit of the mortals who participate therein. [*Id.*]

The *McNulty* court also addressed the issue whether financial contributions at a religious service provided a sufficient basis for invitee status. We find this analysis instructive because the plaintiff in the case at bar similarly alleges that on prior visits to the church she made financial contributions to the church to such an extent that she should be considered an invitee. The *McNulty* court stated:

[N]or would it matter if the plaintiff had alleged that she made a contribution when the collection plate was passed, for this would not have changed her status.... It seems clear to us ... that one who attends a religious edifice for the purpose of attending a religious service, as did the plaintiff in this case, does so "for his own convenience, pleasure or benefit" and is at best a licensee. [*Id.* at 188–189.]

We agree that whether the plaintiff in the instant case previously gave an offering to the church has no bearing on whether she was a licensee or an invitee. Absent a showing that the church's invitation to attend its services was for an essential commercial purpose, Ms. Moeller should be considered a licensee and not an invitee. A person who attends church as a guest enjoys the "unrecompensed hospitality" provided by the church in the same way that a person entering the home of a friend would. *Hambright v. First Baptist Church*, 638 So.2d 865, 868 (Ala., 1994). We conclude that church visitors who are attending church for religious worship are more like social guests (licensees) than business visitors (invitees). The solicitation of entirely voluntary donations by a nonprofit organization is plainly not a commercial activity. Accordingly, a church providing an opportunity for voluntary donations during a religious service that are in no way required to attend the service, i.e., passing a collection plate, does not transform one who attends the church service and elects to make a donation from a licensee into an invitee. Indeed, we imagine that many religious individuals would find it offensive to have their voluntary donations to a church regarded as part of a business or commercial transaction, rather than as a gift intended to aid in various religious good works.

IV. Conclusion

We recognize that a majority of jurisdictions considering the issue have adopted the public invitee definition set forth in § 332 of the Restatement. However, in exercising our common-law authority, our role is not simply to "count heads" but to determine which common-law rules best serve the interests of Michigan citizens. We believe that Michigan is better served by recognizing that invitee status must be founded on a commercial purpose for visiting the owner's premises.

For the above stated reasons, we hold that persons on church premises for other than commercial purposes are licensees and not invitees. Accordingly, we reverse the decision of the Court of Appeals and reinstate the trial court's decision.

WEAVER, C.J., and TAYLOR, CORRIGAN, and MARKMAN, JJ., concurred with YOUNG, J.

MARILYN J. KELLY, J. (dissenting).

I concur with the majority's chronicling of the facts and its statement of the applicable standard of review. I agree, also, with its recitation of the three common-law categories for persons who enter the land or premises of another. However, I dissent from the remainder of the majority's opinion.

The issue is whether individuals who enter another's property for noncommercial purposes are invitees for purposes of determining the standard of care a property owner or possessor owes to them. We have never held that invitee status arises solely where there is a commercial purpose for visiting the owner's premises. Instead, we have long recognized and applied both the commercial-purpose provision and the public-invitee provision of 2 Restatement Torts, 2d, §332 to classify visitors as invitees. The majority's reliance on *McNulty v. Hurley*, 97 So.2d 185 (Fla., 1957) to identify visitors as invitees only when they are visiting for a commercial purpose is misplaced. The majority's action rejects a recognized principle of Michigan law.

A

The common law and the statutes make up a major portion of the law of Michigan. Const. 1963, art. 3, §7.

"The common law does not consist of definite rules which are absolute, fixed, and immutable like the statute law, but it is a flexible body of principles which are designed to meet, and are susceptible of adaption to, among other things, new institutions, public policies, conditions, usages and practices, and changes in mores, trade, commerce, inventions, and increasing knowledge, as the progress of society may require. So, changing conditions may give rise to new rights under the law...." [*Beech Grove Investment Co. v. Civil Rights Comm.*, 380 Mich. 405, 430, 157 N.W.2d 213 (1968), quoting 15A C.J.S., Common Law, §2, pp. 43–44.]

"The Restatement is ... an attempt to categorically recite the content of the common law." *Yoder Co. v. Liberty Mut. Ins. Co.*, 92 Mich.App. 386, 390, 284 N.W.2d 810 (1979). ***

Section 332 of the Restatement is consistent with the common law of Michigan. Our common law, as it pertains to invitees, has been developing since 1872. In numerous cases, we have recognized or applied a rule that is similar to that contained in subsection 332(2). Long ago, in *Hargreaves v. Deacon*, 25 Mich. 1 (1872), this Court recognized a distinction between the duty owed to a trespasser and to one who enters another's property under an inducement or a lawful right. *Hargreaves, supra* at 9. The distinction required something more than mere permission. *Id.* To be entitled to damages, the visitor had to have been invited by the landowner to be on the property. *Id.* at 7.

Notably, for the landowner to incur liability, the *Hargreaves* Court *did not* require that a person be on a landowner's property solely for a commercial purpose. It stated that a suit for damages can lie when the party injured has been induced to come by personal invitation, *or* by employment which brings him there, *or* by resorting there as to a place of business, *or* of general resort held out as open to customers or others whose lawful occasions may lead them to visit there. [*Id.* at 5 (emphasis added).]

Thus, *Hargreaves* formed the basis for recognizing several means by which a person could become an invitee. See *Preston v. Sleziak*, 383 Mich. 442, 450, 175 N.W.2d 759 (1970); *Polston v. S.S. Kresge Co.*, 324 Mich. 575, 578, 37 N.W.2d 638 (1949); *Douglas v. Bergland*, 216 Mich. 380, 387–388, 185 N.W. 819 (1921).

Also long ago, in *Sheldon v. Flint & Pere Marquette R. Co.*, this Court applied the public invitee doctrine, although it did not identify it as such. The plaintiff's decedent was a child induced to enter the defendant's property by a band playing there. *Id.* at 173, 26 N.W. 507. The child had no particular business with the defendant and was not on the property for the pecuniary gain of the defendant. *Id.* at 177, 26 N.W. 507. While there, he was struck by the defendant's train and killed. *Id.* at 174, 26 N.W. 507.

The Court found that the music was naturally calculated to attract a crowd. The defendant should have anticipated that and made provisions to avoid the hazard that resulted in the child's death. *Id.* at 177–178, 26 N.W. 507. It held that a jury question remained whether the defendant had exercised the degree of care owed the plaintiff's decedent under the circumstances. *Id.* at 178, 26 N.W. 507. Notably, the Court did not merely label the child a licensee, despite the absence of any pecuniary benefit to the defendant from the decedent's presence on its property. *Id.* at 177–178, 26 N.W. 507. Thus, we can infer that the Court determined that the decedent could be classified as an invitee on the basis of invitation alone, without a commercial purpose for being on the property.

In 1908, this Court quoted former Justice Cooley in *Blakeley v. White Star Line* 154 Mich. 635, 118 N.W. 482 (1908), to state our common-law definition of an invitee:

> "One is under no obligation to keep his premises in safe condition for the visits of trespassers. On the other hand, when he expressly or by implication invites others to come upon his premises, whether for business *or for any other purpose*, it is his duty to be reasonably sure that he is not inviting them into danger, and to that end he must exercise ordinary care and prudence to render the premises reasonably safe for the visit." [*Blakeley, supra* at 637, 118 N.W. 482, quoting Cooley, Torts, p. 605 (emphasis added).]

> Particularly significant is the fact that Justice Cooley identified two different means by which one could be classified as an invitee: (1) by a finding that the person was *invited* upon the property for business, *or* (2) by a finding that the person was invited for any other purpose. *Id.*

On the basis of Justice Cooley's definition of an invitee, the *Blakeley* Court expressly formulated the applicable rule: "Invitation is sufficient. Pecuniary profit to the owner is not essential." *Id.* at 639, 118 N.W. 482. Thus, in *Blakeley,* we again recognized that our common law does not require a commercial purpose for one to be an invitee. The majority completely ignores the *Blakeley* definition of an invitee. It states that there are several cases that "appear" to support a commercial purpose requirement. Op. at 92. It recognizes that there are cases that are suggestive of the Restatement's public invitee definition. But, it finds that the contours of the definition are difficult to discern. While the contours of the definition to this point may not be a model of clarity, I ask what is difficult to discern regarding the statement in *Blakeley* that "[p]ecuniary profit to the owner is not essential"? *Blakeley, supra* at 639, 118 N.W. 482. From that statement, one can scarcely fail to discern that Michigan law does not require a commercial purpose for someone to be classified as an invitee.

Forty-one years later, in *Polston, supra,* this Court continued to recognize that it could assign invitee status on the basis of invitation alone. It derived the following definition of an invitee:

From *Hargreaves v. Deacon*, [*supra*], it appears that damages for accidental injuries sustained on private premises resulting from the negligence of the owner may not be recovered by one on the theory that he is an invitee "*unless the party injured has been induced to come by personal invitation, or* by employment which brings him there, or by resorting there as to a place of business, or of general resort held out as open to customers," et cetera. [*Polston, supra* at 578, 37 N.W.2d 638 (emphasis added).]

Only after the Court concluded that the plaintiff did not fall within the definition of an invitee did it confer licensee status on him. *Id.*

In *Preston, supra,* we find again that the licensee-invitee distinction does not turn on whether the invitor has the expectation of a pecuniary gain from the invitation. *Id.* at 449–450, 175 N.W.2d 759. "[I]n this state the status of an invitee is tested not only by the theory of economic benefit, *but also upon the concept of invitation.*" *Id.* at 450, 175 N.W.2d 759 (emphasis added).

The majority argues that *Preston* is "internally inconsistent on this point." Op. at 93 However, a close reading of *Preston* indicates that its analysis is actually consistent with our common-law rule and the Restatement definition of a public invitee.

In *Preston*, we considered whether social guests invited to another's home were invitees or licensees. The Court of Appeals had relied on *Genesee Merchants Bank & Trust Co. v Payne* to hold that Michigan law classifies the social guest as an invitee. *Preston, supra* at 447, 175 N.W.2d 759. This Court rejected the *Genesee Merchants Bank* decision and reversed the Court of Appeals. 383 Mich. 442, 175 N.W.2d 759. In so doing, we stated:

> "An invitation may be inferred when there is a common interest or mutual advantage, a license when the object is the mere pleasure or benefit of the person using it. To come under an implied invitation, as distinguished from a mere license, the visitor must come for a purpose connected with the business with which the occupant of the premises is engaged, or which he permits to be carried on there. There must be some mutuality of interest in the subject to which the visitor's business relates, although the particular business which is the object of the visit may not be for the benefit of the occupant. The distinction between a visitor who is a mere licensee and one who is on the premises by invitation turns largely on the nature of the business that brings him there, rather than on the words or acts of the owner which precede his coming." [*Id.* at 448, 175 N.W.2d 759, quoting 3 Cooley, Torts (4th ed.), § 440.]

The majority latches onto the quotation from Cooley as proof that Michigan classifies a visitor as an invitee only when there is a commercial purpose for the visit. Op. at 93. However, the majority ignores the context of the quotation. The *Preston* Court quoted Cooley to preserve the historical distinction between a social guest and invitee. *Preston, supra* at 448, 175 N.W.2d 759. The quotation was not meant to provide the general rule for assigning invitee status to visitors in all other situations.

Later in its opinion, the Court quoted § 332 of the Restatement as the general definition of an invitee. *Id.* at 450, 175 N.W.2d 759. It stated that the Restatement "definition fairly represents the law of this state pertaining to what constitutes the legal status of an invitee." *Id.* at 451, 175 N.W.2d 759 (citations omitted). The Court then identified that the comment accompanying § 332 states that invitee status under the Restatement definition does not apply to social guests. *Id.* at 450–451, 175 N.W.2d 759. A social guest "'does not come as a member of the public upon premises held open to the public for that purpose, and he does not enter for a purpose directly or indirectly connected with business dealings with the possessor.'" *Id.* at 451, 175 N.W.2d 759, quoting 2 Restatement Torts, 2d, § 330, comment h. Thus, the Court held that social guests were not invitees and went on to classify them as licensees. *Id.* at 453, 175 N.W.2d 759.

Comparable Michigan appellate cases decided after *Preston* have focused exclusively on the business invitee provision of § 332. They did not consider the public invitee provision of § 332. In each, however, it was unnecessary to consider the public invitee provision, because invitee status was established on the basis of an economic benefit to the property owner. This is especially true with regard to the cases cited by the majority in which courts have recognized invitee liability for churches. See Op. at 94. In each case this Court or the Court of Appeals classified the visitor as an invitee because the church received a commercial benefit from the visitor's presence. *Id.* There simply was no need to rely on the concept of invitation and apply the public invitee definition.

In order to consider further the public invitee provision of § 332, we had to await a case in which liability was premised on the basis of an injured party being a public invitee. See, e.g., *Roberts v. Auto-Owners Ins. Co.,* 422 Mich. 594, 611, 374 N.W.2d 905 (1985). This case presents that basis, and we should not hesitate to apply the public invitee provision to it.

As identified above, the concept that invitee status is determined by either an economic benefit to, or an invitation by, the property owner is well established in our common law. It has been recognized as the law in Michigan since 1970 in *Preston.* See *Leveque v. Leveque,* 41 Mich.App. 127, 129, 199 N.W.2d 675 (1972); *Sendelbach v. Grad,* 246 N.W.2d 496, 499 (N.D., 1976); 62 Am.Jur.2d, Premises Liability, § 88, p. 442, n. 54. In fact, I would interpret *Preston* as implicitly adopting the Restatement definition of an invitee.

The majority argues that the issue "whether to adopt the Restatement definition of public invitee was not before this Court in *Preston....*" Op. at 95. However, in that case we were required to consider whether a social guest was an invitee or a licensee. *Preston, supra* at 445, 175 N.W.2d 759. In considering that issue, we were obliged to examine the definition of an invitee and a social guest to determine whether the two were compatible. *Id.* at 450–451, 175 N.W.2d 759. We determined that they were not and that the status of a social guest is more consistent with that of a licensee. *Id.* at 451–452, 175 N.W.2d 759. Thus, our discussion of what constitutes an invitee was essential to the resolution of the case.

Accordingly, I find that the issue whether to adopt the Restatement definition of an invitee was squarely before the Court in *Preston.* I would apply *Preston* as precedent, binding on this case.

B

The majority rejects the public invitee provision of § 332 and adopts the reasoning contained in the Florida case of *McNulty, supra,* as more consistent with our state's legal tradition. Op. at 95. In *McNulty,* the Florida Supreme Court held that, to be classified an invitee, one must have been on the property for a material or commercial purpose that benefited the invitor. *Id.* at 188. The Court rejected the plaintiff's argument that the defendant church received a benefit from his presence at a worship service, and labeled him a licensee. *Id.* at 189.

For over a century, Michigan has recognized that one can be classified as an invitee when on an invitor's property for a commercial purpose *or* pursuant to an invitation. See *Hargreaves, supra.* Thus, the *McNulty* decision runs contrary to recognized principles of Michigan law by imposing a commercial purpose requirement to the designation of an invitee. This Court has expressly stated, "Invitation is sufficient. Pecuniary profit to the owner is not essential." *Blakeley, supra* at 639, 118 N.W. 482. Therefore, the majority's reliance on *McNulty* is misplaced.

Furthermore, Florida itself has rejected the *McNulty* decision. See *Post v. Lunney,* 261 So.2d 146 (Fla., 1972). In *Post,* the Florida Supreme Court adopted § 332, including the public invitee provision. *Id.* at 148. It pointed out that the *McNulty* mutual benefit test was too narrow and had the potential to cause unjust results. *Id.* at 149.

For example, it would prohibit recovery for damages due to ordinary negligence to a "window-shopping" visitor to a store, while permitting recovery to a person who made a purchase, however small. To avoid these and similar results, "the economic benefit theory has been strained to the breaking point." [*Id.,* quoting *Smith v. Montgomery Ward & Co.,* 232 So.2d 195, 198 (Fla.App., 1970).]

The Florida court applied the public invitee provision of § 332 to the case. *Id.* at 148. It concluded that the plaintiff was an invitee because she had been invited to enter property opened to members of the public for tours. *Id.* at 148–149.

The recognized law of Michigan is more consistent with the decision in *Post* than it is with the decision in *McNulty.* We have long recognized that one could be an invitee without benefiting the owner or being on the property for a commercial purpose. That principle is contained in the public invitee provision of § 332. Therefore, as the Florida court did in *Post,* this Court should find that the public invitee provision of § 332 is applicable to this plaintiff. The majority recognizes that most jurisdictions have adopted the public invitee definition provided in § 332. However, it states that our role is "not simply to 'count heads.'" Op. at 96. I agree that we should not "simply count heads," but neither should we "bury our heads in the sand" to avoid recognizing that our common law includes the public-invitee definition of an invitee.

C

Michigan's definition of a common-law invitee is identical to that contained in § 332, and § 332 has been, at least implicitly, adopted by *Preston.* However, even if I were to agree with the majority that the Restatement rule is not the law, public policy supports adoption of the Restatement view at this time. As previously stated, our common law is a flexible body of principles and is adaptable to changes in public policy. *Beech Grove, supra.* The application of the public invitee provision to this case is entirely consistent with that view. It is responsive to the public interest that is implicated when premises are opened to the public. Furthermore, § 332 provides greater protection to the public without unduly burdening property owners.

I agree with the Indiana Court of Appeals when it stated:

> The public invitee test set out in Restatement section 332(2) would require that the occupant open his premises to the public or to some broad segment of it. Thus, it would not extend invitee status to social guests. When premises are opened to the public, their use and condition begin to affect the public interest, so that it is reasonable for courts to impose upon the occupant a standard of reasonable care toward those members of the public who enter for the purpose for which they were invited. Prosser, [*Business visitors and invitees,* 26 Minn. L. R. 573, 587 (1942)]. The occupant does not lose control of his property; he can withdraw the invitation or restrict entry as he sees fit. *Id.* Neither does he owe a duty of reasonable care to the public in general. The test would further require that the visitor enter the premises for the particular purpose for which the occupant has encouraged the public to do so. It is this latter fact which raises the inference that the occupant will use reasonable care to keep the premises safe for the visitor.

* * *

Given the public interest involved and our recognition of the implication of safety which arises when the public is encouraged to enter premises for a particular purpose, we conclude that the public invitee test is a proper guide for determining invitee status. [*Fleischer v. Hebrew Orthodox Congregation,* 504 N.E.2d 320, 323 (Ind.App., 1987).]

CONCLUSION

The public invitee provision of § 332 accurately reflects the common law of Michigan. It was adopted by this Court in *Preston* and should be applied here. Furthermore, it reflects the sound public policy of protecting members of the public when premises are open to them.

For the above stated reasons, we hold that persons on church premises for other than commercial purposes are licensees and not invitees. Accordingly, we reverse the decision of the Court of Appeals. We remand this case to the Court of Appeals for consideration of the other issues raised by plaintiff in her appeal which were not resolved by the Court of Appeals in light of its analysis of the present issue.

MICHAEL F. CAVANAGH, J., concurred with MARILYN J. KELLY, J.

Exercise 2-11 Using Policy to Support Legal Arguments

A number of jurisdictions have rejected the common law classifications for land owners and possessors and instead require that an owner, possessor, or occupier of land is held to a duty of reasonable care under all the circumstances. When courts reject a long standing doctrine, or extend or revise a rule of law, they frequently base such decisions on public policy. Therefore, when a lawyer desires to advance a novel theory, or advocate for a shift or change in the law, or for the extension of a rule to a new set of circumstance, she will frequently base such an argument on public policy. Identifying, understanding, and using policy in legal argument is thus an important skill. It is also challenging, because policy arguments are often more complicated than simply applying a set rule or series of cases, because, for example, there may be competing policy interests, requiring not only application of the policy argument advanced by the lawyer, but also an understanding of the relative importance of the various policies that might apply to the scenario, and a basis for arguing to the court that one policy concern is more critical or applicable than another. One of the steps you can take toward acquiring these skills is to learn to recognize a policy argument when it is articulated by the court in an opinion.

A particularly famous case rejecting the common law classifications, and instead requiring a duty of reasonable care, is *Rowland v. Christian*, set out below. As you read *Rowland*, consider:

1. What reasons (including policy based reasons) does the court give for rejecting the common law classifications? Do you agree or disagree with the reasons?

2. What reasons (including policy based reasons) support the use of the common law classifications? Do you agree or disagree with the reasons for maintaining such classifications?

3. What standard would you adopt? Why? What policy or policies support your decision?

Rowland v. Christian

69 Cal.2d 108 (1968)

Plaintiff appeals from a summary judgment for defendant Nancy Christian in this personal injury action.

In his complaint plaintiff alleged that about November 1, 1963, Miss Christian told the lessors of her apartment that the knob of the cold water faucet on the bathroom basin was cracked and should be replaced; that on November 30, 1963, plaintiff entered the apartment at the invitation of Miss Christian; that he was injured while using the bathroom fixtures, suffering severed tendons and nerves of his right hand; and that he has incurred medical and hospital expenses. He further alleged that the bathroom fixtures were dangerous, that Miss Christian was aware of the dangerous condition, and that his injuries were proximately caused by the negligence of Miss Christian.... Miss Christian's affidavit in support of the motion for summary judgment alleged facts showing that plaintiff was a social guest in her apartment when, as he was using the bathroom, the porcelain handle of one of the water faucets broke in his hand causing injuries to his hand and that plaintiff had used the bathroom on a prior occasion. In opposition to the motion for summary judgment, plaintiff filed an affidavit stating that immediately prior to the accident he told Miss Christian that he was going to use the bathroom facilities, that she had known for two weeks prior to the accident that the faucet handle that caused injury was cracked, that she warned the manager of the building of the condition, that nothing was done to repair the condition of the handle, that she did not say anything to plaintiff as to the condition of the handle, and that when plaintiff turned off the faucet the handle broke in his hands severing the tendons and medial nerve in his right hand.

* * *

In the instant case, Miss Christian's affidavit and admissions made by plaintiff show that plaintiff was a social guest and that he suffered injury when the faucet handle broke; they do not show that the faucet handle crack was obvious or even nonconcealed. Without in any way contradicting her affidavit or his own admissions, plaintiff at trial could establish that she was aware of the condition and realized or should have realized that it involved an unreasonable risk of harm to him, that defendant should have expected that he would not discover the danger, that she did not exercise reasonable care to eliminate the danger or warn him of it, and that he did not know or have reason to know of the danger. Plaintiff also could establish, without contradicting Miss Christian's affidavit or his admissions, that the crack was not obvious and was concealed. Under the circumstances, a summary judgment is proper in this case only if, after proof of such facts, a judgment would be required as a matter of law for Miss Christian. The record supports no such conclusion.

Section 1714 of the Civil Code provides: 'Every one is responsible, not only for the result of his willful acts, but also for an injury occasioned to another by his want of ordinary care or skill in the management of his property or person, except so far as the latter has, willfully or by want of ordinary care, brought the injury upon himself.' * * * This code section, which has been unchanged in our law since 1872, states a civil law and not a common law principle. (*Fernandez v. Consolidated Fisheries, Inc.*, 98 Cal.App.2d 91, 96, 219 P.2d 73.)

Nevertheless, some common law judges and commentators have urged that the principle embodied in this code section serves as the foundation of our negligence law.... California cases have occasionally stated a similar view: 'All persons are required to use ordinary care to prevent others being injured as the result of their conduct.' (*Hilyar v. Union Ice Co.*, 45 Cal.2d 30, 36, 286 P.2d 21; *Warner v. Santa Catalina Island Co.*, 44 Cal.2d 310, 317, 282 P.2d 12; see also *Green v. General Petroleum Corp.*, 205 Cal. 328, 333, 270 P. 952, 60 A.L.R. 475; *Perkins v. Blauth*, 163 Cal. 782, 786, 127 P. 50; *McCall v. Pacific Mail S.S. Co.*, 123 Cal. 42, 44, 55 P. 706; *Edler v. Sepulveda Park Apts.*, 141 Cal.App.2d 675, 680, 297 P.2d 508; *Copfer v. Golden*, 135 Cal.App.2d 623, 627–628, 288 P.2d 90; cf. *Dillon v. Legg*, Cal., 69 Cal.Rptr. 72, 76, 441 P.2d 912, 916.) Although it is true that some exceptions have been made to the general principle that a person is liable for injuries caused by his failure to exercise reasonable care in the circumstances, it is clear that in the absence of statutory provision declaring an exception to the fundamental principle enunciated by section 1714 of the Civil Code, no such exception should be made unless clearly supported by public policy. (*Lipman v. Brisbane Elementary Sch. Dist.*, 55 Cal.2d 224, 229–230, 11 Cal.Rptr. 97, 359 P.2d 465; *Muskopf v. Corning Hospital Dist.*, 55 Cal.2d 211, 213 et seq., 11 Cal.Rptr. 89, 359 P.2d 457; *Malloy v. Fong*, 37 Cal.2d 356, 366, 232 P.2d 241.)

One of the areas where this court and other courts have departed from the fundamental concept that a man is liable for injuries caused by his carelessness is with regard to the liability of a possessor of land for injuries to persons who have entered upon that land. It has been suggested that the special rules regarding liability of the possessor of land are due to historical considerations stemming from the high place which land has traditionally held in English and American thought, the dominance and prestige of the landowning class in England during the formative period of the rules governing the possessor's liability, and the heritage of feudalism. (2 Harper and James, The Law of Torts, supra, p. 1432.)

The departure from the fundamental rule of liability for negligence has been accomplished by classifying the plaintiff either as a trespasser, licensee, or invitee and then adopting special rules as to the duty owed by the possessor to each of the classifications. Generally speaking a trespasser is a person who enters or remains upon land of another without a privilege to do so; a licensee is a person like a social guest who is not an invitee and who is privileged to enter or remain upon land by virtue of the possessor's consent, and an invitee is a business visitor who is invited or permitted to enter or remain on the land for a purpose directly or indirectly connected with business dealings between them. (*Oettinger v. Stewart*, 24 Cal.2d 133, 136, 148 P.2d 19, 156 A.L.R. 1221.)

Although the invitor owes the invitee a duty to exercise ordinary care to avoid injuring him (*Oettinger v. Stewart*, supra, 24 Cal.2d 133, 137, 148 P.2d 19, 156 A.L.R. 1221; *Hinds v. Wheadon*, 19 Cal.2d 458, 460–461, 121 P.2d 724), the general rule is that a trespasser and licensee or social guest are obliged to take the premises as they find them insofar as any alleged defective condition thereon may exist, and that the possessor of the land owes them only the duty of refraining from wanton or willful injury. (*Palmquist v. Mercer*, 43 Cal.2d 92, 102, 272 P.2d 26; see *Oettinger v. Stewart*, supra, 24 Cal.2d 133, 137 et seq., 148 P.2d 19, 156 A.L.R. 1221.) The ordinary justification for the general rule severely restricting the occupier's liability to social guests is based on the theory that the guest should not expect special precautions to be made on his account and that if the host does not inspect and maintain his property the guest should not expect this to be done on his account. (See 2 Harper and James, The Law of Torts, supra, p. 1477.)

An increasing regard for human safety has led to a retreat from this position.... *** In refusing to adopt the rules relating to the liability of a possessor of land for the law of admiralty, the United States Supreme Court stated: "The distinctions which the common law draws between licensee and invitee were inherited from a culture deeply rooted to the land, a culture which traced many of its standards to a heritage of feudalism. In an effort to do justice in an industrialized urban society, with its complex economic and individual relationships, modern common-law courts have found it necessary to formulate increasingly subtle verbal refinements, to create subclassifications among traditional common-law categories, and to delineate fine gradations in the standards of care which the landowner owes to each. Yet even within a single jurisdiction, the classifications and subclassifications bred by the common law have produced confusion and conflict. As new distinctions have been spawned, older ones have become obscured. Through this semantic morass the common law has moved, unevenly and with hesitation, towards imposing on owners and occupiers a single duty of reasonable care in all circumstances." (Footnotes omitted.) (*Kermarec v. Compagnie Generale*, 358 U.S. 625, 630–631, 79 S.Ct. 406, 410, 3 L.Ed.2d 550; see also *Jones v. United States*, 362 U.S. 257, 266, 80 S.Ct. 725, 4 L.Ed.2d 697; 2 Harper and James, The Law of Torts, supra, 1430 et seq.; Prosser, Business Visitors and Invitees, 26 Minn.L.Rev. 573; Marsh, The History and Comparative Law of Invitees, Licensees and Trespassers, 69 L.Q.Rev. 182, 359.)

* * *

There is another fundamental objection to the approach to the question of the possessor's liability on the basis of the common law distinctions based upon the status of the injured party as a trespasser, licensee, or invitee. Complexity can be borne and confusion remedied where the underlying principles governing liability are based upon proper considerations. Whatever may have been the historical justifications for the common law distinctions, it is clear that those distinctions are not justified in the light of our modern society and that the complexity and confusion which has arisen is not due to difficulty in applying the original common law rules—they are all too easy to apply in their original formulation—but is due to the attempts to apply just rules in our modern society within the ancient terminology.

* * *

A man's life or limb does not become less worthy of protection by the law nor a loss less worthy of compensation under the law because he has come upon the land of another without permission or with permission but without a business purpose. Reasonable people do not ordinarily vary their conduct depending upon such matters, and to focus upon the status of the injured party as a trespasser, licensee, or invitee in order to determine the question whether the landowner has a duty of care, is contrary to our modern social mores and humanitarian values. The common law rules obscure rather than illuminate the proper considerations which should govern determination of the question of duty.

It bears repetition that the basic policy of this state set forth by the Legislature in section 1714 of the Civil Code is that everyone is responsible for an injury caused to another by his want of ordinary care or skill in the management of his property. The factors which may in particular cases warrant departure from this fundamental principle do not warrant the wholesale immunities resulting from the common law classifications, and we are satisfied that continued adherence to the common law distinctions can only lead to injustice or, if we are to avoid injustice, further fictions with the resulting complexity and confusion. We decline to follow and perpetuate such rigid classifications. The proper test to be applied to the liability of the possessor of land in accordance with section 1714 of the Civil Code is whether in the management of his property he has acted as a reasonable man in view of the probability of injury to others, and, although the plaintiff's status as a trespasser, licensee, or invitee may in the light of the facts giving rise to such status have some bearing on the question of liability, the status is not determinative.

Once the ancient concepts as to the liability of the occupier of land are stripped away, the status of the plaintiff relegated to its proper place in determining such liability, and ordinary principles of negligence applied, the result in the instant case presents no substantial difficulties. As we have seen, when we view the matters presented on the motion for summary judgment as we must, we must assume defendant Miss Christian was aware that the faucet handle was defective and dangerous, that the defect was not obvious, and that plaintiff was about to come in contact with the defective condition, and under the undisputed facts she neither remedied the condition nor warned plaintiff of it. Where the occupier of land is aware of a concealed condition involving in the absence of precautions an unreasonable risk of harm to those coming in contact with it and is aware that a person on the premises is about to come in contact with it, the trier of fact can reasonably conclude that a failure to warn or to repair the condition constitutes negligence. Whether or not a guest has a right to expect that his host will remedy dangerous conditions on his account, he should reasonably be entitled to rely upon a warning of the dangerous condition so that he, like the host, will be in a position to take special precautions when he comes in contact with it.

It may be noted that by carving further exceptions out of the traditional rules relating to the liability to licensees or social guests, other jurisdictions reach the same result … and that the result might even be reached by a continued expansion of the definition of the term 'invitee' to include all persons invited upon the land who may thereby be led to believe that the host will exercise for their protection the ordinary care of a reasonable man (cf. *O'Keefe v. South End Rowing Club*, 64 Cal.2d 729, 737–739, 51 Cal.Rptr. 534, 414 P.2d 830, 16 A.L.R.3d 1). However, to approach the problem in these manners would only add to the confusion, complexity, and fictions which have resulted from the common law distinctions.

The judgment is reversed.

TRAYNOR, C.J., and TOBRINER, MOSK and SULLIVAN, JJ., concur.

BURKE, Justice (dissenting).

I dissent. In determining the liability of the occupier or owner of land for injuries, the distinctions between trespassers, licensees and invitees have been developed and applied by the courts over a period of many years. They supply a reasonable and workable approach to the problems involved, and one which provides the degree of stability and predictability so highly prized in the law. The unfortunate alternative, it appears to me, is the route taken by the majority in their opinion in this case; that such issues are to be decided on a case by case basis under the application of the basic law of negligence, bereft of the guiding principles and precedent which the law has heretofore attached by virtue of the relationship of the parties to one another.

Liability for negligence turns upon whether a duty of care is owed, and if so, the extent thereof. Who can doubt that the corner grocery, the large department store, or the financial institution owes a greater duty of care to one whom it has invited to enter its premises as a prospective customer of its wares or services than it owes to a trespasser seeking to enter after the close of business hours and for a nonbusiness or even an antagonistic purpose? I do not think it unreasonable or unfair that a social guest (classified by the law as a licensee, as was plaintiff here) should be obliged to take the premises in the same condition as his host finds them or permits them to be. Surely a homeowner should not be obliged to hover over his guests with warnings of possible dangers to be found in the condition of the home (e.g., waxed floors, slipping rugs, toys in unexpected places, etc., etc.). Yet today's decision appears to open the door to potentially unlimited liability despite the purpose and circumstances motivating the plaintiff in entering the premises of another, and despite the caveat of the majority that the status of the parties may 'have some bearing on the question of liability …,' whatever the future may show that language to mean.

In my view, it is not a proper function of this court to overturn the learning, wisdom and experience of the past in this field. Sweeping modifications of tort liability law fall more suitably within the domain of the Legislature, before which all affected interests can be heard and which can enact statutes providing uniform standards and guidelines for the future.

I would affirm the judgment for defendant.

McCOMB, J., concurs.

Exercise 2-12 Law Practice

Does the jurisdiction where you intend to practice maintain the common law classifications? If not, what is the duty owed to entrants of land in premises liability cases?

Premises Liability for Third Party Acts

In addition to suits for injuries caused by the possessor's activities or the condition of the premises, owners and possessors are also frequently subject to litigation for injuries caused by the acts of third parties. For example, a person assaulted in a parking lot might sue the owner of the lot for providing inadequate security, or, as you will see in the next few cases, a tenant might sue an owner when he is assaulted by a third party in the common areas of his apartment building, or a student injured by a pedophile while on school grounds might sue the school district. In most of these types of cases the third party who directly caused the harm (the assaulter or pedophile) typically has few or no resources available, including insurance, to pay for any of the injured party's damages, and so the injured party will file suit against other potentially responsible parties (the owner or possessor of the property where the injury occurred) because these parties have sufficient resources to pay for the injury. These parties are sometimes called the "deep pocket."

In the next section you will be asked to consider the factors courts use to determine whether land owners and possessors should be required to take steps to protect persons on their premises from third party criminal acts. In such cases, the existence and extent of duty are both frequently at issue.

Skill Focus: Synthesizing Materials

Remember from Chapter One that sometimes you will need to consult more than one case to develop a complete picture of the rule of law and a complete understanding of its application. For example, sometimes a rule of law will be developed by a series of cases; courts opinions in later cases may use the facts and circumstances of a subsequent case to expand or narrow the rule, clarify the meaning of the rule or one of its components, or add a new or different requirement to the rule. Similarly, when presented with a statute a court may interpret its provisions or explain how the statute applies to the case the court is considering. As a lawyer, it will be your job to figure out how all of the sources fit together to form the rule the court should apply to your case. This is called synthesis — because you are combining materials from several different sources into one unified statement (and explanation) of the rule. As you read material from multiple sources covering the same topic (cases, statutes, regulations, etc.) and make an effort to synthesize the materials, it may help you to consider the following:

1. Does this source add anything new to my understanding of the rule?

2. Does this source change my understanding of the rule?

3. Does this source explain an aspect of the rule that was previously unexplained?

4. Does this source offer any new examples of how the rule should be applied?

Exercise 2-13 Synthesizing Materials to Determine the Existence and Extent of the Duty Owed

To resolve the issues presented by the following problem, you will need to read and synthesize the two cases that are printed after the problem.

Beatrice and Vivian were romantically involved with the same man. This led to several confrontations between the two women, as well as an exchange of threats. One morning Beatrice called the police and reported that a prowler was at the "back part" of her apartment. Officer Horvath, a police officer, and her partner arrived at Beatrice's apartment about ten minutes after receiving the call. The officers did not see anyone near the front door, which, according to the officers, was locked. Immediately after Officer Horvath knocked on the front door, Vivian exited through the rear door of the apartment. When the officers entered Beatrice's apartment, they found Beatrice lying on the floor, stabbed to death. Vivian pled guilty to Beatrice's murder and is currently serving her sentence. The locks on Beatrice's back door were faulty. Beatrice had submitted two service requests to Realty Co. asking it to repair the locks on her back door. Realty Co. failed to repair the locks or to acknowledge Beatrice's requests in any way. Beatrice's killer, Vivian, entered her apartment through the unlocked back door.

Beatrice's mother, on behalf of Beatrice's estate, filed suit against Realty Company, Inc., the leasing company for the apartment, and Levi Brock, the apartment owner, alleging negligence. The basis of the complaint was that Levi and Realty Co., as owner and lessor of the apartment rented to Beatrice, (1) failed to maintain the locks on Beatrice's back door in a safe condition, and (2) failed to take sufficient security measures to protect the tenants in the apartment building.

1. Did Levi Brock and/or Realty Co. owe Beatrice such a duty? Do you need additional information to make this determination? If so, what information do you need?

2. If there was a duty owed, what is the scope of the duty? What actions are necessary? What steps must be taken?

3. If there was a duty owed, what did Levi Brock and/or Realty Co. do that was a breach of their duty?

As you attempt to synthesize the next two cases, it may help you to think about these issues more broadly. In other words, you may want to think more generally about landowner and possessor duties. If so, you could reframe the questions like this:

1. When (in what circumstances) does a landowner or possessor have a duty to protect a person from, or guard against, harm caused by a third party?

2.   What is the extent (scope) of the duty owed by the landowner or possesor? What actions are necessary? What steps must be taken?

Isaacs v. Huntington Memorial Hospital

38 Cal.3d 112, 695 P.2d 653 (1985)

Plaintiff, Mervyn Isaacs, is an anesthesiologist affiliated with defendant, Huntington Memorial Hospital, a private hospital located in Pasadena. On March 26, 1978, at approximately 8:30 p.m., Dr. Isaacs arrived at the hospital with his wife. He parked their car in the hospital's research parking lot which was located across the street from the emergency room and the physicians' entrance to the hospital. The lot was open "to anyone who wished to park there." While his wife was visiting a friend at the hospital, Dr. Isaacs saw some of his patients who were to undergo surgery.

About 10 p.m., Dr. Isaacs, his wife and a family friend left the building and went to the Isaacs' car. While Dr. Isaacs was moving some belongings from the back seat to the trunk, Ms. Isaacs and the friend got into the car. As he was closing the lid to the trunk, Dr. Isaacs was grabbed from behind by a man who held a gun to the doctor's chest. Dr. Isaacs put up his hands and began to turn around very slowly. At that point, the assailant shot the doctor in the chest. The gunman then fled the scene and was never apprehended.

As a result of the shooting, Dr. Isaacs sustained severe injuries, including the loss of a kidney. He and his wife brought an action against the hospital.... The Isaacs alleged that the hospital failed to provide adequate security measures to protect its invitees and licensees against the criminal acts of third persons on its premises. *** [At trial] plaintiffs introduced the following evidence. Harold Bastrup, a security consultant, testified that the hospital was located in a "high crime area." He based this conclusion on incident reports from the hospital and the Pasadena Police Department. Numerous assaults or threatened assaults had occurred on the hospital premises during the three years preceding Dr. Isaacs's shooting.

Among those incidents were several threatened assaults with deadly weapons in the emergency room area across from the research parking lot. In September of 1977, a man pulled out a knife and threatened to cut another person's head off. A security guard, displaying a baton, attempted to talk the assailant into dropping the knife. The guard's efforts were futile until he pulled out his gun. In January of 1977, a man with a knife threatened to assault a person in the hospital emergency room. In March of that same year, a person brandished a rifle in the emergency room. The security guards were able to disarm him.

Plaintiffs also presented evidence of thefts in the vicinity. In August of 1976, a purse snatching occurred near the hospital. In September of 1977, a person grabbed money from a counter in the hospital and ran away.

In addition, a security guard for the hospital testified that incidents involving harassment of persons in the emergency area were "very common." In September of 1977, one such incident, which occurred in front of the emergency room, involved 10 to 12 male adults who were "disturbing the peace [and] drinking."

Testimony was also offered concerning the danger associated with emergency room areas. David Wright, the former director of security at a different hospital, testified that emergency rooms, surrounding areas, and nearby parking lots are the areas with the "highest potential for violent acts." He noted that such areas are "subject to a lot of criminal elements."

Hospital personnel conceded that the emergency room area was frequented by persons under the influence of drugs and alcohol. Dr. Charles Bergquist, who was at the hospital on the night of the shooting, testified that upon entering the hospital that night, "many people [were] milling around ... drinking out of bottles and brown paper packages." Dr. Bergquist described the scene as "scary" and "physically threatening." He also testified that this was not unusual activity.

Plaintiffs also presented evidence concerning security. At the time of the shooting, the hospital had three security guards on duty. One guard was stationed inside the emergency room entrance at the visitor control desk. Another guard was stationed in the employee parking lot, which was located a considerable distance from both the emergency area and the research parking lot. The third guard was on roving patrol on the second floor in one of the buildings.

The guards were unarmed. They wore uniforms and carried flashlights but no nightsticks or mace. Guard dogs were not used.

The hospital also had numerous television cameras at various locations around the hospital to monitor activity in those areas. With the exception of one camera which covered the employee parking lot, all of the cameras were used to view activity inside the hospital.

An escort service was available to protect hospital staff. However, there was conflicting evidence as to whether this service had ever been used by or was known to the doctors.

Evidence was presented concerning the lighting in the research parking lot on the night of the incident. Two lights on the side of the research building, which normally provided some of the light in the research parking lot, were not lit. The testimony as to the lighting conditions in the research parking lot was in conflict. Two witnesses described it as "poor," "dim," and "very dimly lighted." However, two other witnesses said it was "good" and "fair to good."

Finally, plaintiffs presented testimony from two experts in security matters. Both concluded that the hospital's security on the night of the shooting was "totally inadequate." They based their conclusions on (1) the insufficient number of guards, in view of the responsibilities assigned to them and the size of the premises; (2) inadequate administration of the security force; (3) failure to arm the guards with defensive weapons; (4) inadequate television monitoring of the parking lot areas; (5) a lack of any means of communication with the police department on an emergency basis; and (6) an absence of signs warning that the area was guarded. One expert concluded that these aspects rendered the research parking lot "totally devoid of any deterrents or security" on the night of the shooting.

At the close of plaintiffs' case in chief, the hospital moved for nonsuit. The trial court granted the motion and entered judgment in the hospital's favor on the ground that there was insufficient evidence to find the hospital liable.

The court concluded that "plaintiffs failed to introduce evidence essential to prove the following elements of their case: (a) Notice of prior crimes of the same or similar nature in the same or similar portion of defendant's premises; (b) The reasonable foreseeability of the subject crime occurring; (c) The minimum standards of security for premises similar to those of defendant for the period of time and locality involved; [and] (d) Any proof of causation...."

Plaintiffs appeal from that judgment and from the summary judgment entered in favor of Exchange.

I.

The primary question presented by this appeal is whether foreseeability, for the purposes of establishing a landowner's liability for the criminal acts of third persons on the landowner's property, may be established other than by evidence of prior similar incidents on those premises. Since foreseeability is of primary importance in establishing the element of duty (*Weirum v. RKO General, Inc.* (1975) 15 Cal.3d 40, 46, 123 Cal.Rptr. 468, 539 P.2d 36), it is helpful to review the law in this area.

It is well settled that an owner of land has a duty "to take affirmative action to control the wrongful acts of third persons which threaten invitees where the [owner] has reasonable cause to anticipate such acts and the probability of injury resulting therefrom." (*Taylor v. Centennial Bowl, Inc.* (1966) 65 Cal.2d 114, 121, 52 Cal.Rptr. 561, 416 P.2d 793.) This duty is premised on the special relationship between the landowner and the invitee (see Rest.2d Torts, §§ 314A, 315) and the general duty to exercise reasonable care in the management of one's property (see Civ.Code, § 1714, subd. (a);5 *Peterson v. San Francisco Community College Dist.* (1984) 36 Cal.3d 799, 806–807, 205 Cal.Rptr. 842, 685 P.2d 1193).

"It has long been recognized that 'a possessor of land who holds it open to the public for entry for business purposes is subject to liability to members of the public while they are upon the land for such a purpose, for physical harm caused by the accidental, negligent or intentionally harmful acts of third persons ... and by the failure of the possessor to exercise reasonable care to (a) discover that such acts are being done or are likely to be done, or (b) give a warning adequate to enable the visitors to avoid the harm, or otherwise to protect them against it.'" (*Peterson v. San Francisco Community College Dist., supra,* 36 Cal.3d at p. 807, 205 Cal.Rptr. 842, 685 P.2d 1193, quoting Rest.2d Torts, § 344.)

The Restatement Second of Torts, section 344, comment (f) further details the circumstances under which such a duty arises: "Since the [owner of land] is not an insurer of the visitor's safety, he is ordinarily under no duty to exercise any care until he knows or has reason to know that the acts of the third person are occurring, or are about to occur. He may, however, know or have reason to know, from past experience, that there is a likelihood of conduct on the part of third persons in general which is likely to endanger the safety of the visitor, even though he has no reason to expect it on the part of any particular individual. *If the place or character of his business, or his past experience, is such that he should reasonably anticipate careless or criminal conduct on the part of third persons, either generally or at some particular time, he may be under a duty to take precautions against it, and to provide a reasonably sufficient number of servants to afford a reasonable protection.*" (Italics added.)

Whether such a duty exists is a question of law to be determined on a case-by-case basis. (*Weirum v. RKO General, Inc., supra,* 15 Cal.3d at p. 46, 123 Cal.Rptr. 468, 539 P.2d 36.) In considering whether one owes another a duty of care, several factors must be weighed, including: "[T]he foreseeability of harm to the plaintiff, the degree of certainty that the plaintiff suffered injury, the closeness of the connection between the defendant's conduct and the injury suffered, the moral blame attached to the defendant's conduct, the policy of preventing future harm, the extent of the burden to the defendant and consequences to the community of imposing a duty to exercise care with resulting liability for breach, and the availability, cost, and prevalence of insurance for the risk involved. [Citations.] (*Rowland v. Christian* (1968) 69 Cal.2d 108, 113, 70 Cal.Rptr. 97, 443 P.2d 561, 32 A.L.R.3d 496; [citations].)" (*Peterson v. San Francisco Community College Dist., supra,* 36 Cal.3d at p. 806, 205 Cal.Rptr. 842, 685 P.2d 1193.)

It is clear that foreseeability is but one factor to be weighed in determining whether a landowner owes a duty in a particular case. "In this balancing process, foreseeability is an elastic factor. (2 Harper & James [Law of Torts (1956)] §18.2, at p. 1026.) The degree of foreseeability necessary to warrant the finding of a duty will thus vary from case to case. For example, in cases where the burden of preventing future harm is great, a high degree of foreseeability may be required. [Citation.] On the other hand, in cases where there are strong policy reasons for preventing the harm, or the harm can be prevented by simple means, a lesser degree of foreseeability may be required." (*Gomez v. Ticor* (1983) 145 Cal.App.3d 622, 629–630, 193 Cal.Rptr. 600.) Thus, foreseeability is a somewhat flexible concept.

A recent line of Court of Appeal cases has rigidified the foreseeability concept in situations involving a landowner's liability for the criminal acts of third persons against invitees. Those cases have established the rule that "in the absence of prior similar incidents, an owner of land is not bound to anticipate the criminal activities of third persons, particularly where the wrongdoer was a complete stranger to both the landowner and the victim and where the criminal activity leading to the injury came about precipitously." (*Wingard v. Safeway Stores, Inc.* (1981) 123 Cal.App.3d 37, 43, 176 Cal.Rptr. 320; accord *Anaya v. Turk* (1984) 151 Cal.App.3d 1092, 1099, 199 Cal.Rptr. 187; *Riley v. Marcus* (1981) 125 Cal.App.3d 103, 109 & fn. 2, 177 Cal.Rptr. 827; *Jamison v. Mark C. Bloome Co.* (1980) 112 Cal.App.3d 570, 578–580, 169 Cal.Rptr. 399; *Totten v. More Oakland Residential Housing, Inc.* (1976) 63 Cal.App.3d 538, 543, 134 Cal.Rptr. 29; *Rogers v. Jones* (1976) 56 Cal.App.3d 346, 351–352, 128 Cal.Rptr. 404; see also *Jubert v. Shalom Realty* (1982) 135 Cal.App.3d Supp. 1, 6, 185 Cal.Rptr. 641.)

This rule is fatally flawed in numerous respects. First, the rule leads to results which are contrary to public policy. The rule has the effect of discouraging landowners from taking adequate measures to protect premises which they know are dangerous. This result contravenes the policy of preventing future harm. Moreover, under the rule, the first victim always loses, while subsequent victims are permitted recovery. Such a result is not only unfair, but is inimical to the important policy of compensating injured parties (*Peterson v. San Francisco Community College Dist., supra,* 36 Cal.3d at p. 814, 205 Cal.Rptr. 842, 685 P.2d 1193). Surely, a landowner should not get one free assault before he can be held liable for criminal acts which occur on his property.

Second, a rule which limits evidence of foreseeability to prior similar criminal acts leads to arbitrary results and distinctions. (*Mullins v. Pine Manor College* (1983) 389 Mass. 47, 449 N.E.2d 331, 337, fn. 12.) Under this rule, there is uncertainty as to how "similar" the prior incidents must be to satisfy the rule. The rule raises a number of other troubling questions. For example, how close in time do the prior incidents have to be? How near in location must they be? The rule invites different courts to enunciate different standards of foreseeability based on their resolution of these questions.

Third, the rule erroneously equates foreseeability of a particular act with previous occurrences of similar acts. This court has already rejected that notion. "'The mere fact that a particular kind of an accident has not happened before does not ... show that such accident is one which might not reasonably have been anticipated.' [Citation.] Thus, the fortuitous absence of prior injury does not justify relieving defendant from responsibility for the foreseeable consequences of its acts." (*Weirum v. RKO General, Inc., supra,* 15 Cal.3d at p. 47, 123 Cal.Rptr. 468, 539 P.2d 36.)

Finally, the "prior similar incidents" rule improperly removes too many cases from the jury's consideration. It is well established that foreseeability is ordinarily a question of fact. (*Bigbee v. Pacific Tel. & Tel. Co.* (1983) 34 Cal.3d 49, 56, 192 Cal.Rptr. 857, 665 P.2d

947; *Weirum v. RKO General, Inc., supra,* 15 Cal.3d at p. 46, 123 Cal.Rptr. 468, 539 P.2d 36.) "It may be decided as a question of law only if, 'under the undisputed facts there is no room for a reasonable difference of opinion.' [Citations.]" (*Bigbee v. Pacific Tel. & Tel. Co., supra,* 34 Cal.3d at p. 56, 192 Cal.Rptr. 857, 665 P.2d 947.)

There is a general reluctance to remove foreseeability questions from the jury. (See *Cohen v. Southland Corp.* (1984) 157 Cal.App.3d 130, 140–141, 203 Cal.Rptr. 572.) Foreseeability "'is not to be measured by what is more probable than not, but includes whatever is likely enough in the setting of modern life that a reasonably thoughtful [person] would take account of it in guiding practical conduct.' [Citation.] One may be held accountable for creating even '"the risk of a slight possibility of injury if a reasonably prudent [person] would not do so."'" (*Bigbee v. Pacific Tel. & Tel. Co., supra,* 34 Cal.3d at p. 57, 192 Cal.Rptr. 857, 665 P.2d 947.)

Thus, foreseeability is determined in light of all the circumstances and not by a rigid application of a mechanical "prior similars" rule. (Cf. *Bigbee v. Pacific Tel. & Tel. Co., supra,* 34 Cal.3d at pp. 57–58, 192 Cal.Rptr. 857, 665 P.2d 947.) As this court has held, "what is required to be foreseeable is the general character of the event or harm ... not its precise nature or manner of occurrence." (*Ibid.*) Prior similar incidents are helpful to determine foreseeability but they are not necessary. A rule that limits evidence of foreseeability to prior similar incidents deprives the jury of its role in determining that question.

A number of Courts of Appeal have properly recognized that evidence of prior similar incidents is not the sine qua non of a finding of foreseeability. (*Kwaitkowski v. Superior Trading Co.* (1981) 123 Cal.App.3d 324, 329, 176 Cal.Rptr. 494; *Gomez v. Ticor, supra,* 145 Cal.App.3d 622, 630, 193 Cal.Rptr. 600; see also *Cohen v. Southland Corp., supra,* 157 Cal.App.3d 130, 140–142, 203 Cal.Rptr. 572.) These cases express the better view.

In *Kwaitkowski v. Superior Trading Co., supra,* 123 Cal.App.3d 324, 176 Cal.Rptr. 494, the plaintiff was raped and robbed in the lobby of her apartment building. She sued her landlords, alleging that they had notice that (1) the lock of the lobby entrance door was defective at the time of the attack, (2) the apartment building was in a "high crime area," and (3) that an assault and robbery had occurred previously in another common area of the building. The trial court sustained the landlords' demurrer without leave to amend. (*Id.,* at pp. 325–326, 176 Cal.Rptr. 494.)

In reversing the judgment of dismissal, the Court of Appeal noted that "[f]oreseeability does not require prior identical or even similar events." (123 Cal.App.3d at p. 329, 176 Cal.Rptr. 494.) The court reasoned that "[w]hether a given criminal act is within the class of injuries which is reasonably foreseeable depends on the totality of the circumstances and not on arbitrary distinctions...." (*Id.,* at p. 329, 176 Cal.Rptr. 494.) In concluding that the attack was foreseeable, the court focused on the defective nature of the premises (a broken lock), the easy access that strangers had to the interior of the building, the neighborhood in which the apartment building was located, and the prior assault and robbery. (*Id.,* at pp. 328–329, 176 Cal.Rptr. 494.)

Prior incidents, whether similar or not, ... [a]re helpful in establishing foreseeability, but [are] not required to satisfy this element. [O]ther types of evidence may also establish foreseeability, such as the nature, condition and location of the defendant's premises. In analyzing foreseeability in this manner, ... the well-settled rule [is] that "what is required to be foreseeable is the general character of the event or harm ... not its precise nature or manner of occurrence." (*Bigbee v. Pacific Tel. & Tel. Co., supra,* 34 Cal.3d at pp. 57–58, 192 Cal.Rptr. 857, 665 P.2d 947.)

II.

In the present case, this court must determine whether the trial court's invocation of the "prior similar incidents" rule was a proper basis on which to grant defendant's motion for nonsuit.

A judgment of nonsuit removes the case from the trier of fact. For this reason, courts have traditionally taken a very restrictive view of the circumstances under which such a judgment is proper. Thus, it is established that a trial court may not grant a defendant's motion for nonsuit if the plaintiff's evidence would support a jury verdict in the plaintiff's favor. (*Campbell v. General Motors Corp.* (1982) 32 Cal.3d 112, 117–118, 184 Cal.Rptr. 891, 649 P.2d 224; *Ewing v. Cloverleaf Bowl* (1978) 20 Cal.3d 389, 395, 143 Cal.Rptr. 13, 572 P.2d 1155.) ... " 'The mere fact that other inferences adverse to plaintiff might be drawn does not render the inference favorable to plaintiff too conjectural or speculative for consideration [by the jury].' [Citations.]" (*Id.*, at p. 121, 184 Cal.Rptr. 891, 649 P.2d 224.)

The totality of the circumstances in this case strongly suggests that the foreseeability of an assault in the research parking lot should have been submitted to the jury. The hospital was located in a high crime area. Several threatened assaults had occurred in the emergency room area directly across from the research parking lot. There had been thefts in the area. A hospital security guard testified that incidents involving "harassment" were "very common." According to one expert witness, emergency room facilities and surrounding areas are inherently dangerous. Parking lots, by their very nature, create an "especial temptation and opportunity for criminal misconduct...." (Prosser, Torts, *supra*, § 33, p. 174; see *Gomez v. Ticor, supra,* 145 Cal.App.3d at p. 628, 193 Cal.Rptr. 600.)

Further, two of the lights on the building adjacent to the research parking lot, which normally illuminated that area, were not working on the evening Dr. Isaacs was shot. Two witnesses testified that the research parking lot itself had poor lighting. "That a mugger thrives in dark places is a matter of common knowledge." (*Slapin v. Los Angeles International Airport* (1976) 65 Cal.App.3d 484, 488, 135 Cal.Rptr. 296.) In addition, the research parking lot was devoid of any security at the time of Dr. Isaacs's shooting. This contrasted markedly with the security at another parking lot on the hospital's premises, where a security guard was stationed during shift changes and activity was monitored by a television camera. This information, all of which was known or should have been known to the hospital, was sufficient to provide notice of a risk of an assault in the research parking lot.

Under these circumstances, the trial court erred in concluding *as a matter of law* that Dr. Isaacs's assault was not foreseeable. " '[J]ust as we may not rely upon our private judgment on this issue, so the trial court may not impose its private judgment upon a situation, such as this, in which reasonable minds may differ.' [Citation.]" (*Bigbee v. Pacific Tel. & Tel. Co., supra,* 34 Cal.3d at p. 59, 192 Cal.Rptr. 857, 665 P.2d 947.)

It is of no consequence that the injury to plaintiffs was brought about by the criminal acts of a third person. "If the likelihood that a third person may act in a particular manner is the hazard or one of the hazards which makes the actor negligent, such an act whether innocent, negligent, intentionally tortious, or criminal does not prevent the actor from being liable for harm caused thereby." (Rest.2d Torts, § 449; accord *Bigbee v. Pacific Tel. & Tel. Co., supra,* 34 Cal.3d at p. 58, 192 Cal.Rptr. 857, 665 P.2d 947; *Weirum v. RKO General, Inc., supra,* 15 Cal.3d at p. 47, 123 Cal.Rptr. 468, 539 P.2d 36.)

[I]t is evident that the hospital had a duty to take precautions to protect Dr. Isaacs from criminal assaults in the parking lot. The foreseeability of an assault was high in comparison to the minimal burden on the hospital to take security measures to ensure the safety of persons using the research parking lot.

The value to the community of imposing such a duty is manifest.... Although defendant's conduct may have been without moral blame, imposition of liability would further the policy of preventing future harm. The evidence clearly indicates that a duty existed.

Once a court finds that the defendant was under a duty to protect the plaintiff, it is for the factfinder to decide whether the security measures were reasonable under the circumstances. (See *Musgrove v. Ambrose Properties, supra,* 87 Cal.App.3d at p. 53, 150 Cal.Rptr. 722.) The jury must decide whether the security was adequate.

Since the evidence clearly indicates that a duty existed as a matter of law, the trial court erred in removing the case from the jury by granting the hospital's motion for nonsuit.

* * *

VI.

Foreseeability of harm should ordinarily be determined by a jury. That determination calls for the consideration of what is reasonable in light of all the circumstances. One such circumstance is whether the occurrence of prior similar incidents placed the defendant on notice that its security measures were not adequate to prevent harm to persons who use the defendant's premises. While prior similar incidents are helpful to determine foreseeability, they are not required to establish it. Other circumstances may also place the landowner on notice of a dangerous condition. A rule which limits proof of foreseeability to evidence of prior similar incidents automatically precludes recovery to first-injured victims. Such a rule is inherently unfair and contrary to public policy.

Plaintiffs' evidence strongly suggests that the jury could reasonably have concluded that the assault on Dr. Isaacs was foreseeable. Accordingly, the judgment of nonsuit is reversed and the case is remanded to the trial court for further proceedings consistent with the views expressed in this opinion.

As you read the next case, try to synthesize what you learn from the next case with what you've learned from *Issacs*. It may help to consider the following questions:

1. Does the opinion change or alter your view of whether Levi Brock and Realty Co. owed Beatrice any duty? In what way?

2. Does the opinion change or alter your view about the scope of any duty owed to Beatrice? In what way?

3. Does the opinion change or alter your view as to what conduct constituted a breach of duty? In what way?

Yu Fang Tan v. Arnel Management Company

170 Cal.App.4th 1087 (2009)

INTRODUCTION

Plaintiff Yu Fang Tan was shot in an attempted carjacking in the ungated portion of the common area of his apartment complex. He, along with his wife Chun Kuei Chang and son (together, plaintiffs), sued the management company and property owners, defendants Arnel Management Company, Pheasant Ridge Investment Company, and Colima Real Estate Company, for failure to take steps to properly secure their premises' against foreseeable criminal acts of third parties. [T]he trial court ruled that three prior violent crimes against others on the premises' common areas were not sufficiently similar crimes to the one perpetrated on plaintiff to impose a duty on defendants to protect tenants of the apartment complex. The court entered judgment for defendants, and plaintiffs appeal.

[W]e hold that plaintiffs' evidence of three prior violent attacks by strangers in the common areas of the apartment complex were sufficiently similar to the attack on plaintiff to provide substantial evidence of the necessary degree of foreseeability to give rise to a duty on defendants to provide the relatively minimal security measures that plaintiffs seek. Accordingly, we reverse the judgment.

FACTUAL AND PROCEDURAL BACKGROUND

Defendant Arnel Management Company manages the Pheasant Ridge Apartments. Pheasant Ridge is a 620-unit, multi-building apartment complex, with over 1,000 residents, situated on 20.59 acres in Rowland Heights, California. Entrance to the complex is gained from Colima Road. The entrance road bisects the property. The beginning of the entrance road has a grassy median and is bordered on both sides by tennis courts. A little farther up the road lie two open parking lots. One is a visitor lot, located on one side of the entrance road, and the other is the parking lot for the leasing office, located on the other side of the road. Just before the two parking lots, in the middle of the entrance road, sits a "guard shack." Continuing past the two parking lots to the back of the property, the entrance road fans out into a circle by which vehicles can turn left or right through two security gates. The apartments are located beyond the security gates. The gates are remote-control operated. Most of the property's parking spaces lie behind these gates by the apartments.

Plaintiffs moved into Pheasant Ridge in July 2002 and received one assigned parking space. Tenants could pay an additional fee for a garage, but plaintiffs chose not to rent one. At the time they leased the apartment, plaintiffs learned that if they had a second car, they could park it in unassigned parking spaces located throughout the complex, or in one of the two lots for visitors and the leasing office, as long as the car was removed from the leasing office lot before 7:00 a.m.

At around 11:30 p.m. on December 28, 2002, plaintiff arrived home. He drove around the property looking for an open parking space because his wife had parked the family's other car in their assigned space. Unable to locate an available space, plaintiff parked in the leasing office parking lot outside the gated area.

As plaintiff was parking his car, an unidentified man approached him and asked for help. When plaintiff opened his window, the man pointed a gun at plaintiff and told him to get out of the car because the man wanted it. Plaintiff responded, "Okay. Let me park my car first." But the car rolled a little, at which point the assailant shot plaintiff in the neck. The incident rendered plaintiff a quadriplegic.

*** [P]laintiffs' expert UCLA sociology professor Jack Katz, looked at police reports, complaints to the police, property management reports, and records of Pheasant Ridge's security service, PacWest Security Services.... Professor Katz found 10 incidents he viewed as being "particularly significant warning signs," of which three involved "prior violent incidents." All of the incidents involved a sudden attack without warning, late at night, by a stranger on someone who was on the ungated portion of the premises.

The first example of a violent incident occurred just under two years before plaintiffs' attack and involved an assault with a deadly weapon. A guard, who was patrolling on his bicycle around 1:30 a.m., saw someone standing by the maintenance garage. The guard approached the subject and asked him what he was doing. The subject replied he was waiting for a friend. When the guard asked for identification, the subject retrieved an unknown object from his pocket and swung it at the guard. The guard raised his arm in self-protection and received a one and one-half-inch slash on his forearm.

The second example occurred about a year before plaintiff's attack and before the existing gates at the back of the entrance road were installed. The assailants carjacked a car in Santa Monica with what the victim perceived to be a gun. Finding Pheasant Ridge "a good place to rob somebody" because there was no gate to impede their escape, as they told police later, the assailants came onto the property and robbed a tenant at his parking spot. The assailants committed the robbery by blocking the tenant's car, smashing him on the head, and demanding his valuables. They took the tenant's cell phone and other property.

The third violent incident occurred at 3:55 a.m., nine months before the attack on plaintiff. The incident was "also a violent attack, apparently, by strangers in late nighttime in a parking lot," and may have actually been in the leasing office lot. The assailant suddenly and viciously attacked the tenant in the face causing profuse bleeding. Although the victim did not mention a weapon, the police classified the attack [as] an assault with a deadly weapon or force likely to produce great bodily injury.

Professor Katz explained that these three prior incidents all involved "strangers coming in late night, suddenly becoming violent against people they don't know in ungated parking areas." Professor Katz opined that these three incidents "show that the probability is foreseeable here that people on this property will be attacked at some point by a stranger in open parking areas late at night."

Plaintiffs also presented nearly 80 examples of thefts from garages or cars or thefts of cars occurring on the Pheasant Ridge property. The trial court excluded the evidence of these thefts because they did not involve robberies or violent attacks on people.

The trial court asked plaintiffs to "articulate your theory of what additional security measures the defendants were under a duty to have in place in order to prevent the harm" to plaintiff. Accordingly, plaintiffs' counsel stated that the first thing plaintiffs wanted was for defendants to install gates on the entrance roadway before the leasing office and visitor parking lots, rather than at the back of the entrance road. The gates plaintiffs contemplated were "more substantial" than swing-arms; something more akin to the gates defendants had already installed. Counsel explained, "anything that could effectively deter escape is going to help reduce ... the probability of a carjacking occurring." In particular, *counsel declared that plaintiffs were not asking that defendant undertake a measure that would require ongoing surveillance or monitoring, or necessitate the expenditure of significant funds.*

Professor Katz cited research showing that when gates were installed in crime areas, the rate of violent crime went down. The research showed that "offenders who violently attack strangers are in the first instance concerned with their escapes. And, when you put gates in, you—while they can circumvent the gate to get in, they could climb a fence or get around it, they can't anticipate an easy escape.... [T]hey will shy from a crime target that has a gate in favor of one that's ungated. It will shift their focus of attention." Also, gates deter strangers who must explain their presence on the property.

Professor Katz testified that Pheasant Ridge should have ensured that the two objectives (of giving the impression that (1) escape would be impeded and that (2) one's presence on the property would have to be explained) were achieved by having a gate. Professor Katz explained that the effect of gates before the visitor and leasing parking lots would be to block access to all parking spaces and to make escape problematic. He did not eschew a swing-arm that rises and falls as cars enter because criminals could "anticipate on escape that [they] might have to break it and call attention." But, Professor Katz testified, the preferable gate would be "something that is continuous barrier such that if you are on the other side of it, you either have a reason to be there or you don't." Professor Katz also discussed fencing, either four or six feet, depending on the sight lines of the property. However, he explained, because the vast majority of the property is already surrounded by fencing, only a "very small area" of the property would require an extension of the existing barrier, with the result that the extension would be "very minor." *Professor Katz specifically stated he was not recommending that defendants hire security guards or monitor the property.*

At the close of the hearing, the trial court ruled that plaintiffs "failed to demonstrate that enclosing the entire complex, moving the gates, and installing some system or a guard that would let invited guests enter the complex at night, as they propose, would be any less burdensome than providing full-time security guards at night." Therefore, the court observed, in order to impose a duty on defendants, plaintiffs would have to "demonstrate a high degree of foreseeability of the crime committed against [plaintiffs] based upon prior similar incidents of violent crime at Pheasant Ridge."

The three incidents that Professor Katz characterized as "prior violent incidents," the court ruled, "neither singularly nor collectively, make the armed attempted carjacking and attempted murder of Mr. Tan by gunfire foreseeable." The court stated, "Notably, plaintiffs presented no evidence of a prior attempted carjacking, or an attempted murder, or a completed carjacking or murder, or of anyone being shot, or shot at, or reports of gunfire, at Pheasant Ridge." Therefore, the court held, defendants had no duty to take plaintiffs' proposed additional measures to enhance the security in their common areas, including the leasing office parking lot where the crime occurred. The court granted defendants' ensuing motion for judgment on the pleadings and plaintiffs' timely appeal followed.

I. DISCUSSION

a. *Standard of review of a ruling on a motion for nonsuit.*

"Although duty is a legal question, the factual background against which we decide it is a function of a particular case's procedural posture." (*Castaneda v. Olsher* (2007) 41 Cal.4th 1205, 1214, 63 Cal.Rptr.3d 99, 162 P.3d 610 (*Castaneda*).) *** "On review of a judgment of nonsuit, as here, we must view the facts in the light most favorable to the plaintiff[s].

* * *

b. *The duty of landlords to prevent third-party criminal acts on their premises*

To succeed in a negligence action, the plaintiff must show that: (1) the defendant owed the plaintiff a legal duty, (2) the defendant breached the duty, and (3) the breach proximately or legally caused (4) the plaintiff's damages or injuries. (*Ann M., supra,* 6 Cal.4th at p. 673, 25 Cal.Rptr.2d 137, 863 P.2d 207.) The existence of duty is a question of law for the court. (*Id.* at p. 674, 25 Cal.Rptr.2d 137, 863 P.2d 207.)

Our Supreme Court has clearly articulated "the scope of a landowner's duty to provide protection from foreseeable third party [criminal acts].... [It] is determined in part by balancing the foreseeability of the harm against the burden of the duty to be imposed. [Citation.] '"[I]n cases where the burden of preventing future harm is great, a high degree of foreseeability may be required. [Citation.] On the other hand, in cases where there are strong policy reasons for preventing the harm, or the harm can be prevented by simple means, a lesser degree of foreseeability may be required." [Citation.]' [Citation.].... [D]uty in such circumstances is determined by a balancing of 'foreseeability' of the criminal acts against the 'burdensomeness, vagueness, and efficacy' of the proposed security measures.

[Citation.]" (*Ann M., supra,* 6 Cal.4th at pp. 678–679, 25 Cal.Rptr.2d 137, 863 P.2d 207, quoting from *Gomez v. Ticor* (1983) 145 Cal.App.3d 622, 631, 193 Cal.Rptr. 600, disapproved on another point in *Sharon P. v. Arman, Ltd.* (1999) 21 Cal.4th 1181, 1193, 91 Cal.Rptr.2d 35, 989 P.2d 121.)

The higher the burden to be imposed on the landowner, the higher the degree of foreseeability is required. (*Sharon P. v. Arman, Ltd., supra,* 21 Cal.4th at p. 1195, 91 Cal.Rptr.2d 35, 989 P.2d 121, disapproved on other grounds in *Aguilar v. Atlantic Richfield Co.* (2001) 25 Cal.4th 826, 853, fn. 19, 107 Cal.Rptr.2d 841, 24 P.3d 493; *Delgado v. Trax Bar & Grill* (2005) 36 Cal.4th 224, 243, 30 Cal.Rptr.3d 145, 113 P.3d 1159 (*Delgado*); *Castaneda, supra,* 41 Cal.4th at pp. 1213–1214, 63 Cal.Rptr.3d 99, 162 P.3d 610.) A "*high degree* of foreseeability is required in order to find that the scope of a landlord's duty of care includes the hiring of security guards … [because the] monetary costs of security guards is not insignificant" and "the obligation … is not well defined." (*Ann M., supra,* 6 Cal.4th at p. 679, 25 Cal.Rptr.2d 137, 863 P.2d 207, italics added.) The burden of hiring security guards is "so high in fact, that the requisite foreseeability to trigger the burden could rarely, if ever, be proven without prior similar incidents. [Citation.]" (*Wiener v. Southcoast Childcare Centers, Inc.* (2004) 32 Cal.4th 1138, 1147, 12 Cal.Rptr.3d 615, 88 P.3d 517, citing *Ann M., supra,* at p. 679, 25 Cal.Rptr.2d 137, 863 P.2d 207.)

The plaintiff in *Ann M.* was raped by an unknown assailant at her place of employment, a store located in a shopping center. (*Ann M., supra,* 6 Cal.4th at pp. 670–671, 25 Cal.Rptr.2d 137, 863 P.2d 207.) At issue in that case was whether the scope of the duty owed by the shopping center owner to maintain its common areas in a reasonably safe condition included providing security guards in those areas. (*Id.* at p. 670, 25 Cal.Rptr.2d 137, 863 P.2d 207.) The Supreme Court held, under the facts of that case, that the owner did not owe a duty to provide security guards in the common areas. (*Ibid.*) The Court explained that the plaintiff conceded that the prior incidents "were not similar in nature to the violent assault that she suffered. Similarly, none of the remaining evidence presented by Ann M. is sufficiently compelling to establish the high degree of foreseeability *necessary to impose upon Pacific Plaza a duty to provide security guards in the common areas.* Neither the evidence regarding the presence of transients nor the evidence of the statistical crime rate of the surrounding area is of a type sufficient to satisfy this burden." (*Id.* at p. 680, 25 Cal.Rptr.2d 137, 863 P.2d 207, italics added, fn. omitted.)

Next, the Supreme Court held in *Sharon P. v. Arman, Ltd., supra,* 21 Cal.4th 1181, 91 Cal.Rptr.2d 35, 989 P.2d 121, that where there had been no assaults on the premises in 10 years, the plaintiffs' violent third party sexual assault in a commercial underground parking garage was not sufficiently foreseeable to justify requiring the landlord to hire patrolling security guards. (*Id.* at pp. 1185, 1195, 91 Cal.Rptr.2d 35, 989 P.2d 121.) *Sharon P.* rejected the plaintiff's argument for a "per se rule of foreseeability in cases involving underground parking structures." (*Id.* at p. 1192, 91 Cal.Rptr.2d 35, 989 P.2d 121.) It likewise held that seven armed robberies occurring at the bank on the ground floor above the garage were insufficient to impose a duty of care on the defendants to undertake the *onerous security measures of hiring security guards* for the garage. (*Id.* at p. 1195, 91 Cal.Rptr.2d 35, 989 P.2d 121.) *Sharon P.* found that bank robberies "were not sufficiently similar to the sexual assault crime to establish a high degree of foreseeability. Nor would such a duty be found if the assault on plaintiff had occurred in other areas of the office building instead of the garage (e.g., in a common hallway or at plaintiff's place of business)." (*Ibid.*)

More recently, in *Delgado,* one of the bar's two "bouncers" noticed hostile stares between the plaintiff bar patron and other bar patrons and concluded a fight was imminent. The bouncer asked the plaintiff to leave. Once in the parking lot, the plaintiff was accosted by 12 to 20 men. (*Delgado, supra,* 36 Cal.4th at p. 231, 30 Cal.Rptr.3d 145, 113 P.3d 1159.) The Supreme Court held that "only when 'heightened' foreseeability of third party criminal activity on the premises exists—shown by prior similar incidents or other indications of a reasonably foreseeable risk of violent criminal assaults in that location—does the scope of a business proprietor's special-relationship-based duty *include an obligation to provide guards* to protect the safety of patrons. [Citations.]" (*Id.* at p. 240, 30 Cal.Rptr.3d 145, 113 P.3d 1159, fn. omitted.) *Delgado* went on to explain that *Ann M.*'s "progeny … expressly reaffirm the sliding-scale balancing formula … under which we have recognized that, as a general matter, imposition of a high burden requires heightened foreseeability, but a minimal burden may be imposed upon a showing of a lesser degree of foreseeability. [Citations.]" (*Delgado, supra,* 36 Cal.4th at p. 243, 30 Cal.Rptr.3d 145, 113 P.3d 1159.) Such a sliding-scale balancing formula is defined by the Supreme Court by the following principles: "In circumstances in which the burden of preventing future harm caused by third party criminal conduct is great or onerous (as when a plaintiff, such as in *Ann M.,* asserts the defendant had a legal duty to provide *guards or undertake equally onerous measures,* or as when a plaintiff, such as in *Sharon P.* or *Wiener,* asserts the defendant had a legal duty to *provide bright lighting, activate and monitor security cameras, provide periodic 'walk-throughs' by existing personnel,* or provide stronger fencing), heightened foreseeability-shown by prior similar criminal incidents or other indications of a reasonably foreseeable risk of violent criminal assaults in that location-will be required." (*Delgado, supra,* at p. 243, fn. 24, 30 Cal.Rptr.3d 145, 113 P.3d 1159, italics added.) However, the Supreme Court specifically contrasted those "cases in which harm can be prevented by simple means or by imposing merely minimal burdens, only 'regular' reasonable foreseeability as opposed to heightened foreseeability is required." (*Ibid.*)

This analytical approach was confirmed by the Supreme Court in *Castaneda, supra,* 41 Cal.4th 1205, 63 Cal.Rptr.3d 99, 162 P.3d 610: "'First, the court must determine the specific measures the plaintiff asserts the defendant should have taken to prevent the harm. This frames the issue for the court's determination by defining the scope of the duty under consideration. Second, the court must analyze how financially and socially burdensome these proposed measures would be to a landlord, which measures could range from minimally burdensome to significantly burdensome under the facts of the case. Third, the court must identify the nature of the third party conduct that the plaintiff claims could have been prevented had the landlord taken the proposed measures, and assess how foreseeable (on a continuum from a mere possibility to a reasonable probability) it was that this conduct would occur. Once the burden and foreseeability have been independently assessed, they can be compared in determining the scope of the duty the court imposes on a given defendant. The more certain the likelihood of harm, the higher the burden a court will impose on a landlord to prevent it; the less foreseeable the harm, the lower the burden a court will place on a landlord.' [T]he balance of burdens and foreseeability is generally primary to the analysis. [Citation.]" (*Castaneda, supra,* at p. 1214, 63 Cal.Rptr.3d 99, 162 P.3d 610, quoting from *Vasquez v. Residential Investments, Inc.* (2004) 118 Cal.App.4th 269, 285, 12 Cal.Rptr.3d 846, fns. omitted.)

With these rules in mind, we turn to the evidence presented in the instant case.

c. *The trial court erred in finding defendants owed no duty.*

Referring to the first step of the analysis, i.e., the specific security measures that plaintiffs proposed defendants should have taken, the record shows that plaintiffs requested minimal changes: Professor Katz recommended (1) moving the existing security gates from the back of the access road, *or* (2) installing "very similar" gates before the visitor and leasing office parking lots. An additional gate could be "any gate ... —that would *not necessarily* impede climbing over it. It wouldn't have spikes or—or be unusually high. It would just define a property boundary...." "[*v*]*ery similar to the gates they have*...." (Italics added.) Indeed, *Professor Katz did not reject swing-arm gates.* Any gate could remain open during the day to allow business in the leasing office. Plaintiffs clearly stated they were *not* asking for the hiring of a guard or for any form of ongoing surveillance or monitoring. Furthermore, because existing fencing extends around almost the entire perimeter of the property, only a "very minor" extension over a "very small area" would be necessary to close the fencing gap, Professor Katz testified, and could be achieved by merely mounding dirt. Viewing the record as we are required (*Castaneda, supra,* 41 Cal.4th at pp. 1214–1215, 63 Cal.Rptr.3d 99, 162 P.3d 610), the trial court's finding that plaintiffs had proposed "enclosing the entire complex, moving the gates, *and* installing some system *or a guard* that would let invited guests enter the complex at night" overstates the security measures sought. (Italics added.)

The second issue requires the court to analyze how financially and socially onerous the proposed measures would be to the landlord. The measures "could range from minimally burdensome to significantly burdensome under the facts of the case." (*Castaneda, supra,* 41 Cal.4th at p. 1214, 63 Cal.Rptr.3d 99, 162 P.3d 610.) The evidence adduced at the hearing was that the cost to defendants to install the two security gates barricading the two roads at the back of the property was about $13,050. And plaintiffs suggested using the same gates for the front of the property. Although plaintiffs presented no evidence about the cost of extending the fence, notably Professor Katz testified that would necessitate only a "minor extension," because the property is already almost completely surrounded by walls, *and could even involve merely mounding dirt.* As plaintiffs observed, their proposed security measures involved a one-time expenditure and did not require ongoing surveillance of any kind, or the expenditure of significant funds. We disagree with the court that the proposed security measures were onerous.

Turning then to the heart of this case, the third element of foreseeability, plaintiffs demonstrated three prior incidents of sudden, unprovoked, increasingly violent assaults on people in *ungated parking* areas on the Pheasant Ridge premises by strangers in the middle of the night, causing great bodily injury. Professor Katz opined, based on the three incidents, that "the probability is foreseeable here" of plaintiff's attack because in his experience, "you don't get more than this." The evidence of three vicious criminal assaults in the common areas within two years of plaintiff's attack here is more similar and compelling than the evidence in *Ann M., supra,* 6 Cal.4th at page 671, 25 Cal.Rptr.2d 137, 863 P.2d 207 [no evidence landlord had notice of crime on the property], or *Sharon P. v. Arman, Ltd., supra,* 21 Cal.4th at page 1186, 91 Cal.Rptr.2d 35, 989 P.2d 121 [no assaults in 10 years on the premises]. We conclude that plaintiffs presented substantial evidence of prior similar incidents or other indications of a reasonably foreseeable risk of violent criminal assaults on the property so as to impose on defendants a duty to provide the comparatively minimal security measures plaintiffs described.

The court here required a heightened showing of foreseeability necessitating nearly identical prior crimes, in part, because the court perceived the proposed security to be onerous. We have already concluded that the actual measures sought were not especially burdensome under the facts of this case. Thus, the court's ruling is erroneous that where none of these incidents involved guns, shootings, attempted carjackings, or attempted murder, the incidents were not sufficiently similar to meet the heightened standard of foreseeability. We addressed this same issue in *Claxton v. Atlantic Richfield Co., supra,* 108

Cal.App.4th 327, 133 Cal.Rptr.2d 425, where the plaintiff was seriously injured in a vicious, racially motivated attack at a gas station. The record contained evidence of prior robberies, assaults, and gang activity in and around the area. In holding that the plaintiff presented substantial evidence of a reasonably foreseeable risk of violent criminal assaults, we specifically rejected the trial court's ruling requiring evidence of the *same* racially-motivated robberies or assaults as that perpetrated on the plaintiff. We stated, "As set forth in *Ann M.* and *Sharon P.*, the test is prior *'similar'* incidents [citations], not prior *identical* incidents. Therefore, it is immaterial whether any prior robberies or assaults at the station were motivated by racial animus, or were merely garden-variety antisocial behavior. Claxton presented substantial evidence of prior robberies and assaults, as well as other indications of a reasonably foreseeable risk of violent criminal assaults at the station." (*Id.* at p. 339, 133 Cal.Rptr.2d 425, first italics added, second italics in original.) In light of the minimum security measures proposed by plaintiffs here, they have presented substantial evidence of prior, sudden, vicious assaults by a stranger at Pheasant Ridge. It is of no moment that the assaults were not committed with guns where they nonetheless inflicted great bodily injury. Plaintiffs demonstrated a reasonably foreseeable risk of violent criminal assaults on the property.

Perfect identity of prior crimes to the attack on plaintiff is not necessary. Under the Supreme Court's "sliding-scale balancing formula," heightened foreseeability is required to impose a high burden whereas some showing of a "lesser degree of foreseeability" is sufficient where a minimal burden is sought to be imposed on the defendants. (*Delgado, supra,* 36 Cal.4th at p. 243, 30 Cal.Rptr.3d 145, 113 P.3d 1159.) Foreseeability lies on a "continuum from a mere possibility to a reasonable probability." (*Castaneda, supra,* 41 Cal.4th at p. 1214, 63 Cal.Rptr.3d 99, 162 P.3d 610.) Because plaintiffs have only asked for relatively minimal security measures — ones already taken by defendants in another portion of the property — the degree of foreseeability required here is not especially high. As a matter of law, therefore, the three prior incidents cited are sufficiently similar to make the assault on plaintiff foreseeable and to place a duty of care on defendants. Accordingly, the trial court erred in ruling that defendants had no duty of care in this case.

II. DISPOSITION

The judgment is reversed. Defendants to bear the burden of costs on appeal.

Exercise 2-14 To Foresee or Not to Foresee

Recently, some jurisdictions have criticized and/or rejected the use of foreseeability as a factor in determining the existence of a duty for negligence claims. As you read the next case, consider:

1. Should an examination of the existence of duty, in negligence cases based on the acts of third parties, involve consideration of foreseeability of those third party acts? Why or why not?

2. Do you think foreseeability should be considered as part of the determination of any of the following:

   a. Whether a duty was owed?

   b. The extent of the duty owed?

   c. Whether there was a breach of duty?

3. What difference does it make? In other words, why are these issues significant for potential plaintiffs and defendants?

A.W. v. Lancaster County School District

280 Neb. 205, 784 N.W.2d 907 (2010)

C.B., a kindergarten student at Arnold Elementary School in northwest Lincoln, Nebraska, was sexually assaulted in a school restroom during the school day. C.B.'s mother, A.W., sued the Lincoln Public Schools (LPS) on C.B.'s behalf, alleging that LPS' negligence permitted the assault to occur. The district court, however, entered summary judgment for LPS, reasoning that the assault was not foreseeable.

The fundamental issue in this appeal, as framed by the parties, is whether LPS had a legal duty to C.B. to protect him from the assault. But we conclude that our case law has, in the past, placed factual questions of foreseeability in the context of a legal duty when they are more appropriately decided by the finder of fact in the context of determining whether an alleged tort-feasor's duty to take reasonable care has been breached. As a result, we find that the questions of foreseeability presented in this appeal are matters of fact, not of law, and that there is a genuine issue of material fact regarding whether LPS' conduct met its duty of reasonable care. We reverse, and remand for further proceedings.

BACKGROUND ASSAULT OF C.B.

On September 22, 2005, Joseph Siems entered Arnold Elementary School through the main entrance. The door was not locked, but there was a sign next to the entrance informing visitors that they needed to check in with the main office, which was just inside. If they checked in, they would be signed into the building and issued a visitor's nametag. The hallway inside the entrance was visible through glass windows to the two secretaries who worked in the office, and the secretaries were to watch the hallway to make sure that no visitors went past the office without signing in.

Siems went past the office without signing in. Apparently, Siems came in during the lunch hour, when one of the office secretaries was at lunch and the other was making photocopies. One of the regular secretaries was not working that day, and the replacement secretary may not have been instructed to make sure that everyone who came into the building checked in. For whatever reason, no one saw Siems come in the door. But Siems was spotted in the entrance hallway shortly thereafter by a teacher, Kathi Olson. Siems had a cigarette behind his ear and was carrying a backpack; Olson thought he looked out of place. Olson asked Siems if she could help him find anything, but he ignored her. Olson went directly to the office to see if anyone matching Siems' description had signed in.

Two other teachers, Kelly Long and Connie Peters, were monitoring some first graders when they also saw Siems in the hallway. They decided that Long would talk to Siems while Peters stayed with the students. Long saw the contact between Siems and Olson, and when Siems came near, Long asked Siems if she could help him. Siems did not respond, but after the question was repeated, Siems said he needed to use the restroom. Long pointed out a nearby restroom and told Siems that he needed to return to the main office after using the restroom. Siems went toward the restroom, and Long went to her classroom and used the telephone to report the incident to the main office. Long knew that there were no students in that restroom at the time. But Long did not watch Siems to see where he went. Peters saw Siems go into the restroom that Long had indicated, then saw him come out and go back down the hallway. Then she lost sight of him. Although no one saw him, it is apparent that Siems went back down the hallway and into another restroom closer to the main entrance.

One of the school secretaries had seen Siems briefly in the hallway as she was returning from lunch. She answered the telephone when Long called the office. Olson was still there and had just determined that Siems had not signed in. After hearing from Olson and Long, the secretary went to the cafeteria to inform Shannon Mitchell, the administrator in charge of the school at the time. In the meantime, C.B., who was 5 years old, had returned from a trip to the restroom and told his teacher, Susan Mulvaney, that "there was a bad man in the restroom." C.B. later reported that Siems had pulled down C.B.'s pants and briefly performed oral sex on him. Mulvaney stayed at the door of her classroom, next to C.B., and watched the restroom door.

After speaking to the secretary in the cafeteria, Mitchell went to the restroom and saw Siems sitting in a stall. When Mitchell arrived, there were no children in the restroom. Mitchell also saw some children in the hallway approaching the restroom; she prevented them from entering. While doing so, she encountered Mulvaney, who told her what C.B. had said. Mitchell used Mulvaney's telephone to call the office and initiate a "Code Red" lockdown of the school, then went to the office and called the 911 emergency dispatch service.

The Code Red was initiated pursuant to the LPS "Safety and Security Plan" and "Arnold School Emergency Procedures and Security" guidelines that were in effect at the time. Those procedures had been put in place in compliance with LPS "Policy 6411" and "Regulation 6411.1," which required the establishment of district-wide and site-based emergency plans. Generally speaking, the LPS plan required school personnel responding to a trespasser to nonconfrontationally contact the trespasser and, based on what followed, consider calling a Code Red. The Arnold Elementary School procedures explained, generally, the individual responsibilities associated with a Code Red and described the lockdown procedures.

After initiating the Code Red and calling 911, Mitchell went to some benches in the hallway near the restroom and watched the restroom door, along with an assistant principal who was in the building and a school custodian. After being contacted by the assistant principal, Siems left the restroom and then the building, followed by the assistant principal and custodian. The custodian detained Siems as police arrived, and Siems was taken into police custody.

PROCEDURAL HISTORY

C.B.'s mother, A.W., filed this claim against LPS on C.B.'s behalf under the Political Subdivisions Tort Claims Act. As relevant, A.W. alleged that LPS was negligent in failing to have an effective security system and in allowing a stranger to enter C.B.'s school. A.W. alleged that LPS failed to use reasonable care to protect C.B.

LPS filed a motion for summary judgment, supported by evidence of the events described above, Mulvaney's opinion that her actions were reasonable, and the opinion of LPS' director of security that the LPS and Arnold Elementary School emergency procedures were adequate. In response, A.W. adduced evidence of incidents near Arnold Elementary School that had been reported to the Lincoln Police Department between 2001 and 2005, although most of those incidents involved nonviolent crimes and took place outside of school hours.

The district court entered summary judgment for LPS. The court found that Siems' assault of C.B. was not foreseeable and that the police incident reports provided by A.W. were insufficiently similar to Siems' actions to place LPS on notice of the possibility of a sexual assault by an intruder. The court found that LPS had made a prima facie showing that its security plan was adequate and that A.W. had not rebutted that evidence. And the court found that even if the safety and security plan in effect was inadequate, it was exempt from the Political Subdivisions Tort Claims Act as a discretionary function. A.W. appeals.

ASSIGNMENTS OF ERROR

A.W. assigns, consolidated and restated, that the district court erred in finding that (1) LPS did not owe a duty to protect C.B. from the danger of sexual assault by Siems, (2) the sexual assault of C.B. was not reasonably foreseeable, (3) LPS took reasonable steps to protect against foreseeable acts of violence on its premises, (4) Arnold Elementary School had a safety and security plan in effect at the time of the assault which complied with pertinent state law, and (5) the school's safety plan was discretionary.

STANDARD OF REVIEW

Summary judgment is proper if the pleadings and admissible evidence offered at the hearing show that there is no genuine issue as to any material facts or as to the ultimate inferences that may be drawn from those facts and that the moving party is entitled to judgment as a matter of law. *Erickson v. U-Haul Internat.*, 278 Neb. 18, 767 N.W.2d 765 (2009). In reviewing a summary judgment, an appellate court views the evidence in the light most favorable to the party against whom the judgment was granted, giving that party the benefit of all reasonable inferences deducible from the evidence. *Id.*

ANALYSIS

FORESEEABILITY AND DUTY UNDER RESTATEMENT (THIRD) OF TORTS

In order to recover in a negligence action, a plaintiff must show a legal duty owed by the defendant to the plaintiff, a breach of such duty, causation, and damages. *Ehlers v. State*, 276 Neb. 605, 756 N.W.2d 152 (2008). The duty in a negligence case is to conform to the legal standard of reasonable conduct in the light of the apparent risk. *Doe v. Gunny's Ltd. Partnership*, 256 Neb. 653, 593 N.W.2d 284 (1999). The question whether a legal duty exists for actionable negligence is a question of law dependent on the facts in a particular situation. *Id.* But it is for the fact finder to determine, on the facts of each individual case, whether or not the evidence establishes a breach of that duty. See *Heins v. Webster County*, 250 Neb. 750, 552 N.W.2d 51 (1996).

A.W. first argues that LPS had a duty to protect C.B. from the danger of sexual assault, that the sexual assault of C.B. was reasonably foreseeable, and that LPS' response was inadequate to that foreseeable danger. In support of this argument, A.W. relies on the risk-utility test that we have used to determine the existence of a tort duty. See, e.g., *Hughes v. Omaha Pub. Power Dist.*, 274 Neb. 13, 735 N.W.2d 793 (2007). Under that test, we have considered (1) the magnitude of the risk, (2) the relationship of the parties, (3) the nature of the attendant risk, (4) the opportunity and ability to exercise care, (5) the foreseeability of the harm, and (6) the policy interest in the proposed solution. See *id.*

* * *

In previous cases, because the existence of a legal duty is a question of law, we have also treated the foreseeability of a particular injury as a question of law. See *Knoll v. Board of Regents*, 258 Neb. 1, 601 N.W.2d 757 (1999). This places us in the peculiar position, however, of deciding questions, as a matter of law, that are uniquely rooted in the facts and circumstances of a particular case and in the reasonability of the defendant's response to those facts and circumstances.

For that reason, the use of foreseeability as a determinant of duty has been criticized, most pertinently in the recently adopted Restatement (Third) of Torts. Restatement (Third) of Torts: Liability for Physical and Emotional Harm (2010). The Restatement (Third) explains that because the extent of foreseeable risk depends on the specific facts of the case, courts should leave such determinations to the trier of fact unless no reasonable person could differ on the matter. *Id.,* §7, comment *j.* Indeed, foreseeability determinations are particularly fact dependent and case specific, representing "a [factual] judgment about a course of events ... that one often makes outside any legal context." See, *Fazzolari v. Portland School Dist. No. 1J,* 303 Or. 1, 4, 734 P.2d 1326, 1327–28 (1987); W. Jonathan Cardi, *Purging Foreseeability: The New Vision of Duty and Judicial Power in the Proposed Restatement (Third) of Torts,* 58 Vand. L. Rev. 739 (2005). So, by incorporating foreseeability into the analysis of duty, a court transforms a factual question into a legal issue and expands the authority of judges at the expense of juries or triers of fact. See *Gipson v. Kasey,* 214 Ariz. 141, 150 P.3d 228 (2007).

That is especially peculiar because decisions of foreseeability are not particularly "legal," in the sense that they do not require special training, expertise, or instruction, nor do they require considering far-reaching policy concerns. See Cardi, *supra* note 15. Rather, deciding what is reasonably foreseeable involves common sense, common experience, and application of the standards and behavioral norms of the community-matters that have long been understood to be uniquely the province of the finder of fact. See, *Gipson, supra* note 16; Cardi, *supra* note 15.

In addition, we have defined a "duty" as an obligation, to which the law gives recognition and effect, to conform to a particular standard of conduct toward another. See *Schmidt v. Omaha Pub. Power Dist.,* 245 Neb. 776, 515 N.W.2d 756 (1994). Duty rules are meant to serve as broadly applicable guidelines for public behavior, i.e., rules of law applicable to a category of cases. See Cardi, *supra* note 15. But foreseeability determinations are fact specific, so they are not categorically applicable, and are incapable of serving as useful behavioral guides. *Id.* And, as the Arizona Supreme Court explained, "[r]eliance by courts on notions of 'foreseeability' also may obscure the factors that actually guide courts in recognizing duties for purposes of negligence liability." *Gipson, supra* note 16, 214 Ariz. at 144, 150 P.3d at 231, citing Cardi, *supra* note 15; Restatement (Third) of Torts, *supra* note 13, §7.

Instead, as the Restatement (Third) explains, an actor ordinarily has a duty to exercise reasonable care when the actor's conduct creates a risk of physical harm. Restatement (Third) of Torts, *supra* note 13, §7(a). But, in exceptional cases, when an articulated countervailing principle or policy warrants denying or limiting liability in a particular class of cases, a court may decide that a defendant has no duty or that the ordinary duty of reasonable care requires modification. *Id.,* §7(b). A no-duty determination, then, is grounded in public policy and based upon legislative facts, not adjudicative facts arising out of the particular circumstances of the case. See *id.,* §7, comment *b.* And such ruling should be explained and justified based on articulated policies or principles that justify exempting these actors from liability or modifying the ordinary duty of reasonable care. See *id.,* comment *j.* See, also, *Gipson, supra* note 16.

The ensuing complications are illustrated by our reasoning in *Sharkey v. Board of Regents,* in which we relied upon foreseeability in determining a university's legal duty to protect students on its campus from criminal activity. Although invoking our risk-utility test, our decision was grounded entirely in foreseeability. And we reasoned, in the end, that because the evidence showed that violent altercations were not unknown at the location on campus where the plaintiff was attacked, the attack was foreseeable; thus, we held that the university owed a duty "to its students to take reasonable steps to protect against foreseeable acts of violence on its campus and the harm that naturally flows therefrom." *Id.* at 182, 615 N.W.2d at 902.

In other words, we reasoned that because the attack at issue in that case was foreseeable, the defendant had a duty to protect against foreseeable acts of violence. Our reasoning was tautological. It is evident that the university had a landowner-invitee duty to protect against *foreseeable* acts even had the attack in that case *not* been foreseeable. While we purported to be discussing duty, we were in fact assuming the conclusion we claimed to be proving, and we were actually evaluating the sufficiency of the evidence to sustain a conclusion that the university had breached its duty to take reasonable care.

Our mistake was a common one. As the Restatement notes, in a number of cases, courts have rendered judgments under the rubric of duty that are better understood as applications of the negligence standard to a particular category of recurring facts. Restatement (Third) of Torts, *supra* note 13, comment *i*. But the Restatement disapproves that practice and limits the determination of duty to articulated policy or principle, in order to facilitate more transparent explanations of the reasons for a no-duty ruling and to protect the traditional function of the jury as a fact finder. *Id.*, comment *j*. Accord *Thompson, supra*. Simply put, whether a duty exists is a *policy* decision, and a lack of foreseeable risk in a specific case may be a basis for a no-breach determination, but such a ruling is not a no-duty determination. See, *Thompson, supra*; *Behrendt v. Gulf Underwriters Ins. Co.*, 318 Wis.2d 622, 768 N.W.2d 568 (2009); *Gipson, supra*. As the Wisconsin Supreme Court explained, in a negligence case, a defendant's conduct should be examined " "not … in terms of whether … there is a duty to [perform] a specific act, but rather whether the conduct satisfied the duty placed upon individuals to exercise that degree of care as would be exercised by a reasonable person under the circumstances." " See *Behrendt, supra*, 318 Wis.2d at 634, 768 N.W.2d at 574.

To summarize: Under the Restatement (Third), foreseeable risk is an element in the determination of negligence, not legal duty. In order to determine whether appropriate care was exercised, the fact finder must assess the foreseeable risk at the time of the defendant's alleged negligence. The extent of foreseeable risk depends on the specific facts of the case and cannot be usefully assessed for a category of cases; small changes in the facts may make a dramatic change in how much risk is foreseeable. Thus, courts should leave such determinations to the trier of fact unless no reasonable person could differ on the matter. Restatement (Third) of Torts, *supra* note 13, comment *j*. And if the court takes the question of negligence away from the trier of fact because reasonable minds could not differ about whether an actor exercised reasonable care (for example, because the injury was not reasonably foreseeable), then the court's decision merely reflects the one-sidedness of the facts bearing on negligence and should not be misrepresented or misunderstood as involving exemption from the ordinary duty of reasonable care. See *id.*, comment *i*.

We find the reasoning of the Restatement (Third), and our fellow courts that have endorsed it, to be persuasive. See, *Thompson, supra*; *Behrendt, supra*; *Gipson, supra*. The circumstances of this case illustrate how incorporating foreseeability into a duty analysis can confuse the issues. Here, it is not disputed that LPS owed C.B. a duty of reasonable care. The duty of instructors to supervise and protect students is well established under the Restatement (Second) of Torts, the Restatement (Third) of Torts, and our current case law. See Restatement (Second) of Torts §§ 314A and 320, comment *b*. (1965);

Restatement (Third) of Torts, *supra* note 13, §40(b)(5) (Proposed Final Draft No. 1, 2005); see, e.g., *Fu v. State*, 263 Neb. 848, 643 N.W.2d 659 (2002). Instead, the question is whether Siems' assault of C.B. was reasonably foreseeable. That determination involves a fact-specific inquiry into the circumstances that might have placed LPS on notice of the possibility of the assault. Stated another way, it requires us to ask what LPS employees knew, when they knew it, and whether a reasonable person would infer from those facts that there was a danger. Those are *factual* inquiries that should not be reframed as questions of law.

Under the Restatement view, the basic analysis remains the same. The factual question is the same. But, it is properly reframed as a question of fact. LPS owed C.B. a duty of reasonable care. Did LPS, under the facts and circumstances of the case, conduct itself reasonably? Or, more precisely, was Siems' assault of C.B. reasonably foreseeable, such that LPS' duty of reasonable care required it to act to forestall that risk? Such an approach properly recognizes the role of the trier of fact and requires courts to clearly articulate the reasons, other than foreseeability, that might support duty or no-duty determinations. See *Gipson, supra*. And it correctly examines the defendant's conduct, not in terms of whether it had a "duty" to take particular actions, but instead in terms of whether its conduct *breached* its duty to exercise the care that would be exercised by a reasonable person under the circumstances. See *Behrendt, supra*.

We do not view our endorsement of the Restatement (Third) as a fundamental change in our law. It is better understood as rearranging the basic questions that are posed by any negligence case and making sure that each question has been put in its proper place. But it does not change those questions. To say, as we have in the past, that a defendant had no duty, under particular circumstances, to foresee a particular harm is really no different from saying that the defendant's duty to take reasonable care was not breached, under those circumstances, by its failure to foresee the unforeseeable.

But placing foreseeability in the context of breach, rather than duty, properly charges the trier of fact with determining whether a particular harm was, on the facts of the case, reasonably foreseeable — although the court reserves the right to determine that the defendant did not breach its duty of reasonable care, as a matter of law, where reasonable people could not disagree about the unforeseeability of the injury. We have often said that " " " '[t]he risk reasonably to be perceived defines the duty to be obeyed [,]' " " " e.g. *Knoll, supra*, 258 Neb. at 7, 601 N.W.2d at 763, but that proposition should now be understood as explaining how foreseeability helps define what conduct the standard of care requires under the circumstances and whether the conduct of the alleged tort-feasor conforms to that standard. These are determinations reserved for the finder of fact. See *Wilke v. Woodhouse Ford*, 278 Neb. 800, 774 N.W.2d 370 (2009). And the factors of our risk-utility test, which we have employed to determine the existence of a duty, are better applied as possible considerations in determining whether an actor's conduct was negligent. As the Restatement (Third) explains:

> A person acts negligently if the person does not exercise reasonable care under all the circumstances. Primary factors to consider in ascertaining whether the person's conduct lacks reasonable care are the foreseeable likelihood that the person's conduct will result in harm, the foreseeable severity of any harm that may ensue, and the burden of precautions to eliminate or reduce the risk of harm.

Restatement (Third) of Torts, *supra* note 13, §3 at 29.

For the foregoing reasons, we find the clarification of the duty analysis contained in the Restatement (Third) of Torts, §7, to be compelling, and we adopt it. See *Thompson, supra.* We expressly hold that foreseeability is not a factor to be considered by courts when making determinations of duty. See *Gipson, supra.* see, also, *Thompson, supra; Behrendt, supra.*

* * *

REVERSED AND REMANDED FOR FURTHER PROCEEDINGS.

Exercise 2-15 Law Practice

Find the standard for the jurisdiction where you intend to practice — does it consider foreseeability as part of the analysis for determining whether there is a duty owed by land owners and possessors to prevent harm from criminal acts by third parties? What reason or reasons does the court give for the standard it adopts?

(ii) Negligence Per Se — Duty Imposed by Statute

Sometimes a statute may be used to establish the duty owed (and where the statute is violated — that the duty was breached). In such cases two key issues frequently arise — first, whether the statute was actually intended to govern the situation, and second — whether defendant is excused from complying with the statute.

To establish the statute was intended to govern the situation, the court will generally consider whether:

1. The plaintiff is in the class of persons the statute was intended to protect, and

2. The plaintiff suffered the type of harm the statute was intended to prevent.

Sometimes these issues can be determined by looking at the plain language of the statute; however, when a court is not able to determine the intent from the plain language of the statute, the court will look to the legislative history of the statute to make such a determination. When neither of these options provides the court with guidance the court will usually make its best guess as to what the statute was intended to do.

The consequence of finding the statute governs the situation and that defendant violated the statute varies by jurisdiction. In a majority of jurisdictions, the effect is that defendant is said to be ***negligent per se*** — meaning there is a presumption that the defendant breached a duty (because the statute provides the duty and the violation of the statute establishes breach). In most of these jurisdictions the defendant is still allowed to present evidence that there was an acceptable excuse for violating the statute. Acceptable excuses are generally related to the defendant's inability to comply — for example where the defendant lacks the capacity or has made reasonable efforts to comply and has not been able to do so — or for situations where complying with the statute would be more dangerous than not complying — for example, where a driver swerves from her own lane to avoid hitting a child.

In other jurisdictions, violation of the statue provides evidence but not conclusive proof of negligence — meaning the plaintiff may present the statute and evidence of the violation to the jury, who may use the evidence to evaluate whether defendant behaved reasonably under the circumstances; defendants in such jurisdictions are then free to present additional or other evidence that their conduct was reasonable. In other words, in these jurisdictions the standard or duty is to act reasonably under the circumstances, and a violation of a statute is just one piece of the evidence the jury considers in determining whether defendant's conduct was reasonable.

Exercise 2-16 Using Statutes to Establish Duty and Breach

This exercise is based on the same facts set out in exercise 2.13.

The following are relevant provisions of the Housing Code Ordinance in effect in the jurisdiction where the action is filed:

Section 7-1-93 Windows, exterior doors, etc.

Every window, exterior door and basement hatchway shall be reasonably weather tight, watertight and rodent proof and shall be kept in sound working condition and good repair. Locks shall be provided on all exterior doors and all exterior openable windows.

Section 7-1-97 Construction, maintenance, etc., generally, of facilities.

Every facility, piece of equipment or utility which is required under this article shall be so constructed or installed that it will function safely and effectively and shall be maintained in satisfactory working condition.

The statute pursuant to which the ordinances were enacted, reads, in pertinent part:

Legislative declarations and findings of fact.

It is hereby declared that insanitary and unsafe buildings, dwellings and structures of all types and descriptions used for human habitation exist in the incorporated municipalities of this state and that such insanitary and unsafe conditions arise from obsolescence, poor repair, maintenance and the overcrowding and use of such buildings, dwellings and structures used for human habitation and occupancy; and, that such conditions cause an increase in and spread of disease and crime and are damaging and injurious to the inhabitants and general public of such incorporated municipalities.

1. Would defendants Levi Brock and Realty Co. be negligent per se in jurisdictions following the majority rule?

2. What would be the impact of finding defendants negligent per se?

3. What would be the result in a jurisdiction following the minority rule?

4. Do you believe the standards pertaining to premises liability (in the prior section) should apply here (to evaluate duty and breach), rather than the housing ordinances? Why or why not? Would it change the outcome?

Note that although this exercise is based on a premises liability problem, negligence per se may be applicable in a wide variety of circumstances (as many circumstances as there are statutes governing conduct, assuming that plaintiff can establish the required elements).

(iii) Rescuers—Duty Curtailed by Statute

Sometimes legislatures will eliminate or curtail a person's duty to act by eliminating the basis for liability. For example, as described earlier in this chapter, some jurisdictions have enacted Good Samaritan statutes to protect individuals from civil liability for negligence committed during rescues or while voluntarily providing emergency care. For example, a Georgia statute provides:

> Any person, including those licensed to practice medicine and surgery pursuant to the provisions of Chapter 84-9 of the Code of Georgia of 1933 and including any person licensed to render services ancillary thereto, who in good faith renders emergency care at the scene of an accident or emergency to the victim or victims thereof without making any charge therefor, shall not be liable for any civil damages as a result of any act or omission by such person in rendering the emergency care or as a result of any act or failure to act to provide or arrange for further medical treatment or care for the injured person.

And in New Jersey:

> Any individual, including a person licensed to practice any method of treatment of human ailments, disease, pain, injury, deformity, mental or physical condition, or licensed to render services ancillary thereto, or any person who is a volunteer member of a duly incorporated first aid and emergency or volunteer ambulance or rescue squad association, who in good faith renders emergency care at the scene of an accident or emergency to the victim or victims thereof, or while transporting the victim or victims thereof to a hospital or other facility where treatment or care is to be rendered, shall not be liable for any civil damages as a result of any acts or omissions by such person in rendering the emergency care.

N.J. Stat. Ann. Section 2A:62A-1.

Exercise 2-17 Understanding Statutory Language

Notice that neither of the "Good Samaritan" statutes set out above actually state that rescuers and/or emergency care workers do not have a duty (to act reasonably). Can you explain why these statutes are said to have eliminated a rescuer and/or emergency care provider's duty (for purposes of negligence)?

---

(3) Using Circumstantial Evidence — res ipsa loquitur

Sometimes it is not possible for the plaintiff to present direct evidence to establish the defendant's conduct breached the standard of care. For example, imagine that following a routine surgery, plaintiff was discharged from the hospital. After a few days, plaintiff began to feel pain and discomfort in her chest. She went to a nearby urgent care center where they took an x-ray. At right is a copy of the x-ray:

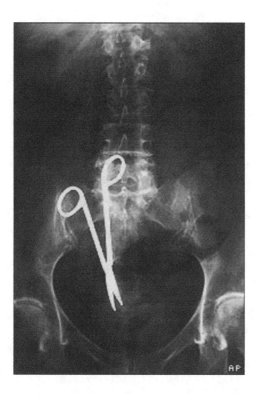

Plaintiff had a second surgery to remove the scissors. Plaintiff comes to your office with the x-ray. She assumes the scissors, which are surgical scissors, were left inside of her during surgery. Since plaintiff was anesthetized during the surgery she does not know how or when they were left inside of her (she can not testify as to how the scissors got there) nor does she know who might be responsible since several doctors and nurses were in the operating room during the surgery. Assuming none of the persons in the operating room admit responsibility for leaving the scissors inside the plaintiff, there is no direct testimony as to how the scissors were left in her chest. Without such testimony plaintiff has no direct evidence that anyone breached the standard of care and so her case would be dismissed for lack of evidence proving the required elements of duty and breach. This would be an unfair result.

To avoid dismissal on these grounds, so that she may present her case to the jury, plaintiff may resort to using a doctrine known as *res ipsa loquitur*, which is Latin for "the thing speaks for itself." Res ipsa loquitur allows plaintiff to establish an inference of negligence, which means she can submit her case to the jury and the jury will decide if the defendant is liable (assuming she can prove causation and damages, which we will discuss in the next section). Although there is some variation, in order for the doctrine to apply, most jurisdictions require plaintiffs to prove: (1) that the accident was of a kind that does not usually occur absent negligence; (2) that the instrumentality that caused the accident was in the exclusive control of the person charged with the negligence; and (3) that the injury suffered was not due to any voluntary act on the part of the plaintiff. If the plaintiff satisfies these elements the trial judge will send the case to the jury to decide whether the plaintiff's evidence is strong enough to support the conclusion that the defendant was negligent. Note that the plaintiff must also prove that the act was the cause of her damages, two topics we will discuss in the next section. It is also important to understand that res ipsa loquitur merely allows the judge to send the case to the jury without direct evidence of negligence;

it does not mean that the defendant loses. The jury will still weigh the evidence and decide if the preponderance of the evidence (the general evidentiary standard for negligence claims) supports plaintiff's claim. In our example it means that the jury must believe that it is more likely than not that the defendant is responsible for leaving the scissors inside of plaintiff (and that this is the cause of the plaintiff's damages).

In our example proving the accident was of a kind that does not usually occur absent negligence would be fairly straightforward; a jury would be able to use common sense to infer that surgical scissors are not ordinarily left inside a person in the absence of negligence. In some cases it will not be within the common experience of the jurors; in those circumstances the plaintiff may introduce evidence, including expert testimony, to fill in the gap in the average juror's experience.

It is somewhat deceiving to say that the second element requires proving that the instrumentality that caused the accident was in the exclusive control of the person charged with the negligence because this general rule is not applicable in all circumstances and is subject to exceptions where the purpose of the doctrine of res ipsa loquitur would otherwise be defeated. For example, in *Ybarra v. Spangard*, 25 Cal. 2d 486 (1944), one of the leading cases on this topic, the plaintiff had surgery to remove his appendix and when he awoke he felt a sharp pain about half way between his neck and right shoulder. The pain spread to the lower part of his arm, and after his release from the hospital the condition grew worse. He was unable to rotate or lift his arm, and developed paralysis and atrophy of the muscles around his shoulder. Plaintiff filed suit, naming as defendants everyone who had been in the operating room. Defendants argued res ipsa loquitur was not applicable because Plaintiff had not shown that the injury was caused by an instrumentality under any of the defendants' control because (1) he had not shown which of the several instrumentalities caused the injury, and (2) he had not shown that any one of the defendants had exclusive control over any particular instrumentality. In rejecting these arguments the court reasoned:

> The present case is of a type which comes within the reason and spirit of the doctrine more fully perhaps than any other. The passenger sitting awake in a railroad car at the time of a collision, the pedestrian walking along the street and struck by a falling object or the debris of an explosion, are surely not more entitled to an explanation than the unconscious patient on the operating table. Viewed from this aspect, it is difficult to see how the doctrine can, with any justification, be so restricted in its statement as to become inapplicable to a patient who submits himself to the care and custody of doctors and nurses, is rendered unconscious, and receives some injury from instrumentalities used in his treatment. Without the aid of the doctrine a patient who received permanent injuries of a serious character, obviously the result of some one's negligence, would be entirely unable to recover unless the doctors and nurses in attendance voluntarily chose to disclose the identity of the negligent person and the facts establishing liability. *See Maki v. Murray Hospital*, 91 Mont. 251, 7 P.2d 228. ***

> We have here no problem of negligence in treatment, but of distinct injury to a healthy part of the body not the subject of treatment, nor within the area covered by the operation. The decisions in this state make it clear that such circumstances raise the inference of negligence and call upon the defendant to explain the unusual result. *See Ales v. Ryan*, 8 Cal.2d 82, 64 P.2d 409; *Brown v. Shortlidge*, 98 Cal.App. 352, 277 P. 134.

The argument of defendants is simply that plaintiff has not shown an injury caused by an instrumentality under a defendant's control, because he has not shown which of the several instrumentalities that he came in contact with while in the hospital caused the injury; and he has not shown that any one defendant or his servants had exclusive control over any particular instrumentality. Defendants assert that some of them were not the employees of other defendants, that some did not stand in any permanent relationship from which liability in tort would follow, and that in view of the nature of the injury, the number of defendants and the different functions performed by each, they could not all be liable for the wrong, if any. ***

But we do not believe that either the number or relationship of the defendants alone determines whether the doctrine of res ipsa loquitur applies. Every defendant in whose custody the plaintiff was placed for any period was bound to exercise ordinary care to see that no unnecessary harm came to him and each would be liable for failure in this regard. Any defendant who negligently injured him, and any defendant charged with his care who so neglected him as to allow injury to occur, would be liable. The defendant employers would be liable for the neglect of their employees; and the doctor in charge of the operation would be liable for the negligence of those who became his temporary servants for the purpose of assisting in the operation. ***

It may appear at the trial that, consistent with the principles outlined above, one or more defendants will be found liable and others absolved, but this should not preclude the application of the rule of res ipsa loquitur. The control at one time or another, of one or more of the various agencies or instrumentalities which might have harmed the plaintiff was in the hands of every defendant or of his employees or temporary servants. This, we think, places upon them the burden of initial explanation. Plaintiff was rendered unconscious for the purpose of undergoing surgical treatment by the defendants; it is manifestly unreasonable for them to insist that he identify any one of them as the person who did the alleged negligent act.

The other aspect of the case which defendants so strongly emphasize is that plaintiff has not identified the instrumentality any more than he has the particular guilty defendant. Here, again, there is a misconception which, if carried to the extreme for which defendants contend, would unreasonably limit the application of the res ipsa loquitur rule. It should be enough that the plaintiff can show an injury resulting from an external force applied while he lay unconscious in the hospital; this is as clear a case of identification of the instrumentality as the plaintiff may ever be able to make.

An examination of the recent cases, particularly in this state, discloses that the test of actual exclusive control of an instrumentality has not been strictly followed, but exceptions have been recognized where the purpose of the doctrine of res ipsa loquitur would otherwise be defeated. Thus, the test has become one of right of control rather than actual control. *See Metz v. Southern Pac. Co.*, 51 Cal.App.2d 260, 268, 124 P.2d 670. In the bursting bottle cases where the bottler has delivered the instrumentality to a retailer and thus has given up actual control, he will nevertheless be subject to the doctrine where it is shown that no change in the condition of the bottle occurred after it left the bottler's possession, and it can accordingly be said that he was in constructive control *Escola v. Coca Bottling Co.*, 24 Cal.2d, 150 P.2d 436. Moreover, this court departed from the single instrumentality theory in the colliding vehicle cases, where two defendants were involved, each in control of a separate vehicle. *See Smith v. O'Donnell*, 215 Cal. 714, 12 P.2d 933; *Godfrey v. Brown*, 220 Cal. 57, 29 P.2d 165, 93 A.L.R. 1092; Carpenter, 10 So.Cal.L.Rev. 170. Finally, it has been suggested that the hospital cases may properly be considered exceptional, and that the doctrine of res ipsa loquitur 'should apply with equal force in cases wherein medical and nursing staffs take the place of machinery and may, through carelessness or lack of skill, inflict, or permit the infliction of injury upon a patient who is thereafter in no position to say how he received his injuries.' *Maki v. Murray Hospital*, 91 Mont. 251, 7 P.2d 228, 231; *see also, Whetstine v. Moravec*, 228 Iowa 352, 291 N.W. 425, 435, where the court refers to the 'instrumentalities' as including 'the unconscious body of the plaintiff.'

In the face of these examples of liberalization of the tests for res ipsa loquitur, there can be no justification for the rejection of the doctrine in the instant case. As pointed out above, if we accept the contention of defendants herein, there will rarely be any compensation for patients injured while unconscious. A hospital today conducts a highly integrated system of activities, with many persons contributing their efforts. There may be, e.g., preparation for surgery by nurses and interns who are employees of the hospital; administering of an anesthetic by a doctor who may be an employee of the hospital, an employee of the operating surgeon, or an independent contractor; performance of an operation by a surgeon and assistants who may be his employees, employees of the hospital, or independent contractors; and post surgical care by the surgeon, a hospital physician, and nurses. The number of those in whose care the patient is placed is not a good reason for denying him all reasonable opportunity to recover for negligent harm. It is rather a good reason for re-examination of the statement of legal theories which supposedly compel such a shocking result.

As *Ybarra* illustrates, the second element can be satisfied without proving exclusive control by the defendant. Thus the element might be more accurately stated as requiring plaintiff to provide evidence establishing the defendant is most likely the one responsible. It is worth noting that by proving the defendant is most likely the one responsible, the plaintiff also satisfies the third and final element, that the incident must not have been due to any voluntary action or contribution on the part of the plaintiff—a requirement meant to eliminate the possibility that it was the plaintiff who was responsible. Note that this third element does not require that plaintiff be completely uninvolved (e.g., unconscious during a surgery) but rather that plaintiff has done nothing to cause her own injury. This is why the requirements for invoking res ipsa are sometimes stated as requiring plaintiff to show: (1) the incident was probably due to negligence, and (2) the defendant was probably the culpable party.

Remember that this does not mean the plaintiff will prevail. Defendant can still submit evidence that he is not the one responsible, or submit no evidence and argue the plaintiff's evidence does not establish he is responsible. The jury is then free to weigh the evidence and determine responsibility. Res ipsa simply allows the judge to send the case to the trier of fact rather than dismiss it for lack of direct evidence of Defendant's responsibility.

Exercise 2-18 A Matter of Law

As you have learned in this section, duty is usually a matter of law—meaning that it is determined by the court at the outset of the litigation. On the other hand, whether the defendant breached the duty is a matter of fact, usually determined by a jury or trier of fact, who applies the relevant standard of care to the facts of the case.

For this exercise you are a clerk for a Judge sitting in the United States District Court in Maryland. You have been asked by the Judge to evaluate the following motions and recommend whether to grant or deny the Defendant's Motion for Summary judgment. The following questions may help guide your analysis:

1. Based on these motions do you believe there is a duty?

2. If you believe there is a duty, what is the duty owed?

3. Is duty the disputed issue?

4. What is the evidence of breach?

5. Is breach the disputed issue?

6. Does res ipsa loquitur apply to this case?

7. If res ipsa loquitur applies, does it allow plaintiff's case to be sent to the jury?

8. If res ipsa loquitur does not apply, has plaintiff presented sufficient evidence to allow the case to be sent to the jury?

---

1   UNITED STATES DISTRICT COURT, DISTRICT OF MARYLAND

2   NORTHERN DIVISION

3

4 Josephine J. O'HAVER,	No. 1:08-CV-01612-AMD
5 Plaintiff,	MEMORANDUM OF LAW IN SUPPORT OF DEFENDANT'S
6 v.	MOTION FOR SUMMARY JUDGMENT
7 THE CHEESECAKE FACTORY RESTAURANTS, INC.,	
8	
9 Defendant.	Date: December 9, 2008.

10

11   *   *   *

12   The Defendant, The Cheesecake Factory Restaurants, Inc. ("Cheesecake Factory"),

13 by its attorneys, … submits this Memorandum of Law in support of its Motion for

14 Summary Judgment, and states:

15   <u>STATEMENT OF UNDISPUTED MATERIAL FACTS</u>

16   The Plaintiff (hereinafter "Plaintiff' or "O'Haver") alleges in this litigation that she

17 was injured while patronizing the Cheesecake Factory Restaurant at Harborplace in

18 downtown Baltimore. Complaint, ¶ 1-3. Allegedly, she was sitting at an outdoor table

1   on a windy day when an umbrella detached from a nearby table and struck her on the
2   head and neck. *Id.;* Deposition of Josephine O'Haver, Exhibit 1 (hereinafter "O'Haver
3   Deposition) at 18. O'Haver believes that her waitress then lifted up the umbrella and
4   said, "It wasn't fastened properly." O'Haver Deposition at 48–49. However, O'Haver
5   admittedly has no reason to believe that anyone associated with the Defendant knew
6   that the umbrella had not been properly secured, if in fact it was not. O'Haver Deposi-
7   tion at 50. Additionally, the Plaintiff has offered no evidence to suggest that the Defen-
8   dant created the condition that injured her (as by improperly fastening the umbrella)
9   or failed to carefully inspect its premises for the existence of such conditions. Addition-
10 ally, Plaintiff has not suggested — and in fact could not suggest — that the umbrella was
11 within the exclusive control of Defendant. These points are significant, because with-
12 out such evidence Plaintiff is unable to prove that Defendant was negligent. The Plain-
13 tiff, who bears the burden of proof, cannot establish all of the elements of her
14 negligence claim. Defendant is entitled to summary judgment.

15 ## LEGAL STANDARD

16   Summary judgment practice in this Court is governed by Rule 56 of the Federal
17 Rules of Civil Procedure. Rule 56 provides that summary judgment "shall be rendered
18 forthwith if the pleadings, depositions, answers to interrogatories, and admissions on
19 file, together with the affidavits, if any, show that there is no genuine issue as to any
20 material fact and that the moving party is entitled to a judgment as a matter of law."
21 *Anderson v. Liberty Lobby,* 477 U.S. 242, 247, 91 L. Ed. 2d 202, 106 S. Ct. 2505
22 (1986). The Court is to consider the facts in the light most favorable to the non-
23 moving party. *Anderson,* 477 U.S. at 255 (1986); *Monumental Paving & Excavating,*
24 *Inc. v. Penn. Manufacturers Ass'n Ins. Co.,* 176 F.3d 794, 797 (4th Cir. 1999). The non-
25 moving party cannot avoid the entry of summary judgment with "mere allegations."
26 *Celotex Corp. v. Catrett,* 477 U.S. 317, 323, 91 L. Ed. 2d 265, 106 S. Ct. 2548 (1986).
27 Instead, the non-moving party must establish the existence of a genuine factual dis-
28 pute, with affidavits or other verified evidence. *Id.*

29 ## ARGUMENT

30   The duty a business owner owes to a person on its premises depends upon the per-
31 son's status at the time of an accident. *Casper v. Cas. F. Smith & Son, Inc.,* 316 Md. 573,
32 578, 560 A.2d 1130 (1989); *Tennant v. Shoppers Food Warehouse Md. Corp.,* 115 Md.
33 App. 381, 387, 693 A.2d 370, 374 (1997). The duty varies based on the visitor's status

as an invitee, a licensee, or a trespasser. *Baltimore Gas & Elec. Co. v. Lane,* 388 Md. 34, 44, 656 A.2d 307 (1995); *Wagner v. Doehring,* 315 Md. 97, 101, 553 A.2d 684 (1989); *Rowley v. Mayor of Balto.,* 305 Md. 456, 464–65, 505 A.2d 494 (1986). The highest duty is owed to business invitees, who enter the proprietor's property for purposes related to the proprietor's business. *Tennant,* 115 Md. App. at 388, 693 A.2d at 374. In this case, it is not disputed that at the time of the incident O'Haver was Defendant's business invitee.

It is also well settled that the owner of a business is not an insurer of its invitees' safety. *Manns v. Giant of Maryland, LLC,* 161 Md. App. 620, 871 A.2d 627, 631 (2005); *Moulden v. Greenbelt Consumer Svcs.,* 239 Md. 229, 210 A.2d 724, 726 (1965). An owner's duty is only to "protect the invitee from injury caused by an unreasonable risk that the invitee would be unlikely to perceive in the exercise of ordinary care for his or her own safety, and about which the owner knows or could have discovered in the exercise of reasonable care." *Tennant,* 115 Md. App. at 388, 693 A.2d at 374 (internal quotations omitted). A business owner is liable for an injury to an invitee only if it knew, or by the exercise of reasonable care could have known, of the condition that caused the injury. *Rawls v. Hochschild, Kohn & Co.,* 207 Md. 113, 117, 113 A.2d 405 (1955); *Tennant,* 115 Md. App. at 389, 693 A.2d at 374. In fact, the invitee bears the burden of proving that the proprietor created the dangerous condition or had actual or constructive knowledge of its existence. *Lexington Market Auth. v. Zappala,* 233 Md. 444, 446, 197 A.2d 147 (1964); *Rehn v. Westfield Am.,* 153 Md. App. 586, 593, 837 A.2d 981, 984 (2003).

It follows that there are only two theories which support a finding of negligence in this case. The first theory is that the Cheesecake Factory created the condition which allegedly resulted in O'Haver's injury, or in other words, that an employee of the Cheesecake Factory failed to properly fasten the umbrella in its stand. The second theory which would permit the Plaintiff to recover would depend on proof that some third party tampered with or improperly fastened the umbrella and the Cheesecake Factory knew, or by the exercise of reasonable care should have known, of the condition and failed to remedy it.

However, O'Haver admitted at her deposition that she has no reason to believe that the Cheesecake Factory knew that the umbrella was not properly secured in its stand. O'Haver Deposition at 50. Therefore under either theory O'Haver must produce some

1 admissible evidence to establish that Cheesecake Factory should and could have discov-
2 ered the condition with the exercise of reasonable care. This Plaintiff cannot do.

3   O'Haver cannot establish that the umbrella was not tampered with — innocently,
4 with no malicious intent implied — by another invitee trying, for example, to adjust
5 the placement of the umbrella at the table. Yet she must do so, because by law she must
6 prove that the Defendant had an adequate opportunity to discover and remedy the
7 condition. Not only is Plaintiff unable to prove how the umbrella came to be in what-
8 ever defective condition she says it was in, but she is also unable to prove when the
9 condition was created. There is no evidence, one way or the other, to show what
10 caused the problem and when it happened, and in the absence of such evidence Plain-
11 tiff's claim fails because she bears the burden of proof.

12   Even if the Plaintiff relies on the inference-permitting doctrine of *res ipsa loquitur*
13 to prove her claims, she cannot succeed because she cannot prove that the umbrella
14 was exclusively within the possession, custody and control of Defendant prior to the
15 incident. *See Chesapeake & Potomac Tel. Co. v. Hicks*, 25 Md. App. 503, 519, 337 A.2d
16 744, 754 (1975) (holding that plaintiff could not recover based on *res ipsa loquitur*
17 where phone booth which electrocuted him was "in a public place, open to public use
18 and readily accessible to intervening forces"); *see also Williams v. McCrory Stores Corp.*,
19 203 Md. 598, 604–05, 102 A.2d 253, 256 (1954) (holding that exclusive control over
20 instrumentality of injury — a chair — was not proven where the chairs were in the
21 temporary use and control of the many business patrons of the restaurant). In this
22 case, as in both *Hicks* and *Williams*, many patrons used the table near the Plaintiffs
23 table. The table and its umbrella were in a public place, open to the public, and read-
24 ily accessible to third parties. It is not permissible under such circumstances to infer
25 negligence on the part of one party — Defendant — and not on the part of the many
26 other parties with access to the umbrella.

27   The party opposing a properly supported motion for summary judgment "may not
28 rest upon the mere allegations or denials of his pleadings," but rather must "set forth
29 specific facts showing that there is a genuine issue for trial." *Bouchat v. Baltimore
30 Ravens Football Club, Inc.*, 346 F.3d 514, 525 (4th Cir. 2003) (interior alteration omit-
31 ted) (quoting FED. R. CIV. P. 56(e)). It is the "affirmative obligation of the trial judge
32 to prevent factually unsupported claims and defenses from proceeding to trial."
33 *Bouchat*, 346 F.3d at 526 (internal quotation marks omitted) (quoting *Drewitt v. Pratt*,

999 F.2d 774, 778–79 (4th Cir. 1993), and citing *Celotex Corp. v. Catrett,* 477 U.S. 317, 323–24, 106 S. Ct. 2548, 91 L. Ed. 2d 265 (1986)). In order to defeat summary judgment, the non-moving party must provide "specific factual support for every element of a claim." *Bouchat,* 346 F.3d at 622. Summary judgment is mandated when the non-moving party, after adequate time for discovery, has failed to make a showing sufficient to establish the existence of an element that is critical to the party's claim, and on which the party will bear the burden of proof at trial. *Celotex,* 477 U.S. at 322–23.

The time for discovery in this case has closed. Plaintiff cannot establish at least one essential element of her claim: that Defendant could and should have discovered the alleged problem with the umbrella with the exercise of ordinary care. She has not proffered a witness who would testify about the standard of care under such circumstances. She cannot say when the condition first occurred or how it was created. She has not sought discovery from Defendant on any of these issues. The only thing she can testify to is that she does not believe Defendant knew of any problem with the umbrella. This will not suffice. O'Haver should not be permitted to submit purely speculative claims to a jury.

CONCLUSION

For the foregoing reasons, the Court should enter summary judgment in Defendant's favor.

Respectfully submitted,

[Attorneys for Defendant]

1 UNITED STATES DISTRICT COURT, DISTRICT OF MARYLAND

2 NORTHERN DIVISION

3

4 Josephine J. O'HAVER,	No. 1:08-CV-01612-AMD
5 Plaintiff,	PLAINTIFF'S RESPONSE TO
	MOTION FOR SUMMARY
6 v.	JUDGMENT
7 THE CHEESECAKE FACTORY	
RESTAURANTS, INC.,	
8 Defendant.	Date: December 22, 2008.
9	

10

11   * * *

12   Now comes the Plaintiff, Ms. Josephine O'Haver, by counsel, [and] hereby responds

13 to the Defendant's Motion for Summary Judgment, and pursuant to Rule 56 of the

14 Federal Rules of Evidence, hereby moves this Honorable Court to deny the Defendant's

15 Motion for Summary Judgment in this matter, and in support thereof states as follows:

16   As the Defendant pointed out in their Memorandum, the duty owed to a person

17 on a business premises depends upon that person's status at the time of the accident.

18 In the case at hand the Defendant has admitted that the Plaintiff was a business invi-

19 tee and that as such they owed her the highest duty possible to someone who enters

20 onto another's property. When dealing with a business invitee the owner has a duty

21 "to 'protect the invitee from injury caused by an unreasonable risk' that the invitee

22 would be unlikely to perceive in the exercise of ordinary care for his or her own

23 safety, and about which the owner knows or could have discovered in the exercise of

24 reasonable care." *Tennant v. Shoppers Food Warehouse Md. Corp.,* 115 Md.App. 381,

25 388, 693 A.2d 370, 374 (1997) (quoting *Casper v. Chas. F. Smith & Son, Inc.,* 316 Md.

26 573, 582, 560 A.2d 1130, 1135 (1989)). Additionally, "[t]he duties of a business invi-

27 tor thus include the obligation to warn invitees of known hidden dangers, a duty to

28 inspect, and a duty to take reasonable precautions against foreseeable dangers." *Ten-*

29 *nant,* 115 Md.App. at 388, 693 A.2d at 374.

30   **REASONABLE DISCOVERY**

31   It is undisputed that the Plaintiff was dining at the Cheesecake Factory Restaurant at

32 Harborplace in Baltimore City when she was struck by an umbrella that detached from

33 a nearby table. It is also undisputed that the umbrella was owned and maintained by

the Cheesecake Factory Restaurant. They are the ones who invited their patrons to dine in an outdoor facility beneath large heavy umbrellas. Finally, the Cheesecake Factory does not dispute that the day in question was windy. Despite these points of agreement, the Defendant has alleged that the Plaintiff cannot establish that (through the exercise of ordinary care) the Defendant could have, and should have, discovered the problem. The Plaintiff disagrees.

The Defendant, by their own admission, concedes that "[The Cheesecake Factory] take[s] precautions to ensure that these umbrellas are appropriately secured and have no control over gusts of wind that are beyond the control of our staff members." Cheesecake Factory letter to Plaintiff's Counsel, ¶ 2, Exhibit 1. This admission in itself shows that the Defendant should have discovered the problem. The Defendant has admitted that they take precautions to secure these umbrellas, yet this umbrella was obviously not secured properly (or it would not have flown up out of its holder).

The Defendant in this case has conceded that they exercise control over the umbrellas by undertaking to inspect them. They obviously were aware of the potential risk of putting these umbrellas outdoors because they did inspect them. Their only allegation was that they cannot control gusts of winds. Nobody expects them to control gusts of wind. But they are expected to take precautions to protect their patrons against those gusts of wind, an obligation they obviously knew they had. Otherwise, why did they inspect the umbrellas?

A business owner has "a duty to inspect, and a duty to take reasonable precautions against foreseeable dangers." *Tennant*, 115 Md.App. at 388, 693 A.2d at 374. It is reasonably foreseeable that on a windy day, an umbrella might be taken away by a gust of wind. The Defendant therefore has a duty to take precautions to ensure that this does not happen, or if it does happen, no invitees are injured in the process. Additionally, the business owner has a duty to inspect. It is not unreasonable to ask a business owner to inspect a foreseeable danger, like the danger present in this case. The Defendant has already conceded that they take precautions to ensure that the umbrellas are secure, however it is obvious that this umbrella had either not been inspected, or it had not been properly inspected. If they did not believe the umbrella could have been properly secured, they should not have invited people to dine outdoors in the first place. The Defendant, through their own admission, has conceded that they should have reasonably discovered the foreseeable danger and problem with the umbrella; therefore, the question should be submitted to a jury.

INDIRECT INFERENCES

The Defendant has also argued that the Plaintiff cannot rely on the doctrine of *res ipsa loquitur* to prove her claims of liability because she cannot prove the umbrella was within the exclusive control of the Defendant. However, the Plaintiff can prove liability without resorting to *res ipsa loquitur*. The umbrella in the case at hand was owned by the Defendant, on the Defendant's property, was erected by the Defendant and flew out of its holder and struck the Plaintiff; these facts are all undisputed. These known facts in and of themselves (without even considering the fact that an employee of the Defendant admitted that the umbrella was not properly secured; Defense Memorandum Exhibit 1, p. 49) are legally sufficient for a jury to conclude that the umbrella was not properly secured, thus making the Defendant liable. The jury is permitted to draw a direct inference from these facts to the conclusion of liability. It is no different than proving a fact by circumstantial instead of direct evidence. The surrounding circumstances in Ms. O'Haver's case clearly show that the umbrella was not properly secured. Therefore, Ms. O'Haver is not required to produce direct evidence on this point. *Res ipsa loquitur* is irrelevant. It is simply a standard negligence case proven in part by circumstantial evidence.

This idea of a direct inference being used to support liability, without the use of *res ipsa loquitur*, has been consistently upheld by Maryland courts. Both the case of *Nalee, Inc. v. Jacobs* and the case of *Cogan Kibler, Inc. v. Vito* are analogous to the case at hand and support the idea that a direct inference may be draw from certain facts to prove liability without the use of the doctrine *of res ipsa loquitur*. *Nalee, Inc. v. Jacobs*, 228 Md. 525, 180 A.2d 677 (1962), *Cogan Kibler, Inc. v. Vito*, 346 Md. 200, 695 A.2d 191 (1997). The court in *Nalee* specifically stated that, "[t]he close resemblance or relationship which may exist between what may be classified as *res ipsa loquitur* cases and cases in which a direct inference of the defendant's negligence may be drawn from particular fact, has been pointed out more than once."

In *Nalee*, the accident occurred in a restaurant when two (2) patrons who were seated on a heavy bench leaned forward, tipping over the bench and causing it to strike another patron. The "plaintiff did not produce evidence directly describing the absence of fastenings between the bench and the restaurant floor, but the absence was proved by inference." *Cogan Kibler, Inc. v. Vito,* 346 Md. at 211, 695 A.2d at 196 (1997) (describing *Nalee,* 228 Md. 525, 180 A.2d 677 (1962)). Even though the Plaintiff offered no actual evidence of the actual fastening of the bench, "the known facts supported the direct inference that the defendant was negligent in failing to have the bench securely fastened to the floor." *Id.* at 211, 196 (1997). This is the same situation in the instant case. The Defendant has argued that the Plaintiff cannot offer facts to support the allegation that the umbrella was improperly secured, but the Plaintiff does not need to offer such facts. These facts may be inferred by the jury based upon the surrounding circumstances. The umbrella was on the Defendant's property, the umbrella was owned by the Defendant and it is common sense that if an umbrella is not secured it could be picked up by the wind. Therefore, the jury can infer that because the umbrella was picked up by the wind it was not secured at all or it was improperly secured.

The court in *Cogan Kibler, Inc.* used the same concept. In *Cogan,* an office worker was injured when she inhaled primer fumes during the renovation and painting of a room adjacent to hers. The primer fumes were passed through the air conditioning system which was connected to the other rooms in the department. The Plaintiff argued that the painter was negligent in failing to ensure that there was adequate ventilation to disperse the primer fumes elsewhere without causing injury to workers in adjacent rooms. The Defendant painter argued (like the Cheesecake Factory) that during the renovation, the air conditioning system was not within their exclusive control, therefore they could not be held liable under the doctrine of *res ipsa loquitur.* However, the Court ruled that the Plaintiff did not need to rely upon *res ipsa loquitur* to support the finding that the painter's negligence was the proximate cause of the Plaintiff injuries. In fact, "[h]ere, Vito did not offer direct evidence describing the absence of sufficient ventilation in the expansion area, but the inference that there was insufficient ventilation is one that the jury could draw." *Cogan Kibler, Inc. v. Vito,* 346 Md. at 211, 695 A.2d at 196 (1997). The fact that the injury occurred can, under appropriate circumstances, justify a jury in concluding that it must have occurred as a result of the Defendant's negligence, even without *res ipsa loquitur.*

If the jury concluded that it was highly unusual for ten percent of the population of the Department to be so adversely affected by the fumes as to require hospital examination, the jury could also infer that any belief by [the Defendant] that there was adequate ventilation under the circumstances was unreasonable.

Id. at 209, 195 (1997).

Again, this is analogous to the instant case. The inference that the umbrella was improperly secured can be clearly drawn from the facts of the case. To prove liability, the Plaintiff need not prove that the umbrella was within the exclusive control of the Defendant, as the Defendant has stated. The Plaintiff can show that the Defendant knew about the potential risk, claimed to have conducted inspections in order to alleviate that risk, and yet failed to adequately inspect this particular umbrella, leading to the Plaintiff's injuries. Because direct inferences can be drawn to support the liability of the Defendant, the question should be submitted to a jury.

RES IPSA LOQUITUR

While the Plaintiff believes that the doctrine of *res ipsa loquitur* need not be used to prove the Defendant's negligence, the Plaintiff can succeed under this theory as well. To successfully prove liability under *res ipsa loquitur,* a plaintiff must "prove three elements: (1) a casualty of a sort which usually does not occur in the absence of negligence; (2) caused by an instrumentality within the defendant's exclusive control; and (3) under circumstances indicating that the casualty did not result from the act or omission of the plaintiff." *Cogan Kibler,* 346 Md. at 209, 695 A.2d at 195 (citing *Dover Elevator Co. v. Swann,* 334 Md. 231, 236–37, 638 A.2d 762, 765 (1994). The Defendant has not challenged the first and third elements of this doctrine. Their entire argument alleges that the Plaintiff cannot meet the second.

The second element of this doctrine deals with the exclusive control of the instrumentality, in this case the umbrella. The Defendant argues that because the umbrella may come within the control of patrons of the restaurant, exclusive control may not be proven or even alleged. To support this allegation, the Defendant has cited two cases in particular, both of which are distinguishable from the case at hand.

The first case upon which the Defendant relies is *Chesapeake & Potomac Tel. Co. v. Hicks,* 25 Md.App. 503, 337 A.2d 744 (1975). In this case, the plaintiff was unable to recover damages under the doctrine of *res ipsa loquitur* for injuries sustained when he was electrocuted by a telephone booth. The court held that because the telephone booth was "in a public place, open to public use and readily accessible to intervening forces," the owner of the telephone booth did not have exclusive control over it. *Id.* at 519, 337 A.2d at 754.

1 This case is easily distinguished from the case at hand due to the location of the in-
2 strumentality. In *Chesapeake* the telephone booth was located outside of a tavern on the
3 sidewalk. *Id.* at 506, 337 A.2d 747. Because the telephone booth was on the sidewalk, it
4 was easily accessible to the public at all times of the day or night. This phone booth,
5 though owned by a private company, was located so that anyone in the public could ac-
6 cess it.

7 The Cheesecake Factory has alleged that the umbrella was "located in a public place,
8 open to the public, and readily accessible to third parties," as the phone booth was in
9 *Chesapeake.* By drawing this comparison between the umbrella and the phone booth, the
10 Defendant has taken the Court's reasoning out of context. The umbrella in the instant
11 case was located at a private restaurant and the phone booth on a public sidewalk.
12 Though the restaurant is open to the public, it is located on private property. The restau-
13 rant has specific hours which it is open to the public and it is not accessible to the public
14 twenty-four (24) hours a day, like a phone booth located on a sidewalk. The umbrella lo-
15 cated inside of a restaurant is only accessible to patrons of the restaurant, while a phone
16 booth on the sidewalk is accessible to any passersby. The Cheesecake Factory has the
17 power to control who has access to the umbrellas and to dictate certain times when they
18 are allowed access. The instrumentalities in these two cases are very easily distinguished
19 from each other. The umbrella in the case at hand is not within the meaning of "located
20 in a public place, open to the public, and readily accessible to third parties," as envi-
21 sioned by the court in *Chesapeake.*

22 Second, the Defendant cites *Williams v. McCrory Stores Corp.*, 203 Md. 598, 102
23 A.2d 253 (1954), a case in which the owner of a restaurant/bar was held not liable for
24 the Plaintiff's injuries when she fell off a bar stool. It was shown that the bar stool was
25 in the temporary use and control of many business patrons, therefore the restaurant
26 owner did not have exclusive control over the bar stool. However, in *Williams,* it was
27 estimated that between "15,000 and 20,000 people come to his store every week ... [a]
28 great many of that crowd occupy the stools at the restaurant counter." *Id.* at 604–605,
29 102 A.2d at 256. While the Defendant has alleged that a number of patrons could have
30 come in contact with the umbrella, there has been no allegation that tens of thousands
31 of patrons could have done so. In fact, the Defendant has offered no evidence to sug-
32 gest that anyone was even sitting at the table from which the umbrella was dislodged (it
33 came from a neighboring table, not Ms. O'Haver's) nor have they offered any evidence

1 stating that anyone was *ever* sitting at that table. If they did produce evidence about the

2 number of patrons who allegedly had access to the table at issue, it would likely result

3 in a factual dispute, thereby defeating the Defendant's Motion for Summary Judgment

4 anyway.

5   Additionally, the accident happened at approximately 12:30 PM and the Cheesecake

6 Factory Restaurant opened at 11:30 AM. Exhibit 2. Because the accident happened

7 merely one (1) hour after the restaurant opened, it would be hard to believe that thou-

8 sands of people were in contact with the umbrella before it fell, making the case at

9 hand distinguishable from *Williams*.

10   Finally, *Williams* was not a typical *res ipsa loquitur* case. In *Williams* there was not even

11 any evidence that the barstool was defective or improperly maintained in the first place.

12 Unlike Ms. O'Haver's case, Williams had nothing to do with a failure to inspect or main-

13 tain. There was absolutely nothing wrong with the stool. A maintenance man even exam-

14 ined it immediately after the plaintiff fell and found it to be in perfect working order.

15 That is not the case for Ms. O'Haver. The umbrella stand clearly was not in perfect work-

16 ing order or else the umbrella never would have blown out. Exclusive control was mean-

17 ingless in *Williams* because even if the defendant had been in exclusive control, there was

18 nothing to "fix." In Ms. O'Haver's case, not only was there something to fix, but the De-

19 fendant knew that failure to do so carried a risk to its customers and yet failed to fulfill

20 their legal obligations anyway.

21   The Defendant has failed to prove why, as a matter of law, *res ipsa loquitur* is not a

22 viable claim. Therefore, the question should be submitted to a jury.

23   WHEREFORE, for all the foregoing reasons the Plaintiff respectfully requests that

24 the Defendant's Motion for Summary Judgment be denied.

25   Respectfully submitted,

26   [Attorneys for Plaintiff]

27

28

29

30

31

32

33

UNITED STATES DISTRICT COURT, DISTRICT OF MARYLAND

NORTHERN DIVISION

Josephine J. O'HAVER,
 	
     Plaintiff,
 	
v.
 	
THE CHEESECAKE FACTORY
RESTAURANTS, INC.,
 	
     Defendant.
	No. 1:08-CV-01612-AMD
	
	DEFENDANT'S REPLY TO
	PLAINTIFF'S RESPONSE TO
	MOTION FOR SUMMARY
	JUDGMENT
	
	Date: January 5, 2009.

* * *

The Defendant, The Cheesecake Factory Restaurants, Inc. ("the Cheesecake Factory") ... pursuant to Rule 56 of the *Federal Rules of Evidence,* respectfully replies to the Plaintiff's Response to its Motion for Summary Judgment ("Plaintiff's Response"), and states as follows:

ARGUMENT

Plaintiff's arguments lack substance.... She argues that a direct inference of liability is permissible because the fact that the umbrella was owned by the Defendant, coupled with the alleged admission of an employee of the Defendant that it was improperly secured, is sufficient to establish negligence. *See* Plaintiff's Response at 4. This is simply not a correct statement of Maryland law. The Plaintiff in this case, whether she wishes to recognize it or not, bears the burden of proving either that the Defendant created the allegedly dangerous condition or had actual or constructive knowledge of its existence. *Lexington Market Auth. v. Zappala,* 233 Md. 444, 446, 197 A.2d 147 (1964); *Rehn v. Westfield Am.,* 153 Md. App. 586, 593, 837 A.2d 981, 984 (2003). Without proof of one of those factors, her claim must fail as a matter of law.

The Plaintiff has offered no such proof. Instead, she admitted at her deposition that she has no reason to believe that the Defendant knew of the condition at all. *See* Defendant's Motion for Summary Judgment at 4. Frankly, the issue is not whether the Defendant had an obligation to inspect, as the Plaintiff trumpets in her Response. Rather, the issue is whether the satisfaction of that obligation under the circumstances presented by this case would have prevented the Plaintiff's accident. On this, the Plaintiff is mute. Perhaps this is because there is simply no evidence from which a jury could conclude that the condition could have been discovered with the exercise of reasonable care.

1   With respect to *res ipsa loquitur,* the Plaintiff confuses the idea of "control" with "ex-
2 clusive control". They are not one and the same, and the theory requires proof of "ex-
3 clusive control". The Defendant is a restaurant located in a public place. Although she
4 argues that the Defendant opened at 11:30 a.m., one hour before the incident at issue
5 (based on a print out of a website made on December 22, 2008—more than three
6 years after the Plaintiff's accident), the Plaintiff assumes that therefore only one hour
7 could have passed between the time that the umbrella became "improperly secured"
8 and the time of the Plaintiff's accident. Such an assumption is inappropriate in this
9 case as the Plaintiff has offered and can offer no proof of when the umbrella became
10 "improperly secured". Nor can the Plaintiff say how the umbrella was "improperly se-
11 cured". Finally, the Plaintiff apparently argues that the Defendant bears the burden of
12 proving that other customers used the table before the Plaintiff did. *See* Plaintiff's Re-
13 sponse at 8. This, again, is not correct: if she wishes to rely on the doctrine of *res ipsa*
14 *loquitur* to prove her case, she, not the Defendant, must establish that the Defendant
15 had exclusive control over the instrumentality at issue. This she cannot do, for all of
16 the reasons previously argued.

17   WHEREFORE, the Defendant, The Cheesecake Factory Restaurants, Inc., respect-
18 fully requests that the Court enter summary judgment in its favor, and requests such
19 additional relief as the Court may deem appropriate.

20   Respectfully submitted,

21   [Attorneys for Defendant]

22

23

24

25

26

27

28

29

30

31

32

33

A Final Note about Duty

As you might have guessed from the materials and exercises in this section, duty issues may arise in a wide variety of circumstances and scenarios. The goal of this section was not to provide you with an exhaustive study of the concept of duty, but rather to equip you with the tools necessary for determining whether a duty exists, and if so, the extent of the duty owed (or standard of care) so that you are able to determine, in any circumstance, whether any particular conduct is a breach of duty, for purposes of evaluating a negligence claim. You've learned that these determinations might involve reviewing cases, statutes, and regulations; researching industry customs and standards; and obtaining opinions from experts. You've also learned that you may need to synthesize materials to accurately portray the law and you may need to learn a new vocabulary to understand the facts of a client's case. The point is that once you understand how to determine: (1) whether a duty exists; (2) the scope of a duty (the standard of care); and (3) whether the conduct in the case is a breach of duty, you are equipped to evaluate these issues in any case that may arise in your practice.

2. Damages

To prove negligence, the plaintiff will also have to establish she suffered damages, which requires proof of the existence and extent of the harm suffered and the amount of money she should be awarded as compensation for that harm. Although damages are usually listed as the final required element for proving a claim for negligence, they are often the first consideration for a plaintiff's lawyer considering whether to take a case, because negligence cases are typically taken on a contingency basis, meaning the lawyer will only be paid if the plaintiff wins at trial or settles the claim for money. Also, for most personal injury cases the plaintiff's lawyer will typically be awarded a percentage of the plaintiff's recovery.

One of a lawyer's most valuable resources is her time; for this reason, when deciding whether to accept a case, a plaintiff's lawyer must consider the amount of time it will take to litigate the plaintiff's claim, the likelihood of recovery, and the amount of damages the plaintiff stands to recover. A lawyer will probably not be willing to accept a case with very little damages, especially one that requires the lawyer to spend substantial hours litigating a claim, because if the lawyer accepts such cases, he or she would not likely be able to earn a living practicing law. This is not to discount the fact that many lawyers will litigate cases with little or no monetary value, or take a case pro bono (without pay) because of the principles of law or fact or social policy considerations involved in the dispute. Absent one of these factors, however, the monetary value of the case, and what the lawyer stands to gain or give up by agreeing to take it, is critical; if it will cost more (in terms of the lawyer's time and other resources) to litigate the case than the lawyer is likely to be able to recover, the lawyer will not usually agree to represent the injured party.

On the other hand the defendant's lawyer, who is not usually paid on a contingency, and who will likely be paid an hourly fee by the client, will probably focus on whether there is a duty that was owed and breached or whether the breach caused any alleged injuries, because if any of these elements can be disproven, the defendant is not liable for any damages—and the case will be dismissed, even if there is significant injury. If liability can be established (or there is some question as to whether it can be established) defendant's lawyer will then be concerned about the extent of damages because it will impact the amount of money that the client will have to pay.

In this text duty and breach are covered first, because those concepts are really the heart of the tort of negligence, while an award of damages is really the remedy for the tort (and thus a topic covered during a third year course usually called Remedies). Also, when you first begin to conceptualize what negligence is, an understanding of how responsibility and liability is determined (e.g., an understanding of risk, duty, and breach) is a better introduction to the tort than a focus on damages, because focusing on damages at the outset might lead you to think that injury is the critical aspect of proving negligence — which is not true. In reality, most of the time lawyers take cases where it is clear the party has suffered a compensable injury, and so the issue is not whether there are damages, but rather how much should be awarded. Finally, although the topic of damages usually comes after causation in the list of elements that must be proven to establish negligence, determining whether the breach caused the damages is easier to do if you first identify the damages and the breach.

Skill Focus: Organizing Material

This section provides you with an important opportunity to consider how you might reorder concepts you learn in law school to suit your purpose. For example, a law student evaluating whether she could establish the elements required for proving a negligence claim might think about them in this order:

1. Identify duty and breach
2. Identify the injury (damages)
3. Look to see whether the breach was the cause of the damages

A lawyer (representing a plaintiff) might think about the elements in this order:

1. Are there provable damages? (if a client has no remedy — i.e. the potential for an award of damages — there is no point in going further) In what amount? Is it worth the time to litigate?
2. Are there other considerations that interest me?
3. Who potentially caused the damages? Will they be able to pay the award? Are they potentially immune? Will I be able to file suit against them?
4. What theory (or theories) of liability will I allege?

A law student writing an exam, or a court writing an opinion will (assuming each of the elements is at issue):

1. Discuss duty
2. Discuss breach
3. Discuss causation
4. Discuss damages, which, in a torts class will not usually be the critical issue — since damages are usually viewed as a remedies topic

This is also the order a plaintiff's lawyer drafting a complaint will likely plead the elements of the cause of action. This illustrates the importance of thinking about the order in which you will present concepts in your examinations and how it might differ from the order topics are presented in your courses (including this one).

Now that you understand where damages might "fit" in your evaluation of a negligence claim, it is time to move on to understanding what they are, and how they are proven.

In a negligence action a plaintiff may be compensated for: property damages; past and future medical expenses; past and future loss of earnings and loss of earning capacity; incidental economic losses; and pain and suffering. Below is a very general overview of each of these types of damages.

When real or personal property is damaged, destroyed or lost courts will usually base a damages award on the diminished fair market value of the property for damaged property, and total fair market value for property that is destroyed or lost. Plaintiff may also be compensated for loss of use of the property, and sometimes for sentimental value. These issues are typically covered in Remedies courses.

Medical expenses include payments to doctors and hospitals, as well as the cost of tests, medical equipment, physical therapy and nursing care. Past medical expenses are easier to establish, because those costs have already been billed by the provider; the more complicated issues, and higher damages awards, usually relate to the costs of future medical care—which can be difficult to prove, since they have not yet occurred. Proof of the need for future medical care usually requires expert testimony, to establish that such care will be necessary.

Lost earnings include past or future wages or business earnings plaintiff did not or will not receive as a result of the injury. Like medical expenses, past losses (which have already been suffered) are easier to prove than future losses. Even more difficult to establish is a loss of earning capacity; loss of earning capacity is a claim for wages from a job plaintiff would have been capable of holding, if the injury had not occurred. To prove lost earning capacity plaintiff must establish that she had the ability, skills and aptitude for such a career. Level and type of education, as well as employment history may be relevant to this determination; for example, if plaintiff dropped out of college prior to the injury, it will be difficult to prove he would have been able to be a lawyer, even if it were his life-long dream. However, a defendant may not reduce liability by arguing that plaintiff had not yet (and so would not have) exploited potential earning capacity; for example, if a plaintiff has a law degree, and at the time of injury is working as a teacher, he may still recover for a loss of an attorney's salary by proving he could have (and would have) gone back to work as a lawyer. In many states the standard for recovering the higher, as yet untapped, earning capacity is that the plaintiff must show it is reasonably certain that he would have ultimately taken the career with higher earning capacity.

Earning capacity issues are especially challenging when the plaintiff is an infant or child. In such cases, courts will often look to evidence of the plaintiff's intelligence and school performance (if such data is available). The careers and achievements of other family members may also be introduced as evidence of the infant or child's earning capacity. Unsupported aspirations, hopes and dreams, however, are not likely going to convince a court that a child would have had a particular career or earning capacity.

Another issue relating to proving earning capacity is proof of the duration of the expected earnings. Some careers last longer than others; for example, the careers of most professional athletes are much shorter than the careers of most doctors. Also, some people live longer than others; there are usually actuarial tables setting out general life expectancy rates. Expert witnesses may be called to provide opinions as to whether plaintiff's life might have been longer or shorter than the life span set out in such tables. Thus, in order to calculate an award for earning capacity the trier of fact must determine plaintiff's life expectancy prior to the injury, as well as the age at which she might have been expected to retire or reduce her workload as a result of age or illness, and the length of the career she expected to have.

Incidental economic losses include those additional monetary expenses plaintiff will incur as a result of the injury. For example, the cost of traveling to a location to receive medical treatment, or the childcare costs plaintiff must pay to have her children cared for while she receives treatment.

The final damages category—pain and suffering—is probably the broadest. This category covers all physical and emotional distress relating to the injury, including distress over reductions in life expectancy and earning capacity, concerns about increased chances of illness as a result of the injury, loss of enjoyment of life, distress over loss of ability to perform daily activities, and other embarrassment, sadness, depression, and discomfort related to the injury. The dollar value of such injuries is subjective—and often difficult to assess.

Exercise 2-19 Evaluating Damages

For this exercise we return to the chapter problem. Below are excerpts from the depositions of Plaintiffs' and Defendants' respective experts. After you review the deposition transcripts, make a list of the damages described by Plaintiffs' expert and a separate list of the damages described by Defendants' expert. Determine:

1. Whether the experts agree on any issues relating to damages;

2. Which issues are in dispute;

3. How the disputed issues might impact the amount of damages awarded to plaintiffs;

4. Whether, based on your reading in this section, there are other damages that might be alleged.

Excerpt from Deposition of Plaintiff's Damages Expert

1   Q Are you aware of the child's current impairments?

2   A Yes.

3   Q What are they?

4   A The child has weakness of all four extremities; has

5   mild to moderate quadriparesis; has hypotonia; has active

6   deep tendon reflexes at plus 2.

7   Clearly Marcus is retarded with respect to language.

8   Essentially nonverbal. He is clearly delayed with respect

9   to psychosocial, adaptive, behavioral, motoric, as well

10   as language communication.

11   He is ambulatory. He is able to walk independently but

12   does it with a wide-based, ataxic gait. So I think

there's a cerebellar component. He clearly, however, requires one-on-one care for his adaptive needs, such as
dressing, feeding, toiletry, personal hygiene, and has
little in the way of independent functioning as it relates to his ability to socialize and interact with his
outside world.

Q And you're aware he has no cerebral palsy?

A Well, he certainly would be classified as a child with
cerebral palsy if by that you mean weakness or compromise
of motor function based upon the central nervous system.
He certainly has central nervous system pathology, and he
certainly has generalized weakness and compromise in
function. I saw significant ataxia. All of these findings,
if you've seen him, would rise to the level of the lay
person's definition of cerebral palsy, which is not a term
that's used by a child neurologist as a rule.

Q Nonetheless, he doesn't have any spasticity?

A No. But a spastic condition is only one kind of cerebral palsy. There are many other kinds in which spasticity does not play a role.

Q. What is his life expectancy?

A This child can be expected to live, if not normal, at
least near normal—a normal lifespan for his demographic
group would be 80 to 85 years. You would expect him,
under these circumstances, to live perhaps 65 to 70
years, given his severe psychomotor retardation—

Q Doctor, you're—go ahead. I'm sorry. I interrupted.
I'm sorry.

A In terms of prognosis he will forever be disabled. He
will not be economically independent He will require probably one-on-one custodial care on a 24-hour basis, which
he is now receiving from his mother. He will require assistance for virtually everything, including feeding,

1 dressing, toiletry, cooking, cleaning, transportation,
2 recreational and social opportunities. He will require on-
3 going special education. He should benefit from occupa-
4 tional/physical therapy once a week for the next ten to
5 fifteen years, through his adolescence.
6   If he develops a seizure disorder, he obviously will
7 need to be seen by a child neurologist, with EEGs and an-
8 ticonvulsant therapy if that's required.
9   He is ambulatory, and I would doubt if he's going to
10 require any significant surgical intervention in either
11 lower extremity, primarily because spasticity has not yet
12 been reported.
13   So his prognosis is that of a child who will be forever
14 dependent upon his environment for his care and support.
15
16
17
18
19
20
21
22
23
24
25
26
27
28
29
30
31
32
33

Excerpt of Deposition of Defendant's Damages Expert

1   Q. Do you have any opinion about his life expectancy?

2   A. Give me a second to think about that one. Here is

3 what I will tell you. If someone asked me about his life

4 expectancy, nobody who has any disease, including neuro-

5 logical disease, has normal life expectancy. That's a

6 statement that I can make.

7   Q. Okay. Well, more likely than not is he going to have

8 a reduction in life expectancy? And if so, based upon

9 what, and by how many days, weeks, months, or years?

10 Defendant's Attorney: Objection. Form.

11 A. More likely than not there will be some reduction,

12 because that's what happens with most metabolic disease.

13 But this is a rare case and I cannot be sure.

14 Q. If, in fact, it turns out that this child does not

15 have a metabolic disorder, there isn't anything else

16 about his health that would lead him to have anything

17 less than a normal life expectancy, is there?

18 A. There will be some reduction in life expectancy, be-

19 cause hypotonia, which is a poor muscle tone may be asso-

20 ciated with some (inaudible) aspiration. But I'm not

21 aware of any studies that have looked into that respect.

22 Q. You would agree with me that this young man should

23 be seeing a physiatrist or a PM&R doctor, wouldn't you?

24 A. Yes.

25 Q. He should be seeing a physiatrist as often as the

26 physiatrist would ask, but at least a couple of times of

27 year until he is an adult, shouldn't he?

28 A. I agree with your first statement. As often as the

29 physiatrist wants to see him, that's how often he should

30 see him.

31

1   Q. Would you agree that he should continue to see a
2 neurologist on at least an annual basis?
3   A. Yes.
4   Q. Do you think that at some point in his later youth
5 or as he approaches adulthood he is also going to need to
6 see an orthopedist and probably have some orthopedic x-
7 rays taken because of his postural instability and the
8 way he moves?
9   A. It is possible.
10   Q. Do you think this young man should be having physi-
11 cal therapy, occupational therapy and speech therapy?
12   A. Yes.
13   Q. Those therapies are necessary outside of the limited
14 amount he is getting in the classroom; correct?
15   A. I don't know how much he is getting in the class-
16 room, but I think a professional, just exactly what I
17 said about physiatry. A professional in those fields, as
18 often as they decide that he needs to be seen, that's how
19 often he should be seen.
20   Q. Do you think it would be useful for Marcus to have
21 if not a physiatrist then some type of a case manager to
22 help him get all of these therapies and treatments that
23 he needs?
24   A. Yes.
25   Q. You would agree with me, wouldn't you, that Marcus
26 will never be able to live on his own?
27   A. Yes.
28   Q. He will always need a caregiver?
29   A. Yes.
30   Q. And that caregiver will have to be somebody who has
31 the experience and knowledge to care for somebody who has
32 among all of his obvious problems the safety issue who
33 can appreciate the safety issues and be able to take care

1 of him and protect him from himself, in essence. Wouldn't

2 you agree with that?

3   A. Yes.

4   Q. That would be somebody along the lines of what? An

5 LPN or an RN?

6   A. There are different people. Again, it depends what

7 is available. There are different kinds of settings, but

8 the principle of what you say is correct.

9   Q. It would need to be somebody more than like a

10 babysitter that you could go out and get?

11   A. There are various settings in which children, young

12 adults and adults like this are taken care of with vari-

13 ous levels of trained personnel. There are residential

14 homes with various levels of trained personnel. Really I

15 can't speak to the exact degree that these people need. I

16 agree completely in principle with what you said as to

17 his needs.

18   Q. So you agree that the average like babysitter, like

19 a college student who is just looking to pick up some

20 money during the summer, you need somebody who is more

21 qualified than that?

22   A. Correct.

23   Q. Would you also agree with me that Marcus will never

24 be gainfully employed?

25   A. Yes.

26   Q. Would you also agree with me that in all likelihood

27 Marcus will never be potty trained?

28   A. I don't know that one way or the other.

29   Q. Do you know that from reading the records and from

30 the information you learned from the family that they

31 have been trying to potty train him for about three years

32 unsuccessfully?

33

1   A. I know that they had tried to potty train him and
2 that it was unsuccessful. That's what I know.
3   Q. Do you think that things like a handheld shower and
4 a bath chair would be useful to help Marcus try to become
5 at least a little bit independent in the personal toi-
6 letry area?
7   A. Yes.
8   Q. Do you think that it would be useful for Marcus to
9 have some type of a communication device to try to train
10 him at least basic things in how to communicate?
11   A. It would be worth a try. I don't know whether it
12 would be successful or not.
13   Q. Was Marcus wearing AFOs when you saw him?
14   A. I don't remember.
15   Q. Your report doesn't reflect one way or another?
16   A. Correct.
17   Q. If his doctors prescribed AFOs, you would have no
18 problem saying he would continue to need those AFOs in-
19 definitely and perhaps forever?
20   A. Whatever the physiatrist says, that's the right an-
21 swer.
22   Q. And you would agree with me that this child will
23 never be able to live out on his own, he's going to re-
24 quire somebody to care for him for his entire life?
25   A. Most likely.
26
27
28
29
30
31
32
33

Exercise 2-20 Calculating the "Value" of Injuries

1. Do you find it challenging to place a monetary value on any of the injuries sustained by plaintiffs in the chapter problem? Which injuries? Why?

2. What monetary value would you place on Marcus' pain and suffering? What monetary value would you place on his parents' pain and suffering? What method would you use to calculate such an award?

3. If you were the plaintiffs' attorney attempting to counsel Marcus' parents about making a settlement demand, how would you discuss the value of Marcus' and his parents' injuries and arrive at a dollar value you could convey to defendants in your demand? What issues might impact Marcus' parents' feelings about the value of the case?

Exercise 2-21 Recovery for Emotional Injuries

Many jurisdictions limit recovery for pain and suffering by placing a cap on the amount of damages plaintiffs may be awarded for noneconomic damages. For example, in Michigan (where our chapter problem is located), the following statute has been enacted:

(1) In an action for damages alleging medical malpractice by or against a person or party, the total amount of damages for noneconomic loss recoverable by all plaintiffs, resulting from the negligence of all defendants, shall not exceed $280,000.00 unless, as the result of the negligence of 1 or more of the defendants, 1 or more of the following exceptions apply as determined by the court pursuant to section 6304.1 in which case damages for noneconomic loss shall not exceed $500,000.00:

(a) The plaintiff is hemiplegic, paraplegic, or quadriplegic resulting in a total permanent functional loss of 1 or more limbs caused by 1 or more of the following:

(i) Injury to the brain.

(ii) Injury to the spinal cord.

(b) The plaintiff has permanently impaired cognitive capacity rendering him or her incapable of making independent, responsible life decisions and permanently incapable of independently performing the activities of normal, daily living.

(c) There has been permanent loss of or damage to a reproductive organ resulting in the inability to procreate.

(2) In awarding damages in an action alleging medical malpractice, the trier of fact shall itemize damages into damages for economic loss and damages for noneconomic loss.

(3) As used in this section, "noneconomic loss" means damages or loss due to pain, suffering, inconvenience, physical impairment, physical disfigurement, or other noneconomic loss.

(4) The state treasurer shall adjust the limitation on damages for noneconomic loss set forth in subsection (1) by an amount determined by the state treasurer at the end of each calendar year to reflect the cumulative annual percentage change in the consumer price index. As used in this subsection, "consumer price index" means the most comprehensive index of consumer prices available for this state from the bureau of labor statistics of the United States department of labor.

Michigan Compiled Laws Annotated Section 600.1483

1. How does this statute impact the plaintiffs' damages?

2. Do you believe such statutes are unfair? Why or why not?

3. Why might such statutes be enacted? What interests do they protect?

In addition to statutory limitations like the one set out above, there are other limitations on recovery for emotional injuries.

It is important at the outset of this discussion to understand that plaintiffs may allege emotional distress damages as one of the types of damages suffered as the result of defendant's negligence, and so long as there are accompanying physical damages there is no issue as to whether plaintiff has a claim for such damages. It is where emotional distress damages are the only injury suffered that the following issues arise.

Historically, victims could not recover for emotional injuries unless they were accompanied by actual physical injury. Courts were skeptical about such injuries and concerned that allowing such claims would result in fraud and limitless liability resulting from any negligent act. Today, proof of physical injury is no longer necessary. However, as courts have attempted to constrain liability for emotional injuries, the development of the law relating to negligence based recovery for emotional distress without physical injury has been far from uniform. As states abandoned the physical injury requirement, many instead required some form of physical impact — meaning contact; in a few states, this requirement still remains. Most states eventually eliminated the impact requirement, and instead limited recovery to those circumstances where the victim was at risk of physical impact; this is sometimes referred to as being within the "zone of danger" and is a recognition that emotional injuries likely exist where a party has been subject to a "near miss."

The Courts divide cases into two types: (1) direct injury cases, meaning cases where the defendant's conduct was directed at the plaintiff; and (2) bystander cases, meaning cases where the defendant's conduct was directed at a third party and plaintiff's injury resulted from witnessing the injury (or effects of the injury) to the third party. The bystander cases created yet another twist, as the "zone of danger" requirement further developed into a split of authority regarding whether it was a zone of physical or psychological danger. In *Dillon v. Legg*, 69 Cal. Rptr. 72 (1968), California became the first jurisdiction to hold that recovery for emotional distress suffered by bystanders was not limited to persons who suffer physical impact or who were in the zone of danger of physical impact. The court in *Dillon* required consideration of three factors:

(1) Whether plaintiff was located near the scene of the accident;

(2) Whether the shock resulted from a direct emotional impact upon plaintiff from the sensory and contemporaneous observance of the accident, as contrasted with learning of the accident from others after its occurrence; and

(3) Whether plaintiff and the victim were closely related, as contrasted with an absence of any relationship or the presence of only a distant relationship.

A majority of states now follow some version of the rule articulated in Dillon.[5]

What may not be evident is that in bystander cases the plaintiff is usually arguing that the duty that is owed is a duty to refrain from acting in a manner that produces emotional distress. This is why such cases usually focus on the issue of duty, rather than damages, and impose limits on emotional distress recovery by finding no duty or a limited duty exists. In such cases courts will use the same factors you learned to consider in the duty section of this chapter. In contrast, in direct injury cases, courts will often find a duty exists based on the relationship between the parties. In such cases the court does not have to consider whether there is a duty to refrain from causing emotional distress; thus, the focus is not on whether there is a duty to refrain from causing emotional distress, but on whether there is actually provable emotional distress (and/or whether emotional distress resulted from a breach). In such cases the analysis will focus on causation and damages, not duty.

States are also split as to whether proof of physical symptoms of the emotional distress is required in order for plaintiff to recover—some jurisdictions require plaintiff have such symptoms in order to recover, while others do not. Also, states that require physical impact or proof of physical symptoms have been willing to carve out exceptions for special circumstances—most frequently for cases involving the mishandling of a corpse of a close relative, predominately because of the belief that it is reasonable to expect emotional injury to result from such circumstances, so proof of physical symptoms, danger or near impact is not necessary to establish the validity of the emotional distress claim.

Exercise 2-22 Law Practice

Given all of the differences in the treatment for emotional distress injuries, your job as a lawyer will be to determine how the jurisdiction where the case is filed treats such cases. For purposes of this exercise, evaluate whether, based on your reading of *Burgess v. Superior Court*, 2 Cal.4th 1064 (1992), Latrice McCoy would have a valid claim for emotional damages. As you read the case, consider:

1. Is Latrice McCoy's claim one for direct injury or bystander injury?

2. What must she prove in order to recover?

    a. Does the jurisdiction require a plaintiff to prove physical impact, or that she was in the "zone of danger" in order to recover?

    b. Does the jurisdiction require proof of physical symptoms in order to recover?

3. Are there any differences between what she must prove for a direct injury vs. bystander injury? Could she have satisfied the requirements for both?

---

5. California now follows a modified version: "In the absence of physical injury or impact to the plaintiff himself, damages for emotional distress should be recoverable only if the plaintiff: (1) is closely related to the injury victim; (2) is present at the scene of the injury-producing event at the time it occurs and is then aware that it is causing injury to the victim and, (3) as a result suffers emotional distress beyond that which would be anticipated in a disinterested witness." *Thing v. LaChusa*, 48 Cal. 3d 633 (1989).

Burgess v. Superior Court

2 Cal.4th 1064 (1992)

This proceeding arises out of the alleged negligent delivery of Joseph Moody II (Joseph). The petitioner (plaintiff) is Julia Burgess (Burgess), Joseph's mother. The real party in interest (defendant) is Narendra Gupta, M.D. (Gupta), the obstetrician who delivered Joseph.

The facts relevant to our decision are not in dispute. On February 26, 1988, Burgess entered labor. She was admitted to the hospital under the care of Gupta, her obstetrician, who had also participated in her prenatal care. At approximately 12:50 p.m., Gupta artificially ruptured Burgess's membranes. Shortly thereafter, according to Burgess, Gupta yelled to the nurse: "Emergency, prolapsed cord." At that point, Burgess "knew that something was wrong" with the delivery. Preparations were begun for a cesarean section.

Approximately 21 minutes elapsed between the time that Gupta diagnosed the cord prolapse and the time Burgess was taken to emergency surgery. During the interim, Gupta was in and out of Burgess' room. According to Burgess, "When he would come back into the room, he would yell, 'Breathe, breathe, because your baby ain't getting enough oxygen.'"

Burgess was placed under general anesthesia for the cesarean section. She was told as she was wheeled out of the recovery room that "something" was wrong with her baby boy. She was given another sedative. The first time she recalls feeling distressed about Joseph's condition was several hours later after she awoke from the sedative.

Joseph was deprived of sufficient oxygen through his umbilical cord for approximately 44 minutes before his delivery. He suffered permanent brain and nervous system damage, allegedly as a result of the deprivation of oxygen. He was not released from Children's Hospital (where he was transferred for specialized treatment) until a month after his birth.

Joseph, Burgess and Joseph Moody (Moody), the father of Joseph, brought suit against Gupta and the hospital. In this suit, Burgess and Moody both sought recovery for emotional distress suffered as a result of the defendants' negligence. Moody's claim was dismissed by the trial court for failure to comply with discovery requests and is no longer at issue. Joseph died during the course of the litigation, allegedly as the result of his injuries.***

Defendants brought a motion requesting summary adjudication that Burgess is not entitled to recover damages for emotional distress from the defendants. The defendants argued that Burgess did not contemporaneously observe Joseph's injury as required by this court in *Thing v. La Chusa, supra*, 48 Cal.3d 644, 257 Cal.Rptr. 865, 771 P.2d 814 (hereafter *Thing*), for recovery in a "bystander" situation and was not a direct victim of Gupta's negligence pursuant to *Molien v. Kaiser Foundation Hospitals* (1980) 27 Cal.3d 916, 167 Cal.Rptr. 831, 616 P.2d 813 (hereafter *Molien*). Relying primarily upon *Thing*, the trial court granted the motion.

Burgess petitioned the Court of Appeal for a writ of mandate vacating the trial court's order. The appellate court granted the writ in a brief decision in which it held that *Thing, supra*, 48 Cal.3d 644, 257 Cal.Rptr. 865, 771 P.2d 814, was not controlling under the facts presented by this case, because Burgess was a "direct victim" rather than a "bystander."

Recognizing the unique relationship between mother and child during pregnancy and childbirth, we granted review in order to address the recurring question of whether a mother can recover damages for the emotional distress suffered as a result of a negligent delivery causing injury to her child.

II. DISCUSSION

A. Because Gupta Owed a Preexisting Duty of Care to Burgess, the Criteria for Recovery of Negligent Infliction of Emotional Distress Enunciated in Thing Are Not Controlling in This Case.

The law of negligent infliction of emotional distress in California is typically analyzed, as it was in this case, by reference to two "theories" of recovery: the "bystander" theory and the "direct victim" theory. In cases involving family relationships and medical treatment, confusion has reigned as to whether and under which "theory" plaintiffs may seek damages for negligently inflicted emotional distress.

Because the use of the "direct victim" designation has tended to obscure, rather than illuminate the relevant inquiry in cases such as the one at hand, we briefly turn our attention to the present state of the law in this area before proceeding to apply this law to the facts that confront us.

We have repeatedly recognized that "[t]he negligent causing of emotional distress is not an independent tort, but the tort of negligence. [Citation.] The traditional elements of duty, breach of duty, causation, and damages apply. ***The distinction between the "bystander" and "direct victim" cases is found in the source of the duty owed by the defendant to the plaintiff. The "bystander" cases, commencing with *Dillon v. Legg* (1968) 68 Cal.2d 728, 69 Cal.Rptr. 72, 441 P.2d 912, and culminating in *Thing, supra,* 48 Cal.3d 644, 257 Cal.Rptr. 865, 771 P.2d 814, address "the question of duty in circumstances in which a plaintiff seeks to recover damages as a percipient witness to the injury of another." (*Christensen, supra,* 54 Cal.3d at p. 884, 2 Cal.Rptr.2d 79, 820 P.2d 181.) These cases "all arise in the context of physical injury or emotional distress caused by the negligent conduct of a defendant with whom the plaintiff had no preexisting relationship, and to whom the defendant had not previously assumed a duty of care beyond that owed to the public in general." (*Ibid.,* emphasis added.) In other words, bystander liability is premised upon a defendant's violation of a duty not to negligently cause emotional distress to people who observe conduct which causes harm to another.

Because in such cases the class of potential plaintiffs could be limitless, resulting in the imposition of liability out of all proportion to the culpability of the defendant, this court has circumscribed the class of bystanders to whom a defendant owes a duty to avoid negligently inflicting emotional distress. These limits are set forth in Thing as follows: "In the absence of physical injury or impact to the plaintiff himself, damages for emotional distress should be recoverable only if the plaintiff: (1) is closely related to the injury victim, (2) is present at the scene of the injury-producing event at the time it occurs and is then aware that it is causing injury to the victim and, (3) as a result suffers emotional distress beyond that which would be anticipated in a disinterested witness." (48 Cal.3d at p. 647, 257 Cal.Rptr. 865, 771 P.2d 814.)

In contrast, the label "direct victim" arose to distinguish cases in which damages for serious emotional distress are sought as a result of a breach of duty owed the plaintiff that is "assumed by the defendant or imposed on the defendant as a matter of law, or that arises out of a relationship between the two." (*Marlene F., supra,* 48 Cal.3d at p. 590, 257 Cal.Rptr. 98, 770 P.2d 278.) In these cases, the limits set forth in *Thing, supra,* 48 Cal.3d 644, 257 Cal.Rptr. 865, 771 P.2d 814, have no direct application. (*Marlene F., supra,* 48 Cal.3d at p. 589, fn. 4, 257 Cal.Rptr. 98, 770 P.2d 278; *Christensen, supra,* 54 Cal.3d at pp. 890–891, 2 Cal.Rptr.2d 79, 820 P.2d 181.) Rather, well-settled principles of negligence are invoked to determine whether all elements of a cause of action, including duty, are present in a given case.

Much of the confusion in applying rules for bystander and direct victim recovery to the facts of specific cases can be traced to this court's decision in *Molien*, which first used the "direct victim" label. In that case, we answered in the affirmative the question of whether, in the context of a negligence action, damages may be recovered for serious emotional distress unaccompanied by physical injury. (*Molien, supra*, 27 Cal.3d at pp. 927–931, 167 Cal.Rptr. 831, 616 P.2d 813.)

In so holding, we found that a hospital and a doctor owed a duty directly to the husband of a patient, who had been diagnosed incorrectly by the doctor as having syphilis and had been told to so advise her husband in order that he could receive testing and, if necessary, treatment. (*Molien, supra*, 27 Cal.3d at p. 923, 167 Cal.Rptr. 831, 616 P.2d 813.) We reasoned that the risk of harm to the husband was reasonably foreseeable and that the "alleged tortious conduct of the defendant was directed to him as well as to his wife." (Id. at pp. 922–923, 167 Cal.Rptr. 831, 616 P.2d 813.) Under such circumstances we deemed the husband to be a "direct victim" and found the criteria for bystander recovery not to be controlling. (Id. at p. 923, 167 Cal.Rptr. 831, 616 P.2d 813.)

The broad language of the *Molien* decision coupled with its perceived failure to establish criteria for characterizing a plaintiff as a "direct victim" rather than a "bystander," has subjected *Molien* to criticism from various sources, including this court. (E.g., *Thing, supra*, 48 Cal.3d at pp. 658–664, 257 Cal.Rptr. 865, 771 P.2d 814.) The great weight of this criticism has centered upon the perception that *Molien* introduced a new method for determining the existence of a duty, limited only by the concept of foreseeability. To the extent that *Molien, supra*, 27 Cal.3d 916, 167 Cal.Rptr. 831, 616 P.2d 813, stands for this proposition, it should not be relied upon and its discussion of duty is limited to its facts. As recognized in Thing, "[I]t is clear that foreseeability of the injury alone is not a useful 'guideline' or a meaningful restriction on the scope of [an action for damages for negligently inflicted emotional distress.]" (48 Cal.3d at p. 663, 257 Cal.Rptr. 865, 771 P.2d 814.)

Nevertheless, other principles derived from *Molien, supra*, 27 Cal.3d 916, 167 Cal.Rptr. 831, 616 P.2d 813, are sound: (1) damages for negligently inflicted emotional distress may be recovered in the absence of physical injury or impact, and (2) a cause of action to recover damages for negligently inflicted emotional distress will lie, notwithstanding the criteria imposed upon recovery by bystanders, in cases where a duty arising from a preexisting relationship is negligently breached. (*Christensen, supra*, 54 Cal.3d at pp. 890–891, 2 Cal.Rptr.2d 79, 820 P.2d 181; *Marlene F., supra*, 48 Cal.3d at pp. 590–591, 257 Cal.Rptr. 98, 770 P.2d 278.) In fact, it is this later principle which defines the phrase "direct victim." That label signifies nothing more.

Gupta, however, has succumbed to the confusion in this area by failing to recognize that the distinction between bystander and direct victim cases is found in the source of the duty owed by the defendant to the plaintiff. Gupta argues, relying upon *Ochoa v. Superior Court*, (1985) 39 Cal.3d 159, 172–173, 216 Cal.Rptr. 661, 703 P.2d 1 (hereafter *Ochoa*), that, when the emotional distress for which damages are claimed is "purely derivative" of the injury of another, the plaintiff may only recover such damages by satisfying the criteria for bystander recovery. Gupta claims that Burgess's damages are "derivative" because he owed no duty of care to Burgess to avoid injuring her child. Therefore, she may recover for her emotional distress, if at all, only as a bystander. We disagree.

In *Ochoa*, the parents sought damages for the emotional distress that they suffered from witnessing the defendants' failure to provide adequate medical care to their son, who was incarcerated. We held that the parents could state a claim for such damages, but only as bystanders, not as direct victims. In so holding we stated, "the defendants' negligence ... was directed primarily at the decedent, with Mrs. Ochoa looking on as a helpless bystander as the tragedy of her son's demise unfolded before her." (*Ochoa, supra,* 39 Cal.3d at pp. 172–173, 216 Cal.Rptr. 661, 703 P.2d 1.) In *Ochoa* the defendants had no preexisting relationship with the parents upon which to premise a duty of care; therefore, Mrs. Ochoa was necessarily in the position of a bystander with respect to her son's health care. The source of the duty, rather than the "derivative nature" of the injuries suffered by Mrs. Ochoa, was determinative.

In contrast to the facts of *Ochoa* and *Molien,* we are presented in this case with a "traditional" plaintiff with a professional negligence cause of action. Gupta cannot and does not dispute that he owed a duty of care to Burgess arising from their physician-patient relationship. (6 Witkin, Summary of Cal.Law (9th ed. 1988) Torts, § 776, p. 116 ["Liability for malpractice arises where there is a relationship of physician-patient between the plaintiff and the defendant doctor; the relationship gives rise to the duty of care. [Citations.]"].) Rather, Gupta contends that, while his alleged negligence resulting in injury to Joseph breached a duty of care owed to Joseph, it did not breach a duty of care owed to Burgess. In other words, Gupta claims that the scope of the duty of care owed to Burgess was limited to avoiding physical injury to her during her prenatal care and labor; it did not extend to avoiding injury to her fetus and the emotional distress that would result from such an injury. The origin of these mutually exclusive duties to Burgess and Joseph is apparently Gupta's unsupported assertion that Burgess and Joseph were two separate patients, because his actions could physically injure one and not the other.

To accept Gupta's argument would require us to ignore the realities of pregnancy and childbirth. Burgess established a physician-patient relationship with Gupta for medical care which was directed not only to her, but also to her fetus. The end purpose of this medical care may fairly be said to have been to provide treatment consistent with the applicable standard of care in order to maximize the possibility that Burgess's baby would be delivered in the condition in which he had been created and nurtured without avoidable injury to the baby or to Burgess. (Cf. *Cunningham et al., Williams Obstetrics, supra,* at p. 1.) Moreover, during pregnancy and delivery it is axiomatic that any treatment for Joseph necessarily implicated Burgess's participation since access to Joseph could only be accomplished with Burgess' consent and with impact to her body.

In addition to the physical connection between a woman and her fetus, there is an emotional relationship as well. ***Any negligence during delivery which causes injury to the fetus and resultant emotional anguish to the mother, therefore, breaches a duty owed directly to the mother.

Thus, as the Court of Appeal correctly determined in this case, the failure by Burgess to satisfy the criteria for recovery under *Thing, supra,* 48 Cal.3d 644, 257 Cal.Rptr. 865, 771 P.2d 814, does not end the inquiry. The alleged negligent actions resulting in physical harm to Joseph breached a duty owed to both Joseph and Burgess. Burgess was unavoidably and unquestionably harmed by this negligent conduct. (*Christensen, supra,* 54 Cal.3d at pp. 886–887, 890–891, 2 Cal.Rptr.2d 79, 820 P.2d 181 [in upholding cause of action to recover damages for emotional distress arising out of improperly performed funeral services, this court recognized that the emotional state of the bereaved plaintiffs dictated that the duty of care assumed by those providing funeral services included not merely performing cremations, but performing them in a dignified and respectful manner]; *Marlene F., supra,* 48 Cal.3d at p. 591, 257 Cal.Rptr. 98, 770 P.2d 278 [in upholding a cause of action by a mother to recover damages for emotional distress arising out of the sexual molestation of her son by a therapist, who was treating both mother and son for intrafamily problems, this court recognized that the therapist's action breached a duty of care to the mother since it would directly injure her and cause her severe emotional distress and would harm the intrafamily relationship under his care].)

As in Marlene F., once the scope of the duty of care assumed by Gupta to Burgess is understood, Burgess' claim for emotional distress damages may simply be viewed as an ordinary professional malpractice claim, which seeks as an element of damage compensation for her serious emotional distress. The elements of a claim for professional negligence incorporate a specific standard of care into the elements of a negligence claim. "The elements of a cause of action in tort for professional negligence are: (1) the duty of the professional to use such skill, prudence and diligence as other members of his profession commonly possess and exercise; (2) a breach of that duty; (3) a proximate causal connection between the negligent conduct and the resulting injury; and (4) actual loss or damage resulting from the professional's negligence. [Citations.]" (*Budd v. Nixen* (1971) 6 Cal.3d 195, 200, 98 Cal.Rptr. 849, 491 P.2d 433.) A plaintiff in a case of medical malpractice may recover damages for emotional distress. (See *Marlene F., supra*, 48 Cal.3d at pp. 591, fn. 6, 257 Cal.Rptr. 98, 770 P.2d 278 (lead opn. of Arguelles, J.), 599 (conc. opn. of Eagleson, J.); *Molien, supra*, 27 Cal.3d at pp. 930–931, 167 Cal.Rptr. 831, 616 P.2d 813; 2 *Louisell & Williams, Medical Malpractice, supra*, at ¶ 18.11.)

Moreover, contrary to Gupta's assertions, the imposition of liability in this case would not be an unprecedented extension of the law. We note that our holding has been foreshadowed by several decisions of our Courts of Appeal. Although relying upon differing theories to support claims for damages for emotional distress suffered by mothers whose children were harmed or died as a result of obstetrical malpractice, the majority of our appellate courts, which have considered the issue, have ruled in favor of a mother's right to plead and prove such damages. (*Newton v. Kaiser Foundation Hospitals, supra*, 184 Cal.App.3d 386, 228 Cal.Rptr. 890 [parents of a child left partially paralyzed as a result of the application of allegedly excessive use of traction during birth may recover damages for emotional distress suffered]; *Andalon v. Superior Court, supra*, 162 Cal.App.3d 600, 208 Cal.Rptr. 899 [reversal of partial summary judgment of parents' claim for damages for emotional distress arising from defendant's failure to prenatally diagnose Down's Syndrome]; *Sesma v. Cueto, supra*, 129 Cal.App.3d 108, 181 Cal.Rptr. 12 [reversal of partial summary judgment of mother's claim for damages for emotional distress arising out of death of her child during birth]; *Johnson v. Superior Court, supra*, 123 Cal.App.3d 1002, 177 Cal.Rptr. 63 [demurrer sustained to mother's cause of action for negligent infliction of emotional distress, but right to recover emotional distress suffered as result of stillbirth held to be part of mother's pending malpractice claim]; but see *Martinez v. County of Los Angeles, supra*, 186 Cal.App.3d 884, 231 Cal.Rptr. 96 [parents of a child who allegedly suffered brain damage during birth could not recover damages for their emotional distress incurred primarily as a result of "restructuring their lives" to care for the child]; *Hurlbut v. Sonora Community Hospital, supra*, 207 Cal.App.3d 388, 254 Cal.Rptr. 840 [parents of child severely brain damaged during birth could not recover damages for their emotional distress under a bystander theory; no other theory was presented at trial].)

As the majority of lower courts have recognized, *Thing, supra*, 48 Cal.3d 644, 257 Cal.Rptr. 865, 771 P.2d 814, does not control recovery by a mother for emotional distress suffered as a result of the negligent injury of her child during labor and delivery. Under the facts of this case, Burgess is not a "bystander" for purposes of bringing a claim for compensation for damages for her serious emotional distress. Burgess is permitted to recover these damages as a result of the breach of the duty of care arising from the physician-patient relationship between Gupta and Burgess. Gupta's negligent breach of this duty is sufficient to satisfy the elements of a claim for professional malpractice on Burgess' behalf.

B. Lack of Physical Injury Does Not Defeat Burgess's Claim.

Gupta also seeks to win summary adjudication by negating the damage element of Burgess's claim. To accomplish this end, Gupta contends that Burgess has not alleged that she suffered physical injury.

Gupta's argument is unpersuasive. First, Gupta overlooks the fact that Burgess has pled injury to her "nervous system and person." Gupta presented no evidence to dispute this alleged physical injury. Rather, Gupta confined his motion to the argument that Burgess's claim fails because she did not suffer any physical injury that was wholly unrelated to the emotional distress stemming from Joseph's injuries. In other words, the source of Burgess's injuries relegated her to "bystander" status. For the reasons set forth above, this contention fails.

Moreover, even if Burgess had failed to allege physical injuries, physical injury is not a prerequisite for recovering damages for serious emotional distress, especially when, as here, there exists a "guarantee of genuineness in the circumstances of the case." (*Molien, supra*, 27 Cal.3d at pp. 928–930, 167 Cal.Rptr. 831, 616 P.2d 813, citation and internal quotation marks omitted.) Serious emotional distress itself satisfies the damage element of Burgess's cause of action.

* * *

III. DISPOSITION

For the reasons set forth herein, we hold that Burgess is not required to satisfy the criteria for recovery as a bystander and may state a claim for damages for serious emotional distress arising from the negligent delivery of her child.... Therefore, the judgment of the Court of Appeal is modified to direct the superior court, in addition to reversing its order of summary adjudication, to enter an order in accordance with the views expressed herein.

Exercise 2-23 Emotional Distress Claims and Noneconomic Damage Caps

Although the Michigan Statute in exercise 2-21, applies to "the total amount of damages for noneconomic loss recoverable by all plaintiffs, resulting from the negligence of all defendants" not all statutes imposing damage caps contain such limiting language. For example, compare the language from the Michigan statute, with this language from California Civil Code section 3333.2.:

(a) In any action for injury against a health care provider based on professional negligence, the injured plaintiff shall be entitled to recover noneconomic losses to compensate for pain, suffering, inconvenience, physical impairment, disfigurement and other nonpecuniary damage.

(b) In no action shall the amount of damages for noneconomic losses exceed two hundred fifty thousand dollars ($250,000).

In interpreting this statute, California courts have held the $250,000 limit on noneconomic damages applies separately to each plaintiff because the statute focuses on the "injured plaintiff" who is entitled to recover noneconomic losses in an amount not to exceed $250,000, and nothing in the statute limits the defendant's total liability to that amount. In order to limit the defendant's total liability to $250,000 for all claims arising from a single act of professional negligence, the statute would have to state that the cap applies to the total amount of noneconomic damages arising from a "single act of negligence" or "a single injury-causing incident." Instead the statute places a cap on the recovery for each injured person.

In jurisdictions where statutory limits allow each plaintiff to recover damages for the amount up to the cap, parties (usually relatives of the physically injured party) are more likely to file independent claims, including claims for emotional distress. Does the difference between the Michigan and California statutes help to explain why Latrice McCoy (whose case is governed by Michigan law) did not file her own claim for emotional distress? Which do you believe is the fairer approach — Michigan's or California's?

3. Causation

In addition to proving defendant owed plaintiff a duty, breached that duty, and that plaintiff suffered injuries, a plaintiff in a negligence case must show that that the defendant's breach is what caused her injuries. In other words, a plaintiff might be injured, and defendant might have a legal duty, which he breached, and still defendant might not be liable for negligence, because in order to be negligent the defendant's breach of duty must be the cause of the plaintiff's injury (damage). Proving causation involves two distinct concepts: factual cause and proximate cause — both of which must be proven in order to establish liability.

a. Factual Cause — The "but for" Test

Factual cause (also sometimes referred to as actual cause or cause-in-fact) is usually determined by the "but for" test — meaning the plaintiff must prove that "but for" the defendant's breach, the plaintiff would not have been damaged (injured). The "but for" tests requires you to imagine what would happen if you removed defendant's breach from the scenario. If the injury would still have occurred, then defendant is not the "but for" or factual cause of the plaintiff's injury; conversely, if in the absence of defendant's breach the injury would not have occurred, then defendant is the "but for" or factual cause of plaintiff's injury.

To understand this concept (and to be able to determine whether there is factual cause), it may help you to do the following.

1. Identify the defendant's breach of duty.

2. Identify the injury (damages) for which plaintiff seeks redress.

3. Determine whether the injury (damages) would still exist if you removed the breach from the equation. If the answer is no, then defendant's breach is the factual cause of the plaintiff's damages.

An example will probably help to make this clear. Returning to the problem set out in exercise 2.13 (*Beatrice (via her estate) v. Realty Co*), this process would require you would do the following:

1. Identify the breach. *In the exercise it was the failure to put locks on the apartment door.*

2. Identify the damages for which plaintiff seeks redress. *In the exercise it was compensation for the Beatrice's death resulting from being murdered by an intruder in her apartment.*

3. Determine whether the injury would still exist [*whether defendant would still have been murdered in her apartment*] if defendant had not breached his duty [*if defendant had put locks on the apartment door*].

   a. If the answer is no, [*Beatrice would be alive if the locks were there*] then defendant's breach is the "but for" or factual cause of plaintiff's damages.

   b. If, however, the damages would still have occurred [*the intruder would still have entered and killed Beatrice or, stated another way, Beatrice would still be murdered*] even if there was no breach [*the locks were on the door*], then the breach [*failure to put the locks on the door*] would not be the "but for" or factual cause of the plaintiff's injury.

Exercise 2-24 Proving Factual Cause

Evaluate whether the following testimony, if given in *Beatrice v. Realty Co*, would impact plaintiff's ability to prove factual cause.

   Officer Horvath testified that it was his opinion that Vivian entered and exited through the rear door of the apartment.

   Realty Co and Levi Brock presented evidence that during the criminal trial Vivian testified that she entered the apartment through the front door.

   Beatrice's next door neighbor and the Realty Co. maintenance man testified that, immediately after Beatrice was killed, the locks on the back door were tested and were found to be in good working order.

If all of the testimony set out above is offered, and the defendants request a nonsuit (a judgment that the evidence is insufficient and the case should not go to the jury) on the basis that plaintiff cannot prove factual cause—what result?

Exercise 2-25 Law Practice

Imagine you represent the plaintiff in *Beatrice v. Realty Co*. Upon receiving the defendant's motion for nonsuit, the court encourages the parties to make another attempt at settling the case. It is your job to explain to Beatrice's mother the factual causation issues in the case and to help her evaluate the strengths and weakness of her claim. What would you say to her? Would you recommend taking a settlement offer? Why or why not? For what amount?

---

b. Factual Cause—The Substantial Factor Test

The "but for" test works well for single defendant, single event situations; however in multiple defendant or multiple event situations, it has limitations.

In situations where two or more breaches jointly cause an injury, any one of which *operating alone* could have been sufficient to cause the result, under the "but for" test all of the defendants might be able to escape liability on the grounds that the harm would have occurred without each of their conduct. For example, imagine that two different companies—A and B—dumped toxic waste into a town's water supply and the toxic wasted caused a variety of injuries to the town's residents. Under a "but for" analysis, company A could argue that the injuries would still have occurred even if they had not dumped toxic waste into the water supply, because company B's dumping would have caused the injuries. Company B could make the same argument. Neither would be the "but for" cause of the injuries. Both would escape liability for the dumping. As you can see, this would lead to illogical results—because injured parties (like the town residents) would never be able to prove factual cause in such situations.

In such cases, the "but for" test is not used. Rather, the defendant's conduct is deemed a cause of the injury if it is a substantial factor in bringing about the plaintiff's harm. This is called the "substantial factor" test. Note that in situations where neither party's conduct alone could have caused the injury, and both contributed to it, the "but for" test would still apply. For example, if neither company dumped a sufficient amount of toxic waste in the water supply to cause injury, but the combination of the two companies dumping toxic wasted did, then each would be a "but for" cause of the injury, because "but for" either company dumping the waste, no injury would have resulted. It is only when both companies *operating alone* could have caused the injury that the "but for" test does not apply.

Another type of situation where the "but for" test proves problematic is in cases where plaintiff is able to establish that several defendants committed a breach, and that one of the breaches caused her harm, but she cannot ascertain which one. For example, imagine plaintiff's mother took medication during pregnancy. Many years later plaintiff discovered that the medication is the cause of plaintiff's serious medical condition. Two different companies manufactured the drug at the time plaintiff's mother took the medication, but plaintiff does not know which one manufactured the pills actually ingested by her mother. Neither plaintiff nor anyone else can determine which of the two manufacturers is responsible. Both manufacturers produced identical injury causing pills. One manufacturer's pills were ingested by her mother; the other company's pills were not. Although we know one of the manufacturers caused the harm, neither can be held responsible. In such cases, courts allow plaintiff to sue both manufacturers. To establish factual cause, plaintiff must prove that either manufacturer could have caused the harm (without proving exactly which of the manufacturers it was), essentially showing that either could have been the "but for" cause, and that one of them was. At this point the burden of proof shifts to the defendants (the manufacturers) to prove that they could not have been the one to cause the harm (i.e. that they could not have manufactured the pill ingested by Plaintiff's mother). If the manufacturer(s) are not able to satisfy this burden, they will be held liable. Usually in these cases manufacturers are liable in proportion to their market share (the percentage of their total sales) of the medication in question.

Exercise 2-26 Selecting and Applying the Appropriate Test to Determine Factual Cause

In each of the following scenarios determine whether the "but for" or the substantial factor test is appropriate. Then, using the appropriate test, determine whether defendant's breach was a factual cause of plaintiff's injury.

a. Gas Company failed to provide warnings of odor fade (the odorant added to natural gas to warn of the presence of natural gas may be absorbed by steel pipes — making the gas undetectable). Plumber released what he thought was regular air (because it was odorless) and then attempted to mend a pipe with a blow torch, which, because of the presence of gas, caused an explosion. Is Gas Company's failure to warn a factual cause of the explosion? What if there was no evidence that, had the gas company issued such a warning, Plumbers would have been aware of it?

b. Employees of a contractor were hired to install hardwood flooring. While on the job, they caused a house fire by discarding cigarettes into a garbage can. Is Contractor's negligent supervision of Employees the factual cause of the house fire?

c. Daycare Provider did not adequately supervise or fence a playground area at a day care center. Unknown children entered the property through the unfenced area and caused injury to a child by throwing rocks at his head. Is Daycare Provider's failure to supervise or fence the area the factual cause of child's injury?

d. Superstore negligently sold bullets to Troubled Teen, who used them to shoot several of his classmates, his teachers and himself. Is Superstore's negligent sale of bullets the factual cause of the shootings?

e. Construction Company constructed a building that did not conform to city building codes. The building would have collapsed during an "ordinary" earthquake. The building did collapse, but as the result of an earthquake of such magnitude that no building survived the quake — even those that conformed to city building codes. Is Construction Company's failure to build in accordance with city building codes the factual cause of the buildings collapse?

f. Company negligently designed and maintained an airstrip which caused the crash of a small airplane. The plane was carrying Surgeon, who was killed, and thus unable to perform a life saving surgery on Patient, who died. Is Company's negligence the factual cause of Patient's death?

g. Doctor negligently performed a vasectomy, resulting in the birth of Serial Killer, who eventually grew up and went on to kill several hundred women. Is Doctor's negligence the factual cause of the serial killings?

h. Manufacturer is one of a number of companies that manufacture insulation products containing asbestos. Manufacturer failed to warn Worker of the dangers involved in handling products containing asbestos. Worker, an insulation installer, was exposed to asbestos over a thirty-three year period. It is impossible to determine which particular exposure resulted in producing Worker's injuries, which include asbestosis. It is certain that Worker's injuries were incurred by inhaling dust from insulation products. On many occasions, Worker was exposed to the products of every one of the companies that manufacture asbestos. The effect of exposure to asbestos is cumulative; each exposure results in an additional and separate injury. Even the most recent exposures could have added to or accelerated Worker's overall condition. Asbestosis does not usually manifest itself until at least fifteen years after initial exposure. Is Manufacturer the factual cause of Worker's asbestosis?

i.   Surfer and Picnicker were independently building a bonfire on the beach. Each one failed to properly extinguish their respective bonfires before leaving the beach. Due to unusually high winds and dry conditions sparks from both bonfires escaped their sites and began a fire. The two fires burned out of control, eventually joining together to create one fire that burned down an entire condominium complex. Either of the out of control fires alone would have destroyed the condominium complex. Is Surfers failure to properly extinguish his bonfire a factual cause of the destruction of the condominium complex?

As you can see from some of the examples in the factual cause exercises, if factual cause were the only requirement for proving causation in a negligence action, there could be liability in some cases that would seem unfair or even illogical. For example, holding the doctor who negligently performed a vasectomy liable for the acts of a grown up serial killer, because "but for" the failed vasectomy the child would not have existed and grown up to kill others, stretches liability a bit too far. This is why, in addition to factual cause, the plaintiff must also show that the defendant's breach of duty was the proximate, as opposed to remote, cause of the resulting injuries.

---

c. Proximate Cause

Proximate cause is often characterized as a means by which courts are able to place practical limits on liability as a matter of policy—usually by cutting off liability in cases where the defendant's breach is a distant link in the chain of causation leading to plaintiff's injury. Proximate cause allows a judgment to be made that the defendant's conduct, although a factual cause, is so insignificant that no one would think of it as a cause for which a defendant should be held responsible.

In most cases plaintiffs sue defendants that are closely connected with their injury, and proximate cause is not a hotly contested issue. However, for those times where it is contested, it is important to understand how to address such issues. Most courts use foreseeability as the standard for measuring the defendant's scope of liability, meaning defendants are only liable for the foreseeable consequences of their breach of duty—which may involve considering both the foreseeable types of injuries one would expect from such a breach, as well as the foreseeable types of victims. Returning to our earlier example, from exercise 2.13, this would mean that the plaintiff's damages [death from murder in her apartment] must be closely connected with—or a foreseeable outcome of—defendant's breach [not installing locks on the apartment door] in order to say that the breach was a proximate cause of the plaintiff's injury. Often, these kinds of cases (suits against others for criminal acts of third parties) present interesting issues of foreseeability—which we saw during our review of such cases in the previous section of this chapter.

Courts will sometimes engage in a discussion of whether a third party's intervening act or conduct was the immediate cause of the injury, and thus a superseding (or in some cases, supervening, which is the same thing) cause of plaintiff's injury, which "cuts off" or eliminates defendant's liability. These courts frequently have rules about when an intervening act is or is not a superseding cause. For example, for many courts, a defendant is still liable if the third party's negligence was reasonably foreseeable; or the third party's act, as viewed by a reasonable person knowing the then-existing circumstances, was not highly extraordinary; or the third party's conduct was not extraordinarily negligent and was a normal consequence of the situation created by defendant. The reality is that even where courts employ such language and tests, viewing proximate cause in the language of intervening and superseding acts, they are really using foreseeability to determine liability—so don't let the language (and labels) used in such cases confuse you.

It can sometimes be helpful, in evaluating whether defendant's breach was a proximate cause of plaintiff's injury, to ask yourself whether the plaintiff's injury is the type you would have expected to result from the defendant's breach. If the answer is yes, then the intervening act does not likely cut off liability. Another way to approach the issue is to identify the defendant's breach, and then stop to consider what result (outcome) you would expect to result from such a breach; then skip ahead to the injury and see if it is what you expected—if so, then the defendant will probably be liable even if there were other intervening events. If not (you didn't expect such an outcome, or it seems really surprising to you), then proximate cause likely does not exist. You might want to try these techniques on the next set of exercises. If you do, it is important to understand that when you think about the outcome one might expect to flow from defendant's breach you must be somewhat specific about the type of injury and/or victims. For example, you would not want to characterize the likely injury resulting from failing to provide locks on the door as broadly as "injuries to persons inside the apartment" (which could provide nearly limitless liability), nor would you want to characterize it as "violent crimes committed against tenants in the apartment" (which would limit liability for many injuries that would likely be closely connected with the breach). Defining the scope is sometimes tricky—which is what makes this an interesting area when the issue does arise. Also remember that where it is a close call, the question will go to the trier of fact (usually a jury), who will ultimately decide whether the injury was a foreseeable consequence of the breach; your job, as both a law student and a lawyer, will be to understand when it is clear and when it is not, and to make the best argument you can that the result is or is not foreseeable, based on the facts.

There is one final point you should understand—the "eggshell" or "thinskull" plaintiff principle, which is an exception to the general approach requiring foreseeability. Essentially the doctrine can be summed up with the frequently stated sentiment: "the defendant takes the plaintiff as he finds the plaintiff." This means that if the plaintiff suffers a greater injury than other members of the general public would have suffered in the same situation, the defendant still must pay for the harm caused. Imagine, for example, defendant kicked plaintiff in the shins. Ordinarily such a kick would have caused a person to suffer minor injuries, such as a bruise; instead, because plaintiff had a degenerative disease making her bones as brittle as eggshells, she suffered major injuries in the form of several broken bones. Defendant is liable for the broken bones. This doctrine appears to be an exception to the general principle requiring foreseeability because defendant ends up being liable for unforeseeable injuries. However, another way to view the scenario is to understand that injury must be foreseeable but the extent or severity of the injury need not be. In other words, since it was foreseeable that kicking someone in the shins would result in injury, the defendant is being held liable for causing that foreseeable injury, even though the injury turns out to be unforeseeably severe.

Exercise 2-27 Evaluating Proximate Cause

In each of the following examples, determine whether the defendant's breach proximately caused the plaintiff's damages.

a. Worker is an employee of Company. Per Company's instructions, Worker was using gasoline to clean machinery, in an eight by ten foot room containing a gas heater lit with an open flame. A rat escaped from the machinery (soaked in the gasoline cleaner) and attempted to hide under the gas heater. The rat burst into flames causing the heater to explode, killing Worker. Is Company liable for Worker's death?

b. Church hired Pastor despite evidence Pastor had previously molested adolescent boys. Pastor subsequently molested Boy. Boy then molested his younger sister. Is Church liable for younger sister's injuries?

c. Worker on a road construction crew, run by City, was instructed to stand next to open traffic on a busy highway, with only a sawhorse as a barrier to protect him from traffic. Driver had an epileptic seizure as a result of failing to take his medicine. During the seizure Driver's car plowed through the barrier and into Worker, who was seriously injured. Is City liable for Worker's injuries?

d. Driver hit Pedestrian, who was crossing the sidewalk. Pedestrian broke her leg and was taken to Hospital for treatment. Doctor, who was treating Pedestrian for the broken leg, committed malpractice, resulting in Pedestrian having her leg amputated. Is Driver liable for Pedestrian's injuries (including amputation)?

e. Landlord failed to install security gates or lights in an underground parking garage in an apartment complex in a high crime neighborhood. Tenant was raped in the parking garage. Is Landlord liable for the rape?

f. Driver was not paying attention and rear-ended Teen's car at a stoplight. Although she suffered no physical injuries, immediately after the impact she began to behave in a bizarre manner, so she was taken to a hospital where she was diagnosed as suffering from a schizophrenic reaction, resulting from the auto accident. Is Driver liable for her injuries?

Exercise 2-28 Understanding Historical Context

Based upon the readings thus far, you may be wondering whether foreseeability is part of the "test" for duty, proximate cause, or both. The roots of this discussion may well lie in perhaps the most famous Torts case ever written, *Palsgraf v. Long Island Railroad*, 162 N.E. 99, 99–105 (N.Y. 1928).[6] In that case, Helen Palsgraf

---

6. Seriously—Google it—there is even a YouTube video featuring LEGO™ mini figures, in case the description here isn't satisfying enough.

was standing on a platform of defendant's railroad waiting for her train. While she was waiting, two men ran forward to board a different train that was leaving the station. One of the men was carrying a package. As he jumped aboard the car he appeared to lose his footing so a guard on the train reached forward to help him in, while another guard on the platform pushed him from behind. The package he was carrying was dislodged and fell. The package contained fireworks, which exploded and knocked down some scales at the other end of the platform, many feet away. The scales struck Mrs. Palsgraf, causing injuries, for which she sued.

At the time of the *Palsgraf* decision, proximate cause extended liability to all "directly traceable" consequences. In writing for the majority, Judge Benjamin Cardozo (then justice of New York's highest court, later Supreme Court Justice) looked to the duty element as a basis to restrict liability, and held Mrs. Palsgraf was not a foreseeable plaintiff and could not recover. He had this to say:

> The conduct of the defendant's guard, if a wrong in its relation to the holder of the package, was not a wrong in its relation to the plaintiff, standing far away. Relatively to her it was not negligence at all. Nothing in the situation gave notice that the falling package had in it the potency of peril to persons thus removed. Negligence is not actionable unless it involves the invasion of a legally protected interest, the violation of a right. 'Proof of negligence in the air, so to speak, will not do.' Pollock, Torts (11th Ed.) p. 455....

> If no hazard was apparent to the eye of ordinary vigilance, an act innocent and harmless, at least to outward seeming, with reference to her, did not take to itself the quality of a tort because it happened to be a wrong, though apparently not one involving the risk of bodily insecurity, with reference to someone else.... 'The ideas of negligence and duty are strictly correlative.' *Bowen, L. J., in Thomas v. Quartermaine*, 18 Q. B. D. 685, 694. The plaintiff sues in her own right for a wrong personal to her, and not as the vicarious beneficiary of a breach of duty to another.

* * *

> Here, by concession, there was nothing in the situation to suggest to the most cautious mind that the parcel wrapped in newspaper would spread wreckage through the station. If the guard had thrown it down knowingly and willfully, he would not have threatened the plaintiff's safety, so far as appearances could warn him. His conduct would not have involved, even then, an unreasonable probability of invasion of her bodily security. Liability can be no greater where the act is inadvertent.

Judge Andrews, writing for the dissent, rejected the view that a duty is owed only to foreseeable victims:

> Is [negligence] a relative concept—the breach of some duty owing to a particular person or to particular persons? Or, where there is an act which unreasonably threatens the safety of others, is the doer liable for all its proximate consequences, even where they result in injury to one who would generally be thought to be outside the radius of danger? This is not a mere dispute as to words. We might not believe that to the average mind the dropping of the bundle would seem to involve the

probability of harm to the plaintiff standing many feet away whatever might be the case as to the owner or to one so near as to be likely to be struck by its fall. If, however, we adopt the second hypothesis, we have to inquire only as to the relation between cause and effect. We deal in terms of proximate cause, not of negligence.

But we are told that 'there is no negligence unless there is in the particular case a legal duty to take care, and this duty must be one which is owed to the plaintiff himself and not merely to others.' Salmond Torts (6th Ed.) 24. This I think too narrow a conception. Where there is the unreasonable act, and some right that may be affected there is negligence whether damage does or does not result. That is immaterial. Should we drive down Broadway at a reckless speed, we are negligent whether we strike an approaching car or miss it by an inch. The act itself is wrongful. It is a wrong not only to those who happen to be within the radius of danger, but to all who might have been there — a wrong to the public at large. *** 'The measure of the defendant's duty in determining whether a wrong has been committed is one thing, the measure of liability when a wrong has been committed is another.' *Spade v. Lynn & B. R. Co.*, 172 Mass. 488, 491, 52 N. E. 747, 748 (43 L. R. A. 832, 70 Am. St. Rep. 298). Due care is a duty imposed on each one of us to protect society from unnecessary danger, not to protect A, B, or C alone.

It may well be that there is no such thing as negligence in the abstract. 'Proof of negligence in the air, so to speak, will not do.' In an empty world negligence would not exist. It does involve a relationship between man and his fellows, but not merely a relationship between man and those whom he might reasonably expect his act would injure; rather, a relationship between him and those whom he does in fact injure. If his act has a tendency to harm someone, it harms him a mile away as surely as it does those on the scene. *** Every one owes to the world at large the duty of refraining from those acts that may unreasonably threaten the safety of others. Such an act occurs. Not only is he wronged to whom harm, might reasonably be expected to result, but he also who is in fact injured, even if he be outside what would generally be thought the danger zone. There needs be duty due the one complaining, but this is not a duty to a particular individual because as to him harm might be expected. Harm to some one being the natural result of the act, not only that one alone, but all those in fact injured may complain. We have never, I think, held otherwise.... Unreasonable risk being taken, its consequences are not confined to those who might probably be hurt.

Even so, Judge Andrews recognized that some limit on the scope of liability was necessary, and viewed proximate cause as the vehicle for imposing such limits:

> [W]hen injuries do result from our unlawful act, we are liable for the consequences. It does not matter that they are unusual, unexpected, unforeseen, and unforeseeable. But there is one limitation. The damages must be so connected with the negligence that the latter may be said to be the proximate cause of the former.

These two words have never been given an inclusive definition. What is a cause in a legal sense, still more what is a proximate cause, depend in each case upon many considerations, as does the existence of negligence itself. Any philosophical doctrine of causation does not help us. A boy throws a stone into a pond. The ripples spread. The water level rises. The history of that pond is altered to all eternity. It will be altered by other causes also. Yet it will be forever the resultant of all causes combined. Each one will have an influence. How great only omniscience can say. You may speak of a chain, or, if you please, a net. An analogy is of little aid. Each cause brings about future events. Without each the future would not be the same. Each is proximate in the sense it is essential. But that is not what we mean by the word. Nor on the other hand do we mean sole cause. There is no such thing.

Should analogy be though helpful, however, I prefer that of a stream. The spring, starting on its journey, is joined by tributary after tributary. The river, reaching the ocean, comes from a hundred sources. No man may say whence any drop of water is derived. Yet for a time distinction may be possible. Into the clear creek, brown swamp water flows from the left. Later, from the right comes water stained by its clay bed. The three may remain for a space, sharply divided. But at last inevitably no trace of separation remains. They are so commingled that all distinction is lost.

As we have said, we cannot trace the effect of an act to the end, if end there is. Again, however, we may trace it part of the way. A murder at Serajevo may be the necessary antecedent to an assassination in London twenty years hence. An overturned lantern may burn all Chicago. We may follow the fire from the shed to the last building. We rightly say the fire started by the lantern caused its destruction.

A cause, but not the proximate cause. What we do mean by the word 'proximate' is that, because of convenience, of public policy, of a rough sense of justice, the law arbitrarily declines to trace a series of events beyond a certain point. This is not logic. It is practical politics. Take our rule as to fires. Sparks from my burning haystack set on fire my house and my neighbor's. I may recover from a negligent railroad He may not. Yet the wrongful act as directly harmed the one as the other. We may regret that the line was drawn just where it was, but drawn somewhere it had to be. We said the act of the railroad was not the proximate cause of our neighbor's fire. Cause it surely was. The words we used were simply indicative of our notions of public policy. Other courts think differently. But somewhere they reach the point where they cannot say the stream comes from any one source.

Take the illustration given in an unpublished manuscript by a distinguished and helpful writer on the law of torts. A chauffeur negligently collides with another car which is filled with dynamite, although he could not know it. An explosion follows. A, walking on the sidewalk nearby, is killed. B, sitting in a window of a building opposite, is cut by flying glass. C, likewise sitting in a window a block away, is similarly injured. And a further illustration: A nursemaid, ten blocks away, startled by the noise, involuntarily drops a baby from her arms to the walk. We are told that C may not recover while A may. As to B it is a question for court or jury. We will all agree that the baby might not. Because, we are again told, the chauffeur had no reason to believe his conduct involved any risk of injuring either C or the baby. As to them he was not negligent.

But the chauffeur, being negligent in risking the collision, his belief that the scope of the harm he might do would be limited is immaterial. His act unreasonably jeopardized the safety of any one who might be affected by it. C's injury and that of the baby were directly traceable to the collision. Without that, the injury would not have happened. C had the right to sit in his office, secure from such dangers. The baby was entitled to use the sidewalk with reasonable safety.

The true theory is, it seems to me, that the injury to C, if in truth he is to be denied recovery, and the injury to the baby, is that their several injuries were not the proximate result of the negligence. And here not what the chauffeur had reason to believe would be the result of his conduct, but what the prudent would foresee, may have a bearing—may have some bearing, for the problem of proximate cause is not to be solved by any one consideration. It is all a question of expediency. There are no fixed rules to govern our judgment. There are simply matters of which we may take account. We have in a somewhat different connection spoken of 'the stream of events.' We have asked whether that stream was deflected—whether it was forced into new and unexpected channels. *Donnelly v. H. C. & A. I. Piercy Contracting Co.*, 222 N. Y. 210, 118 N. E. 605. This is rather rhetoric than law. There is in truth little to guide us other than common sense.

There are some hints that may help us. The proximate cause, involved as it may be with many other causes, must be, at the least, something without which the event would not happen. The court must ask itself whether there was a natural and continuous sequence between cause and effect. Was the one a substantial factor in producing the other? Was there a direct connection between them, without too many intervening causes? Is the effect of cause on result not too attenuated? Is the cause likely, in the usual judgment of mankind, to produce the result? Or, by the exercise of prudent foresight, could the result be foreseen? Is the result too remote from the cause, and here we consider remoteness in time and space. *Bird v. St. Paul & M. Ins. Co.*, 224 N. Y. 47, 120 N. E. 86, 13 A. L. R. 875, where we passed upon the construction of a contract—but something was also said on this subject. Clearly we must so consider, for the greater the distance either in time or space, the more surely do other causes intervene to affect the result. When a lantern is overturned, the firing of a shed is a fairly direct consequence. Many things contribute to the spread of the conflagration—the force of the wind, the direction and width of streets, the character of intervening structures, other factors. We draw an uncertain and wavering line, but draw it we must as best we can.

Once again, it is all a question of fair judgment, always keeping in mind the fact that we endeavor to make a rule in each case that will be practical and in keeping with the general understanding of mankind.

Here another question must be answered. In the case supposed, it is said, and said correctly, that the chauffeur is liable for the direct effect of the explosion, although he had no reason to suppose it would follow a collision. 'The fact that the injury occurred in a different manner than that which might have been expected does not prevent the chauffeur's negligence from being in law the cause of the injury.' But the natural results of a negligent act—the results which a prudent man would or should foresee—do have a bearing upon the decision as to proximate cause. We have said so repeatedly. What should be foreseen? No human foresight would suggest that a collision itself might injure one a block away. On the contrary, given an explosion, such a possibility might be reasonably expected. I think the direct connection, the foresight of which the courts speak, assumes prevision of the explosion, for the immediate results of which, at least, the chauffeur is responsible.

It may be said this is unjust. Why? In fairness he should make good every injury flowing from his negligence. Not because of tenderness toward him we say he need not answer for all that follows his wrong. We look back to the catastrophe, the fire kindled by the spark, or the explosion. We trace the consequences, not indefinitely, but to a certain point. And to aid us in fixing that point we ask what might ordinarily be expected to follow the fire or the explosion.

This last suggestion is the factor which must determine the case before us. The act upon which defendant's liability rests is knocking an apparently harmless package onto the platform. The act was negligent. For its proximate consequences the defendant is liable. If its contents were broken, to the owner; if it fell upon and crushed a passenger's foot, then to him; if it exploded and injured one in the immediate vicinity, to him also as to A in the illustration. Mrs. Palsgraf was standing some distance away. How far cannot be told from the record—apparently 25 or 30 feet, perhaps less. Except for the explosion, she would not have been injured. We are told by the appellant in his brief, 'It cannot be denied that the explosion was the direct cause of the plaintiff's injuries.' So it was a substantial factor in producing the result—there was here a natural and continuous sequence—direct connection. The only intervening cause was that, instead of blowing her to the ground, the concussion smashed the weighing machine which in turn fell upon her. There was no remoteness in time, little in space. And surely, given such an explosion as here, it needed no great foresight to predict that the natural result would be to injure one on the platform at no greater distance from its scene than was the plaintiff. Just how no one might be able to predict. Whether by flying fragments, by broken glass, by wreckage of machines or structures no one could say. But injury in some form was most probable.

Under these circumstances I cannot say as a matter of law that the plaintiff's injuries were not the proximate result of the negligence.

Courts continue to cite both the majority and dissenting opinions from *Palsgraf*, and to define the scope of liability in terms of both duty and proximate cause—using foreseeability in both contexts as the standard for establishing limits on liability.

1. As you hopefully remember from the duty section of this chapter, duty is usually determined as a matter of law, and is an issue resolved by the court, while proximate cause is determined by the trier of fact (usually

the jury). The main criticism leveled at those courts using foreseeability as a limit on the duty owed is that allowing courts to consider foreseeability as part of determining duty removes a factual consideration (i.e., determining what was foreseeable under the circumstances) from the jury. How might this impact a party's case (having a judge, rather than a jury, decide an issue)?

2. In light of this section, review your responses to the questions preceding *A.W. v. Lancaster County School District*. Has your opinion changed? Why or why not?

3. Do you agree with Cardozo, Andrews or neither? Why?

Exercise 2-29 Analyzing Causation and Evaluating Expert Opinions

For this exercise we return to the chapter problem. Below are relevant excerpts of the transcripts from Plaintiffs' and Defendants' expert witness depositions. Based on your understanding of the materials in this section, review the deposition transcripts to evaluate causation from both perspectives.

Excerpt from Deposition Transcript of Plaintiffs' Expert Witness

1   Q. What is your opinion in this case?

2   A My opinion is that Marcus sustained, during labor and

3   delivery, which has been or will be described by both de-

4   fense and plaintiff obstetricians as being abnormal in the

5   sense that there was a tachysystole or hyperstimulation,

6   tetanic contractions, frequent late decelerations, evi-

7   dence for hypoxia with a falling scalp pH during labor, at

8   some point after 1700 and thereafter, there was, I be-

9   lieve, sufficient reduction in perfusion to the watershed,

10 basal ganglia, cerebellum, cerebral cortex bilaterally,

11 together with hypoglycemia that was documented soon after

12 delivery, that this is a combination principally of lack

13 of perfusion; secondarily, significant hypoglycemia.

14   Q What are the pertinent facts of this case that are

15 important to your opinion?

16   A The pertinent facts include, number one, the abnormal

17 labor, which has been and will be well-documented by the

18 obstetrical experts; the fact the child was delivered, and

1 although it was given Apgars of 7 over 8—and an Apgar of
2 7 in a term baby is not normal, but nonetheless these are
3 Apgar scores that are not compatible with the narrative
4 notes immediately upon delivery. In the DR they describe
5 marked reduction in tone and reflexes, acrocyanosis, and
6 shallow breathing. These narrative findings would not allow
7 a scoring of 7 at one minute and 8 at five minutes. Never-
8 theless, there was significant depression and compromise of
9 this newborn from the beginning.
10   There was a reported venous cord pH, which is maternal
11 circulation, that revealed mild to moderate metabolic
12 acidosis with a base excess of minus 7 and a pH of 7.21.
13 We have a normal placenta, based upon placental pathol-
14 ogy. Nothing to suggest inflammatory response, such as
15 chorioamnionitis.
16   We have, then, a child who was quite sick in the newborn
17 from the very beginning. There was an acute encephalopathy
18 with, I believe, seizure activity. There was hypoglycemia,
19 as I indicated earlier, first documented at 1945, the child
20 having been delivered at 1816. Probably was hypoglycemic
21 the entire time and remained hypoglycemic despite initial
22 therapy. The child had tremors, was jittery, with multiple
23 entries into the records, and had seizure-like activity,
24 about which nothing was done, as a matter of fact. For ex-
25 ample, an EEG was not obtained, and the child was not
26 treated for a suspect seizure disorder. The child was hy-
27 potonic, limp, had a weak cry. And this is a continual
28 theme during admission.
29   There was respiratory distress, primarily characterized
30 by shallow breathing. There was acrocyanosis. There were
31 multiple episodes of desaturation. There were at least
32 three episodes of bradycardia. There was apnea. The child
33 was described as being very sleepy, lethargic on numerous

1 occasions. There was difficulty in feeding, in nippling.
2 The child would not open his eyes. There was hyperbiliru-
3 binemia, up to 15.5. The NRBCs, an indicator of bone mar-
4 row hypoxia, was elevated.
5   So the combination of a mild to moderate metabolic aci-
6 dosis that was present on further blood gases, together
7 with depression and compromise from the beginning follow-
8 ing delivery, together with his acute encephalopathy in
9 the context of a labor described as being tetanic, hyper-
10 stimulated, tachysystole with frequent late decelera-
11 tions, rising baseline, reduced beat-to-beat variability
12 after 1700—the combination of those factors have per-
13 suaded me that this is an injury that occurred at the
14 end of labor and delivery.
15   Q Just so I understand, you're saying there's a combi-
16 nation of hypoglycemia and HIE. Is that fair to say?
17   A I think you've misrepresented what I said. I said
18 that the primary pathogenesis is poor perfusion. And
19 I've said that there is a secondary phenomenon in which
20 there was a period of sustained hypoglycemia at levels
21 that will have a deleterious effect upon the brain.
22   Q But the point is here we're talking about alleged hy-
23 poxic injury; is that correct?
24   A No. You continue to misrepresent what I've said.
25 We're talking about injury to the brain because of poor
26 perfusion, which is supplemented by hypoglycemia.
27   Q Well, what caused the injury? The perfusion or the
28 hypoglycemia?
29   A The perfusion is the primary pathogenesis.
30   Q Did you mention a part of the brain that should be in-
31 jured because of this perfusion?
32   A It's very unpredictable. It may be a very small part
33 of the brain, or it may be widespread. In this case it

1 involves both hemispheres. It involves the watershed. It

2 involves the basal ganglia. It involves the cerebellum.

3   Q And you, of course, would expect to find evidence of

4 damage to the basal ganglia or the cerebellum on MRI

5 findings?

6   A You may or you may not. In this case there is signifi-

7 cant pathology of the basal ganglia, of the pons, of the

8 midbrain on T2 flare images. There is significant damage of

9 the anterior and posterior limbs of the internal capsule,

10 as well as diffuse atrophy in both cerebral hemispheres.

11   Q What are you basing that on?

12   A The MRI.

13   Q You said the main injury for the child is perfusion,

14 yes?

15   A Yes.

16   Q This perfusion theory, is it in the literature?

17   A It is not a theory. Perfusion is the sine qua non for

18 damage to the central nervous system if it is inter-

19 rupted. And it has been addressed many thousands of times

20 in the literature, both in the experimental as well as in

21 the clinical literature.

22   Q Okay. We're not talking about HIE here. Is that how I

23 understand it?

24   A What do you mean by "HIE"?

25   Q Hypoxic ischemic encephalopathy. You're saying

26 there's a perfusion problem, which is complicated after

27 delivery by hypoglycemia; is that correct?

28   A There is a perfusion compromise towards the end of

29 labor and delivery that was further compromised by hypo-

30 glycemia after delivery.

31   Q But even though you mention hypoglycemia, you said

32 earlier the injury was because of the perfusion?

33

1   A That is the primary pathogenesis. A secondary patho-
2 genesis would be hypoglycemia.

3   Q Okay. So we're talking about an ischemic injury?

4   A Yes—with the late decelerations, the tetanic contrac-
5 tions, the hyperstimulation. These all compromise the
6 ability of the fetal heart to pump adequate cardiac output
7 to the brain, which, at its maximum, will be about 25
8 percent. These are all ischemic injuries.

9   Q Okay. That's what I needed to know. In your review
10 I'm assuming you reviewed the newborn admission?

11   A Yes.

12   Q I'm going to hand you that, the newborn assessment I
13 want to go over it with you. Now, we're talking about a
14 perfusion problem, but I'd like to go over, I guess, a
15 few other things.

16   Number one, neurological: It's noted that the child is
17 responsive to pain. Is that consistent with a perfusion
18 problem?

19   A Yes. Being responsive to pain is a very, very late
20 reflex in terms of neurological injury. You may have a
21 devastated brain and still be pain-responsive.

22   Q All right. His reflexes: He's got all of them. He's
23 got root, suck, swallow, gag, grasp, and Moro. Is that
24 consistent with a hypoxic injury?

25   A This is not credible based upon the subsequent exami-
26 nations in which there was a minimal Moro, very poor
27 Moro. The child was not sucking well and was having diffi-
28 culty swallowing. So this admission is not—this neuro-
29 logical admission is not compatible with the findings that
30 came before or the findings that came following over a
31 number of days.

32

33

1 Q Okay. I accept your skepticism. We move along.

2 Seizures: It says he doesn't have any. You said he had

3 some—

4 A This is on admission. This is a one—this is at 2110

5 on 10/22. The child, throughout the course, was jittery,

6 had tremors, and had seizure-like activity. You're taking

7 a single snapshot at 2110 and trying to make more of it

8 than you possibly can. In any event, having said that,

9 the neurological findings in this admission are not com-

10 patible with this child's clinical course.

11 Q Okay. And just—I want to step back because you said

12 he was jittery and had seizure-like activity. Isn't that

13 something you'd expect with a hypoglycemic child?

14 A No, because by that time he was no longer hypo-

15 glycemic. This was long after he had his hypoglycemia

16 corrected. On 10/25 he was described as being jittery. At

17 that time his blood sugar was 68. He was described as

18 showing seizure-like movements. This is on 10/25, three

19 days after delivery. On 10/23 he had tremors, again with

20 a blood sugar that was not in the seriously depressed

21 range. Those are two examples of this child's condition.

22 Again, on 10/24 the child was jittery. Again, between 10/

23 22 and 10/23, jittery. So there are entries from 10/22

24 through 10/25 where Marcus was jittery, and on 10/25 they

25 finally used the term "seizure-like movements."

26 Q Is jitteriness the same thing as having a seizure?

27 A It may be.

28 Q And it may not be?

29 A Sometimes it is, sometimes it isn't.

30 Q His heart rate?

31 A He had shallow respirations, and those persisted, and

32 yet they described his respiratory rate as within normal

33 limits, chest expansion—in other words, his pulmonary

1 system was described as normal despite the fact that he

2 had shallow respirations. So there's an inconsistency

3 there between the admission at 2110 and what was de-

4 scribed earlier and later.

5   Q Under "Gastrointestinal, Urinary," he voided? Do you

6 see that?

7   A Yes. There is nothing about the GI or elimination

8 system that appears to be unusual or abnormal.

9   Q I'm just curious because usually when the body is

10 trying to respond to a lack of oxygen, doesn't it

11 preferably send oxygen to the brain and away from organs

12 like the kidney, from the skin, from the lungs, from the

13 intestines?

14   A You don't mean oxygen; you mean blood flow.

15   Q Well, blood flow with—

16   A And yes, blood flow can be shunted. The normal cardiac

17 output percent to brain is between 21 and 23 percent In

18 periods when there's compromise in blood flow, that will

19 increase to 25 percent And sometimes the other organs

20 will experience reduced blood flow, and on occasion they

21 will become ischemic.

22   In this case that was never evaluated. The kidney func-

23 tion studies, liver function studies were never evalu-

24 ated, so we don't know if there was any compromise with

25 respect to ischemia in those two organs.

26   Q Well, with the kidneys we'd look at the BUN and the

27 creatinine, wouldn't we?

28   A I did not make a note of the BUN or creatinine, so

29 either it was normal or it was not performed.

30   Q So that would, again, rule against any kidney damage?

31   A If it was not performed, we wouldn't know.

32   Q But If it was performed—

33

1 A If it was performed and done in a timely manner, then
2 it would be against a renal ischemia.

3 Q Right Just—I think there's one, perhaps, last thing.
4 His color is pink at this time, and he was born at 1816,
5 so about three hours later, roughly. So would you expect
6 a child who has had a perfusion problem, which I think is
7 synonymous with having shock, really, being pink?

8 A Yes, because by the time that this child was examined
9 by this nursing staff, there was most likely adequate 02
10 saturation. And as long as your saturation is above 75
11 percent, you're going to have a pink child.

12 Q You talked about—you looked at the mother's—the ve-
13 nous pH, and you determined that was a metabolic acidosis?

14 A Mild to moderate.

15 Q Okay. You said it was a respiratory acidosis. You did
16 say that?

17 A Yes. I think there's a significant respiratory acido-
18 sis component.

19 Q Okay. Now, with an ischemic injury what kind of find-
20 ings would we expect to see on head imaging?

21 A Very unpredictable. It may be focal, multifocal, gen-
22 eralized. May be arterial. May be in the watershed. May
23 be limited to the basal ganglia, limited to the cerebel-
24 lum, limited to the parasagittal cortical strips. Very
25 unpredictable.

26 Q But nonetheless, we would expect some sort of head
27 finding, on the MRI, yes?

28 A Usually. Not always, but usually.

29 Q You'd expect a disturbance in the myelination pattern?

30 A You may have that, depending upon the localization.

31 Q Well, the premature brain, it's not mature, and it's
32 still growing. So if there is an injury, that would af-
33 fect the myelination pattern. More likely than not, you

1 should see a disturbance in the myelination pattern if
2 there had been an ischemic injury?
3   A If it's severe enough and dependent upon its location.
4   Q And you would, of course, see lesions as well with
5 respect to the basal ganglia, the occipital cortex, what-
6 ever; you would still see lesions?
7   A Depending upon the degree, you may. Not always, but
8 often. Again, depending upon the degree.
9   Q Did you see either in this case, myelination or le-
10 sions?
11   A The MRI that I reviewed indicated widespread pathology
12 in both cortex and white matter, including the myelin,
13 with abnormal increased signaling on the T2 flare images in
14 white matter, subcortical, periventricular, corti-
15 comedullary junction, in both hemispheres.
16   In addition, there was increased T2 flare signaling in
17 the gray matter, such as the thalamic cuclei, the basal
18 ganglia. In addition, there was also increased signaling
19 in the midbrain long tracks, the cerebral peduncles, and
20 the basis pontis.
21   There was widespread secondary Wallerian and transsy-
22 naptic degeneration, and this is identifiable on the MRI
23 that was done on April 4th, 2000. The result was general-
24 ized—moderately generalized cortical and central atrophy,
25 in which there's enlargement of the lateral ventricles,
26 right more than left, enlargement of the subarachnoid
27 spaces, the anterior interhemispheric fissure, the sylvian
28 fissures. There's reduced gyral volume with increased sul-
29 cation. There's a thinning of the corpus callosum, with
30 all of its constituent parts present.
31   So we have widespread pathology on the MRI.
32
33

1   Q We talked about the basal ganglia and the changes—you

2 would—would it be—you would characterize that as le-

3 sions, would you? I want to understand what—

4   A They're abnormal.

5   Q Would you call them lesions?

6   A Yes.

7   Q Now, with an ischemic injury don't we expect some

8 sort of edema initially?

9   A You may have edema initially.

10   Q I mean, it's usually—correct me if my chronology is

11 wrong. You have a hit, an ischemic hit, yes? And then you

12 get—you may or may not get edema, yes?

13   A Depending upon the severity and depending upon the

14 volume that's involved.

15   Q Okay. But—and you may or may not get edema, but if

16 you do get edema, does it stay or does it go away?

17   A Oh, it disappears, usually by 96 hours to—certainly

18 by 10 days you will no longer see visually, on a routine

19 MRI, edema.

20   Q What happened—I mean, when the edema goes away, be it

21 in 10 days or whatever we want to call it, does a cyst

22 develop?

23   A Depends upon the nature of the injury. It may or may

24 not. In this case what you have is compromise in brain

25 growth. And that brain growth, at six months of age, re-

26 veals significant atrophy.

27   This would not be an issue had they done an imaging

28 study in the newborn period, as they should have in

29 1999, since we had a child who was neurologically abnor-

30 mal; we had a child who had suspect seizure activity.

31 They should have done both an EEG and an imaging study,

32 at least a CT, and certainly, if that were abnormal,

33 then an MRI. These studies were not done. As a matter of

1 fact, he had a pediatric neurological consultation, and

2 they were not even recommended by someone who should

3 have known better.

4   Q Okay. I guess I just wanted to follow up the question

5 regarding edema and it goes away, may or may not have a

6 cyst I understand nothing is certain. If a cyst were to

7 develop, would you more likely than not expect them to de-

8 velop within the first two weeks or by three or four weeks?

9   A You may begin to see areas of atrophy within 10 to 14

10 days, particularly if it's in the periventricular region.

11 Generally speaking, it takes a bit longer than that.

12   Q So generally speaking, more likely it's usually about

13 three to four weeks?

14   A You cannot generalize, and I won't do that.

15   Q Okay. But you said we may see it within the first two

16 weeks, but—

17   A I didn't say that. I said by 10 to 14 days—and if I

18 didn't say that, I meant to say by 10 to 14 days you may

19 begin to see some areas of atrophy. Certainly you will

20 begin to see them after that. But it is impossible to

21 generalize because it depends upon the local situation,

22 the severity, the volume, and the nature of the injury.

23   Q Okay. Is there anything remarkable about this EEG?

24   A It was done because they were looking for seizure ac-

25 tivity. I assume they queried the youngster's staring

26 spells, were satisfied that the EEG did not reveal evi-

27 dence for seizure. And this was an important therapeutic

28 decision not to treat. This, by the way, is another piece

29 of clinical evidence against a D-2-hydroxyglutaric

30 aciduria.

31   Q Please tell me how. How is that? How does it go

32 against D-2—

33

1   A Because all of the neonatal-onset D-2—and this is a
2 very rare condition—with severe psychomotor retardation
3 have had ongoing seizure disorders.
4   Q All of them?
5   A There are fifteen reported cases.
6   Q Okay. And do you base your conclusion the child does
7 not have D-2-hydroxyglutaric aciduria on anything else?
8   A The level of D-2 that was obtained. That level is
9 simply too low to allow for a phenotype as severely im-
10 paired as this child.
11   Q Would it be reasonable, given these labs, given the
12 child's presentation, for someone to conclude that "I
13 can't specifically say, but this child does have a meta-
14 bolic disorder"?
15   A If somebody did not know the facts of labor and de-
16 livery and the newborn period and was simply presented
17 with a child like this youngster, a metabolic evaluation
18 is in order.
19   Q If the doctor who did the fibroblast studies, was to
20 testify at trial that his testing did not rule out all
21 mitochondrial disorders, would you change your opinion?
22   A It's impossible to rule out all mitochondrial disor-
23 ders. They are developing as we speak in terms of disor-
24 ders of one of the metabolic pathways. And they're
25 discovering a wide variety of mitochondrial DNA disor-
26 ders, whether they're elimination syndromes or depletion
27 syndromes, syndromes of poor organization, or any of the
28 other general categories of a mitochondrial DNA disorder.
29 So this is an impossibility. Suffice it to say, fortu-
30 nately, they're very rare because most embryos with such
31 a disorder do not survive.
32   Having said that, we have excluded those that they have
33 considered, including D-2, based upon direct urinary evi-

1 dence. And we're left with what I consider to be the sim-
2 plest and the clearest explanation for Marcus's condi-
3 tion: a highly disordered labor and delivery, which
4 resulted in an acute encephalopathy and newborn period.

5   Q Okay. Just—I just want to make sure I have your
6 opinion correctly. It's your feeling that the child had
7 a perfusion problem, and later on, hypoglycemia was a
8 secondary element?

9   A It is not a feeling.

10   Q The point—my understanding is that the child—because
11 he's an infant of a diabetic mother, he's going to have—
12 he has hypoglycemia. We looked at the record. His first
13 glucose volume was 14, and he had the hyperbilirubinemia
14 and that the stress of the labor made the hypoglycemia
15 worse and that the injury to the child was the hypo-
16 glycemia. Does that make any sense to you?

17   A I think hypoglycemia played a role as a secondary
18 pathogenetic mechanism, yes. And I've expressed that on
19 several occasions earlier in this deposition.

20   Q Does hypoglycemia make hypoxia worse, or is it that
21 hypoxia makes hypoglycemia worse?

22   A Let's talk in terms of ischemia. There is a synergis-
23 tic relationship between hypoglycemia and poor perfusion,
24 whereby the focus or the target can be made worse if the
25 two are together in a synergistic fashion than if only
26 one was there. They may act synergistically in an adverse
27 fashion.

28   Q If they act synergistically, would the injury that
29 you would expect to see be an ischemic injury?

30   A Yes.

31   Q And just so I understand, I mean his hypoglycemic
32 value, is it just because he was a child of a gesta-
33

1 tional diabetic mother, or it is that fact plus the fact
2 of the labor?

3   A This was a baby of a diabetic mom, and infants of di-
4 abetic moms frequently have hypoglycemia. A stressed baby
5 of a diabetic mom would have greater difficulties with hy-
6 poglycemia as a general rule.

7   Q So that is the more likely reason why he was hypo-
8 glycemic?

9   A In my opinion the primary factor is the fact that he
10 is a baby of a diabetic mom, however, and I want to be
11 sure the record is clear, that a baby who has undergone a
12 significant period of intrauterine acidosis as was the
13 case with this baby, would tolerate the hypoglycemia less
14 well and the hypoglycemia would have a higher likelihood
15 of producing permanent neurological injury. In other
16 words, if you add to a component of asphyxia or in-
17 trauterine acidosis a component of post birth hypo-
18 glycemia the two would have an additive effect in terms
19 of any problems that one would encounter neurologically
20 so far as the baby is concerned.

21   Q Is that your opinion here?

22   A I think the hypotonia is seen in cases where you com-
23 bine newborn—a newborn who was acidotic prior to deliv-
24 ery who is somewhat asphyxiated at delivery, and then
25 gets a second hit to the brain, if you will, in the form
26 of significant and symptomatic hypoglycemia.

27   Q He is going to get a second hit. Where is that hit
28 going to be?

29   A The hypoglycemia tends to affect primarily the brain
30 and tends to affect primarily the cortical portions of
31 the brain.

32   Q Just so I understand, it is because the child is of
33 a gestational diabetic mother and because of the stress

1 of the labor which caused the really low glucose values

2 when he was born?

3   A Yes.

4   Q Just so I understand your opinion, your feeling is

5 that Marcus suffered hypoglycemia during the neonatal

6 period?

7   A Yes.

8   Q And it was that in combination with the labor course

9 which leads to his current impairments?

10   A That is my opinion.

11

12

13

14

15

16

17

18

19

20

21

22

23

24

25

26

27

28

29

30

31

32

33

Excerpt from Deposition Transcript of Defendant's Expert Witness

1   Q. Is your opinion that Marcus Ricks most likely has a

2 2-hydroxyglutaric aciduria?

3   A. My opinion is that he most likely has it.

4   Q. Is that diagnosis made exclusively based upon the

5 one—I think it was a urine report?

6   A. It is based on the urine report and the compatible

7 clinical picture and radiological material. You could not

8 possibly diagnose hydroxyglutaric aciduria from a pic-

9 ture, an image or an exam, but you could rule it out as

10 an only diagnosis from those tests. So in order to make

11 the diagnosis and rule out other possibilities, that's

12 why you need the whole picture.

13   Q. In your mind, sir, is his clinical picture compati-

14 ble with any other diagnosis?

15   A. If we take the whole clinical picture, the history,

16 the physical, the lab, the radiology, I think it is com-

17 patible with a metabolic disease. It could be multiple

18 metabolic diseases, but I think the metabolic disease

19 that it probably is is 2-hydroxyglutaric aciduria because

20 of the urine test.

21   Q. How many times have you diagnosed your own patients

22 or patients you have consulted on with 2-hydroxyglutaric

23 aciduria?

24   A. I don't think I have my own patient with this dis-

25 ease.

26   Q. Well, how many cases of D-2-hydroxyglutaric aciduria

27 are you aware of in the world?

28   A. I would say maybe less than twenty.

29   Q. Have you ever, as a treating doctor, made that diag-

30 nosis of any patient?

31   A. No.

1   Q. I am going to show you a document that I am marking
2 as Exhibit X. Is this the report upon which you formu-
3 lated your opinion about the 2-hydroxyglutaric aciduria?
4   A. Yes.
5   Q. On that report, the creatinine level is 9; correct?
6   A. In the urine, yes.
7   Q. It specifically says on the report that a urine speci-
8 men containing less than 25 milligrams per deciliter crea-
9 tinine may be too dilute for accurate testing; correct?
10   A. Which page does it say that on?
11   Q. At the bottom of the first page.
12   A. Yes, it says that.
13   Q. That's also done from this urine sample, isn't it?
14   A. I think we have been talking about the organic acid
15 screen.
16   Q. Right, but that's a urine screen?
17   A. I think what we have been talking about until now is
18 a urine screen.
19   Q. I want to make sure. The report upon which you base
20 your opinion, you know that it says that it may be too
21 dilute to be accurate based upon the creatinine level; is
22 that fair?
23   A. Correct, that's fair.
24   Q. On the second page of that document, it noted that
25 the excretion of 2-hydroxyglutaric acid was 54?
26   A. Correct.
27   Q. It's specifically noted in this report that they
28 couldn't tell, that it was not possible to differentiate
29 D and L forms, didn't they?
30   A. Yes.
31   Q. They also say that excretions of D-2 are typically
32 markedly elevated and the range they give is 600 to
33 7,000; correct?

1 A. What they say exactly is that the excretions of D-2-
2 hydroxyglutaric acid is typically, but not always,
3 markedly elevated (range 600-7,000).
4 Q. Based upon the range that they give, Marcus' 2-
5 hydroxyglutaric acid level was far below what they consider
6 the range to make the diagnosis of 2-hydroxyglutaric
7 aciduria, isn't it?
8 A. Far below the typical range, yes.
9 Q. Then it goes on further after it talks about the L-2
10 to say "These findings are difficult to correlate and could
11 be coincidental," don't they?
12 A. Right. They say they need clinical information.
13 Q. So we've got something that's reported to be far
14 below what they consider the typically normal range, it
15 could be coincidental and the specimen has far too lit-
16 tle creatinine for them to say it's an accurate test,
17 but yet that's what you rely upon to formulate the 2-
18 hydroxyglutaric aciduria diagnosis as the most likely
19 diagnosis?
20 A. I do, yes, along with the history, the physical and
21 the MRI; so right, alone that's one thing, but we need
22 all of the rest and that's why we need all the rest.
23 Q. What in the history tells you that this is 2-
24 hydroxyglutaric aciduria?
25 A. The clinical picture is compatible with that diagno-
26 sis. The features that are compatible are hypotonia,
27 macrocephaly, MRI findings, increased succinate, one
28 episode of decreased bicarb and elevation of lactate and
29 pyruvate.
30 Q. What part of the physical exam leads you to make
31 this diagnosis?
32 A. What is compatible, not diagnostic, but compatible
33 is the hypotonia.

1 Q. Although these are comparable with the diagnosis you

2 made, they are also compatible with many other things,

3 aren't they?

4 A. Yes.

5 Q. The MRI findings, although based upon your interpre-

6 tation of the film may be compatible, it's also compatible

7 with many other things, isn't it?

8 A. Yes.

9 Q. What was the report of the MRI? What did the report

10 of the MRI say?

11 A. The MRI on 4/4/00 showed mild diffuse brain atrophy.

12 That was my understanding of their summary.

13 Q. What does diffuse brain atrophy mean?

14 A. The definition of brain atrophy is brain shrinkage.

15 Q. So they saw diffuse meaning all around the brain

16 that it had shrunk?

17 A. I don't know what they saw.

18 Q. In light of the fact that we know the creatinine

19 level was 9 and it needs to be 25 to be accurate, in

20 light of the fact that the lab says that these findings

21 are difficult to correlate and could be coincidental and

22 the fact that the 2 hydroxy level was only elevated to 54

23 when their elevated range is 600 to 7,000, how can you

24 say more likely than not this is what his problem is?

25 A. The typical is in that range, but then there are

26 others one presumes who are atypical and the answer to

27 your question, and we know this, but what it says is typ-

28 ically but not always.

29 Q. But he doesn't fit square into the range of D-2, of

30 2-hydroxyglutaric aciduria to come to that conclusion,

31 does he, because his level is only 54?

32 A. He does not fit into the typical range for 2-

33 hydroxyglutaric aciduria, correct.

1   Q. Here's my question to you then. This, at least po-
2 tentially, is a sample that according to the lab, is too
3 dilute and the level of 2-hydroxyglutaric acid, by this
4 lab's report, is far less than it would need to be to
5 make a diagnosis of 2-hydroxyglutaric aciduria, and the
6 report specifically says that this finding could be coinci-
7 dental. Taking all of those things together, how do you
8 come to the conclusion that more likely than not this
9 child has a diagnosis that less than thirty people of the
10 billions and billions in the world have?
11 Defendant's Attorney: Objection. Form.
12   A. Because the clinical picture, the radiological pic-
13 ture are consistent. The clinical features patients pres-
14 ent with—ataxia, hypotonia and seizures, so he has the
15 hypotonia and he is certainly incoordinated which would
16 qualify to what most people talk about when they say
17 ataxia so he has really two of the three features that
18 they talk about. But my answer goes beyond that. There
19 are many features here that are not typical or that are
20 compatible with multiple diseases and really what we have
21 to do is take everything and try to put it in one unified
22 whole. That's what I'm trying to do, and this is the best
23 unified whole that I can put it into.
24   Q. Would you expect to see a baby who was floppy at
25 birth if they had poor perfusion as a result of acidosis
26 and hypoxia?
27   A. Yes, I would not expect the baby to be hypotonic.
28   Q. Hypotonic is otherwise defined as floppy?
29   A. Yes.
30   Q. So if there's a floppy baby at birth, you would say
31 the reason they're floppy is because of some metabolic
32 disorder and not because of a lack of oxygen during the
33 labor and delivery process; is that correct?

1   A. Yes. Let me clarify.

2   There are cases in which due to hypoxia the baby may

3   be hypotonic for a transient period, almost always

4   within a three- to six-month period that is converted to

5   a spasticity.

6   So there could be a small amount of like a limited pe-

7   riod of hypotonia, but then it changed into hypertonia or

8   spasticity later on, which didn't happen in this case.

9   Q. But we're not even talking about this case I'm ask-

10 ing at birth, if a baby is hypotonic, you would say that

11 that would not be related to or could not be related to,

12 in your opinion, decreased oxygen during the labor and

13 delivery period?

14 A. It is possible that on a single exam after birth,

15 somebody can be hypotonic due to hypoxia, but they cannot

16 remain hypotonic over an extended period of time.

17 Q. Isn't it most likely that a baby who has decreased

18 oxygen during the labor period is going to be born floppy

19 and have low tone or hypotonia?

20 A. They can be. They can be depressed, yes, in the im-

21 mediate period after birth.

22 Q. It's not that they can be, they most likely are,

23 aren't they?

24 A. Yes, they are.

25 Q. And likewise, a baby who's not properly oxygenated

26 would have decreased respirations or would be depressed,

27 correct?

28 A. Yes.

29 Q. That doesn't mean they have a metabolic disorder,

30 does it?

31 A. No, not necessarily.

32

33

1 Q. I assume you have some opinion as to why you think
2 that Marcus Ricks does not fit a hypoxic ischemic en-
3 cephalopathy etiology.
4 A. I do.
5 Q. Let me ask you this. Does he support an etiology of
6 birth asphyxia?
7 A. No.
8 Q. Do you have some opinion as to what caused the find-
9 ings that you noted on the MRI?
10 A. Yes.
11 Q. What is that?
12 A. His metabolic disease.
13 Q. How does a metabolic disease cause the findings you
14 noted on MRI?
15 A. It affects cell distribution, placement, number, all
16 of the above.
17 Q. Does it cause cells not to form or does it cause
18 formed cells to die?
19 A. I don't know that in this particular case.
20 Q. I'm not asking you in this particular case. I'm ask-
21 ing you about a metabolic disease. Do metabolic diseases
22 that cause cell changes in the brain, are they cells that
23 die or are they cells that don't ever grow so there is
24 holes where they should be or what is it?
25 A. It could be either. There are examples of both.
26 Q. In Marcus' case, could you tell from looking at the
27 MRI if that was dead cells you were seeing in the brain
28 or something else?
29 A. I saw no evidence of dead cells. That doesn't mean
30 for sure that there are not some dead cells, but I saw no
31 evidence. That was what I was trying to say when I said
32 that I didn't see any parenchymal change so I did not see
33 any scar in that brain.

1   Q. Do you think there is any HIE at all present in
2 this case?
3   A. No.
4   Q. Tell me why you think it's not due to a hypoxic is-
5 chemic injury.
6   A. One is I don't think that he had a significant event
7 to damage his brain. He had variable decelerations. There
8 was a question of a late component. He had a scalp pH that
9 is first normal and then abnormal, low at 7.04, but his
10 Apgar scores are good and he had a blood gas done which
11 does not show any metabolic acidosis after he is born.
12   For those reasons, I think that he did not have signifi-
13 cant insult of the kind that's going to damage the brain.
14 Two is that although he had—
15   Q. I'm sorry. Before you go on, what blood gas are you
16 referring to?
17   A. Blood gas at 18:53.
18   Q. So you're referring to that arterial blood gas?
19   A. Correct.
20   Q. Okay. Sorry. Continue on.
21   A. Two, although he has tremors and hypotonia in the
22 newborn period, he starts to feed relatively early. He is
23 feeding well—I'll tell you exactly when. He has got a
24 lusty cry on 10/23 and on the initial PO1 note, intern
25 note, the child was taking formula, 20 cc's every three
26 hours, the note on the day that the child is born. The
27 child is feeding early and the child has a good cry, so
28 these findings are a point against the kind of severe en-
29 cephalopathy that will cause the kind of very severe cog-
30 nitive retardation that this child has. That's number two.
31   Number three is that although there is no question that
32 he has very significant motor findings, his cognitive re-
33 tardation is out of proportion to his motor findings. He

1 has worse cognitive abilities than he has motor abilities
2 which is again a point against a hypoxic ischemic insult
3 where usually the motor findings are worse than the cogni-
4 tive findings.
5   Four, he has got no scar on his brain on MRI, perhaps
6 one of the most significant findings. I would think that
7 with this child if this was HIE, I would expect to see
8 severe scarring on the brain.
9   Five, his motor finding is hypotonia, not hypertonia.
10 There is one kind of hypoxic ischemic injury at birth in
11 which you can have hypotonia but, one, he didn't have that
12 kind clinically and, two, he doesn't have the changes on
13 MRI that you would see with that kind.
14   Six, he has got the metabolic changes which include not
15 only that one value which is not in the usual or typical
16 range but also the elevated succinic acid, the decreased
17 bicarb and the elevated lactate and pyruvate which are
18 all compatible with, though not diagnostic of, his meta-
19 bolic disease.
20   Q. Let's go back to the beginning. You said he didn't
21 have any significant event, that there were variable de-
22 celerations with a late component. Is that your interpre-
23 tation of the fetal monitor strip?
24   A. No. I'm taking it from the record.
25   Q. I want you to assume for this question, sir, that
26 for the last three hours before Marcus Ricks was born, he
27 had late decelerations with every contraction and these
28 late decelerations lasted for, they were prolonged which I
29 think by definition they last more than a minute or two,
30 and I want you to further assume that there will be tes-
31 timony at trial that during this last three hours, this
32 baby was hypoxic and became acidotic as is evidenced by
33 the decrease in pH on the scalp pHs. Would that have any

1 impact on your opinion that there was nothing significant

2 that happened during the labor and delivery process?

3   A. What I said was not that there was nothing signifi-

4 cant but that there wasn't an event large enough to dam-

5 age the brain, yes.

6   Q. So you don't think that three hours of hypoxia and

7 acidosis is enough to damage the brain?

8   A. Not when the child comes out with an Apgar of 7, 8

9 and has no metabolic acidosis on the blood gas.

10   Q. The Apgar scores, if I told you the Apgar scores

11 were five and six, would that change your opinion?

12   A. My opinions depend on the data. Make any change in

13 the data, I'll rethink my opinions.

14   Q. If Marcus was having seizures in the neonatal period

15 as described by seizure-like activity and staring spells—

16 spell or spells. I don't remember if it's noted more than

17 once—would that change your opinion about Marcus' injury?

18   A. Again, change the facts and I'll reevaluate, but the

19 short answer is no. He has symptoms in the neonatal pe-

20 riod. No one is denying that he has brain symptoms.

21   The question is what is causing them. Is it a metabolic

22 disease or is it hypoxic ischemic injury? This is what it

23 boils down to. For the reasons that I have told you, I

24 think it's not HIE, and I do think it's metabolic.

25   Q. Do you see any notes in the neonatal period where he

26 was not feeding well or did not have a good suck?

27   A. Yes.

28   Q. During what time period was that?

29   A. There is a neurology note with Dr. Walker on 10/28,

30 and that note says that there was some concern about the

31 suck the first day and thereafter there was a better

32 suck. After three days, there was a good suck with some

33 variability.

1   Q. Does that imply to you that it wasn't normal during
2 that whole first at least three days?

3   A. It wasn't completely normal. Yes, it does.

4   Q. If a patient has birth asphyxia, they could have or
5 they are more likely than the average child to have hypo-
6 glycemia?

7   A. Yes.

8   Q. If somebody has hypoglycemia, can that cause injury
9 to the brain?

10   A. It can, but neonates tolerate hypoglycemia a little
11 better than adults and if it's going to do it it would be
12 associated with seizures at the time.

13   Q If a child has birth asphyxia, that could lead to or
14 predispose the child to have hypoglycemia which could re-
15 sult in some brain injury?

16   A. It is possible.

17   Q. If that happened, would you expect the child to have
18 mental retardation?

19   A. It could be a consequence. To be clear, I don't
20 think that's what happened here, but if we are speaking
21 hypothetically, it is a possibility.

22   Q. Do you have any other opinions in this case?

23   A. No.

24   Q. Do you think that the hypoglycemia caused any prob-
25 lems to this child?

26   A. No, I don't.

27   Q. Hypoglycemia is a metabolic disorder, isn't it?

28   A. Yes.

29   Q. You think it was not that metabolic disorder but some
30 other that caused his problem?

31   A. Yes.

32

33

4. Defenses

Traditionally there were two defenses to negligence: contributory negligence and assumption of risk. Both defenses completely barred a plaintiff's recovery. Today nearly all states have replaced contributory negligence with some type of comparative fault. As jurisdictions have converted from contributory negligence to comparative fault, they have adopted a number of different approaches to incorporating the doctrine of assumption of risk, the topics covered in this section.

a. Contributory Negligence and Comparative Fault

Contributory negligence is really just negligence on the part of the plaintiff; where plaintiff fails to exercise ordinary care for her own safety, and such failure is a contributing cause of the plaintiff's injury, she is contributorily negligent. Under the traditional rule, if defendant was able to prove plaintiff's contributory negligence plaintiff's recovery would be barred; plaintiff would recover nothing.

In all but a few states contributory negligence has been replaced by comparative fault. This is also sometimes called comparative negligence. In a comparative fault system if a defendant proves plaintiff's contributory negligence the jury weighs the fault of the plaintiff against the fault of the defendant and apportions liability by assigning each party a percentage reflecting the amount the party is at fault. The plaintiff's damages are then reduced by the percentage of plaintiff's fault. For example, let's assume a jury determined defendants were 75% responsible for plaintiff's harm and plaintiff was 25% responsible for her own harm. If plaintiff's total damages are $100,000, plaintiff's award will be reduced by 25%. Plaintiff will receive $75,000. Put another way damages are calculated as follows:

value of plaintiff's injury	X	percentage of defendant's fault	=	plaintiff's damages award
$100,000	X	75%	=	$75,000

There are two different approaches to comparative fault. The first is called pure comparative fault. In a pure comparative fault jurisdiction the plaintiff may recover regardless of her degree of fault. For example, if plaintiff is determined to be 99% at fault, she may recover 1% of her damages. Using the example above, this would mean she would receive $1,000.

The second form of comparative fault is called modified comparative fault. In a modified comparative fault jurisdiction the plaintiff may only recover if her percentage of fault is below a certain threshold. In some jurisdictions plaintiff will not recover if her negligence is *equal to* defendant's negligence (her negligence is 50% or greater). In other jurisdictions plaintiff will not recover if her negligence *exceeds* defendant's negligence (50.1% or greater). This might seem like a distinction without a difference, but in many cases juries believe the parties are equally at fault (50% each); in such cases plaintiffs recover half of their damages in the "exceeds" jurisdictions, but recover nothing in the "equal to" jurisdictions.

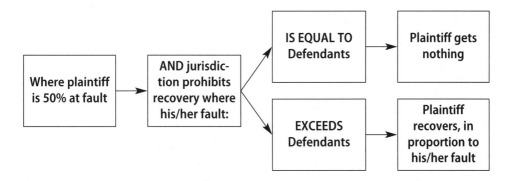

Finally, you should be aware that many lawyers use the term contributory negligence to describe comparative fault. When you hear a lawyer use the term contributory negligence and you are practicing in a comparative fault jurisdiction, the term contributory negligence is likely being used to indicate the comparative fault of the parties is being evaluated, rather than to indicate the plaintiff's recovery is completely barred.

Exercise 2-30 Identifying the Applicable Standard

Review the following jury instruction to determine which standard the jurisdiction applies, then redraft the instruction so that it might be used in a jurisdiction that follows a different standard.

> The defendant has the burden of proof on her claim that the plaintiff was negligent and that such negligence was a proximate cause of plaintiff's injury.
>
> If your verdict is for the plaintiff and you find that the negligence of both parties was a proximate cause of plaintiff's injury, then you must determine the degree of such negligence, expressed as a percentage, attributable to each party.
>
> Negligence on the part of the plaintiff does not bar recovery by plaintiff against the defendant for damages for economic loss. However, the percentage of negligence attributable to the plaintiff will be used by the court to reduce the amount of damages for economic losses that you find were sustained by plaintiff.
>
> Negligence on the part of the plaintiff does not bar recovery by plaintiff against the defendant for damages for noneconomic loss unless plaintiff's negligence is more than 50 percent. If the plaintiff's negligence is more than 50 percent, your verdict will be for the defendant as to plaintiff's claim for damages for noneconomic loss. Where the plaintiff's negligence is 50 percent or less, the percentage of negligence attributable to plaintiff will be used by the court to reduce the amount of damages for noneconomic loss that you find were sustained by plaintiff.

b. Assumption of Risk

When a plaintiff assumes a risk it means the plaintiff knows the risks of the activity and is willing to take those risks and be responsible for any resulting consequences. When a party assumes the risk of an activity, they give up their right to compensation for injuries that result from the risk they have taken. The critical areas of inquiry for determining whether a plaintiff assumed a risk are: (1) Did the plaintiff know the risks? and (2) Did the plaintiff voluntarily assume them?

Express assumption of risk is an advance agreement between the plaintiff and defendant as to what risks plaintiff assumes. If you have ever engaged in activities like sky diving, bungee jumping or rock climbing you have probably entered into such an agreement—perhaps by signing a waiver and release acknowledging the risks associated with such activities and releasing the party providing the service from liability. In these types of cases, the first issue—whether plaintiff knew of the risks—is usually a question of whether the waiver and release clearly stated the risk that caused the injury. In such cases, courts will usually strictly construe the waiver and release, reading it very narrowly, because the party seeking to avoid liability (the drafter of the waiver) has the burden of making sure that the risk, including the magnitude and consequences of that risk, are clear. The second issue—whether plaintiff voluntarily assumed the risk—arises where there is an argument that the plaintiff had no real choice, other than to sign the waiver and release. This does not mean that because a party must sign a release or forgo sky diving, that the waiver (assumption of risk) is involuntary. The voluntary choice in that situation is to sky dive or not to sky dive—and the plaintiff can forgo skydiving or sign the waiver. Sometimes, for public policy reasons, courts will not enforce such waivers. For example, where hospitals have attempted to require a waiver and release as a condition of treating a patient, courts have been unwilling to enforce such waivers; although you could argue that requiring such a waiver is just like the sky diving issue—the choice is to forgo the medical attention or sign the release—most courts recognize that foregoing an essential service (like medical care) is not a real choice.

Implied assumption of risk exists where a party's behavior indicates he knew the risks and was willing to suffer any resulting consequences. For example, if a person watches several other people slip and fall in an attempt to climb a set of icy stairs, we can imply from his choice to climb the stairs that he assumes the risk that he too will slip and fall. In other words, a party impliedly assumes the risk when he voluntarily engages in an activity with knowledge of its risks.

Under a contributory negligence system, both express and implied assumption of the risk would bar recovery by the plaintiff, meaning plaintiff would recover nothing—zero. As jurisdictions have abandoned contributory negligence and adopted comparative fault they have altered the defense of assumption of risk. Most jurisdictions still retain express assumption of risk as a complete defense to negligence under the rationale that if a party specifically consents to the harm or risk of harm, they should not recover when that harm occurs. Implied assumption of risk, however, has a much more complicated past and present. To understand how the doctrine is currently treated it is important to first understand the ways courts categorize (and label) implied assumption of risk.

Some courts use the terms primary and secondary implied assumption of risk to categorize the type of risk assumed. Primary assumption of risk is the term applied to circumstances where defendant has a limited or no duty or has not breached a duty. For example, imagine defendant owns and operates an ice rink and plaintiff is injured when another skater collides into her. In such a case plaintiff's injury is caused by an inherent risk of the activity—if you ice skate in a rink full of other ice skaters, other ice skaters may run into you. Similarly, if one football player is injured as a result of being tackled by another football player, we would say that the injured player assumed the risk of injury inherent in playing football. These are both examples of primary assumption of the risk. You might be wondering at this point why courts do not resolve these issues by simply saying the defendant did not breach any duty—in both of these examples, there has been no breach; this would be a valid observation, and in fact, there are legal commentators that would agree with you. However, the term primary assumption of risk continues to be the label applied to such situations because courts reason that the agreement to participate in an activity where there is a limited duty is an assumption of the risk of potential injury resulting from the reduced duty of care.

Secondary implied assumption of risk is the label given to those circumstances where defendant has breached a duty, and plaintiff engages in an activity with knowledge of the defendant's negligence. For example, if the plaintiff borrows the defendant's car with knowledge that defendant has not repaired the car's faulty brakes, plaintiff knows about and voluntarily assumes the risk of injury resulting from defendant's negligent maintenance of the car.

Other courts characterize implied assumptions of risk as either reasonable or unreasonable. For example, in our car borrowing hypothetical, if the plaintiff was borrowing the car to run to the grocery store for snacks, it might be unreasonable to assume the risks of driving the car with faulty brakes. On the other hand, if plaintiff was borrowing the car to take someone that was having a heart attack to the emergency room, the risk might be a reasonable one.

Understanding the ways courts characterize implied assumption of risk should help you to understand the different ways courts apply the implied assumption of the risk doctrine in comparative fault jurisdictions. Here is a summary of the different approaches courts have used:

- In some jurisdictions, all types of implied assumption of risk are still a complete defense, and where she has impliedly assumed the risk, plaintiff may not recover for her injuries. These jurisdictions reason that because assumption of risk is essentially consent to the possibility of being injured from the activity, plaintiff should not be compensated when the injury she anticipated and agreed to actually occurs.

- Some jurisdictions absorb unreasonable assumptions of risk into the comparative fault analysis, treating it as a partial, but not complete defense, meaning plaintiff's recovery may be reduced according to comparative fault principles. In these jurisdictions, reasonable implied assumptions of risk remain a complete defense, barring recovery. Courts in these jurisdictions rationalize that an unreasonable assumption is evidence of plaintiff's negligence, while a reasonable assumption is more like consent. If you have trouble buying into the rationalization for this paradox you are in good company—many legal scholars and commentators are similarly critical of this approach.

- Still other jurisdictions completely incorporate implied assumption of risk into their comparative fault analysis, but have a different view of what that means. Some of these jurisdictions have totally abolished implied assumption of risk as a defense, on the grounds that once implied assumption of risk is made part of the calculation of fault, rather than acting as a complete defense, it is a superfluous doctrine. In other words, these courts reason that in evaluating plaintiff's fault, reasonable implied assumptions of risk would never be the basis for reducing the plaintiff's award (since a reasonable assumption is not evidence of fault) and unreasonable implied assumptions of risk are really just evidence of plaintiff's own negligence, which is already part of what a comparative fault analysis requires. Since consideration of unreasonable assumptions of risk would be redundant and consideration of reasonable assumptions would be meaningless, the doctrine serves no independent purpose.

• Other jurisdictions incorporating implied assumption of risk into the comparative fault calculation have been unwilling to abolish the doctrine entirely, and instead allow both primary and secondary implied assumptions (reasonable and unreasonable) to be considered as part of the evaluation of whether plaintiff's recovery should be reduced. Such courts reason that even though a reasonable assumption of risk is not evidence of fault, it is evidence the plaintiff agreed to be responsible for injuries that would result from the risk, and since the point of comparative fault is to allocate responsibility for injury, it should be part of the calculation.

Exercise 2-31 Identifying Risks

The Snake River Rafting Company is in the business of providing outdoor adventure experiences. One of their experiences is a guided rafting trip down the Snake River in Wyoming. They would like you to review the waiver and release they provide to all persons who take their river rafting trip down the Snake River. They would like to know if it is sufficient to protect them from claims by persons who might be injured on such trips, and whether there is any language you would add, delete, or revise. You may want to begin this process by identifying the most common ways persons are injured from such activities.

Acknowledgement of Risks

According to Wyoming State Law: Any person who takes part in any sport or recreational opportunity assumes the inherent risks in that sport or recreational opportunity, whether those risks are known or unknown, and is legally responsible for any and all damage, injury or death to himself or other persons or property that results from the inherent risks in that sport or recreational opportunity. "Inherent risks" are those dangers or conditions which are characteristic of, intrinsic to, or an integral part of any sport or recreational opportunity.

Although Snake River Rafting Company has taken reasonable steps to provide you with appropriate equipment and skilled guides so you can enjoy an activity for which you may not be skilled, we wish to remind you that this activity is not without risk. Certain risks cannot be eliminated without destroying the unique character of this activity. The same elements that contribute to the unique character of this activity can be causes of loss or damage to your equipment, or accidental injury, illness, or in extreme cases, permanent trauma or death. We do not want to frighten you or reduce your enthusiasm for this activity, but we do think it is important for you to know in advance what to expect and to be informed of the inherent risks. These risks include, but are not limited to: personal injury due to entering or exiting a vessel, being thrown from a vessel or capsizing due to collision or water conditions. These injuries may include cuts, bruises, hypothermia, broken bones, head injury, and in extreme cases, death.

The Snake is a complex river to float. The beauty and lack of whitewater lulls floaters into inattentiveness. A tangle of channels and constant shifting of logjams present difficulties found on few whitewater rivers. Accidents are common. Typically, spring flows will be muddy, extremely cold, and very high, increasing the difficulty of all river sections. As snowmelt diminishes, volume decreases and waters clear. In spite of reduced flow, the current stays deceptively strong. Logjams and tight turns remain.

The advanced level section of the river, from Deadman's Bar to Moose Landing, is the most challenging stretch of river and most accidents occur here. The river drops more steeply, with faster water than in other sections south of Pacific Creek. Complex braiding obscures the main channel and strong currents can sweep boaters into side channels blocked by logjams.

By signing this document I am indicating I am aware that outdoor activities entail risks of injury or death to myself. I also understand the description of these risks is not complete and that other unknown or unanticipated risks may result in injury or death. I agree to assume responsibility for the risks identified herein and those risks not specifically identified. My participation in this activity is purely voluntary, no one is forcing me to participate, and I elect to participate in spite of the risks.

In addition to comparative fault and assumption of risk, other defenses may be used to limit or bar plaintiff's recovery. For example, immunity, which we studied in the first chapter may also be a defense to negligence (or any other tort); as we saw in Chapter One a lawyer should always research potential immunity claims, to be certain a client's case will not be dismissed at the outset of the litigation. Another common defense, which is applicable to all causes of action, is a defense that the Statute of Limitations bars the action.

c. Statute of Limitations

A statute of limitations is a rule that limits the amount of time a party has to file a claim. These limits vary depending on the jurisdiction and type of claim. If a plaintiff fails to file her claim within the application limitations period, her claim is barred, making it a complete defense to liability. To calculate the statute of limitations you must know the rules in your jurisdiction regarding when the statute begins to run and whether the limitations period may be tolled for any reason, as well as what the limitations period is for each of the causes of action in the case.

Exercise 2-32 Statutory Deconstruction —
Determining the Limitations Period

Examine the following statutes to determine the statute of limitations for the chapter problem (*McCoy v. Henry Ford Health Systems*) and for exercise 2.13 (*Beatrice v. Realty Co.*). Be sure to answer the following questions:

1.   When did the limitations period begin to run?

2.   When did it expire?

3.   What, if anything, would toll the limitations period?

5805. Injuries to persons or property

(1) A person shall not bring or maintain an action to recover damages for injuries to persons or property unless, after the claim first accrued to the plaintiff or to someone through whom the plaintiff claims, the action is commenced within the periods of time prescribed by this section.

(2) Subject to subsections (3) and (4), the period of limitations is 2 years for an action charging assault, battery, or false imprisonment.

(3) The period of limitations is 5 years for an action charging assault or battery brought by a person who has been assaulted or battered by his or her spouse or former spouse, an individual with whom he or she has had a child in common, or a person with whom he or she resides or formerly resided.

(4) The period of limitations is 5 years for an action charging assault and battery brought by a person who has been assaulted or battered by an individual with whom he or she has or has had a dating relationship.

(5) The period of limitations is 2 years for an action charging malicious prosecution.

(6) Except as otherwise provided in this chapter, the period of limitations is 2 years for an action charging malpractice.

(7) The period of limitations is 2 years for an action against a sheriff charging misconduct or neglect of office by the sheriff or the sheriff's deputies.

(8) The period of limitations is 2 years after the expiration of the year for which a constable was elected for actions based on the constable's negligence or misconduct as constable.

(9) The period of limitations is 1 year for an action charging libel or slander.

(10) Except as otherwise provided in this section, the period of limitations is 3 years after the time of the death or injury for all actions to recover damages for the death of a person, or for injury to a person or property.

(11) The period of limitations is 5 years for an action to recover damages for injury to a person or property brought by a person who has been assaulted or battered by his or her spouse or former spouse, an individual with whom he or she has had a child in common, or a person with whom he or she resides or formerly resided.

(12) The period of limitations is 5 years for an action to recover damages for injury to a person or property brought by a person who has been assaulted or battered by an individual with whom he or she has or has had a dating relationship.

(13) The period of limitations is 3 years for a products liability action. However, in the case of a product that has been in use for not less than 10 years, the plaintiff, in proving a prima facie case, shall be required to do so without benefit of any presumption.

(14) An action against a state licensed architect or professional engineer or licensed professional surveyor arising from professional services rendered is an action charging malpractice subject to the period of limitation contained in subsection (6).

(15) The periods of limitation under this section are subject to the applicable period of repose established in section 5839.1

(16) The amendments to this section made by the 2011 amendatory act that added this subsection apply to causes of action that accrue on or after the effective date of that amendatory act.

(17) As used in this section, "dating relationship" means frequent, intimate associations primarily characterized by the expectation of affectional involvement. Dating relationship does not include a casual relationship or an ordinary fraternization between 2 individuals in a business or social context.

5838a. Medical malpractice claim; accrual; definitions; limitations

(1) For purposes of this act, a claim based on the medical malpractice of a person or entity who is or who holds himself or herself out to be a licensed health care professional, licensed health facility or agency, or an employee or agent of a licensed health facility or agency who is engaging in or otherwise assisting in medical care and treatment, whether or not the licensed health care professional, licensed health facility or agency, or their employee or agent is engaged in the practice of the health profession in a sole proprietorship, partnership, professional corporation, or other business entity, accrues at the time of the act or omission that is the basis for the claim of medical malpractice, regardless of the time the plaintiff discovers or otherwise has knowledge of the claim. As used in this subsection:

(a) "Licensed health facility or agency" means a health facility or agency licensed under article 17 of the public health code, Act No. 368 of the Public Acts of 1978, being sections 333.20101 to 333.22260 of the Michigan Compiled Laws.

(b) "Licensed health care professional" means an individual licensed or registered under article 15 of the public health code, Act No. 368 of the Public Acts of 1978, being sections 333.16101 to 333.18838 of the Michigan Compiled Laws, and engaged in the practice of his or her health profession in a sole proprietorship, partnership, professional corporation, or other business entity. However, licensed health care professional does not include a sanitarian or a veterinarian.

(2) Except as otherwise provided in this subsection, an action involving a claim based on medical malpractice may be commenced at any time within the applicable period prescribed in section 58051 or sections 5851 to 5856,2 or within 6 months after the plaintiff discovers or should have discovered the existence of the claim, whichever is later. However, except as otherwise provided in section 5851(7) or (8), the claim shall not be commenced later than 6 years after the date of the act or omission that is the basis for the claim. The burden of proving that the plaintiff, as a result of physical discomfort, appearance, condition, or otherwise, neither discovered nor should have discovered the existence of the claim at least 6 months before the expiration of the period otherwise applicable to the claim is on the plaintiff. A medical malpractice action that is not commenced within the time prescribed by this subsection is barred. This subsection does not apply, and the plaintiff is subject to the period of limitations set forth in subsection (3), under 1 of the following circumstances:

(a) If discovery of the existence of the claim was prevented by the fraudulent conduct of the health care professional against whom the claim is made or a named employee or agent of the health professional against whom the claim is made, or of the health facility against whom the claim is made or a named employee or agent of a health facility against whom the claim is made.

(b) There has been permanent loss of or damage to a reproductive organ resulting in the inability to procreate.

(3) An action involving a claim based on medical malpractice under circumstances described in subsection (2)(a) or (b) may be commenced at any time within the applicable period prescribed in section 5805 or sections 5851 to 5856, or within 6 months after the plaintiff discovers or should have discovered the existence of the claim, whichever is later. The burden of proving that the plaintiff, as a result of physical discomfort, appearance, condition or otherwise, neither discovered nor should have discovered the existence of the claim at least 6 months before the expiration of the period otherwise applicable to the claim is on the plaintiff. A medical malpractice action that is not commenced within the time prescribed by this subsection is barred.

5851. Disabilities of infancy or insanity at accrual of claim; year of grace; tacking; removal of infancy disability; medical malpractice exception; application to imprisonment disability

(1) Except as otherwise provided in subsections (7) and (8), if the person first entitled to make an entry or bring an action under this act is under 18 years of age or insane at the time the claim accrues, the person or those claiming under the person shall have 1 year after the disability is removed through death or otherwise, to make the entry or bring the action although the period of limitations has run. This section does not lessen the time provided for in section 5852.1

(2) The term insane as employed in this chapter means a condition of mental derangement such as to prevent the sufferer from comprehending rights he or she is otherwise bound to know and is not dependent on whether or not the person has been judicially declared to be insane.

(3) To be considered a disability, the infancy or insanity must exist at the time the claim accrues. If the disability comes into existence after the claim has accrued, a court shall not recognize the disability under this section for the purpose of modifying the period of limitations.

(4) A person shall not tack successive disabilities. A court shall recognize only those disabilities that exist at the time the claim first accrues and that disable the person to whom the claim first accrues for the purpose of modifying the period of limitations.

(5) A court shall recognize both of the disabilities of infancy or insanity that disable the person to whom the claim first accrues at the time the claim first accrues. A court shall count the year of grace provided in this section from the termination of the last disability to the person to whom the claim originally accrued that has continued from the time the claim accrued, whether this disability terminates because of the death of the person disabled or for some other reason.

(6) With respect to a claim accruing before the effective date of the age of majority act of 1971, Act No. 79 of the Public Acts of 1971, being sections 722.51 to 722.55 of the Michigan Compiled Laws, the disability of infancy is removed as of the effective date of Act No. 79 of the Public Acts of 1971, as to persons who were

at least 18 years of age but less than 21 years of age on January 1, 1972, and is removed as of the eighteenth birthday of a person who was under 18 years of age on January 1, 1972.

(7) Except as otherwise provided in subsection (8), if, at the time a claim alleging medical malpractice accrues to a person under section 5838a2 the person has not reached his or her eighth birthday, a person shall not bring an action based on the claim unless the action is commenced on or before the person's tenth birthday or within the period of limitations set forth in section 5838a, whichever is later. If, at the time a claim alleging medical malpractice accrues to a person under section 5838a, the person has reached his or her eighth birthday, he or she is subject to the period of limitations set forth in section 5838a.

(8) If, at the time a claim alleging medical malpractice accrues to a person under section 5838a, the person has not reached his or her thirteenth birthday and if the claim involves an injury to the person's reproductive system, a person shall not bring an action based on the claim unless the action is commenced on or before the person's fifteenth birthday or within the period of limitations set forth in section 5838a, whichever is later. If, at the time a claim alleging medical malpractice accrues to a person under section 5838a, the person has reached his or her thirteenth birthday and the claim involves an injury to the person's reproductive system, he or she is subject to the period of limitations set forth in section 5838a.

(9) If a person was serving a term of imprisonment on the effective date of the 1993 amendatory act that added this subsection, and that person has a cause of action to which the disability of imprisonment would have been applicable under the former provisions of this section, an entry may be made or an action may be brought under this act for that cause of action within 1 year after the effective date of the 1993 amendatory act that added this subsection, or within any other applicable period of limitation provided by law.

(10) If a person died or was released from imprisonment at any time within the period of 1 year preceding the effective date of the 1993 amendatory act that added this subsection, and that person had a cause of action to which the disability of imprisonment would have been applicable under the former provisions of this section on the date of his or her death or release from imprisonment, an entry may be made or an action may be brought under this act for that cause of action within 1 year after the date of his or her death or release from imprisonment, or within any other applicable period of limitation provided by law.

(11) As used in this section, "release from imprisonment" means either of the following:

(a) A final release or discharge from imprisonment in a county jail.

(b) Release on parole or a final release or discharge from imprisonment in a state or federal correctional facility.

Skill Focus: Creating Issues Checklists

When you complete a unit of study, it is a good idea to review the unit and create a list of potential issues you should look for when you evaluate a set of facts. Many practice guides provide practitioners in various specialties with such lists, so that they do not miss issues when evaluating a case or forget any important steps during litigation, and many lawyers develop such lists for themselves based on their own practice experiences. Successful law students often use similar lists to help them evaluate an essay examination. In this way, law school essay exams mirror law practice. For this unit your list might look something like this:

Is the existence of duty an issue?

Is it a circumstance where courts have found no duty (e.g., rescuers)?

    Is it a failure to act vs. taking action?

    Does a statute limit liability?

    Is there a relationship?

    What are the reasons for or against establishing a duty? (e.g., Do the social costs outweigh the social benefits?)

    Is this claim for emotional injury by a bystander?

If a duty exists, what is the standard of care?

    Reasonable person?

    Professional?

    Premises liability?

        Common law classifications?

        Reasonable person?

        Harm by third parties?

    Statutory?

        Does it establish Negligence per se?

            If so, what is the effect?

Is there a breach?

    Is there direct evidence of breach?

        If no, does res ipsa loquitur apply

Was the breach the cause of the plaintiff's injuries?

    Was the breach a factual cause of the injuries?

        Was it the "but for" cause?

        Was it a substantial factor?

        Were there concurrent causes?

        Can market share be used?

    Was the breach the proximate cause of the plaintiff's damages? (is it too remote?)

What are the plaintiff's damages?

Are there any limitations on her damages?

    Is there a damage cap?

    Are they exclusively emotional distress damages?

        Direct vs. bystander?

Did plaintiff contribute to her own injury?

> Does the jurisdiction apply contributory negligence or comparative fault?
>
>> If comparative fault, pure or modified?
>>
>> How much is recovery reduced?

Did plaintiff assume any risk of injury?

> Was it an express assumption?
>
> Was it an implied assumption?
>
>> Will the implied assumption be considered? (which approach does the jurisdiction follow?)

Is the claim barred by failure to file within the statute of limitations?

You might want to note a few things about the list. First, it is set up to mirror the order issues would be addressed (written) on an examination, rather than the order the issues were covered in the chapter, because the point of the list is to help find issues during an exam. Law school texts and classes sometimes cover issues in the order it makes sense to learn them, not necessarily the order it makes sense to write them on an exam. Law school faculty expect that you will spend time organizing the issues into the order that is appropriate for writing; this is usually one of the steps they are referring to when they say you should create an "outline" (the other is to fill in this list of issues with the corresponding rules). Next, note that the list is not all-inclusive; you may want to add other issues to the list. An issues list is meant to help you remember to look for issues. As you practice issue spotting you may notice that there are particular issues you forget; adding those issues to your list will help ensure you do not forget them the next time you evaluate a fact pattern.

You may want to use this list to help you spot the issues in the sample essay examination set out in the next exercise.

Exercise 2-33 Preparing for Essay Examinations—
Spotting the Issues

Jaquilla owns a roving pastry business named "Torte Die For." As part of her business, she uses a large van that functions much like an old fashioned ice cream truck in that she drives it around to various neighborhoods, selling pastries from the van. Her pastries were reviewed in "Gourmazing" magazine; the magazine described Jaquilla's tortes (a small cake or pie) as "the most delectable dessert on the continent." The magazine review created a huge demand for Jaquilla's Tortes—which would sell out within minutes of her arrival at the various locations she frequented.

Jaquilla hired several drivers and purchased multiple vans, to try to keep up with the demand. Demand continued to exceed supply. She had been following the same route for years, but once people became aware of her daily route they began lining up early, before she arrived. This created many hazards, including road blocks, as people swarmed the vans, trying to purchase one of Jaquilla's tortes.

In response to the overzealous crowds, Jaquilla abandoned her practice of following the same route each day. She and her drivers began to tweet their locations (a process of sending out an instant electronic message to a group of subscribers). The tweet would include the location and time that the van would arrive at a given location and would be sent out approximately 30 minutes before the van's arrival.

Petra received one of Jaquilla's tweets. She desperately needed of one of Jacquila's tortes to impress her foodie friends. Petra jumped into her car and raced to the tweeted location to purchase a torte. Petra knew from experience that she had less than 30 minutes to make it to the location — or the tortes would be gone. In her haste to get to the location, Petra caused an accident, which injured Quinn.

The accident also caused a delay in traffic while the roadway was shut down and cleared of debris from the car accident. Ricarda, who was stuck in traffic, and was unable to move from the roadway, was forced to give birth to her first child in the back of her car, on the side of the roadway. Ricarda's baby, Nola, was born with the umbilical cord wrapped around her neck, which deprived Nola of oxygen for a sufficient amount of time to cause extensive brain damage. Assume that if the accident had not occurred, Ricarda would have made it to the hospital for Nola's birth, where Nola would have been delivered via Cesarean section and the brain damage would not have occurred.

Discuss:

1. Jaquilla's potential liability for Petra, Quinn, Ricarda, and Nola's injuries.

2. Petra's potential liability for Quinn, Ricarda and Nola's injuries

---

Skill Focus: Law School Essay Examinations

Law school essay examinations mirror practice in that you are given a hypothetical client problem, in the form of a story, which is usually referred to as "the facts" or "the fact pattern." Similarly, clients have a personal story that forms the bases for each case. The client's story will not usually come in as tidy a form as a law school essay exam, but must instead be derived from witness interviews, documents, depositions, etc. Either way, your job (as a lawyer and a law student) is to evaluate the facts and determine what legal issues are presented, what standards (rules) should be applied to resolve the issues, and what the likely result will be when that standard is applied to the facts. In order to justify your prediction on a law school exam (or persuade a court as a lawyer), you must explain the basis for your opinion, which means explaining which facts were significant to your decision and why they were significant — much the way courts do in their opinions when they explain the basis for a decision. Often law school fact patterns are written so that the likely outcome is very unclear (this, too, mirrors real practice). This means there will be very good arguments that the result could go either way. Your job on a law school exam is to articulate both arguments and then make a prediction as to which one is likely to win (and why). Your job as a lawyer is similar, you must be able to anticipate counter arguments so that you are prepared to respond to and refute them.

This form of analyzing a legal problem is called IRAC. This term is also used as a shorthand reference for the format used for writing answers to legal problems—on exams and in practice. It may help you to see it this way:

I   the legal **issue** presented

R   the **rule** (standard) that should be applied to resolve the issue

A   the **application** of the standard to the facts

C   the **conclusion** you predict the court will make

The problem with the term IRAC is that it leads to a good deal of confusion among law students because of some common misunderstandings about what exactly it means to "IRAC" an exam answer. For example:

IRAC does not mean writing the labels "I," "R," "A," "C" or "Issue," "Rule," "Application," "Conclusion," on the parts of your answer.

IRAC does not mean writing one IRAC per exam or even one IRAC per broad issue. Each legal concept should be addressed separately. For example, if the issue is whether there was negligence (a very broad issue) you would be required to consider several narrower issues in order to address that broad issue (namely duty, breach, causation, and damages). Note that each of these narrower issues might require consideration of even narrower issues; for example duty might require consideration of whether a duty exists and if so, what is the scope of that duty. Each of these issues requires a separate IRAC. The structure of your answer would look something like this:

Negligence

    Rule for negligence (requires duty, breach, causation, damages)

        Duty?

            Rule for duty (existence and scope)

                Existence?

                    Rule for existence

                    Application of stated rule

                    Conclusion re: existence of duty

                Scope?

                    Rule for scope

                    Application of stated rule

                    Conclusion re: scope

            Conclusion re: duty

        Breach?

            Rule for breach

            Application of stated rule

            Conclusion re: breach

        Causation?

            Rule for causation (factual and proximate)

                Factual cause?

Rule for factual cause

Application of stated rule

Conclusion re: factual cause

Proximate cause?

Rule for proximate cause

Application of stated rule

Conclusion re: proximate cause

Conclusion re: causation

Damages?

Rule for damages

Application of stated rule

Conclusion re: damages

Conclusion re: negligence

Notice that the structure of this answer is really: IR IRIRACIRAC IRAC IRIRACIRAC IRAC C. The IRACs for duty, breach, causation and damages form the "A" of the broader issue of negligence; the IRACs for scope and extent form the "A" for the issue of duty. As you can see, the term IRAC includes a number of different structural variations.

IRAC does not mean the "I," "R," "A," and "C" are treated equally. The "I," "R," and "C" are necessary components, but they are not as heavily weighted as the "A" because the A is where a student demonstrates understanding of the material and the ability to apply concepts to future problems. This does not mean you can ignore the "I," "R," and "C," because, for example, you cannot do the A(nalysis) unless you spot the I(ssue) and know the correct R(ule) that will be applied. Rather, it means that you should spend the most time on the A section because it is where you will demonstrate that you can do more than recite the law; it is where you demonstrate you can use the law to resolve the issues — in the fact pattern and in future cases involving clients.

IRAC does not mean there is a "one size fits all" approach to law school essay writing. There are variations with respect to what is required, and these variations may be exam specific and/or professor specific. For example, the "I" may require stating the issue broadly (e.g., is D negligent), and then stating each of the narrow issues required to resolve that broader issue (e.g., Did D owe P a duty? What was the standard of care? Was D's conduct a breach of the standard of care? etc.). This might be the case where facts in the fact pattern indicate each of these narrower issues requires consideration. On the other hand the "I" may only require stating a very narrow issue (Does a manufacturer of insulation products containing asbestos have a duty to protect the family members of it's workers from injury from asbestos?). This might be the case where only that issue is contained in the call, or where a professor expects you to limit your discussion on exams to the aspect of the case that is most likely to be contested. Some professors prefer issues in the form of a question, while others might allow you to use a word or phrase to identify an issue (e.g., breach of duty). Some might want the issue in the form of a heading, and some might want it in the form of a sentence at the start of the paragraph addressing the issue. It is important to understand that these are all variations of the same task—stating the issue. Similar variations exist for the "R." For example the "R" might consist of the words from a statute, a rule statement from a case, a broad or narrow holding from a case, or a rule or holding that represents several synthesized cases (which might require you to articulate holdings, facts and rationales to explain the "rule"). While it might frustrate you at first, becoming comfortable with the skill of responding to individual faculty preferences will prepare you for practice, because judges will often have differing preferences (for example, some judges like for you to two hole punch documents delivered to their chambers, or to deliver a filed copy of any motions directly to their courtrooms). Also, lawyers must adapt their format to fit the circumstances, which is why it is useful to learn to adapt your IRAC format to fit the task you are given on an essay exam.

Exercise 2-34 Preparing for Essay Examinations—
Drafting an Answer Using IRAC

Using what you've learned thus far, draft an answer to exercise 2.33. Be sure to use the IRAC format.

Chapter Three

Advocating for Extension, Modification or Imposition of a Rule — Strict Liability

Objectives

Learning and Study Skills

Refine ability to deconstruct rules

Improve the "A" in IRAC by explaining the reasons for a conclusion

Apply or distinguish a case in order to answer a question posed on an essay examination

Law Practice Skills

Deconstruct and apply statutes

Understand how to obtain evidentiary support for a claim or defense

Use public policy to make an argument that a rule should be extended, modified or imposed

Understand and apply the factors courts use or consider when determining whether to impose strict liability

Evaluate policy arguments used by courts to justify a decision to impose (or reject) strict liability

Synthesize legal authority

Use synthesized authority to strengthen a legal argument

Apply and distinguish legal authority based on policy and facts

Understand how to analyze a problem using a factors test (rather than a rule with elements)

Understand and apply the rules of causation to a new context

Be able to sufficiently explain the reason(s) for a conclusion to convince a court to adopt the conclusion

Substantive Legal Knowledge

State the factors a court will consider to determine whether an animal is wild or domestic

State the factors courts use or consider when determining whether to impose strict liability

State the factors from the Restatement (Second) Torts for determining whether an activity is abnormally dangerous

State the potential effect(s) of imposing strict liability on a class of activities

Introduction

As you have seen from the first two chapters, plaintiff will usually be required to establish some fault on the part of the defendant in order to prevail on her tort claims. For some activities or categories of conduct, however, a plaintiff does not need to establish fault in order to recover. Defendant may be liable where he exercised reasonable or even extraordinary care. As a result, the imposition of strict liability usually reduces the frequency of such activities, and/or the number of persons who choose to participate in such activities, because such reduction is the only way for an actor engaging in such activities to reduce or limit liability. Since the effect of imposing strict liability is usually the reduction or elimination of the activity, such a standard is applied to a very narrow range of activities, typically (1) certain categories of animals; and (2) abnormally dangerous activities.

If defendant's conduct falls within one of the categories for which there is strict liability, plaintiff need only prove that the activity is one for which defendant is strictly liable, that defendant engaged in such activity, and that defendant's activity caused plaintiff's injury. For purposes of establishing causation, plaintiff must show that the "thing" which made the activity dangerous is what resulted in the plaintiff's harm—a concept we will cover in the final section of this chapter. As you might suspect, litigation in this area is typically centered on whether the activity defendant is engaged in is one for which defendant is strictly liable. This involves either (1) an evaluation of whether a defendant's activity is covered by a definition (e.g., a statute, or common law rule); or (2) an evaluation of whether there are policy reasons to impose strict liability on the class of activities defendant is engaged in. For example, where a state has enacted a statute imposing liability on owners of wild animals, the litigation may involve whether defendant's animal is "wild" within the meaning of a statute—this would be an example of the first type of evaluation. If the state has no statute or common law rule which classifies ownership of wild animals as one for which strict liability applies, or if the state uses negligence or some other standard to impose liability, litigation may involve consideration of whether, for policy reasons, a jurisdiction should impose such liability—this would be an example of the second type of evaluation.

It might help to approach a strict liability problem in this way:

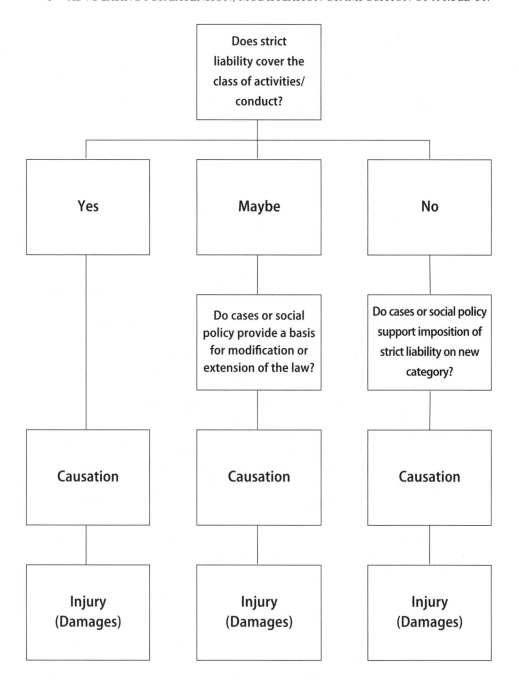

A. Strict Liability for Animals

Generally speaking, strict liability is based on whether an animal is classified as livestock, wild or domestic. Strict liability is generally imposed for damage caused by trespassing livestock, unless the trespass is onto land abutting a highway where the animals are being herded, or the jurisdiction requires the landowner bringing the claim to have fenced her property, and she has not done so. Usually, owners and possessors of wild animals are strictly liable for damages caused by the animals. Public zoos are an exception to this rule, since they are generally held to a negligence standard. For the most part, keepers of domestic animals are liable only if the keeper knew or should have known of the animals dangerous propensities. There is, however, variation among the states with regard to dogs. Many states have adopted a true strict liability standard for dog bites, imposing liability without regard to whether the dog's owner did anything wrong with respect to protecting others, or whether the owner had any reason to be aware that the dog might bite.

Exercise 3-1 Strict Liability for Dog Bites

This exercise will help you to understand the different approaches jurisdictions have adopted to govern liability for dog bites. Your task will be to evaluate the dog owner's liability for the following problem under the three different statutory schemes set out at the end of the fact pattern.

Defendants are the owners of Travis, a mixed-breed dog, who appears to be part Labrador Retriever and part American Pit Bull Terrier. Travis is 14 years old and has never exhibited aggressive characteristics toward people or other dogs. Travis routinely escapes from the backyard where he lives, even though his owners have taken substantial and frequent measures to contain him. Usually when Travis escapes one of the neighbors finds him roaming the neighborhood streets, puts him back into his yard, and leaves a note for Travis' owners letting them know that Travis was roaming the neighborhood. During one of these "escapes" Travis bit Alva, a four-year-old girl, who lives in Travis' neighborhood. Alva knew Travis from a previous encounter; Alva's mom is one of the neighbors that had returned Travis after one of his many "escapes." According to Alva, she called Travis by name because she planned to lead him home. Travis came running toward her, jumped on her and bit her in the stomach several times. No one else saw the event. The bite caused life threatening injuries and Alva underwent several hours of surgery at the local children's hospital. It took her several weeks to recover, and she will have permanent scarring and damage to her stomach, requiring several additional surgeries over her lifetime.

Evaluate whether Travis' owners are liable under each of the following statutes; the three statutes represent three different approaches states have taken to regulate domestic animals — more specifically, dogs.

§ 11-2003. Liability for Dog Bites

(A) The owner of a dog which bites a person when the person is in or on a public place or lawfully in or on a private place, including the property of the owner of the dog, is liable for damages suffered by the person bitten, regardless of the former viciousness of the dog or the owner's knowledge of its viciousness.

(B) A person is lawfully in or on the private property of the owner of a dog within the meaning of this article when an invitee or guest, or when in the performance of a duty imposed upon him by law of the state or United States, or by ordinances of a municipality in which such property is located.

(C) Proof of provocation of the attack by the person injured shall be a defense to the action for damages. The issue of provocation shall be determined by whether a reasonable person would expect that the conduct or circumstances would be likely to provoke a dog.

§ 313 Liability of Animal Owners

The owner of a dog is strictly liable for damages for injuries to persons or property caused by the dog and which the owner could have prevented and which did not result from the injured person's provocation of the dog.

§ 982811 Liability of Dog Owners

A dog owner is liable for injuries the dog inflicts only if the owner harbors the dog with actual or constructive knowledge that the dog has vicious or dangerous propensities. A dangerous propensity is a tendency of the animal to do any act that might endanger the safety of persons or property.

Exercise 3-2 Obtaining Evidentiary Support

What evidence might you be able to obtain that would support your argument that Travis had dangerous propensities, as required by § 982811? Would any of the following help? Why or why not? How might you obtain such evidence?

Travis' breed and size

Complaints brought to his owner's attention

Proof that Travis is kept on a tight leash or chain

A warning sign on his owner's premises (e.g., "Beware of Dog")

Exercise 3-3 Imposing Strict Liability

Recently, the imposition of strict liability has been the subject of some media attention as the result of litigation relating to the regulation of pit bulls.

John Gibeaut, A Bite Worse Than Its Bark: Maryland Puts Pit-Bull Owners on Liability Notice, ABA Journal (September 2012)

After sending strong signals for more than a decade, the Maryland Court of Appeals told pit bull owners—and their landlords—they can be held strictly liable for dog attacks on people. (For now, the ruling has been stayed, pending the outcome of a motion for reconsideration.)

Not surprisingly, pit bull owners and their advocates pressed the alarm button and persuaded state legislators to convene a task force aimed at overriding the decision in *Tracey v. Solesky*. For liability to attach under the old law, the owner needed knowledge of a particular dog's past aggressive behavior.

"All pet owners are responsible for their pets, not just owners of pit bulls," says Tina Regester, a spokeswoman for the Maryland Society for the Prevention of Cruelty to Animals. The SPCA opposes laws that single out certain breeds as particularly vicious.

In a pair of 1998 cases, Maryland's highest court said it considers pit bulls inherently dangerous and hinted that strict liability was imminent.

The cases involved attacks by dogs ominously named Trouble and Rampage. A child was killed in the attack blamed on Rampage.

The next chance arrived at the court last fall in the 2007 mauling of Dominic Solesky, 10, who underwent five hours of lifesaving surgery. The offending canine was less ominously named Clifford, but the issue was presented squarely enough to make Maryland one of about a dozen states that impose liability without knowledge of past attacks.

But in ruling the way it did, the Maryland court almost certainly made dog-bite cases more litigious and perhaps harder to maintain. That's because the court, without offering guidance, applied the decision not only to purebred pit bulls, but to mixed breeds that may have some pit bull lineage.

While the American Kennel Club and the American Dog Breeders Association recognize three lines of bull terriers, mixed breeds can be endless—though most are characterized by muscular builds and large, broad heads. But how much pit bull must a specimen contain to make the owner strictly liable for the damage it does?

"That's the million-dollar question," Regester says. "It's not just a specific breed of dog but a group of dogs."

And the evidence may be hard for plaintiffs to come by.

"Oftentimes, an examination isn't possible because the dog already has been put down," says *Solesky* plaintiffs' lawyer Kevin A. Dunne of Baltimore. Animal control authorities already had put Clifford down against the owner's wishes before Dunne got the case, though the defendants at trial agreed the dog was a pit bull.

Dunne also expects breed identification to be hotly litigated in future cases. Otherwise, an owner may stand virtually defenseless. While no one is going to drag a dog carcass into a courtroom, necropsy reports and photographs may be available, especially if the case involves law enforcement.

Dunne says plaintiffs also may obtain the information they need through records of licensing and rabies shots, in addition to veterinarian visits, all of which routinely inquire about an animal's breed.

"Nobody's going to put down 'nothing,'" he says.

The debate over whether to impose strict liability on pit bull owners, possessors and others highlights an important skill—using public policy to argue for or against the imposition of strict liability.

For this exercise you have been retained to represent defendant Dorothy Tracey in her appeal to the Maryland Supreme Court to overturn the appellate court's decision (set out below) to impose strict liability on owners and possessors of pit bulls. Since this is the only question certified by the Supreme Court, please limit your discussion to this issue. Be sure to consider:

1. What are your client's strongest arguments?

2. What are plaintiffs' strongest arguments?

3. How will you respond to plaintiffs' arguments?

4. Do you believe owners of pit bull should be strictly liable? Why or why not?

Tracey v. Solesky
2012 WL 3759036, (Md. Ct. App. 2012)

NOTICE: THIS OPINION HAS NOT BEEN RELEASED FOR PUBLICATION
IN THE PERMANENT LAW REPORTS. UNTIL RELEASED,
IT IS SUBJECT TO REVISION OR WITHDRAWAL.

In Maryland the vicious mauling of young children by pit bulls occurred as early as 1916. *Bachman v. Clark,* 128 Md. 245; 97 A. 440 (1916). In that case, a ten-year-old boy, John L. Clark, was playing on the north side of a street when a pit bull ("bull terrier") came across the street from its owner's property and attacked him, inflicting serious injuries. The pit bull refused to release the boy until a witness picked up a [small piece of timber] and struck the dog, killing it. Similar to the testimony in the present case by the boy's mother, in that old case the mother described the aftermath of the attack on her child as follows:

> ... [H]e was unconscious, in such a condition that she did not know whether he was living or dead ... Blood all over him.

Id. at 247, 97 A.2d at 440.

Over the last thirteen years, there have been no less than seven instances of serious maulings by pit bulls upon Maryland residents resulting in either serious injuries or death that have reached the appellate courts of this State, including the two boys attacked by the pit bull in the present case.[1] Five of the pit bull attacks in Maryland have been brought to the attention of this Court, and two have reached the Court of Special Appeals.

The first two attacks to reach this Court were reported in *Shields v. Wagman, et al.,* 350 Md. 666, 714 A.2d 881 (1998), where a pit bull attacked a business invitee at a strip shopping center and later attacked a tenant. Both attacks took place in the parking area of the strip-shopping center owned and maintained by the landlord. The pit bull was kept by its owner, also a tenant who operated an automobile repair business on leased premises.

In the first instance, Ms. Shields took her car to the parking area for repairs, and as she exited her car and approached the leased premises, the pit bull broke through the door and attacked her, inflicting serious injuries. *Id.,* at 670, 714 A.2d at 883.[2] In the second instance, the pit bull was not restrained and chased another tenant in the shopping center, Mr. Johnson, onto the roof of a car in the parking lot and attacked him, again inflicting serious injuries. As a result, Mr. Johnson had several surgeries to his arm, lost sensation in that arm, and was impaired in his ability to perform certain duties related to his job. *Id.,* at 671, 714 A.2d at 883. This Court held that the landlord in that case had

---

1. In addition to the maulings in Maryland, there have been at least two instances of serious maulings by pit bulls that have reached the appellate courts of the District of Columbia, *infra,* since 2005. Accordingly, within a hundred mile radius there have been nine serious mauling appellate cases involving pit bulls within the last thirteen years.

2. In the hospital she underwent emergency surgery and was hospitalized for a week. She later had to return to the hospital for further surgeries. She lost four months of work.

actual knowledge that the pit bull (whose name was Trouble) was dangerous and had the right to cause the removal of the pit bull from the premises but failed to do so, and in not so doing, had negligently allowed the attacks to occur on the parking premises controlled by the landlord. *Id.,* at 690, 714 A.2d. 892–893.

The third case decided by this Court just two months later, *Matthews v. Amberwood Associates Limited Partnership, Inc.,* 351 Md. 544, 719 A.2d 119 (1998), involved a situation where a pit bull (named Rampage) attacked a child inside a tenant's apartment killing the child. We found that because the landlord's employees had reported Rampage's aggressiveness and viciousness on prior occasions to management personnel, that knowledge was imputed to the landlord even though the attack occurred in the premises leased to the tenant. *Id.,* at 588–59, 719 A.2d. 125–26. Accordingly, because the landlord had the right not to renew the lease or to remove the pit bull under a "no pets" provision in the lease, he could be held liable. *Ibid.*

In *Moore v. et al., v. Myers,* 161 Md.App. 349, 868 A.2d 954 (2005), a case originating out of Prince Georges County, the Court of Special Appeals was faced with a factual situation in which an unleashed and unrestrained pit bull chased a twelve year old girl into a street where she was run over by an automobile and suffered two broken arms, a broken leg, and a fractured jaw.[3] At the time, Prince Georges County had adopted statutes specific to pit bulls that, among other things, required owners of pit bulls to keep the dogs in enclosures or leashed at all times. *Id.,* at 364, 868 A.2d at 962. Based primarily on a violation of those statutes, the Court of Special Appeals held the owner of the pit bull liable. *Id.,* at 367, 868 A.2d at 964.

In *Ward v. Hartley,* 168 Md.App. 209, 895 A.2d 1111(2006) (in which the relevant party in the lawsuit was the landlord), a taxi driver was dispatched to pick up a passenger for transportation to the Kennedy Kreiger Institute. When he knocked on the door to the leased premises, he heard someone tell children not to open the door. He stepped back and at the same time a child opened the door and a pit bull came charging out as he heard someone yell "Get the dog." He hit the pit bull with some rolled-up paper he had in his hand and the pit bull grabbed his foot. He then ran to his cab with the pit bull still holding onto his foot and, with the pit bull still attached, climbed on top of the car. A police car appeared on the scene, and as it did, two boys ran out of the house laughing and pulled the dog off of the cabdriver's foot. The cab driver's foot was severely injured and required surgery. *Id.,* at 213, 895 A.2d at 1113. There was no evidence in the case that the landlord knew that a pit bull was being kept on the premises until he heard about the incident with the cab driver. The Court of Special Appeals, in holding for the landlord, opined: "Keeping a pit bull did not violate any covenant of the lease, nor did it violate any law or ordinance. No provision of the lease gave the landlord control over any portion of the rental premises. Thus, appellees had no duty to inspect the premises." *Id.,* at 217, 895 A.2d at 1115.

The present case involves an attack by a pit bull named Clifford. Notwithstanding his relatively benign name, Clifford possessed the aggressive and vicious characteristics of both Trouble and Rampage. He escaped twice from an obviously inadequate small pen[4]

---

3. Apparently, the son of the owner 'sicced' the pit bull on three girls, one of whom was the victim.

4. The pen was described as being 4 feet high with no overhanging ledge and an open area at the top. Clifford jumped out of the top of the pen-at least twice on the day of the attacks. In *Matthews v. Amberwood, supra,* at 563, we quoted language from the New Mexico case of *Garcia v. Village of Tijeras,* 108 N.M. 116, at 119–121, 767 P.2d 355 (1988) that "... extraordinary measures are required for confining American Pit Bull Terriers, such as a *six* [emphasis added] foot chainlink fence with an overhanging ledge to keep the dogs from jumping out, ..."

and attacked at least two boys at different times on the same day.[5] The second young boy was Dominic Solesky. As a result of his mauling by Clifford, Dominic initially sustained life threatening injuries and underwent five hours of surgery at Johns Hopkins Hospital to address his injuries, including surgery to repair his femoral artery. He spent seventeen days in the hospital, during which time he underwent additional surgeries, and then spent a year in rehabilitation.[6]

Here, the trial court granted a judgment for the defendant landlord at the close of the Plaintiff's case on the grounds that, according to the trial judge, the evidence was insufficient to permit the issue of common law negligence to be presented to the jury. On the state of the common law relating to dog attacks in existence at that time, the trial court was correct. The plaintiff took an appeal to the Court of Special Appeals and that court reversed the trial court, finding that the evidence had been sufficient to create a valid jury issue as to the extent of the landlord's knowledge as to Clifford's dangerousness in respect to the then common law standards in dog attack negligence cases.

* * *

We ... establish in this case, and prospectively, a strict liability standard in respect to the owning, harboring or control of pit bulls and cross-bred pit bulls in lieu of the traditional common law liability principles that were previously applicable to attacks by such dogs. We shall direct the Court of Special Appeals to reverse the trial court and send this case back to that court. ***

We are modifying the Maryland common law of liability as it relates to attacks by pit bull and cross-bred pit bull dogs against humans. With the standard we establish today (which is to be applied in this case on remand), when an owner or a landlord is proven to have knowledge of the presence of a pit bull or cross-bred pit bull (as both the owner and landlord did in this case) or should have had such knowledge, a *prima facie* case is established. It is not necessary that the landlord (or the pit bull's owner) have actual knowledge that the specific pit bull involved is dangerous. Because of its aggressive and vicious nature and its capability to inflict serious and sometimes fatal injuries, pit bulls and cross-bred pit bulls are inherently dangerous.[7]

The Old Common Law

In the early Maryland case of *Goode v. Martin*, 57 Md. 606, 609–612 (1882), which involved an attack by a Newfoundland dog and a "small terrier," the Court stated certain

---

5. After he attacked the first boy, the pit bull's owner apparently restrained the dog and put him back in the pen he had just jumped out of, whereupon, in a short period of time the pit bull jumped out of the pen again and attacked the second boy, Dominic.

6. The first boy attacked, Scotty Mason, was described after the attack on him as he appeared before his mother (an assistant States Attorney for Baltimore City) as:

> He was hysterical. He was bloody from about the chest area up. His face was covered in blood. He was crying. He didn't look like Scotty. I thought he had been hit by a baseball bat....

* * *

> Well, he was unable to talk. He was so hysterical, but the two older boys told me he had been attacked by a dog, and I was frankly shocked ...

7. We are, of course, aware that such dogs can, and sometimes do, become well mannered pets in respect to their own human families as pointed out in some of the briefs. The question, however, is not whether they are maiming or killing their owners or members of the owners' families (although sometimes they do), it is the degree to which they are attacking others, and the seriousness of the injuries caused, in comparison with the rate of dog attacks (and types of injuries) in respect to all breeds of dogs.

inferences that could then be made against *an owner* in a case such as the present case. There the Court first said: "In order to render the owner liable in damages to any one bitten by his dog, it must be proved not only that the dog was fierce, but that the owner had knowledge that he was fierce. To this effect are all the authorities. [citations omitted]." But later in its opinion, the Court stated:

> But we think the appellant is right in his contention that the defendant may be presumed to have knowledge that his dogs were fierce and dangerous, from the fact that he was accustomed to keep them tied during the day-time. In *Perry v. Jones*, 1 *Espinasse*, 452, Lord KENYON held from the fact that the owner kept his dog tied and did not permit him to run at large, it must be presumed that he had knowledge that the dog was vicious, unruly and not safe to be permitted to go abroad.... So, in the case now before us, we think the fact that the appellee kept his dogs tied during the day and let them loose at night, furnishes proof that he knew it would endanger his neighbors to permit them to be unfastened.... The evidence ought to be left to the jury as tending to prove the temper and vicious disposition of the dogs, and the knowledge of the appellees thereto, and it was therefore error in the Judge of the Circuit Court to take the case from the jury, and the judgment appealed from will be reversed and a new trial be awarded.[8]

Martin 57 Md. at 611–12.

In *Bachman v. Clark, supra,* we stated the then common law standard in relation to dog attacks:

> At common law, the owner of a dog is not liable for injuries caused by it, unless it has a vicious propensity and notice of that fact is brought home to him. But when it is once established that the dog is of a vicious nature, and that the person owning or keeping it has knowledge of that fact, the same responsibility attaches to the owner to keep it from doing mischief as the keeper of an animal naturally ferocious would be subject to, and proof of negligence on the part of the owner is unnecessary. This is the recognized and well settled law of this state [citation omitted].

Clark, 128 at 247, 97 A. 440 at 441 (citation omitted).

This standard has been acknowledged and sometimes criticized in treatises, nonetheless, it has generally persisted. *See Harper, James and Gray on Torts,* Section 14.9, at 291 (3rd ed., 2007)

> This rule has been criticized as to actual damage done by animals with known propensities therefore, such as attacks on birds and poultry by cats, but any such change in the law will most likely come from legislative enactment, *although there is no necessary reason to prevent courts from making such modifications without the aid of a statute* [emphasis added].

Harper, further comments that:

---

8. It is questionable whether this early modification to the old common law rule would have been applied by that Court had that era been subject to the population, traffic and congestion of modern-urban life and to the numerous statutes forbidding the running loose of dogs and the requirements that they be leashed or under control, such as is generally prevalent to some degree in many jurisdictions at the present time. We have previously noted that "The fact that the dogs here were kept in an enclosure in a suburban area in a day when legal restrictions frequently forbid a dog's running at large cannot have the same significance that the matter of enclosure had in 1916 and 1882." *Mcdonald v. Burgess,* 254 Md. 452, 258, 255 A.2d 299, 302 (1969)

The common law has for many years made a distinction between animals ferae naturae and animals mansuetae natura, or between wild animals and domestic animals.

* * *

It thus appears that one keeps dangerous animals at one's peril, that is, at strict liability, but otherwise as to animals 'not dangerous.' As to the former class, it is no defense that the keeper employed reasonable care, or even a high degree of diligence to prevent their escape. Liability is independent of any fault on the part of the owner.

* * *

He may keep such animals, if he will, but if he has notice of their danger to human beings..., he cannot keep them, even carefully, at the risk of others. He has introduced an unusual danger into the community and he does so at his own risk.

Id. at Section 14.11.

Modifying the Common Law

In *Ireland v. State*, 310 Md. 328, 331–332, 529 A.2d 365–366 (1987) we discussed the basic framework of the Court's role in establishing and modifying common law rules:

> The determination of the nature of the common law as it existed in England in 1776, and as it then prevailed in Maryland either practically or potentially, and the determination of what part of the common law is consistent with the spirit of Maryland's Constitution and her political institutions, are to be made by this Court.
>
> > "Whether particular parts of the common law are applicable to our local circumstances and situation, and our general code of laws and jurisprudence, is a question that comes within the province of the Courts of Justice, and is to be decided by them. The common law, like our Acts of Assembly, are subject to control and modification of the Legislature, and may be abrogated, or changed as the General Assembly may think most conducive to the general welfare; so that no great inconvenience, if any, can result from the power deposited with the judiciary to decide what the common law is, and its applicability to the circumstances of the State, and what has become obsolete from non-user or other cause. *State v. Buchanan*, 5 H. & J. 317, 365–66 (1821)."

Because of the inherent dynamism of the common law, we have consistently held that it is subject to judicial modification in the light of modern circumstances or increased knowledge.... *Id.* at 331–332, 529 A.2d at 366.

More recently, in *Mayor & City Council of Baltimore, et al. v. Clark,* 404 Md. 13, 944 A.2d 1122 (2008) ... we held that, "It is well settled that, where the General Assembly has announced public policy, the Court will decline to enter the public policy debate, even when it is the common law that is at issue *and the Court certainly has the authority to change the common law* [italics added]." *Id.* at 38, 944 A.2d at 1135. *** "Generally, changes in the common law are applied prospectively, as well as to the case triggering the change in the common law."

* * *

Strict Liability Standards in Pit Bull Attack Cases

We began our modification of the old common-law rule with respect to dog attack cases with our strong dicta in *Matthews, supra,* highlighting the particular characteristics of pit bulls and cross-bred pit bulls. There we explained the difference between pit bulls and other breeds of dogs when we noted:

> Thus, the foreseeability of harm in the present case was clear. The extreme dangerousness of this breed, as it has evolved today, is well recognized. 'Pit bulls as a breed are known to be extremely aggressive and have been bred as attack animals.' *Giaculli v. Bright,* 584 So.2d 187, 189 (Fla.App.1991). Indeed, it has been judicially noted that pit bull dogs 'bite to kill without signal' (*Starkey v. Township of Chester,* 628 F.Supp. 196, 197 (E.D.Pa.1986)), are selectively bred to have powerful jaws, high insensitivity to pain, extreme aggressiveness, a natural tendency to refuse to terminate an attack, and a greater propensity to bite humans than other breeds. The "Pit Bull's massive canine jaws can crush a victim with up to two thousand pounds (2,000) of pressure per square inch — three times that of a German Sheppard or Doberman Pinscher." *State v. Peters,* 534 So.2d 760, 764 (Fla.App.1988) *review denied,* 542 So.2d 1334 (Fla.1989). *See also Hearn v. City of Overland Park,* 244 Kan. 638, 650, 647, 722 P.2d 758, 768, 765, *cert. denied* 493 U.S. 976, 110 S.Ct. 500, 107 L.Ed.2d 503 (1989) ('pit bull dogs represent a unique health hazard ... [possessing] both the capacity for extraordinarily savage behavior ... [a] capacity for uniquely vicious attacks ... coupled with an unpredictable nature" ... and that "of the 32 known human deaths in the United States due to dog attacks ... [in the period between July 1983 and April 1989], 23 were caused by attacks by pit bull dogs." Pit bull dogs have even been considered as weapons. *See State v. Livingston,* 420 N.W.2d 230 (Minn.App.1998) (for the purpose of first degree murder); *People v. Garraway,* 187 A.D.2d 761, 589 N.Y.S.2d 942 (1992) (upholding conviction of pit bull's owner of criminal weapon in the third degree).

> * * *

> .... And the Albuquerque Humane Society reported that no other breed of dog has "ever caused the kinds of injuries or exhibited the aggressive behavior shown by American Pit Bull Terriers ... [and the humane society does not] adopt out pit bull dogs because of their potential for attacks on other animals and people"); [some citations in this paragraph omitted].

Matthews, 351 Md. At 562–63 & n. 4, 719 A.2d at 127–128 & n. 4 (emphasis added).

However, we also stated in *Matthews* that:

> .... Under the present circumstances, however, where a landlord retained control over the matter of animals in the tenant's apartment, coupled with the knowledge of past vicious behavior by the animal, *the extremely dangerous nature of pit bull dogs,* and the foreseeability of harm to persons and property in the apartment complex, the jury was justified in finding that the landlord had a duty to the plaintiffs and that the duty was breached. The following principle set forth in *Prosser and Keeton on the Law of Torts,* Sec. 4 at 25 (5th ed.1984), is applicable here:

>> 'The 'prophylactic' factor of preventing future harm has been quite important in the field of torts. The courts are concerned not only with the compensation of the victim, but with admonition of the wrongdoer. When the decisions of the courts are known, and defendants realize that they may be held liable, there is of course a strong incentive to prevent the occurrence of the harm. Not infrequently one reason for imposing liability is the deliberate purpose of providing that incentive.'

Id. at 570, 719 A.2d at 131–132 (emphasis added).

Because the issue of strict liability was not expressly raised on appeal, we decided *Matthews* on regular common law negligence requirements. However, the language of that case clearly forecasted the direction the Court might take in the proper case. This is that case.

Soon after we decided *Matthews,* a "special report" was published in the Journal of the American Veterinary Medical Association noting that:

> From 1979 through 1996, dog attacks resulted in more than 300 dog-bite related fatalities in the United States. Most victims were children. Studies indicate, … that pit bull-type dogs were involved in approximately a third of human … [fatalities] during the 12 year period from 1981 through 1992.…[9]

See, 217 Journal of the American Veterinary Medical Association, no. 6, September 15, 2000, at 836. The report went on to state: "… the data indicates that Rottweilers and pit bull type dogs accounted for 67% of human DBRF ["dog bite related fatalities"] in the United States between 1979 and 1996". *Id.,* at 839. "It is extremely unlikely that they accounted for anywhere near 60% of dogs in the United States during that same period and, thus, there appears to be a breed-specific problem with fatalities." *Ibid.*[10]

An abstract from a recent article published in the *Annals of Surgery,* entitled "*Mortality, Mauling, and Maiming by Vicious Dogs*" which explored maiming and deaths due to dog attacks noted that:

> Abstract
>
> **OBJECTIVE:** Maiming and death due to dog bites are uncommon but preventable tragedies. We postulated that patients admitted to a level 1 trauma center with dog bites would have severe injuries and that the gravest injuries would be those caused by pit bulls.
>
> **DESIGN:** We reviewed the medical records of patients admitted to our level 1 trauma center with dog bites during a 15-year period. We determined the demographic characteristics of the patients, their outcomes, and the breed and characteristics of the dogs causing the injuries.
>
> **RESULTS:** Our Trauma and Emergency Surgery Services treated 228 patients with dog bite injuries; for 82 of those patients the breed of the dog involved was recorded (29 were injured by pit bulls)[29 out of 82]. Compared with attacks by other breeds of dogs, attacks by pit bulls were associated with a higher median injury Severity Scale score (4 vs. 1; $P=0.002$), a higher risk of an admission Glasgow Coma Scale score of 8 or lower (17.2% vs. 0%; $P=0.006$), higher median hospital charges ($10,500 vs. $7200/$P=0.0003$); and a higher risk of death (10.3% vs. 0%; ($P=0.041$).

---

9. The figures also indicated that during a 12 year period ending in 1992, almost half of fatalities were caused by Rottweilers. More recent data indicates that currently more fatalities are caused by pit bulls than by Rottweilers. This may reflect the increasing popularity of pit bulls, i.e., more pit bulls—more attacks. Other issues such as training, use by persons in the illegal drug trade, etc., may also be causative factors.

10. The on-line publication *Animal People,* www.animalpeoplenews.org, estimates that pit bulls make up approximately 5% of the total dog population in the United States partly based upon surveys of for sale advertisements. The breed breakdowns at 62 animal shelters holding 5,236 dogs indicated that 23% of the dogs so held were pit bulls. These figures, if accurate, support an inference that pit bulls end up in animal shelters at a much larger ratio than their overall ratio within the total dog population.

CONCLUSIONS: Attacks by pit bulls are associated with higher morbidity rates, higher hospital charges, and a higher risk of death than are attacks by other breeds of dogs. Strict regulation of pit bulls may substantially reduce the U.S. mortality rates related to dog bites.

John K. Bini et al., *Mortality, Mauling, and Maiming by Vicious Dogs,* 253 Annals of Surgery, no. 4, May 2011.

The Center for Disease Control, in at least one of its *"Morbidity and Mortality"* Weekly Reports (MMWR) has noted that:

From 1979 through 1994, attacks by dogs resulted in 279 deaths of humans in the United States ... (1, 2) Such attacks have prompted widespread review of existing local and state dangerous-dog laws, including proposals for adoption of breed-specific restrictions to prevent such episodes (3).

The "Editorial Note" following the Weekly Report noted that

during 1979–1996, fatal dog attacks occurred in 45 states. In 1986, nonfatal dog bites resulted in an estimated 585,000 injuries that required medical attention or restricted activity; in that year, dog bites ranked 12th among the leading causes of nonfatal injuries in the United States. In 1994, an estimated 4.7 million persons (1.8% of the U.S. population) sustained a dog bite, of these, approximately 800,000 (0.3%) sought medical care for the bite.

46 MMWR Weekly no. 21, *Dog-Bite Related Fatalities — United States 1995–1996,* May 30, 1997, pp. 463–466.

Although the Center for Disease Control did not recommend breed-specific regulation[11] it did state: "... laws for regulating dangerous or vicious dogs should be promulgated and enforced vigorously."

Cases from other jurisdictions that address the inherent viciousness of pit bulls often involve the constitutionality of certain dog control regulations, or criminal cases where dog owners have been charged with using pit bulls as dangerous weapons. For example, in *City of Toledo v. Tellings,* 114 Ohio St.3d 278, 280–283, 871 N.E.2d 1152 (2007), the Ohio Supreme Court, reversing an intermediate appellate court, upheld most of Toledo's breed-specific regulations involving pit bulls. Tellings had challenged the constitutionality of that section of the statute that included pit bulls in the "vicious dog" category and stated that the "ownership, keeping, or harboring of a vicious dog" violated the regulations. Vicious dogs were defined in the statute to include pit bulls.

The Ohio court went on to state:

The trial court cited the substantial evidence supporting its conclusion that pit bulls, compared to other breeds, cause a disproportionate amount of danger to people. The chief dog warden of Lucas County testified that (1) when pit bulls attack, they are more likely to inflict severe damage to their victim than other breeds of dogs, (2) pit bulls have killed more Ohioans than any other breed of dog, (3) Toledo police officers fire their weapons in the line of duty at pit bulls

---

11. The Center did attach a chart of the breed-specific dog-attack fatalities it had recorded between 1979 and 1996. That chart showed that of the 279 fatal attacks in this country in that period, 79 were by pit bulls or pit bull crosses. Rottweilers accounted for 29 deaths.

more often than they fire weapons at people and other breeds of dogs combined, (4) pit bulls are frequently shot during drug raids because pit bulls are encountered more frequently in drug raids than any other dog breed. The trial court also found that pit bulls are 'found largely in urban settings where there are crowded living conditions and a large number of children present,' which increases the risk of injury caused by pit bulls.

The evidence presented in the trial court supports the conclusion that pit bulls pose a serious danger to the safety to citizens. The state and the city have a legitimate interest in protecting the citizens from the degree of danger posed by this breed of domestic dog.

Tellings, 871 N.E.2d at 1157 (emphasis added). *See also Bess v. Bracken County Fiscal Court*, 210 S.W.3d 177, 182 (2006 Ky.App.) ("Here, the determination by the Bracken County Fiscal Court that pit bull terriers have "inherently vicious and dangerous propensities" was certainly not unreasonable given the evidence in support of that finding.").

In *The Florida Bar v. Pape* and *The Florida Bar v. Chandler*, 918 So.2d 240, at 242 and 245, (2005 Fla.) cases, two Florida attorneys were disciplined for using an image of a pit bull in their advertising because it was misleading, and also portrayed an inappropriate message. Although the disciplinary case itself was unusual, relevant for our purposes here is the following statement by the Supreme Court of Florida:

In this case we impose discipline on two attorneys for their use of television advertising devices that violate the Rules of Professional Conduct. These devices, which invoke the breed of dog known as the pit bull, demean all lawyers and thereby harm both the legal profession and the public's trust and confidence in our system of justice.

* * *

In addition, the image of a pit bull and the on-screen display of the words "PIT BULL" ... are not relevant to the selection of an attorney. The referee found that the qualities of a pit bull as depicted by the logo are loyalty, persistence, tenacity, and aggressiveness. We consider this as a charitable set of associations that ignores the darker side of the qualities often also associated with pit bulls: malevolence, viciousness, and unpredictability. Further, although some may associate pit bulls with loyalty to their owners ... even the perception of loyalty may be unwarranted. In June, a twelve-year old boy was mauled to death in San Francisco by his family's two pit bulls.... That same month a Bay Area woman suffered severe injuries in an attack by her nine-year-old pit bull.... A St. Louis man was killed in May by his two pit bulls that had "no apparent history of aggression and [were] described as well kept [source citations in paragraph omitted.]

Pit bulls have a reputation for vicious behavior that is borne of experience.

Id., at 241, 245 & n. 4.

Although the District of Columbia Court of Appeals found for the landlord on the basis that he had no right to terminate the lease in the case of *Campbell v. Noble*, 962 A.2d 264, 264–265 (2008 D.C.App.), the Court described the magnitude of the injuries suffered by a boy hired to clean up dog waste from pit bulls:

.... The dogs then began to attack Elijah, biting him in the face and body.... Elijah was raced to the hospital, where he underwent nine hours of surgery. Since the attack, Elijah has had physical and psychological difficulties. He had to relearn how to balance and walk, and has had terrible nightmares about the attack; he also no longer has a right ear. His left ear was surgically reattached.

McNeely v. United States, 874 A.2d 371. (2005 D.C.App.), arose out of a vicious attack by two pit bulls. McNeely, the owner of the dogs, was criminally charged and convicted of two counts of violating the "Pit Bull and Rottweiler Dangerous Dog Designation Emergency Act of 1996 (the "Pit Bull Act") that imposed certain requirements on a breed-specific basis relating to pit-bulls. McNeely challenged the statute on several grounds including "... that the Act constitutes an impermissible strict liability statute." *McNeely, supra,* at 375.

The facts of the attack are described as follows:

> At approximately 1:00 a.m. on May 13, 1996, Helen Avery carried a bag of spoiled food to the trash can behind her home. As she replaced the can lid, Avery saw two dogs appear from under the steps of her back porch. The dogs charged towards her, forcing Avery to seek an escape by scaling a fence to her neighbor's yard. Unfortunately, she did not evade the dogs quickly enough: one of them seized Avery by the back of her leg and pulled her off the fence, while the other dog jumped on top of her as she fell backwards. During the ensuing attack, skin, muscle, and nerve tissues were bitten off from various parts of her body, including her leg and both arms; one of her toes was nearly bitten off, and she lost a large amount of blood. The attack finally ended when Avery's son, Jerrel Bryant, and two other men successfully chased the dogs off by beating them with an ax and baseball bat.

In arguing that a denial of a motion to dismiss be upheld, the government stated that all that was required to be proven under the statute was that the owner knew the dog was a pit bull. The District of Columbia Court of Appeals agreed and upheld the conviction, and noted further, as related to the basic *scienter* requirement under the statute, that all that was required to be shown was that the pit bulls had attacked without provocation and the owner knew "that the dogs he owned were pit bulls." *Id.*

Multiple constitutional issues and other arguments were raised by pit bull advocates[12] in a challenge to a pit bull strict liability statute in the case of *The Colorado Dog Fanciers, Inc. et al. v. The City and County of Denver,* 820 P.2d 644 (Colo.1991). The Supreme Court of Colorado in upholding the statute at issue, opined, in relevant part:

> Since section 8-55 allows the determination that a dog is a pit bull based on non-scientific evidence, the dog owners assert that they are denied substantive due process. The city, however, is not required to meet its burden of proof with mathematical certainty of scientific evidence. Therefore, even though section 8-55 permits a finding of pit bull status to be based on expert opinion or on nonscientific evidence, such a procedure does not violate the dog owner's due process rights.

---

12. Some are similar to the arguments made in the appellant or *amicus'* briefs filed in the present case by supporters of pit bulls. In light of Maryland's situation, we find those particular arguments unpersuasive. We have fully reviewed and considered all the briefs.

We recognize the problems that exist when breed specific legislation is proposed—which is opposed by pit bull breeders, owners and fanciers. Such opposition has been present for many years. Our opinion in the present case does not ban pit bulls, but puts a greater responsibility for vicious dogs where pit bull advocates have long argued it should be—with the owners and others who have the power of control over such dogs. Our opinion imposes greater duties by reducing the standards necessary to hold owners and others liable for the attacks of their pit bulls.

The dog owners also assert that the city ordinance treats all pit bulls and substantially similar dogs as inherently dangerous and is, therefore, unconstitutionally overbroad. This contention is without merit.

* * *

The dog owners argue that the ordinance violates the Equal Protection Clause by creating an irrational distinction between one who owns a dog with the physical characteristics of a pit bull and one who owns a dog lacking those characteristics.

* * *

.... The trial court found that pit bull attacks, unlike attacks by other dogs, occur more often, are more severe, and are more likely to result in fatalities. The trial court also found that pit bulls tend to be stronger than other dogs, often give no warning signals before attacking, and are less willing than other dogs to retreat from an attack, even when they are in considerable pain. Since ample evidence exists to establish a rational relationship between the city's classification of certain dogs as pit bulls, and since there is a legitimate governmental purpose in protecting the health and safety of the city's residents and dogs, the trial court correctly concluded that the ordinance did not violate the dog owner's right to equal protection of the laws.

Id., at 649–652 (internal citations and footnotes omitted).

Harper, supra, notes that at least the following states have some form of state-strict liability statute in which the finding of dangerousness of the particular attacking dog is not necessary to establish the elements of negligence: Arizona, Florida, Illinois, Iowa, New Jersey, Nebraska, Oklahoma, Connecticut, Wisconsin and Ohio. There are also indications in the literature that California, South Carolina and the District of Columbia also have some form of strict liability statute relating to dogs. Additionally, some of the cases and other authority we have examined concern local animal control laws, some of which are breed-specific.

The sources and discussions above, coupled with our extensive dicta in *Matthews, supra,* and the numerous instances of serious and often fatal attacks by pit bulls throughout the country, and especially in Maryland, persuades us that the common law needs to be changed in order that a strict liability standard be established in relation to attacks by pit bull and cross-bred pit bull mixes.

CONCLUSION

We hold that upon a plaintiff's sufficient proof that a dog involved in an attack is a pit bull or a pit bull mix, and that the owner, or other person(s) who has the right to control the pit bull's presence on the subject premises (including a landlord who has the right and/or opportunity to prohibit such dogs on leased premises as in this case) knows, or has reason to know, that the dog is a pit bull or cross-bred pit bull mix, that person is strictly liable for the damages caused to a plaintiff who is attacked by the dog on or from the owner's or lessor's premises.[13] This holding is prospective and applies to this case and causes

---

13. The appellee attempted to make the argument that the landlord had sufficient control over the alley behind the house such as to make the alley part of the landlord's and lessee's premises. He is incorrect. The language he asserts affords that right of control is the same as, or similar to, language contained in most deeds of conveyance in this state. It merely gives to the grantee whatever rights the grantor had in the alley. In the case of alleys improved, maintained or accepted by public entities, the primary right that language gives to an adjacent landowner is to be able to make a claim to the center of the roadway if the public body ever closes the alley or sufficiently abandons it. Until that time, adjacent landowners have ingress and egress rights along with the general public. Generally,

of action accruing after the date of the filing of this opinion. Upon remand to the trial court, it shall apply in this case the modifications to the common law herein created.

JUDGMENT OF THE COURT OF SPECIAL APPEALS AFFIRMED FOR THE REASONS HEREIN STATED; THAT COURT IS DIRECTED TO REMAND THE CASE TO THE TRIAL COURT FOR A RETRIAL CONSISTENT WITH THE NEW COMMON LAW PRINCIPLES HEREIN ADOPTED; COSTS IN THIS COURT AND IN THE COURT OF SPECIAL APPEALS TO BE PAID BY THE APPELLANT.

Dissenting Opinion by GREENE, J., which HARRELL and BARBERA, JJ., join.

I respectfully dissent:

Today, the majority holds that a pit bull or any dog with a trace of pit bull ancestry (determined by what means the majority opinion leaves us entirely in the dark)[14] shall be deemed hence forth vicious and inherently dangerous as a matter of law. Thus, an owner, keeper, or landlord with control over a tenant's premises can be held strictly liable for harm a pit bull or mixed-breed pit bull[15] causes to third parties. ***

One author has described the common law standard of strict liability in dog bite cases in the following way:

> For centuries, dogs have been known as a companion to man[kind]. As such, they were considered harmless; and if they did, in fact, possess dangerous characteristics, it was considered abnormal. Consequently, the owner of a dog was not strictly liable for a dog bite, unless he had reason to know the dog was abnormally dangerous. Being abnormally dangerous was often characterized as having a tendency to attack human beings, whether the attack was in anger or in play. The owner's liability was in keeping a dog after gaining knowledge of its propensity for abnormally vicious behavior. Thus, the requirement of scienter was a hurdle plaintiffs needed to overcome in order to proceed with a lawsuit. (Footnotes omitted.)

Lynn A. Epstein, *There Are No Bad Dogs, Only Bad Owners: Replacing Strict Liability with a Negligence Standard in Dog Bite Cases*, 13 Animal L. 129, 132 (2006). Believing that the traditional common law principles of strict liability applicable to dog bite cases are inadequate, the majority modifies the common law. In the present case, the Court of Special Appeals reversed the trial court and remanded the case for a new trial, and the majority affirms

---

they do not have the right to control the public way. As we are holding that liability follows a pit bull when it leaves its abode to launch an attack, control of the alley is not an issue. In this case, it is clear that the pit bull twice left its enclosure on the lessee's/landlord's property to attack two boys. Accordingly, the pit bull attacked the two boys *from* the subject property.

If the owner had taken the pit bull to the supermarket or on a day trip to the beach in Ocean City, and while there, the pit bull attacked someone, the attack would not have been on or '*from*' the leased premises. While the owner's responsibility remains clear, liability, if any, on the part of the landlord in such a situation seems much more remote.

14. The majority opinion delivers an unenlightening and unworkable rule regarding mixed-breed dogs. How much "pit bull" must there be in a dog to bring it within the strict liability edict? How will that be determined? What rationale exists for any particular percentage of the genetic code to trigger strict liability?

15. Mixed-breed pit bulls are dogs "with heritages including any percentage of recognized pit-bull breeds[.]" Kristen E. Swann, Note, *Irrationality Unleashed: The Pitfalls of Breed-Specific Legislation*, 78 UMKC L.Rev. 839, 853 (2010). To the extent that the majority discusses "cross-bred" pit bulls, we note that, for purposes of the issues considered herein, the term "cross-bred" will be treated the same as "mixed-breed" in the context of this discussion.

that judgment, but for a different reason than that given by our brethren on the intermediate appellate court. According to the majority, if on remand the plaintiff can prove that the owner or landlord had knowledge of Clifford's presence on the leased premises and that Clifford is a "pit bull or cross-bred pit bull," or if the plaintiff can prove that the owner or landlord should have had such knowledge, the plaintiff will have established a *prima facie* case of strict liability for any harm caused. *See* Maj. slip op. at 9.

Until today, the common law in Maryland was that the owner or keeper of a dog or other domestic animal would be held strictly liable for injuries caused by that animal, provided the plaintiff could show that the owner or keeper "had knowledge of [the animal's] disposition to commit such injury [.]" *Twigg v. Ryland,* 62 Md. 380, 385 (1884) (noting that "[t]he gist of the [strict liability] action is the keeping [of] the animal after knowledge of its mischievous propensities"). Likewise, until today, a landlord would be held liable to a third party for an attack by a tenant's animal where the landlord had knowledge of the animal's presence on the leased premises and knowledge of its vicious propensities, and the landlord maintained control over the leased premises. *Matthews v. Amberwood Assocs. Ltd. P'ship, Inc.,* 351 Md. 544, 570, 719 A.2d 119, 131–32 (1998); *see Shields v. Wagman,* 350 Md. 666, 690, 714 A.2d 881, 892–93 (1998). *Scienter,* or knowledge, is defined as "[a] degree of knowledge that makes a person legally responsible for the consequences of his or her act or omission; the fact of an act's having been done knowingly, esp. as a ground for civil damages or criminal punishment." *Black's Law Dictionary* 1373 (8th ed.2004). Under Maryland law, "the owner's [strict] liability arises from exposing the community to a known dangerous beast rather than any negligence in keeping or controlling his animal." *Slack v. Villari,* 59 Md.App. 462, 473, 476 A.2d 227, 232 (1984) (citing William L. Prosser, *Handbook of the Law of Torts* § 76, at 499 (4th ed.1971)). The burden is on the plaintiff to establish "that the owner [or keeper of the animal] knew, or by the exercise of ordinary and reasonable care should have known, of the inclination or propensity of the animal to do the particular mischief that was the cause of the harm." *Herbert v. Ziegler,* 216 Md. 212, 216, 139 A.2d 699, 702 (1958) (citations omitted). If the plaintiff fails to show the owner or keeper's *scienter,* or knowledge, of the animal's propensity to cause the very harm inflicted, recovery for the harm caused by the animal will be denied. *See Twigg,* 62 Md. at 386.

With regard to this theory of strict liability, the mere fact that a dog is kept in an enclosure or is otherwise restrained is not sufficient to show the owner or keeper's knowledge of the animal's vicious propensities or inclination to bite people. *McDonald v. Burgess,* 254 Md. 452, 458, 255 A.2d 299, 302 (1969); *see Ward v. Hartley,* 168 Md.App. 209, 218, 895 A.2d 1111, 1116 (2006), *cert. denied,* 394 Md. 310, 905 A.2d 844 (2006). Furthermore, in accordance with the well-settled common law standard of strict liability, the breed of the dog, standing alone, has never been considered a sufficient substitute for proof that a *particular* dog was dangerous or had a violent nature. *See McDonald,* 254 Md. at 460, 255 A.2d at 303; *Slack,* 59 Md App. at 476, 476 A.2d at 234. Specifically, in *McDonald,* we held that the mere fact that the dog in question belonged to a specific breed, which "can and often does behave in a very vicious manner," was insufficient to hold the owner legally responsible for his German shepherd attacking another person. *McDonald,* 254 Md. at 460–61, 255 A.2d at 303. In that case, "[t]here [wa]s nothing in the record to demonstrate that the particular dog alleged to have caused the injury ... was of a violent or oppressive nature" and that the defendant had the requisite *scienter. Id.* Thus, in order to hold the owner or keeper of a dog strictly liable, there must be a showing that the *particular* dog, in that case a German shepherd, was of a violent nature and that the owner or keeper of the dog knew, or by the exercise of ordinary care should have known, of the dog's inclination or propensity to do the particular mischief that was the cause of the harm. *McDonald,* 254 Md. at 456–60, 255 A.2d at 301–03.

Furthermore, until today, this Court has never announced a theory of strict liability predicated upon the alleged knowledge of the owner, keeper, or landlord of the premises, based upon assumptions about a particular breed of an animal, where a dog of that breed caused an injury to another human being. Ordinarily, the owner, keeper, or landlord of the premises, would be strictly liable in a dog bite case where the responsible party was in a position to anticipate the harm; primarily, because he or she had sufficient knowledge of the dog's vicious propensities or inclination and would thereby be in a position to take corrective action. *See Bachman v. Clark,* 128 Md. 245, 248, 97 A. 440, 441 (1916). Under the new rule announced today, however, the only corrective action an owner, keeper, or landlord could possibly take to avoid liability for the harm caused to another by a pit bull or mixed-breed pit bull is not to possess or allow possession of this specific breed of dog on the premises. Conversely, any other breed of dog in the possession of the owner or on premises controlled by the landlord, no matter how violent, apparently, would be judged by a different standard. As a result of the majority opinion, it is unclear as to what standard should be applied prospectively to owners and landlords for the liability of other breeds of dogs kept on the premises.

Although this Court has authority to alter the common law, we have been reluctant to do so because of the principle of *stare decisis,* which we have confirmed "promotes the evenhanded, predictable, and consistent development of legal principles, fosters reliance on judicial decisions, and contributes to the actual and perceived integrity of the judicial process." *DRD Pool Serv., Inc. v. Freed,* 416 Md. 46, 63, 5 A.3d 45, 55 (2010) (quoting *Livesay v. Balt. Cnty.,* 384 Md. 1, 14, 862 A.2d 33, 40–41 (2004)). We have changed or modified the common law when the prior decision was "clearly wrong and contrary to established principles[,]" *State v. Adams,* 406 Md. 240, 259, 958 A.2d 295, 307 (2008) (quotation omitted), *cert. denied,* 556 U.S. 1133, 129 S.Ct. 1624, 173 L.Ed.2d 1005 (2009), or when precedent has been superseded by significant changes in the law or facts. *Harrison v. Montgomery Cnty. Bd. of Educ.,* 295 Md. 442, 459, 456 A.2d 894, 903 (1983) (allowing departure from *stare decisis* when there are "changed conditions or increased knowledge, [such] that the rule has become unsound in the circumstances of modern life, a vestige of the past, no longer suitable to our people").

Consistent with our precedent, there is no good reason to modify the common law in this case. Modern circumstances and knowledge gleaned from the literature regarding "pit bulls" have not substantially changed since 1998 when we decided *Matthews* and *Shields.* The majority relies upon a *Report* issued after our decisions in *Matthews* and *Shields* that is published in the Journal of the American Veterinary Medical Association and indicates that "pit bull-type dogs were involved in approximately a third of human ... [fatalities] reported during the [twelve]-year period from 1981 through 1992[.]" *See* Jeffrey J. Sacks et al., *Breeds of Dogs Involved in Fatal Human Attacks in the United States Between 1979 and 1998,* 217 J. Am. Veterinary Med. Ass'n 836, 836 (2000) [hereinafter *Veterinary Medical Association Report*]. This information was certainly available prior to publication of the *Veterinary Medical Association Report.* The Report does not recommend strict liability as a potential solution to the problem of attacks by pit bull dogs. *See Veterinary Medical Association Report, supra,* at 839–40. In fact, the *Report* questions the success of breed-specific liability requirements and urges the consideration of factors completely unrelated to the breed or appearance of dogs, including their socialization, training, size, sex, and reproductive status. *See id.* The *Veterinary Medical Association Report* warns that dog bite data can be misleading. *See Veterinary Medical Association Report, supra,* at 838. Moreover, other reports question the use of dog bite statistics and emphasize that such statistics do not provide an accurate portrayal of dogs that bite. *See* Stephen Collier, *Breed-Specific Legislation and the Pit Bull Terrier: Are the Laws Justified?*, 1 J. Veterinary Behavior 17, 18 (2006); Bonnie V. Beaver et al., *A Community Approach to Dog Bite Prevention*, 218 J. Am. Veterinary Med. Ass'n 1732, 1733 (2001).

Public knowledge and the hysteria regarding pit bulls is no more prevalent now than it was in 1998 when *Matthews* and *Shields* were decided. *See* Collier, *supra*, at 17–18 (discussing a trend in several countries, including the United States, of the media portraying the pit bull breed with "lurid and sensational accounts of its background, capabilities, and character" and the lasting effects of that depiction). A 2011 Report entitled *Mortality, Mauling, and Maiming by Vicious Dogs*, cited by the majority, notes that "[s]trict regulation of pit bulls may substantially reduce the U.S. mortality rates related to dog bites." John K. Bini et al., *Mortality, Mauling, and Maiming by Vicious Dogs*, 253 Annals Surg. 791, 791 (2011). The author recommends regulation, however; he does not specifically suggest imposing strict liability in tort. Bini et al., *supra*, at 796. Furthermore, strict regulation does not equate to strict liability in tort. In the field of regulation, for example, the direct focus is on the owner's behavior, sterilization, socialization, supervision, breeding practices, educational outreach to potential dog owners, and screening of potential owners. *See* Jamey Medlin, *Pit Bull Bans and the Human Factors Affecting Canine Behavior*, Comment, 56 DePaul L.Rev. 1285, 1304–1318 (2007) (suggesting laws designed to target human behavior related to treatment of dogs, including sterilization, breeder licensing programs, screening programs, and community outreach). With regard to dog bite statistical information, some experts express doubt that it is even possible to calculate dog bite rates for a particular breed of dog or to compare rates between breeds because many dogs are unregistered or unlicensed. See Safia Gray Hussain, *Attacking the Dog Bite Epidemic: Why Breed-Specific Legislation Won't Solve the Dangerous-Dog Dilemma*, Note, 74 Fordham L.Rev. 2847, 2870–71 (2006) (referencing Beaver et al., *supra*, at 1733).

According to some experts, there are more than twenty-five breeds of dogs commonly mistaken for pit bulls. Hussain, *supra*, at 2870. Notwithstanding this empirical evidence, the majority relies upon the assumption that all pit bulls are inherently dangerous. In this record, there is no evidence from expert witnesses to support the proposition that pit bulls or pit bull mixed-breeds are inherently dangerous. It appears that the media has demonized pit bulls as gruesome fighting dogs and has not revealed the long history of pit bulls as family dogs with passive behaviors. *See* Medlin, *supra*, at 1288–1290 (discussing the role of pit bulls as family pets in the early twentieth century in contrast to public perception today); Lynn Ready, *Pit-Bull Terrier Therapy Dogs Provide Great Service to Their Community*, Best Friends Animal Society Pit Bull Terrier Initiatives (Apr. 28, 2011), http://network.bestfriends.org/initiatives/pitbulls/17100/news.aspx. The majority also assumes that breed-specific rules, as opposed to behavior modification rules, are a better approach to controlling the problem of dog bites caused by pit bulls and mixed-breed pit bulls that attack humans. Again, the empirical evidence is in dispute. Some experts conclude that breed-specific liability rules provide a superficial sense of security because many factors completely unrelated to the breed or appearance of dogs affect their tendency toward aggression, including early experience, socialization, training, size, sex, and reproductive status. *See* Sacks et al., *supra*, at 839–40.

In those states referenced by the majority as examples of jurisdictions where the strict liability standard has been applied in the manner the majority announces today, it was clearly the legislatures of those states that enacted specific legislation to address the problem of harm caused by pit bulls and mixed-breed pit bulls. For example, the majority relies upon *City of Toledo v. Tellings*, in which the Supreme Court of Ohio upheld Toledo's breed-specific legislation with regard to "pit bulls." *Tellings,* 871 N.E.2d 1152, 1159 (Ohio 2007) (holding that "the state of Ohio and the city of Toledo have a legitimate interest in protecting citizens from the dangers associated with pit bulls, and that R.C. 955.11(A)(4)(a)(iii) and 955.22 and Toledo Municipal Code 505.14 are rationally related to that interest and are constitutional"). Likewise, in Colorado, the District of Columbia, Florida, and Kentucky, strict liability statutes addressing liability for injuries caused by dogs were enacted by the respective state legislatures. Rebecca F. Wisch, *Quick Overview of Dog Bite Strict Liability Statutes,* Michigan State University College of Law Animal Legal & Historical Center (May 2006, updated 2010), http://www.animallaw.info/articles/qvusdogbiteslstatutes.htm. In each of those jurisdictions, the courts have followed the lead of state legislatures rather than legislating from the bench. *See, e.g., Colo. Dog Fanciers, Inc. v. City & Cnty. of Denver,* 820 P.2d 644, 646 (Colo.1991) (evaluating the constitutionality of the " 'Pit Bulls Prohibited' ordinance"); *McNeely v. United States,* 874 A.2d 371, 380 (D.C.2005) (concluding that "the Pit Bull Act is sufficiently definite to comport with the demands of the Constitution's Due Process Clause and that the Council [of the District of Columbia] created through the Act a constitutional strict liability felony, without requiring a culpable state of mind, so long as it is proved that the defendant knew he or she owned a pit bull"); *State v. Peters,* 534 So.2d 760, 761–62 (Fla.Dist.Ct.App.1988) (upholding a local ordinance regulating the ownership of pit bulls); *Bess v. Bracken Cnty. Fiscal Ct.,* 210 S.W.3d 177, 179–80 (Ky.Ct.App.2006) (recognizing the "right of state legislatures to exercise their police power to regulate dog ownership" and upholding a local county ordinance banning possession of pit bull terriers).

Given the nature of the extensive social problem of regulating pit bulls and mixed-breed pit bulls, the majority elects to focus on the breed of the dog involved, rather than on the behavior of the dog, the owner, and the landlord. The issues raised involving breed-specific regulation are not appropriate for judicial resolution; rather, those issues are best resolved by the Maryland General Assembly, as that branch of government is better equipped to address the various issues associated with regulation of pit bulls and mixed-breed pit bulls. For example, some experts indicate that the term "pit bull" does not describe any one particular breed of dog; instead, it is a generic category encompassing the American Staffordshire Terrier, the Staffordshire Bull Terrier, and the American Pit Bull Terrier. *See* Hussain, *supra,* at 2851–52. Neither the American Kennel Club nor the United Kennel Club recognizes all three breeds, and the breed descriptions and standards provided by the two organizations differ. *Id.* It is difficult for courts, therefore, both to determine whether a particular dog should be categorized as a pit bull and to differentiate between pit bulls and other breeds. Hussain, *supra,* at 2852; Karyn Grey, *Breed-Specific Legislation Revisited: Canine Racism or the Answer to Florida's Dog Control Problems?,* Comment, 27 Nova L.Rev. 415, 432 (2003) (positing that "the evidentiary method for determining when a dog is a pit bull or pit bull mix can be confusing and difficult"). In addition, the connection between a dog's appearance and the actual breed is tenuous, according to some experts. *See* Victoria L. Voith, *Shelter Medicine: A Comparison of Visual and DNA Identification of Breeds of Dogs,* Proceedings of Annual AVMA Convention (July 11–14, 2009), http://www.nathanwinograd.com/linked/misbreed.pdf (finding that there is discrepancy between breed determination based on physical attributes and scientific determinations). Taking into consideration the lack of evidence in the record of this case with regard to the landlord's knowledge of the vicious propensities of the dog, the conflicting studies about how best to control the dog bite "epidemic" mentioned herein, and the problems inherent in defining what constitutes a "mixed-breed" pit bull, the matter of creating a new standard of liability is fraught with problems and is beyond the sphere of resolution by any appellate court.

Judges HARRELL and BARBERA have authorized me to state that they join in the views expressed in this dissenting opinion.

ON MOTION FOR RECONSIDERATION

Opinion by WILNER, J., which ADKINS, J., joins.

On April 26, 2012, the Court filed an Opinion in this case holding, by a four-to-three vote, that, "upon a plaintiff's sufficient proof that a dog involved in an attack is a pit bull or a pit bull mix, and that the owner, or other person(s) who has the right to control the pit bull's presence on the subject premises (including a landlord who has the right and/ or opportunity to prohibit such dogs on leased premises as in this case) knows, or has reason to know, that the dog is a pit bull or cross-bred pit bull mix, that person is strictly liable for the damages caused to a plaintiff who is attacked by the dog on or from the owner's or lessor's premises" (bolding added). Notwithstanding a dissent by Judge Greene, joined in by Judges Harrell and Barbera, I joined the majority Opinion, authored by Judge Cathell.

On May 25, 2012, the petitioner, Dorothy Tracey filed a motion for reconsideration, complaining that the imposition of a "new duty" on landlords was fundamentally unfair and unconstitutional as applied to her. An answer to the motion was filed by the respondents. As to the Court's holding with respect to pit bulls, I would deny the motion. For the reasons stated in Judge Cathell's Opinion, I do not believe that a "new duty" was created or that there is anything unconstitutional or unfair about holding Ms. Tracey liable for the gruesome damage done to Dominic Solesky by a pit bull that she knowingly, and with obvious reservations, allowed her tenant to keep on her property.

The Opinion is not as dramatic and pervasive as the motion claims. It does not prohibit the ownership or breeding of pit bulls; it does not require that persons who own such dogs get rid of them. By imposing long-standing principles of common law strict liability for what is now clearly foreseeable damage done by those dogs, it simply requires that those who possess them or permit them to be on their property take reasonable steps to assure that they do not run loose or otherwise are in a position to injure other people.

That said, having re-read the briefs, relevant portions of the record extract, and the dissent, I am now convinced that, on the record before us, the application of the Court's holding of strict liability to cross-bred pit bulls was both gratuitous and erroneous. I would grant the motion for reconsideration, in part, to delete any reference to cross-bred pit bulls (*i.e.*, part pit bull and part some other breed of domestic dog), so that the Court's holding would apply only to pit bulls that are not cross-breds. There are two reasons for my change in position. First, there was never any assertion, suggestion, or finding in this case that the dog was a cross-bred—was anything other than a pit bull. Second, it is not at all clear what "cross-bred" really means—whether it is limited to the offspring of two pure-bred dogs of different breed, so that the offspring is, in effect, half of one and half of the other, or includes succeeding generations bred from cross-bred parents.

The complaint filed in the Circuit Court alleged that the dog that mauled young Dominic was a "pit bull terrier." The lease allowed the tenant to keep "2 pit bull dogs." Although Ms. Tracey's answer to the complaint is not in the record extract, it does not appear that she ever contested that the dog was a pit bull terrier or asserted that it was a cross-bred. The case proceeded on the premise that dog was a pit bull terrier and not a cross-bred. Unlike the situation in *Ward v. Hartley*, 168 Md.App. 209, 220 (2006), there was not even a suggestion that the dog *might* be a cross-bred. The acknowledgment that the dog was a "pit bull" or "pit bull terrier" remained at the appellate level. Throughout Ms. Tracey's brief, the dog is referred to as a pit bull. The prior cases cited in the majority Opinion all involved pit bulls. There is no suggestion in any of them (except a brief reference in *Wade v. Hartley*) that the dog in question was or might have been a cross-bred.

In short, the question of whether strict liability should apply to cross-breds was never in the case—was never asserted or argued. By gratuitously including them, the Court has opined on an issue that was never raised or argued.

Because the cross-bred issue was never raised, there is no discussion about what the term includes. It appears that some dog-breeding organizations treat cross-breds as synonymous with hybrids. Some recognize as a cross-bred, or a hybrid, only the offspring of pure-bred parents. Others, while claiming that the intended benefits of crossbreeding accrue only to the first generation, acknowledge what is a matter of common knowledge anyway—that it is not uncommon for cross-breds to mate with pure-breds or with other cross-breds, creating dogs that may have elements of several breeds in varying proportions. In imposing strict liability for cross-breds, some greater certainty is required. Is it intended that a dog be classified as a cross-bred pit bull if only one of its grandparents (or great-grandparents, or great-great grandparents) was a pure-bred pit bull?

A motion for reconsideration gives each judge of the Court an opportunity to take another look at the issue and to rethink the position formerly asserted. Because of the care that each judge, individually and collaboratively with his or her colleagues, takes before reaching a conclusion, it is rare that a motion for reconsideration will be found persuasive, and so they are rarely granted. On reflection, however, I am now convinced that the majority (of which I was a part) erred in gratuitously applying strict liability to cross-breds, when that issue was never in the case, and, through this opinion on the motion for reconsideration, I disassociate myself with that aspect of the majority Opinion. Any extension of strict liability to cross-breds (or to any other breed of dog), other than by legislative action, should await a case in which that issue is fairly raised.

I am authorized to state that Judges HARRELL, GREENE, ADKINS, and BARBERA join in this Opinion on reconsideration, with the caveat that Judges HARRELL, GREENE, and BARBERA maintain their dissent to the extension of strict liability to the owners of pit bulls and to the owners of property who permit tenants to keep pit bulls on their property. Chief Judge BELL and Judge CATHELL would deny the motion for reconsideration.

ON MOTION FOR RECONSIDERATION

ORDER

ROBERT M. BELL, Chief Judge.

For the reasons stated in Judge Wilner's Opinion on Reconsideration, it is, by the Court of Appeals of Maryland this 21st day of August 2012, ORDERED:

1. That the motion for reconsideration is granted in part and denied in part; and

2. That the Opinions filed April 26, 2012, are amended to delete any reference to cross-breds, pit bull mix, or cross-bred pit bull mix.

Exercise 3-4 Born to Be Wild?

Since strict liability is imposed for damages caused by wild animals, keepers of animals not traditionally considered domestic may find themselves in the position of arguing that their "pet" is not a wild animal. Such was the case for the ferret owners in *Gallick v. Barto*, 828 F.Supp. 1168 (1993):

[W]e believe that there are general considerations which lead to the conclusion that a ferret is a wild animal.

First, ferrets have been kept by humans for some time basically because of their propensity to attack small animals ... and ferrets serve that purpose only because of their ferocity. For this reason, many authorities have warned against keeping ferrets as pets. "Some animals should never be pets. Turtles, poisonous snakes, chimpanzees, skunks, *ferrets,* and other *wild animals* bite and carry diseases. Furthermore, as this type of animal matures, it can become aggressive, ..." Bruce A. Epstein, *Pets Can Play Important Part in Child's Growth,* St. Petersburg Times, November 25, 1989, at 2 (emphasis added). In 1986, Dr. Kenneth Kizer, then-director of the California Health Department, stated that there had been several documented instances in which savage attacks by ferrets had led to the death or maiming of babies. He attributed the attacks to the possibility that babies had odors similar to those of suckling rabbits. Jon Van, *Ferret Fad Dangerous, Vets Told,* Chicago Tribune, September 7, 1986, Section C at 1. Joining Dr. Kizer in his position were the American Veterinary Medical Association and the Humane Society of the United States. *Id.*

Several states do not allow residents to possess ferrets, while others put limits on ferret ownership.... [I]n Maine, a ferret is not permitted off the premises of the owner unless caged, leashed, or otherwise under the actual physical control of the owner, and the seller of a ferret must provide the following written notification:

A. Ferrets have been known to attack humans, particularly children, for no reason and without warning.

B. There is no proven vaccine for rabies in ferrets nor is there an accepted procedure for judging a rabid ferret without sacrificing the ferret. A ferret which bites a person may be immediately seized and put to death by the State in order to obtain necessary test samples.

Me.Rev.Stat.Ann. tit. 7, § 3966 (West 1993).

Defendants argue that the court should apply the following distinction:

Domestic animals include those which are tame by nature, or from time immemorial have been accustomed to the association of man, or by his industry have been subjected to his will, and have no disposition to escape his dominion.

Wild animals comprehend those wild by nature, which, because of habit, mode of life, or natural instinct, are incapable of being completely domesticated, and require the exercise of art, force, or skill to keep them in subjection.

Brief in Support of Defendants', Bruce Barto and Betty Barto, Motion for Summary Judgment at 5 (quoting *Com. v. Johnson*, 31 Som.L.J. 195, 208 (C.P.1975), which in turn cited C.J.S. *Animals* § 3.

As noted above, ferrets have been known to return to a feral state upon escaping, and have done so in large numbers in New Zealand. Novak, *supra*. Obviously, an animal which has a propensity to bite, which has traditionally been kept for the purpose of hunting rabbits and rats, and which will savagely attack small children without provocation is not an animal capable of being completely domesticated. It appears that people have kept ferrets as house pets only in recent years, and it cannot be said that they have been accustomed to this type of association "from time immemorial." At best, ferrets' natural predisposition to attack has been used as a tool by humans in ridding themselves of rodents and other pests. The instincts of a ferret clearly are not such as would allow it to be completely domesticated.

Defendants also cite *Andrews v. Smith, supra*, which distinguishes between wild animals such as "a tiger or a venomous reptile" and "horses, oxen and dogs." Certainly, the former are wild and the latter are domestic. The problem with such a simple distinction is that so many animals fall between the categories which these examples clearly delineate. For example, dogs may be domestic, but there are dogs, such as pit bulls, doberman pinschers, and rottweilers, the hazard of keeping which cannot be denied. Moreover, there are wild animals, such as box turtles or iguanas, which may be harmless in captivity. ***

[D]efendants argue that the facts of this case indicate that the ferrets owned by Miller and Long were domestic. They focus on the fact that the ferrets were permitted to roam about the house, that the cage was used only for food and water bowls, and that ferrets are sold in pet stores.

First, whether *these particular* ferrets were tame is not the issue, since a wild animal may be tame without changing its essential nature. A case cited by defendants, *Johnson, supra,* supports this conclusion. In that case, the defendants acquired two African leopard cubs, had them declawed and tamed, and accustomed them to captivity. The Court of Common Pleas of Somerset County held that their essential nature as wild cats remained unchanged. *Id.* at 208–209.

Second, the facts of this case do not necessarily support the contention that the ferrets were tame. A wild animal may be permitted to roam outside of its cage. There is no indication that they were permitted outside of the residence and would return when called or otherwise summoned. Moreover, two of the ferrets apparently were caged at the time of the attack ...

In sum, we are of the view that ferrets are an inverse of the types of dogs we have noted above. A pit bull may be considered a domestic animal because dogs generally are considered domestic animals. Therefore, a pit bull is a domestic animal with dangerous propensities.

A ferret, on the other hand, is a wild animal which people may, to a point, be successful in keeping in their home. Therefore, a ferret is a wild animal with domestic propensities. However, those propensities do not change its essential character as a wild animal. We hold that a ferret is a wild animal.

Based on *Gallick v. Barto*, 828 F.Supp. 1168 (1993), and the following information from the U.S. Food and Drug Administration, determine whether a turtle is a wild animal.

According to the U.S. Food and Drug Administration (FDA) website (http://www.fda.gov/forconsumers/consumerupdates/ucm048151.htm):

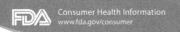

FDA Consumer Health Information
www.fda.gov/consumer

Pet Turtles: Cute But Contaminated with Salmonella

Centers for Disease Control and Prevention

The little glassy-eyed creatures may look cute and harmless, but small turtles can make people very ill. Turtles commonly carry bacteria called Salmonella on their outer skin and shell surfaces.

People can get Salmonella by coming in contact with
· turtles or other reptiles (lizards, snakes)
· amphibians (frogs, salamanders, newts)
· the habitats of reptiles or amphibians

Salmonella can cause a serious or even life-threatening infection in people, even though the bacteria do not make reptiles or amphibians sick. An example is the 2007 death of a four-week-old baby in Florida linked to Salmonella from a small turtle. The DNA of the Salmonella from the turtle matched that from the infant.
People infected with Salmonella may have diarrhea, fever, stomach pain, nausea, vomiting, and headache. Symptoms usually appear 6 to 72 hours after contact with the bacteria and last about 2 to 7 days. Most people recover without treatment, but some get so sick that they need to be treated in a hospital.

Because young children are more vulnerable to the effects of Salmonella, since 1975, FDA has banned the sale of turtles with a shell less than four inches long.

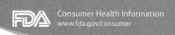

All reptiles and amphibians are commonly contaminated with Salmonella. But it is the small turtles that most often are put in contact with young children, where consequences of infection are likely to be severe.

Who Is at Risk?

Anyone can get Salmonella infection, but the risk is highest in

• infants
• young children
• elderly people
• people with lowered natural resistance to infection due to pregnancy, cancer, HIV/AIDS, diabetes, and other diseases

"All reptiles and amphibians are commonly contaminated with Salmonella," says Joseph C. Paige, D.V.M., a Consumer Safety Officer in the Food and Drug Administration's (FDA's) Center for Veterinary Medicine. "But it is the small turtles that most often are put in contact with young children, where consequences of infection are likely to be severe." Because of this health risk, since 1975, FDA has banned the sale of small turtles with a shell less than four inches long.

"Young children are ingenious in constructing ways to infect themselves," says Paige. "They put the small turtles in their mouths or, more often, they touch the turtles or dangle their fingers in the turtle tank water and then put their hands in their mouths. Also, sometimes the tanks and reptile paraphernalia are cleaned in the kitchen sink, and food and eating utensils get cross-contaminated."

Surfaces such as countertops, table tops, bare floors, and carpeting can also become contaminated with the bacteria if the turtle is allowed to roam on them. The bacteria may survive for a long period of time on these surfaces.

Infection From Turtles and Frogs on the Rise

Infectious disease specialists estimate that banning small turtles prevents 100,000 Salmonella infections in children each year in the United States. But disturbingly, Salmonella infections still occur because some pet shops, flea markets, street vendors, and online stores still sell small turtles.

From May 1, 2007, to January 18, 2008, the Centers for Disease Control and Prevention (CDC) received reports of Salmonella infection in 103 people—most of them children—in 33 states. Fortunately, there were no deaths. However, 24 people were so sick that they landed in the hospital. The investigation showed that most of the sick people were exposed to a turtle (touching, feeding, cleaning habitat, changing water) shortly before they got sick. Two teenaged girls who became ill had been swimming in an unchlorinated, in-ground pool where the family's pet turtles had also been allowed to swim.

Health officials found that the strain of Salmonella that caused the outbreak in people was the same strain found on many of the turtles (or their habitats) belonging to those who became ill.

More recently, frogs were the source of an outbreak of Salmonella infection. As of Dec. 30, 2009, CDC has received reports of infection in 85 people in 31 states due to contact with water frogs, including African dwarf frogs. Water frogs commonly live in aquariums or fish tanks. The outbreak, which affected mostly children, likely began in April 2009, and some infected people needed to be hospitalized.

Advice for Consumers

• Don't buy small turtles or other reptiles or amphibians for pets or as gifts.
• If your family is expecting a child, remove any reptile or amphibian from the home before the infant arrives.
• Keep reptiles and amphibians out of homes with children under 5 years old, the elderly, or people with weakened immune systems.
• Do not clean aquariums or other supplies in the kitchen sink. Use bleach to disinfect a tub or other place where reptile or amphibian habitats are cleaned.
• Always wash hands thoroughly with soap and water after touching any reptile or amphibian, its housing, or anything (for example, food) that comes in contact with the animal or its housing.
• Watch for symptoms of Salmonella infection, such as diarrhea, stomach pain, nausea, vomiting, fever, and headache. Call your doctor if you or your family have any of these symptoms. FDA

Find this and other Consumer Updates at www.fda.gov/ForConsumers/ConsumerUpdates

Sign up for free e-mail subscriptions at www.fda.gov/consumer/consumerenews.html

B. Abnormally Dangerous Activities

The abnormally dangerous activity doctrine was originally applied to cases where a hazardous activity or condition maintained on a defendant's property created a risk of injury to a neighbor's person or property by escaping from defendant's property. The doctrine was first articulated in the English case of *Rylands v. Fletcher*, which continues to remain influential today. *Rylands* involved a dispute between neighboring landowners. The defendants hired contractors who negligently constructed a reservoir on land located above a number of vacant mine shafts. The defendants themselves were unaware of the shafts, and were found not to have been negligent. When the reservoir was partially filled it burst through one of the underlying shafts, causing water to flow into the plaintiff's coal mine, causing considerable damages. The trial court found for the defendants. On appeal, the trial court decision was reversed. The appellate decision was subsequently upheld by the House of Lords:

> The Defendants, treating them as the owners or occupiers of the close on which the reservoir was constructed, might lawfully have used that close for any purpose for which it might in the ordinary course of the enjoyment of land be used; and if, in what I may term the natural use of that land, there had been any accumulation of water, either on the surface or underground, and if, by the operation of the laws of nature, that accumulation of water had passed off into the close occupied by the Plaintiff, the Plaintiff could not have complained that that result had taken place. If he had desired to guard himself against it, it would have lain upon him to have done so, by leaving, or by interposing, some barrier between his close and the close of the Defendants in order to have prevented that operation of the laws of nature.

* * *

> On the other hand if the Defendants, not stopping at the natural use of their close, had desired to use it for any purpose which I may term a non-natural use, for the purpose of introducing into the close that which in its natural condition was not in or upon it, for the purpose of introducing water either above or below ground in quantities and in a manner not the result of any work or operation on or under the land,—and if in consequence of their doing so, or in consequence of any imperfection in the mode of their doing so, the water came to escape and to pass off into the close of the Plaintiff, then it appears to me that that which the Defendants were doing they were doing at their own peril; and, if in the course of their doing it, the evil arose to which I have referred, the evil, namely, of the escape of the water and its passing away to the close of the Plaintiff and injuring the Plaintiff, then for the consequence of that, in my opinion, the Defendants would be liable. ***

> The same result is arrived at on the principles referred to by Mr. Justice *Blackburn* in his judgment, in the Court of Exchequer Chamber, where he states the opinion of that Court as to the law in these words: "We think that the true rule of law is, that the person who, for his own purposes, brings on his land and collects and keeps there anything likely to do mischief if it escapes, must keep it in at his peril; and if he does not do so, is *prima facie* answerable for all the damage which is the natural consequence of its escape. He can excuse himself by shewing that the escape was owing to the Plaintiff's default; or, perhaps, that the escape was the consequence of *vis major*, or the act of God; but as nothing of this sort exists here, it is unnecessary to inquire what excuse would be sufficient. The general rule, as above stated, seems on principle just. The person whose grass or corn is eaten down by the escaping cattle of his neighbour, or whose mine is flooded by the water from his neighbour's reservoir, or whose cellar is invaded by the filth of his neighbour's privy, or whose habitation is made unhealthy by the fumes and noisome vapours of his neighbour's alkali works, is damnified without any fault of his own; and it seems but reasonable and just that the neighbour who has brought something on his own property (which was not naturally there), harmless to others so long as it is confined to his own property, but which he knows will be mischievous if it gets on his neighbour's, should be obliged to

make good the damage which ensues if he does not succeed in confining it to his own property. But for his act in bringing it there no mischief could have accrued, and it seems but just that he should at his peril keep it there, so that no mischief may accrue, or answer for the natural and anticipated consequence. And upon authority this we think is established to be the law, whether the things so brought be beasts, or water, or filth, or stenches."

Exercise 3-5 Extending, Modifying and Rejecting Strict Liability

This exercise contains two decisions—one rejecting and one adopting the strict liability doctrine articulated in *Rylands*. As you read the cases consider:

1. What justifications does each court provide for adopting or rejecting strict liability?

2. Do you agree or disagree with the decisions?

3. Is there a way to reconcile the three decisions? In other words, is there any policy or other rationale that would explain the result in all three?

Apply what you learn to resolve the following problem:

Cameron lived in Ocean View Hills, California, in a hilltop home overlooking the ocean. Ocean View Hills has almost no flat land available for building and so most of the homes are situated on terraced lots cut into the hills. Recently, following a month of unusually heavy rain, the hillside under some of the homes along the hilltop collapsed and those hilltop homes slid down the hillside into other homes below, destroying all of the homes involved. While many areas in Southern California had often experienced similar landslides as the result of heavy rain, this was a first for Ocean View Hills.

Most of the homes involved in the landslides had been built in the early 1940s as single story, three to five bedroom homes. In the past decade some of the homes in the neighborhood had been purchased by new owners who had remodeled the homes, substantially increasing the size of the homes by adding several stories and tripling or quadrupling the footprint of the home (the square footage of the first story). Cameron owned one such home, which he had remodeled from a cozy three bedroom beach cottage into a three story, twenty-two room modern architectural marvel.

Mitchell lived in one of the homes below Cameron's. During the landslides Cameron's home slid off of the hilltop, down the hill and into Mitchell's home, destroying them both. There is evidence that the collapse of the hillside was due, at least in part, to the added weight of the recently remodeled homes, including Cameron's, although no amount of reasonable care in the construction of the home would have prevented the landslide. Also, as a result of their size and weight, the recently remodeled, larger homes, like Cameron's, traveled further down the hillside than the older, smaller homes; the larger homes caused substantially more destruction as a result. For example, Mitchell's is the only home on his "terrace level" of the hillside that was destroyed, since his neighbors lived below the original, smaller homes, that did not make it as far down the hill as Cameron's home.

Should Cameron be strictly liable to Mitchell for the damages caused by Cameron's home sliding down the hilltop? What are the arguments for and against imposing strict liability?

Skill Focus: Applying and Distinguishing Cases Part Three

Remember from Chapter One that where the jurisdiction has not yet decided an issue, the lawyer has two goals: (1) to persuade the court to adopt authority from other jurisdictions, and (2) to persuade the court that the authority to be adopted results in a favorable decision to the lawyer's client. In Chapter One we focused on the second part. In this chapter we will do both.

Remember that applying and distinguishing cases requires you to find similarities and/or differences between the facts or social policies at play in a client's case and the facts or social policies the court considered in making their decision in the precedent case. You may want to review the skill focus in Chapter One for further discussion of this topic.

Remember: to apply a case a lawyer would identify the similarities (facts, policy, reasoning) with the precedent case and the client's case and convince the court that those similarities were the basis for the court's decision, so the result should be the same in the client's case. To distinguish a case a lawyer would identify differences (facts, policy, reasoning) between the precedent case and the client's case and convince the court that those differences mean that the result should be different in the client's case.

Where a jurisdiction has not yet adopted a rule, you must take it one step further. You must convince the court that the particular rule you want the court to adopt (e.g., imposing strict liability) is actually itself good social policy. In other words, in addition to considering what was important to the court's decision in the authority you want the court to apply (and whether those facts, set of facts, policy, or other reasons are similar or different from your client's) you also have to think about why the rule they applied was actually a good one—and why it is the best choice among the possible options. This is the question the court will consider when it is faced with whether to adopt a rule of law.

Turner v. Big Lake Oil Co.

128 Tex. 155 (1936)

The primary question for determination here is whether or not the defendants in error, without negligence on their part, may be held liable in damages for the destruction or injury to property occasioned by the escape of salt water from ponds constructed and used by them in the operation of their oil wells. The facts are stated in the opinion of the Court of Civil Appeals (62 S.W.(2d) 491), and will be but briefly noted in this opinion.

The defendants in error in the operation of certain oil wells in Reagan county constructed large artificial earthen ponds or pools into which they ran the polluted waters from the wells. On the occasion complained of, water escaped from one or more of these ponds, and, passing over the grass lands of the plaintiffs in error, injured the turf, and after entering Garrison draw flowed down the same into Centralia draw. In Garrison draw there were natural water holes, which supplied water for the livestock of plaintiffs in error. The pond, or ponds, of water from which the salt water escaped were, we judge from the map, some six miles from the stock water holes to which we refer. The plaintiffs in error brought suit, basing their action on alleged neglect on the part of the defendants in error in permitting the levees and dams, etc., of their artificial ponds to break and overflow the land of plaintiffs in error, and thereby pollute the waters to which we have above referred and injure the turf in the pasture of plaintiffs in error. The question was submitted to a jury on special issues, and the jury answered that the defendants in error did permit salt water to overflow from their salt ponds and lakes down Garrison draw and on to the land of the plaintiffs in error. However, the jury acquitted the defendants in error of negligence in the premises.

* * *

[T]he immediate question presented is whether or not defendants in error are to be held liable as insurers, or whether the cause of action against them must be predicated upon negligence. We believe the question is one of first impression in this court, and so we shall endeavor to discuss it in a manner in keeping with its importance.

Upon both reason and authority we believe that the conclusion of the Court of Civil Appeals that negligence is a prerequisite to recovery in a case of this character is a correct one. There is some difference of opinion on the subject in American jurisprudence brought about by differing views as to the correctness or applicability of the decision of the English courts in *Rylands v. Fletcher*, L.R. 3 H.L. 330.

* * *

In *Rylands v. Fletcher* the court predicated the absolute liability of the defendants on the proposition that the use of land for the artificial storage of water was not a natural use, and that, therefore, the landowner was bound at his peril to keep the waters on his own land. *Rylands v. Fletcher*, L.R. 3, H.L. 330; *City Water Power Co. v, Fergus Falls*, Ann.Cas.1912A, 110, note; 27 R.C.L. p. 1206, s 124. This basis of the English rule is to be found in the meteorological conditions which obtain there. England is a pluvial country, where constant streams and abundant rains make the storage of water unnecessary for ordinary or general purposes. When the court said in *Rylands v. Fletcher* that the use of land for storage of water was an unnatural use, it meant such use was not a general or an ordinary one; not one within the contemplation of the parties to the original grant of the land involved, nor of the grantor and grantees of adjacent lands, but was a special or extraordinary use, and for that reason applied the rule of absolute liability. This conclusion is supported by the fact that those jurisdictions which adhere to the rule in *Rylands v. Fletcher* do not apply that rule to dams or reservoirs constructed in rivers and streams, which they say is a natural use, but apply the principle of negligence. 27 R.C.L. p. 1207, s 125. In other words, the impounding of water in stream-ways, being an obvious and natural use, was necessarily within the contemplation of the parties to the original and adjacent grants, and damages must be predicated upon negligent use of a granted right and power; while things not within the contemplation of the parties to the original grants, such as unnatural uses of the land, the landowner may do only at his peril. As to what use of land is or may be a natural use, one within the contemplation of the parties to the original grant of land, necessarily depends upon the attendant circumstances and conditions which obtain land, necessarily depends upon the attendant or the initial terms of those grants.

In Texas we have conditions very different from those which obtain in England. A large portion of Texas is an arid or semiarid region. West of the 98th meridian of longitude, where the rainfall is approximately 30 inches, the rainfall decreases until finally, in the extreme western part of the state, it is only about 10 inches. This land of decreasing rainfall is the great ranch or livestock region of the state, water for which is stored in thousands of ponds, tanks, and lakes on the surface of the ground. The country is almost without streams; and without the storage of water from rainfall in basins constructed for the purpose, or to hold waters pumped from the earth, the great livestock industry of West Texas must perish. No such condition obtains in England. With us the storage of water is a natural or necessary and common use of the land, necessarily within the contemplation of the state and its grantees when grants were made, and obviously the rule announced in *Rylands v. Fletcher*, predicated upon different conditions, can have no application here.

Again, in England there are no oil wells, no necessity for using surface storage facilities for impounding and evaporating salt waters therefrom. In Texas the situation is different. Texas has many great oil fields, tens of thousands of wells in almost every part of the state. Producing oil is one of our major industries. One of the by-products of oil production is salt water, which must be disposed of without injury to property or the pollution of streams. The construction of basins or ponds to hold this salt water is a necessary part of the oil business. In Texas much of our land was granted without mineral reservation to the state, and where minerals were reserved, provision has usually been made for leasing and operating. It follows, therefore, that as to these grants and leases the right to mine in the usual and appropriate way, as, for example, by the construction and maintenance of salt water pools such as here involved, incident to the production of oil, was contemplated by the state and all its grantees and mineral lessees, that being a use of the surface incident and necessary to the right to produce oil. 40 Corpus Juris, p. 752, s 74.

From the foregoing it is apparent that we decline to follow and apply in this case the rule of absolute liability laid down in *Rylands v. Fletcher*....

* * *

The judgments of the Court of Civil Appeals and of the district court are affirmed.

Cities Service Co. v. State

312 So.2d 799 (1975)

This is an interlocutory appeal from a partial summary judgment on liability entered against the appellant.

The appellant, Cities Service Company (Cities Service), operates a phosphate rock mine in Polk County. On December 3, 1971, a dam break occurred in one of Cities Service's settling ponds. As a result, approximately one billion gallons of phosphate slimes contained therein escaped into Whidden Creek and thence into the Peace River, thereby killing countless numbers of fish and inflicting other damage.

Appellee, The State of Florida (State), filed suit against Cities Service seeking injunctive relief as well as compensatory and punitive damages arising out of the dam break. ***

The determination of this appeal necessarily requires the consideration of the doctrine of strict liability for the hazardous use of one's land which was first announced in *Rylands v. Fletcher*, 1868, L.R. 3 H.L. 330. In that case the defendants, who were millowners, had constructed a reservoir upon their land. The water broke through into the shaft of an abandoned coal mine and flooded along connecting passages into the adjoining mine of the plaintiff. When the case reached the Exchequer Chamber, Justice Blackburn said:

> 'We think that the true rule of law is that the person who for his own purposes brings on his land and collects and keeps there anything likely to do mischief if it escapes, must keep it at his peril, and if he does not do so he is prima facie answerable for all the damage which is the natural consequences of its escape.'

This statement was limited in the House of Lords to the extent that Lord Cairns said that the principle applied only to a 'nonnatural' use of the defendant's land as distinguished from 'any purpose for which it might in the ordinary course of the enjoyment of land be used.'

* * *

While the application of the doctrine has not been specifically passed upon by the appellate courts of Florida, an early Supreme Court case implies its acceptance. In *Pensacola Gas Co. v. Pebbly* (1889) 25 Fla. 381, 5 So. 593, the plaintiff claimed damages which resulted when a neighboring landowner constructed a gas works and allowed refuse to spill out onto the land and sink through the sand into the common water thereby polluting the plaintiff's well. The trial court apparently charged the members of the jury that the plaintiff would be entitled to a verdict if they determined that the plaintiff's wells were rendered unfit for use by the defendant without regard to the question of negligence. In affirming a judgment for the plaintiff, the Supreme Court said:

> 'The appellant gas company had the right to use the water in and about the gas-works as they pleased, but they had no right to allow the filthy water to escape from their premises, and to enter the land of their neighbors. It was the duty of the company to confine the refuse from their works so that it could not enter upon and injure their neighbors, and if they did so it was done at their peril; the escape of the refuse filthy water being in itself an evidence of negligence on the part of the gas company.'

Among the cases cited for this proposition was *Ball v. Nye*, 99 Mass. 582, which was one of the early American decisions approving the strict liability doctrine of *Rylands v. Fletcher*.

There are two reported circuit court decisions on the subject, both coincidentally arising out of the escape of phosphatic wastes from a reservoir maintained in connection with a phosphate mining operation. In 1953, the Circuit Court of Hillsborough County refused to apply the doctrine of *Rylands v. Fletcher* in *Ague v. American Agricultural Chemical Company*, Cir.Ct. Hillsborough Co. 1953, 5 Fla.Supp. 133. Yet, sixteen years later the same court in *Caldwell v. American Cyanamid Co.*, Cir.Ct. Hillsborough Co. 1969, 32 Fla.Supp. 163, adopted the doctrine as limited to the non-natural use of land and denied a motion to dismiss the allegations of the complaint alleging strict liability.

In early days it was important to encourage persons to use their land by whatever means were available for the purpose of commercial and industrial development. In a frontier society there was little likelihood that a dangerous use of land could cause damage to one's neighbor. Today our life has become more complex. Many areas are overcrowded, and even the non-negligent use of one's land can cause extensive damages to a neighbor's property. Though there are still many hazardous activities which are socially desirable, it now seems reasonable that they pay their own way. It is too much to ask an innocent neighbor to bear the burden thrust upon him as a consequence of an abnormal use of the land next door. The doctrine of *Rylands v. Fletcher* should be applied in Florida.

There remains, however, the serious question of whether the impounding of phosphate slime by Cities Service in connection with its mining operations is a non-natural use of the land. In opposition to the State's motion, Cities Service filed an affidavit of the manager of the plant where the dam break occurred. The affidavit points out that the property is peculiarly suitable for the mining of phosphate and that the central Florida area of which Polk County is the hub is the largest producer of phosphate rock in Florida. It further appears that Florida produced over 80% of the nation's marketable phosphate rock and one-third of the world production thereof in 1973. The affidavit goes on to explain that the storing of phosphate slimes in diked settling ponds is an essential part of the traditional method of mining phosphate rock. Hence, Cities Service argues that its mining operations were a natural and intended use of this particular land.

There have been many American cases which have passed upon the question of whether a particular use of the land was natural or non-natural for the purpose of applying the *Rylands v. Fletcher* doctrine. Thus, *Prosser, Supra*, states at page 510:

> The conditions and activities to which the rule has been applied have followed the English pattern. They include water collected in quantity in a dangerous place, or allowed to percolate; explosives or inflammable liquids stored in quantity in the midst of a city; blasting; pile driving; crop dusting; the fumigation of part of a building with cyanide gas; drilling oil wells or operating refineries in thickly settled communities; an excavation letting in the sea; factories emitting smoke, dust or noxious gases in the midst of a town; roofs so constructed as to shed snow into a highway; and a dangerous party wall.

> On the other hand the conditions and activities to which the American courts have refused to apply *Rylands v. Fletcher*, whether they purport to accept or to reject the case in principle, have been with few exceptions what the English courts would regard as a 'natural' use of land, and not within the rule at all. They include water in household pipes, the tank of a humidity system or authorized utility mains; gas in a meter, electric wiring in a machine shop, and gasoline in a filling station; a dam in the natural bed of a stream; ordinary steam boilers; an ordinary fire in a factory; an automobile; Bermuda grass on a railroad right of way; a small quantity of dynamite kept for sale in a Texas hardware store, barnyard spray in a farmhouse; a division fence; the wall of a house left standing after a fire; coal mining operations regarded as usual and normal; vibrations from ordinary building construction; earth moving operations in grading a hillside; the construction of a railroad tunnel; and even a runaway horse. There remain a few cases, including such things as water reservoirs or irrigation ditches in dry country, or properly conducted oil wells in Texas or Oklahoma, which are un-doubtedly best explained upon the basis of a different community view which makes such things 'natural' to the particular locality. The conclusion is, in short, that the American decisions, like the English ones, have applied the principle of *Rylands v. Fletcher* only to the thing out of place, the abnormally dangerous condition or activity which is not a 'natural' one where it is. (Emphasis supplied)

* * *

In the final analysis, we are impressed by the magnitude of the activity and the attendant risk of enormous damage. The impounding of billions of gallons of phosphatic slimes behind earthen walls which are subject to breaking even with the exercise of the best of care strikes us as being both 'ultrahazardous' and 'abnormally dangerous,' as the case may be.

This is not clear water which is being impounded. Here, Cities Service introduced water into its mining operation which when combined with phosphatic wastes produced a phosphatic slime which had a high potential for damage to the environment. If a break occurred, it was to be expected that extensive damage would be visited upon property many miles away. In this case, the damage, in fact, extended almost to the mouth of the Peace River, which is far beyond the phosphate mining area described in the Cities Service affidavit. We conclude that the Cities Service slime reservoir constituted a non-natural use of the land such as to invoke the doctrine of strict liability.

Ordinarily, the determination of whether or not a particular structure or method of operation is natural or non-natural is one which would require the trial court's evaluation of all of the pertinent factors at a trial. However, we believe that in this case the liability may be properly determined by way of summary judgment.... From the transcript of the testimony taken in connection with the injunction proceedings, it is evident that despite the best of care, earthen dams enclosing phosphate settling ponds do give way from time to time without explanation. All of the assertions of Cities Service relative to the need to maintain settling ponds in its mining operations, the suitability of the land for this purpose and the importance of phosphate to the community as well as to the world at large may be accepted at face value. Admitting the desirability of phosphate and the necessity of mining in this manner, the rights of adjoining landowners and the interests of the public in our environment require the imposition of a doctrine which places the burden upon the parties whose activity made it possible for the damages to occur.

Affirmed.

Exercise 3-6 Applying Factors

A number of jurisdictions have adopted Restatement Torts (Second) § 520, which proposes consideration of the following factors to determine whether an activity is abnormally dangerous:

(a) Whether the activity involves a high degree of risk of some harm to the person, land or chattels of others;

(b) Whether the harm which may result from it is likely to be great;

(c) Whether the risk cannot be eliminated by the exercise of reasonable care;

(d) Whether the activity is not a matter of common usage;

(e) Whether the activity is inappropriate to the place where it is carried on; and

(f) The value of the activity to the community.

1. What is the difference between a rule with factors and a rule with elements?

2. Would application of these factors explain the result in *Turner*? In *Cities Services*?

3. Would application of these factors change your analysis of the problem set out in exercise 3-5?

4. Do you believe such a rule provides greater certainty (or better guidance) to attorneys evaluating whether an activity is abnormally dangerous? Consider the following cases:

Klein v. Pyrodyne Corp.

117 Wash.2d 1 (1991)

The plaintiffs in this case are persons injured when an aerial shell at a public fireworks exhibition went astray and exploded near them. The defendant is the pyrotechnic company hired to set up and discharge the fireworks. The issue before this court is whether pyrotechnicians are strictly liable for damages caused by fireworks displays. We hold that they are.

* * *

FIREWORKS DISPLAYS AS ABNORMALLY DANGEROUS ACTIVITIES

The Kleins contend that strict liability is the appropriate standard to determine the culpability of Pyrodyne because Pyrodyne was participating in an abnormally dangerous activity. This court has addressed liability for fireworks display injuries on one prior occasion. In *Callahan v. Keystone Fireworks Mfg. Co.*, 72 Wash.2d 823, 435 P.2d 626 (1967), this court held that a pyrotechnician could maintain a negligence suit against the manufacturer of the defective fireworks. The issue as to whether fireworks displays are abnormally dangerous activities subject to strict liability was not raised before the court at that time, and hence remains open for this court to decide.

The modern doctrine of strict liability for abnormally dangerous activities derives from *Fletcher v. Rylands,* 159 Eng.Rep. 737 (1865), *rev'd,* 1 L.R.-Ex. 265, [1866] All E.R. 1, 6, *aff'd sub nom. Rylands v. Fletcher,* 3 L.R.-H.L. 330, [1868] All E.R. 1, 12, in which the defendant's reservoir flooded mine shafts on the plaintiff's adjoining land. *Rylands v. Fletcher* has come to stand for the rule that "the defendant will be liable when he damages another by a thing or activity unduly dangerous and inappropriate to the place where it is maintained, in the light of the character of that place and its surroundings." W. Keeton, D. Dobbs, R. Keeton & D. Owen, *Prosser and Keeton on Torts* § 78, at 547–48 (5th ed. 1984).

The basic principle of *Rylands v. Fletcher* has been accepted by the Restatement (Second) of Torts (1977). *See generally Prosser and Keeton* § 78, at 551 (explaining that the relevant Restatement sections differ in some respects from the *Rylands* doctrine). Section 519 of the Restatement provides that any party carrying on an "abnormally dangerous activity" is strictly liable for ensuing damages. The test for what constitutes such an activity is stated in section 520 of the Restatement. Both Restatement sections have been adopted by this court, and determination of whether an activity is an "abnormally dangerous activity" is a question of law. *New Meadows Holding Co. v. Washington Water Power Co.,* 102 Wash.2d 495, 500, 687 P.2d 212 (1984); *Langan v. Valicopters, Inc.,* 88 Wash.2d 855, 567 P.2d 218 (1977); *Siegler v. Kuhlman,* 81 Wash.2d 448, 502 P.2d 1181 (1972), *cert. denied,* 411 U.S. 983, 93 S.Ct. 2275, 36 L.Ed.2d 959 (1973).

Section 520 of the Restatement lists six factors that are to be considered in determining whether an activity is "abnormally dangerous". The factors are as follows:

(a) existence of a high degree of risk of some harm to the person, land or chattels of others;

(b) likelihood that the harm that results from it will be great;

(c) inability to eliminate the risk by the exercise of reasonable care;

(d) extent to which the activity is not a matter of common usage;

(e) inappropriateness of the activity to the place where it is carried on; and

(f) extent to which its value to the community is outweighed by its dangerous attributes.

Restatement (Second) of Torts § 520 (1977). As we previously recognized in *Langan v. Valicopters, Inc., supra,* 88 Wash.2d at 861–62, 567 P.2d 218 (citing Tent. Draft No. 10, 1964, of comment (f) to section 520), the comments to section 520 explain how these factors should be evaluated:

Any one of them is not necessarily sufficient of itself in a particular case, and ordinarily several of them will be required for strict liability. On the other hand, it is not necessary that each of them be present, especially if others weigh heavily. Because of the interplay of these various factors, it is not possible to reduce abnormally dangerous activities to any definition. The essential question is whether the risk created is so unusual, either because of its magnitude or because of the circumstances surrounding it, as to justify the imposition of strict liability for the harm that results from it, even though it is carried on with all reasonable care.

Restatement (Second) of Torts § 520, comment *f* (1977). Examination of these factors persuades us that fireworks displays are abnormally dangerous activities justifying the imposition of strict liability.

We find that the factors stated in clauses (a), (b), and (c) are all present in the case of fireworks displays. Any time a person ignites aerial shells or rockets with the intention of sending them aloft to explode in the presence of large crowds of people, a high risk of serious personal injury or property damage is created. That risk arises because of the possibility that a shell or rocket will malfunction or be misdirected. Furthermore, no matter how much care pyrotechnicians exercise, they cannot entirely eliminate the high risk inherent in setting off powerful explosives such as fireworks near crowds.

The dangerousness of fireworks displays is evidenced by the elaborate scheme of administrative regulations with which pyrotechnicians must comply. Pyrotechnicians must be licensed to conduct public displays of special fireworks. WAC 212-17-220. To obtain such a license, the pyrotechnician must take and pass a written examination administered by the director of fire protection, and must submit evidence of qualifications and experience, including "participation in the firing of at least six public displays as an assistant, at least one of which shall have been in the current or preceding year." WAC 212-17-225. The pyrotechnician's application for a license must be investigated by the director of fire protection, who must confirm that the applicant is competent and experienced. WAC 212-17-230. Licensed pyrotechnicians are charged with ensuring that the display is set up in accordance with all rules and regulations. WAC 212-17-235. Regulations also govern such matters as the way in which the fireworks at public displays are constructed, stored, installed, and fired. WAC 212-17-305, -310, -315, and -335. The necessity for such regulations demonstrates the dangerousness of fireworks displays.

Pyrodyne argues that if the regulations are complied with, then the high degree of risk otherwise inherent in the displays can be eliminated. Although we recognize that the high risk can be reduced, we do not agree that it can be eliminated. Setting off powerful fireworks near large crowds remains a highly risky activity even when the safety precautions mandated by statutes and regulations are followed. The Legislature appears to agree, for it has declared that in order to obtain a license to conduct a public fireworks display, a pyrotechnician must first obtain a surety bond or a certificate of insurance, the amount of which must be at least $1,000,000 for each event. RCW 70.77.285, .295.

The factors stated in clauses (a), (b), and (c) together, and sometimes one of them alone, express what is commonly meant by saying an activity is ultrahazardous. Restatement (Second) of Torts § 520, comment *h* (1977). As the Restatement explains, however, "[l]iability for abnormally dangerous activities is not ... a matter of these three factors alone, and those stated in Clauses (d), (e), and (f) must still be taken into account." Restatement (Second) of Torts § 520, comment *h* (1977); *see also New Meadows Holding Co. v. Washington Water Power Co., supra,* 102 Wash.2d at 504, 687 P.2d 212 (Pearson, J., concurring) ("strict liability ... may not be imposed absent the presence of at least one of the factors stated in clauses (d), (e), and (f)").

The factor expressed in clause (d) concerns the extent to which the activity is not a matter "of common usage". The Restatement explains that "[a]n activity is a matter of common usage if it is customarily carried on by the great mass of mankind or by many people in the community." Restatement (Second) of Torts § 520, comment *i* (1977). As examples of activities that are not matters of common usage, the Restatement comments offer driving a tank, blasting, the manufacture, storage, transportation, and use of high explosives, and drilling for oil. The deciding characteristic is that few persons engage in these activities. Likewise, relatively few persons conduct public fireworks displays. Therefore, presenting public fireworks displays is not a matter of common usage.

Pyrodyne argues that the factor stated in clause (d) is not met because fireworks are a common way to celebrate the 4th of July. We reject this argument. Although fireworks are frequently and regularly enjoyed by the public, few persons set off special fireworks displays. Indeed, the general public is prohibited by statute from making public fireworks displays insofar as anyone wishing to do so must first obtain a license. RCW 70.77.255.

The factor stated in clause (e) requires analysis of the appropriateness of the activity to the place where it was carried on. In this case, the fireworks display was conducted at the Puyallup Fairgrounds. Although some locations—such as over water—may be safer, the Puyallup Fairgrounds is an appropriate place for a fireworks show because the audience can be seated at a reasonable distance from the display. Therefore, the clause (e) factor is not present in this case.

The factor stated in clause (f) requires analysis of the extent to which the value of fireworks to the community outweighs its dangerous attributes. We do not find that this factor is present here. This country has a long-standing tradition of fireworks on the 4th of July. That tradition suggests that we as a society have decided that the value of fireworks on the day celebrating our national independence and unity outweighs the risks of injuries and damage.

In sum, we find that setting off public fireworks displays satisfies four of the six conditions under the Restatement test; that is, it is an activity that is not "of common usage" and that presents an ineliminably high risk of serious bodily injury or property damage. We therefore hold that conducting public fireworks displays is an abnormally dangerous activity justifying the imposition of strict liability.

This conclusion is consistent with the results reached in cases involving damages caused by detonating dynamite. This court has recognized that parties detonating dynamite are strictly liable for the damages caused by such blasting. *See Foster v. Preston Mill Co.,* 44 Wash.2d 440, 443, 268 P.2d 645 (1954); *see also Bringle v. Lloyd,* 13 Wash.App. 844, 537 P.2d 1060 (1975); *Erickson Paving Co. v. Yardley Drilling Co.,* 7 Wash.App. 681, 502 P.2d

334 (1972). There are a number of similarities between fireworks and dynamite. Both activities involve licensed experts intentionally igniting for profit explosives that have great potential for causing damage. Moreover, after the explosion no evidence remains as to the original explosive. The notable difference between fireworks and dynamite is that with fireworks the public is invited to watch the display and with dynamite the public is generally prohibited from being near the blasting location. Because detonating dynamite is subject to strict liability, and because of the similarities between fireworks and dynamite, strict liability is also an appropriate standard for determining the standard of liability for pyrotechnicians for any damages caused by their fireworks displays.

PUBLIC POLICY AND STRICT LIABILITY FOR FIREWORKS DISPLAYS

Policy considerations also support imposing strict liability on pyrotechnicians for damages caused by their public fireworks displays, although such considerations are not alone sufficient to justify that conclusion. Most basic is the question as to who should bear the loss when an innocent person suffers injury through the nonculpable but abnormally dangerous activities of another. In the case of public fireworks displays, fairness weighs in favor of requiring the pyrotechnicians who present the displays to bear the loss rather than the unfortunate spectators who suffer the injuries. In addition,

> [t]he rule of strict liability rests not only upon the ultimate idea of rectifying a wrong and putting the burden where it should belong as a matter of abstract justice, that is, upon the one of the two innocent parties whose acts instigated or made the harm possible, but it also rests on problems of proof:
>
>> One of these common features is that the person harmed would encounter a difficult problem of proof if some other standard of liability were applied. For example, the disasters caused by those who engage in abnormally dangerous or extra-hazardous activities frequently destroy all evidence of what in fact occurred, other than that the activity was being carried on. Certainly this is true with explosions of dynamite, large quantities of gasoline, or other explosives.

Siegler v. Kuhlman, 81 Wash.2d 448, 455, 502 P.2d 1181 (1972), *cert. denied,* 411 U.S. 983, 93 S.Ct. 2275, 36 L.Ed.2d 959 (1973) (quoting Peck, *Negligence and Liability Without Fault in Tort Law,* 46 Wash.L.Rev. 225, 240 (1971)). In the present case, all evidence was destroyed as to what caused the misfire of the shell that injured the Kleins. Therefore, the problem of proof this case presents for the plaintiffs also supports imposing strict liability on Pyrodyne.

* * *

CONCLUSION

We hold that Pyrodyne Corporation is strictly liable for all damages suffered as a result of the July 1987 fireworks display. Detonating fireworks displays constitutes an abnormally dangerous activity warranting strict liability. Public policy also supports this conclusion.... Therefore, we affirm the decision of the trial court.

Cadena v. Chicago Fireworks Mfg. Co.

297 Ill.App.3d 945 (1998)

Plaintiffs ... appeal from an order of the circuit court granting summary judgment in favor of defendant City of Chicago Heights (City). ***

On July 3, 1991, Chicago Fireworks Manufacturing Company, who is not a party to this appeal, conducted a Fourth of July fireworks display at Bloom Township High School in the City of Chicago Heights. The City's administrator, Enrico Doggett (Doggett), was in charge of coordinating all activities surrounding the fireworks display. *** During the fireworks display, one of the fireworks misfired and landed in the crowd which had gathered to view the display, injuring the Cadenas....

In response to the City's motion for summary judgment, the Cadenas argued that: the City was engaged in an ultrahazardous activity and was therefore strictly liable for any injuries caused by the fireworks display. *** In reply, the City contended that: Illinois case law did not support plaintiffs' argument that the use of fireworks was an ultrahazardous activity. ***

Illinois courts have either implicitly or explicitly adopted the Restatement (Second) of Torts (Restatement) in analyzing whether an activity should be considered ultrahazardous. *** Section 520 sets forth the following factors to be considered in determining whether an activity is abnormally dangerous or ultrahazardous:

"(a) existence of a high degree of risk of some harm to the person, land or chattels of others;

(b) likelihood that the harm that results from it will be great;

(c) inability to eliminate the risk by the exercise of reasonable care;

(d) extent to which the activity is not a matter of common usage;

(e) inappropriateness of the activity to the place where it is carried on; and

(f) extent to which its value to the community is outweighed by its dangerous attributes."

Restatement (Second) of Torts § 520 (1977).

"The terms 'ultrahazardous,' 'abnormally dangerous,' or 'intrinsically dangerous,' as traditionally used, refer to that type of danger which is inherent in the instrumentality itself at all times and do not mean danger which arises from mere casual or collateral negligence of others with respect to it under the particular circumstances." *Fallon,* 148 Ill.App.3d at 935, 102 Ill.Dec. 479, 500 N.E.2d 101. The *Miller* court, in holding that the use of firearms is not an ultrahazardous activity, described the following approach in analyzing whether an activity should be considered ultrahazardous:

"While all of these [Restatement] factors are important and should be considered, ordinarily the presence of more than one factor, but not all of them, will be necessary to declare the activity ultrahazardous as a matter of law so as to hold the actor strictly liable. The essential question is whether the risk created is so unusual, either because of its magnitude or because of the circumstances surrounding it, as to justify the imposition of strict liability even though the activity is carried on with all reasonable care. [Citation.] Considerations of public policy also enter prominently into the decisions by our courts to impose strict liability (at least in product liability cases). [Citation.] Particular consideration is also given to the appropriateness of the activity to the place where it is maintained, in light of the character of the place and its surroundings * * *." *Miller,* 272 Ill.App.3d at 270, 209 Ill.Dec. 311, 651 N.E.2d 239.

Based on the factors listed in section 520 of the Restatement, we find that the displaying of fireworks is not an ultrahazardous activity. While plaintiffs argue that because the detonation of explosives has been found to be ultrahazardous and fireworks are a form of explosives, therefore this court should find that fireworks displays constitute an ultrahazardous activity, this comparison alone is not enough to support a finding that a fireworks display is an ultrahazardous activity under an analysis of the factors listed in section 520 of the Restatement. While factors (a) and (b) of the Restatement are arguably met because there exists a high degree of risk of some harm to a person during a fireworks display, and the likelihood that the harm that results from it will be great because of the explosive nature of fireworks, the other factors listed in the Restatement are not met. Under factor (c), the exercise of reasonable care in displaying fireworks will significantly reduce the risks involved. Moreover, section (c) does not require the reduction of *all* risk, and indeed, there exists significant risk using a firearm, an activity which this court has previously determined is not an ultrahazardous activity. *Miller,* 272 Ill.App.3d at 270–71, 209 Ill.Dec. 311, 651 N.E.2d 239. Under factor (d), while displaying fireworks is not a common activity undertaken by a large amount of individuals, certainly many individuals view them and many municipalities display fireworks. Thus, fireworks displays *are* a matter of common usage. Under factor (e), we assume that the location was appropriate for the fireworks display in the absence of factual allegations in plaintiffs' complaint specifically describing the area as inappropriate for fireworks displays. See *Miller,* 272 Ill.App.3d at 271, 209 Ill.Dec. 311, 651 N.E.2d 239. Lastly, we determine, based on the fact that the general public enjoys fireworks displays to celebrate every July 4, they are of some social utility to communities. Therefore, we find that the value of the fireworks display is not outweighed by its dangerous attributes. Accordingly, we find that a fireworks display is not an ultrahazardous activity as a matter of law.

* * *

We further briefly note that we find plaintiffs' contention, that other jurisdictions have found the displaying of fireworks to be an ultrahazardous activity, unpersuasive. As the City argues, only one jurisdiction has explicitly found that such activity is ultrahazardous. See *Klein v. Pyrodyne Corporation,* 117 Wash.2d 1, 810 P.2d 917 (1991). We decline to follow *Klein,* and disagree with that court's determination that the risk involved in fireworks displays cannot be sufficiently reduced and that the value of fireworks displays to the community does not outweigh their dangerous attributes. While the other jurisdictions that plaintiffs cite do state that fireworks are *dangerous,* such a determination is not enough to find that the displaying of fireworks is an ultrahazardous activity.

* * *

For the reasons stated, the judgment of the circuit court is affirmed.

Affirmed.

Exercise 3-7 Improving the "A" in IRAC — Explaining Your Reasoning

Frequently feedback on student essay exams contains statements indicating that the analysis is "cursory" or "conclusory" (or it may simply contain the statement "why?"). Students may struggle to understand (1) what such feedback means, and (2) how to "fix" the problem.

Simply stated, each of these comments is meant to communicate to a student that he or she is not explaining the reasons or basis for his or her conclusion. The problem may exist, at least in part, because the "analysis" students read in court opinions does not always model the type of "analysis" expected in exams. For example, in *Cardenas,* the court's "analysis" of factor c, "inability to eliminate the risk by the exercise of reasonable care" was as follows:

> Under factor (c), the exercise of reasonable care in displaying fireworks
> will significantly reduce the risks involved. Moreover, section (c) does

not require the reduction of *all* risk, and indeed, there exists significant risk using a firearm, an activity which this court has previously determined is not an ultrahazardous activity.

This type of "analysis" would likely receive a very low grade from a law school professor because it does not really explain why reasonable care would eliminate the risk, it simply concludes that (1) all risk does not have to be eliminated, and (2) reasonable care eliminated a sufficient amount. Compare the analysis above, with the analysis of the same factor from the decision in *Lipka v. DiLungo*, 26 Conn. L. Rptr. 654 (2000):

> (c) Inability to eliminate the risk by the exercise of due care. Connecticut General Statute § 29-357, is a legislative determination that the risk associated with fireworks displays will be reduced by the exercise of due care. That risk, however, will not be eliminated. Fireworks are, by definition, explosive devices, and incidents of injuries to spectators of carefully conducted municipal displays will occasionally occur. Conn.Gen.Stat. § 29-359 recognizes this fact by requiring persons conducting lawful fireworks displays to "furnish proof of financial responsibility to satisfy claims for damages" resulting from such displays. This supports the conclusion that an unavoidable risk remains in the case of a lawful fireworks display. Factor (c) is established here.

1. What differences are there between this paragraph and the "analysis" in *Cardenas*?

2. Which one is better? Why?

3. Could this paragraph be improved? How?

4. Find the analysis of this same factor in *Klein*. Did you have trouble isolating the analysis of factor (c) from the analysis of other factors? Why or why not? Is the issue identified more clearly in the preceding paragraph from *Lipka*? Does identifying the specific issue you are addressing make it easier for the reader to follow?

5. When you read cases (in this text and other classes), be sure to evaluate the court's analysis to determine whether it is "conclusory." Where it is, try re-writing the analysis to reflect the type of analysis you will be expected to do on essay examinations and in practice.

6. How does this apply to your own writing?

C. Causation

Once a plaintiff establishes that strict liability applies to the defendant's conduct, her next hurdle is to prove causation. The plaintiff's injury must result from that which makes the activity abnormally dangerous, or plaintiff will not be entitled to recover.

For example, in *Foster v. Preston Mill Co.*, 268 P.2d 645 (1954), plaintiffs sued a blasting operation for injury resulting from the noise and vibrations. Plaintiffs, who operated a mink farm, claimed the noise frightened their mink to such an extent that the older mink killed their young. The court held that because the damage suffered was not the kind of harm that was within the scope of the abnormal risk posed by blasting activity there was no liability (for the cause of action based on strict liability).

Exercise 3-8 Evaluating Causation

What would be the result under the statutes set out in exercise 3-1, if a plaintiff sued for injury resulting from tripping and falling over a dog?

Chapter Four

The "Burden" of Proof: Marshalling the Evidence — Strict Products Liability

Objectives

Learning and Study Skills

Practice case reading skills

Write an essay examination answer to a strict products liability problem

Law Practice Skills

Be able to present complex factual and legal material in an accessible form

Determine whether expert testimony is needed and how such testimony would help the trier of fact

Evaluate witness testimony to determine whether a party has satisfied their burden of proof for the elements of a claim or defense

Examine a witness to elicit information that establishes the elements of a claim or defense

Understand how interrogatories are used to obtain evidence to help prove a claim or defense

Understand the difference between direct and circumstantial evidence, and how circumstantial evidence is used to prove elements of a strict products liability claim

Understand the reasons courts classify items as products or non products

Determine who should be named as a defendant in a suit based on strict products liability

Be able to identify whether a product has a manufacturing, design and/or warning defect

Determine whether a warning is adequate

Understand how allegations of product misuse impact proof of causation

Apply a deconstructed rule or statute to solve a problem

Apply and distinguish legal precedent

Synthesize materials

Find and utilize research relating to products that are the subject of an action for strict products liability

Substantive Legal Knowledge

State the requirements for proving a cause of action for strict products liability, including:

How courts determine whether an item is a product;

The rule for determining whether defendant was a seller, manufacturer or distributor of an injury causing product

The tests courts employ to determent whether there is a defect in:

Manufacturing

Design

Warning

The methods available for proving a defect existed when a product left the defendant's control

Introduction

When a product injures someone there are several potential causes of action a plaintiff may allege. The plaintiff may allege that the seller, manufacturer or distributor of the product was negligent, or breached a warranty under the uniform commercial code or misrepresented information about the product, or is strictly liable for placing a defective product in the stream of commerce. This collective set of causes of action is sometimes referred to as "products liability." This chapter will focus on the strict liability based cause of action, which is also referred to as "products liability." To avoid confusion in this chapter, any time the term products liability appears, it is a reference to the strict liability based cause of action—the only cause of action covered in this chapter.

Strict products liability, in reality, is not truly strict liability—where the plaintiff need simply prove the category of conduct is covered by strict liability (i.e., making and distributing products), injury and causation. To establish liability based on a cause of action for strict products liability plaintiff must also prove the product was defective. More specifically, to prevail in a modern strict products liability suit a plaintiff must prove:

(1) The item causing the injury is one that is classified as a product;

(2) The defendant was a seller, manufacturer or distributor of the product that injured plaintiff;

(3) The product was defective, at the time the product left the defendant's control;

(4) The product defect caused the plaintiff's harm.

The elements for establishing a prima facie case vary based on both the jurisdiction and the particular type of product defect at issue in the case, but generally speaking most jurisdictions require some version of these elements. In this chapter we will consider each of these requirements, and you will use what you learn to evaluate the chapter problem.

Chapter Problem

As part of a "go green" initiative, BookCo began manufacturing books using elephant dung paper. Elephant dung paper can be manufactured without the harsh (and environmentally unfriendly) chemicals and bleaches normally used in the paper production process. Also, elephant dung is a renewable source of raw material, unlike wood pulp, the traditional raw material for paper, the use of which depletes forests. This makes elephant dung paper an environmentally responsible alternative to ordinary paper.

BookCo desired to use locally "produced" elephant dung because, in addition to the benefits described above, it decreases BookCo's carbon footprint because it substantially reduces the amount of energy necessary for transporting the elephant dung. The dung used in BookCo's manufacturing process is from local elephants—usually elephants traveling with a local circus (hereafter, the "circus elephants").

Elephants are poor digesters of their food and over 50% of what they eat is excreted in their dung. In addition to their regular diet of fruits and vegetables, the circus elephants consume a substantial quantity of peanuts because many circus patrons feed elephants peanuts, erroneously believing elephants like peanuts. Peanuts make up about 10–15% of the circus elephants diet. This is far more than the average amount of peanuts in a typical elephant's diet. A typical elephant's diet contains between 0–2% peanut products (meaning there are many elephants that do not consume any peanuts or peanut products as part of their diet).

BookCo could purchase and import enough peanut-free elephant dung from Africa and Asia to make their product, although it would substantially increase production costs of the dung paper, as well as substantially increase BookCo's carbon footprint.

Sierra purchased a paper journal manufactured by BookCo using elephant dung paper. The label contained the following statement: "This product was manufactured using 100% elephant dung paper. There are no toxic chemicals used in our paper-making process. No Bleach. No Acids."

Sierra is highly allergic to peanuts (an allergy that affects approximately 2% of the population). While Sierra was writing in her BookCo journal, she began to experience an allergic reaction to the peanut fibers in the elephant dung paper. She was able to dial 911 before her airway began to swell, her blood pressure dropped and she lost consciousness. Luckily, she was rescued. She spent 24 hours in the hospital and was released. She suffered no further injuries.

Sierra's reaction was extreme. She suffered what is known as anaphylactic shock, an allergic reaction in which the release of histamine causes swelling, difficulty in breathing, heart failure, circulatory collapse, and sometimes death. Most peanut allergy sufferers will experience some minor level of discomfort, including skin rashes, stuffy or runny noses, and/or gastrointestinal problems (like nausea and vomiting) if they come into contact with peanut particles.

In the food industry it is standard to warn consumers if a food (1) contains (or may contain) peanuts; or (2) is manufactured on equipment that manufactures other products with peanuts; or (3) is produced in a facility that also processes peanuts. No such standard warning exists in the book industry.

1. Is the Item that Caused the Injury a Product?

The first issue to consider is whether the item is one that is classified as a product. The modern trend in product liability actions is for courts to define what does (and does not) constitute a product based solely on the jurisdiction's social policy. To make matters more challenging, some of the "products" recognized by one jurisdiction will be excluded by other jurisdictions applying identical policy considerations. This means that in order to persuade a court to classify an item as a product, and bring the claim under the umbrella of strict products liability a lawyer must do more than recite appropriate social policy. She must use the facts and available evidence in the case to show the applicability of the social policies to her particular case—similar to what you practiced in Chapter Three, in arguing for the applicability of strict liability to other activities. When determining whether an item is a product (and strict liability should apply) courts have considered a number of social policy concerns, including: American competitiveness worldwide; accident prevention; insurance costs; and whether regulatory systems such as worker's compensation, medical insurance, and administrative regulations of health and safety provide sufficient protections and safety incentives.

The chart below contains examples of items courts have defined as products (for which there is strict liability) and non products (for which there is no claim for strict liability). As you consider these examples, and the reading, ask yourself why courts might have classified the items this way (i.e., what social policy reasons may exist for such classifications).

Product	Non Product
• a bus shelter • leased cars or planes • roofing material installed and made part of a roof • video games • heating and air systems attached to a building • aeronautical charts • component parts (separately or assembled with other component parts) • prefabricated buildings • mass produced housing • live animals	• financial lease agreements • custom-made and/or partially completed goods • "how-to" books and textbooks • video games • private swimming pools • a water slide and other improvements to real property • a glass shower door in an apartment • a condominium • a rental housing complex • commercial premises • live animals

Some items may be specifically excluded from the definition of products. For example, in most jurisdictions human blood and human tissue are not considered "products." Services are also not considered products, even if the service provided relates directly to a product. For example, if someone inspects and repairs a machine, they are a provider of a product-related service, rather than the provider of a product. If however, the same repairer replaces a component part on a machine with a new part, the replacement of the part constitutes sale of a product (the part). Note that the repair itself still constitutes a service.

In some cases the surrounding circumstances may dictate whether an item may be considered a product. For example, when a suit is based on the information contained within a book, most courts will not impose strict liability for fear that it would significantly infringe on free speech. On the other hand, some courts have imposed strict products liability in cases involving information contained in maps and navigational charts. As you read the next two cases, think about why (for purposes of imposing strict liability) there might be a distinction between information in a book and information contained in a map or navigational chart:

Way v. Boy Scouts of America
856 S.W.2d 230, 238–39 (Tex.Ct.App.1993)

Jan Way, individually and on behalf of the estate of Rocky William Miller, deceased, sued the Boy Scouts of America, National Shooting Sports Foundation, Inc., and Remington Arms Company, Inc. claiming that a supplement on shooting sports published in *Boys' Life* magazine caused the death of her son. Way's twelve-year-old son, Rocky, read the supplement on shooting sports and was later killed when the rifle he and several friends were playing with accidentally discharged. The trial court granted appellees' motions for summary judgment. Appellant contends the trial court erred in granting summary judgment. Because we conclude that Texas law does not recognize a cause of action for publication of an article or advertisement that causes harm under these circumstances, we affirm the trial court's judgment.

BACKGROUND

Included in the September 1988 edition of *Boys' Life* magazine was an advertising supplement on shooting sports, sponsored by National Shooting Sports Foundation Inc., in which Remington Arms Company, Inc., placed an advertisement. Included in the sixteen-page supplement were advertisements for firearms and ammunition manufacturers. With the various manufacturer advertisements, the supplement contained the following articles: *How it Feels to Carry Our Flag at the Olympics, Experience Biathlon, Qualify for a Presidential Sports Award, Earn Your Straight Shooter Award,* and *Getting Started in the Shooting Sports.* These articles supplied information about earning merit badges for shooting; the biathlon, an Olympic shooting sport; the Presidential Sports Award, which can be earned for accomplishments in the shooting sports; and getting started in the shooting sports. The supplement also included a checklist on firearm safety.

After reading the September supplement and obtaining information on shooting sports, Rocky and several of his friends located an old rifle and a .22-caliber cartridge. On November 19, 1988, Rocky was killed when the rifle accidentally discharged.

Jan Way sued the Boy Scouts of America, National Shooting Sports Foundation, Inc., and Remington Arms Company, Inc., for the death of her son. Way based her action on theories of negligence and strict products liability, claiming negligent publication of supplemental material in *Boys' Life* magazine and that the information contained in the supplement made the magazine a defective product. She alleged her son was motivated to experiment with the rifle and cartridge as a direct result of the supplemental edition to the September 1988 edition of *Boys' Life* magazine published by the Boy Scouts of America.

The Boy Scouts of America and the National Shooting Sports Foundation filed motions for summary judgment alleging: (1) Texas law does not recognize a cause of action for negligent publication, and no duty was owed to plaintiff; (2) there was no duty to warn of the allegedly dangerous nature of the supplement; (3) no special duty was owed to plaintiff, a minor; (4) no statute was violated; (5) *Boys' Life* magazine and the supplement are not "products"; and (6) the claims are barred by the First Amendment of the United States Constitution and article I, section eight of the Texas Constitution. Remington Arms' motion for summary judgment asserted: (1) no duty; (2) the First Amendment of the United States Constitution; and (3) article I, section eight of the Texas Constitution.

The Texas Supreme Court has adopted the theory of strict tort liability as the rule applicable to defective products that cause physical harm to persons. *McKisson v. Sales Affiliates, Inc.,* 416 S.W.2d 787, 789 (Tex.1967). The very essence of a products liability cause of action is the existence of a *product*.

Way relies on *Brocklesby v. United States,* 767 F.2d 1288 (9th Cir.1985), *cert. denied,* 474 U.S. 1101, 106 S.Ct. 882, 88 L.Ed.2d 918 (1986); *Saloomey v. Jeppesen & Co.,* 707 F.2d 671 (2d Cir.1983); and *Fluor Corp. v. Jeppesen & Co.,* 170 Cal.App.3d 468, 216 Cal.Rptr. 68 (1985), to support her contention that the advertising supplement was a product. These three cases are factually distinguishable from the present case.

All three cases involved aircraft charts and flight maps that erroneously depicted data necessary for the navigation and operation of an airplane. In those cases, the charts were physically used in the operation of the aircraft at the time of the accident. The inaccurate data directly caused or was alleged to have caused the accidents in question in the same manner in which a broken compass or an inaccurate altimeter would have caused a plane to crash.

Here, Way is not complaining about the physical properties of the supplement. She alleges the ideas and information contained in the magazine encouraged children to engage in activities that were dangerous. These are intangible characteristics, not tangible properties. The Ninth Circuit explained the distinction between tangible and intangible aspects of a publication as follows:

> A book containing Shakespeare's sonnets consists of two parts, the material and the print therein, and the ideas and expression thereof. The first may be a product, but the second is not. The latter, were Shakespeare alive, would be governed by copyright laws; the laws of libel, to the extent consistent with the First Amendment; and the laws of misrepresentation, negligent misrepresentation, negligence, and mistake. These doctrines applicable to the second part are aimed at the delicate issues that arise with respect to intangibles such as ideas and expression. Products liability law is geared to the tangible world.

Winter v. G.P. Putnam's Sons, 938 F.2d 1033, 1034 (9th Cir.1991). In *Winter,* the plaintiffs consulted *The Encyclopedia of Mushrooms* in gathering and cooking mushrooms. After eating the mushrooms, they became sick. The plaintiffs analogized their case to the ones involving defective aeronautical charts to support their cause of action for products liability. The *Winter* court rejected this argument. The court found the aeronautical charts to be highly technical tools similar to a compass. In contrast, the court found the *Encyclopedia of Mushrooms* to be like a book on how to use a compass or aeronautical chart. The court further found that although the chart itself is like a physical product, the how-to-use book is pure thought and expression. The court concluded there was no basis for a products liability action.

Additionally, in *Herceg v. Hustler Magazine,* a diversity case applying Texas law, the court summarized the law in this area as follows:

> Plaintiffs' claims under strict liability are without support in existing case law.
> The Court is aware of no court which has held that the content of a magazine

or other publication is a product. Rather, they have held to the contrary. *Herceg*, 565 F.Supp. at 803.

We conclude that the ideas, thoughts, words, and information conveyed by the magazine and the shooting sports supplement are not *products*.

Way additionally contends: (1) the magazine was dangerous in the design of its content because the inclusion of the commercial shooting supplement rendered the product unreasonably dangerous; and (2) appellees had a duty to furnish adequate warnings and instructions for the safe use of the product. Because we find the content of the magazine and supplement are not products within the meaning of the Restatement (Second) of Torts, these contentions are also without merit.

We conclude the trial court did not err in granting appellees' motions for summary judgment. We have determined that Way cannot prevail on any of her pleaded theories. Therefore, we need not discuss appellees' affirmative defenses. We affirm the trial court's judgment.

The *Way* court distinguished the following case (and cases like it). Do you agree that there is a distinction between the map at issue in the next case and the periodical at issue in *Way*? Why?

Aetna Cas. & Sur. Co. v. Jeppesen & Co.

642 F.2d 339, 341–42 (9th Cir.1981)

This appeal is taken from judgment granting Aetna Casualty and Surety Company indemnity from Jeppesen & Company for money paid by Aetna in settlement of wrongful death actions filed by representatives of passengers killed in a plane crash. We reverse.

On November 15, 1964, a Bonanza Airlines plane crashed in its approach to Las Vegas, Nevada, on a flight from Phoenix, Arizona. All on board were killed. Wrongful death claims filed on behalf of the passengers were settled by Bonanza, with Aetna as Bonanza's insurer paying to the extent of Bonanza's coverage.

Jeppesen publishes instrument approach charts to aid pilots in making instrument approaches to airports. Aetna contends that the chart for the Las Vegas Airport was defective, and that product defect was the cause of the crash. Asserting product liability on the part of Jeppesen, it brought this action in the District Court for the District of Nevada as Bonanza's subrogee, seeking to recover from Jeppesen the sums it has paid in settlement of the wrongful death claims. Following bench trial, the court found that the chart was defective; that the defect was the proximate cause of the crash; that Bonanza was negligent in failing to discover the defect and alert its pilots; and that the crew members were not negligent in relying on the defective chart. The court apportioned damages between Bonanza and Jeppesen on the basis of its findings of comparative fault: 80 percent to Jeppesen and 20 percent to Bonanza. It is from that judgment that Jeppesen has taken this appeal.

Jeppesen contends that the record does not support the court's finding that the instrument approach chart was defective. Jeppesen approach charts depict graphically the instrument approach procedure for the particular airport as that procedure has been promulgated by the Federal Aviation Administration (FAA) after testing and administrative approval. The procedure includes all pertinent aspects of the approach such as directional heading, distances, minimum altitudes, turns, radio frequencies and procedures to be followed if an approach is missed. The specifications prescribed are set forth by the FAA in tabular form. Jeppesen acquires this FAA form and portrays the information therein on a graphic approach chart. This is Jeppesen's "product." The parties do not dispute that the information thus contained in Jeppesen's Las Vegas approach chart is in all respects accurate. The defect, if any, is in the graphic presentation of that information.

Each chart portrays graphically two views of the proper approach. The top portion is the "plan" view, depicted as if one were looking down on the approach segment of the flight from directly above. The bottom portion depicts the "profile" view, presented as a side view of the approach with a descending line depicting the minimum allowable altitudes as the approach progresses. The plan view is regarded as a superior method of presenting course and course changes; the profile view as a superior method of presenting altitude and altitude changes. Each chart thus conveys information in two ways: by words and numbers, and by graphics.

The plan view correctly shows the minimum altitude at a distance of 15 miles from the Las Vegas Airport as 6,000 feet. The profile view does not extend beyond three miles from the airport. Both plan and profile views correctly show the minimum altitude at a distance of three miles from the airport as 3,100 feet. The "defect" in the chart consists of the fact that the graphic depiction of the profile, which covers a distance of three miles from the airport, appears to be drawn to the same scale as the graphic depiction of the plan, which covers a distance of 15 miles. In fact, although the views are the same size, the scale of the plan is five times that of the profile.

Aetna produced as witness an aviation psychologist, who testified that most Jeppesen approach charts have the same or roughly the same scale for both plan and profile views; that a pilot and navigator would come to take this for granted, and, when faced with the Las Vegas chart would assume that the altitude shown on the profile as proper for three miles distant would, reading it as drawn to the same scale as the plan, be proper for 15 miles distant. The theory of Aetna was that the crash was due to pilot reliance on this faulty assumption, invited by the difference in scale. It contends that this difference in scale created a conflict between the information conveyed by the graphics of the chart and that conveyed in words and numbers, and that this conflict rendered the chart defective.

Jeppesen disputed Aetna's claim that it was the custom of the chartmakers to draw the profile and plan views to the same scale. In addition, Jeppesen produced experienced pilots as witnesses who testified that they had never made assumptions such as those attributed to the Bonanza flight crew, and had never heard of any pilots who had. Jeppesen contends that Aetna has failed completely to make out a case of product defect. We cannot agree.

While the information conveyed in words and figures on the Las Vegas approach chart was completely correct, the purpose of the chart was to translate this information into an instantly understandable graphic representation. This was what gave the chart its usefulness, this is what the chart contributed to the mere data amassed and promulgated by the FAA. It was reliance on this graphic portrayal that Jeppesen invited.

The trial judge found that the Las Vegas chart "radically departed" from the usual presentation of graphics in the other Jeppesen charts; that the conflict between the information conveyed by words and numbers and the information conveyed by graphics rendered the chart unreasonably dangerous and a defective product.

Under Nevada law a plaintiff can recover for injuries caused by use of a product with a defective design which makes it unsafe for its intended use, so long as the plaintiff is unaware of the defect at the time of use. On these facts, we conclude that the court's finding that the product was defective is not clearly erroneous.

Exercise 4-1 Synthesizing and Applying Material

1. How is the information contained in the Jeppesen chart different from the information contained in a "how to" manual? How is it similar?

2. Should a video game be classified as a product? Why or why not?

3. Based on your reading can you list examples of items you previously viewed as "products" that would not be classified as such?

4. What policy reasons cause courts to characterize items as products or non products?

Exercise 4-2 Classifying Products

There has been significant litigation surrounding the classification of electricity as a product. The weight of authority currently supports extending strict liability to electrical utilities. Courts have generally found that once the electricity passes through the customer's meter, it is considered a product in the stream of commerce, and is subject to strict liability; however, before the electricity reaches the meter and is made available to the customer, courts have held that it is not a product in the stream of commerce. Most of the cases refusing to extend strict liability involve injuries from accidental contact with a power line. The courts are split on the issue of whether stray voltage should be treated as a product. Some courts have held that high-voltage electrical power is a "product," but that it has not been "sold" until it has passed through a customer's meter. A small number of courts have held strict liability inapplicable to electricity regardless of whether the harm was caused before or after the electricity passed through the customer's meter. What might explain the differences in characterization of electricity as a product or non product?

In *James v. Meow Media, Inc.,* 300 F.3d 683 (6th Cir. 2002), the plaintiffs argued that since "electricity" is a "product" for purposes of strict liability, and internet sites are nothing more than communicative electrical pulses, internet sites should be a product since there is no relevant difference between the internet transmissions and the electricity. Assuming the argument was made in a jurisdiction that classifies electricity as a product, do you agree with the plaintiff's argument?

2. Was the Defendant a Commercial Seller or Distributor of the Product that Injured Plaintiff?

If the injury causing item is a product, the next step for the plaintiff's lawyer is to identify the parties potentially responsible for distributing and selling the product (the potential defendants). To establish liability, a plaintiff must be able to prove the potential defendant (a) is engaged in the business of selling or otherwise distributing the specific type of product that injured the plaintiff; (b) is not immune from liability; and (c) manufactured, sold or distributed the actual product that injured the plaintiff. Each of these issues will be addressed separately in this section.

a. Was the Defendant Engaged in the Business of Selling or Otherwise Distributing the Product that Injured Plaintiff?

In determining whether a suit is appropriate, the first consideration is whether the potential defendant is engaged in the business of selling or otherwise distributing the product that harmed the plaintiff—meaning they must be a commercial seller or distributor of the product (rather than a private seller).

To qualify as a commercial seller or distributor the defendant does not need to be engaged exclusively, or even primarily, in selling or otherwise distributing the product, but it must be engaged in more than occasional or casual sales or distribution. To be held liable, the commercial seller must also be in the business of selling the specific type of products that harmed the plaintiff.

Exercise 4-3 Identifying Commercial Sellers and Distributors

Would any of the following qualify as a commercial seller or distributor (and for what products)?

1. A private owner of a car who sells it to another
2. A regular eBay seller
3. A movie theater's sales of popcorn and candy
4. A "snack shack's" sales of candy at weekly youth sporting events (soccer, baseball, etc.)
5. A gas station that does car repair work and sells parts and tires

---

Lialiblity is not limited to the party that sold plaintiff the product. Any party in the chain of distribution (manufacturer, wholesaler, retailer, etc.) is liable for injury caused by the sale of a defective product. This includes nonmanufacturing sellers and distributors. This is true even when such nonmanufacturing sellers or distributors are not the ones that made the product defective and are not in a position to prevent defects from occurring. The restatement and the case that follows illustrate this well established principle.

§ 20. Definition Of "One Who Sells Or Otherwise Distributes"

(a) One sells a product when, in a commercial context, one transfers ownership thereto either for use or consumption or for resale leading to ultimate use or consumption. Commercial product sellers include, but are not limited to, manufacturers, wholesalers, and retailers.

(b) One otherwise distributes a product when, in a commercial transaction other than a sale, one provides the product to another either for use or consumption or as a preliminary step leading to ultimate use or consumption. Commercial nonsale product distributors include, but are not limited to, lessors, bailors, and those who provide products to others as a means of promoting either the use or consumption of such products or some other commercial activity.

(c) One also sells or otherwise distributes a product when, in a commercial transaction, one provides a combination of products and services and either the transaction taken as a whole, or the product component thereof, satisfies the criteria in Subsection (a) or (b).

§ 14. Selling Or Distributing As One's Own A Product Manufactured By Another

One engaged in the business of selling or otherwise distributing products who sells or distributes as its own a product manufactured by another is subject to the same liability as though the seller or distributor were the product's manufacturer.

Exercise 4-4 Proof that Defendant is a Seller, Distributor or Manufacturer of the Product

The following is a transcript of the deposition of the president of XYZ CORP, a defendant in a products liability action which alleges plaintiff was injured by XYZ CORP's defectively manufactured widgets. As you review the testimony:

1. Determine why counsel is asking each of the questions

    a. What is counsel attempting to prove?

    b. Why is that at issue?

2. Determine whether the testimony is sufficient to establish that XYZ CORP is a:

    a. Commercial seller, or

    b. Distributor, or

    c. Manufacturer, of:

    d. Widgets

3. Are there other questions you should ask? What are they?

4. Will plaintiff potentially have evidence that would help prove this issue? What might that evidence be?

```
1    [Q] What is your occupation?

2    [A] I am president of XYZ CORP.

3    [Q] How would you describe the business of your company?

4    [A] We manufacture various mechanical parts.

5    [Q] Do you manufacture widgets as part of your business?

6    [A] We do. Widgets are probably the most widely used of

7  all the mechanical parts, and we manufacture thousands

8  each year.

9    [Q] What do you do with the widgets and other mechani-

10 cal parts you manufacture?

11   [A] We sell them.

12   [Q] To whom do you sell them?

13
```

1   [A] Wholesalers and other distributors. We also sell
2 some directly to industrial users.
3   [Q] How many widgets did your company sell during the
4 last calendar year?
5   [A] I believe we sold roughly two hundred fifty thousand
6 widgets during the last calendar year.
7   [Q] How many different sales transactions did that in-
8 clude?
9   [A] I couldn't give you an exact number. It is probably
10 in the thousands.
11   [Q] Did those transactions occur all at once or were
12 they spaced out over the entire year?
13   [A] They were spaced out over the entire year.
14   [Q] Do you know what your company's gross revenues were
15 last year from sales of widgets?
16   [A] Yes, roughly.
17   [Q] What were they? The gross revenues from widget sales?
18   [A] They were in the neighborhood of one hundred and
19 twenty five thousand dollars.
20
21
22
23
24
25
26
27
28
29
30
31
32
33

As you read the following case, think about whether you believe it is a good idea to allow suits against retailers, distributors and wholesalers when the manufacturer caused the defect. Remember that in these cases, the manufacturer will likely have to indemnify the other seller/distributors.

Vandermark v. Ford Motor Company

34 Cal.Rptr. 723 (1964)

In October 1958 plaintiff Chester Vandermark bought a new Ford automobile from defendant Lorimer Diesel Engine Company, an authorized Ford dealer doing business as Maywood Bell Ford. About six weeks later, while driving on the San Bernardino Freeway, he lost control of the car. It went off the highway to the right and collided with a light post. He and his sister, plaintiff Mary Tresham, suffered serious injuries. They brought this action for damages against Maywood Bell Ford and the Ford Motor Company, which manufactured and assembled the car. They pleaded causes of action for breach of warranty and negligence. The trial court granted Ford's motion for a nonsuit on all causes of action and directed a verdict in favor of Maywood Bell on the warranty causes of action. The jury returned a verdict for Maywood Bell on the negligence causes of action, and the trial court entered judgment on the verdict. Plaintiffs appeal.

Vandermark had driven the car approximately 1,500 miles before the accident. He used it primarily in town, but drove it on two occasions from his home in Huntington Park to Joshua Tree in San Bernardino County. He testified that the car operated normally before the accident except once when he was driving home from Joshua Tree. He was in the left-hand west-bound lane of the San Bernardino Freeway when traffic ahead slowed. He applied the brakes and the car 'started to make a little dive to the right and continued on across the two lanes of traffic till she hit the shoulder. Whatever it was then let go and I was able to then pull her back into the road.' He drove home without further difficulty, but before using the car again, he took it to Maywood Bell for the regular 1,000-mile new car servicing. He testified that he described the freeway incident to Maywood Bell's service attendant, but Maywood Bell's records do not indicate that any complaint was made.

After the car was serviced, Vandermark drove it in town on short trips totaling approximately 300 miles. He and his sister then set out on another trip to Joshua Tree. He testified that while driving in the right-hand lane of the freeway at about 45 to 50 miles per hour, 'the car started to make a little shimmy or weave and started pulling to the right. * * * I tried to pull back, but it didn't seem to come, so I applied my brakes gently to see if I could straighten her up, but I couldn't seem to pull her back to the left. So, I let off on the brakes and she continued to the right, and I tried again to put on the brakes and she wouldn't come back, and all of a sudden this pole was in front of me and we smashed into it.' Plaintiff Tresham testified to a substantially similar version of the accident. A witness for plaintiffs, who was driving above 200 feet behind them, testified that plaintiffs' car was in the right-hand lane when he saw its taillights come on. The car started to swerve and finally skidded into the light post. An investigating officer testified that there were skid marks leading from the highway to the car.

Plaintiffs called an expert on the operation of hydraulic automobile brakes. In answer to hypothetical questions based on evidence in the record and his own knowledge of the braking system of the car, the expert testified as to the cause of the accident. It was his opinion that the brakes applied themselves owing to a failure of the piston in the master cylinder to retract far enough when the brake pedal was released to uncover a bypass port through which hydraulic fluid should have been able to escape into a reservoir above the master cylinder.

Failure of the piston to uncover the bypass port led to a closed system and a partial application of the brakes, which in turn led to heating that expanded the brake fluid until the brakes applied themselves with such force that Vandermark lost control of the car. The expert also testified that the failure of the piston to retract sufficiently to uncover the bypass port could have been caused by dirt in the master cylinder, a defective or wrong-sized part, distortion of the fire wall, or improper assembly or adjustment. The trial court struck the testimony of the possible causes to the failure of the piston to retract, on the ground that there was no direct evidence that any one or more of the causes existed, and it rejected plaintiffs' offer to prove that all of the possible causes were attributable to defendants. These rulings were erroneous, for plaintiffs were entitled to establish the existence of a defect and defendants' responsibility therefore by circumstantial evidence, particularly when, as in this case, the damage to the car in the collision precluded determining whether or not the master cylinder assembly had been properly installed and adjusted before the accident.

Accordingly, for the purposes of reviewing the nonsuit in favor of Ford and the directed verdict in favor of Maywood Bell on the warranty causes of action, it must be taken as established that when the car was delivered to Vandermark, the master cylinder assembly had a defect that caused the accident. Moreover, since it could reasonably be inferred from the description of the braking system in evidence and the offer of proof of all possible causes of defects that the defect was owing to negligence in design, manufacture, assembly, or adjustment, it must be taken as established that the defect was caused by some such negligence.

Ford contends, however, that it may not be held liable for negligence in manufacturing the car or strictly liable in tort for placing it on the market without proof that the car was defective when Ford relinquished control over it. Ford points out that in this case the car passed through two other authorized Ford dealers before it was sold to Maywood Bell and that Maywood Bell removed the power steering unit before selling the car to Vandermark.

In *Greenman v. Yuba Power Products, Inc.*, 59 Cal.2d 57, 62, 27 Cal.Rptr. 697, 700, 377 P.2d 897, 900, we held that 'A manufacturer is strictly liable in tort when an article he places on the market, knowing that it is to be used without inspection for defects, proves to have a defect that causes injury to a human being.' Since the liability is strict it encompasses defects regardless of their source, and therefore a manufacturer of a completed product cannot escape liability by tracing the defect to a component part supplied by another. (*Goldberg v. Kollman Instrument Corp.*, 12 N.Y.2d 432, 437, 240 N.Y.S.2d 592, 191 N.E.2d 81.) Moreover, even before such strict liability was recognized, the manufacturer of a completed product was subject to vicarious liability for the negligence of his suppliers or subcontractors that resulted in defects in the completed product. (*Dow v. Holly Manufacturing Co.*, 49 Cal.2d 720, 726–727, 321 P.2d 736; *Ford Motor Co. v. Mathis*, 5 Cir., 322 F.2d 267, 273; *Boeing Airplane Co. v. Brown*, 9 Cir., 291 F.2d 310, 313; see Rest., Torts, s 400.) These rules focus responsibility for defects, whether negligently or nonnegligently caused, on the manufacturer of the completed product, and they apply regardless of what part of the manufacturing process the manufacturer chooses to delegate to third parties. It appears in the present case that Ford delegates the final steps in that process to its authorized dealers. It does not deliver cars to its dealers that are ready to be driven away by the ultimate purchasers but relies on its dealers to make the final inspections, corrections, and adjustments necessary to make the cars ready for use. Since Ford, as the manufacturer of the completed product, cannot delegate its duty to have its cars delivered to the ultimate purchaser free from dangerous defects, it cannot escape liability on the ground that the defect in Vandermark's car may have been caused by something one of its authorized dealers did or failed to do.

Since plaintiffs introduced or offered substantial evidence that they were injured as a result of a defect that was present in the car when Ford's authorized dealer delivered it to Vandermark, the trial court erred in granting a nonsuit on the causes of action by which plaintiff sought to establish that Ford was strictly liable to them. Since plaintiffs also introduced or offered substantial evidence that the defect was caused by some negligent conduct for which Ford was responsible, the trial court also erred in granting a nonsuit on the causes of action by which plaintiffs sought to establish that Ford was liable for negligence.

Plaintiffs contend that Maywood Bell is also strictly liable in tort for the injuries caused by the defect in the car and that therefore the trial court erred in directing a verdict for Maywood Bell on the warranty causes of action. Maywood Bell contends that the rule of strict liability in the *Greenman* case applies only to actions against manufacturers brought by injured parties with whom the manufacturers did not deal.

Retailers like manufacturers are engaged in the business of distributing goods to the public. They are an integral part of the overall producing and marketing enterprise that should bear the cost of injuries resulting from defective products. (*See Greenman v. Yuba Power Products, Inc.,* 59 Cal.2d 57, 63, 27 Cal.Rptr. 697, 377 P.2d 897.) In some cases the retailer may be the only member of that enterprise reasonably available to the injured plaintiff. In other cases the retailer himself may play a substantial part in insuring that the product is safe or may be in a position to exert pressure on the manufacturer to that end; the retailer's strict liability thus serves as an added incentive to safety.

Strict liability on the manufacturer and retailer alike affords maximum protection to the injured plaintiff and works no injustice to the defendants, for they can adjust the costs of such protection between them in the course of their continuing business relationship. Accordingly, as a retailer engaged in the business of distributing goods to the public, Maywood Bell is strictly liable in tort for personal injuries caused by defects in cars sold by it.

The judgment of nonsuit in favor of Ford Motor Company is reversed. The judgment in favor of Maywood Bell Ford on the negligence causes of action is affirmed and in all other respects the judgment in favor of Maywood Bell Ford is reversed.

If you disagree with the decision to allow suits against nonmanufacturing sellers and distributors, you may side with those states that have enacted legislation preventing such suits, which is the next question to address in deciding whether to name a party as a defendant.

---

b. Will the Defendant Have Immunity?

Liability in most cases is ultimately passed on to the manufacturer responsible for creating the product defect. However, nonmanufacturing sellers or distributors that are sued must still devote resources to defending such suits (and seeking indemnification). In some states legislation has been enacted that provides immunity (from suits based on strict products liability) for nonmanufacturing sellers or distributors. The immunity statutes are based on the notion that preventing suits against nonmanufacturing sellers or distributors saves the time and costs associated with defending such suits.

Exercise 4-5 Statutory Immunity

As you read the following statute, think about these questions:

1. What if a nonmanufacturing seller or distributor is dismissed from an action at the beginning of the lawsuit, because it appears that the manufacturer will be able to pay the judgment, but at some point during the suit the manufacturer becomes insolvent?

2. Should the plaintiff be left to suffer the loss uncompensated?

3. What safeguards should be included in these types of statutes?

4. What other issues might arise in states that provide immunity to nonmanufacturing sellers or distributors?

5. Does the statute effectively resolve these issues?

735 Illinois Compiled Statutes Annotated 5/§ 2-621. Product liability actions.

(a) In any product liability action based on any theory or doctrine commenced or maintained against a defendant or defendants other than the manufacturer, that party shall upon answering or otherwise pleading file an affidavit certifying the correct identity of the manufacturer of the product allegedly causing injury, death or damage. The commencement of a product liability action based on any theory or doctrine against such defendant or defendants shall toll the applicable statute of limitation and statute of repose relative to the defendant or defendants for purposes of asserting a strict liability in tort cause of action.

(b) Once the plaintiff has filed a complaint against the manufacturer or manufacturers, and the manufacturer or manufacturers have or are required to have answered or otherwise pleaded, the court shall order the dismissal of a product liability action based on any theory or doctrine against the certifying defendant or defendants, provided the certifying defendant or defendants are not within the categories set forth in subsection (c) of this Section. Due diligence shall be exercised by the certifying defendant or defendants in providing the plaintiff with the correct identity of the manufacturer or manufacturers, and due diligence shall be exercised by the plaintiff in filing an action and obtaining jurisdiction over the manufacturer or manufacturers.

The plaintiff may at any time subsequent to the dismissal move to vacate the order of dismissal and reinstate the certifying defendant or defendants, provided plaintiff can show one or more of the following:

(1) That the applicable period of statute of limitation or statute of repose bars the assertion of a cause of action against the manufacturer or manufacturers of the product allegedly causing the injury, death or damage; or

(2) That the identity of the manufacturer given to the plaintiff by the certifying defendant or defendants was incorrect. Once the correct identity of the manufacturer has been given by the certifying defendant or defendants the court shall again dismiss the certifying defendant or defendants; or

(3) That the manufacturer no longer exists, cannot be subject to the jurisdiction of the courts of this State, or, despite due diligence, the manufacturer is not amenable to service of process; or

(4) That the manufacturer is unable to satisfy any judgment as determined by the court; or

(5) That the court determines that the manufacturer would be unable to satisfy a reasonable settlement or other agreement with plaintiff.

(c) A court shall not enter a dismissal order relative to any certifying defendant or defendants other than the manufacturer even though full compliance with subsection (a) of this Section has been made where the plaintiff can show one or more of the following:

(1) That the defendant has exercised some significant control over the design or manufacture of the product, or has provided instructions or warnings to the manufacturer relative to the alleged defect in the product which caused the injury, death or damage; or

(2) That the defendant had actual knowledge of the defect in the product which caused the injury, death or damage; or

(3) That the defendant created the defect in the product which caused the injury, death or damage.

(d) Nothing contained in this Section shall be construed to grant a cause of action on any legal theory or doctrine, or to affect the right of any person to seek and obtain indemnity or contribution.

(e) This Section applies to all causes of action accruing on or after September 24, 1979.

Exercise 4-6 Naming Responsible Parties as Defendants

What reasons might exist for plaintiff to maintain an action against both the immediate seller-dealer of the product and against the manufacturer even where the immediate seller may be liable under the strict tort liability doctrine? Consider the following:

Plaintiff was injured because of brake hose failure. Plaintiff filed an action against the dealer and the manufacturer, and failed to appeal from a ruling dismissing the complaint as to the manufacturer. Plaintiff then tried to introduce into evidence recall letters from the manufacturer stating that the hose in question was subject to fatigue and rupture after extensive usage and should be immediately replaced. These letters were seemingly an admission of defective manufacture or design (and admissions by a party are admissible evidence). However, the evidence was held inadmissible against the dealer (the only remaining defendant), since the admission was made by a nonparty (the manufacturer) and was therefore not an admission by a party (the dealer).

Exercise 4-7　Law Practice

Has the jurisdiction where you intend to practice enacted any legislation limiting or barring actions against non-manufacturer sellers?

---

c. Did Defendant Sell, Distribute or Manufacture the Specific Product that Caused Plaintiff's Injury?

If the defendant is in the business of selling or otherwise distributing the type of product that injured plaintiff, and if the defendant is not protected by a statute such as the one in the previous section, the final hurdle is to establish that the defendant manufactured, sold or distributed the actual product that caused injury. Since products are often destroyed in the injury causing event, this can sometimes present difficulties. Although in certain cases circumstantial evidence may be used to establish the identity of the manufacturer or the seller of a defective product, such evidence must establish that it is reasonably probable, rather than merely possible, that the defendant was the source of the allegedly defective product.

As you read the next case, identify each witness and the testimony presented. Based on that collective testimony decide whether you believe it is reasonably probable that the defendant was the seller or manufacturer of the injury causing product. Why or why not?

Healey v. Firestone Tire & Rubber Company

87 N.Y.2d 596, 663 N.E.2d 901 (1996)

Plaintiff was severely injured when struck in the head by a part of a multipiece truck tire rim which explosively separated when the tire which had just been inflated on it was dropped by an employee of defendant All-Inn Trucking, Inc. Carl J. Lange, plaintiff's expert, examined and inventoried rims on All-Inn trucks and plaintiff's expert O.J. Hahn examined the rims on all 10 of All-Inn's trucks and those stored on its premises. Hahn identified three rims, all manufactured and designed by defendants Firestone Tire & Rubber Company and Bridgestone/Firestone, Inc. (collectively referred to as Firestone), as being the only rims of All-Inn that could have been involved in the accident. This theory was based on the assertion that the rims evidenced signs of substantial "chording", i.e., being distorted and out of round, which Hahn opined was the cause of the explosive separation of the rim involved in plaintiff's accident. According to plaintiff, the three rims were marked for identification and left in the custody of All-Inn's expert pursuant to an understanding with the trucking company's insurance carrier that they would be preserved.

Plaintiff commenced this action against Firestone and All-Inn. The causes of action against Firestone were grounded in negligence and strict products liability under both manufacturing defect and design defect theories. Approximately a year later, it was disclosed that All-Inn had lost the three rims identified by plaintiff's expert Hahn as the possible instrumentalities for the rim involved in the accident.

Firestone then moved for summary judgment, asserting that it was undisputed that the multipiece rim which plaintiff alleged caused the accident was irretrievably lost and that, therefore, plaintiff's evidence was insufficient as a matter of law to establish the identity of the manufacturer of the offending rim or that a defect in that product caused the accident. Supreme Court denied Firestone's motion, concluding that there was sufficient circumstantial evidence to implicate Firestone as the manufacturer of the accident-causing rim. The court further concluded that a triable issue of fact was presented that the rim's defective design was the cause of its explosive separation, based upon plaintiff's expert Hahn's opinion excluding any other possible cause.

A majority at the Appellate Division agreed with Supreme Court that plaintiff had submitted sufficient circumstantial evidence to permit the inference that Firestone made the accident rim, the Court also held that, as to the plaintiff's design defect strict products liability cause of action, Firestone was not prejudiced by the disappearance of the suspect rims identified by plaintiff's expert, since the actual design of the product could be independently established. The Court however, concluded that the disappearance of the rims "fatally prejudiced" Firestone's defense against plaintiff's negligence and manufacturing defect causes of action and, therefore, modified Supreme Court's order by dismissing those claims, leaving intact only the design defect cause of action. [This case] presents two issues: (1) whether there was sufficient evidence to identify Firestone as the manufacturer of the offending rim, and (2) whether the plaintiff's inability to identify the actual rim involved in the accident fatally prejudiced Firestone in defending plaintiff's claim that the accident was due to the design of the rim and not another cause.

We reverse. This case presents no exception to the general rule that one of the necessary elements plaintiff in a strict products liability cause of action must establish by competent proof is that it was the defendant who manufactured and placed in the stream of commerce the injury-causing defective product (see, *Hymowitz v. Lilly & Co.*, 73 N.Y.2d 487, 504, 541 N.Y.S.2d 941, 539 N.E.2d 1069, cert. denied 493 U.S. 944, 110 S.Ct. 350, 107 L.Ed.2d 338; *Morrissey v. Conservative Gas Corp.*, 285 App.Div. 825, 136 N.Y.S.2d 844, affd. 1 N.Y.2d 741, 152 N.Y.S.2d 289, 135 N.E.2d 45).

The identity of the manufacturer of a defective product may be established by circumstantial evidence (see, *Taylor v. General Battery Corp.*, 183 A.D.2d 990, 991, 583 N.Y.S.2d 325; *Otis v. Bausch & Lomb*, 143 A.D.2d 649, 650, 532 N.Y.S.2d 933; *Prata v. National R.R. Passenger Corp.*, 70 A.D.2d 114, 118, 420 N.Y.S.2d 276, appeal dismissed 48 N.Y.2d 975; 1 Weinberger, New York Products Liability s 8:05). Moreover, circumstantial evidence may sufficiently demonstrate the maker's identity, notwithstanding the destruction of the allegedly defective product after use (see, *Taylor v. General Battery Corp., supra*; *Otis v. Bausch & Lomb, supra*).

The circumstantial evidence of identity of the manufacturer of a defective product causing personal injury must establish that it is reasonably probable, not merely possible or evenly balanced, that the defendant was the source of the offending product (see, *D'Amico v. Manufacturers Hanover Trust Co.*, 173 A.D.2d 263, 266, 569 N.Y.S.2d 962; see also, *Vecta Contract v. Lynch*, 444 So.2d 1093 [Fla Ct App 4th Dist], review denied 453 So.2d 44; *Naden v. Celotex Corp.*, 190 Ill.App.3d 410, 415, 137 Ill.Dec. 821, 824, 546 N.E.2d 766, 769 [circumstantial evidence in a products liability case "must justify an inference of probability as distinguished from mere possibility"]). Speculative or conjectural evidence of the manufacturer's identity is not enough (*D'Amico v. Manufacturers Hanover Trust Co., supra*; *Perez v. New York Tel. Co.*, 161 A.D.2d 191, 192, 554 N.Y.S.2d 576; *Sosa v. Joyce Beverages*, 159 A.D.2d 335, 337, 552 N.Y.S.2d 612).

Plaintiff's proof was insufficient to establish any reasonable probability that a Firestone rim caused plaintiff's accident. Biassi, who was on the All-Inn premises when the accident occurred, testified at his presuit deposition that the rim that explosively separated and injured plaintiff was a three-piece rim. There was uncontested evidence that at least six companies in addition to Firestone made three-piece truck tire rims. These Firestone rims were distributed under the brand name "Accu-Ride." In 1986, however, Firestone ceased making rims, having sold its rim manufacturing assets and rim design to an unrelated company called Accuride Corporation.

Biassi also testified at his deposition that the accident rim was reassembled the day after the incident and was either installed on one of All-Inn's trucks or placed against the wall of a shed at the trucking company's premises. Biassi emphatically denied present knowledge of the whereabouts of the particular rim involved in the accident. He kept no records of his purchases of rims, stating that rims were usually acquired in used condition "from guys selling rims, guys coming by" or from truckers going out of business.

Notably, at his deposition, Biassi was not asked whether, nor did he confirm that, the accident rim was still in the possession of All-Inn when the deposition took place some five weeks after the accident. Indeed, in a subsequent affidavit Biassi averred that tires and rims on the All-Inn trucks were changed frequently because of severe use on equipment primarily driven to haul dirt and gravel over rough terrain, and that broken and worn-out rims were discarded without any inventory control. Thus, Biassi's evidence raised a substantial question as to whether the actual rim that explosively separated to cause plaintiff's injuries remained in the possession of All-Inn during the subsequent inspections of the rims on its trucks and at its premises by plaintiff's experts.

The foregoing evidentiary gap was not filled by the affidavit of Lange, plaintiff's expert, who conducted an examination and inventory of rims at All-Inn's premises and on its trucks. He examined a total of 89 rims, of which he identified 85 as "FIRESTONE-designed Accu-Ride 5o Radial Commander" (emphasis supplied). Lange gave reasons for excluding the remaining four rims as suspects in causing plaintiff's accident. Lange, however, did not examine an unspecified number of inside tandem rims on the All-Inn trucks.

Moreover, as already noted, the rims Lange described as "FIRESTONE-designed Accu-Ride" could well have included rims manufactured by Accuride Corporation after the 1986 sale of all of Firestone's truck tire rim-making operations.

Equally unavailing to prove identity of the manufacturer was the affidavit of plaintiff's expert Hahn regarding his examination of the rims on all 10 of All-Inn's trucks and the spare rims on its premises. It is true that Hahn identified three specific rims as being capable of causing plaintiff's accident because of their physical condition and that he established that those rims were definitely manufactured by Firestone from the markings on them. Hahn, however, described the rims he examined on six of the 10 All-Inn trucks as being "of the Accu-Ride 5o Radial Commander three-piece type", in contrast to the "FIRESTONE-manufactured" rims he described finding on other trucks or in storage on the premises.

The foregoing was the only evidence relevant to the identification of Firestone as the manufacturer of the actual accident rim, and it was insufficient to establish any reasonable probability that Firestone made the offending product. Of primary significance, no reasonable inference could be drawn from Biassi's deposition and affidavit that the accident-causing rim was retained by All-Inn so as to have been available for subsequent inspection and identification by plaintiff's experts. The affidavit of those experts could not cure this defect in proof. Indeed, their averments were insufficient even to establish a definite likelihood that a significant preponderance of the rims they inspected were actually manufactured by Firestone. Consequently, plaintiff has failed to raise a triable issue of fact on the identity of Firestone as the manufacturer of the allegedly defective product in this case (*see, Franov v. Exxon Co.,* 178 A.D.2d 327, 328, 577 N.Y.S.2d 392, lv. dismissed, 80 N.Y.2d 822, 587 N.Y.S.2d 894, 600 N.E.2d 621; *D'Amico v. Manufacturers Hanover Trust Co.,* 173 A.D.2d at 267, 569 N.Y.S.2d 962, *supra; cf. Prata v. National R.R. Passenger Corp.,* 70 A.D.2d 114, 420 N.Y.S.2d 276, *supra*).

Our disposition of this issue renders discussion of the second issue unnecessary. Accordingly, the order of the Appellate Division should be reversed, summary judgment should be granted dismissing the complaint in its entirety as against defendants Firestone Tire & Rubber Company and Bridgestone/Firestone, Inc.

Exercise 4-8 Identifying the Manufacturer

How would you go about determining the manufacturer of a particular product? What resources would you use? Under what circumstances would you need expert testimony?

---

3. Can Plaintiff Prove the Product was Defective at the Time it Left the Defendant's Control?

In this section, we will explore two issues: (1) proving that the injury causing product was defective and (2) proving that the defect existed at the time the product left the defendant's control. The first issue — proving the product was defective — requires an understanding of the three categories of product defects as well as an understanding of the problems relating to proving a product was defective. To prove that the product is defective the plaintiff must establish that at the time of distribution or sale, the product was defectively **designed**, defectively **manufactured**, or contained an **inadequate warning or instructions**.

> Design defect
>
> The test for *design defect* is dependent on the jurisdiction and type of product. In some cases the plaintiff must prove that the risks created by the product outweighed the utility of the product, making the product unreasonable dangerous; this is referred to as the risk/utility test. In some cases (and jurisdictions) the plaintiff is also required to establish that the foreseeable risks of harm posed by the product could have been reduced or avoided by the adoption of a reasonable alternative design, and because of the omission of the alternative design the product was not reasonably safe; this consideration is sometimes included in the risk/utility assessment and is sometimes a stand alone test known as the feasible alternative design test. In some cases (and jurisdictions) the plaintiff must show that the product did not conform to the ordinary expectations of a consumer and was therefore unreasonably dangerous; this is called the consumer expectation test.
>
> Manufacturing defect
>
> To prove a product had a *manufacturing defect*, the plaintiff must establish that the product was not manufactured according to its intended design and

was unreasonably dangerous as a result. Manufacturing defects arise when products do not conform to the manufacturer's specifications (the product's "blueprint").

Warning defect

To prove a product is defective because of *inadequate instructions or warnings*, the plaintiff must prove the foreseeable risks of harm posed by the product could have been reduced or avoided by providing reasonable instructions or warnings, and because of the failure to provide the instructions or warnings, the product was not reasonably safe. Note that an effective warning may not absolve the defendant of liability; where the product could have been made safe without impairing utility or cost, simply warning about the danger will not usually suffice.

We will explore each of these defects in greater detail in this section.

In addition to understanding the law related to establishing a defect, proving there was a defect usually requires developing knowledge and expertise in a number of other areas including: an understanding of the product design and specifications; industry standards relating to the product; and an understanding of the manufacturing and distribution processes. It also requires an evaluation of the available evidence, including an assessment of who may possess the relevant evidence and how to obtain it. This will ultimately include an assessment of what is admissible, a topic covered in Evidence texts and courses, but that is beyond the scope of this textbook. Instead, we will focus on the type of evidence that might be available to the client (direct and/or circumstantial evidence, lay or expert testimony, etc.) in proving a defect existed and leave the question of whether it will actually be admissible to your Evidence course.

It is a good idea to begin to think about how you would go about obtaining information about a product (the design and manufacturing process) because this type of fact investigation is critical in product liability cases. For example, in order to prove or disprove the alleged defect you will need to be able to understand the product sufficiently to depose experts for the opposing side and present the design and manufacturing issues to a judge or jury in a way that makes it understandable. If you are a plaintiff's lawyer you will likely not have unlimited resources, or even immediate access to experts while you are making your initial assessment of the claim. If you are the defendant's lawyer it is helpful to understand the business and product of your client (which, among other benefits, goes a long way to establishing trust in the attorney client relationship). These are just a few of the reasons it is important to be able to find information about your product and understand the design and manufacturing process. For each of the products in this chapter you might want to explore the potential sources of product information available to you, to help you develop this skill.

The second issue covered in this chapter—proving the defect existed at the time it left the defendant's control—is another common hurdle in product liability lawsuits; in other words, the problem facing an attorney filing a products liability suit is whether she can present sufficient evidence that the plaintiff's injury was caused by a defective condition that was present when the product left the hands of the defendant. There may not be a person that is able to testify from personal knowledge that a particular product was sold in a defective condition. The result is that many courts allow both the existence of the defect and that the defect existed at the time of purchase to be established by circumstantial, rather than direct, evidence. This means that the court will allow a case to go to the jury if the plaintiff can produce enough evidence to raise a reasonable inference that the defective condition of the product existed at the time of sale. The Restatement explains it this way:

§ 3. Circumstantial Evidence Supporting Inference of Product Defect

It may be inferred that the harm sustained by the plaintiff was caused by a product defect existing at the time of sale or distribution, without proof of a specific defect, when the incident that harmed the plaintiff:

a) was of a kind that ordinarily occurs as a result of product defect; and

b) was not, in the particular case, solely the result of causes other than product defect existing at the time of sale or distribution.

For example, frequently in defective products litigation, the allegedly defective product has been destroyed, and is therefore not available for inspection or production at trial. In some cases this might be fatal to the plaintiff's case because without the product she does not have sufficient evidence to show that the product that caused injures her was defective. This leaves her with the option of introducing circumstantial evidence to provide her case. For example, she can introduce evidence of how the product functioned at the time of injury (e.g., testimony by witnesses that the tire came apart while she was driving), which allows the jury to infer the product was defective (since tires don't usually do that unless something is defective). She may produce a product that is identical (or nearly so) to the actual injury causing product and then introduce testimony that certain defects (present in the duplicate product) were characteristic of the entire line of products manufactured by the defendant, which allows the jury to infer that the product that injured the plaintiff was also defective. However, if she chooses this method, the trial court must determine whether there is sufficient similarity between the product at issue and the duplicate product, and the court may exclude the duplicate product (and testimonial evidence) on the grounds that the duplicate product is not sufficiently similar to the product actually at issue. Finally, plaintiff might also introduced evidence in the form of a qualified witness who had an opportunity to examine the product between the time the injury occurred and the time of the products disappearance, and the jury may infer from this testimony that the product was defective.

Exercise 4-9 Circumstantial Evidence

Review the facts and testimony from *Vandermark v. Ford Motor Company*, and determine whether the evidence that the product was defective, at the time it left the manufacturer's control, was direct or circumstantial evidence.

Exercise 4-10 Identifying Evidentiary Support

Using what you've learned so far, how might you establish that the products described below were defective, at the time they left the manufacturer?

a. Mike purchased a new blender. Mike used the blender approximately 10 times, exclusively for making fruit smoothies. While he was making a smoothie, the blender suddenly shattered. A piece of glass struck Mike's eye, causing harm.

b. Ben was riding his brand new bicycle. When he approached a stop sign he attempted to stop the bicycle by applying the brakes, but the bicycle did not slow down. Luckily Ben jumped off the bicycle just before it rolled into oncoming traffic. Ben sustained some relatively minor injuries, including a fractured wrist. The bicycle was crushed by a large truck and dragged for several feet, destroying the frame and brake assembly.

c. Jack purchased a new ABC Electric Power Screwdriver. He inserted the bit for the appropriate screw size and turned the power button on. The bit shot out of the tool and lodged itself in Jack's arm, causing serious injury. Two weeks after purchasing the electric screwdriver, Jack believed the tool was making too much noise and brought it to the Acme Tool Repair Shop to check it out. Acme removed the mechanism that held the bit, examined it, and then reassembled it. Finding no problem, Acme returned the tool to Jack.

Skill Focus: The Value and Purpose of Expert Testimony

The particulars about expert testimony are covered in most Evidence courses and are beyond the scope of this text; however, a basic understanding of the need for, and availability of, expert testimony will aid in your understanding of how to handle a products liability action — since experts frequently provide the testimony that establishes there was a defect.

In Chapter Two you identified information from expert witness depositions, and in so doing, you saw how expert testimony can provide evidence to establish the elements of a cause of action. In this chapter you will take the next step and consider additional questions — whether (and how) expert testimony might aid the jury (essentially making the initial decision about what expertise you might need).

When admitting expert testimony, the court must determine (1) that the case is one in which the trier of fact will be assisted by expert testimony, usually because the particular issue lies outside the knowledge and experience of the average layperson, and (2) that the witness possesses such specialized knowledge or skill that their testimony will assist the jury in understanding the evidence. If an issue is not within the common knowledge of an ordinary person it may be necessary for the plaintiff to introduce expert testimony in order to establish a prima facie case. Generally speaking, a witness does not need to possess any particular or specific academic qualifications to qualify as an expert witness. Under Federal Rule of Evidence 702, "If scientific, technical or other specialized knowledge will assist the trier of fact to understand the evidence or to determine a fact in issue, a witness qualified as an expert by knowledge, skill, experience, training or education, may testify thereto in the form of an opinion or otherwise." The expert's opinion may be based on first hand evidence or facts or data presented to him at the trial, provided it is the type of information reasonably relied upon by experts in the field in forming such opinions. The data may include verbal or written statements of others, reports or texts. A party may also introduce evidence of experiments conducted prior to trial if they can show that the experiment replicates a "substantial similarity to conditions at the time in question." The court may refuse to permit expert testimony if the expert is not qualified in the area for which testimony is sought, or does not have sufficient basis for the expert's opinion. Once a person is qualified and testifies as an expert, the jury determines what weight is to be given to their testimony; the jury is free to credit or disregard any expert's testimony.

As you read the cases in the next section, try to determine:

(1) What type of defect(s) are alleged by the plaintiff;

(2) Whether there are any resources available to you that provide information about the product (you may want to search for information about each product and find out more about the design, engineering, industry standards, etc.);

(3) What evidence—direct and/or circumstantial—is available to prove the defect existed at the time the product left the defendant's control; and

(4) Whether expert testimony is necessary to prove (a) there was a defect, and/or (b) the defect existed at the time the product left the defendant's control.

Dico Tire, Inc. v. Cisneros

953 S.W.2d 776, 780–99 (Tex. App. 1997)

This is a negligence and product liability case. Appellee, Roger Cisneros, sued appellant, Dico Tire, Inc., for injuries he sustained when a tire exploded as he was repairing it. At the time of the accident, Cisneros was a tire service repairman for E.B. Creager Tire & Battery, Inc. On May 22, 1992, he was sent to a construction site to repair a tire on a front-end loader. He first put a small amount of air into the tire to find the leak and then deflated the tire. After separating the tire from the wheel, he noticed that the tire had previously been patched at least three times. Cisneros patched the new hole and remounted the tire on the rim. He seated, or locked, the tire's beads against the steel flange of the rim by inserting four to five pounds of air pressure into the tire. Once the beads appeared to be seated, Cisneros continued to inflate the tire to thirty-five pounds while monitoring air pressure gauges. This pressure was well within the maximum of fifty pounds for which the tire was rated. During the inflation, Cisneros stood the tire upright on the ground, resting it on the tread. Cisneros did not use the safety restraining device which was available in his truck.

After the tire was inflated, the tire and wheel assembly fell flat on the ground. Cisneros recapped the valve stem which was facing up. Then, as Cisneros was leaning forward to reach under the tire to lift it up, the side to the ground blew off the wheel. The force of the expelled air propelled the tire upward into Cisneros' face, causing him to fly backwards. Cisneros claims that at this point one side of the tire was free of the wheel assembly.

Cisneros' nose and lip were cut open and several of his teeth were damaged. He was transported to a hospital emergency room where he was treated by a plastic surgeon. Eventually, Cisneros was also treated by a dentist, a neurologist, and an ear, nose, and throat specialist.

Cisneros sued Dico, alleging that the tire was defectively manufactured because the bead bundles deformed during the manufacturing process. He also alleged that a defective design caused the bead bundles to be susceptible to deformation during manufacture. In addition, Cisneros contended that other designs were available to protect against deformation in the manufacturing process and that the alternate designs reduced the risk of an explosive blow off, even when a deformation occurs. Cisneros further asserted that Dico was negligent in its post-manufacture inspection of the tire because a reasonably prudent inspection would have disclosed the defect.

Dico answered and alleged that Cisneros' own negligence was the proximate cause of the accident. The jury found that design and manufacturing defects in the tire were producing causes and that Dico's negligence was the proximate cause of the accident. The jury also found that Cisneros was not negligent.

A defectively designed product is one that is unreasonably dangerous as designed, taking into consideration the utility of the product and the risk involved in its use. *Turner v. General Motors Corp.*, 584 S.W.2d 844, 847 n. 1, 851 (Tex.1979). Design defect cases are not based on consumer expectancy, but on the manufacturer's design of a product which makes it unreasonably dangerous, even though not flawed in its manufacture. *Ford Motor Co. v. Pool*, 688 S.W.2d 879, 881 (Tex.App.-Texarkana 1985), *aff'd in part on other grounds, rev'd in part on other grounds*, 715 S.W.2d 629 (Tex.1986). Whether a product was defectively designed requires a balancing by the jury of its utility against the likelihood of and gravity of injury from its use. *Caterpillar, Inc.*, 911 S.W.2d at 383–84; *Boatland of Houston, Inc. v. Bailey*, 609 S.W.2d 743, 746 (Tex.1980). We evaluate whether a product has a design defect in light of the economic and scientific feasibility of safer alternatives. *Caterpillar Inc.*, 911 S.W.2d at 384; *see Boatland*, 609 S.W.2d at 746. If there are no safer alternatives, a product is not unreasonably dangerous as a matter of law. *Caterpillar Inc.*, 911 S.W.2d at 384; *see Boatland*, 609 S.W.2d at 748.

To recover for a manufacturing defect, the plaintiff must show a manufacturing flaw which renders the product unreasonably dangerous; that the defect existed at the time the product left the seller, and that the defect was the producing cause of the plaintiff's injuries. *Pool*, 688 S.W.2d at 881; *Fitzgerald Marine Sales v. LeUnes*, 659 S.W.2d 917, 918 (Tex.App.-Fort Worth 1983, writ dism'd). An unreasonably dangerous product is one that is dangerous to an extent beyond that which would be contemplated by the ordinary consumer, with the ordinary knowledge common to the community as to its characteristics. *Turner*, 584 S.W.2d at 846–47. A manufacturing defect exists when a product does not conform to the design standards and blueprints of the manufacturer and the flaw makes the product more dangerous and therefore unfit for its intended or foreseeable uses. *USX Corp. v. Salinas*, 818 S.W.2d 473, 483 n. 8 (Tex.App.-San Antonio 1991, writ denied); *Pool*, 688 S.W.2d at 881. The manufacturing defect theory is based upon a consumer expectancy that a mass-produced product will not differ from its counterparts in a manner which makes it more dangerous than the others. *USX Corp.*, 818 S.W.2d at 477 n. 2; *Pool*, 688 S.W.2d at 881.

Cisneros testified that after inflating the tire with four or five pounds of pressure, the bead appeared to be seated next to the wheel's flange. He then inflated the tire to thirty-five pounds of pressure, recapped the valve stem, and leaned down to pick up the tire. As he was bent over the tire, it exploded and hit him in the face. According to Cisneros, one side of the tire was over the flange after the explosion. Testimony from other witnesses supports Cisneros' claims. Harry Cobb, a sales representative present at the construction site when the accident occurred, testified that he heard a loud popping noise and saw Cisneros fly backward while the tire bounced about ten feet. Cobb also testified that Cisneros' face, nose, and mouth appeared to be injured. Creager Tire employees, who saw the tire and wheel assembly after the accident, testified that one bead of the tire was separated from the wheel. Ricardo Martinez, assistant service manager for Creager, testified that he had no doubt that the tire blew off the flange.

Walter Harm, an engineer for Uniroyal Tire Company, testified about the design, man-ufacture, and testing of tire products. Harm has an economics degree from Wayne State University, a chemical engineering degree from William State University, and has completed some graduate work in chemical engineering at Wayne State. The entire thirty-one years of his professional career has been spent working for Uniroyal. Harm held the positions of tire construction engineer, materials engineer, research engineer, automotive manager for original equipment, and senior engineer for tire reliability. In these positions, Harm engineered the component parts of tires, evaluated new products, and tested tires to failure (burst testing) to determine how the components related to the cause. At one point in his career, Harm supervised quality control by inspecting tires before and after curing. When faulty tires were returned by customers during this period, Harm checked them for component failures. Harm also has experience in developing the materials that go into the make-up of component parts. He has performed materials failure testing and has issued production specifications for materials.

Harm described the wheel at issue as a single-piece wheel and the tire as a multistrand weftless bead tire. He used a videotape provided by Dico to explain the process of building the tire. Harm explained that a tire's plies are wrapped around rings of wires, or beads, located on both of the tire's inner edges. The circumference of the bead is smaller than the wheel's flange, or outer edge. The strength of bead wires is meant to prevent the tire from blowing over the flange.

Harm also explained how a tire like the one at issue would be mounted onto a wheel. According to Harm, one bead is placed over the flange as far as it will go. The remainder of the bead is lubricated and then forced onto the wheel. This bead falls into the narrow drop center of the wheel, allowing the process to be repeated with the other bead. Next, the tire is slightly inflated to seat the beads against the flanges. During this process, the beads trap air and move away from the narrow drop center out onto the larger portion of the wheel until they are locked against the flange. Once the beads appear to be seated, the inflation process can continue pursuant to the manufacturer's specifications.

Harm testified that there are two possible causes for a tire bead to blow over the flange; a broken bead or a defective bead. In this case, x-rays eliminated the possibility that broken beads caused the accident. Harm explained, however, that a defective bead can give the appearance of being seated by hanging up. If the hang-up goes unnoticed, then the tire can blow over the flange in some instances.

Harm testified that cording, or bead hang-ups, are a normal part of the inflation procedure. A hang-up occurs when a portion of the bead does not move uniformly along the wheel out to the flange. Generally, a hang-up will release itself causing a popping sound as the wires in the bead hit against the flange. On occasion a hang-up will cause the tire to have the appearance of being seated because the air pressure forces the tire's side wall over the flange, hiding the fact that the bead did not move as it should have. Some hang-ups result in tire failure when the forces exerted on the tire are not spread evenly on all wires and a weakened portion of the bead blows over the flange. If the inflated tire were lying flat on the ground and the underside of the tire blew over the flange, the entire wheel assembly would be forced upward as air is expelled from the tire against the ground. A tire with thirty-five pounds of pressure could be projected upward ten to twenty feet.

In Harm's opinion, a hang-up of a defective bead caused the explosion at issue. The explosive release of air against the ground forced the tire and wheel assembly up into Cisneros' face as he was leaning over the tire. Harm based his opinion on his thirty-one years of experience in the tire industry, his training, his knowledge, and the evidence presented. He relied on testimony that the tire was inflated within the specified operating pressures, that the bead appeared to be seated, that there was a loud explosion, and that after the event one bead was over the flange. Harm stated that he found no abnormalities during his inspection of the wheel assembly. However, x-rays revealed that the bead wires were not tightly wound and formed gaps. He explained that as wires gapped during curing, rubber flowed in to fill the spaces. When this happens, the tire has a dished out appearance and feel along its circumference. Harm testified that he could see and feel the defect in the bead. Because of the defect, the wires were not supplying the strength required to hold the bead on the wheel, and the bead slipped over the flange causing an explosive release of air pressure. Harm testified that the tire blew off the flange at this point in time, as opposed to the times prior or subsequent to the particular mounting procedure at issue, because the hang-up involved a weak spot which could not withstand the exerted pressures.

Harm testified that by design, the bead is supposed to be a tightly wound bundle of wires, symmetrical in shape, following a definite pattern, and laying in a definite layer of the tire. He explained, however, that during vulcanization, or curing, the wire ends can unwind and move within the liquid rubber if they are not secured. To prevent unwinding, Uniroyal uses tie-downs which are squares of woven fabric wound around the bead wires to keep them secure. Other methods of reducing the risks caused by loose wires included using a computer controlled hex design for greater uniformity in strength throughout the bead, or using a larger diameter wire to increase the tensile strength of the bead. These methods could also be combined. Harm stated that the three methods were in use in the tire industry, that they would reduce the risk of injuries, and that they would not decrease the tire's utility. Harm testified that the risk of injury from defective beads could also be reduced if the manufacturer visually and manually inspected each tire after curing. If a manufacturer made these inspections, defective tires would be rejected before leaving the manufacturer's possession.

Harm testified that Dico does not include tie-downs for bead wires in the design of its multistrand weftless tire. The tire at issue was described as such a tire. X-rays, viewed by the jury, showed that the wires in this tire were not as tightly wound as they should have been and gaps appeared between the wires. Harm opined that because the wires were encased in rubber and could not shift after the curing procedure was completed, they moved during the manufacturing process. Harm also testified that he could feel and see "dishouts" along the entire circumference of the tire. For this reason, it was his opinion that the bead was defective at the time the tire left Dico's possession. According to Harm, the tire was unreasonably dangerous as designed and manufactured.

Harm also reviewed the deposition testimony of Clarence E. Erickson, a Dico engineer. Erickson's testimony showed that Dico did not have a manual post-cure inspection process for each tire. Erickson's deposition testimony was read to the jury and showed that Dico did not inspect its beads after curing was completed. A videotape showing Dico's manufacturing process, played during Harm's testimony, did not show a manual inspection procedure. Harm testified that if Dico had operated in an ordinary and prudent manner as a reasonable tire company should, they would have a post-cure inspection procedure. Harm testified that Dico's failure to properly inspect finished tires was negligence. If Dico had inspected its finished tires, the defect at issue could have been found during a hand inspection, and the tire at issue would have been rejected.

Dico contends that Harm's testimony was without probative value because it varied materially from the facts that were related by Cisneros. Specifically, Dico asserts that Cisneros claimed that the bead was properly seated and that Harm rejected this fact in developing his theory as to how the accident occurred. The record, however, shows Cisneros testified that the bead appeared to be seated. We conclude that Cisneros' testimony does not vary materially from the facts on which Harm relied.

After reviewing the substance of Harm's testimony, we find that it establishes the reasonable probability that a defective bead in a Dico tire caused Cisneros' injuries. The testimony was derived from Harm's thirty-one years in the tire industry spent in design, production, testing, and quality control. Harm's testimony is based on demonstrable facts rather than assumptions, possibility, surmise, and speculation. We conclude, therefore, that Harm's testimony is reliable proof of design and manufacturing defects as well as of Dico's negligence. Moreover, portions of Harm's testimony were similar to testimony provided by other witnesses.

Clarence Erickson, a retired Dico tire engineer, testified that a tightly wound bead bundle has more strength than one with gaps. He agreed that there was an explosive separation of the tire from the rim and did not dispute the fact that the tire and wheel assembly was propelled off the ground. Erickson admitted that a Dico tire with a defective bead which allowed the tire to blow over the flange would absolutely create a dangerous condition. He also testified that the danger would not be one contemplated by the ordinary user. Moreover, Erickson viewed x-rays of the tire at issue. He explained that the underlap moved through the wires. Erickson claimed this was not an unusual occurrence because that was the way Dico made these tires.

Ronald Walker, who had extensive expertise in the area of tire failure analysis, testified that if the bottom side of a tire were not properly seated and the tire was inflated to thirty-five pounds, then a tireman would be in danger if he leaned over the tire. If an explosion occurred at that point, the tireman would be injured. Walker also testified that hang-ups were common occurrences that can affect the construction of the tire by creating weaknesses. Walker opined that one portion of the bead on the tire at issue abraded against the edge of the wheel well, while another portion got "ready to come up over the flange" as pressure was added. At that point, the tire rapidly deflated, the tire and wheel assembly was launched, and the bead came off the wheel.

We hold that the evidence is legally sufficient to support the jury's findings on the issues of negligence, design defect, and manufacturing defect.

Exercise 4-11 Legally Sufficient Evidence

Much of the "evidence" students are exposed to in law school texts is appellate court summaries of evidence presented at trial. These evidentiary summaries are very different in form from actual evidence presented during trial, as you will see in this exercise. Below is a trial transcript of the plaintiff's expert witness' testimony in a products liability suit against the manufacturer of a truck tire, alleging defective manufacture of the tire.[1] Based on what you have learned so far, evaluate whether the plaintiff has met her burden of proof for any of the elements of her products liability claim. You may want to mark the places where testimony about each element is elicited.

---

1. The transcript is an edited compilation of the transcripts set out in 39 Am. Jur. Proof of Facts 2d 209 §§ 11–15.

1   [Q] At my request, did you examine the tire in this

2 case?

3   [A] I did, at least what remains of it.

4   [Q] Could you identify that tire for the jury, please?

5   [A] This is the tire, or what is left of it, Plain-

6 tiff's Exhibit [A] It is a bias ply tire manufactured by

7 _____. As you can see, it has no tread on it. The

8 tread has completely separated from the tire.

9   [Q] Does the separation of the tread from the tire mean

10 that the tire has failed?

11   [A] Yes, most certainly.

12   [Q] Could you describe the tire in terms of construction?

13   [Witness steps down from witness stand to demonstrate

14 tire description]

15   [A] This tire has a 12-ply rating. That doesn't mean

16 that it has to have 12 plies. It actually has six body

17 plies—nylon cord plies running in a bias direction from

18 bead to bead. The beads are located on either side of the

19 tire. The bead is the hard rim on the inside perimeter of

20 a tire that fits over the wheel rim to hold the tire in

21 place. There are three plies going in one direction and

22 three in the other, which is why it is called a bias ply-

23 constructed tire. On this particular tire, there is a

24 breaker ply that extends across the crown of the tire

25 from curb guard to curb guard.

26   [Q] What did you do during your examination?

27   [A] I placed the tire on a spreading machine where I

28 carefully examined the tire under intense light and magni-

29 fication. I measured the hardness of the rubber at various

30 random locations with a durometer. I also carefully exam-

31 ined the tube, flap, and rim which accompanied the tire.

32   [Q] During your examination of this tire and its parts,

33 did you take any photographs?

1   [A] I did.

2   [Photographs authenticated and received in evidence.]

3   [Q] Can you describe to the jury the area of failure in
4   this tire?

5   [A] Yes. This photograph is taken looking directly
6   [demonstrating] into the rupture where the hole is
7   through the tire. One way in which you can identify a
8   heat-generated rupture is the fact that at each end of
9   the elongated hole there is usually a "Y" configuration
10 where the cords have broken on the bias of the tire. If
11 this were an impact break where the tire had hit a curb
12 or some other object I would expect an "X" type break,
13 which would join at the very center. As you can see from
14 looking at the photographs and the tire, there is an
15 elongated hole here with two "Ys" which do not intersect
16 at the center.

17 [Q] Is there any evidence in that photograph of the
18 heat generated in this tire?

19 [A] Yes. Allow me to demonstrate with the tire, and
20 then I will show you on the photograph. This tire had a
21 considerable amount of heat generated all through it. The
22 heat was caused by friction on the road and by a tread
23 separation which was chafing or rubbing against the tire
24 cords themselves. On a large truck, the heat can go as
25 high as 400 or 450 degrees Fahrenheit. When this happens,
26 the tire loses its flexibility and the rubber changes its
27 appearance. The cords become brittle and they feel like
28 cardboard. Here is the point [indicating area on tire],
29 as I see it, where some of the greatest amount of heat
30 was generated. It can be seen by what we call in the in-
31 dustry "chafe and polish." Chafe is the condition of
32 friction between the tread and the cords which are moving
33 while the tire is rotating through its footprint. If you

1 take the palms of your hands and rub them together you
2 will find that heat is generated. A truck tire carrying a
3 load and going down the highway at 55 miles per hour can
4 reach a temperature that will actually melt the tire
5 cords. If the temperature is over, say, 250 degrees
6 Fahrenheit, synthetic nylon and thermal type cords will
7 begin to lose their tensile strength, and by that I mean
8 stretching strength. The strength of the cords becomes
9 minimal as the temperature rises. They will actually melt
10 at 450 degrees. This tire contains cords in this rupture
11 area which actually melted, and that conclusively shows
12 that temperatures above 400 degrees Fahrenheit and proba-
13 bly 450 degrees were achieved in this tire. Right through
14 here [demonstrating] is where the greatest temperature
15 was reached.
16   [Q] What caused the heat you have been describing?
17   [A] The friction of the tread that was loose around the
18 tire builds the temperature within the tire cords. As you
19 can see, the tread is completely gone although the tire
20 is still in one piece.
21   [Q] Using the photographs, can you show us any of these
22 cords which melted?
23   [A] Yes. Plaintiff's Exhibit D is a close-up picture of
24 the cords that have ruptured. I have placed three arrows
25 on the enlargement to show the cords which have actually
26 melted and fused together. There are thousands of fila-
27 ments in each of these cords. If you cut the cord, you
28 look at something like a shaving brush end. But these
29 tire cords have actually melted together and they look
30 like a solid piece.
31   [Q] Do you have an opinion as to what caused this tire
32 to separate?
33   [A] I do.

1   [Q] Please state that opinion to the jury.

2   [A] Tires don't normally separate. There must be a rea-
3   son for the separation. In this case it was initiated and
4   caused by a manufacturing defect in this tire. It is my
5   opinion that the defect here was in the form of air en-
6   trapments, air pockets, that were built in during the man-
7   ufacture of the tire at the factory by the manufacturer.

8   [Q] Please explain to the jury how, in your opinion,
9   air entrapments were manufactured into this tire.

10   [A] Let me briefly describe some generalities regarding
11   tire manufacturing. Many people assume that to make a
12   tire you simply pour rubber into a mold, heat it, cure
13   it, and then take it out as a tire with a tread design
14   that looks like this tire here in the courtroom. Actu-
15   ally, making a tire is a very painful process and not au-
16   tomatic at all. There are somewhere between 12 and 30
17   individual component parts of uncured rubber and plies
18   made on a production line. These are cut to size for each
19   specific size and type of tire. Then, at one point, there
20   is one person who is totally responsible for building the
21   entire tire from start to finish. The component parts are
22   brought to him and he begins building on what we call flat
23   implant ply, the second ply, the beads, and flip-ups.
24   Step-by-step, he physically builds a tire by laminating
25   these pieces together.

26   [Q] What do you mean by "laminating"?

27   [A] A piece of plywood is an example. You laminate or
28   bond together one piece to another. The tread of a tire is
29   laminated to the top ply. Originally all of these are sep-
30   arate pieces.

31   [Q] Please continue.

32   [A] If you'll notice around the circumference of the
33   sidewall of the tire there is a one-inch strip here which

1 is called a curb guard. We will use that as a reference

2 point to indicate where the problem originated. Here [in-

3 dicating] is the junction point of the sidewall and the

4 tread which, as you can see, are made of different compo-

5 nents. The breaker ply which I earlier described to you

6 does not go down into the sidewall but stops about this

7 point [indicating] near the curb guard. This is a logical

8 place for a tire builder who is assembling these tires to

9 create and trap air, and in my opinion, that is what hap-

10 pened with this tire. The air pockets are still in the

11 tire and can be observed.

12   [Q] Can you show the air pockets to the jury?

13   [A] If I use this small spotlight, it will give them a

14 better view of the pockets. As you can see, there is a

15 small "flap" here from which the tread is torn. It varies

16 in size along the circumference of the tire and is jagged

17 due to the tearing which took place. You can pull this

18 flap back, like so [demonstrating], and you can see these

19 strips running along inside here which are cleaner and

20 shinier than the rest of the tire and have a different

21 appearance. They have no tire cord markings on them. This

22 is evidence of air entrapments. Air entrapments usually

23 show up clean and shiny. These pockets are located inter-

24 mittently all around the tire. They are like a channel

25 circumferentially going around the tire. You can see and

26 feel these air pockets.

27   [Q] Do you have any photographs that could further

28 demonstrate the air pockets?

29   [A] Yes. On Plaintiff's Exhibit D you can see where the

30 arrows are pointing toward the air entrapments. The rest

31 of the area has cord markings and is muddy colored, but

32 the pocket marks are black and shiny showing where the

33 entrapment has occurred and was molded into the tire.

1   [Q] And you said these entrapments are located

2 throughout the circumference of the tire?

3   [A] Yes. Approximately 40 percent of the circumference

4 in the area of the curb guard has evidence of air pocket-

5 ing behind it.

6   [Q] And it is your opinion that these air pockets were

7 manufactured into this tire?

8   [A] That is my opinion.

9   [Q] What evidence do you have that shows that the air

10 pockets you have just described and demonstrated caused

11 the ultimate failure of this tire?

12   [A] If we go back to the piece of tread which we dis-

13 cussed earlier, even though it is the only piece we have,

14 I gained some important information from my examination

15 of that.

16   [Q] Please take this piece of tread and show us what you

17 learned from your examination.

18   [A] If you will look at the outer surface of the tread,

19 you can see an erratic wear pattern. There is a combina-

20 tion of what we call heel-and-toe step wear. The pattern

21 of wear across the tread is not even. You can actually

22 see dipping here [demonstrating].

23   [Q] What is the importance of an erratic wear pattern?

24   [A] It could indicate many things. Misalignment, for

25 instance. However, because the tread has completely sepa-

26 rated from the tire, the conclusion I came to for the er-

27 ratic tread wear was due to the fact that it adheres or

28 sticks to the tire in some locations, and in other loca-

29 tions, such as here [demonstrating] it tears away from

30 the tire. As the tire was rotating in service, prior to

31 the time of failure, there were areas that were sticking

32 well and other areas that were loose. This intermittent

33 looseness resulted in the erratic tread wear.

1   [Q] Does the underside of that piece of tread have any

2 significance to you?

3   [A] Yes.

4   [Q] What is that?

5   [A] There are places underneath that show it tore away

6 from the tire. You have areas of impression of the tire

7 cords which mean that in those areas you had adhesion at

8 the time of failure, but you also have areas of chafe and

9 polish.

10   [Q] Could you explain the difference?

11   [A] Here [demonstrating], we have an image of the tire

12 cords. This actually pulled away some of the breaker

13 strip, while in this area it can be observed that the im-

14 pression of the tire cords has been rubbed off. That is

15 what we call chafe and polish. It is somewhat shiny. That

16 is the area which was loose and was chafing together when

17 the tire failed. The chafing caused the polishing effect

18 that we see.

19   [Q] Is there evidence of chafe and polish on the casing?

20   [A] Yes. Again around the entire outer periphery you

21 have conclusive evidence of chafing, polishing, separa-

22 tion, and a resulting heavy heat buildup. The tar paper-

23 ish kind of surface here is where heat has actually

24 destroyed the properties of the tire cord and rubber

25 within this surface.

26   [Q] Would you describe the chafe as uniform or erratic?

27   [A] Erratic.

28   [Q] Does that have any significance?

29   [A] Yes. It means the plies were adhering in some parts

30 and separated in some parts. This type of separation is

31 typical of what a tire with this type defect exhibits just

32 prior to failure.

33

1   [Q] Did these air pockets get into any other area of
2   the tire that might have contributed to the ultimate
3   failure?
4   [A] Yes. The air pockets located here along the curb
5   guard will cause a build up in heat as the tire rotates
6   on the road. Under any type of increase in temperature
7   these air pockets will begin to expand. As the tire goes
8   through its footprint, it flexes. For example, if you look
9   at the bottom of this tire, when it gets a load on it, it
10   goes through a flexing condition [demonstrating]. As it
11   flexes, the air pockets are encouraged, so to speak, to
12   expand. The air pockets expand upward and across the
13   crown because the tire is flexing. So, for example, as the
14   tire goes 18,000 or 20,000 miles it begins to separate
15   more and more. It's like a cavity in a tooth. If you
16   don't do something to correct it, it's only going to get
17   worse. As the tire in question separated, the friction of
18   the moving of the tread against the outer ply caused a
19   deterioration of these plies. High pressure from air
20   within the casing, which was about 85 pounds per square
21   inch, overcame the strength of the weakened-by-tempera-
22   ture tire cords, and the tire simply exploded.
23   [Q] And, in your opinion, the origin of all that was
24   the air pockets?
25   [A] That is correct.
26
27
28
29
30
31
32
33

Exercise 4-12 Thinking Like a Jury

You might have heard that law school teaches you to "think like a lawyer." While this is a useful skill, you may also want to learn to "think like a jury" if you are preparing a case for or presenting a case at trial. For example, when you read the testimony in exercise 4-11, did you experience any confusion? Where? Why? Do you think a jury might be similarly confused? How might you eliminate that confusion?

Remember, as you read the next series of cases you should consider:

(1) What type of defect(s) are alleged by the plaintiff;

(2) Whether there are any resources available to you that provide information about the product (You may want to search for information about each product and find out more about the design, engineering, industry standards, etc.);

(3) What evidence—direct and/or circumstantial—is available to prove the defect existed at the time the product left the defendant's control; and

(4) Whether expert testimony is necessary to prove (a) there was a defect, and/or (b) the defect existed at the time the product left the defendant's control.

Based on the last two exercises, you might also think about how you would elicit the appropriate evidence and how you (or your experts and other witnesses) would present the evidence to the jury so that it is understandable.

Jurls v. Ford Motor Co.

752 So.2d 260 (La. App. 2 Cir. 2000)

Plaintiffs, Danny D. Jurls and Betty Jean Jurls, appeal a judgment dismissing their products liability action against Ford Motor Company ("Ford"). The trial court granted Ford's motion for directed verdict at the close of the plaintiffs' presentation of their case to the jury. We now reverse the trial court's judgment and remand for further proceedings.

FACTS

Danny Jurls ("Jurls") purchased a 1989 Ford Ranger pick-up truck from a Ford dealership in September 1989. The vehicle was a demonstrator model with approximately 5,000 miles on the odometer and came equipped with a cruise control system. Jurls drove the vehicle for two months, logging about 2,000 miles, prior to the accident at issue. No mechanical problems occurred during this time.

The accident at issue occurred on November 14, 1989, during Jurls' return home to Bossier City from work. Jurls was employed as a teacher at Princeton Elementary School in Haughton, Louisiana. Jurls typically traveled to and from work along Interstate 20 ("I-20"). The accident occurred as Jurls exited I-20 at Airline Drive in Bossier City. Jurls testified that he set the cruise control at 65 m.p.h. for his drive along I-20. Upon entering the city limits of Bossier City, he reduced his speed to 55 m.p.h. As he approached the Airline Drive exit, Jurls applied the brakes to slow down before entering the exit ramp.

Jurls testified that he felt his speed was under control and that he did not remove his foot from the brake pedal. Then, Jurls felt the vehicle increase in speed as though coasting. He pressed down on the brake pedal twice to no avail. He believed that the brakes on his vehicle had gone out. Jurls then attempted to slow the vehicle by pressing the clutch and shifting gears from fifth to second. The engine began "screaming." Believing that the vehicle would kill him, Jurls turned the key off. The steering column stiffened as the vehicle entered the intersection at Airline Drive, and Jurls "just kind of folded up ... and rode with it." The vehicle crossed the intersection on a red light and flipped three or four times, seriously injuring Jurls and totaling the vehicle.

Deborah Oswald, a passenger in a vehicle traveling northbound on Airline Drive, witnessed the accident. Oswald first noticed Jurls traveling on the I-20 off-ramp. Oswald testified that it appeared as though the vehicle was increasing in speed and as though Jurls could not stop the vehicle. However, Jurls was able to maintain sufficient control of his vehicle to go around other vehicles without hitting them. Oswald heard Jurls say that he could not stop his vehicle. Additionally, Nancy John Chance, the driver of the vehicle in which Oswald was riding, also testified that she saw Jurls' vehicle on the off-ramp and that it did not appear to be slowing and that it did not look like Jurls could stop it. Chance also heard Jurls say immediately after the accident that the brakes would not work.

When paramedics and police arrived at the accident scene, Jurls told them that the brakes would not stop the vehicle. Officer Kevin Ross of the Bossier City Police Department investigated the accident. Officer Ross' testimony regarding his investigation corroborates Jurls' version of how the accident occurred. Although Jurls initially believed that the brakes on his vehicle had failed, he learned shortly after the accident that the brakes worked. Jurls then came to believe that the cruise control system must have malfunctioned. Phillip J. Mijka, a design analysis engineer employed by Ford, inspected Jurls' vehicle in January 1990.

Mijka's inspection first eliminated the possibility of a linkage problem with either the engine or accelerator as a cause of the accident. With linkage eliminated as a possible problem, Mijka agreed with Jurls' counsel that only two possibilities remained: either the cruise control did not respond or Jurls' foot remained on the accelerator. Mijka then conducted a visual inspection of the cruise control system, checking the speedo cable routing, wiring in the engine compartment, and the connections using a screw driver test. All checked out fine. Mijka then used a cruise control analyzer, also referred to as a rotunda device, which uses an auxiliary battery source to check the brake and clutch switches. This test indicated that the brake and clutch switches made an electrical connection or circuit when moved. The vacuum dump valve was tested by sucking on it and by applying a vacuum gauge. Both tests appeared positive. However, all parts of the cruise control system could not be tested. Mijka could not test the servo operator because the vehicle could not be started. Also, the amplifier could not be tested, and the speed sensor could not be located, possibly due to damage from the accident. Mijka testified that after his inspection, he determined that at least four systems were operating which could have disengaged the cruise control: the off switch on the cruise control, the brake switch, the clutch switch, and the dump valve. However, Mijka admitted that if the system computer, which was not tested, was not working, then neither the signal from the clutch or brake switch may have disengaged the cruise control.

After Mijka's inspection, Jurls hired a repairman to remove the cruise control components from the vehicle before it was scrapped. The cruise control parts were stored in a garage owned by a friend of Jurls and later turned over to Jurls' attorney. Jurls and his wife filed suit against Ford for damages, alleging that the vehicle's cruise control system was defective. After withstanding two summary judgment motions, the matter proceeded to trial before a jury. In addition to the testimony of Jurls, Officer Ross, the two witnesses to the accident, and Mijka, the record also includes the testimony of two additional witnesses called by the plaintiffs.

Victor DeClerc, a design analysis engineer employed by Ford, was called by the plaintiffs on cross-examination, as was Mijka. On the Tuesday before trial, DeClerc tested the parts of the cruise control system that had been removed after the accident. Plaintiffs' counsel first questioned DeClerc about the meaning of "overspeeding" as that term was used in a 1989 Ford shop manual. DeClerc explained that the term was used in the context of testing the speed control of a vehicle raised on a hoist and not being driven. Declerc was not aware that the shop manual also contained a caution regarding overspeeding in the context of a road test. When informed of this fact, DeClerc explained that the caution applied to technicians working on vehicles with speed control problems and that drivers would not, in all likelihood, see such problems. DeClerc also testified that though he researched various reports to get a global picture on overspeeding, he did no specific research on complaints of cruise control problems with Ford.

DeClerc tested the parts remaining from Jurls' cruise control system by placing them on another 1989 Ford Ranger. DeClerc was unable to test the dump valve, the speed sensor, or the wiring from Jurls' vehicle; he was able to test the amplifier and servo mechanism which had not been tested by Mijka. Though the test vehicle would not start at first due to problems with the clutch switch from Jurls' vehicle, DeClerc's test of the cruise control system revealed no malfunction. DeClerc did testify that the engine noise heard by Jurls when he attempted to shift gears could result from only two possibilities: the cruise control or Jurls' foot inadvertently placed on the accelerator.

Testifying on the plaintiffs' behalf was Donnie Tuminello who qualified as an expert in automobile mechanics. The most likely cause of the accident, according to Tuminello, was failure of the dump valve to release when the brakes were pressed and disengage the cruise control, thereby resulting in overspeeding. Tuminello discussed the overspeeding caution included in the Ford shop manual and believed that the problem mentioned in the manual was what happened in this instance — the cruise control did not disengage when Jurls applied the brakes.

Tuminello agreed with Mijka and Declerc that the overspeeding, as indicated by the engine noise when Jurls attempted to shift gears, resulted from either the cruise control or Jurls' inadvertently pressing the accelerator. Tuminello participated in Declerc's testing of the cruise control parts from Jurls' vehicle. Although Tuminello did not criticize the testing when conducted, at trial he stated that the test using the substitute Ford Ranger was not a valid test of the cruise control system because all the parts from Jurls' vehicle were not available. Tuminello mentioned that the amplifier, the "brain of the system," could not be properly tested because the schematic was not available from Ford. Tuminello also believed that the fuses from Jurls' vehicle were not tested. Although Tuminello stated that he did not believe Ford made a defective part, he later explained the comment by stating that Ford does not make a defective product, but that there had to be a defect in order for the cruise control system in the Jurls' vehicle to have malfunctioned.

At the close of the plaintiffs' case, Ford moved for a directed verdict. The trial court found that the plaintiffs failed to prove the existence of a defect and that reasonable minds could not conclude that there was a defect in the vehicle when it left the manufacturer. The trial judge also indicated that he would not allow the matter to go before a jury only to try to get sympathy for the plaintiffs because Ford is a large corporation. Plaintiffs appeal the judgment dismissing their claim against Ford and contend that the evidence was sufficient to allow the jury to reasonably conclude that the accident was caused by a defect in their vehicle's cruise control system.

DISCUSSION

A manufacturer is liable for damages proximately caused by an unreasonably dangerous product when the damages arose from a reasonably anticipated use of the product. La. R.S. 9:2800.54(A). A product may be unreasonably dangerous in construction or composition, in design, or because of the lack of an adequate warning or the failure to conform to an express warranty. La. R.S. 9:2800.54.

In their petition for damages, the plaintiffs alleged there was a defect in either the design or manufacture of the Ford Ranger and that Ford failed to warn that the cruise control system could malfunction as it did. Having waived both the design defect and failure to warn claims at trial, the plaintiffs' remaining theory is that of a manufacturing defect under La. R.S. 9:2800.55 which states: A product is unreasonably dangerous in construction or composition if, at the time the product left its manufacturer's control, the product deviated in a material way from the manufacturer's specifications or performance standards for the product or from otherwise identical products manufactured by the same manufacturer.

We cannot infer the existence of a defect solely from the fact that an accident occurred. Ashley, supra. However, a manufacturing defect may be established by circumstantial evidence under the evidentiary doctrine of res ipsa loquitur. *Kampen v. American Isuzu Motors, Inc.*, 119 F.3d 1193 (5 th Cir.1997), vacated on other grounds, 157 F.3d 306 (5 th 1998); *Williams v. Emerson Elec. Co.*, 909 F.Supp. 395 (M.D.La.1995); *Randolph v. General Motors Corp.*, 93 1983 (La.App. 1st Cir.11/10/94), 646 So.2d 1019), writ denied, 95-0194 (La.3/17/95), 651 So.2d 276; *State Farm Mut. Auto. Ins. Co. v. Wrap-On Co., Inc.*, 626 So.2d 874 (La.App. 3rd Cir.1993), writ denied, 93-2988 (La.1/28/94), 630 So.2d 800. The res ipsa loquitur doctrine means that the circumstances surrounding an accident are so unusual as to give rise to an inference of negligence or liability on the part of the defendant. Under such circumstances, the only reasonable and fair conclusion is that the accident resulted from a breach of duty or omission on the part of the defendant. *State Farm, supra.* Jurisprudence has relaxed the exclusive control element associated with res ipsa loquitur. *Williams, supra; Spott v. Otis Elevator Co.*, 601 So.2d 1355 (La.1992); *State Farm, supra; Lucas v. St. Frances Cabrini Hospital*, 562 So.2d 999 (La.App. 3d Cir.1990), writ denied, 567 So.2d 101, 567 So.2d 103 (La.1990).

The plaintiffs were not able to point to any specific defect which resulted in a malfunction of the cruise control system. However, the plaintiffs' expert, Donnie Tuminello, was able to point to possible causes for the alleged malfunction. Tuminello initially believed the most likely cause of the accident was the dump valve which failed to reduce pressure in the vacuum tank when the brake was applied and disengage the cruise control. Tuminello also suggested at trial that the cruise control malfunction could have resulted from some problem with either the amplifier or the clutch switch. While the tests performed on the available cruise control components by Ford's experts revealed no negative results, Tuminello's testimony called into question the absolute reliability of the tests performed to discover what may have malfunctioned in Jurls' vehicle at the time of the accident. Neither Mijka nor DeClerc was able to test all the components of the cruise control system either due to damage from the accident or because the repairman hired by Jurls to remove the parts after the accident failed to remove all necessary components. Particularly relevant to our consideration of whether the directed verdict was properly granted is that all the experts—Mijka, DeClerc, and Tuminello—agreed that the engine noise heard by Jurls could only have been caused by one of the two following options: either Jurls inadvertently had his foot on the accelerator rather than the brake, or the cruise control system was engaged. No evidence shows that Jurls' foot was on the accelerator rather than on the brake.

Circumstantial evidence may be sufficient under the facts of a case to establish a manufacturing defect for purposes of liability under the LPLA. We note that the LPLA imposes liability on a manufacturer for "a characteristic of the product" that renders it unreasonably dangerous, and not a "specific" characteristic. See *Williams, supra,* at FN3.

The trial court also relied upon our decision in *Ashley, supra,* as a basis for its ruling. However, there are factual distinctions between the case *sub judice* and *Ashley, supra. Ashley* involved an older vehicle which had been driven 75,621 miles. While a mechanic who examined the vehicle in *Ashley* after the accident found the throttle open beyond the normal idling position, the plaintiff did not specifically recall whether she stepped on the accelerator or the brake. The sudden acceleration accident in *Ashley* occurred after the plaintiff came to a stop then proceeded to turn left, a maneuver which would have required her to accelerate, thereby increasing the likelihood that the plaintiff actually had her foot on the accelerator rather than on the brake. In the case *sub judice,* the vehicle was new with approximately 7,000 miles on the odometer at the time of the accident. The accident occurred only two months after Jurls purchased the vehicle. Both immediately after the accident and at trial, Jurls was adamant that he applied the brakes and that the vehicle would not stop. The manner in which the accident occurred suggests the likelihood that Jurls would have been applying his brakes to slow the vehicle as it negotiated the exit from I-20. Based on these distinctions, we believe the circumstantial evidence in the present case is greater than that in *Ashley, supra,* and deserving of close scrutiny by a jury.

While the evidence put forth by the plaintiff in the present case is not overwhelming and not certain to result in a favorable verdict, we cannot say that it is so overwhelmingly deficient as to preclude the possibility that reasonable minds might find that the Ford Ranger was unreasonably dangerous under the LPLA. The absence of expert testimony indicating a specific defect in the vehicle is not dispositive of liability. A jury might infer that the product was unreasonably dangerous from the circumstantial evidence presented. The outcome is for the jury to decide. Therefore, we find that the trial court erred in granting a directed verdict in favor of Ford in this matter.

CONCLUSION

For the reasons discussed, we reverse the trial court's dismissal of the plaintiffs' action against Ford and remand for further proceedings consistent with this opinion. REVERSED AND REMANDED.

WILLIAMS, J., dissenting.

Because the plaintiffs failed to present evidence to establish that the particular cruise control system installed in this specific vehicle materially deviated from the manufacturer's specifications or performance standards, I respectfully dissent.

A manufacturer shall be liable to a claimant for damage caused by an unreasonably dangerous product during a reasonably anticipated use. LSA-R.S. 9:2800.54. *Ashley v. General Motors Corp.,* 27,851 (La.App.2d Cir.1/24/96), 666 So.2d 1320. A product is unreasonably dangerous in construction if, at the time it left the control of the manufacturer, the product deviated in a material way from the manufacturer's specifications or performance standards, or if the product deviated from otherwise identical products made by the same manufacturer. LSA-R.S. 9:2800.55.

In the present case, the majority attempts to circumvent the plaintiffs' burden of presenting some evidence that the product deviated from manufacturer specifications by relying on the evidentiary doctrine of res ipsa loquitur. This doctrine is a rule of circumstantial evidence in which negligence is inferred because in common experience the incident in question would not ordinarily occur in the absence of negligence. However, if there is an equally plausible explanation for the occurrence, then application of the doctrine is defeated. *McDowell v. Don Bohn Ford, Inc.*, 99-238 (La.App. 5 th Cir. 7/27/99), 739 So.2d 950. The circumstantial evidence presented must exclude reasonable hypotheses with a fair amount of certainty. *Weber v. Fidelity & Casualty Ins. Co.*, 250 So.2d 754, 259 La. 599 (1971).

As an example of "circumstantial" evidence, the majority refers to the testimony of Tuminello, a retired auto mechanic. However, even if applying the *res ipsa loquitur* doctrine, Tuminello's recitation of "possible causes" for the alleged cruise control malfunction is not sufficient to establish an inference of liability because he was unable to exclude with a fair amount of certainty the reasonable hypothesis that Jurls was negligent in pressing the accelerator.

The plaintiffs argue that the witness testimony established a factual issue for the jury because DeClerc, Mijka and Tuminello all agreed that if the engine made a loud roaring noise when Jurls pressed the clutch, the two possible explanations were that his other foot was pressing down on the accelerator pedal, or that the cruise control was holding the throttle open. However, such testimony merely indicates two alternative reasons for the described racing of the engine, and does not relieve plaintiffs of their statutory burden to present evidence that the cruise control materially deviated from Ford's specifications.

In support of its reasoning, the majority cites the case of *State Farm Mutual Auto. Ins. Co. v. Wrap-On Co., Inc.*, 626 So.2d 874 (La.App. 3 rd Cir.1993), in which a fire caused damage to property, and the owner and his insurer sued the manufacturer of heating tape for pipes, alleging that the product was unreasonably dangerous and had caused the fire. Expert testimony ruled out all other sources of the fire and identified physical evidence such as burn marks on pipes, allowing an inference that the heat tape had malfunctioned and caused the fire.

Here, in contrast, the plaintiffs' expert failed to identify any physical evidence of malfunction and the majority itself has pointed out that the expert testimony suggests that in addition to a cruise control problem, an equally possible cause of the roaring engine noise was the plaintiff's inadvertent pressing of the gas pedal. Because there is an equally plausible explanation for the occurrence, the doctrine of res ipsa loquitur is inapplicable and the majority's reliance thereon is misplaced.

Expert testimony based on speculation, conjecture and mere possibilities cannot support a judgment. *Lott v. Lebon*, 96-1328 (La.App. 4th Cir. 1/15/97), 687 So.2d 612, writs denied, 97-0359, 97-0414 (La.3/21/97), 691 So.2d 92, 95. Despite Tuminello's earlier affidavit opinion that the accident was caused by a vacuum dump valve malfunction, during trial he suggested that the cruise control did not work because of a possible problem with the amplifier. Although Tuminello acknowledged that he had not tested the amplifier and could not specify any physical evidence of amplifier failure, Tuminello speculated that there was "a possibility of some condition in that amplifier that could cause" a malfunction and that there were "a lot of things that could have happened" to the amplifier.

Another possibility raised by Tuminello was that the clutch switch had malfunctioned, preventing the deactivation of the cruise control. He supported this suggestion by pointing out that the test vehicle would not start after the clutch from the Jurls vehicle was installed. Despite his stated concern about the clutch, at trial Tuminello maintained that he could not remember whether pressing the clutch had deactivated the cruise control during the test. However, Tuminello was able to recall that the brake had deactivated the cruise control and he acknowledged that he could not dispute DeClerc's testimony that the clutch had disengaged the system as well.

Although plaintiffs' expert witness mentioned several possible problems which could have affected operation of the cruise control under the circumstances of the accident, Tuminello's testimony was speculative at best and thus is not sufficient to support a jury finding that any of the cruise control components of the Jurls' 1989 pickup truck deviated in a material way from Ford's performance standards. To the contrary, the evidence shows that each of the cruise control parts which were tested functioned properly.

In an attempt to support their allegation that the cruise control was defective, the plaintiffs introduced into evidence a Ford service manual, which recognized the possibility of overspeeding, a condition where the throttle is held open. However, the plaintiffs did not present any evidence that their truck exhibited the problem described in the manual, other than the occurrence of the accident itself. A factfinder may not infer the existence of a defect in a product based solely on the fact that an accident occurred. *Jaeger v. Automotive Casualty Insurance Co.*, 95-2448 (La.App. 4 th Cir. 10/9/96), 682 So.2d 292, writ denied, 96-2715 (La.2/7/97), 688 So.2d 498.

The majority ignores the plaintiffs' burden of proof and apparently imposes upon defendant the burden of establishing that all of the cruise control parts worked properly. However, it is the plaintiffs who have the burden of proving by a preponderance of the evidence that a material deviation from the norm rendered the product unreasonably dangerous.

Although the plaintiffs proved that an accident occurred and that Danny Jurls sustained injuries, the plaintiffs failed to satisfy their burden of proving that the cruise control system in their pickup truck was unreasonably dangerous due to a material deviation from Ford's product specifications, as required by the Louisiana Products Liability Act. Consequently, the record in this case does not contain evidence, even when viewed in the light most favorable to plaintiffs, from which a reasonable juror could infer that the accident was caused by a defect in the cruise control of the plaintiffs' vehicle. Therefore, I cannot say that the trial court abused its discretion in granting the defendant's motion for a directed verdict. Accordingly, I would affirm the district court's judgment.

Woodin v. J.C. Penney Co., Inc.

427 Pa.Super. 488, 629 A.2d 974 (1993)

In this action to recover fire damage attributed by plaintiffs to a defectively manufactured freezer cord, the trial court set aside a verdict for the plaintiffs and entered judgment n.o.v. in favor of the defendant seller and manufacturer. Plaintiffs appealed. We affirm.

Early in 1979, Robert and Alice Woodin purchased a chest type freezer from J.C. Penney Company, Inc. The freezer had been manufactured by White Consolidated Industries, Inc. It was delivered by Penney's employees and placed in the northeast corner of the utility room located on the first floor of the Woodin home. The utility room was approximately eighteen (18) feet wide and eight (8) feet long, had wood panelled walls and a plywood floor finished with Armstrong linoleum. The back of the freezer was placed along the east wall of the room, and the left end of the unit was positioned along the north wall. Only two and one-half (2 1/2) feet of unoccupied space existed between the right end of the freezer and the south wall of the room. Because the power cord, which extended from the unit's compressor in the back, left corner of the freezer, was of insufficient length, an extension cord was used to connect the freezer to the electrical outlet located at the southeast corner of the room.

For more than eight years the freezer operated continuously without complaint. On December 2, 1987, the Woodins left their home at or about 9:30 a.m. A fire was reported about noon. Alleging that the fire had been caused by a defect in the power cord, the Woodins filed suit against J.C. Penney, which, in turn, joined White, the manufacturer, as an additional defendant.

At trial, the plaintiffs relied on the testimony of expert witnesses that the fire had been caused by a short circuit in the power cord near the unit's compressor. The defendants contended, however, that the fire had not originated in the area of the compressor and that it could not have been started by a short circuit in the power cord. A jury returned a verdict for the plaintiffs for $67,850.00, the amount of the damages stipulated by the parties. The trial court overruled the jury's verdict because there was an absence of evidence identifying any defect in the cord of the freezer and because the verdict, therefore, could be based on nothing but speculation.

It is well settled that in order to recover on a theory of strict product liability, a plaintiff must prove that (1) the product was defective; (2) the defect was the proximate cause of the plaintiff's injuries; and (3) the defect existed at the time it left the manufacturer's control. *Berkebile v. Brantly Helicopter Corp.*, 462 Pa. 83, 93–94, 337 A.2d 893, 898 (1975); *Roselli v. General Electric Co.*, 410 Pa.Super. 223, 229, 599 A.2d 685, 688 (1991), allocatur granted, 530 Pa. 645, 607 A.2d 255 (1992), appeal discont'd, January 11, 1993. Generally, a plaintiff will produce direct evidence of a product's defective condition. In those cases where the plaintiff is unable to prove the precise nature of the product's defect, however, he may, in some cases, rely on the "malfunction theory" of product liability. *Rogers v. Johnson & Johnson Products, Inc.*, 523 Pa. 176, 182, 565 A.2d 751, 754 (1989). The malfunction theory allows the plaintiff to use circumstantial evidence to establish a defective product. In *Rogers v. Johnson & Johnson Products, Inc., supra,* the court stated: [The malfunction theory] permits a plaintiff to prove a defect in a product with evidence of the occurrence of a malfunction and with evidence eliminating abnormal use or reasonable, secondary causes for the malfunction. [The plaintiff is relieved] from demonstrating precisely the defect yet it permits the trier-of-fact to infer one existed from evidence of the malfunction, of the absence of abnormal use and of the absence of reasonable, secondary causes. *Id.* (citations omitted). Although proof of a specific defect is not essential to establish liability under this theory, the plaintiff cannot depend upon conjecture or guesswork. "The mere fact that an accident happens, even in this enlightened age, does not take the injured plaintiff to the jury." *Stein v. General Motors Corp.*, 58 D. & C.2d 193, 203 (Bucks 1972), aff'd, 222 Pa.Super. 751, 295 A.2d 111 (1972).

The freezer in the instant case had functioned flawlessly for more than eight (8) years. Appellants testified that they had at no time observed wearing or deterioration of the power cord. In *Kuisis v. Baldwin-Lima-Hamilton Corp.*, 457 Pa. 321, 319 A.2d 914 (1974), the Supreme Court stated as follows:

We recognize that, as a general rule, "prolonged use of a manufactured article is but one factor, albeit an important one, in the determination of the factual issue whether [a defect in design or] manufacture proximately caused the harm." The age of an allegedly defective product must be considered in light of its expected useful life and the stress to which it has been subjected. In most cases, the weighing of these factors should be left to the finder of fact. But in certain situations the prolonged use factor may loom so large as to obscure all others in a case. Professor Prosser has summarized the position generally taken by the courts on this question: "[Lapse of time and long continued use] in itself is not enough, even when it has extended over a good many years, to defeat the recovery where there is satisfactory proof of an original defect; but when there is no definite evidence, and it is only a matter of inference from the fact that something broke or gave way, the continued use usually prevents the inference that the thing was more probably than not defective when it was sold." *Id.* at 336, 319 A.2d at 923 (citations omitted).

Here, there was no evidence to identify any defect in the freezer cord at the time the freezer was sold. Thus, the occurrence of the fire alone did not give rise to an inference of a defect at the time of manufacture. Richard Brugger, a professional engineer, expressed the opinion that the cord was "not adequate." However, he conceded that he had never examined an undamaged freezer cord, and when the damaged cord which had been attached to appellants' freezer was shown to him, he was unable to identify any defect therein. His opinion, he said, was based on evidence that a short circuit had occurred in the power cord, but he conceded that short circuits can and frequently do occur during fires because the intense heat generated by an external fire destroys wire insulation.

Under these circumstances, we agree with the trial court that the evidence was insufficient to prove a defect in the cord at the time of manufacture and sale of the freezer unit. Where, as here, the freezer had functioned flawlessly during eight (8) years of continuous operation and plaintiffs' evidence was unable to identify any specific defect therein, the jury could not properly infer the existence of a defect from the occurrence of a fire. The jury's verdict, therefore, as the trial court appropriately observed, could only be a product of speculation. There was no evidence to support a finding that the freezer was defective when sold.

McCabe v. American Honda Motor Co.
100 Cal. App. 4th 1111, 123 Cal. Rptr. 2d 303 (2002)

Plaintiff Lucille McCabe appeals from a judgment entered in a products liability action after the trial court granted summary judgment for defendants American Honda Motor Company, Incorporated and Saturn of the Valley, Incorporated (Saturn). McCabe was injured when the driver's side air bag in her Honda Civic failed to deploy in a frontal collision with another car. McCabe sued Honda, the air bag's manufacturer, and Saturn, the reseller, alleging the air bag was defective in both its manufacture and its design.

FACTUAL AND PROCEDURAL BACKGROUND

On September 2, 1999, while traveling westbound in her Civic, McCabe came to a full stop in the left turn lane of a controlled intersection and waited for a break in oncoming traffic to make a left turn. According to McCabe, as the light turned yellow and she prepared to make her left turn, a Cadillac traveling eastbound at a "high speed" collided "head on" with her Civic. Although the Civic was equipped with a driver's side air bag, the air bag did not deploy in the crash. McCabe, who suffered damage to her face and teeth in the accident when her head slammed against the steering wheel, sued Honda and Saturn, alleging the Civic's air bag was defective in its design and/or manufacture.

Honda moved for summary judgment, arguing that the air bag performed in accordance with its intended design. Honda included with its motion the 1995 owner's manual for the Civic, advising the consumer that the air bag system is designed to inflate only "in a severe frontal collision" comparable to "a crash into a parked car at 25 [miles per hour]," and will not inflate "in a moderate frontal collision, or during a rear impact, side impact, or a roll-over even if the impact is severe." The owner's manual also included an illustration depicting the "frontal collision range" to span from the outside corner of one front headlight to the outside corner of the other.

Honda also included the expert declaration of Mary Christopherson, a Honda staff engineer involved in the design and testing of automotive air bags. Christopherson explained that determining whether an air bag should have deployed after a given collision required "an analysis of the angle of impact and the longitudinal deceleration experienced by the vehicle in the collision as compared with the severity of a 12 [miles per hour] full frontal impact." According to Christopherson, the air bag is designed to deploy "when the crash sensors predict in the first moments of a collision that the deceleration of the vehicle along its longitudinal axis will be more severe than a full frontal barrier impact at or above 12 [miles per hour]," and is designed not to deploy if the "longitudinal deceleration of the vehicle is less severe than a full frontal barrier impact below 8 [miles per hour]." In addition, the "'frontal collision range' for deployment is defined as an impact with a principal direction of force that is within 30 degrees of the centerline of the vehicle. Air bags are not intended to deploy in impacts in which the principle [sic] force vector is outside the 30 degree range, unless the crash severity is so severe that the longitudinal deceleration of the vehicle exceeds the severity of a 12 [miles per hour] full frontal barrier impact."

Christopherson reconstructed the accident based on the "physical damage to the vehicles as depicted in the photographs," and concluded the "left front corner of the Civic made initial contact with the left front wheel area of the Cadillac" at a 35-degree frontal collision range, outside the "30 degree frontal collision range" required for the air bag to deploy. She determined the longitudinal component of the crash was approximately four miles per hour, "very clearly less severe" than a 12-mile-per-hour "full frontal barrier impact" in which the air bag is designed to deploy. Based on the foregoing, Christopherson opined that the air bag system performed as designed, and there was "no evidence of a defect."

McCabe's Opposition

In opposition to the summary judgment motion, McCabe maintained the Cadillac collided with her Civic "head on." McCabe included photographs of the Civic showing extensive damage to the left front hood area and to the left side of the car and claimed the collision occurred within the frontal collision range identified in the owner's manual. McCabe also included witness testimony, including her own and that of the Cadillac's driver, that the Cadillac was traveling at a speed at or in excess of 35 miles per hour when it collided with her Civic. McCabe testified she purposely purchased a car with an air bag for safety reasons and expected the air bag would deploy in a high-speed head-on collision like the one in this case.

Honda's Reply and the Trial Court's Ruling

In reply, Honda observed that McCabe offered no expert testimony refuting Christopherson's expert opinion that the air bag performed in accordance with its intended design. Honda argued that the consumer expectation test set forth in *Barker v. Lull Engineering Co.* (1978) 20 Cal.3d 413, 143 Cal.Rptr. 225, 573 P.2d 443 (Barker), permitting a plaintiff to prove a design defect with circumstantial evidence that the product performed below the safety standard an ordinary consumer would expect, did not apply to the deployment of an air bag, which, it maintained, involved sophisticated technology and was outside the ordinary experience of the consumer.

The trial court granted summary judgment for Honda, reasoning that, by omitting from her opposition any expert testimony contravening Christopherson's declaration, McCabe had failed to produce evidence sufficient to raise a triable issue of fact as to whether the air bag should have deployed under the circumstances of this accident. The court concluded, without explanation, that the consumer expectation test, permitting a plaintiff to establish a design defect without resort to expert testimony, was inapplicable to the circumstances of this case.

McCabe contends (1) the trial court erred in concluding the consumer expectation test for defective design was inapplicable under the facts of this case; and (2) under the consumer expectation test, she raised triable issues of fact as to whether the air bag's design was defective.

DISCUSSION

California recognizes two distinct categories of product defects: manufacturing defects and design defects. (*Barker, supra*, 20 Cal.3d at pp. 429–430, 143 Cal.Rptr. 225, 573 P.2d 443.) A manufacturing defect exists when an item is produced in a substandard condition. (*Barker*, at p. 429, 143 Cal.Rptr. 225, 573 P.2d 443; *see, e.g., Lewis v. American Hoist & Derrick Co.* (1971) 20 Cal.App.3d 570, 580, 97 Cal.Rptr. 798 [manufacturer's failure to comply with its own design specifications regarding assembly of crane showed manufacturing defect].) Such a defect is often demonstrated by showing the product performed differently from other ostensibly identical units of the same product line. (*Barker*, at p. 429, 143 Cal.Rptr. 225, 573 P.2d 443.)

A design defect, in contrast, exists when the product is built in accordance with its intended specifications, but the design itself is inherently defective. (*Barker, supra*, 20 Cal.3d at p. 429, 143 Cal.Rptr. 225, 573 P.2d 443.) In Barker, the Supreme Court recognized two tests for proving design defect. The "consumer expectation test" permits a plaintiff to prove design defect by demonstrating that "the product failed to perform as safely as an ordinary consumer would expect when used in an intended or reasonably foreseeable manner." (*Id.* at pp. 426–427, 143 Cal.Rptr. 225, 573 P.2d 443, italics omitted.) This test, rooted in theories of warranty, recognizes that implicit in a product's presence on the market is a representation that it is fit to do safely the job for which it was intended. (*Barker*, at p. 430, 143 Cal.Rptr. 225, 573 P.2d 443; *see also Soule v. General Motors Corp.* (1994) 8 Cal.4th 548, 566, 34 Cal.Rptr.2d 607, 882 P.2d 298 (*Soule*) ["ordinary users or consumers of a product may have reasonable, widely accepted minimum expectations about the circumstances under which it should perform safely. Consumers govern their own conduct by these expectations, and products on the market should conform to them"].) If the facts permit an inference that the product at issue is one about which consumers may form minimum safety assumptions in the context of a particular accident, then it is enough for a plaintiff, proceeding under the consumer expectation test, to show the circumstances of the accident and "the objective features of the product which are relevant to an evaluation of its safety" (*Soule*, at p. 564, 34 Cal.Rptr.2d 607, 882 P.2d 298), leaving it to the fact-finder to "employ '[its] own sense of whether the product meets ordinary expectations as to its safety under the circumstances presented by the evidence.'" (*Soule, supra*, 8 Cal.4th at p. 563, 34 Cal.Rptr.2d 607, 882 P.2d 298; *Campbell v. General Motors Corp.* (1982) 32 Cal.3d 112, 126, 184 Cal.Rptr. 891, 649 P.2d 224.) Expert testimony as to what consumers ordinarily "expect" is generally improper. (*Soule*, at p. 567, 34 Cal.Rptr.2d 607, 882 P.2d 298 [expert testimony as to what laypersons may expect from product improperly invades province of jury].) An exception exists where the product is in specialized use with a limited group of consumers. In such cases, "if the expectations of the product's limited group of ordinary consumers are beyond the lay experience common to all jurors, expert testimony on the limited subject of what the product's actual consumers do expect may be proper." (*Soule,* supra, 8 Cal.4th at p. 568, fn. 4, 34 Cal.Rptr.2d 607, 882 P.2d 298.)

The second test for design defect is known as the "risk-benefit test." Under this test, products that meet ordinary consumer expectations nevertheless may be defective if the design embodies an "'excessive preventable danger.'" (*Barker, supra,* 20 Cal.3d at p. 430, 143 Cal.Rptr. 225, 573 P.2d 443; *Soule, supra,* 8 Cal.4th at p. 567, 34 Cal.Rptr.2d 607, 882 P.2d 298.) To prove a defect under this test, a plaintiff need only demonstrate that the design proximately caused the injuries. Once proximate cause is demonstrated, the burden shifts to the defendant to establish that the benefits of the challenged design, when balanced against such factors as the feasibility and cost of alternative designs, outweigh its inherent risk of harm. (*Barker,* at p. 431, 143 Cal.Rptr. 225, 573 P.2d 443; *Soule,* at p. 562, 34 Cal.Rptr.2d 607, 882 P.2d 298.)

The two tests provide alternative means for a plaintiff to prove design defect and do not serve as defenses to one another. A product may be defective under the consumer expectation test even if the benefits of the design outweigh the risks. *(Curtis v. State of California ex rel. Dept. of Transportation* (1982) 128 Cal.App.3d 668, 690–691, 180 Cal.Rptr. 843.) On the other hand, a product may be defective if it satisfies consumer expectations but contains an excessively preventable danger in that the risks of the design outweigh its benefits. (*Barker, supra,* 20 Cal.3d at p. 430, 143 Cal.Rptr. 225, 573 P.2d 443.)

Whether a plaintiff may proceed under the consumer expectation test or whether design defect must be assessed solely under the risk-benefit test is dependent upon the particular facts in each case. (*Soule, supra,* 8 Cal.4th at p. 566, 34 Cal.Rptr.2d 607, 882 P.2d 298.) Because "'[i]n many situations ... the consumer would have no idea how safe the product could be made,'" the consumer expectation test is "reserved for cases in which the everyday experience of the product's users permits a conclusion that the product's design violated minimum safety assumptions and is thus defective regardless of expert opinion about the merits of the design." (*Id.* at pp. 562, 567, 34 Cal.Rptr.2d 607, 882 P.2d 298.) For example, "the ordinary consumers of modern automobiles may and do expect that such vehicles will be designed so as not to explode while idling at stoplights, experience sudden steering or brake failure as they leave the dealership, or roll over and catch fire in two-mile-per-hour collisions."

Some products "cause injury in a way that does not engage its ordinary consumers' reasonable minimum assumptions about safe performance. For example, the ordinary consumer of an automobile simply has 'no idea' how it should perform in all foreseeable situations, or how safe it should be made against all foreseeable hazards." (*Soule,* supra, 8 Cal.4th at pp. 566–567, 34 Cal.Rptr.2d 607, 882 P.2d 298.) In those cases, where plaintiff's theory of defect seeks to examine the behavior of "obscure components under complex circumstances" outside the ordinary experience of the consumer, the consumer expectation test is inapplicable; and defect may only be proved by resort to the risk-benefit analysis. (*Id.* at p. 570, 34 Cal.Rptr.2d 607, 882 P.2d 298 [where automobile collision resulted in left front wheel breaking free, collapsing rearward and smashing floorboard into driver's feet, it was error to instruct jury with consumer expectation test; proper test for defect is risk-benefit because behavior of obscure component parts during complex circumstances of accident not within ordinary experience of consumer]; *Morson v. Superior Court* (2001) 90 Cal.App.4th 775, 793–795, 109 Cal.Rptr.2d 343 [consumer expectation test inapplicable to assess defect in latex glove where chemical in the rubber caused allergic reactions in those sensitive to latex; the allergenicity of the rubber is "'a matter beyond the common experience and understanding'" of the product's consumers].)

Whether a product is within the everyday experience of ordinary consumers and thus susceptible to a consumer expectation analysis cannot be determined by looking at the product in isolation, but rather must be considered in the context of the facts surrounding its failure. The critical question is whether the "circumstances of the product's failure permit an inference that the product's design performed below the legitimate, commonly accepted minimum safety assumptions of its ordinary consumers." (*Soule*, supra, 8 Cal.4th at pp. 568–569, 34 Cal.Rptr.2d 607, 882 P.2d 298, italics added.)

The critical question, in assessing the applicability of the consumer expectation test, is not whether the product, when considered in isolation, is beyond the ordinary knowledge of the consumer, but whether the product, in the context of the facts and circumstances of its failure, is one about which the ordinary consumers can form minimum safety expectations. (*Soule*, supra, 8 Cal.4th at pp. 568–569, 34 Cal.Rptr.2d 607, 882 P.2d 298.) If the facts permit such an inference, it is error to conclude the consumer expectation test is inapplicable as a matter of law. (*See id.* at p. 568, 34 Cal.Rptr.2d 607, 882 P.2d 298.)

In this case, drawing all inferences and resolving all conflicts in favor of the nonmoving party, we find summary judgment was improperly granted because numerous triable issues of material fact exist as to the circumstances of the accident. In reversing summary judgment, we do not hold either that the consumer expectation test applies as a matter of law or that the test was satisfied in this case. In putting forth its own version of the accident, the defense will be free to argue to the fact finder that the consumer expectation test is not applicable in this case because the performance of the air bag in this type of collision is not the type of product performance about which consumers may have reasonable minimum safety expectations. We hold simply that, based on the evidence presented, and resolving all factual inferences in favor of the nonmoving party, there is sufficient evidence from which a jury could infer that the failure of an air bag to deploy under the facts and circumstances advanced by McCabe violates commonly held minimum safety assumptions within the every day experience of ordinary consumers. For this reason, summary judgment was improper.

Honda's summary judgment motion fails for another reason. A claim of design defect may be proved under the consumer expectation theory (if applicable) or the risk benefit theory. The tests are not mutually exclusive, and a plaintiff may proceed under either or both. Under the risk-benefit theory, McCabe need only show the design caused her injuries; if so, the burden shifts to the defendant to prove the benefits of the design outweigh its inherent risks. (*See Bresnahan v. Chrysler Corp.*, supra, 32 Cal.App.4th at p. 1565, 38 Cal.Rptr.2d 446.) McCabe provided evidence of causation when she testified the failure of the air bag to deploy forced her head to crash into the steering wheel, resulting in facial and dental injuries. Honda did not dispute McCabe's evidence of causation, nor did it provide any evidence as to the relative risks-benefits of the air bag's design. On summary judgment, it was Honda's burden to negate McCabe's claim of design defect. Honda's failure to provide any evidence negating design defect under the alternative risk-benefit theory also mandates reversal of the order granting summary judgment.

The judgment is reversed. The matter is remanded for further proceedings not inconsistent with this opinion.

Exercise 4-13 Elements of Proof

Below is a list of elements of proof for defective airbag claims. As you review the list, consider:

1. What aspects of this list are inapplicable under the court's decision in *McCabe*? Will they be inapplicable in every defective airbag case? Why or why not?

2. What element(s) are at issue in *McCabe*?

3. Which elements do you think are frequently the most difficult to prove in defective airbag cases?

_____ Airbag system was sold in defective condition unreasonably dangerous to user

    _____ Defect in design

        _____ Gravity of danger posed by airbag system's design

        _____ Likelihood of injury resulting from danger posed by airbag system's design

        _____ Feasibility of safer alternative design

            _____ Effect of alternative design on user

            _____ Financial cost of alternative design

            _____ Design available at time airbag system was manufactured

        _____ Dangerousness not known to or readily discoverable by ordinary user

            _____ Airbag system was dangerous beyond extent contemplated by ordinary user with ordinary knowledge of system's characteristics

            _____ Failure of airbag system to comply with industry standards

    _____ Defect in manufacturing

        _____ Subject airbag system or component differs from others of same model

        _____ Airbag system as designed differs from airbag system and as manufactured

---

As you read the next two cases, remember to consider:

(1) What type of defect(s) are alleged by the plaintiff;

(2) Whether there are any resources available to you that provide information about the product (You may want to search for information about each product and find out more about the design, engineering, industry standards, etc.);

(3) What evidence—direct and/or circumstantial—is available to prove the defect existed at the time the product left the defendant's control; and

(4) Whether expert testimony is necessary to prove (a) there was a defect, and/or (b) the defect existed at the time the product left the defendant's control.

You may also want to consider:

(5) What are the elements of proof for each of the alleged defects?

Rawlings Sporting Goods Co., Inc. v. Daniels
619 S.W.2d 435 (Tex. Civ. App. 1981)

This is an appeal by defendant Rawlings from $1,500,000 judgment against it in favor of plaintiff Daniels in a products liability and negligence case. Plaintiff Daniels sued defendant Rawlings alleging plaintiff sustained injuries on August 20, 1974, during football practice; that plaintiff was wearing a Rawlings helmet when he was in collision with another player; that the helmet rather than deflecting the blow and absorbing the shock, caved in, causing massive head and brain injuries to plaintiff; that the helmet as manufactured by defendant was defective; and exposed plaintiff to an unreasonable risk of harm. Plaintiff further alleged defendant was negligent in failing to warn of the protective limitations of the helmet, which was a proximate cause of plaintiff's injuries.

Plaintiff was quarterback on the Franklin High School football team. On August 20, 1974, while participating in team practice, he was involved in a "head to head" collision with a teammate. The collision caused an indentation in plaintiff's helmet. Plaintiff turned the helmet into the coach and continued with practice. The next day, August 21, plaintiff returned to practice. While participating in such practice he passed out. He was taken to a Bryan hospital, and then to a Houston hospital, where his condition was diagnosed as a subdural hematoma. After the subdural hematoma had been surgically evacuated he returned to school on September 14, 1974. Plaintiff's injury resulted in severe permanent brain damage drastically reducing his abilities.

Plaintiff was wearing the helmet manufactured by defendant when he had the head to head collision. The helmet indented inward some 1½ to 2 inches. There is evidence that if a helmet receives a blow and doesn't deflect it, but instead indents in, that the helmet was defective; and defendant's own witnesses testified that if a helmet indented an inch and a half and came in contact with the wearer's skull that considerable force was transmitted to and focused on the wearer's skull at that point.

All the evidence is that the purpose of the helmet was to protect the wearer's head from injury. There is evidence that if a football helmet indents it is not performing its function, that it is "defective headgear". Another witness, a professional athletic trainer testified: "I don't want a football helmet that is going to cave in" and "I don't want it to give at all".

Dr. Moiel who performed the surgery on plaintiff, testified that skull contact by the plastic portions of the helmet can cause a brain injury such as suffered by plaintiff; that plaintiff had a large blood clot over the left side of the brain; that plaintiff "had obviously had a bruise to his head and to his brain which resulted in several things; first becoming unconscious due to a concussion, bruising the right side of the brain, which reflected the EEG abnormalities on the right and then, developed a blood clot on the opposite side of the brain, the left side, all as a result of the same accident or injury". And Dr. Omaaya, a witness for defendant, testified that a collision of two football players sufficient to cause the indentation of the helmet of one and a half inches over the right temporal area would be sufficient to cause a subdural hematoma, and that this was true even if the contact was not sufficient to bruise the skull.

It is our view there is ample evidence from which the jury could conclude that the indented helmet was defective because it failed to perform its intended purpose, to protect the wearer from head injuries.

All the evidence is that the primary purpose of a football helmet is to protect against "head" or "brain" injuries of the wearer of the helmet. Defendant has known for a long time that a helmet will not protect against brain injury and against subdural hematoma;

that almost all fatal football injuries result from head and neck injuries; and that when a person uses a football helmet for its intended purpose of protecting the head while playing football, that there is still a significant risk of brain injury. In spite of this knowledge defendant made an election, a conscious decision, not to warn users that the helmet would not protect the brain from this type of injury.

Every manufacturer has a duty to warn of dangers in the use of its product of which it knows or should know. *Crocker v. Winthrop Lab., Div. of Sterling Drug, Inc.*, Tex., 514 S.W.2d 429; *Bristol-Myers Co. v. Gonzales*, Tex., 561 S.W.2d 801; *Technical Chemical Co. v. Jacobs*, Tex., 480 S.W.2d 602; *Air Shields, Inc. v. Spears*, Tex.Civ.App. (Waco) NRE, 590 S.W.2d 574.

We think defendant had a duty to warn that its helmet would not protect against head and brain injuries. Where there is no warning, as here, the presumption is that the user would have read an adequate warning. *Technical Chemical Co. v. Jacobs, supra.* And plaintiff's father affirmatively testified he would not have consented to plaintiff's playing had he been aware the helmet would not have protected against brain injury.

The danger to plaintiff was not inherent in the helmet, but in the use of the helmet. We think liability arises when a product is manufactured and marketed for protection of the consumer, the consumer buys the product, relying on it for his protection, while engaged in a generally dangerous activity, the manufacturer fails to warn of known limitations in the protective abilities of its product with which the user is not equally familiar, and as a result, the consumer is injured while using the product.

The rationale supporting a duty to warn is clear. The consumer is encouraged to participate in dangerous activity because of his confidence in the protective ability of the product. The manufacturer on the other hand, has superior knowledge of the limitations of the product. Where it is foreseeable that a consumer will rely on the product, thus exposing himself to a risk he might have avoided had he known the limitations, there is a duty to warn. Here the failure to warn was negligence. A product that does not include a warning is dangerously defective. In the instant case the jury was authorized to believe that a proximate cause of plaintiff's injury was the absence of a warning of the limitations of his helmet sufficient to prevent his reliance upon its protective capacities.

Defendant admitted that it never made any attempt to warn potential users of the limitations of its helmets; that it had known for a long time that the helmets will not protect against brain injuries; that it made the "conscious decision" not to tell people the helmet would not protect against subdural hematomas; that the company "elected" not to warn that the helmets would not protect against head injuries, in spite of the knowledge that laymen believe that the purpose of the helmet is to protect the head. A witness for defendant testified that 30 to 40 deaths occur each year from subdural hematomas received in football; that parents do not have this detailed knowledge, and that "it is the responsibility of the manufacturer to explain that".

Defendant asserts that it exercised care in manufacturing the helmet; but there is no evidence of any care whatsoever being exercised in the matter of failure to warn of the helmet's limitation.

In the instant case, defendant fully understood the dangers which were incidental to the use of its helmets. Testimony of defendant's own witnesses revealed defendant knew: 1) A practical helmet could not be designed that would prevent all head injuries; 2) there are limitations on the protection capabilities of any helmet; 3) it has been known for a long time that helmets will not protect against all brain injuries; 4) defendant's helmets would not protect against all subdural hematomas; 5) laymen believe the purpose of the helmet is to protect the head; 6) almost all fatal football injuries are related to head and neck injuries; 7) 200,000 to 4 million football players are injured each year; 8) you can receive a brain injury while in a helmet that performs all the functions that it was designed to perform; 9) the helmet has severe limitations on protecting the brain; it will not protect against subdural hematomas; 10) total football deaths are between 30 and 40 a year from subdural hematoma; 11) parents of high school players don't have this detailed knowledge of the dangers of subdural hematoma.

There is evidence that since 1960 almost all fatal injuries from playing football have been as a result of head or neck injuries; that in spite of the helmets being worn, the injury sustained by plaintiff, subdural hematoma, can occur, and that the foregoing was well known to defendant.

In spite of all the facts known to defendant, it made a conscious business decision not to warn of this grave danger.

Viewing all the circumstances in this case, and the entire record, we think the jury authorized to find defendant grossly negligent. AFFIRMED.

Pavlides v. Galveston Yacht Basin

727 F.2d 330 (5th Cir. 1984)

Sam Pavlides and four of his chums set out on a fishing trip in Pavlides' Robalo 236 motorboat. Four of them, including Pavlides, never returned: they died while attempting to swim to safety from their swamped boat. The fifth, Anthony Moustakelis, made it to an adjacent oil rig.

On this appeal, the decedents' estates challenge the trial court's conclusion that the manufacturer of the boat, AMF Slickcraft Boat Division, Inc. (AMF) was not strictly liable for defects in design, manufacture or marketing. We conclude that the trial court applied an erroneous measure of the duty to warn, one unduly prejudicial to plaintiffs. Therefore, we remand for the trial court to reconsider the evidence under the correct standard, and to make further rulings as necessary, in accordance with this opinion.

After launching Pavlides' Robalo 236 from the Galveston Yacht Basin, the five fishermen involved in this case filled the boat's fuel tank and motored out into the Gulf of Mexico to fish. They made fast to one oil rig, fished for about 15 minutes, then moved to another-a trip of about five minutes. After some 15 minutes at the second rig, Moustakelis noticed about an inch and a half of water in the stern of the boat, but Pavlides told him not to worry. However, as the boat continued to take on water through the bilge the men became concerned. Pavlides attempted to use the bilge pump and the radio, but neither worked since by then water had flooded the batteries in the rear of the boat. The men then attempted to start the engines and self-bail the boat, as Pavlides had been instructed by the salesman to do should the bilge take on water. They accidentally cast off from the rig with only one engine working; shortly after, the operating engine failed, indicating that water had reached its air intake. Moustakelis testified that at that point they felt it was too dangerous to open the bilge access port and try to identify the problem. Expert testimony at trial established that trying to locate the cause of the water entering the bilge and replacing the bilge drain plug from either the inside or the outside of the boat would be a very hazardous undertaking once the bilge was flooded.

As the now-powerless boat drifted back past the rig, Moustakelis abandoned ship and swam to it. The other four men remained in the boat, trying to bail it manually as it continued to sink by the stern. Three of the decedents then put on life jackets and tried to swim to the rig but were swept back by the current. The fourth, Jack Nikolaides, swam without a life preserver to within a few feet of the rig, but the current prevented him from reaching it. According to Moustakelis' testimony, at that time only the forward portion of the boat was above water, but it had not turned over.

Moustakelis lost sight of the men and the boat as they continued to drift away from him. He could not tell whether the boat had capsized or not when he lost sight of it. Moustakelis was rescued several hours later by a private boat and the Coast Guard was then called to the scene. They found the Robalo 236 some six hours after the accident, by which time it had fully capsized. The bodies of two of the decedents were found; the other two are presumed dead. The Coast Guard report lists the causes of death as drowning, with hypothermia a contributing factor due to the 56-degree water temperature.

The Robalo 236

Plaintiffs' strict liability arguments require a fairly extensive discussion of the design, manufacture and marketing of the Robalo 236 ("R-236"). The R-236, which went on the market in 1974, was the first "Robalo" designed, manufactured and marketed by AMF. However, the "Robalo" name already enjoyed a wide and excellent reputation: previous "Robalo" models had been made and marketed by the Robalo Company, an individually-owned Florida concern engaged in the manufacture of pleasure boats for deep sea fishing. The Robalo boats made by the Florida concern had acquired a reputation for safety arising from the boats' "fully-foamed" construction, meaning that all of the void spaces in the hull were filled with foam flotation material so that the boats had no void bilge space. This made these Robalos virtually "unsinkable." All models made by the Robalo Company had drain holes in the stern side of the boat designed to allow water which accidentally entered the cockpit or engine well to run out when the boat was slowly moving forward, thus "self-bailing" the boat. Although one of these drain holes, the "sump" hole, was below the waterline, no drain holes on any Robalo made by the Florida concern led into void bilge space.

AMF acquired the Robalo Company in the early 1970s, shortly after it had acquired the Slickcraft Company, a Michigan-based manufacturer engaged in making boats for fishing on the Great Lakes. The Slickcraft line was not fully-foamed; in these boats the bilge space was wholly or partly void.

AMF merged the corporate structures of Robalo and Slickcraft, but since the two lines sold to distinct markets, AMF continued to market "AMF Robalo" boats and "AMF Slickcraft" boats. However, in response to the request of a fishermen's association that AMF build a 23-foot boat for Michigan lake fishing, AMF decided to market a new model which would resemble the Robalo 230 (a 23-foot, fully-foamed boat) with the addition of a cutty cabin.

The resulting design, which AMF marketed both under the name "Robalo 236" and under the name "Slickcraft 236", was not a fully-foamed boat, but rather had a large void space in the bilge with a through-hull bilge drain in the rear of the bilge below the waterline. The bilge drain could be plugged either from the inside, by reaching in through the bilge access port to the bottom of the bilge (a distance of about three feet), or from the outside, by reaching down between the engines. If the plug was inserted from the inside, it was not visible from the outside, and vice versa.

The void bilge space in the R-236 meant that, unlike all other Robalos, the R-236 was not completely self-bailing. Water which entered the bilge—through the bilge drain or in any other manner—could only be removed normally by operating the bilge pump. The R-236 was not equipped with an automatic bilge pump that would commence bailing when water reached a certain level in the bilge, nor was it equipped with any warning device to notify occupants of the presence of water in the bilge.

Tests conducted by plaintiffs' expert on Pavlides' R-236 after the accident showed that when the bilge drain plug was removed, the covered, enclosed bilge space would fill with water in about 11 minutes, at which time water would first be visible on deck. Experts on both sides testified that the only way an operator of the R-236 would be aware of water in the bilge before it appeared on deck was that when the boat was underway, it would feel heavy to an experienced sailor.

Once the bilge was filled with water, moreover, there was a good chance that the bilge pump would not function since by that time the batteries might well be flooded—as happened in today's case. The undisputed expert testimony was that it would be extremely difficult and dangerous to attempt to determine the cause of water entering through the bilge or to replace the bilge drain plug from either the inside or outside when water was rapidly filling the cockpit through the flooded bilge. In the post-accident tests, the R-236 filled with water and developed a list to starboard in less than four minutes after water appeared on the deck of the boat. At this point in the test the four men on board were unable to stop the boat from capsizing. The test was terminated to prevent injury to the crew, the testing facility or the boat. Obviously, water would reach the air intake of the engines, shutting them down, during these few minutes (as happened here).

The sales literature furnished by AMF is, to say the least, misleading as to the design of the R-236. The "AMF Robalo 236 Outboard Specifications" in the sales pamphlet state that the R-236 is "85 percent closed-cell foam," suggesting that the boat is foamed to 85 percent of capacity with closed-cell foam. In fact, the evidence showed that the boat is only about 25 percent foamed. The salesman's testimony at trial established that a buyer could not determine how much flotation material there was on the R-236 by examining the boat. Indeed, plaintiffs' expert testified that it would be necessary to cut open the boat to determine what percent of it was in fact foamed.

With the R-236, AMF furnished a "Robalo Owner's Manual," a copy of which was given to Sam Pavlides by the salesman. The Manual does not describe the design of the R-236, unique among Robalos; nor does it mention that the R-236 has a void bilge space, a bilge drain and a bilge drain plug. It does not indicate that the bilge drain plug could come off accidentally; it does not say how an operator is supposed to be aware of the bilge filling with water; it does not state that when water appears on deck in the rear of the cockpit it could well mean that the bilge is flooded and that in consequence the electrical system, including the bilge pump, is in immediate danger of failing and that the engines may shortly fail as well. Nor does it note that replacing the bilge drain plug when the bilge is full of water is a very difficult and hazardous procedure. The only reference in the Manual to "drain plugs" or through-hull openings occurs in Pre-Launch Procedure C:

> Whether you keep your boat in the water during the boating season or remove it after each trip, we advise following a routine check list to prevent problems and possible safety hazards.
>
> **1. Through Hull Fittings.** You should be familiar with all through hull fittings. Check each one before launching to make sure no damage has occurred in transit or that no obstructions to ports or openings have resulted from floating debris.
>
> **2. Drain Plugs.** Make certain indicated lower drain plugs are in place. Generally the outboard motor well upper drain plugs as well as the control tube through drain plug are left out of the drain tubes when under way to allow deck water to flow overboard. Drain plugs can be tightened by turning the center screw clockwise.

These instructions refer to Robalo fully-foamed boats and not to the R-236, but could easily be misinterpreted to apply to the R-236 as well. Like the boat illustrated in the Manual, the R-236 has four drain holes in the stern. However, while the only below-waterline hole shown in the Manual is a "sump" hole—which can be left open with no danger—the corresponding below-waterline hole in the R-236 is the bilge drain which, as noted above, poses a serious risk if left unplugged.

The statements in the Manual regarding what to do if water appears in the boat are similarly misleading. The sole instruction on this point states: "[I]f water in the boat appears excessive, open the upper drain plugs."

Sam Pavlides brought his R-236 from Fred and Ralph Lester, employees of the Redwing Boat Company [an AMF dealer]. Fred Lester testified at trial that he told Sam Pavlides that the R-236 was "unsinkable." Fred and his brother Ralph took Pavlides out into the Galveston Yacht Basin to demonstrate the boat. Before launching it, they installed the various drain plugs. According to Ralph's deposition: "We told him the boat was self-bailing. We backed it down in the water, got some water on deck, showed Sam that in 30, 40 seconds the water had already dissipated out through the rear drain holes.... The three holes in back.... Q: Above the water line? A: Yes, sir.... We showed him that by slowly accelerating, the water runs aft." Fred Lester also testified that they told Pavlides that the bilge would also self-bail if the boat was "under forward motion" so he should start the engines if water was coming in the bilge.

The Lesters also explained the boat's electrical system, including the bilge pump switch, to Pavlides. According to their testimony, however, neither of the Lesters told Pavlides that the bilge plug could fall out accidentally and that the bilge would then fill with water in a very short period of time. Nor, according to their testimony, did they tell him how he could know if the bilge was filling with water. They did not warn him of the specific dangers which would be the almost inevitable result of the bilge's filling: that the bilge pump might short out and that in a few minutes water would reach the air intake of the engines, causing them to fail. They did not tell him—because, so they testified, they did not know—that if the bilge flooded the R-236 would fill with water in less than four minutes after water appeared on deck.

Failure to Warn: Standard of Adequate Warning

Strict liability for failure-to-warn is founded on twin principles of social utility and the right of the individual to determine his own fate. On the one hand, the manufacturer's duty to instruct and warn as to all hazards which as an expert he could foresee is derived from the notion that a warning that costs the manufacturer little can prevent severe losses by enabling users to avert harm. *Reyes v. Wyeth Laboratories*, 498 F.2d 1264, 1274–75 (5th Cir.), cert. denied, 419 U.S. 1096, 95 S.Ct. 687, 42 L.Ed.2d 688 (1974). But also, the user has an individual right to this knowledge. As we stated in a leading products liability case: "Any … product user has a right to decide whether to expose himself to the risk." *Borel*, 493 F.2d at 1106.

It is a fundamental principle of the law of product liability in this Circuit that a manufacturer has a responsibility to instruct consumers as to the safe use of its product and to warn consumers of dangers associated with its product of which the seller either knows or should know at the time the product is sold. *Borel*, 493 F.2d at 1088–90; see Restatement (Second) of Torts, Section 402 A. comment j. In assessing what hazards are foreseeable, a manufacturer is held to the status of an expert. *Borel*, 493 F.2d at 1089. The lack of adequate warnings renders a product defective and unreasonably dangerous even if there is no manufacturing or design defect in the product. *Martinez v. Dixie Carriers, Inc.*, 529 F.2d 457, 465–66 (5th Cir.1976); *Reyes*, 498 F.2d at 1272–73.

We have repeatedly held that in order for a warning to be adequate, it must provide "a complete disclosure of the existence and extent of the risk involved," *Alman Brothers Farms & Feed Mill, Inc. v. Diamond Laboratories, Inc.*, 437 F.2d 1295, 1303 (5th Cir.1971). A warning must (1) be designed so it can reasonably be expected to catch the attention of the consumer; (2) be comprehensible and give a fair indication of the specific risks involved with the product; and (3) be of an intensity justified by the magnitude of the risk. *Bituminous Casualty Corp. v. Black & Decker Manufacturing Co.*, 518 S.W.2d 868, 872–73 (Tex.Civ.App.-Dallas, 1974), writ ref'd n.r.e.

The question of whether or not a given warning is legally sufficient depends upon the language used and the impression that such language is calculated to make upon the mind of the average user of the product. Id. at 873 (emphasis added).

Since the warning is intended to be adequate for the "average user" of the product, the adequacy of the warning must be evaluated together with the knowledge of the ultimate users of the product. Where, for example, a product is marketed solely to professionals experienced in using the product, the manufacturer may rely on the knowledge which a reasonable professional would apply in using the product. *See Martinez*, 529 F.2d at 465–67 (where product was marketed exclusively for use by experienced professionals, industrial manufacturer could tailor its warnings accordingly). Where, however, the product is marketed to the general public, the manufacturer must tailor the warning to the man-in-the-street, *Borel*, 493 F.2d at 1092–93 (dangers of asbestos dust not well enough known to insulation workers to reduce manufacturer's duty to warn). Thus, contrary to the trial court's view, a manufacturer does not generally have the right to assume that persons using a complex product know how it is to be used.

In concluding as a matter of law that a manufacturer could make such an assumption in general, and in applying that assumption to the instant case, the trial court erred. The evidence clearly showed that the R-236 was marketed to the general public; no restrictions were imposed on its sale by AMF. Therefore, AMF had the duty to provide a warning that gave consumers with no special knowledge of how to operate the R-236 adequate information about all particular and nonobvious hazards associated with its operation.

The trial court's finding that "any reasonably prudent boater must have known that it was unsafe to operate the boat with a bilge space open to ocean water" betrays a second, related misconception as to the standard of adequacy: a warning must advise the user of the specific nature and extent of the risk involved. The danger involved with the R-236 was not so much that it was unsafe to leave the bilge drain unplugged as that the accidental slipping out of the plug could set in motion a catastrophic sequence of events which if not arrested immediately would inevitably result in the boat's submerging. An ordinary consumer could not be expected to infer that this sequence of events would occur even if he did realize that the bilge drain should be plugged.

AMF, on the other hand, should have foreseen this danger and warned of it. The depositions of AMF's experts and their testimony at trial established that AMF knew or should have known that it was possible for bilge plugs to come out at sea, and that if this happened in the R-236 the occupants of the boat might not realize that the bilge was flooding until a substantial amount of water entered the bilge, since the boat was not equipped with a warning device or an automatic bilge pump. AMF knew that loss of the bilge drain plug at sea presented a "severe hazard." More specifically, AMF knew, or should have known, that if the bilge filled with water the battery box would flood, causing the bilge pump to fail. AMF also knew that the R-236 was not self-bailing as the other Robalos were, and that consequently it could swamp. Finally, AMF knew, or should have known, that if the boat swamped sufficiently the water would reach the air intakes and shut off the engines. Holding AMF to the legally mandated standard of expertness, we find that the manufacturer should reasonably have foreseen that a disaster like that which happened here could occur if warnings adequate to inform an ordinary person of the specific danger were not given. Consequently, it had a commensurate duty to provide such a warning.

The information provided by AMF on the R-236—the Owner's Manual and the sales pamphlet containing the specifications—does not mention the void bilge of the R-236, the bilge drain or the hazards of bilge flooding. Therefore, under the standard of Borel and cases following it, this material provides a legally insufficient warning to the average Robalo buyer of the potential dangers associated with use of the R-236.

Where inadequate warnings are provided, the law presumes that a user would have read warnings provided and acted to minimize the risk to himself. *Reyes*, 498 F.2d at 1287. In the absence of evidence to the contrary, therefore, the manufacturer's failure to warn is held to be a producing cause of the accident. Id. at 1281–82. In the instant case, a conclusion that AMF failed adequately to warn plaintiffs of the dangers of the R-236 design would give rise to a presumption that had an adequate warning been provided, they would have acted so as to minimize the risk. Had Pavlides been adequately warned, he might not have bought an R-236 at all, or he might have installed a warning device or automatic bilge pump to avert the danger of water accumulating in the bilge unbeknownst to the occupants of the boat.

The judgment below is reversed and the case is remanded for further proceedings in accordance with this opinion.

REVERSED and REMANDED.

The duty to warn is really two separate duties, (1) the duty to provide information about hidden dangers and (2) the duty to provide information about how to use the product safely. The key issue that arises when there is a potentially defective warning is whether the warning was adequate. This standard applies whether there was no warning given at all, or whether there was a warning, but the plaintiff claims it was not sufficient. Adequacy is determined in light of all of the facts and circumstances. As you consider whether a warning is adequate it might help to think about the following questions:

1. What information should be conveyed?
    a. What is a reasonable amount and type of information that should be given to a consumer about the product?
    b. How will the product be used?
    c. What are the risks?
    d. Does the warning convey those risks?
    e. Does the warning convey the ways to avoid those risks?
    f. Are there instructions for how to use the product safely?
2. How should that information be communicated?
    a. Will it be understood by those that need the information?
    b. Is it appropriately conspicuous?
3. To whom should the information be communicated?
    a. Who are the foreseeable users?

    b.   Who might be harmed by the product?

    c.   Is the information likely to reach those persons?

Exercise 4-14 Adequacy of Warning Label

Based on what you have learned about warnings thus far, consider the following and decide whether the warning is adequate or defective. Also, as you evaluate the claim consider (1) What evidence could the plaintiff introduce that would support the claim that the warning was inadequate? and (2) What evidence could the Defendant introduce that would negate the plaintiff's claim that the warning was inadequate?

Smile, Inc. manufactures "Fresh Breath," a combination mouth wash and fluoride rinse for minty fresh breath and healthy teeth. "Fresh Breath" is meant to be swished in the mouth and spit out, not swallowed. If swallowed it is highly toxic for animals and children. The "Fresh Breath" bottle is a 24 oz. clear plastic bottle with a child-proof cap that is approximately 8 inches tall and 2 inches wide. "Fresh Breath" comes in several flavors and colors including, Minty Blue, Cinnamon Red, and Spearmint Green. On the front label is a picture of a large smile. On the back of the bottle is a 2 x 2 inch graphic of the traditional skull and cross bones that looks like this:

Just under the skull and crossbones is the following warning, in 14-point type: "DANGER. HIGHLY TOXIC IF SWALLOWED.

Bob had a bottle of "Fresh Breath" on the counter of his bathroom. Bob does not have children. Bob's sister was visiting from out of state with her five-year-old son, Stan, who is Bob's nephew. Stan had never been to Bob's house before. While Stan was using the bathroom he spotted Bob's bottle of Cinnamon Red "Fresh Breath" on the counter. Thinking it was his favorite fruit punch, Stan drank the "Fresh Breath" and died.

Exercise 4-15 Obtaining Evidence — Drafting Interrogatories

Interrogatories, as you will learn in Civil Procedure, are one of the discovery devices parties use to obtain information from opposing parties. Law firms may keep "banks" of interrogatories and practice guides contain suggestions and standard questions; for this reason new lawyers often have some guidance in drafting such requests, and may be lulled into a false sense of competency. It is very important that you carefully review and adapt the template to each individual case. The sample interrogatories below represent such a template.[2] Your task is to use the sample to guide you in drafting a set of interrogatories on behalf of the plaintiffs in exercise 4-14. You may want to begin by creating a list of what must be proven to establish liability and any defenses. It may also help to ask yourself what each question is attempting to ascertain and whether that is at issue in your case.

1	<div align="center">**DEFINITIONS**</div>
2	A. PLAINTIFF means _____ *[name]*
3	B. DEFENDANT means _____ *[name]*, including all of its agents
4	and employees.
5	C. OCCURRENCE means the incident described in paragraph
6	_____ of PLAINTIFF'S complaint.
7	D. THE PRODUCT means the product that allegedly caused PLAIN-
8	TIFF'S injury, as described in paragraph _____ of PLAINTIFF'S complaint.
9	E. SIMILAR PRODUCTS means other products manufactured by DE-
10	FENDANT that are substantially similar to THE PRODUCT either in their design
11	or in their intended use. SIMILAR PRODUCTS includes products that are of the
12	same model or design as THE PRODUCT.
13	F. COMPARABLE PRODUCTS means products manufactured by per-
14	sons or businesses other than DEFENDANT that are substantially similar to THE
15	PRODUCT either in their design or in their intended use.
16	G. IDENTIFY a person means to state his or her full name, address,
17	and telephone number; his or her occupation; the name, address, and telephone
18	number of his or her employer, if known; and any professional or employment
19	relationship to DEFENDANT.
20	H. IDENTIFY a business entity means to give that entity's full name and
21	its principal address and telephone number.

---

2. These sample interrogatories are an edited version of the model interrogatories set out in: 8 Am. Jur. Proof of Facts 3d 547 and, because they focus on defective warnings, are not intended to be a complete set of interrogatories for use in a products liability case.

INTERROGATORIES

Dangers Known to Manufacturer

1. Describe all hazards and dangers in THE PRODUCT of which DEFENDANT knew before the OCCURRENCE.

2. Describe all hazards and dangers in SIMILAR PRODUCTS of which DEFENDANT knew before the OCCURRENCE.

3. For each hazard and danger described in response to Interrogatories 1 and 2, state how DEFENDANT gained knowledge of the hazard, IDENTIFY the agent or employee who first acquired such knowledge, and state when such knowledge was acquired.

4. For each hazard and danger described in response to Interrogatories 1 and 2, describe the probable cause of the hazard or danger and the possible results of the hazard or danger that DEFENDANT foresaw.

5. For each hazard and danger described in response to Interrogatories 1 and 2, state when and how DEFENDANT informed the owner of THE PRODUCT of the hazard or danger before the OCCURRENCE.

6. IDENTIFY each person with an M.D. or Ph.D. degree now or ever in DEFENDANT'S employ who has had as part of his or her duties the evaluation or review of evaluations of the safety of SIMILAR PRODUCTS.

7. For each person identified in response to Interrogatory 6, describe his or her specific duties to DEFENDANT and the dates of those duties.

8. If DEFENDANT consulted with any scientist, physician, or other technical or medical personnel as to the safety of THE PRODUCT or SIMILAR PRODUCTS before the OCCURRENCE, IDENTIFY each such person consulted and state the date of each consultation and the information that was received from each consultant.

Safety Features and Precautions

9. List each safety feature included in or located on THE PRODUCT.

10. List each safety feature included in or located on SIMILAR PRODUCTS.

11. Describe the purposes of each safety feature listed in response to Interrogatories 9 and 10.

12. For each safety feature listed in response to Interrogatories 9 and 10, state the date, place, persons involved (indicating relationship to DEFENDANT), substance, and results of each test made on SIMILAR PRODUCTS to determine the effectiveness of the safety feature.

13. For each safety feature that was not included in THE PRODUCT but that was known to DEFENDANT at the time of DEFENDANT'S involvement with THE PRODUCT, describe the feature, explain why the feature was not included in THE PRODUCT, and state the additional cost per unit of including the safety feature.

14. If DEFENDANT took any other precaution before the OCCURRENCE to prevent injuries to users of THE PRODUCT and SIMILAR PRODUCTS, in addition to the safety features listed in response to Interrogatories 9 and 10, describe each such additional precaution, including the specific hazards and dangers intended to be averted by the precaution, how the precaution altered THE PRODUCT, how the product user was made aware of the precaution, and the date on which the precaution was taken or initiated.

15. With respect to each precaution described in response to Interrogatory 14, IDENTIFY the agent or employee of DEFENDANT who first discovered or learned of the need for the precaution, and IDENTIFY the agent or employee of DEFENDANT who directed that the precaution be taken.

16. Describe each precaution that was taken by DEFENDANT to prevent injuries to users of SIMILAR PRODUCTS after the OCCURRENCE, in addition to the safety features and precautions described in response to Interrogatories 9–14.72

Instructions and Warnings About Injury-Causing Product

17. Describe each label, direction, instruction, manual, and other writing that was distributed with THE PRODUCT as marketed by DEFENDANT, including the full text of the writing, the colors and sizes of type used, and the position of the writing on THE PRODUCT or on or in the package in which THE PRODUCT was marketed by DEFENDANT.

18. Describe all warnings, directions, instructions, and other printed materials that were sent or distributed by DEFENDANT to PLAINTIFF or to the owner of THE PRODUCT between the date of the sale of THE PRODUCT by DEFENDANT and the date of the OCCURRENCE.

19. Describe all warnings that were given by DEFENDANT to PLAINTIFF before the OCCURRENCE and that concerned the use of THE PRODUCT or SIMILAR PRODUCTS, in addition to the warnings described in response to Interrogatories 17 and 18.

20. *[If plaintiff was not the owner of the product:]* Describe all warnings that were given by DEFENDANT to the owner of THE PRODUCT before the OCCURRENCE and that concerned the use of THE PRODUCT or SIMILAR PRODUCTS, in addition to the warnings described in response to Interrogatories 17 and 18.

21. Describe all materials printed or published by or for DEFENDANT that refer to the uses, safety, or side effects of THE PRODUCT, in addition to the materials described in response to Interrogatories 17–20.

22. IDENTIFY each person who has custody of records relating to the writings and warnings described in response to Interrogatories 17–21.

23. If any agent or employee of DEFENDANT personally instructed PLAINTIFF as to the use or operation of THE PRODUCT, state the substance of each such instruction and the date on which it was given, and IDENTIFY all persons who gave such instructions.

Instructions and Warnings About Similar Products

24. Describe all labels, directions, instructions, manuals, and other printed materials that were distributed with SIMILAR PRODUCTS marketed by DEFENDANT in the three years immediately preceding the OCCURRENCE.

25. Describe all warnings, directions, instructions, and other printed materials concerning SIMILAR PRODUCTS that were sent to purchasers or users of SIMILAR PRODUCTS between the date of the sale of THE PRODUCT by DEFENDANT and the date of the OCCURRENCE.

26. If DEFENDANT uses or has used sales representatives in connection with the marketing of SIMILAR PRODUCTS, describe all instructions given to such sales representatives with respect to the uses, safety, and side effects of SIMILAR PRODUCTS.

27. If DEFENDANT intends or expects that the dealer who sells SIMILAR PRODUCTS will ordinarily provide the purchaser with additional information or instructions about the use of the product, describe the nature and content of such information and instructions.

28. Describe the source from which and manner in which the dealer is intended or expected to obtain the ability to provide the information, instructions, and demonstrations described in response to Interrogatory 27.

29. If, before the OCCURRENCE, DEFENDANT issued to wholesale or retail distributors of SIMILAR PRODUCTS any warnings or instructions concerning any haz-

ard related to the use of such products, state the text of each such warning or instruction, when the warning or instruction was issued, the form of the warning or instruction, and the person or class of persons to whom each such warning or instruction was
issued.

30. With respect to each warning and instruction identified in response to Interrogatory 29, IDENTIFY the person or persons who have custody of documents and
records relating to the warning or instruction.

31. If DEFENDANT has issued any warnings or taken any precautions as a result of
complaints received by DEFENDANT, or accidents or injuries brought to the attention
of DEFENDANT, from users of SIMILAR PRODUCTS, describe the nature of the action taken and the defect or hazard to which the action was addressed.

32. State the date each action described in response to Interrogatory 31 was taken,
and IDENTIFY each person who directed or authorized the action.

33. Describe each activity DEFENDANT has undertaken to warn owners or users of
SIMILAR PRODUCTS of the potential hazards and dangers of such products, in addition to the activities described in response to Interrogatories 24–31.

34. Describe each activity DEFENDANT has undertaken to warn the public of possible dangers in the use of SIMILAR PRODUCTS, in addition to the activities described in response to Interrogatories 24–31.

35. IDENTIFY the person who has charge of the labeling of SIMILAR PRODUCTS.

36. With respect to each label, insert, and other printed matter relating to the use of
SIMILAR PRODUCTS that has accompanied such products as placed on the market,
IDENTIFY the person or persons who have custody of a copy of the printed matter.

37. Describe all materials printed or published by or for DEFENDANT that refer to
the uses, safety, or side effects of SIMILAR PRODUCTS, in addition to the materials
described in response to Interrogatories 24–34.

38. For each item described in response to Interrogatory 37, state the date it was distributed and the manner in which it was distributed, and IDENTIFY its author.

39. IDENTIFY DEFENDANT'S advertising agents who are employed or used in
connection with the promotion of SIMILAR PRODUCTS.

40. With respect to each advertising agent identified in response to Interrogatory 39,
give a summary of all instructions given to the agent regarding the uses, safety, and
side effects of SIMILAR PRODUCTS.

Remedial Measures

41. Describe all instructions and warnings that were included with SIMILAR PRODUCTS marketed by DEFENDANT after the OCCURRENCE, extending up to the present time.

42. If, after the OCCURRENCE, DEFENDANT issued to wholesale distributors, retail distributors, or consumer purchasers of SIMILAR PRODUCTS any warnings or instructions concerning any hazard related to the use of such products, state the full text of each such warning or instruction, when the warning or instruction was issued, the form of the warning or instruction, and the person or class of persons to whom the warning or instruction was issued.

43. IDENTIFY each person who has custody of documents and records relating to the warnings and instructions described in response to Interrogatory 42.

Warnings Issued by Other Manufacturers

44. If DEFENDANT knows of any warnings or instructions used by manufacturers of COMPARABLE PRODUCTS, state the full text of each such warning or instruction, the form in which it was given, the name and address of the person or corporation who used the warning or instruction, the dates when the warning or instruction was used or given, and the persons or classes of persons to whom the warning or instruction was given.

4. Causation and Injury

A complete discussion of causation, damages, comparative fault and assumption of the risk, which we covered in Chapter Two, is not warranted here, since there is virtually no difference in terms of the application of those principles to causes of action for strict products liability. You may wish to review those sections and apply those principles to the exercises and problems in this chapter, in order to gain practice applying the concepts in the context of strict products liability.

There are two issues that frequently arise in products liability actions that are worth special attention: (1) the presumption that plaintiff would have read and heeded an adequate warning; and (2) the requirement that defendants must anticipate foreseeable misuse of their products.

a. Presumption plaintiff would "read and heed" an adequate warning

In proving that an inadequate warning was the cause of the plaintiff's injury, two issues of proof exist. First, whether an adequate warning would have been read and heeded even if it had been provided, and, second, whether an adequate warning would have prevented the plaintiff's injury even if it had been read and heeded. People frequently neglect to thoroughly read directions or heed warnings. For example, the warnings on some boxes of fabric softening sheets indicate that use of such sheets will remove flame retardant on children's pajamas—a point that manufacturers and sellers do not stress in their advertising, and many people are surprised to learn.

Once a plaintiff proves that a warning was inadequate, some courts consider it unfair to place an additional burden on the plaintiff to prove that the inadequacy of the warning actually caused the injury, partly because such a requirement would often prevent recovery because it would require pure speculation. Therefore, many jurisdictions presume that a user would have read an adequate warning. Under this view, in the absence of evidence rebutting the presumption, once a plaintiff proves the warning was inadequate, a jury may find that the inadequate warning was the cause of the plaintiff's injury, without the need for further proof. Defendant may present evidence tending to prove plaintiff was careless, or knew of the risk and disregarded it; in such cases, the jury will weigh the evidence and make a determination as to causation.

b. Anticipating foreseeable misuse

Misuse is related to causation in that defendants may claim that the plaintiff's misuse, and not the product defect, was the cause of the plaintiff's injury. However, defendant must offer proof of something more than an exercise of poor judgment or failure to use common sense. Defendant must prove plaintiff used the product in an unintended *and* unforeseeable way. This requires proof that plaintiff's use (and misuse) could not have been reasonably anticipated.

Exercise 4-16 Anticipating Misuse

Should the manufacturer of each of the products below anticipate the following "misuses" of their products?

Driving automobiles faster than the posted speed limit

Driving automobiles while intoxicated

Standing on a chair to reach an item from a high shelf

Standing on the top step of a ladder

Mixing energy drinks with alcohol (for consumption)

Inhaling nitrous oxide from a can of whipped cream

Using an ungrounded extension cord for an item that has a grounded plug

Wiping a child's face with disinfectant wipes

Opening a can of paint with a screwdriver

A child hanging on the side of a shopping cart

Using fabric softener sheets in loads of laundry that contain children's pajamas

Wearing a seatbelt under the arm rather than over the shoulder

If you answered "yes" for any of the above misuses consider whether:

1. The manufacturer should be required to warn against such dangers (are they hidden or obvious)?

2. Is warning sufficient, or is redesign necessary (because the risks outweigh the utility, etc.)?

Exercise 4-17 Essay Exam Practice

For additional essay exam practice, write an answer to the chapter problem and exercise 4-14.

Chapter Five

Putting It All Together—Representing the Defendant in a Defamation Action

---

Objectives

Learning and Study Skills

Refine reflective learning skills

Organize materials to reflect understanding of material

Use organized materials as a framework for understanding additional information

Use cases to enhance existing knowledge

Law Practice Skills

Spot issues in pleadings

Use a secondary source to:

    Obtain background information,

    Gain familiarity with an area of law

    Put primary sources in context

    Guide research

    Refine understanding of issues presented

    Organize information

Use case law to enhance existing knowledge

Understand when further research may be necessary

Organize materials in order to effectively evaluate a client's case

Evaluate strengths and weaknesses in a client's case

Adapt learning to evaluate new cases

Understand a case sufficiently to prepare a client for deposition

Develop an awareness of and empathy for client feelings and emotions

Understand how a client's anxiety and other emotions may impact the client's case

Be able to apply law of defamation to a set of facts and circumstances to predict the outcome of a case or issue

Understand what evidence is required to prove a cause of action for defamation

Understand the burden of proof for pleading the prima facie case of defamation

Understand what evidence is required to establish an affirmative defense in a defamation action

Understand the burden of proof for pleading affirmative defenses

Understand when Constitutional issues arise and how that might impact pleading and proving a defamation claim

Understand the difference between pleading and proving truth as an affirmative defense, and proving falsity as an element of the cause of action for defamation

Substantive Legal Knowledge

Be able to state elements of the prima facie case of defamation

Be able to define the terms "slander" and "libel"

Be able to state the elements required for proving affirmative defenses of:
qualified privilege; and
absolute privilege

Be able to state the requirements for proving actual malice

Be able to state the factors a court may consider when evaluating whether a person is a public official

Be able to state the factors a court may consider when evaluating whether a person is a public figure

Be able to state the factors a court will consider when evaluating whether a statement pertains to a matter of public concern

Introduction

Usually a defendant is notified that he or she is being sued by being served with the plaintiff's complaint.[1] The defendant then has a relatively short time to respond (often 30 days from the time of service); for a defendant's attorney this time may be even shorter if defendant waits several days (or longer) to contact an attorney. Within that relatively short time, a defendant's attorney must accumulate enough information about the law and facts to determine the best course of action. The most common responses to a complaint are to file either an Answer or a Motion to Dismiss for Failure to State a Claim.

---

1. Sometimes the parties will engage in preliminary settlement discussions, or there will be statutory notice provisions that will provide defendant with some notice of the action before the complaint is served.

In order to determine the best course of action, and draft either of these documents, the defense attorney must evaluate whether (1) plaintiff has alleged sufficient facts to prove each of the required elements for each cause of action and (2) what affirmative defenses might be alleged. Frequently, especially when a lawyer is very new, this determination will involve learning a new area of law. When a case presents an issue not previously litigated by the attorney, it requires the same skills, which are used to expand the attorney's knowledge about the area of law.

This chapter will guide you through the process of learning a new area of law the way a lawyer might approach such a task. Therefore, this chapter is arranged differently than prior chapters. The materials in this chapter are not arranged by topic, the way they usually appear in law school texts, but instead are arranged by source of information, the way they might appear to a lawyer.

It will be your job to synthesize the materials, select the information you believe is relevant, and arrange the concepts so that they help you analyze your client's case and complete whatever task is required. In other words, this chapter will help you to learn a previously unfamiliar area law and then to apply that newly acquired knowledge to the task you need to perform. The questions at the start of each section will help you with each step so that you will be able to effectively represent your client.

Before you begin it may be helpful to understand some differences between learning the law from a law school text, and learning the law from the materials that will be available to you as a lawyer. For example, thus far each of the statutes and cases in this text has addressed a single issue or narrow range of related issues, and the issues have been identified, at least broadly, by the headings or the accompanying text. The materials have also been organized for you so that cases, statutes and other materials were covered in the order that would best help you to understand the topic, and issues were kept separate from one another. This is different from law practice for several reasons. First, cases do not usually contain introductory material designed to acquaint you with the topic, to help you develop knowledge before reading the case. When lawyers want to read about an area of law they are not familiar with, they must find such introductory material themselves; lawyers frequently look to sources other than cases for this information. For example, lawyers will sometimes use secondary sources, specifically practice guides, to acquaint themselves with basic legal principles in an unfamiliar area.

Practice guides usually contain state specific and practice area specific information about the law; for example, most states have practice guides for state civil procedure, personal injury law and criminal law. Practice guides also direct lawyers to useful cases and/or statutes and provide helpful pointers about difficulties attorneys litigating such cases might encounter. When you read a practice guide your job will usually be to form a checklist or outline of the issues you will need to consider—both substantive legal issues and procedural issues, much like the issues checklists and outlines you've been creating for each of the topics you have studied in this text. After you understand the basic legal principles, you will then find and review applicable statutes and cases and integrate what you learn from those cases and statutes into your understanding of the basic legal principles, further developing your understanding of what you will need to prove or disprove, to effectively represent your client.

This might surprise you, because so much of the learning in law school is derived from cases. In fact, law students frequently begin their research process by performing a search for cases on one of the legal research websites; the problem with this approach is that if you do not yet understand the basic legal principles your research may result in a large number of marginally relevant cases and you will likely spend significant time reading irrelevant material, or cases that do not solve the precise issues you need to address and resolve in your client's case. By first taking the time to understand the basic principles and develop a framework for the topic, your research will yield better results in the form of cases and other sources that address the specific legal issues you are interested in learning about, and you will have a means for organizing what you find. Additionally, practice guides will frequently provide you with advice for avoiding the most common mistakes made by new practitioners.

Another difference between prior sections of this text and law practice is that unlike the edited cases in this text (and most other texts), most unedited cases contain a discussion of multiple issues. This results in two key differences between reading cases in a law school text and reading cases as a lawyer. The first is that edited cases in a law school text allow you to focus on one issue at a time, whereas actual cases require you to think about several issues simultaneously, because a case may cover more than one topic (or issue) that is relevant to your client's problem. The second difference is that edited cases in law school remove issues that are not relevant to the topic covered, whereas actual cases may contain irrelevant information in the form of a legal issue you do not presently need to resolve (or the case may be entirely irrelevant to your client's case). In this chapter, rather than assuming the issues in the cases are relevant, you will have to determine which aspects of the case (if any) are relevant to your problem. This mirrors law practice in that lawyers frequently must sort through material and identify what is relevant and what is not. This applies not only to cases but also to practice guides, statutes, documents, and virtually everything else you will read as a lawyer.

As you begin this task, keep in mind that your ultimate goal is to put the materials together in such a way that they (1) help you understand the law, as well as the strengths and weaknesses of your client's case, and (2) allow you to explain the law and facts of your case to the relevant audience—e.g., judge, jury, mediator, client or opposing counsel—in order to achieve your goal—e.g., prevailing on a motion, settling the claim, preparing for deposition, etc.

Chapter Problem

You represent defendants Robyn Wong and Cooperative Child Care for Single Parents (CCCSP) in an action for defamation by Alan Strickland.[2] The clients contacted your law firm just a few days before the deadline to answer, and plaintiff's counsel would not grant an extension of time to respond. Another associate was assigned the task of drafting an answer, which is contained in the file. You will be handling this matter from this point forward. The exercises in this chapter are designed to assist you in representing your clients—your first task is to familiarize yourself with the documents in the file, which are set out below. The first page is an email from the Associate who reviewed the complaint with Ms. Wong during the initial client meeting:

---

2. The materials in this problem are based on similar facts contained in *Hill v. Hill*, a California Performance Exam administered in July 1987.

Re: Strickland v. Wong

I met with Robyn Wong when she came to the office with the complaint. I thought you might want to know some of the things she related to me, because I am not sure the information is contained in any of the documents in the file.

According to Wong, she is in charge of background and reference checks for CCCSP, and she is paid for doing this service. CCCSP also subscribes to a background check reporting service which does the criminal and credit check. According to Wong, CCCSP is a non-profit organization that provides afterschool care to the children of its members. Every parent member must provide care two days per month, which allows the organization to charge fees that are slightly lower than the market rate.

The plaintiff is a pediatric dentist. His son Viktor goes to school with Wong's children. At some type of school function Wong ran into the plaintiff's ex-wife. Apparently, Wong mentioned to the ex-wife that the plaintiff was applying to CCCSP, and the ex-wife went on something of a rant. She told Wong that plaintiff was a child abuser, that he had to go to court ordered counseling, and that she had to leave him and ended up leaving Viktor with him just to get away, which is how plaintiff wound up with custody.

Wong reported the ex-wife's statements to the Board, both orally during the meeting and in writing, in the form of a report to the Board. The report was circulated during the meeting, and since it is an open meeting, a few of the members who were present, but not on the Board, received copies. She also thinks that the members who were present may have shown the report to other members, because she has had one or two people who were not present at the meeting ask her about it.

Wong said that after plaintiff's application for membership was denied, the plaintiff called her. She said she felt badly about what happened, especially because all of his references were wonderful and everything checked out. During the call she told plaintiff about his ex-wife's statement; she told him that although she had to report it, she felt the board had overreacted. She thinks the board was being overly cautious because the members all have children in the program.

In the same conversation plaintiff told her that he and the ex-wife had a very tumultuous marriage because every time he would spank Victor, she would call him abusive. I asked Wong if she knew what the spanking entailed and she said she didn't get into it with him, because he was so upset, and he had already been denied membership. Plaintiff also told Wong that the only counseling he did was the counseling to try to save the marriage. Wong said both parties seem to be pretty hostile about one another.

She left a copy of the application and releases signed by the plaintiff as well as a copy of her memo to the board—which are all in the file. She also mentioned that a number of the members are no longer taking their kids to the plaintiff's dental practice, and that she hopes it isn't because of her report.

Based on some preliminary research, I've drafted an answer for your review. Please let me know if you need anything else.

1   SUPERIOR COURT OF NORTH CAROLINA

2   GENERAL COURT OF JUSTICE, DURHAM COUNTY

3

4 Alan STRICKLAND, an individual,   No. 09CVS0111303

5   Plaintiff,   COMPLAINT

6 v.

7 Robyn WONG and Cooperative
   Child Care for Single Parents,
8 a non-profit entity,

9   Defendants.

10

11

12   COMPLAINT

13   The plaintiff, Alan Strickland, complaining of the defendants, Robyn Wong and Co-

14 operative Child Care for Single Parents, says and alleges the following:

15   THE PARTIES

16   1. The plaintiff, Alan Strickland, is a citizen and resident of Durham County,

17 North Carolina.

18   2. The defendant, Cooperative Child Care for Single Parents ("Defendant CCCSP"),

19 is a private non-profit partnership organized and existing under the laws of the State of

20 North Carolina, with its main office in Durham, North Carolina.

21   3. The defendant, Robyn Wong ("Defendant Wong"), is a citizen and resident of

22 Durham County, North Carolina.

23   4. At all relevant times, Defendant Wong was a member of the Board of Directors of

24 Defendant CCCSP.

25   FACTS COMMON TO ALL CAUSES OF ACTION

26   5. Plaintiff is a pediatric dentist, and his ability to succeed and prosper in his busi-

27 ness, profession and means of livelihood is critically dependent upon his stature and

28 his business reputation, both as a business person and as a person that is trustworthy

29 with regard to the care of children.

30   6. For fifteen years, Plaintiff built, developed and earned a professional reputation

31 as a skilled, dedicated and trustworthy pediatric dentist.

32

33

1   7. In April 2010, Plaintiff separated from and then divorced Jocelyn Smessler-

2 Strickland. Plaintiff was awarded primary physical and legal custody of the couple's

3 son, Viktor.

4   8. In May 2010, Plaintiff, in an effort to provide support and care for Viktor, ap-

5 plied for membership with Defendant CCCSP.

6   9. CCCSP members are single parents who provide after-school care to each other's

7 children as part of a cooperative service.

8   10. As part of the screening process for membership in CCCSP, Plaintiff submitted

9 an application. In the application Plaintiff provided references and a signed release au-

10 thorizing CCCSP to verify the information submitted with his application.

11   11. Defendant Wong was assigned to verify Plaintiff's information, and conduct

12 Plaintiff's background screening.

13   12. Plaintiff's application was denied.

14   13. During an event held at the elementary school attended by Viktor Strickland and

15 Defendant Wong's child, Plaintiff's ex-wife, Jocelyn Smessler-Strickland informed

16 Wong that Strickland had "abused Viktor and had sought psychiatric counseling".

17   14. Defendant Wong knowingly made false, defamatory and slanderous statements

18 to the board when she repeated Jocelyn Smessler-Strickland's statements to board

19 members.

20   15. In June 2010, Plaintiff was informed by other member of CCCSP that Defen-

21 dant Wong reported her findings, including Jocelyn Smessler-Strickland's statement, in

22 a written report to the CCCSP Executive Board, which was circulated to CCCSP mem-

23 bers who were present during a monthly Board meeting.

24   16. Neither Defendant Wong, nor Defendant CCCSP made an attempt to verify the

25 accuracy of Jocelyn Smessler-Strickland's statements.

26   17. The written report containing Jocelyn Smessler-Strickland's statements was false,

27 defamatory and slanderous, and Defendants knew the statements in the report were

28 defamatory and slanderous.

29   18. Defendant Wong uttered the statements and submitted the report while acting as

30 agent for Defendant CCCSP.

31   **FIRST CAUSE OF ACTION: SLANDER PER SE**

32   19. Plaintiff hereby realleges and incorporates by reference the preceding paragraphs

33 of this Complaint.

20. The statements described above in paragraphs 13–15 were slanderous per se in that the slanderous character of these statements is clear and obvious from the words alone that were used and were defamatory statements about Plaintiff with respect to his business, profession and means of livelihood, and that the statements accused Plaintiff of a crime.

21. These slanderous statements were published in that Defendant Wong knowingly communicated these slanderous statements to third persons, including the CCCSP Executive Board.

22. Defendant Wong and Members of the CCCSP Executive Board knowingly communicated these slanderous statements to third persons, including CCCSP members.

23. The slanderous statements were false.

24. The slanderous statements described above were known to be false by Defendant Wong and Defendant CCCSP at the time the statements were made.

25. The slanderous statements directly and proximately caused Plaintiff to suffer actual damages in the form of ridicule, humiliation, public contempt, loss of reputation, damage to his business, profession and means of livelihood, and monetary, economic and business loss in the form of patients withdrawing from Plaintiff's pediatric dental practice.

26. Based upon the slanderous and defamatory statements and for the reasons stated above, Defendants Wong and CCCSP are liable to the plaintiff for slander per se, and the plaintiff is entitled to recover compensatory damages in an amount to be determined by a jury, but in any event, in amount in excess of Ten Thousand Dollars.

SECOND CAUSE OF ACTION: SLANDER

27. Plaintiff hereby realleges and incorporates by reference paragraphs 1–18 of this Complaint, and he pleads the Second Cause of Action in the alternative to the First Cause of Action.

28. The statements described above were slanderous in that the slanderous and injurious character of these statements is evident when the statements are explained by extrinsic evidence of the circumstances surrounding and preceding these statements.

29. The statements described above were defamatory statements about Plaintiff with respect to his business, profession and means of livelihood.

30. These slanderous statements were published in that Defendant Wong knowingly communicated these slanderous statements to third persons, including the CCCSP Executive Board.

31. Defendant Wong and Members of the CCCSP Executive Board knowingly communicated these slanderous statements to third persons, including CCCSP members, and did so further knowing that the third persons would repeat the statements to others.

32. Upon information and belief, persons who heard the statements or read Defendant Wong's report, reasonably understood that Defendant Wong's statements subjected Plaintiff to public ridicule, contempt and/or disgrace.

33. The defamatory statements were false.

34. At the time Defendants made and distributed the false and defamatory statements they knew that these statements were false.

35. The slanderous statements directly and proximately caused Plaintiff to suffer actual damages in the form of ridicule, humiliation, public contempt, loss of reputation, and further, these statements directly and proximately caused Plaintiff to suffer special damages in an amount in excess of Ten Thousand Dollars, including but not limited to out-of-pocket expenses incurred in an effort to mitigate the damages caused by these statements, loss of past and future income from diminished clientele at his pediatric dental practice, and loss of earning capacity in his business, profession and means of livelihood.

36. Based upon the slanderous and defamatory statements Defendants are liable to the plaintiff for slander per quod, and the plaintiff is entitled to recover compensatory damages, including the above-described special damages, in an amount to be determined by a jury, but in any event, in amount in excess of Ten Thousand Dollars.

THIRD CAUSE OF ACTION: LIBEL PER SE

37. Plaintiff hereby realleges and incorporates by reference paragraphs 1–18 of this Complaint.

38. Defendant Wong reduced the defamatory statements to writing when she put them in the memorandum she distributed to the CCCSP Executive Board.

39. The defamatory statements were published in writing in the memorandum Defendant Wong distributed to the CCCSP Executive Board.

40. Defendant CCCSP, by and through Wong and the CCCSP Executive Board, distributed the written defamatory statement to CCCSP members, as described above in paragraphs 13–16.

41. The libelous and defamatory statements directly and proximately caused Plaintiff to suffer actual damages in the form of ridicule, humiliation, public contempt, loss of reputation, damage to his business, profession and means of livelihood, and monetary, economic and business loss.

42. Based upon the libelous and defamatory statements, and for the reasons stated above, Defendants are liable to Plaintiff for libel per se, and Plaintiff is entitled to recover compensatory damages in an amount to be determined by a jury, but in any event, in amount in excess of Ten Thousand Dollars.

FOURTH CAUSE OF ACTION: LIBEL PER QUOD

43. Plaintiff hereby realleges and incorporates by reference the preceding paragraphs of this Complaint, and he pleads the Fourth Cause of Action in the alternative to the Third Cause of Action.

44. The defamatory and injurious character of the statements described above are evident when these statements are explained by extrinsic evidence of the circumstances surrounding and preceding these statements.

45. The statements described above were defamatory statements about Plaintiff with respect to his business, profession and means of livelihood.

46. The defamatory statements were published by the defendants in that Defendant Wong and Defendant CCCSP, by and through Wong and the CCCSP Executive Board, knowingly communicated these statements to third persons, and did so further knowing that the third persons would spread the statements to others.

47. The defamatory statements were false.

48. At the time she made the false and defamatory statements Defendant Wong knew that these statements were false. At the time Defendant CCCSP, by and through Wong and the CCCSP Executive Board, made the false and defamatory statements Defendant CCCSP knew that these statements were false.

49. The libelous and defamatory statements directly and proximately caused Plaintiff to suffer actual damages in the form of ridicule, humiliation, public contempt, loss of reputation, and further, these statements directly and proximately caused Plaintiff to suffer special damages in an amount in excess of Ten Thousand Dollars, including but

1 not limited to out-of-pocket expenses incurred in an effort to mitigate the damages

2 caused by these statements, loss of past and future income from diminished clientele at

3 his pediatric dental practice, and loss of earning capacity in his business, profession

4 and means of livelihood.

5   50. Based upon the libelous and defamatory statements, and for the reasons stated

6 above, Defendants are liable to the plaintiff for libel per quod, and the plaintiff is enti-

7 tled to recover compensatory damages, including the above-described special damages,

8 in an amount to be determined by a jury, but in any event, in amount in excess of Ten

9 Thousand Dollars.

10   **JURY TRIAL DEMANDED**

11 **PLAINTIFF RESPECTFULLY DEMANDS A JURY TRIAL ON ALL ISSUES OF**

12 **FACT SO TRIABLE.**

13   **WHEREFORE**, Plaintiff, Alan Strickland, respectfully prays to the Court:

14   1. That he have and recover of the Defendants, compensatory damages, including

15 special damages, in an amount to be determined by a jury, but in any event in an

16 amount in excess of ten thousand dollars ($10,000.00);

17   2. For the costs of this action, including interest, to the extent permitted by law;

18   3. For reasonable attorney's fees when permitted by law; and

19   4. For such, other and further relief which the Court deems equitable, just and

20 proper.

21   RESPECTFULLY SUBMITTED, this the 23rd day of January, 2011.

22

23

24

25

26

27

28

29

30

31

32

33

1 **SUPERIOR COURT OF NORTH CAROLINA**

2 **GENERAL COURT OF JUSTICE, DURHAM COUNTY**

3

4 Alan STRICKLAND, an individual,   No. 09CVS0111303

5   Plaintiff,   **ANSWER OF DEFENDANTS WONG AND COOPERATIVE**

6 v.   **CHILD CARE FOR SINGLE PARENTS**

7 Robyn WONG and Cooperative Child Care for Single Parents,

8 a non-profit entity,

9   Defendants.

10

11

12   <u>ANSWER</u>

13 NOW COME Defendants, and answer the Complaint as follows:

14   **FIRST DEFENSE**

15 The Plaintiff's Complaint fails to state claims upon which relief may be granted.

16   **SECOND DEFENSE**

17 Some or all of Plaintiff's claims are untimely under the applicable statute(s) of

18 limitations.

19   **THIRD DEFENSE**

20 To the extent that the Plaintiff has attempted to state a claim for defamation, slander

21 and/or slander per se, libel per se and/or libel per quod, Defendants plead the affirma-

22 tive defense of truthfulness as to any statement(s) found to have been made by any of

23 the Defendants or anyone that is determined to be their agent.

24   **FOURTH DEFENSE**

25 To the extent that Plaintiff has attempted to state a claim for defamation, slander

26 and/or slander per se, libel per se and/or libel per quod, any alleged statement(s) were

27 not published, nor did any statement(s) damage Plaintiff's reputation.

28   **FIFTH DEFENSE**

29 To the extent that Plaintiff has attempted to state a claim for defamation, slander

30 and/or slander per se, libel per se and/or libel per quod, for communications among

31 and between Defendants or anyone determined to be their agent, Defendants plead

32 the affirmative defense of qualified privilege because such statements were made in

33 good faith on subjects which the person communicating had a right and/or duty to

communicate, and were made to a person having a corresponding interest or duty in the communication.

SIXTH DEFENSE

In response to the separately numbered paragraphs of the Complaint, Defendants further answer as follows:

1. Admitted.

2. Admitted.

3. Admitted.

4. Admitted on information and belief.

5. Defendants lack sufficient information upon which to form a belief as to the truthfulness of the allegation and it is therefore denied.

6. Defendants lack sufficient information upon which to form a belief as to the truthfulness of the allegation and it is therefore denied.

7. Defendants lack sufficient information upon which to form a belief as to the truthfulness of the allegation and it is therefore denied.

8. Defendants lack sufficient information upon which to form a belief as to the truthfulness of the allegation and it is therefore denied.

9. Admitted.

10. Admitted.

11. Admitted.

12. Admitted.

13. Defendants lack sufficient information upon which to form a belief as to the truthfulness of the allegation and it is therefore denied.

14. Denied.

15. Defendants lack sufficient information upon which to form a belief as to the truthfulness of the allegation and it is therefore denied.

16. Denied.

17. Denied.

18. Admitted.

19. Restates allegations.

20. Denied.

21. Denied.

22. Denied.

23. Denied.

24. Denied.

25. Denied.

26. Denied.

27. Restates allegations.

28. Denied.

29. Denied.

30. Denied.

31. Denied.

32. Denied.

33. Denied.

34. Denied.

35. Denied.

36. Denied.

37. Restates allegations.

38. Denied.

39. Denied.

40. Denied.

41. Denied.

42. Denied.

43. Restates allegations.

44. Denied.

45. Denied.

46. Denied.

47. Denied.

48. Denied.

49. Denied.

50. Denied.

Defendants admit that Plaintiff seeks the relief requested and requests a jury trial, but deny that any judgment or relief should be granted to Plaintiff.

Defendants deny any and all allegations contained in Plaintiff's Complaint, express or implied, that are not expressly and unequivocally admitted in this Answer.

Wherefore, Defendants pray for judgment as follows:

1 | 1. That Plaintiff takes nothing by her Complaint, and that the Complaint be dismissed in its entirety;

2. That Defendants be awarded the attorneys' fees that they reasonably incur in defending this case;

3. That Defendants be awarded costs and expenses in the manner and to the extent permitted by law; and

4. For such other and further relief as the Court may deem just and proper.

Respectfully submitted,

Attorneys for Defendants

CCCSP

Cooperative Care for Children of Single Parents

APPLICATION

1. Applicant Information

Name: **ALAN**   **JOHN**   **STRICKLAND**
       (First)   (Middle)   (Last)

Address: **2002 TO PRES.**   **2413 ARBOL DR.**   **DURHAM**   **NC 27708**
         (Mo/Yr)   (Street)   (City)   (Zip/State)

Phone: **919-555-1706**   Email: **AJSTRICKLAND@PEDDDS.COM**

Name(s) of Child(ren) living with you:

Name: **VIKTOR**   **ALAN**   **STRICKLAND**
      (First)   (Middle)   (Last)
Please indicate whether you have legal custody: ☒ yes ☐ no ☒ primary ☐ joint
Please indicate whether this child will be enrolled in CCCSP ☒ yes ☐ no ☐

Name: **N/A**
      (First)   (Middle)   (Last)
Please indicate whether you have legal custody: ☐ yes ☐ no ☐ primary ☐ joint
Please indicate whether this child will be enrolled in CCCSP ☐ yes ☐ no ☐

Name: **N/A**
      (First)   (Middle)   (Last)
Please indicate whether you have legal custody: ☐ yes ☐ no ☐ primary ☐ joint
Please indicate whether this child will be enrolled in CCCSP ☐ yes ☐ no ☐

Name(s) of Child(ren) not living with you:

Name: **N/A**
      (First)   (Middle)   (Last)
Please indicate whether you have legal custody: ☐ yes ☐ no ☐ primary ☐ joint
Please indicate whether this child will be enrolled in CCCSP ☐ yes ☐ no ☐

Name: **N/A**
      (First)   (Middle)   (Last)
Please indicate whether you have legal custody: ☐ yes ☐ no ☐ primary ☐ joint
Please indicate whether this child will be enrolled in CCCSP ☐ yes ☐ no ☐

Name: **N/A**
      (First)   (Middle)   (Last)
Please indicate whether you have legal custody: ☐ yes ☐ no ☐ primary ☐ joint
Please indicate whether this child will be enrolled in CCCSP ☐ yes ☐ no ☐

Marital Status: ☐ separated ☒ divorced ☐ never married ☐ widowed ☐ other (please explain): _____

Monthly income (amount and sources): **$10,000   DENTAL PRACTICE**

Name: _____ALAN STRICKLAND_____

2. List your previous employers. Include approximate date, organization's name and address, type of work you performed, name of supervisor and phone number. *(Attach a separate page, if necessary.)*

Date: Organization: Type of Work: Supervisor: Phone:

1997 to PRES.   ALAN STRICKLAND, D.D.S. SELF-EMPLOYED DENTIST   919-555-7300

_____

_____

3. List your highest earned academic degree (and/or professional license). Include date, organization's name and address, type of degree (license), and phone number.

Date: Organization: Type of Degree: Phone:

1994   UNC DENTAL SCHOOL   D.D.S.   919-555-6701 × 157

4. Please provide the names and phone numbers of three personal references not related to you.

Name: Home Phone: Work Phone:

REBECCA FLANIGAN   919-555-2312   919-555-6211
HILARY BURGESS   919-555-5621   919-555-0713
MIKE DOUBET   919-555-5309   919-555-8721

5. Have you ever been charged with or committed a crime (regardless of age), including criminal traffic violations?   ☐Yes ☒No

   If yes, please explain: *(attach a separate page, if necessary)*_____

   _____

   _____

6. Is there anything in your past or present that would prohibit you from effectively working with children or other members?   ☐Yes ☒No

   If yes, please explain: *(attach a separate page, if necessary)*_____

   _____

   _____

7. Each member is required to work 2 days each month for each child enrolled. By submitting this application you indicate your willingness to do so. Please list any days or times that are inconvenine for you. The center is open for before school care from 6:00-8:30 a.m. and for after school care from 3:00-6:00 p.m.

   LATE AFTERNOONS ON MONDAYS AND WEDNESDAYS

   _____

   _____

Applicant's Signature___Alan Strickland_____ Date 5/31/2010

CCCSP

Cooperative Care for Children of Single Parents

SCHOOL AGE CHILD INFORMATION FORM

Child's Name: __VIKTOR STRICKLAND__

Does your child have a nickname? ☒ Yes ☐ No
If yes, what is it: __VIK__

Name of School: __DURHAM ELEMENTARY__

Pediatrician: __DR. SMYTHE   919 - 555 - 3719__

Emergency contact: __JOCELYN SMESSLER - STRICKLAND__
                                                         __919-555-2103__

What language is spoken in your home: __ENGLISH__

Does your child have any food sensitivities? ☐ Yes ☒ No
If yes, please identify: _____

Does your child make new friends easily? __YES__
What activities does your child enjoy? __SOCCER__

How do you handle discipline in your home? __GROUNDING AND SPANKING__

What characteristics in your child's development would you like:
Encouraged? __FOCUS AND RESPONSIBILITY__

Discouraged? __TALKING BACK TO ADULTS__

Please provide any other information relating to your child that would
be helpful in understanding and caring for your child: _____

Date: __5/31/10__   __Alan Strickland__
         D M Y   Parent/Guardian signature

CCCSP

Cooperative Care for Children of Single Parents

AUTHORIZATION TO RELEASE INFORMATION RELATING TO BACKGROUND CHECK

Print Name: ___ALAN___ ___JOHN___ ___STRICKLAND___
            (First)   (Middle)   (Last)

Former Name(s) and Dates Used:
___NONE___

Current Address Since: _6/02_ _2413 ARBOL DR._ _DURHAM_ _N.C._ _27705_
                       (Mo/Yr)   (Street)   (City)   (Zip/State)

Previous Address From: _____
                        ((Mo/Yr)   (Street)   (City)   (Zip/State)

Social Security Number: __867-00-53091__

Date of Birth: _11/13/68_   Telephone Number: _919-555-1706_

Drivers License Number/State: _7613250_ _NC_

The information contained in this application is correct to the best of my knowledge. I hereby authorize **CCCPS** and its designated agents and representatives to conduct a comprehensive review of my background causing a consumer report and/or an investigative consumer report to be generated for membership and/or volunteer purposes. I understand that the scope of the consumer report/ investigative consumer report may include, but is not limited to the following areas: verification of social security number; current and previous residences; employment history, education background, character references; civil and criminal history records from any criminal justice agency in any or all federal, state, county jurisdictions; driving records, birth records, and any other public records, and reports from credit agencies to verify credit rating. I further authorize any individual, company, firm, corporation, or public agency (including the Social Security Administration and law enforcement agencies), and educational institution to divulge any and all information, verbal or written, pertaining to me, to **CCCPS** or its agents. I further authorize the complete release of any records or data pertaining to me which the individual, company, firm, corporation, or public agency may have, to include information or data received from other sources. I hereby release **CCCPS**, its agents, officials, representative, or assigned agencies, including officers, employees, or related personnel both individually and collectively, from any and all liability for damages of whatever kind, which may, at any time, result to me, my heirs, family, or associates because of compliance with this authorization and request to release. This authorization shall be valid in original or copy form.

Signature: _Alan Strickland_   Date: _5/31/10_

Cooperative Care for Children of Single Parents

AUTHORIZATION TO RELEASE HEALTHCARE INFORMATION

Child's Name: **VIKTOR STRICKLAND** Date of Birth: **11/13/68**

Parent's Name: **ALAN STRICKLAND** Social Security #: **867-00-53091**

I request and authorize **DR. SMYTHE** to
release healthcare information of the Child and Parent named above to:

Name: **CCCSP**

Address: **123 MAIN ST.**

City: **DURHAM** State: **NC** Zip Code: **27708**

This request and authorization applies to:

☐ Healthcare information relating to the following treatment, condition, or dates: _____

_____

☒ All healthcare information

☐ Other: _____

☒ Yes ☐ No   I have the power to authorize the release of such information with respect to any minor listed
in this form, and I hereby grant such authorization with respect to the Child listed above.

☒ Yes ☐ No   No other person's authorization is necessary with respect to any minor listed in this form.

Parent Signature: *Alan Strickland* Date Signed: **5/31/10**

THIS AUTHORIZATION EXPIRES NINETY DAYS AFTER IT IS SIGNED.

Cooperative Care for Children of Single Parents

To: CCCSP Executive Board

From: Robyn Wong, Board Member, Applications and Admissions Chair

Regarding: Application of Alan Strickland (for child: Viktor Strickland)

Mr. Strickand submitted all releases and a completed application. I contacted sources directly or obtained the information from CGI Inc., a record verification service provider, to verify the accuracy of the information provided.

Mr. Strickland's education, residence, marital status, and other information was accurate. According to CGI Inc., he did not have any criminal record, is not listed in the child abuse registry, does not have any civil judgment against him, and has an excellent credit rating.

Mr. Strickland's references consisted of two current members, and one non-member who is a parent of another child at the school Viktor Strickland attends. They all said basically the same thing. He is a great dentist, frequent volunteer at the school, very dependable, a nice person and is great with their kids.

Mr. Strickland seems well qualified and I would recommend him for membership.

I feel compelled to pass on one piece of information, although I am not sure what to make of it. Last week I ran into Mr. Strickland's ex-wife, Jocelyn, at a school event. Both Viktor Strickland and my children attend the same school, and the school was holding a fundraiser. I happened to mention to Jocelyn that Mr. Strickland was applying for CCCSP membership. Jocelyn seemed very agitated. She asked me if I knew that Mr. Strickland was an abuser. According to Jocelyn, he abused Viktor, to the point that Viktor needed medical treatment. Jocelyn also said that Mr. Strickland had to attend court ordered counseling, and that she left him, and gave him custody of Viktor just so she could get away.

The family court records contain very little, other than the judgment awarding custody to Mr. Strickland, and a general order for all parties to seek counseling. I really think this is just a case of an angry ex-wife and I am not sure I would put much stock into it. In fact, when I called Mr. Strickland to confirm that his application was ready for submission to the board, I didn't even ask him about it.

Exercise 5-1 Using Practice Guides to Develop Knowledge and Understanding

This exercise contains an excerpt from the Tort Lawyers Fictitious Guide to Personal Injury Practice in North Carolina.[3] Use the excerpt to (1) develop your understanding of the law; (2) create an outline and checklist of the issues you will likely encounter in your representation of Defendants Wong and CCCSP (legal issues, procedural issues, and factual issues); (3) create a list of the cases you believe you should read in order to further develop your understanding; (4) make note of which of these cases will most likely provide guidance about your particular case (as opposed to general information about the tort of defamation); and (5) make notes of any particular problems you believe you (and your client) will face. In making note of the problems you may face be sure to consider the substantive law, procedural requirements, and factual ambiguities (or areas where you need to investigate or seek clarification).

I. Common Law Defamation

Defamation compensates a plaintiff for injury to her reputation. Counsel should be aware of the tensions between the plaintiff's right to be compensated for such injury and defendant's right to free speech. Constitutional constraints are covered in section VI of this chapter.

A. The prima facie case

Defamation requires proof that: (1) the defendant made a defamatory statement; (2) the defamatory statement was of and concerning the plaintiff; and (3) the defamatory statement was published to a third party. The plaintiff must also plead and prove that the defamatory statement caused damages; for a discussion of damages see section V of this chapter.

(1) Defamatory Statement

Generally speaking, a statement is defamatory if it tends to adversely affect a person's reputation. Thus, a statement is defamatory if it subjects the plaintiff to hatred, scorn, ridicule, contempt or disgrace; deters others from associating with the plaintiff; or lowers the plaintiff in the estimation of the community. Mere insults, hyperbole, pure opinion and obvious jokes do not amount to defamation.

> [I.A.1.a] In determining whether a statement can be reasonably interpreted as stating actual facts about an individual for purposes of a defamation action, courts look to the circumstances in which the statement is made; specifically, courts consider whether the language used is loose, figurative, or hyperbolic language, as well as the general tenor of the article. *Craven v. Cope*, 656 S.E.2d 729 (N.C. Ct. App. 2008).

---

3. No such guide actually exists, although there are several practice guides that cover personal injury law in North Carolina; also, most states have similar guides. This section is intended to simulate the materials and information in such guides; toward that end, a majority of the case summaries (the one or two lines about each case) are printed much as they appear in Strong's North Carolina Index 4th, and where there are altered, or they do not appear in Strong's, they are drafted to mimic that style.

[I.A.1.b] Author's statements in magazine article about his experience with his automobile insurance company and claims adjustor after the theft of his car, in which author claimed the adjustor intended to take him to the gas chamber and that her actions were equivalent to those taken by former Soviet security police, constituted hyperbolic language that no reasonable reader could take literally, and thus, the statements did not amount to libel. *Daniels v. Metro Magazine Holding Co., L.L.C.*, 634 S.E.2d 586 (N.C. Ct. App. 2006).

A statement need not be defamatory "on its face." The plaintiff is permitted to offer evidence to show that listeners or readers would understand its' defamatory meaning.

[I.A.1.c] Letter from insurance company to its' customers informing them that insurance company had recently refrained from allowing its' employees to visit Plaintiff's body shop was capable of defamatory meaning since the letter could be interpreted as indicating body shop had an unsafe condition on the premises. *Pack Bros. Body Shop, Inc. v. Nationwide Mut. Ins. Co.*, 01 CVS 805, 2003 WL 21017395 (N.C. Super. Jan. 10, 2003).

[I.A.1.d] Letter stating plaintiff was being suspended without pay, while defendant investigated who had authored a defamatory letter that had circulated through the workplace, could be reasonably interpreted as imputing wrongdoing on the part of plaintiff. *Cummings v. Lumbee Tribe of N. Carolina*, 590 F. Supp. 2d 769, 772 (E.D.N.C. 2008)

[I.A.1.e] CNN report that source had been taking medication for a nervous disorder for ten years could have given the impression that source was mentally ill and required medication that he was no longer taking, creating false impression that source's use of (or need for) medication was the cause of CNN's erroneous story on Operation Tailwind. The Ninth Circuit held that statements, although perhaps "true" when viewed in isolation, could create an overall false impression when considered in context. *Van Buskirk v. Cable News Network, Inc.*, 284 F.3d 977, 984–85 (9th Cir. 2002).

(2) Identifying the Plaintiff

The defamatory statement must be "of and concerning" the plaintiff, meaning the statement must refer to some ascertained or ascertainable person and that person must be the plaintiff. *Arnold v. Sharpe*, 296 N.C. 533, 539, 251 S.E.2d 452, 456 (1979). Where the statement identifies the allegedly defamed party by name this requirement is plainly satisfied. Where the statement does not expressly name the plaintiff, the plaintiff must present evidence that establishes she is the subject of the defamatory statement ("colloquium"). For example, where the statement identifies the allegedly defamed party by title or other designation, plaintiff must plead and prove that a reasonable listener would have understood the title or other designation referred to plaintiff.

If the statement refers to a group or to unnamed members of a group, the size of the group in question will be relevant for determining whether this requirement is satisfied. The larger the group, the less likely it is that a court will permit an action for defamation from group members.

[I.A.2.a] Defamatory statements were "of or concerning" plaintiffs where advertisement made reference to "[Plaintiff's] law firm," claiming the "law firm" had committed unethical business practices. The reference to "[Plaintiff's] law firm" maligned each of the four attorneys in the firm. The court also held identification of the actual name of the law firm was readily ascertainable from the reference to "[Plaintiff's] law firm." *Boyce & Isley v. Cooper*, 153 N.C.App. 25 (2002).

[I.A.2.b] A defamatory statement referring to misconduct by "someone" in a group of nine persons did not support an action for defamation by a member of that group because the reference was too vague to indicate any of the individual members of that group. *See Chapman v. Byrd,* 124 N.C.App. 13, 17, 475 S.E.2d 734, 737 (1996), *disc. review denied,* 345 N.C. 751, 485 S.E.2d 50 (1997).

[I.A.2.c] Members of an eleven-member jury could maintain a cause of action for libel where the defamatory statement imputed misconduct to the entire jury. Where a statement defames a small group or class of persons in its entirety, any member of that class may pursue an action for defamation, despite the fact that the statement fails to specifically identify that particular individual. *Carter v. King,* 174 N.C. 549, 553, 94 S.E. 4, 6 (1917).

The plaintiff must be alive at the time the defamatory statement is made. An action for defamation is personal and a dead person cannot suffer reputational injury.

[I.A.2.d] Administrator of decedent's estate did not have a cause of action for the defamation against commercial photographer employed by a coroner to photograph the scene of a head-on collision between an automobile driven by the decedent and a truck owned by the coroner agent, for allegedly making and distributing defamatory pictures falsely depicting conditions at the wreck, since action did not survive decedent. *Gillikin v. Bell*, 254 N.C. 244, 118 S.E.2d 609 (1961).

(3) Publication

In order to form the basis of an action for libel or slander, it is necessary that the defamatory matter be communicated to some person or persons other than the person defamed. The statement need only be communicated to one person other than the plaintiff to satisfy this requirement.

Publication may be intentional or negligent. If defendant knew or should have known there was an unreasonable risk that defamatory matter would be communicated to a third party, or could have reasonably anticipated the defamatory matter would be communicated to a third party, defendant will be held liable for the publication. *Alley v. Long*, 209 N.C. 245, 183 S.E. 294 (1936).

[I.A.3.a] When a third person overhears a statement there is a publication, even when the person making the defamatory remarks cannot see and is not conscious of the third person's presence. *Alley v. Long*, 209 N.C. 245, 183 S.E. 294 (1936).

[I.A.3.b] Proof of the mere possibility that someone might have overheard the words is insufficient. *Tyer v. Leggett*, 246 N.C. 638, 99 S.E.2d 779 (1957).

Those who "republish" a statement, by repeating it to another, are liable as if they were the original publisher. In other words, a defendant may not avoid liability by attributing a defamatory statement to another person. Even where a defendant is merely repeating a statement made by another, he is liable if the statement he repeats is defamatory. Restatement (Second) of Torts, § 578 (1976).

B. Libel and Slander

Defamation encompasses the separate torts of libel and slander. *Pierce v. Atlantic Group, Inc.*, 724 S.E.2d 568 (N.C. Ct. App. 2012). "Slander" is oral defamation. "Libel" is written defamation. When defamatory words are spoken with the intent that the words be reduced to writing, and the words are in fact written, the publication is both "slander" and "libel."

[I.B.a] Defamatory radio broadcast presents potential claim for libel. *Woody v. Catawba Valley Broad. Co.*, 272 N.C. 459, 462, 158 S.E.2d 578, 581 (1979).

(1) Slander per se

Where a plaintiff pleads and proves slander per se, damages are, as a matter of law, presumed. For all other slanderous statements, special damage must be alleged and proved by the plaintiff. Such special damages are considered a required element of the tort. For a further discussion of damages, see section V.

Slander per se is a false statement that is orally communicated to a third person and amounts to: (1) an accusation that the plaintiff committed a crime involving moral turpitude; (2) an allegation that impeaches the plaintiff in his trade, business, or profession; or (3) an imputation that the plaintiff has a loathsome disease. *Kinesis Advertising, Inc. v. Hill,* 652 S.E.2d 284 (N.C. Ct. App. 2007). North Carolina appears to have abandoned the traditional common law position that the imputation of unchastity in a woman is slander per se.

Ordinarily a person may not maintain an action for a slander if he invited or procured the statement or the statement was invited or procured by a person acting on his behalf, especially when the statement is induced so that suit may be brought thereon.

[I.B.1.a] False words imputing to a businessperson conduct that is derogatory to his character as a businessperson are actionable per se. *Losing v. Food Lion, L.L.C.,* 648 S.E.2d 261 (N.C. Ct. App. 2007).

[I.B.1.b] Felony child abuse is a crime of "moral turpitude" for purposes of action for slander per se. *Dobson v. Harris,* 134 N.C. App. 573, 521 S.E.2d 710 (1999), decision rev'd on other grounds, 352 N.C. 77, 530 S.E.2d 829 (2000).

[I.B.1.c] A wife's assertions that her husband had sex with the family dog were slander per se. *Kroh v. Kroh,* 152 N.C. App. 347, 567 S.E.2d 760 (2002), review denied, 356 N.C. 673, 577 S.E.2d 120 (2003).

[I.B.1.d] Statements concerning plaintiff's academic credentials amounted to allegations that impeached plaintiff in his profession. *Raymond U v. Duke University,* 91 N.C. App. 171, 371 S.E.2d 701, 49 Ed. Law Rep. 410 (1988),

[I.B.1.e] Alleged slander on the part of a school superintendent with respect to whether employee of board of education voluntarily resigned or was fired in dispute over preparation of payroll was not actionable per se. A false statement which is alleged to impeach one's trade or profession must do more than merely injure a person in his business; it must touch the plaintiff in his special trade or occupation and must contain an imputation necessarily hurtful in its effect on his business. *Tallent v. Blake,* 57 N.C. App. 249, 291 S.E.2d 336, 4 Ed. Law Rep. 306 (1982).

[I.B.1.f] North Carolina has long recognized the harm that can result from false statements that impeach a person in that person's trade or profession. Such statements are defamation per se; the mere saying or writing of the words is presumed to cause injury, and there is no need to prove any actual injury. *Hien Nguyen v. Taylor*, 723 S.E.2d 551 (N.C. Ct. App. 2012).

(2) Libel

Pictures, caricatures, signs and other written or printed materials, including written or printed words, may be libelous. Libel is generally divided into three classes: (1) publications that are obviously defamatory; (2) publications that have two possible interpretations, one of which is defamatory and the other of which is not; and (3) publications that are not obviously defamatory, but that become defamatory when considered with innuendo, colloquium, and explanatory circumstances. *Griffin v. Holden*, 636 S.E.2d 298 (N.C. Ct. App. 2006). Where a publication is obviously defamatory, meaning that is defamatory "on its face" it is libel "per se." Where extrinsic, explanatory evidence is needed to show defamatory impact, the statement is libel "per quod." The law presumes that general damages result from an unauthorized publication which is libelous per se; such damages are not required to be proven by evidence. For a further discussion of damages, see section V.

In determining whether a publication is libelous per se, the court will consider the publication in context and ascribe meaning based on how the publication would be naturally understood by ordinary persons. *Holleman v. Aiken*, 668 S.E.2d 579 (N.C. Ct. App. 2008). To be libelous per se, the words must have but one meaning and that meaning must be such that a court can presume as a matter of law that the statement tends to disgrace and degrade the defamed party or hold him up to public hatred, contempt, or ridicule or cause him to be shunned and avoided. *Holleman v. Aiken*, 668 S.E.2d 579 (N.C. Ct. App. 2008). In evaluating whether a statements is libelous per se the statement will be considered in the context of the document in which it is contained, stripped of all insinuations, innuendo, colloquium, and explanatory circumstances. *Nucor Corp. v. Prudential Equity Group, LLC*, 659 S.E.2d 483 (N.C. Ct. App. 2008).

Where the statement is not libelous per se, and it is capable of having both a defamatory meaning and a non-defamatory meaning, it is for the jury to determine which of the two was intended and so understood by those to whom it was addressed or by whom it was heard. *Hien Nguyen v. Taylor*, 684 S.E.2d 470 (N.C. Ct. App. 2009).

To prevail under a theory of libel per quod, plaintiff must plead and prove (1) defendant knowingly made a publication or communication to a third person; (2) defendant intended the publication or communication to be defamatory; and (3) those to whom it was published understood it to be defamatory. *Holleman v. Aiken*, 668 S.E.2d 579 (N.C. Ct. App. 2008). Thus, libel per quod, requires proof of injury and special damage. *Griffin v. Holden*, 636 S.E.2d 298 (N.C. Ct. App. 2006). Emotional distress and mental suffering alone are not sufficient to establish a basis for relief in cases based exclusively on libel per quod.

II. Privileged Communications

Even where a statement is found to be actionable as libel or slander, the law regards certain communications as privileged, and defendant may not be held liable for making such statements. Whether a communication is privileged is a question of law for the court and not for the jury, unless the circumstances of the publication are in dispute, in which case it is a mixed question of law and fact. Privilege is an affirmative defense which must be specially pleaded in the answer, and the burden is on defendant to establish facts sufficient to support such a plea.

A. Qualified privilege

When a communication is made: (1) on a subject matter in which the declarant has an interest, right or duty, (2) to a person having a corresponding interest, right or duty, (3) on a privileged occasion, and (4) in a manner and under circumstances fairly warranted by the occasion and duty, right or interest, the statement is qualifiedly privileged. *Kinesis Advertising, Inc. v. Hill*, 652 S.E.2d 284 (N.C. Ct. App. 2007). Stated another way, the essential elements for a qualified privilege to exist as a defense to a claim for libel are: good faith, an interest to be upheld, a statement limited in its scope to this purpose, a proper occasion and publication in an appropriate manner and to the proper parties only. Thus a qualified or conditional privilege may be lost by proof of actual malice on defendant's part and by excessive publication.

[II.A.a] An official report by an investigator of a church, published in the official organ of the church, is qualifiedly privileged. *Herndon v. Melton*, 249 N.C. 217, 105 S.E.2d 531 (1958).

[II.A.b] A letter written by the chairman of a major political party to the Governor and a letter written by the chairman to the State Board of Elections, criticizing election officials in the conduct of an election, are qualifiedly privileged. *Ponder v. Cobb*, 257 N.C. 281, 126 S.E.2d 67 (1962).

[II.A.c] Allegedly defamatory statements made by SBI agent to the sheriff charged with safekeeping plaintiff in the county jail pending extradition were qualifiedly privileged since both the agent who arrested plaintiff and the sheriff had an interest in and duty with reference to the safekeeping of plaintiff, and the statements made by the agent might be useful to the sheriff in carrying out his responsibilities. *Towne v. Cope*, 32 N.C. App. 660, 233 S.E.2d 624 (1977).

(1) Loss of privilege — proof of actual malice

Actual malice may be proven by evidence of ill-will or personal hostility, or by showing that declarant published the defamatory statement with knowledge that it was false, with reckless disregard for the truth or with a high degree of awareness of its probable falsity. The burden of proving malice is on the plaintiff, since there is a presumption that the author made the statements in good faith and without malice. If the plaintiff cannot meet his burden of showing actual malice, privilege bars any recovery for the communication, even if it is false. A plaintiff is permitted to prove actual malice by circumstantial evidence.

[II.A.1.a] When an otherwise defamatory communication is made in pursuance of a political, judicial, social, or personal duty, an action for libel or slander will not lie, even where the statement is false, unless plaintiff proves actual malice. However, mother failed to overcome presumption of good faith where she did not present evidence of child abuse, and instead relied on bare allegations and suspicion. *Dobson v. Harris*, 352 N.C. 77, 530 S.E.2d 829 (2000).

[II.A.1.b] Wife's statements to the Department of Social Services that her husband molested her sons were made with actual malice, thereby negating any defense of privilege where: audiotapes offered by the wife contained no evidence from which a reasonable person could conclude that sexual misconduct had occurred; both sons testified that the husband had not molested them; both sons testified they had informed the wife, when she inquired, that her husband had not molested them in any way; and the trial court found as fact that the husband had not molested either son and that the wife knew her statements were false when she made them. *Kroh v. Kroh*, 152 N.C. App. 347, 567 S.E.2d 760 (2002)

(2) Loss of privilege — proof of excessive publication

Excessive publication may be proven by evidence defendant communicated information beyond the scope of the interest to be upheld or in a manner or to more persons then were necessary.

> [II.A.2.a] Statements made by defendant's employees in investigating charges of sexual misconduct were privileged since there was no evidence that the employees spoke to anyone outside of those who had a corresponding interest in the communication and were part of the investigative process. *Troxler v. Charter Mandala Center, Inc.*, 89 N.C. App. 268, 365 S.E.2d 665 (1988).

> [II.A.2.b] An attorney's letters to purchasers of automobile manufacturer's buyback vehicles, which allegedly stated that a class action suit had been filed against the manufacturer for alleged violations of the state's lemon law, and that the purchasers could have been defrauded by the manufacturer, were subject to a qualified privilege against the manufacturer's claim for libel per se; the attorney had a legitimate interest in obtaining information from the purchasers as clients in their own actions against the manufacturer, the purchasers had an interest in determining whether the manufacturer had complied with the lemon law, the communications took place in private letters, and the letters were sent in good faith and without malice or excessive publication. *Daimlerchrysler Corp. v. Kirkhart*, 148 N.C. App. 572, 561 S.E.2d 276 (2002), writ denied, review denied, 356 N.C. 668, 577 S.E.2d 113 (2003) and review dismissed, 356 N.C. 668, 577 S.E.2d 112 (2003).

> [II.A.2.c] Statements made by insurance company defendant's agent to plaintiff's uncle and first cousin accusing plaintiff of the misappropriation of funds belonging to defendant were not qualifiedly privileged, since neither the uncle nor the cousin had any interest or duty with reference to the subject of the agent's statements. *Stewart v. Nation-Wide Check Corp.*, 279 N.C. 278, 182 S.E.2d 410 (1971).

B. Absolute Privilege

A defendant may escape liability for certain defamatory statements, even where such statements are false, or made with ill-will or for a malicious purpose.

(1) Judicial proceedings

The general rule is that a defamatory statement made in the course of a judicial proceeding is absolutely privileged and will not support a civil action for defamation, even if it is made with express malice. *Jones v. Coward*, 666 S.E.2d 877 (N.C. Ct. App. 2008). An absolute privilege exists not only for statements made during an ongoing judicial proceeding but also for communications that are related to such judicial proceedings, including statements made in connection with a proposed judicial proceeding. *Harris v. NCNB Nat. Bank of North Carolina*, 85 N.C. App. 669, 355 S.E.2d 838 (1987). The court must decide as a matter of law whether the alleged defamatory statements are sufficiently related to a proposed or ongoing judicial proceeding. *Jones v. Coward*, 666 S.E.2d 877 (N.C. Ct. App. 2008). The test for relevancy is generous; however, a mere allegation that the libelous matter was filed with the clerk of the Superior Court does not show conclusively that it was uttered during the course of, or in relation to, a judicial proceeding.

[II.B.1.a] Legitimate argument to the jury comes within the rule of absolute privilege. *Wall v. Blalock*, 245 N.C. 232, 95 S.E.2d 450, 61 A.L.R.2d 1297 (1956).

[II.B.1.b] Libel claim based on warrant charging plaintiff with refusing to obey an order of a police officer to move her vehicle, was barred by privilege, since a "judicial proceeding" encompassed the warrant from the time of its issuance through plaintiff's trial. *Jones v. City of Greensboro*, 51 N.C. App. 571, 277 S.E.2d 562 (1981) (overruled on other grounds by, *Fowler v. Valencourt*, 334 N.C. 345, 435 S.E.2d 530 (1993)).

[II.B.1.c] A debt collection letter threatening criminal prosecution was protected by an absolute privilege because the letter was between the parties' attorneys, involved a judicial proceeding, and the allegedly defamatory statements were relevant to the proceeding. *Burton v. NCNB Nat. Bank of North Carolina*, 85 N.C. App. 702, 355 S.E.2d 800 (1987).

[II.B.1.d] Allegedly slanderous statements made by defendant dentist about plaintiff dentist were absolutely privileged where the statements were made to an attorney during a pre-deposition conference in a dental malpractice case and the statements were relevant and pertinent to the pending malpractice litigation. *Rickenbacker v. Coffey*, 103 N.C. App. 352, 405 S.E.2d 585 (1991).

[II.B.1.e] Statements or questions by an attorney to a potential witness regarding a suit in which attorney was involved were privileged, where the statement or question was sufficiently relevant to the subject matter of the controversy. *Jones v. Coward*, 666 S.E.2d 877 (N.C. Ct. App. 2008).

[II.B.1.f] An attorney in North Carolina is absolutely privileged to publish defamatory matter in preliminary communications related to a proposed judicial proceeding, if the material is relevant to the anticipated litigation and published to persons significantly interested in the litigation. *Andrews v. Elliot*, 109 N.C. App. 271, 426 S.E.2d 430 (1993).

(2) Legislative proceedings

Legislators are not liable for defamatory statements made during debate on the floor of the legislature. This includes knowingly false statements. *Hutchinson v. Proxmire*, 443 U.S. 111 (1979).

IV. Other Defenses

A. Truth as a defense

Truth is an absolute or complete defense to a claim of defamation, whether the claim is for libel or slander, and regardless of whether the statement was made in bad faith, or for a malicious purpose or because of the ill will of the publisher. Defendant may not be held liable if the defamatory statement was true, even if plaintiff proves the elements establishing defamation.

Also, a defendant may not be held liable for defamation for presenting a true account of events regardless of what someone might conclude from that account. *Entravision Communications Corp. v. Belalcazar*, 99 S.W.3d 393 (Tex. App. Corpus Christi 2003). However, liability will still exist when there is an omission of material facts, or a misleading presentation or juxtaposition of true facts. *Scripps Texas Newspapers, L.P. v. Belalcazar*, 99 S.W.3d 829 (Tex. App. Corpus Christi 2003).

A mere belief that a false statement is true is not a defense. *Hart v. Bennet*, 267 Wis. 2d 919, 2003 WI App 231, 672 N.W.2d 306 (Ct. App. 2003). However, an honest belief in the truth of the defamatory statement may support a qualified privilege.

> [IV.A.a] Employee did not have a claim for defamation where supervisor noted in employee's work history that there were prior allegations of sexual harassment since Employee admitted he had been accused of sexual harassment at work. *Meyerson v. Harrah's East Chicago Casino*, 67 Fed. Appx. 967 (7th Cir. 2003) (applying Indiana law).

(1) Substantial truth is sufficient

The defendant is not required to prove literal truth; substantial truth is the standard. Whether a statement is substantially true is a question of fact, and is for the jury to determine, unless the court concludes no reasonable jury could find that the statement was false.

> [IV.A.1.a] Statements by doctors that a university researcher threatened staff members with acids were not slanderous because evidence that researcher was mixing acid and another substance together and placing the hot and smoking flask in the staff members hands was sufficient to establish statements were substantially true. *Kwan-Sa You v. Roe*, 97 N.C. App. 1, 387 S.E.2d 188 (1990).

> [IV.A.1.b] Where the term "gunman" was used to describe a Plaintiff who admittedly had a gun in his possession during a standoff with police officers, it was a fair representation of the full truth, even though Plaintiff did not "wield" or "brandish" a gun. *White v. Town of Chapel Hill*, 899 F. Supp. 1428, 1438 (M.D.N.C. 1995) aff'd, 70 F.3d 1264 (4th Cir. 1995).

(2) Burden of proof lies with the defendant

Since truth is an affirmative defense it is not the plaintiff's initial burden to show that an allegedly defamatory statement is false. *Williams v. Boyle*, 72 P.3d 392 (Colo. Ct. App. 2003), as modified on denial of reh'g, (Feb. 6, 2003); *Stringer v. Wal-Mart Stores, Inc.*, 151 S.W.3d 781 (Ky. 2004). Defendant has the burden of proving truth; if the defendant fulfills this burden, she has a complete defense to an action for defamation.

Note that this is a substantial difference between common law defamation claims and defamation claims that must conform to constitutional constraints; in cases with constitutional implications, plaintiff bears the burden of establishing that the statement is false, as part of her prima facie case. For further discussion, see Constitutional Defamation, section VI.

(3) Republisher must prove truth of original statement

In those situations where a person repeats another's defamatory statement, the republisher must prove that the original statement is true, even if the defamatory statement was attributed to another at the time of publication. It is not sufficient to prove that the person quoted made the statement. *Erickson v. Jones Street Publishers, L.L.C.*, 368 S.C. 444, 629 S.E.2d 653 (2006).

B. Inadequate notice and request for retraction

(1) Notice requirements

At least five days before plaintiff brings a civil action for libel against a newspaper or periodical, plaintiff must serve the defendant notice, in writing, specifying the article and the statements which plaintiff alleges to be false and defamatory. N.C. Gen. Stat. Ann. § 99-1. This requirement does not apply to anonymous communications and publications. N.C. Gen. Stat. Ann. § 99-1

At least five days before plaintiff brings a civil action for libel or slander, for the publishing, speaking, uttering, or conveying by words, acts, or in any other manner, a defamatory statement through any radio or television station, the plaintiff must serve defendant notice, in writing, specifying the time of and the words or acts which plaintiff alleges to be false and defamatory. N.C. Gen. Stat. Ann. § 99-1. This requirement does not apply to anonymous communications and publications. N.C. Gen. Stat. Ann. § 99-1.

A letter written by plaintiff and received by defendant, that contains a demand for retraction and apology, and clearly specifies an article in which alleged false and defamatory statements are plainly indicated, constitutes sufficient notice. N.C. Gen. Stat. Ann. § 99-1.

(2) Relevant only for limiting damages

The requirement that plaintiff provide defendant notice and an opportunity for retraction are relevant solely to the issue of punitive damages and are not relevant for determining whether plaintiff has alleged a cause of action for libel. Thus, an action for libel may proceed, and compensatory damages may be recovered, even if notice has not been given. *Roth v. Greensboro News Co.*, 217 N.C. 13, 6 S.E.2d 882 (1940).

If an article (1) is published in good faith; (2) its falsity is due to an honest mistake of the facts; (3) there are reasonable grounds for believing that the statements in the article are true; and (4) within 10 days after the service of notice a full and fair correction, an apology and retraction is published, in the same editions or corresponding issues of the newspaper or periodical in which the article appeared, and in as conspicuous a place and type as was the original article, then the plaintiff may recover only actual damages. N.C. Gen. Stat. Ann. § 99-2.

C. Immunity

In certain circumstances defendant may have immunity from liability for making defamatory statements.

(1) Immunity for Employers

Where requested by a prospective employer, a current or former employer who discloses information about a current or former employee's job history or job performance, to a prospective employer is immune from civil liability and is not liable in civil damages for the disclosure or any resulting consequences. N.C. Gen. Stat. Ann. § 1-539.12.

This immunity is lost if the plaintiff shows by a preponderance of the evidence that: (1) the information disclosed by the current or former employer was false; and (2) the employer providing the information knew or reasonably should have known that the information was false. N.C. Gen. Stat. Ann. § 1-539.12.

(2) Reports of Suspected Child Abuse

Individuals making a report of suspected child abuse or neglect to the department of social services have immunity from criminal or civil liability, including liability for slander. This immunity is only available if the individual makes the report in good faith. The individual's good faith is presumed. N.C. Gen. Stat. Ann. § 7B-309.

[IV.C.2.a] Plaintiff mother failed to overcome the presumption of good faith when she failed to present any evidence but instead relied on bare allegations and suspicion. *Dobson v. Harris*, 352 N.C. 77, 530 S.E.2d 829 (2000).

V. Damages

For slander per se, damages are conclusively presumed and do not have to be alleged or proved. Similarly, the law presumes that general damages actually and proximately result from an unauthorized publication which is libelous per se; such damages are not required to be proven by evidence. In both types of cases, the amount of such damages is determined by the jury. As a practical matter counsel should be aware that although no evidence is required in such circumstances, juries are not likely to award substantial damages in the absence of proof such damages were suffered. Counsel who fail to present evidence of damages may not be satisfied with the award.

For a defamation claim, compensatory damages include (1) pecuniary loss, direct or indirect, or special damages; (2) damages for physical pain and inconvenience; (3) damages for mental suffering; and (4) damages for injury to reputation. *Hien Nguyen v. Taylor*, 723 S.E.2d 551 (N.C. Ct. App. 2012).

For publications which are not defamatory per se, but which become defamatory when considered in connection with innuendo, colloquium and explanatory circumstances, special damages must be alleged and proven. *Flake v. Greensboro News Co.*, 212 N.C. 780, 195 S.E. 55 (1938); *Tallent v. Blake*, 57 N.C. App. 249, 291 S.E.2d 336, 4 Ed. Law Rep. 306 (1982). Special damage, as that term is used in the law of defamation, means pecuniary loss. *Williams v. Rutherford Freight Lines, Inc.*, 10 N.C. App. 384, 179 S.E.2d 319 (1971); *Stutts v. Duke Power Co.*, 47 N.C. App. 76, 266 S.E.2d 861 (1980). Thus, emotional distress and mental suffering are not alone sufficient to establish a basis for relief in cases requiring proof of special damage. Additionally, some special damage must have occurred by the time the action is filed. *Tallent v. Blake*, 57 N.C. App. 249, 291 S.E.2d 336, 4 Ed. Law Rep. 306 (1982).

> [V.a] Plaintiff's claim alleging slander by school superintendent with respect to whether employee of board of education voluntarily resigned or was fired in dispute over preparation of payroll was dismissed for failure to state a claim because nothing in plaintiff's evidence indicated she was ever denied employment, sustained pecuniary loss, or incurred medical expenses before filing an action. *Tallent v. Blake*, 57 N.C. App. 249, 291 S.E.2d 336, 4 Ed. Law Rep. 306 (1982).

> [V.b] Where defamatory material is published in good faith, and within 10 days after the service of the notice of impending suit, a full and fair correction, apology and retraction is published in the same manner as was the original material, the plaintiff may recover only actual damages. If the defendant does not retract and correct after such notice, punitive damages may also be awarded. *Pentuff v. Park*, 194 N.C. 146, 138 S.E. 616, 53 A.L.R. 626 (1927).

Defendant is liable for damages resulting from a secondary publication or repetition which is the natural consequence of the original publication.

VI. Constitutional Constraints

In order to recover for defamation, public officials and public figures are required to prove, by clear and convincing evidence, (1) the allegedly defamatory statement is false; and (2) defendant published the statement with actual malice. *New York Times Co. v. Sullivan*, 376 U.S. 254, 84 S. Ct. 710, 11 L. Ed. 2d 686 (1964); *Curtis Publishing Co. v. Butts*,

388 U.S. 130 (1967). Actual malice requires proof that defendant knew the statement was false or acted with reckless disregard for whether it was false. Proving that the allegedly defamatory statement was published with reckless disregard requires the plaintiff to offer sufficient evidence to establish that the defendant entertained serious doubts as to the truth of the publication. *St. Amant v. Thompson*, 390 U.S. 727 (1968).

> [VI.a] Actual malice requires more than just a failure to investigate, but a deliberate decision not to acquire information that would confirm the falsity, amounting to a purposeful avoidance of the truth, would likely be sufficient. *Harte-hanks Communications, Inc. v. Connaughton*, 491 U.S. 657 (1989).

> [VI.b] Deliberate alteration of quotations, by itself, does not establish actual malice. *Masson v. New Yorker Magazine*, 501 U.S. 496 (1991).

The requirement that plaintiff prove falsity and actual malice is intended to curtail the chilling effect a defamation action may have on speech relating to matters of public concern. *New York Times Co. v. Sullivan*, 376 U.S. 254, 84 S. Ct. 710, 11 L. Ed. 2d 686 (1964).

> [VI.c] Even where advertisement is defamatory and contains factual inaccuracies, because "debate on public issues should be uninhibited, robust, and wide-open" a public official may not recover unless he proves actual malice. *New York Times Co. v. Sullivan*, 376 U.S. 254, 270, 84 S.Ct. 710, 11 L.Ed.2d 686, 701 (1964).

Where a plaintiff is a private person, the subject matter of the defamatory matter must be analyzed to determine whether it deals with a matter of public concern. *See Gertz v. Robert Welch, Inc.*, 418 U.S. 323 (1974); *Dun & Bradstreet v. Greenmoss Builders, Inc.*, 472 U.S. 749 (1985). Where the defamatory matter deals with a matter of public concern, and plaintiff seeks to recover damages for actual injury, the plaintiff must prove falsity and that defendant did not act as a reasonable prudent person in attempting to confirm the accuracy of the information. If, however, plaintiff seeks presumed or punitive damages, she must prove falsity and actual malice. Whether a matter is of public concern is decided on a case by case basis. For further discussion of private persons and matters of public concern, see section VI.3.

A. Public Officials, Public Figures & Matters of Public Concern

Because of the heightened requirements for pleading and proving a defamation cause of action in such cases, the threshold question in any defamation action is whether the matter involves a public official, a public figure or a matter of public concern.

(1) Public officials

Public officials are those persons who exercise substantial governmental power or authority and are positioned to affect policy. *Rosenblatt v. Baer*, 383 U.S. 75 (1966). There is some debate as to how far the meaning of the term public official may extend, and whether and to what extent it covers those employed in government-run services. It has been applied to include an Internal Revenue Service agent (*Angel v. Ward*, 43 N.C. App. 288 (1979)); a deputy sheriff of Forsyth County (*Cline v. Brown*, 24 N.C. App. 209 (1974)); a physician in a mental commitment proceeding (*Hall v. Piedmont Publ'g Co.*, 46 N.C. App. 760 (1980)); and a town manager (*Varner v. Bryan*, 113 N.C. App. 697 (1994)).

There are certain limitations on how far the *New York Times* standard extends. For example, a public official does not necessarily maintain that designation for life. *See, e.g. Redmond v. Sun Publishing Co.*, 239 Kan. 30, 716 P.2d 168 (1986); *Lewis v. Coursolle Broadcasting*, 127 Wis. 2d 105, 377 N.W.2d 166 (1985). Also, the defamatory material must relate to the plaintiff's "conduct, fitness or role" as a public official, in order for the New York Times rule to apply. *Griffin v. Holden*, 180 N.C. App. 129, 135, 636 S.E.2d 298, 303 (2006).

> [VI.A.1.a] Physician in a mental commitment proceeding required to prove actual malice to recover for defamatory statements relating to his official conduct. *Hall v. Piedmont Publ'g Co.*, 46 N.C. App. 760 (1980).

> [VI.A.1.b] A town manager required to prove actual malice where allegedly defamatory statements were made by defendant town council members in a review given to him after his termination. *Varner v. Bryan*, 113 N.C. App. 697 (1994).

If the plaintiff is categorized as a public official, and the statement relates to her conduct, fitness, or role, as a public official, then she must prove, by clear and convincing evidence, falsity and actual malice to successfully maintain an action for defamation. If she does, then presumed and punitive damages may be awarded, without fear of trampling on the First Amendment.

(2) Public figures

Public figures must also plead and prove falsity and actual malice in order to recover for defamation. The test for determining whether a plaintiff is a public figure is far from clear. In *Gertz v. Robert Welch, Inc.*, 418 U.S. 323 (1974), the Supreme Court, in attempting to provide some guidance on this issue made it clear that public figure status should attach only to those persons who have assumed some role of importance in the resolution of issues of general or public interest. According to the Court, the public-figure determination requires "looking to the nature and extent of an individual's participation in the particular controversy giving rise to the defamation." In *Gertz*, the Court divided public figures into two groups: (i) general purpose public figures and (ii) limited-purpose public figures.

(i) general purpose public figures

To establish that plaintiff is a general purpose public figure defendant must convince the court that plaintiff has achieved such pervasive fame or notoriety that she has become a public figure for all purposes and in all contexts. In finding plaintiff to be a public figure, the court will likely evaluate whether plaintiff voluntarily thrust herself to the forefront of a public controversy, in order to influence its' outcome, and whether she has voluntarily exposed herself to increased risk of injury from defamatory falsehoods. The court will also likely consider whether plaintiff enjoys significantly greater "access to the channels of effective communication" and has a more realistic opportunity to counteract false statements than a private person would. *Gertz v. Robert Welch, Inc.*, 418 U.S. 323 (1974). Counsel should be aware that the Court has determined that socially prominent people are not public figures merely because certain aspects of their lives are highly publicized. *Time, Inc. v. Firestone*, 424 U.S. 448 (1976).

> [VI.A.2.i.a] Candidate for public office qualifies as "public figure" for defamation purposes. *Boyce & Isley v. Cooper*, 153 N.C. App. 25 (2002), writ denied, review denied, appeal dismissed, 580 S.E.2d 361 (2003) and cert. denied, 540 U.S. 965, 124 S. Ct. 431, 157 L. Ed. 2d 310 (2003).

> [VI.A.2.i.b] Prominent attorney representing family of young man killed by police officer was not a public figure where he did not discuss the litigation with the press. Even though he had been active in community and professional affairs; had served as an officer of local civic groups and professional organi-

zations; published several books and articles on legal subjects; and was well known in some circles, he had achieved no general fame or notoriety in the community. *Gertz v. Robert Welch, Inc.*, 418 U.S. 323 (1974).

[VI.A.2.i.c] Wife in high-profile divorce case was not a public figure even where she was prominent in social circles and often in newspapers. *Time, Inc. v. Firestone*, 424 U.S. 448 (1976).

[VI.A.2.i.d] Researcher who was singled out and ridiculed by Senator was private figure because he did not invite public attention and comment merely because he was recipient of federal grants. *Hutchinson v. Proxmire*, 443 U.S. 111 (1979).

Those persons who are public figures for all purposes will have to satisfy the New York Times test in virtually all defamation cases in which they are a plaintiff. However, public figures, like public officials, may escape the limitations of the New York Times test if the subject matter of the defamatory material is completely unrelated to their public-figure status.

(ii) limited-purpose public figures

Defendant may establish plaintiff is a limited-purpose public figure by proving plaintiff voluntarily injected herself into a particular public controversy. In such cases, plaintiff becomes a public figure for a limited range of issues.

[VI.A.2.ii.a] Plaintiff doctor was limited public figure for purposes of important public controversy surrounding in vitro fertilization, where plaintiff's agent repeatedly acknowledged there was national controversy about infertility treatment, plaintiff thrust himself into vortex of controversy and admitted that he had spent every spare moment trying to stop debate, wrote to several politicians, hired personal lobbyist, procured services of public relations agent to enhance public image, and provided newspaper with his side of debate. *Gaunt v. Pittaway*, 139 N.C. App. 778, 534 S.E.2d 660 (2000).

[VI.A.2.ii.b] One of the first female fighter pilots was limited public figure for purposes of public controversy about women in combat. *Lohrenz v. Donnelly*, 350 F.3d 1272 (D.C. Cir. 2003).

[VI.A.2.ii.c] Air-traffic controller who was on duty at the time of a plane crash became a public figure in that context. *Dameron v. Washington Magazine*, 779 F.2d 736 (D.C. Cir. 1985).

[VI.A.2.ii.d] CEO of nation's largest cooperative market was declared limited public figure for issues relating to supermarket industry. *Waldbaus v. Fairchild Publications, Inc.*, 627 F.2d 1287 (D.C. Cir. 1986).

[VI.A.2.ii.e] Stepfather of murdered child was limited purpose public figure, for purposes of his defamation action alleging that he was falsely charged with the murders of his stepson and two other children because issues involved were matter of public concern; stepfather publicly advocated his lack of involvement in the murders well before defendants made the alleged defamatory statements; stepfather had full access to the media; and stepfather attempted to influence public opinion and the authorities. *Hobbs v. Pasdar*, 682 F. Supp. 2d 909 (E.D. Ark. 2009).

[VI.A.2.ii.f] Where there was no evidence showing high school athlete voluntarily injected himself into a controversy regarding "sportsmanship" court refused to hold amateur athletes are public figures when they participate voluntarily in public sporting events. *Wilson v. Daily Gazette Co.*, 588 S.E.2d 197, 207 (W. Va. 2003).

[VI.A.2.ii.g] Football player for the University of Alabama was public figure for purposes of comments relating to play on the field because player voluntarily played sport before thousands of persons—including spectators and sportswriters—so he necessarily assumed the risk that these persons would comment on the manner in which he performed. *Holt v. Cox Enterprises*, 590 F. Supp. 408, 412 (N.D. Ga. 1984).

It is also possible that plaintiff may be classified as an involuntarily public figure, where she has been involuntarily injected into a public controversy or issue, but involuntary public figures are rare.

[VI.A.2.ii.h] Airport controller on duty during plane crash was involuntary public figure. *Dameron v. Washington Magazine, Inc.*, 779 F.2d 736, 742–43 (D.C.Cir.1985).

[VI.A.2.ii.j] Wife of famous television host Johnny Carson held to be an involuntary public figure. *Carson v. Allied News Co.*, 529 F.2d 206, 210 (7th Cir.1976).

[VI.A.2.ii.k] Security guard accused of Olympic bombing held to be involuntary public figure. *Atlanta Journal-Constitution v. Jewell*, 251 Ga.App. 808, 555 S.E.2d 175, 186 (2002).

As with public officials, public figures may escape the limitations of the *New York Times* rule if the subject matter of the defamatory material is wholly unrelated to the public issue or controversy giving rise to their public-figure status.

(3) Matters of public concern

Where a plaintiff is a private person, the subject matter of the defamatory matter must be analyzed to determine whether it deals with a matter of public concern. *See Gertz v. Robert Welch, Inc.*, 418 U.S. 323 (1974); *Dun & Bradstreet v. Greenmoss Builders, Inc.*, 472 U.S. 749 (1985). Where the defamatory matter deals with a matter of public concern, and plaintiff seeks to recover damages for actual injury, the plaintiff must prove (1) falsity and (2) that defendant did not act as a reasonable prudent person in attempting to confirm the accuracy of the information. If, however, plaintiff seeks presumed or punitive damages, she must prove falsity and actual malice.

Whether a matter is "of public concern" is decided on a case by case basis. Generally speaking, matters of public concern are those "relating to any matter of political, social, or other concern to the community" and matters of private concern are those that address matters only of personal interest. *Connick v. Myers*, 461 U.S. 138, 143, 103 S. Ct. 1684, 1688, 75 L. Ed. 2d 708 (1983). The court will consider the "content, form and context" of the statement. *Dun & Bradstreet v. Greenmoss Builders, Inc.*, 472 U.S. 749 (1985). The statement does not have to be about a matter of national importance in order to be a matter of public concern. It may be sufficient to establish the speech concerns a relatively small segment of the general public. *Levinsky's, Inc. v. Wal-Mart Stores, Inc.*, 127 F.3d 122 (1st Cir. 1997).

[VI.A.3.a] Defamatory statements addressed a matter of public concern where the matter: (1) was discussed throughout the community, nationally on CNN and Fox News and internationally; (2) was the subject of public study, discussed at the Council of Government, and State Universities; and (3) that local Visitors

Bureau received calls from other states asking about the matter. *Neill Grading & Const. Co., Inc. v. Lingafelt*, 168 N.C. App. 36, 45, 606 S.E.2d 734, 740 (2005).

[VI.A.3.b] Suit by private plaintiffs against nonmedia defendants arising out of a false credit report respecting plaintiff's business did not involve matters of public interest or concern. *Dun & Bradstreet v. Greenmoss Builders, Inc.*, 472 U.S. 749 (1985).

[VI.A.3.c] Broadcast statements that long-distance truckers pose risks to other drivers on the nation's highways unquestionably involved a matter of public concern. *Veilleux v. Nat'l Broad. Co.*, 206 F.3d 92, 108 (1st Cir. 2000).

Exercise 5-2 Summarizing and Organizing Materials

Based on your reading from the practice guide, answer the following questions:

1. What must a plaintiff plead and prove in order to establish a claim for defamation? Be sure to consider:

   a. Are there different requirements for pleading libel v. slander?

   b. Are there differences between actions based on statements that are defamatory "per se" v. "per quod"?

   c. When does the *New York Times* standard apply?

   d. How does application of the *New York Times* standard change plaintiff's pleading requirements?

   e. When must the plaintiff allege special damages?

2. What affirmative defenses are available to defendants in a defamation action?

3. What must defendants plead and prove to establish each of the affirmative defenses?

Exercise 5-3 Using Information from a Practice Guide to Identify Issues and Direct Research

1. What are the disputed issues in *Strickland v. Wong* (your case)?

2. Which cases cited in the practice guide are most likely to provide you with additional information about these disputed issues?

3. What do you hope to find in each of these cases? In other words, what could the cases contain that would be helpful to your clients?

4. What do you hope you will not find in each of these cases? In other words, what could the cases contain that would be harmful to your clients?

Exercise 5-4 Using Cases to Enhance Existing Knowledge

After completing exercise 5-3, question 2, compare your selections with the cases reprinted in the next section. These selected cases are the cases from the practice guide that, based on the information contained in the practice guide, are likely to have direct application to Defendants Wong and CCCSP's case.

These cases are not as heavily edited as the materials in prior chapters. They may address one or more of the issues in your case, and they may contain irrelevant information. They are reprinted in the order in which you might have selected them from the practice guide, and are not necessarily organized by issue or significance. Your assignment is to determine what is useful, and integrate what you learn from the cases and statutes into the outline or issues list you developed using exercises 5-1 and 5-3.

As you read these cases, they will likely generate a number of additional issues you will need to consider and address, therefore, keep track of:

1. Issues you will likely need to discuss with your clients, including areas of weakness you expect plaintiff's counsel to probe;

2. Thoughts you have about the strengths and weaknesses of your clients' case;

3. Evidence you will need to obtain during discovery, which may include documents and testimony (from depositions and interviews).

Dobson v. Harris

134 N.C. App. 573, 521 S.E.2d 710 (1999)

On 3 May 1997, plaintiff visited a J.C. Penney store in Oak Hollow Mall in High Point, North Carolina, to retrieve an item she had purchased previously under the store's layaway plan. She brought her fifteen-month-old daughter with her. Defendant Holly Harris (Harris), an employee of defendant J.C. Penney Company, Inc. (Penney's), attempted to assist plaintiff. When plaintiff indicated that she did not have her store receipt for the item on layaway, Harris asked plaintiff her name. Harris apparently misheard plaintiff's response, for she brought plaintiff an item that was being held for a different customer. However, neither plaintiff nor Harris realized the misunderstanding until plaintiff had already written a check. Plaintiff then noticed the error and began to berate Harris, who apologized and obtained the correct item. Because the correct item was more expensive than the one Harris earlier produced, plaintiff was obligated to write another check for the difference in price. Plaintiff demanded an apology from Harris for causing plaintiff to have to write two checks. Although Harris apologized, plaintiff stormed out, indicating that she would call Harris's supervisor to complain.

While Harris was sorting out the mistake with the merchandise, plaintiff's daughter became restive. Plaintiff, apparently exasperated, yelled at the child, picked her off the counter where she had been sitting, and set her back down hard. Accounts of the incident differ as to the violence of plaintiff's act and whether the child's head was near a sharp edge. Allegedly concerned by plaintiff's display and actions toward her child, Harris reported her account of events to a representative of the Guilford County Department of Social Services (DSS). Upon request, Harris provided the representative with plaintiff's name, address, and other identifying information, which she obtained from plaintiff's check. An investigator for DSS advised plaintiff that a complaint had been filed against her. The investigation ultimately was terminated when DSS was unable to substantiate Harris's complaint.

Plaintiff brought suit claiming slander *per se*.... In her complaint, plaintiff alleged (1) that Harris falsely reported that plaintiff abused and neglected her child while in Penney's and (2) that Penney's was liable to plaintiff for the actions of its employee pursuant to the doctrine of *respondeat superior.* Defendants filed a joint answer in which they contended that Harris's observation of plaintiff's treatment of her child justified Harris's report to DSS. Defendants' answer also raised several defenses, including the qualified privilege established by N.C. Gen.Stat. § 7A-550 (1995, repealed 1 July 1999). Plaintiff then filed an affidavit denying assertions of fact made in defendants' answer. When defendants failed to answer plaintiff's interrogatories completely, plaintiff moved to compel their response. Defendants moved for summary judgment, and on 2 July 1998, the Honorable W. Erwin Spainhour granted defendants' motion for summary judgment without hearing plaintiff's motion to compel. Plaintiff appeals.

* * *

A moving party is entitled to summary judgment if it can establish that no claim for relief exists or that the claimant cannot overcome an affirmative defense or legal bar to the claim. *See Boone v. Vinson,* 127 N.C.App. 604, 606–07, 492 S.E.2d 356, 357 (1997) (citation omitted), *disc. review denied,* 347 N.C. 573, 498 S.E.2d 377 (1998). Accordingly, plaintiff must forecast evidence of the elements of slander *per se* ... to survive summary judgment in her case against Harris. In her case against Penney's, plaintiff must first show liability on the part of Harris, then establish that Penney's is responsible for the acts of Harris. We review plaintiff's claims seriatim.

Slander *per se*

Slander *per se* is a form of defamation in which the defendant makes a false oral communication to a third person that (1) harms the plaintiff's trade, business, or profession; (2) conveys that the plaintiff has a loathsome disease; or (3) states that the plaintiff has committed a crime involving moral turpitude. *See Phillips v. Winston-Salem/Forsyth County Bd. of Educ.,* 117 N.C.App. 274, 450 S.E.2d 753 (1994), *disc. review denied,* 340 N.C. 115, 456 S.E.2d 318 (1995). Here, Harris's allegation of child abuse qualifies as slander *per se,* if at all, under the last category. "'Moral turpitude involves an act of inherent baseness in the private, social, or public duties which one owes to his fellowmen or to society, or to his country, her institutions and her government.'" *Averitt v. Rozier,* 119 N.C.App. 216, 218, 458 S.E.2d 26, 29 (1995) (quoting *State v. Mann,* 317 N.C. 164, 170, 345 S.E.2d 365, 369 (1986)). Whether child abuse is a crime of moral turpitude is an issue of first impression in North Carolina. Review of cases outside North Carolina reveals that few states have considered the issue, and decisions in those states are split. *Compare People v. Williams,* 169 Cal.App.3d 951, 215 Cal.Rptr. 612 (1985) (holding convictions of moral turpitude include those involving child abuse),1 *In Re Wortzel,* 698 a.2d 429 (d.C.1997) (holding felony child abuse is a crime of moral turpitude), and *State v. Austin,* 84 S.D. 405, 172 N.W.2d 284 (1969) (holding misdemeanor child abuse is a crime of moral turpitude), *with Bazzanella v. Tucson City Court,* 195 Ariz. 372, 988 P.2d 157, 1999 WL 398929 (Ct.App.1999) (holding misdemeanor child abuse is not a crime of moral turpitude).

Further complicating our decision is the fact that plaintiff's complaint contains ambiguities in its allegations that (1) Harris reported both that the child was abused and neglected and (2) that "there was a severe injury to [the child's] head." Accusations of abuse and neglect allegedly made by Harris may be covered by N.C. Gen.Stat. §7A-517(1), and (21) (Cum.Supp.1998, repealed 1 July 1999) (defining "Abused juveniles" and "Neglected juvenile" under the former North Carolina Juvenile Code), or N.C. Gen.Stat. §14-318.4 (1993) (making child abuse a felony). Further, the allegation that "there was a severe injury to [the child's] head" may mean either that a pre-existing injury was observed or that an injury was inflicted in the presence of Harris. However, because this matter is before us to review the grant of a motion for summary judgment, all conflicts are resolved against the moving party. *See Aune v. University of North Carolina,* 120 N.C.App. 430, 462 S.E.2d 678 (1995), *disc. review denied,* 342 N.C. 893, 467 S.E.2d 901 (1996). We therefore view allegations in the light most favorable to plaintiff and hold that statements allegedly made by Harris communicated that plaintiff had committed an act or acts that constituted a violation of N.C. Gen.Stat. §14-318.4 (1993). We further hold that violation of section 14-318.4 is a crime of moral turpitude and conclude that plaintiff alleged slander *per se* and forecast evidence sufficient to withstand Harris's motion for summary judgment.

Harris nevertheless contends that she is protected by the qualified privilege codified in N.C. Gen.Stat. §7A-550 (1995, repealed 1 July 1999). That statute provides both civil and criminal immunity to defendants who in good faith report suspected child abuse; it also establishes a rebuttable presumption that reports are made in good faith. *Id.* A plaintiff may overcome this presumption by showing that a defendant acted with actual malice. *See Davis v. Durham City Schools,* 91 N.C.App. 520, 523, 372 S.E.2d 318, 320 (1988) (citation omitted).

Actual malice may be proven by evidence of ill-will or personal hostility on the part of the declarant[.] [It may also be proved] by a showing that the declarant published the defamatory statement with knowledge that it was false, with reckless disregard for the truth or with a high degree of awareness of its probable falsity. *Kwan-Sa You v. Roe,* 97 N.C.App. 1, 12, 387 S.E.2d 188, 193 (1990) (citations omitted). If plaintiff cannot meet his burden of showing actual malice, the qualified privilege operates as an absolute privilege and bars any recovery for the communication, even if the communication is false. *Clark v. Brown,* 99 N.C.App. 255, 263, 393 S.E.2d 134, 138 (second citation omitted), *disc. review denied,* 327 N.C. 426, 395 S.E.2d 675 (1990). "The question whether the evidence in the record in a defamation case is sufficient to support a finding of actual malice is a question of law." *Harte-Hanks Communications, Inc. v. Connaughton,* 491 U.S. 657, 685, 109 S.Ct. 2678, 2694, 105 L.Ed.2d 562, 587 (1989) (citation omitted).

Because this is an appeal from summary judgment, the record reflects no resolution of facts in controversy. Accordingly, in reviewing the decision of the trial court, this Court must determine from the record on appeal whether "the pleadings, depositions, answers to interrogatories, and admissions on file together with the affidavits, if any," N.C. Gen.Stat. §1A-1, Rule 56(c) (1990), when viewed in the light most favorable to plaintiff, indicate reckless disregard for the truth, knowledge of falsity, or a high degree of awareness of its probable falsity. *See Clark,* 99 N.C.App. at 263, 393 S.E.2d at 138. Plaintiff is permitted to prove actual malice by circumstantial evidence, *see Harte-Hanks,* 491 U.S. at 657, 109 S.Ct. at 2680, 105 L.Ed.2d at 562, and her affidavit adamantly denies Harris's allegations of abusive behavior. When viewed in a light most favorable to plaintiff, this affidavit forecasts some evidence indicating that Harris reported plaintiff with knowledge that the report was false. Plaintiff's and defendants' conflicting accounts establish that there is a genuine issue of material fact to be determined by a jury. We therefore reverse the trial court with regard to its grant of summary judgment on plaintiff's slander *per se* cause of action against Harris.

Harris is only liable to plaintiff if Harris reported child abuse with actual malice. However, Harris's statements, if made with actual malice, were outside the scope of her employment, eliminating liability on the part of Penney's. *See Troxler v. Charter Mandala Center*, 89 N.C.App. 268, 271–72, 365 S.E.2d 665, 668–69, *disc. review denied*, 322 N.C. 838, 371 S.E.2d 284 (1988). Consequently, summary judgment was properly granted in favor of defendant Penney's on the issue of slander *per se*.

We reverse the trial court's grant of summary judgment and remand this case on plaintiff's claim against defendant Harris for slander *per se*.

Kroh v. Kroh
152 N.C. App. 347, 567 S.E.2d 760 (2002)

This appeal by defendant wife arises from a civil judgment against her stemming from her illegal wiretapping of her plaintiff husband's in-home conversations and actions. She presents the following issues on appeal: ... [(I)] Did the trial court properly exclude veterinary reports that the wife contends support her allegations of bestiality against the husband? [(II)] Did the trial court err in finding the wife liable for slander *per se* for her statements to various individuals concerning her suspicions that her husband was having sex with the family dog and molesting her children? ... [W]e affirm the exclusion of the veterinary reports for failure of the wife to authenticate the exhibits, and affirm in part, and vacate and remand in part, the trial court's bench judgment on the husband's slander *per se* claims.

Thomas and Teresa Kroh married in 1992 and separated in early December 1998. During the marriage and at the time of the alleged acts giving rise to this action in November and December 1998, the couple lived together along with Teresa Kroh's thirteen and ten year old sons from a prior marriage. At all relevant times, Thomas Kroh worked as a police officer with the Greensboro Police Department.

On numerous occasions throughout the marriage, Teresa Kroh accused Thomas Kroh of having affairs with other women; these accusations became more frequent during the spring and early fall of 1998. In early November 1998, unbeknownst to her husband, Teresa Kroh placed tape recorders in the family home, and later placed a video camera in the home. As a result, she obtained audio and video recordings from these devices without her husband's knowledge. In a conversation before Thanksgiving in November 1998, Teresa Kroh accused her husband of having sexual relations with the family dog, and claimed to have captured the event on tape. Her husband subsequently informed her that he wished to end the marriage.

Around the first of December 1998, Teresa Kroh reported to the State Bureau of Investigation that her husband had engaged in sexual conduct with the family dog, and had molested her two minor sons. The next day, she telephoned her husband's sister, Nancy Dowell, and told Ms. Dowell that Thomas Kroh had molested their two minor sons and had been having sex with the family dog. Around the same time, Teresa Kroh telephoned her husband's long-time friend, Richard Herrin, and stated to him that her husband had engaged in sex with the family dog. When Herrin and her husband's co-worker, Steve Hollers, went to retrieve some of her husband's belongings from the family home, Teresa Kroh stated to Herrin, in the presence of Hollers, not to allow her husband near Herrin's dogs.

In March 1999, Thomas Kroh brought this action against Teresa Kroh alleging causes of action against her for (1) abuse of process, (2) defamation, (3) violation of North Carolina's Electronic Surveillance Act, Art. 16 of Chapter 15A of the General Statutes (N.C. Gen.Stat. §§ 15A-286 *et seq.* (2001)), and (4) intentional infliction of emotional distress. He later amended his complaint to add a cause of action for negligent infliction of emotional distress. Teresa Kroh answered, asserting various affirmative defenses, including the truth of her allegations.

On 7 January 2000, Superior Court Judge Howard R. Greeson, Jr., granted summary judgment in favor of Thomas Kroh on his claims under the Electronic Surveillance Act and awarded $1,000.00 in compensatory damages under G.S. § 15A-296. Following a bench trial on the remaining claims, Judge Greeson found Teresa Kroh liable for slander *per se,* and awarded Thomas Kroh $20,000 in compensatory damages, $60,000 in punitive damages for slander *per se,* and $5,000 in punitive damages for violation of the Electronic Surveillance Act. This appeal followed.

*** [W]e address the issue of whether the trial court erred in finding Teresa Kroh liable for slander *per se* for her statements to various individuals concerning her suspicions that her husband was having sex with the family dog and molesting her children. We answer: No, because the trial court's findings are supported by competent evidence and those findings in turn support the conclusions of law.

> Appellate review of findings of fact "made by a trial judge, without a jury, is limited to ... whether there is competent evidence to support the findings of fact." A trial court's conclusions of law, however, are reviewable *de novo* on appeal.

Lee Cycle Ctr., Inc. v. Wilson Cycle Ctr., Inc., 143 N.C.App. 1, 9, 545 S.E.2d 745, 750 (internal citations omitted), *affirmed,* 354 N.C. 565, 556 S.E.2d 293 (2001).

The record on appeal in this case shows that Teresa Kroh's assignments of error on this issue state merely that the "trial court erred in its findings of fact and conclusions of law" and cite the trial court's entire judgment entered 28 December 2000, without directing this court's attention to any specific findings or conclusions made by the trial court. "Where no exception is taken to a finding of fact by the trial court, the finding is presumed to be supported by competent evidence and is binding on appeal." *Koufman v. Koufman,* 330 N.C. 93, 97, 408 S.E.2d 729, 731 (1991). Therefore, we need only determine whether the trial court's findings of fact support its conclusions of law supporting liability for slander *per se. See Harris v. Walden,* 314 N.C. 284, 333 S.E.2d 254 (1985).

"False accusations of crime or offenses involving moral turpitude are actionable as slander *per se.*" *Dobson v. Harris,* 352 N.C. 77, 79, 530 S.E.2d 829, 832 (2000). However, N.C. Gen.Stat. § 7B-301 (2001) imposes an affirmative duty upon anyone "who has cause to suspect" child abuse or neglect to report such conduct to the county Department of Social Services. Furthermore, N.C. Gen.Stat. § 7B-309 (2001) provides immunity from civil liability to those who report such conduct in accordance with G.S. § 7B-301, "provided that the person was acting in good faith." The reporter's "good faith" is to be presumed "[i]n any proceeding involving liability [.]" *Id.* In other words, these statutes:

> relieve[] the defendant of the burden of going forward with evidence of her good faith and impose[] upon the plaintiff the burden to go forward with evidence of the defendant's bad faith or malice.

Dobson, 352 N.C. at 83, 530 S.E.2d at 835.

In this case, not only did Teresa Kroh allege that Thomas Kroh had molested her minor children, she also asserted that he had sex with the family dog. Assuredly, any such statements regarding the family dog would not be privileged under the plain language of G.S. §7B-301 which concerns the abuse or neglect of children. Therefore, Teresa Kroh's statements to Nancy Dowell, Richard Herrin, and additional statements in the presence of Steve Hollers concerning acts between Thomas Kroh and the family dog which the trial court found to constitute slander *per se, see Dobson,* were not protected by any qualified privilege under G.S. §7B-309. Furthermore, statements to anyone other than persons with the county Department of Social Services concerning allegations that Thomas Kroh molested her minor sons would not be protected under G.S. §7B-309's provision of qualified immunity since that statute concerns reports to the county Department of Social Services.

Thus, the remaining question is whether the trial court properly found that Teresa Kroh's statements to the Department of Social Services were made with actual malice, thereby negating any defense of privilege under G.S. §7B-309. *See* N.C. Gen.Stat. §1D-5 (2001) (defining malice as "a sense of personal ill will toward the claimant that activated or incited the defendant to perform the act or undertake the conduct that resulted in harm to the claimant"); *see also Dobson,* 352 N.C. at 86, 530 S.E.2d at 837 (to overcome G.S. §7B-309's good-faith presumption, plaintiff must show defendant acted with actual malice). We conclude that the record on appeal supports the trial court's determination that Teresa Kroh acted with actual malice, thus negating any qualified immunity she otherwise would have enjoyed under G.S. §7B-309 for her statements to the Department of Social Services.

The trial court found as fact in its 28 December 2000 judgment that the audiotapes offered by Teresa Kroh "contained no evidence from which a reasonable person could conclude that sexual misconduct had occurred." Both of Teresa Kroh's minor sons testified that Thomas Kroh had not molested them in any way; both sons also testified that they had informed Teresa Kroh, when she inquired, that Thomas Kroh had not molested them in any way. The trial court found as fact that Thomas Kroh had not molested either of Teresa Kroh's minor sons, and that Teresa Kroh knew those statements were false when she made them. The trial court found that Teresa Kroh made these statements "maliciously and with the intent to injure [p]laintiff." Furthermore, the trial court conspicuously failed to find that Teresa Kroh's testimony was credible, and found instead that Teresa Kroh's conduct had been "cruel, wicked and with evil intent." As Teresa Kroh did not except to these findings of fact, they are deemed binding on appeal. *See Koufman.*

The trial court thus concluded that Teresa Kroh's statements "were made with the knowledge that they were false ... [or] with [] reckless disregard for the[ir] truth or a high degree of awareness of the probability of [their] falsity." Additionally, the trial court concluded that Thomas Kroh had proven by clear and convincing evidence that Teresa Kroh's statements were made with malice as defined in G.S. §1D-5.

Upon a careful review of the record and the evidence before the trial court, we conclude that the trial court's factual findings support its conclusion that Teresa Kroh's statements to the Department of Social Services were made with the knowledge that they were false or with reckless disregard as to their truth or falsity. The trial court's findings that Teresa Kroh's statements were made "maliciously and with the intent to injure" Thomas Kroh, and that Teresa Kroh's conduct in the matter had been "cruel, wicked and [done] with evil intent," support the trial court's conclusion that Teresa Kroh's statements were made with actual "malice" as defined in G.S. §1D-5, thus depriving her of any alleged qualified immunity under G.S. §7B-309. Accordingly, we affirm the trial court's conclusion that Teresa Kroh was liable to Thomas Kroh for slander *per se* in connection with her statements made to the Department of Social Services, the State Bureau of Investigation, Nancy Dowell, Richard Herrin and Steve Hollers.

*** [W]e affirm the trial court's exclusion of the veterinary reports proffered by Teresa Kroh at trial, and affirm the trial court's findings of fact and conclusions of law in its 28 December 2000 judgment, including its conclusion that Teresa Kroh acted with actual malice and therefore was not entitled to the "good faith" presumption under G.S. § 7B-309. In addition, we affirm the trial court's award of compensatory and punitive damages to Thomas Kroh on his slander *per se* claims.

Tallent v. Blake

57 N.C. App. 249, 291 S.E.2d 336 (1982)

Plaintiff instituted this action to recover actual and punitive damages resulting from "slanderous and defamatory statements" made by defendant. Defendant's answer asserted truth as a defense.

Plaintiff's evidence tended to show that she worked for the School Food Service of the Cleveland County Board of Education. She did secretarial work and bookkeeping. She prepared checks for the School Food Service employees by using the computer in the central office of the Board of Education; however, she did so under the direction of Peggy Fuller. Peggy Fuller was the computer operator for the Board of Education, and she prepared the payroll checks for all employees other than those in the School Food Service. Plaintiff was not trained to operate the computer, she could not operate it on her own, and she was afraid of it. Peggy Fuller resigned her position effective 30 April 1980. On 1 May 1980, plaintiff was asked to use the computer to prepare the payroll for all ten-month employees of the Board. She responded that she did not know how to do this. Later that day, plaintiff was summoned to the office of defendant, Jerry Lee Blake, who was the superintendent of the county school system. Plaintiff told defendant that she did not know how to do the payroll. Defendant told plaintiff that she would do the job requested as best she could or else. Plaintiff testified that she asked defendant whether "or else" meant that she would be fired, that defendant said that it did, and that she left defendant's office with the understanding that she had been fired. Defendant, who was called to testify for plaintiff, testified that he told plaintiff that "or else" meant that she would be choosing not to work for the Board, that plaintiff then said that she quit, and that he regarded plaintiff as having resigned from her job. Michael Goforth, a reporter for the *Shelby Daily Star*, telephoned defendant on 2 May 1980 to ask some questions. Defendant told the reporter that two people had resigned and that "[a]ny claim Mrs. Tallent was fired is false." This statement was quoted in a newspaper article.

Defendant moved for a directed verdict at the close of plaintiff's evidence. Among other grounds, he argued that his statement to the reporter was in no way slanderous or defamatory and that plaintiff had failed either to allege or prove special damages. The trial judge allowed a directed verdict as to plaintiff's claim for punitive damages, but he otherwise denied the motion. Defendant presented no evidence and renewed his motion which again was denied.

The judge submitted two issues as to liability, which were stated and answered as follows:

1. Did the defendant, Jerry Lee Blake, slander the plaintiff, Rhonda Walker Tallent?

[Yes.]

2. Were the statements concerning the plaintiff, Rhonda Walker Tallent, true?

[No.]

The jury set actual damages at $1,500.00. Defendant moved for judgment notwithstanding the verdict based upon the same arguments previously presented. The judge denied the motion and entered judgment on the verdict.

On appeal, defendant presents and argues six assignments of error, but the six assignments are based upon only three exceptions. These exceptions are to the denial of a directed verdict at the close of plaintiff's evidence, the denial of a directed verdict at the close of all evidence, and the denial of judgment notwithstanding the verdict. The standards applicable to a motion for a directed verdict and to a motion for judgment notwithstanding the verdict are the same. *Dickinson v. Pake*, 284 N.C. 576, 201 S.E.2d 897 (1974); *Nytco Leasing, Inc. v. Southeastern Motels, Inc.*, 40 N.C.App. 120, 252 S.E.2d 826 (1979). All the evidence which supports plaintiff's claim must be taken as true and must be considered in the light most favorable to plaintiff, giving her the benefit of every reasonable inference which legitimately may be drawn therefrom, with contradictions, conflicts and inconsistencies being resolved in plaintiff's favor. The issue is whether the evidence, when considered in that manner, is sufficient for submission to the jury. *Id.* Defendant's six assignments of error therefore present but a single issue. However, we must examine the record carefully in order to refine that issue.

Plaintiff asserts in her brief, "[T]his is not a case of slander. It is, rather, a case of libel *per se.*" We cannot agree. The term defamation includes two distinct torts, libel and slander. In general, libel is written while slander is oral. Prosser, Law of Torts (4th ed. 1971), § 111, p. 737. Libel, being criminal in origin, always was regarded as the greater wrong, and greater responsibility was attached to it. "It was accordingly held that some kinds of defamatory words might be actionable without proof of any actual damage to the plaintiff if they were written, where such damage must be proved if they were spoken. [Footnote omitted.] This remains the chief importance of the distinction." *Id.* § 112, p. 752. *Accord, Kindley v. Privette*, 241 N.C. 140, 84 S.E.2d 660 (1954). The distinction between libel and slander is sometimes a difficult one to make. For example, an interview given to a newspaper reporter may support an action for libel as well as slander. The speaking of defamatory words to a newspaper reporter will support an action for slander. However, the speaking of such words to a reporter also will support an action for libel if the speaker intends that his words be embodied forthwith in a physical form and the words are subsequently so embodied. *Bell v. Simmons*, 247 N.C. 488, 101 S.E.2d 383 (1958).

The present case concerns a statement made by defendant to a reporter that was then quoted in a newspaper article. Under the above principles, plaintiff might have been able to pursue both theories, libel and slander, against defendant. However, plaintiff's case was tried solely on the theory of slander; no issue as to libel was submitted. In fact, plaintiff did not present the newspaper article in evidence. The jury instructions have not been included in the record, and we must assume that the judge correctly instructed the jury in accordance with the issue submitted, the issue of slander. The argument on defendant's motion for a directed verdict has been included in the record. The argument was in terms of slander. The theory upon which the case was tried must prevail in considering the appeal, interpreting the record, and determining the validity of exceptions. *Paul v. Neece*, 244 N.C. 565, 94 S.E.2d 596 (1956). A party may not acquiesce in the trial of his case upon one theory below and then argue on appeal that it should have been tried upon another. *Bryan Builders Supply v. Midyette*, 274 N.C. 264, 162 S.E.2d 507 (1968). To put it more colorfully, "the law does not permit parties to swap horses between courts in order to get a better mount in the Supreme Court." *Weil v. Herring*, 207 N.C. 6, 10, 175 S.E. 836, 838 (1934). This is true with respect to a motion for directed verdict.

In passing upon a trial judge's ruling as to a directed verdict, we cannot review the case as the parties might have tried it; rather, we must review the case as tried below, as reflected in the record on appeal. *See Feibus & Company, Inc. v. Godley Construction Co.*, 301 N.C. 294, 271 S.E.2d 385 (1980). This case was tried on the theory of slander, and plaintiff has not appealed or assigned as error the trial judge's failure to submit an issue as to libel. Therefore, plaintiff may not argue the law of libel on appeal.

In the present case, then, the issue for our decision is whether the evidence, when considered in the light most favorable to plaintiff, was sufficient for submission to the jury on the theory of slander. In arguing below that the evidence was insufficient, defendant stated, among other grounds, that his statement was not defamatory and that plaintiff had failed to prove special damages. We rest our decision on the second of these grounds.

Slander may be actionable *per se* or only actionable *per quod*. Special damages must be pleaded and proved in the latter case, but not the former. *Badame v. Lampke*, 242 N.C. 755, 89 S.E.2d 466 (1955); *Williams v. Rutherford Freight Lines, Inc.* and *Willard v. Rutherford Freight Lines, Inc.*, 10 N.C.App. 384, 179 S.E.2d 319 (1971). There are four categories of slander actionable *per se*.

> Decisions in this State generally limit false statements which may be classified as actionable *per se* to those which charge plaintiff with a crime or offense involving moral turpitude, impeach his trade or profession, or impute to him a loathsome disease. (A fourth category has been added by statute; that is, statements charging incontinency to a woman. G.S. 99-4).

Williams v. Rutherford Freight Lines, Inc. and *Willard v. Rutherford Freight Lines, Inc., supra* at 388, 179 S.E.2d at 322. The alleged slander in the present case can be actionable *per se* only if it comes under the second category listed above, *i.e.*, statements which impeach one's trade or profession. In order to come within this category of slander, a false statement must do more than merely injure a person in his business. The false statement "(1) must touch the plaintiff in his special trade or occupation, and (2) must contain an imputation necessarily hurtful in its effect on his business." *Badame v. Lampke, supra*, 242 N.C. at 757, 89 S.E.2d at 468. The present statement, at its worst, indicates that plaintiff lied in relating the circumstances under which she left her job with the Board of Education. Such a statement does not impeach the plaintiff's occupation.

> North Carolina cases have held consistently that alleged false statements made by defendants, calling plaintiff "dishonest" or charging that plaintiff was untruthful and an unreliable employee, are not actionable per se. *See Satterfield v. McLellan Stores*, 215 N.C. 582, 2 S.E.2d 709 (1939); *Ringgold v. Land*, 212 N.C. 369, 193 S.E. 267 (1937). Such false statements may be actionable *per quod*; if so, some special damages must be pleaded and proved. *Ringgold, supra*.

Stutts v. Duke Power Co., 47 N.C.App. 76, 82, 266 S.E.2d 861, 865 (1980). We conclude that the evidence in the present case did not show a slander actionable *per se* and, thus, that plaintiff's evidence, in order to withstand defendant's motions for directed verdict and judgment notwithstanding the verdict, had to show special damages.

In the law of defamation, special damage means pecuniary loss. Emotional distress and humiliation alone are not enough to support a claim actionable *per quod*. *Williams v. Rutherford Freight Lines, Inc.* and *Willard v. Rutherford Freight Lines, Inc., supra*. Furthermore, "where, as here, it is essential that some special damage must occur before a claim is actionable, *at least some special damage must have occurred by the time the action is instituted*." *Id.* 10 N.C.App. at 390–91, 179 S.E.2d at 324 (emphasis added). *Accord, Scott v. Harrison*, 215 N.C. 427, 2 S.E.2d 1 (1939); *Crawford v. Barnes*, 118 N.C. 912, 24

S.E. 670 (1896). The *Scott* case was an action for slander in which the plaintiff alleged that as a result of the slander, her husband, a high school principal, had been required to accept as a condition of re-election to his position that he would not seek re-election in the future. The Supreme Court stated as follows:

> It is suggested that the condition imposed upon plaintiff's husband at the time of his re-election might eventually lead to his unemployment and result in damage to her. This, we think, is too remote and speculative for present consideration. Newell, Slander and Libel, 4th Ed., section 746, quotes *DeGrey, C. J.*, in *Onslow v. Horne*, 3 Wils., 177, 2 W. Bl., 750: "I know of no case where ever an action for words was grounded upon eventual damages which may possibly happen to a man in a future situation;" and refers to the established rule that the damages must have accrued before the institution of the suit.

Scott v. Harrison, supra, 215 N.C. at 431, 2 S.E.2d at 3. The *Crawford* case was an action for slander in which the Supreme Court upheld dismissal because "[t]he special damage alleged, to-wit, the loss of the election of the plaintiff to Congress, did not accrue, according to the complaint, till 6 November, and the summons was issued 17 September. The damage not having accrued before the summons issued, the action cannot be maintained." *Crawford v. Barnes, supra*, 118 N.C. at 915–16, 24 S.E. at 671.

The alleged slander in the present case occurred on 2 May 1980. Plaintiff instituted her action on 13 May 1980. The evidence reveals no special damages resulting from the alleged slander at that time. The loss of plaintiff's job with the Board of Education, of course, resulted from the events of 1 May 1980, not from the alleged slander of 2 May 1980. Plaintiff testified that she sought other employment, but she was not sure of the dates involved. She was not sure whether she had sought other employment at the time she filed this action. Plaintiff testified that she did not receive employment in May 1980, that she received employment in June 1980 which she held for only two weeks and lost by "mutual agreement" and that she received employment in August 1980 that she was still holding at the time of trial. There is nothing in her testimony to indicate that she ever was denied employment because of the alleged slander by defendant. Plaintiff also testified that she fell behind in monthly payments on various accounts in June and July of 1980, and that in October 1980 she filed "a Chapter Thirteen, which is part of the Bankruptcy Code, in which I made monthly payments to the Court to pay off my debts." This testimony shows no pecuniary loss, and it involves events occurring after institution of this action on 13 May 1980. Finally, plaintiff testified that she suffered worry, loss of sleep, and emotional problems that led her to go to a doctor for medication in June and July of 1980. Special damages include illness sufficient to require medical care and expense. *See Bell v. Simmons, supra.* However, plaintiff's testimony shows no such damages before 13 May 1980 and fails to show the amount of any medical expenses incurred thereafter.

Therefore, plaintiff failed to show special damages sufficient to support a claim for slander actionable *per quod*, and defendant's motions for directed verdict and judgment notwithstanding the verdict should have been allowed.

Reversed.

Towne v. Cope

32 N.C. App. 660, 233 S.E.2d 624 (1977)

This is a civil action wherein the plaintiff, Donald M. Towne, seeks to recover from the defendant, Kenneth Cope, $75,000 compensatory and $150,000 punitive damages for defamation. In his complaint plaintiff alleged that on 20 August 1974 defendant, an agent of the State Bureau of Investigation, with malice made the following defamatory statements of and concerning plaintiff to Blain Stalcup, Sheriff of Cherokee County:

> "That guy is nutty as a fruitcake, he is a right wing radical, an extremist, and he has tried to bribe a witness in New Hampshire; that when the children were taken from the plaintiff they had welts and bruises on their bodies where they had been beaten, and that they were dirty and half-starved, and had lice in their hair and insect bites all over them; that plaintiff had run out on $27,000.00 in debts in New Hampshire; that plaintiff was apt to be violent, to use a gun and that a letter existed saying that plaintiff would kill the said minor children and himself if plaintiff's former wife ever attempted to locate the plaintiff."

Defendant filed a 12(b)(6) motion to dismiss for failure to state a claim upon which relief can be granted. In his motion defendant set up the affirmative defense of qualified privilege. The court considered matters outside the pleadings and treated the motion as one for summary judgment. The uncontroverted evidence offered in support of and in opposition to the motion establishes the following facts:

On 18 August 1974 Bruce Cheney, Chief of Police in Gilford, New Hampshire, contacted the North Carolina State Bureau of Investigation concerning the possibility that the plaintiff, who was under indictment in New Hampshire for the abduction of his three children, was residing in western North Carolina. Defendant located plaintiff in Murphy, North Carolina, where he was teaching pre-school children at "Free Methodist Church." On 20 August 1974 defendant, accompanied by Chief Cheney and Sergeant Gene Rogers of the Belknap County, New Hampshire, Sheriff's Department, served a fugitive arrest warrant on plaintiff at the church. Plaintiff would not waive extradition to New Hampshire, and defendant took him to the Cherokee County jail. Defendant turned plaintiff over to Sheriff Blain Stalcup and left, but returned later and made the alleged defamatory statements to Sheriff Stalcup. Defendant then fingerprinted and photographed the plaintiff and departed.

After a hearing on the motion in Jackson County on 22 March 1976, the court on 23 April 1976 made specific and detailed "findings of fact," stated separately its conclusions of law based thereon, and entered summary judgment for defendant.

Plaintiff appealed.

*** Since it is not necessary, even inadvisable in most cases, for the trial court in ruling on a motion for summary judgment to find the facts specially and state separately its conclusions of law as in a trial before the judge without a jury, *Wall v. Wall*, 24 N.C.App. 725, 212 S.E.2d 238 (1975), we do not rule specifically on plaintiff's numerous assignments of error based on exceptions to the findings and conclusions made in this case. Rather, we go directly to the question of whether the alleged slanderous statements made by the defendant to the Sheriff were qualifiedly privileged, and whether the record discloses that there are no genuine issues of material fact and defendant is entitled to judgment as a matter of law.

It is the occasion of the publication of the alleged defamation that is privileged, *Ponder v. Cobb*, 257 N.C. 281, 126 S.E.2d 67 (1962), and the burden is on the defendant to prove the affirmative defense of qualified privilege by establishing facts sufficient to show that the publication was made on a privileged occasion. *Stewart v. Check Corp.*, 279 N.C. 278, 182 S.E.2d 410 (1971).

Conditional or qualified privilege is based on public policy. It does not change the actionable quality of the words published, but merely rebuts the inference of malice that is imputed in the absence of privilege, and makes a showing of falsity and actual malice essential to the right of recovery.

"A qualified or conditionally privileged communication is one made in good faith on any subject matter in which the person communicating has an interest, or in reference to which he has a right or duty, if made to a person having a corresponding interest or duty on a privileged occasion and in a manner and under circumstances fairly warranted by the occasion and duty, right, or interest. The essential elements thereof are good faith, an interest to be upheld, a statement limited in its scope to this purpose, a proper occasion, and publication in a proper manner and to proper parties only. The privilege arises from the necessity of full and unrestricted communication concerning a matter in which the parties have an interest or duty." 50 Am.Jur.2d Libel & Slander s 195, pp. 698–699 (1970).

Where the occasion is privileged, the presumption of law is that the defendant acted in good faith, and the burden is on the plaintiff to prove that the publication was made with actual malice in order to destroy the qualified privilege. *Stewart v. Check Corp., supra*; *Ponder v. Cobb, supra*; *Ramsey v. Cheek*, 109 N.C. 270, 13 S.E. 775 (1891).

"Whether the occasion is privileged is a question of law for the court, subject to review, and not for the jury, unless the circumstances of the publication are in dispute, when it is a mixed question of law and fact." *Ramsey v. Cheek*, supra, at 274, 13 S.E. at 775.

There is no dispute as to the circumstances of the publication in this case. It was made by one law enforcement officer who had just arrested the plaintiff to another law enforcement officer who was charged with the safekeeping of plaintiff in the Cherokee County jail. Both the defendant and the Sheriff had an interest in and duty with reference to the safekeeping of plaintiff while he awaited extradition to New Hampshire. The statements made by the defendant to the Sheriff concerning plaintiff's alleged mental state and political persuasion, and concerning the facts surrounding plaintiff's alleged abduction of his three children and subsequent arrest in North Carolina might be useful to Sheriff Stalcup in carrying out his responsibilities as Sheriff of Cherokee County. Therefore, the record establishes that the alleged statements were made on a qualifiedly privileged occasion, and summary judgment for defendant was appropriate unless the record discloses, as plaintiff contends, a genuine issue exists as to whether the statements were made with actual malice on the part of defendant in which case plaintiff could recover even if the occasion were privileged.

"... When a motion for summary judgment is made and supported as provided in this rule (Rule 56), an adverse party may not rest upon the mere allegations or denials of his pleading, but his response by affidavits or as otherwise provided in this rule, must set forth specific facts showing that there is a genuine issue for trial. If he does not so respond, summary judgment, if appropriate, shall be entered against him." G.S. 1A-1, Rule 56(e).

In the present case defendant supported his motion for summary judgment by establishing the affirmative defense of qualified privilege. Even though plaintiff, thereafter, had the burden of setting forth specific facts "by affidavits or otherwise" showing a genuine issue exists as to whether defendant made the alleged statements with actual malice, he relied simply on the allegations in his complaint to show malice. Therefore summary judgment was appropriately entered against him.

Plaintiff contends the court erred in "entertaining" the motion for summary judgment and entering an order thereon when the motion had not been "docketed" with the Clerk of Superior Court of Cherokee County, the county in which the action had been commenced. While G.S. 1A-1, Rule 5(d) requires that a motion for summary judgment "shall be filed with the court," we find no prejudicial error in the court's hearing and ruling on defendant's motion for summary judgment since the record discloses the following statement of the court:

"Inasmuch as copies of the defendant's Motion for Summary Judgment, Memorandum in support of Motion for Summary Judgment and Addendum to the Memorandum in support of the Motion for Summary Judgment were filed with Judge Lacy Thornburg, Residing Judge for Cherokee County, and Wesley F. Talman, Jr., Attorney for the Plaintiff, and that all parties were put on notice, or had reason to know, of the fact that the defendant had made a Motion for Summary Judgment, the Court therefore considered that the Motion for Summary Judgment and supporting affidavits and documents were sufficiently filed with the Court in this case."

* * *

Summary judgment for defendant is affirmed.

Troxler v. Charter Mandala Center, Inc.

89 N.C. App. 268, 365 S.E.2d 665 (1988)

On 28 January 1986, plaintiff filed suit against Charter Medical Executive Corporation (Charter Medical) and his employer, Charter Mandala Center, Inc. (Mandala), a wholly owned subsidiary of Charter Medical. The complaint sought recovery for slander and intentional infliction of emotional distress arising out of statements by defendants' employees that plaintiff, while working as a mental health worker, had sexual relations with a minor female patient at Mandala's hospital. On 24 April 1987, defendants filed a motion for summary judgment. The motion was granted on 15 May 1987. Plaintiff appeals.

The record reveals that on or about 18 January 1985, plaintiff's co-worker, Gregory Holthusen (Holthusen), met after work hours with his shift supervisor, Nancy Davis (Davis). Holthusen reported to Davis that several months earlier another co-worker, Thomas Kennedy (Kennedy), had told him that plaintiff and four other workers had engaged in sexual relations with a minor female patient. After receiving counsel from Davis, Holthusen reported the information to the head nurse who in turn reported it to the director of nursing. The director informed the hospital administrator, Alan Erbe (Erbe). Erbe subsequently contacted his immediate supervisor, an employee of Charter Medical in St. Louis, Missouri, who instructed Erbe how to proceed.

An investigation was initiated and those persons allegedly involved were interviewed. Plaintiff was interviewed and denied any sexual misconduct. During the course of the investigation, Erbe notified personnel at Charter Medical in Atlanta. He also contacted the local police and protective services. Charter Medical sent an investigative team to Mandala's hospital.

On 22 January 1985, plaintiff was suspended from his job pending the investigation. In March 1985, Mandala terminated plaintiff's employment.

In a sworn affidavit filed by plaintiff, Kennedy denied ever talking to Holthusen about the alleged sexual misconduct. He further stated in his affidavit that Holthusen was bitter towards blacks who were receiving promotions ahead of Holthusen and specifically towards plaintiff who had been promoted. In an affidavit filed by defendant, Holthusen stated that Kennedy had related to him the charges concerning plaintiff and that Holthusen reported the charges out of concern for the welfare of the patients.

In their answer, defendants raise the affirmative defense of qualified privilege. They also assert that Holthusen's alleged slanderous statements cannot be imputed to them because he was outside the scope of his employment when the statements were made to Davis.

Plaintiff ... contends that the circumstances under which Holthusen first related to Davis the alleged sexual misconduct did not constitute a "privileged occasion" and the qualified privilege defense is inapplicable. Second, plaintiff contends that the defense of qualified privilege, if it existed, was lost by excessive publication and malice on the part of Holthusen and Erbe.... We reject plaintiff's arguments and affirm the trial court's order.

A trial court shall grant summary judgment "if the pleadings, depositions, answers to interrogatories, and admissions on file, together with the affidavits, if any, show that there is no genuine issue as to any material fact and that any party is entitled to a judgment as a matter of law." G.S. 1A-1, Rule 56(c); *Keesing v. Mortgage Corp.*, 278 N.C. 523, 180 S.E.2d 823 (1971). In ruling on the motion, the court must consider the evidence in the light most favorable to the non-movant. *Walker v. Westinghouse Electric Corp.*, 77 N.C.App. 253, 335 S.E.2d 79 (1985), *disc. rev. denied*, 315 N.C. 597, 341 S.E.2d 39 (1986). The non-movant must be given all favorable inferences which may reasonably be drawn from the facts proffered. *English v. Realty Corp.*, 41 N.C.App. 1, 254 S.E.2d 223, *disc. rev. denied*, 297 N.C. 609, 257 S.E.2d 217 (1979); *Whitley v. Cubberly*, 24 N.C.App. 204, 210 S.E.2d 289 (1974). Therefore, any documents presented which support the movant's motion must be strictly scrutinized while the non-movant's papers are regarded with indulgence. *Miller v. Snipes*, 12 N.C.App. 342, 183 S.E.2d 270, *cert. denied*, 279 N.C. 619, 184 S.E.2d 883 (1971).

The record contains two affidavits which are in direct conflict with each other. Kennedy's affidavit, furnished by plaintiff, states that Kennedy never talked to Holthusen and that Holthusen was resentful and bitter toward plaintiff. Holthusen's affidavit, furnished by defendant, states that Kennedy told him that plaintiff and others had sexual relations with a minor female patient and that he reported the story to his supervisor after normal working hours.

It is apparent to this court that plaintiff has attempted to put forth two conflicting arguments. On the one hand, plaintiff has argued that defendants are liable under *respondeat superior* because Holthusen was acting within the scope of his employment. On the other hand, plaintiff has argued that defendant's employee, Holthusen, was motivated by malice and resentment. If we accept Kennedy's statement, Holthusen would be outside the scope of his employment and defendants are not liable under the doctrine of *respondeat superior*. If we accept Holthusen's statement, he would be within the scope of employment and the defense of qualified privilege would apply. Defendant is entitled to summary judgment under either theory.

*** If we assign every favorable inference to Kennedy's affidavit and thus accept it as true, then Holthusen's statements to Davis were to further a malicious purpose of his own and are thus outside the scope of his employment [and defendants are not liable].

Even if we accepted Gregory Holthusen's affidavit that he was acting out of concern for patient welfare and found him to be within the scope of his employment, defendant would still be entitled to summary judgment because Holthusen then had a qualified privilege for his allegations regarding plaintiff.

> 'A qualified or conditionally privileged communication is one made in good faith on any subject matter in which the person communicating has an interest, or in reference to which he has a right or duty, if made to a person having a corresponding interest or duty on a privileged occasion and in a manner and under circumstances fairly warranted by the occasion and duty, right or interest.'

Gibby v. Murphy, 73 N.C.App. 128, 132–133, 325 S.E.2d 673, 676 (1985), *quoting, Stewart v. Check Corp.,* 279 N.C. 278, 285, 182 S.E.2d 410, 415 (1971). A "privileged occasion" arises "'when for the public good and in the interests of society one is freed from liability that would otherwise be imposed on him by reason of the publication of defamatory matter.'" *Ponder v. Cobb and Runnion v. Cobb and Rice v. Cobb,* 257 N.C. 281, 295, 126 S.E.2d 67, 78 (1962), *quoting* 53 C.J.S., Libel and Slander, section 87, pp. 142 and 143.

The health care industry plays a vital and important role in our society. It plays a critical part in helping us to maintain our physical and mental well-being. We as a society, therefore, are interested in the quality and trustworthiness of the care which the medical community provides.

In response to society's concern, defendants, as owners and operators of medical facilities, have an interest in fostering public confidence in their ability to provide safe and expert patient care and treatment. Part of the task of fostering such confidence involves hiring and maintaining a skilled and trustworthy staff and investigating any allegations of patient abuse or mistreatment by members of that staff. Thus, the statements made by the employees (other than Holthusen) of Mandala and Charter Medical in investigating the charges of sexual misconduct were privileged.

Holthusen, an employee of defendant who was directly responsible for patient care, had an ethical if not employment-based duty to report any allegations of abuse. If his affidavit is taken as true, he was protecting the public interest as well as the interests of the patients and defendants. In this context, the allegations reported by Holthusen to his immediate supervisor and to similarly interested personnel were made on a "privileged occasion." If he was within the scope of his employment, he had qualified privilege. Additionally, because Holthusen, according to his affidavit, was acting to further defendants' business, he would be within the scope of his employment and the privilege which freed him of liability would be imputed to defendants. *See generally Morrison v. Kiwanis Club,* 52 N.C.App. 454, 279 S.E.2d 96, *disc. rev. denied,* 304 N.C. 196, 285 S.E.2d 100 (1981).

On previous occasions our courts have held that allegations made during the course of investigations are privileged. *See Jones v. Hester,* 260 N.C. 264, 132 S.E.2d 586 (1963) (corporate president's investigation of employee held to be privileged); *Hartsfield v. Hines,* 200 N.C. 356, 157 S.E. 16 (1931) (defendant's investigation of corporate mismanagement held to be privileged); *Gattis v. Kilgo,* 140 N.C. 106, 52 S.E. 249 (1905) (investigation of charges against college president by board of trustees held to be privileged); *Pressley v. Can Company,* 39 N.C.App. 467, 250 S.E.2d 676, *disc. rev. denied,* 297 N.C. 177, 254 S.E.2d 37 (1979) (employment evaluation report by defendant's agent and sent to defendant's manager held to be privileged). The undisputed facts here make clear the privileged nature of the communications made by Erbe, the hospital administrator. The record shows that Erbe only made statements regarding plaintiff to protective services, an agency to which he was legally bound to report (*See* G.S. 7A-543), to the police, to supervisory personnel at Charter Medical and to personnel who were part of the investigation process.

Plaintiff has asserted that defendants' qualified privilege was lost because of Erbe's malice toward plaintiff and excessive publication. We do not agree. Plaintiff has put forth no evidence that Erbe spoke to anyone outside of those who had a corresponding interest in the communication and were part of the investigative process. Nor did he provide any evidence to show malice other than an alleged statement by Erbe to plaintiff that plaintiff was facing a possible prison term. On its face, such a statement can hardly be said to indicate malice.

Finally, plaintiff contends that statements made by defendants' employees and the alleged manner in which they were communicated constituted an intentional infliction of emotional distress. We disagree. The entire record is devoid of any evidence of outrageous conduct on the part of defendants' employees. To the contrary, the record shows that defendant's administrator received information concerning sexual abuse of a minor in its care. Erbe had a duty to the patients and to defendant to investigate these charges. He was further bound, under G.S. 7A-543, to report these allegations to protective services. All of the people with whom he spoke were part of the investigative process. Given these circumstances, Erbe's conduct cannot be considered outrageous or extreme.... Defendants here conducted a confidential and necessary investigation to protect patients under their care.

Affirmed.

Kwan-Sa You v. Roe

97 N.C. App. 1, 387 S.E.2d 188 (1990)

The following facts do not appear to be disputed. In 1977 plaintiff began working as assistant professor of pediatrics in the Pediatric Metabolism Laboratory at Duke University. Plaintiff had been hired for the position by Dr. Charles R. Roe, director of the laboratory and one of the defendants here. On 24 May 1982 defendant Roe sent a letter to plaintiff purporting to dismiss him as of 1 April 1983; a copy of this letter was sent to Dr. Katz, Chairman of the Department of Pediatrics. Pursuant to an administrative appeal plaintiff's employment was extended until 1 October 1983.

Plaintiff alleges that in the interim several meetings and discussions about plaintiff took place with and among the various defendants. On 3 September 1982 plaintiff met with Dr. Roe to discuss the letter of termination. Defendant Byrd, Administrative Assistant to the Division of Pediatric Metabolism, was also in attendance and took the minutes of the 3 September 1982 meeting. During the meeting Dr. Roe accused plaintiff of failing to divulge certain reagent recipes used in the laboratory. Plaintiff denied these allegations. Dr. Roe informed plaintiff that if he did not comply with the request to turn over these recipes and train technical personnel to make the reagents by 7 September 1982 plaintiff's privileges in the Pediatric Metabolism Laboratory would be terminated.

On 23 September 1982 plaintiff met with Dr. Roe and Robert Metcalf, an administrator of Duke University. This meeting was to "explore the options available to Dr. You." Ms. Byrd took the minutes of this meeting also. It is apparent from the record that plaintiff had been offered laboratory space by a Dr. Clark and that during this meeting plaintiff refused to say whether he would accept the offer. Dr. Roe was adamant that plaintiff would not be allowed to use laboratory space and facilities in the Pediatric Metabolism Laboratory. However, he allowed plaintiff to remain on the premises through 29 September 1982 when plaintiff was scheduled to meet with Dr. Katz.

Plaintiff alleges that at approximately 1:00 p.m. on 30 September 1982 he arrived at his office and found a locksmith changing the locks on his office door as well as the other doors in the laboratory. Later that afternoon Dr. Katz told plaintiff to remove his materials from his office. Plaintiff also alleges that on or about 28 October 1982 Dr. Katz wrote plaintiff a letter informing him that he no longer had any duties in or access to the Pediatric Metabolism Laboratory.

Plaintiff also alleges that on or about 30 September 1982 defendants Roe, Katz, Byrd, Corinne Houpt, Jeffrey Houpt and Stoudemire made false and slanderous statements concerning plaintiff's mental condition. Plaintiff alleges that these statements were all "maliciously or willfully, wantonly and recklessly made." Plaintiff alleges he was involuntarily committed as a result of these statements and that his professional reputation was damaged. ***

Defamation.

(1) Slander.

Plaintiff alleges that statements made by various defendants were false, and were maliciously made to discredit plaintiff. Specifically, plaintiff argues that defendants Roe, Katz and Byrd made the following "untrue and defamatory statements" about him:

1. He was threatening staff members of the Pediatric Metabolism Laboratory with acids;

2. He was making bombs in the laboratory;

3. He had a history of violently abusing his wife; [and]

4. He wrote letters to his wife threatening to kill her and the children.

Plaintiff argues that these statements constitute slander per se because they involve allegations of moral turpitude. The defendants have asserted in defense the truth of the statements and a qualified privilege in making the statements. Plaintiff asserts that the facts before the trial court raised a genuine issue regarding the truth of the statements and the declarants' actual malice.

The record before us shows that the statements related above were true. There is evidence that plaintiff acted peculiarly on two occasions when in the laboratory, mixing acid and another substance together and placing the hot and smoking flask in the employees' hands. These instances were the basis of the statement that plaintiff was threatening employees with acid. The statement regarding a bomb also has a basis in fact. Although the facts tend to show that the statement was a misunderstanding of what plaintiff meant, there is no dispute that plaintiff stated that "the bomb has been dropped" and the "wires are burning." The statements regarding plaintiff's abuse of his wife and threats to her and their children are also based on fact. There is plenary evidence in the record to support the statements that plaintiff had abused his wife physically and had written threatening letters to her while she was out of the country. Because we find no facts that raise a genuine issue regarding the statements' truthfulness, we need not discuss defendants' assertion of a qualified privilege and plaintiff's assertion of actual malice.

(2) Libel.

Plaintiff argues in his brief that the termination letter written by Dr. Roe constituted libel per se because it tended to impeach plaintiff in his trade or profession. The letter stated that plaintiff was being terminated because he abandoned his responsibilities as assistant director of the clinical laboratory, he was reluctant to push himself toward grant deadlines and he was unwilling to provide recipes of ingredients to the technical staff. Plaintiff has alleged that Dr. Roe maliciously communicated these false charges to Dr. Katz to justify plaintiff's termination. Defendant Roe asserted as his defense the truth of the matters asserted and that his statements were protected by a qualified privilege. Plaintiff argues that actual malice on defendant's part defeats the defense of qualified privilege.

Plaintiff has raised a genuine issue of fact on the defense of qualified privilege.

> A qualified or conditionally privileged communication is one made in good faith on any subject matter in which the person communicating has an interest, or in reference to which he has a right or duty, if made to a person having a corresponding interest or duty on a privileged occasion and in a manner and under circumstances fairly warranted by the occasion and duty, right, or interest.

The essential elements thereof are good faith, an interest to be upheld, a statement limited in its scope to this purpose, a proper occasion, and publication in a proper manner and to proper parties only. The privilege arises from the necessity of full and unrestricted communication concerning a matter in which the parties have an interest or duty.

Pressley v. Continental Can Co., 39 N.C.App. 467, 469–70, 250 S.E.2d 676, 678, *disc. rev. denied*, 297 N.C. 177, 254 S.E.2d 37–38 (1979). Plaintiff has raised an issue of Dr. Roe's good faith. Where a statement is libel per se, that is, "a false written statement which on its face is defamatory," *Robinson v. Nationwide Ins. Co.*, 273 N.C. 391, 393, 159 S.E.2d 896, 899 (1968), there is a presumption of malice. *Stewart v. Nation-Wide Check Corp.*, 279 N.C. 278, 284, 182 S.E.2d 410, 414 (1971). However, a finding of qualified privilege rebuts the inference of malice and makes it necessary for the plaintiff to prove actual malice before he can recover. *Id.* at 285, 182 S.E.2d at 414–15.

Actual malice may be proven by evidence of ill-will or personal hostility on the part of the declarant, see *Ponder v. Cobb*, 257 N.C. 281, 294, 126 S.E.2d 67, 76 (1962), or by a showing that the declarant published the defamatory statement with knowledge that it was false, with reckless disregard for the truth or with a high degree of awareness of its probable falsity. *Ward v. Turcotte*, 79 N.C.App. 458, 460, 339 S.E.2d 444, 446–47 (1986). Here there is also an issue of fact whether there was personal hostility between plaintiff and Dr. Roe. Plaintiff alleges and asserts in his deposition that Dr. Roe and he had been "at odds" for some time prior to receiving the letter of termination. Plaintiff alleges that this personal hostility was the basis for his termination. However, plaintiff also argues that Dr. Roe wanted to change the focus of research in the laboratory and for that reason Dr. Roe wanted to terminate plaintiff. This evidence is sufficient to raise a genuine issue of material fact whether Dr. Roe's statements were made without good faith or probable cause and therefore constituted actual malice. For this reason we hold that summary judgment was improvidently granted on this issue.

In summary, the orders of the trial court granting summary judgment on the [issue of slander is] affirmed.... However, those portions of the orders that grant summary judgment in favor of the various defendants on the claims based on libel, ... are vacated and the cause is remanded for further proceedings in the trial court. All other assignments of error have been abandoned by plaintiff.

Affirmed in part, vacated in part and remanded.

White v. Town of Chapel Hill

899 F. Supp. 1428, 1438 (M.D.N.C. 1995)

A review of the record in this case, including numerous depositions, reveal the following facts. Slightly after 5:30 p.m. on May 19, 1992, members of the Chapel Hill Police Department responded to a 911 call reporting a hostage situation in an apartment complex at an apartment occupied by Plaintiff William K. White and his then fiance, Rhonda Allen, two individuals with a history of substance abuse and mental illness. When the police arrived, Ms. Allen was outside the apartment. She related to James Hugerich, supervisor of the Crisis Unit and a trained police negotiator, that she had come home that day and found Plaintiff's journal notes expressing suicidal and homicidal thoughts. She had some of the notes with her. Hugerich read these notes which stated that Plaintiff wanted to drive down Interstate 85 and "blow away" certain persons and that Plaintiff could "blow his brains all over the wall," and which expressed Plaintiff's belief that Plaintiff was lethal to others. Hugerich was familiar with both Plaintiff and Ms. Allen, and had been to Plaintiff's apartment in 1991 as a result of an individual committing suicide in the apartment. At that time, Hugerich accompanied Plaintiff and Ms. Allen to the hospital emergency room so that they could be seen by a psychiatrist. As a result of that incident, Hugerich was aware that Plaintiff and Allen were allegedly alcoholics, and that she apparently suffered from a multiple personality disorder.

After showing Hugerich Plaintiff's journal entries, Allen explained to Hugerich that she was concerned that Plaintiff was dangerous, both to himself and others, and that after finding the journal she had confronted Plaintiff and called a psychiatrist at Duke Hospital and that Plaintiff had talked to the psychiatrist on the telephone. She said that Plaintiff had then become angry at her and began to choke and threaten her, and that she kicked him in the stomach and fled the apartment with the notes. She advised that he was carrying a .44 caliber revolver and handcuffs and had very little sleep or food for the last week and a half.

After reading the notes and conferring with Sabrina Garcia, a psychologist who also was a member of the Crisis Unit at the scene, Hugerich made telephone contact with the Plaintiff about 6:00 p.m. and asked him what had happened. Plaintiff advised Hugerich that Allen had been hospitalized two weeks previously and that her therapist advised him to make sure that he did not allow her to harm herself or Plaintiff, and since that time he had his .44 caliber revolver loaded and strapped to his side, in addition to his handcuffs. He confirmed that he had had very little sleep or food. He said that the day's episode began by Allen reading his notes, over-reacting and calling Duke Hospital, and threatening him with psychiatric hospitalization. A scuffle ensued, and Allen kicked him in the stomach where he had numerous staples from a surgery that removed a tumor and part of his pancreas and intestines. According to Plaintiff, Allen has a multiple personality disorder and, at the time of the scuffle, Allen had assumed one of her "alters," a 19-year-old, 6'3", 235-pound male, "Michael," whose physical strength Plaintiff could not match.

Plaintiff indicated he wanted the police to go away and leave him alone, and that, although he had no explanation for his journal notes, he was not suicidal or homicidal. Plaintiff insisted that he had a right to possess his gun and to remain in his apartment. Hugerich agreed and assured him that the police were not going to rush the apartment. Hugerich advised Plaintiff that the police were concerned for Plaintiff's own safety and for others in the crowded apartment complex. Hugerich had several telephone discussions with Plaintiff over a period of nearly six hours concerning securing the gun and getting help for Plaintiff. Plaintiff stated that he did not have to come out of his apartment in the absence of a warrant, and Hugerich assured the Plaintiff that the police did not have an arrest warrant for him, that he had done nothing wrong, and that they only wanted to help him. Finally, Plaintiff indicated that he had been working with Dr. Reisner of Duke Hospital towards a psychiatric commitment and gave Hugerich permission to talk to Dr. Reisner. Hugerich contacted Dr. Reisner, who arranged for the Plaintiff to be seen by a psychiatrist at the Duke emergency room. Hugerich advised Plaintiff of his arrangements with Dr. Reisner, and Plaintiff also talked with Dr. Reisner on the telephone.

Plaintiff testified that the pain in his side became more intense and that because of the pain he agreed to come out of his apartment and to go with Hugerich to the hospital for treatment of his injuries. Plaintiff and Hugerich agreed that Plaintiff would come out of the sliding glass door to the apartment with his finger through the open chamber of the pistol and with his hands up, that Hugerich would drive up in front of the apartment, open the trunk to his car, Plaintiff would put the pistol in the trunk, and that they would drive to the Duke Hospital emergency room.

Hugerich testified that at the agreed upon time, 11:15 p.m., he drove to the designated spot in front of the apartment and got out of his car. He said that Plaintiff was delayed in exiting the sliding door, that Plaintiff turned toward the door and remained facing the door for approximately sixty seconds, and that when Plaintiff turned around and faced the car, his hands were down at his sides and the gun was not visible. At that moment, other officers took Plaintiff to the ground and secured him with handcuffs. Plaintiff was taken to the Duke Hospital emergency room, where he was seen by Dr. Mary Soderstrom, who evaluated Plaintiff, made findings, and ordered that Plaintiff be involuntarily committed.

Plaintiff filed this action against the Town of Chapel Hill, and against Chief Ralph Pendergraph, Captain Greg Jarvis, both of whom were present at the scene, and law enforcement officers John Doe I–IV, individually and in their official capacities. Plaintiff pleads one federal constitutional claim under 42 U.S.C. § 1983 with three bases—violations of the First, Second, and Fourth Amendments. Plaintiff also pleads four state-law claims—assault and battery, intentional infliction of emotional distress, false imprisonment, and defamation.

Defendants have moved for summary judgment, arguing that no unconstitutional or tortious conduct occurred, and that even if Plaintiff's constitutional rights were violated, the Town of Chapel Hill is not liable under *Monell v. Department of Social Services*, 436 U.S. 658, 98 S.Ct. 2018, 56 L.Ed.2d 611 (1978), and the individual Defendants have qualified immunity.

* * *

D. *Defamation*

Plaintiff alleges that Defendants referred to Plaintiff as a "gunman" when speaking with the press. Plaintiff claims that this allegation, and other, non-specified allegations, brought Plaintiff into disrepute in the community and, therefore, is actionable as slander. As an example of the alleged effect of Defendants' alleged statements to the press, Plaintiff claims that he was requested to leave his apartment complex; however, that request was later rescinded. Plaintiff alleges no other particular damages resulting from Defendants' allegedly defamatory statements.

In order for Plaintiff to establish a claim for slander *per se* against a Defendant, Plaintiff must demonstrate that (1) Defendant spoke base or defamatory words which tended to prejudice Plaintiff in his reputation, office, trade, business or means of livelihood or hold him up to disgrace, ridicule or contempt; (2) the statement was false; and (3) the statement was published or communicated to and understood by a third person. *West v. King's Dep't Store, Inc.*, 321 N.C. 698, 703, 365 S.E.2d 621, 624 (1988) (citations omitted).

Truth is a complete defense to a claim of slander. *Parker v. Edwards*, 222 N.C. 75, 78, 21 S.E.2d 876, 878 (1942). Plaintiff argues that the use of the word "gunman" to describe him was false as he did not "wield" or "brandish" a gun. Webster's Dictionary defines "gunman" as, *inter alia*, "[a] man armed with a gun." *Webster's II New Riverside University Dictionary* (1988). Allegedly slanderous statements are to be considered in context. *See Tyson v. L'eggs Products, Inc.*, 84 N.C.App. 1, 13–14, 351 S.E.2d 834, 842 (1987). In the present case, the "gunman" statement and other unspecified statements are alleged to have been made during and after a long stand-off with Plaintiff who admittedly had a gun in his possession. If the statements that were made were a fair representation of the full truth, Plaintiff's claim for slander is barred. *See Parker*, 222 N.C. at 78, 21 S.E.2d at 878–79. Given the understood meaning of the word "gunman," and the circumstances under which the statements were alleged to have been made, the court finds that no reasonable jury could find that the alleged statements were false.

In addition, Plaintiff presents no evidence that a third person heard and understood any of the allegedly defamatory statements. "[A] mere possibility that someone might have heard the alleged [defamatory statements] is not enough" to proceed with a claim of slander. *West*, 321 N.C. at 704, 365 S.E.2d at 625 (citing *Tyer v. Leggett*, 246 N.C. 638, 641, 99 S.E.2d 779, 782 [1957]). For these reasons, taking the evidence in the light most favorable to Plaintiff, Plaintiff cannot proceed with his defamation claim against Defendants.

In sum, in examining Plaintiff's state-law tort claims, the court finds that no genuine issues of material fact exist and, taking the evidence in the light most favorable to Plaintiff, Defendants are entitled to judgment as a matter of law.

An order and judgment in accordance with this memorandum opinion shall be entered contemporaneously herewith.

ORDER AND JUDGMENT

For the reasons set forth in the memorandum opinion filed contemporaneously herewith,

IT IS ORDERED AND ADJUDGED that Defendants' motions for summary judgment as to all of Plaintiff's claims are **GRANTED** and this action is **DISMISSED** with prejudice.

Losing v. Food Lion, L.L.C.
648 S.E.2d 261 (N.C. Ct. App. 2007)

A defendant is entitled to summary judgment when he has shown that the plaintiff cannot overcome an affirmative defense. Because we find that the defendant here definitively proved the affirmative defenses of truth, to slander *per se;* and expiration of the statute of limitations, to invasion of privacy; we affirm the trial court's grant of summary judgment.

On 28 January 2005, Plaintiff Mervyn D. Losing filed a complaint against his employer, Food Lion, LLC, and his direct supervisor, Food Lion district manager Robert Jones, alleging defamation, negligent infliction of emotional distress, negligence, and invasion of privacy, stemming from a drug test of Mr. Losing on 11 December 2001. According to Mr. Losing, he was selected by Food Lion and Mr. Jones for a random drug test soon after returning to work following an accident and injury suffered during the course and scope of his employment. The drug test returned as "substituted," meaning that it was not consistent with human urine. Under Food Lion's substance abuse policy, a "substituted" urine sample was considered a positive screen. A confirmation test conducted by the laboratory facility used by Food Lion likewise found that the sample from Mr. Losing was not consistent with human urine. In accordance with Food Lion's zero tolerance policy, Mr. Jones then fired Mr. Losing from his position at Food Lion on 18 December 2001. However, Mr. Losing exercised his right to a retest, which returned negative. Food Lion ultimately admitted that the initial result was a false positive and reinstated Mr. Losing to his previous position with the same salary and back pay. *** Mr. Losing contends that Mr. Jones made statements concerning his failed drug test to other Food Lion employees, including that he tested positive, substituted non-human urine in the drug test, and was fired for failing the drug test.

Following answers filed by Food Lion and Mr. Jones, Mr. Losing voluntarily dismissed with prejudice his claim for negligent infliction of emotional distress on 19 December 2005.

On 29 June 2006, Food Lion filed an amended motion for summary judgment, arguing that Mr. Losing had failed to establish a *prima facie* case for defamation, negligence, or invasion of privacy, and that such claims were also precluded by qualified privilege, an independent intervening cause, and the statute of limitations, respectively, among other affirmative defenses. Several affidavits, including that of Mr. Jones, were submitted with Food Lion's motion for summary judgment, as well as the interrogatories, requests for admissions, and documents produced during discovery prior to the filing of the motion. On 13 July 2006, the trial court granted Food Lion's motion for summary judgment with prejudice, ordering that Mr. Losing should recover nothing from Food Lion as to any of his causes of action.

Preliminarily, we observe that summary judgment is properly granted when the evidence, viewed in the light most favorable to the non-moving party, shows no genuine issue of material fact. *Bruce-Terminix Co. v. Zurich Ins. Co.*, 130 N.C.App. 729, 733, 504 S.E.2d 574, 577 (1998) (citation omitted); *see also* N.C. Gen.Stat. § 1A-1, Rule 56(c) (2005). Additionally, a defendant may show he is entitled to summary judgment by: "(1) proving that an essential element of the plaintiff's case is non-existent, or (2) showing through discovery that the plaintiff cannot produce evidence to support an essential element of his or her claim, or (3) showing that the plaintiff cannot surmount an affirmative defense." *Draughon v. Harnett Cty. Bd. of Educ.*, 158 N.C.App. 705, 708, 582 S.E.2d 343, 345 (2003) (internal quotation and citation omitted), *aff'd per curiam*, 358 N.C. 137, 591 S.E.2d 520, *reh'g denied*, 358 N.C. 381, 597 S.E.2d 129 (2004).

In his appeal, Mr. Losing argues that summary judgment was improper because a genuine issue of material fact remains as to each element of his claim against Food Lion for (I) slander *per se*....

I.

First, Mr. Losing argues that a genuine issue of material fact remains as to each element of his claim for slander *per se* against Food Lion, such that summary judgment was improper. We disagree.

Under North Carolina law, "slander *per se*" is "an oral communication to a third party which amounts to (1) an accusation that the plaintiff committed a crime involving moral turpitude; (2) an allegation that impeaches the plaintiff in his trade, business, or profession; or (3) an imputation that the plaintiff has a loathsome disease." *Boyce & Isley, PLLC v. Cooper*, 153 N.C.App. 25, 29–30, 568 S.E.2d 893, 898 (2002) (quotation and citation omitted), *disc. review denied, dismissed*, 357 N.C. 163, 580 S.E.2d 361, *cert. denied*, 540 U.S. 965, 124 S.Ct. 431, 157 L.Ed.2d 310 (2003). "False words imputing to a merchant or business man conduct derogatory to his character and standing as a business man and tending to prejudice him in his business are actionable, and words so uttered may be actionable *per se*." *Id.* at 30, 568 S.E.2d at 898 (quotation and citation omitted). Thus, an essential element of a slander *per se* claim based on defaming an individual's business reputation is that the statements are false; truth is therefore an affirmative defense to such a claim. *Long v. Vertical Technologies, Inc.*, 113 N.C.App. 598, 602–03, 439 S.E.2d 797, 801 (1994) ("[I]n order to be actionable, the defamatory statement must be false. The truth of a statement is a complete defense.").

In the instant case, Mr. Losing specifically alleged in his complaint that Mr. Jones had made statements including, but not limited to:

a. That [Mr. Losing] had been fired for substituting non human urine on a drug test.

b. That he had failed a drug test.

c. That he was failing to follow store operating procedures.

d. That he was fired over a drug test.

e. That, through Brian Sloan, you need to get [Mr. Losing's] attorney, he can get you off of a drug test.

In his deposition statements, Mr. Losing refers to the "rumors ... around the whole store" after he was fired, which he acknowledges were recounted to him by others. He admits that he never heard Mr. Jones tell anyone that his sample showed non-human urine; rather, his "evidence" that Mr. Jones made the slanderous statements is that "if him [sic] and I are in the room and I'm told I have non-human urine and I'm being fired for it, there's only two people in that room. Just him and me [sic]. I told nobody."

In his brief to this Court, Mr. Losing states that, "[t]he simple question is whether or not [Mr.] Losing failed a drug test. If [Mr.] Losing did fail a drug test, then truth would be a defense." Nevertheless, Mr. Losing asserts that the drug test was not "completed" after the initial test and confirmation test conducted by Food Lion. Rather, Mr. Losing contends that the drug test was not "completed" until he exercised his right to the retest and found that the original results had been false positives. We find this argument to be without merit.

The evidence in this case is incontrovertible that Mr. Losing did, under the terms of Food Lion's substance abuse policy, fail a drug test. Although the result was ultimately shown to have been a false positive, the fact remains that a finding of a "substituted" sample constituted a failed test under Food Lion's policy. Mr. Losing's result was of a "substituted" sample; therefore, he failed the test. Under the express terms of Food Lion's zero tolerance policy, Mr. Losing was then fired for failing a drug test. These were all true statements, notwithstanding the underlying falsity of the positive drug test.

Moreover, in the depositions submitted to the trial court for consideration of Food Lion's motion for summary judgment, Mr. Losing recounted that Mr. Jones told him, "I'm going to have to fire you for non-human urine that came back-non-human urine on a drug test. I have to fire you because it's a positive drug test." Likewise, Mr. Losing admitted in one of his depositions that he was suspended for a week in March 2002 for "failure to follow store operating procedures." Even assuming *arguendo* that Food Lion has *respondeat superior* liability for statements made about Mr. Losing by Mr. Jones— and even acknowledging that such statements might have been uncalled—for, unfair, and perhaps cruel gossip—any statements made by Mr. Jones regarding Mr. Losing's failing a drug test due to non-human urine, being fired for such, and failing to follow store procedures were still strictly true. As such, they are not slanderous *per se.*

Nor is Mr. Losing's claim that Brian Sloan's alleged statement to "get [Mr. Losing's] attorney, he can get you off of a drug test [ ]" slanderous. Such an assertion does not rise to the level of alleging "conduct derogatory to [Mr. Losing's] character and standing as a business man," nor does it "tend [ ] to prejudice him in his business." *Boyce & Isley*, 153 N.C.App. at 30, 568 S.E.2d at 898. For that reason, we have "held consistently that alleged false statements made by defendants, calling plaintiff 'dishonest' or charging that plaintiff was untruthful and an unreliable employee, are not actionable *per se.*" *Tallent v. Blake*, 57 N.C.App. 249, 253, 291 S.E.2d 336, 339–40 (1982) (quotation and citation omitted).

In sum, the statements objected to by Mr. Losing do not rise to the level of slander *per se.* Moreover, the statements were all true, even if Mr. Losing subsequently showed that they were based on a false underlying premise. As such, because Mr. Losing could not overcome the affirmative defense of truth, we must uphold the trial court's grant of summary judgment to Food Lion.

Affirmed.

Exercise 5-5 Integrating Information

1. What additional information did you learn from reading the cases?

2. How does that information connect with what you learned from the practice guide?

3. Did any of the cases contain information that is helpful to your clients? Explain.

4. Did any of the cases contain information that is harmful to your clients? Explain.

5. Did any of the cases contain information that you would like to further explore?

6. Do you have any questions about the law (as it pertains to your clients) that are unresolved? Is further research warranted?

7. What are the disputed issues in *Strickland v. Wong* (your case)?

Exercise 5-6 Evaluating the Evidence — Creating a Discovery Plan

Based on your reading so far, make a list of what plaintiff will need to prove at trial in order to establish Defendants Wong and CCCSP are liable. What evidence do you currently possess that might negate one or more of these items? What additional evidence could you obtain that might help you?

Make a list of what you must prove in order to establish each of the defenses you've pleaded in the answer. For each of the items you must prove, determine what evidence you already have. Next determine whether there is additional evidence you need obtain, in order to meet your burden of proof at trial. For the evidence you do not yet possess, determine how you will obtain that evidence during discovery—i.e., determine who possesses the evidence (your clients, a witness, the plaintiff, etc.) and in what form (documents, testimony, etc.).

Exercise 5-7 Identifying Weaknesses — Preparing for Your Client's Deposition

You will be meeting with Defendant Robyn Wong to prepare her for her deposition. Please prepare an outline or memorandum detailing the items you plan to cover during this meeting, and an explanation for why you plan to cover each item. For this exercise you do not need to worry about the necessary general instructions (e.g., what to bring, what to wear, that the client will be under oath, etc.), rather you should focus on those things impacting the substance of the client's testimony (which may include the client's anxiety about being deposed). After your client's deposition you plan to file a motion for summary judgment based on qualified privilege, unless there is information uncovered during deposition that impacts your assessment of the likelihood you would prevail on such a motion (which at this point, you think is pretty likely).

The following excerpt from *Preparing Your Client For Deposition*, 2 No. 2 Prac. Litigator 41 (March 2001), will help you complete your task:

Effective deposition preparation requires that you reduce your client's anxiety with information and practice.

YOUR CLIENT'S DEPOSITION is important. Your opponents have read all the books on discovery and know this. Your opponents will go after the unfiltered facts. They will be looking to uncover those memory gaps, inconsistencies, improbabilities, embarrassments, weaknesses, and flaws present in every case. They will test your case and your client. They will be looking for ammunition for their dispositive motion, for tough settlement talks, and, if necessary, for trial.

Your client is anxious ("characterized by extreme uneasiness of mind or brooding fear about some contingency"). Let's face it, you're anxious, too. (The "contingency" you're brooding about may be your fee.) To resort to the barbarity of sports metaphor, this could be the ball game.

Your client's anxiety is rational, grounded in life experience and common sense, exacerbated by the myth and mystery of the litigation process. You need empathy and understanding. Your client may be thinking this:

"This litigation involves high stakes. Truth, justice, honor, principle, reputation, and money are on the line. Omigod, what if I lose!?

Lawyers are to be feared and distrusted. At least the other side's lawyers. I've seen the movies and TV shows. They have these sneaky lawyer tricks to make you look bad. Or like a liar. Or like an idiot. What did I get myself into!?

They can ask me anything. Are they going to show that I did something wrong? Or embarrassing? Or stupid? Did I make mistakes? What if I forget something? What did I get myself into!?

I'm going to have to speak in front of all these people, lawyers and the other side and a court reporter. I hate that. I've read the polls; people fear public speaking second only to death. What did I get myself into!?

Those opposing lawyers are nasty. Will they yell at me? Insult me? Badger me? Can my lawyer protect me? Am I strong enough to stand up to this kind of abuse? What did I get myself into!?

Where am I supposed to go for this deposition? What time? Where do I park? What do I wear? What should I bring? Who'll be there? How long will this take? What did I get myself into!?"

Your job is to alleviate this anxiety, and to harness its energy for productive purposes. You accomplish this through effective preparation. Effective preparation consists of four steps:

• First, you must prepare yourself;

• Second, you must directly address your client's anxiety;

• Third, you must alleviate your client's anxiety with information, about the law, the litigation, the discovery process, and exactly what is expected of your client; and

• Fourth, you must alleviate your client's anxiety by demonstrating his ability to be an effective witness. You accomplish this in three ways: practice, practice, practice.

PREPARE YOURSELF • To effectively prepare your client, you must first prepare yourself. You need to know everything there is to know: the law, the facts, your theory of the case,

your opponent's theory, and how all these things mesh. You need a plan. You need to know how you will support your theory, how your opponent will support his, and how each of you will respond to the other. You need mastery of the details: what the witnesses will say, what the documents say, the who, what, where, when, why and how. You need to know what is important and what is not, and that sometimes what seems unimportant at first proves to be very important in the end. So, your preliminary task may be summed up in a simple rule: know everything.

Ethical Responsibilities

Perfect knowledge is not enough. You must be confident in the legitimacy of your role and objectives. You are an advocate for your client. This carries some ethical responsibility. Under the applicable ethical rules you've got to be competent, prepared and diligent. You've got to keep your client informed about the litigation and sufficiently educated to make informed decisions. You are obligated to "act with commitment and dedication to the interests of the client and with zeal in advocacy upon the client's behalf." You've got to be loyal to your client. At the same time, you have a responsibility to the truth; a lawyer may not knowingly offer evidence that the lawyer knows to be false or falsify evidence, or counsel or assist a witness to testify falsely. [citations omitted]

"Coaching" the Client

These ethical responsibilities are entirely consistent with "coaching" your client to present truthful testimony clearly, logically, and persuasively. In "Preparing Witnesses," *The Litigation Manual: A Primer for Trial Lawyers* (John G. Koetl, ed., ABA 2d ed. 1989) at 469, David H. Berg writes: "There are lawyers who refuse to woodshed witnesses at all, who just throw them up on the stand and let them tell their story. Their clients most often are referred to as 'appellants.'" Berg continues: "Everyone who testifies has to be woodshedded. It is probably unethical to fail to prepare a witness, and it is undoubtedly cruel to subject anyone to cross-examination without preparation." For more on this, see Stuart M. Israel, "Coaching Witnesses," Vol. 10, No. 3 Labor and Employment Lawnotes 10 (Fall 2000) and Stuart M. Israel, "The Ethics of Witness Preparation," Vol. 9, No. 2 Labor and Employment Lawnotes 6 (Summer 1999) (available at http:// www.icle.org/sections/labor/lawnotes/index.htm).

Once you have the prerequisites—perfect knowledge and confidence that preparation is a worthy and ethical endeavor—you're ready to prepare your client for the modern substitute for medieval dispute resolution by personal combat, the deposition.

ADDRESS YOUR CLIENT'S ANXIETY • Malone and Hoffman identify the witness' "level of confidence about his ability to perform in the deposition environment" as the "primary factor affecting the witness's performance." David M. Malone and Peter T. Hoffman, *The Effective Deposition: Techniques and Strategies that Work*, at 155 (NITA, 2d ed. 1996). They conclude that the "primary goal" of witness preparation is to "take burdens off of the witness's shoulders so that he can focus only on the substance of his answers."

Acknowledge the Witness's Anxiety

To accomplish this, you should build confidence first by directly addressing and acknowledging the legitimacy of your client's anxiety. Once that is done, you can move on to substance, technique and practice. You might begin like this:

Pat, you may be nervous about your deposition. It's natural. Everybody gets nervous. A deposition puts you in an unusual situation, sitting in a conference room answering questions in front of a bunch of people listening to your every word, with a court reporter preserving it all for posterity. Who wouldn't be nervous?

We're going to prepare you for your deposition. When we're done, you are going to be ready. You'll understand exactly what to expect. You'll understand the process and you'll be prepared to be an effective witness. You'll even know where to park.

Our preparation may not eliminate all your nervousness, but when we've finished you'll have the confidence that you are ready and prepared to do a great job. Okay, that's our objective, to get you ready. Any questions so far?

EDUCATE YOUR CLIENT · You will build your client's confidence with information. Mystery breeds anxiety. Here are some things you might want to discuss with your client (not the details and technicalities, but the concepts).

* * *

How Depositions Are Used

At trial for impeachment and as substantive evidence (Fed. R. Civ. P. 32; MCR 2.308(A)) and in support of summary judgment motions (Fed. R. Civ. P. 56(c), (e).

The Cross-Examiner's Deposition Objectives

• Discover facts about the case;

• Discover facts about your client;

• Assess your client as a witness and an opponent;

• Obtain and preserve facts and admissions for use in motions and at trial;

• Find bias, interest and other things that can be argued to diminish your client's credibility;

• Identify documents;

• Commit your client to testimony; and

• Obtain material for impeachment.

* * *

[An] Overview of the Case

Moving from the mundane and generic to the sublime and specific, give your client a framework for comprehending the litigation. This includes an overview of the applicable law, the opposing theories of the case, the significant issues, and what needs to be communicated clearly to support your client's objectives. Your explanation needn't be overly detailed or technical; key issues will naturally arise during your preparation and practice. Your explanation should, however, give your client the foundation for understanding how the parts fit into the whole. For example:

Pat, as you know, our main claim is that you were terminated from your job because of your age in violation of the law that prohibits age discrimination. Our theory is that that Ralph Cheatham decided to fire you because he thinks people older than 50 are dinosaurs. We're going to prove this in various ways. We're going to show that Cheatham made remarks showing age bias. We're going to show that you were replaced by a 27-year-old whose credentials don't measure up to yours. We're going to show you had a solid work record. We're going to prove our case with witnesses like your co-workers, and with documents and, most importantly, with your testimony. You are going to have the chance to tell it like it is, and to show the justice of your case.

Now, you know the company says you were terminated for poor work performance. They say you messed up the Cameron project. They say this is a legitimate, non-discriminatory reason for firing you. Cheatham really emphasized the Cameron project at his deposition. I'm sure that's going to be a principal focus of your deposition. We have to be fully prepared to explain what happened and that the whole mess was Cheatham's fault, so we'll be spending a lot of time discussing the Cameron project. We'll be reviewing all the pertinent documents, all the Cameron project paperwork. We want to show that the Cameron project is just a pretext, that you really were fired because of your age. Okay, any questions about this so far?

Exercise 5-8 Adapting Learning to Evaluate New Claims

For each of the following scenarios determine which cases from the practice guide would likely be most useful to your representation of the client. Be sure you are able to explain why. If the cases you choose are different from the cases you selected for the chapter problem, explain why you've made different choices.

a. Janice's seventeen year old daughter, Laura, was murdered. The morning after Laura's body was found the newspaper ran a story which, among other things, quoted Laura's doctor as saying "there simply was no family support to encourage Laura to continue her education." Laura was a high school drop-out, but Janice had always encouraged her to pursue her G.E.D. The doctor claims she told the newspaper that Laura lacked *financial* (not family) support to continue her education. Although an editor usually reviews each story before final publication and verifies the accuracy of the printed information, in this case, no one other than the reporter read the entire story before it was published. Is Newspaper liable for defamation?

b. As part of the background investigation for a magazine article Reporter was writing about prostitution in City, Reporter interviewed City Police Chief. The article was published in CITY Magazine and contained the following statement: "In City, according to City Police Chief, 'prostitution is practically nonexistent.' 'There's an overabundance of it free from personnel at the military base, from some wives and daughters of military men who are overseas for long periods and some girls from college in City who provide plenty of it. Prostitution has never really been a problem.' And it was apparent from his tone of voice and slightly defensive posture that he did not want the press to make it into one." As a result of the article and the statements attributed to him, residents of City, and the Commander of the military base have demanded that City Police Chief be removed from his office. City Police Chief sued CITY Magazine and Reporter, claiming the statements are false and defamatory. City Council, who has been tasked with determining whether City Police Chief should be removed from office, contacted you to assess the likelihood City Police Chief will prevail in his defamation action.

c. Kraufman is a prominent local real estate developer and builder in City. While he was engaged in negotiations with the City Council to obtain a zoning variance that would allow him to construct high-density housing on land he owned, the City was attempting to purchase a different tract of Kaufman's land in order to build a new high school. The concurrent negotiations provided both parties considerable leverage and created substantial local controversy. Several members of the community retained

Attorney to file an injunction to stop the City Council from granting a variance. Attorney drafted a settlement demand letter, in which he called Kraufman's negotiations "blackmail" and threatened to file a lawsuit requesting the injunction if City Council caved to Kraufman's demands. Kraufman sued for libel, seeking both compensatory and punitive damages, claiming Attorney's letter imputed to him the crime of blackmail. What is the likelihood that Kraufman will prevail?

d. During an interview with Court TV a reporter asked Attorney about Psychiatrist, a doctor that had testified against Attorney's client, in client's trial for the murder of client's parents. Psychiatrist had recently informed the public she was planning to write a book on the subject. Attorney told the reporter Psychiatrist was "mentally unbalanced" and "a terrible witness who was disliked by the jury." He accused her of hunting publicity, stating: "this thing is being broadcast world-wide and it brings out the Looney Tunes. And this is one of the Looney Tunes." He added that "in the criminal case, she had the audacity to submit a bill of $100,000," but the court "laughed at her and gave her zero." He concluded by stating that the description "of the nuts growing on trees" in California was "not that far off." What is Attorney's best defense if he is sued by Psychiatrist?

e. Recruiter is one of three recruiting coordinators for University, a large public college with a wildly popular, nationally recognized basketball program. His job is to recruit players for University's basketball program. Recently, college recruiting has received national attention because of an NCAA investigation which resulted in fines, suspension and removal of personnel at a large number of colleges as a result of such colleges committing recruiting violations. In fact, University has been placed on probation because the NCAA determined it committed substantial violations, including "payoffs to a college player and various criminal activities." Recruiter contacted you because as far as his conduct goes, these statements are not true. Evaluate Recruiter's claim for defamation.

f. Newspaper published a story that Raymond, a local man who won the lottery, was being sued by his girlfriend, who claimed she was entitled to half of the winnings. The woman who sued was actually his neighbor. Raymond is married. Will Raymond have to plead and prove special damages in order to recover?

g. Singer owns and operates a nightclub where she regularly performs as the star attraction. She advertises her performances approximately 200 times a year in local print media, proclaiming herself the "most electrifying one-woman show on the entertainment scene" and "superstar of stage, screen, television and radio." LIFETV, a television network, aired a story referring to Singer as a "stripper-turned-singer." Singer sued LIFETV for defamation. LIFETV based the story on information that Singer had been employed by a strip club. Singer was in fact employed by the strip club, but as a bartender, and not as one of the club's exotic dancers. Evaluate Singer's claim for defamation.

Exercise 5-9 Reflection and Revision

Consider whether the outline or issues checklist you developed in exercises 5-1 and 5-3 helped you to evaluate the scenarios in exercise 5-7. Consider how you might revise your outline or issues checklist to help you evaluate future client problems. Do the following charts reflect your understanding of the topic? How do they differ from the one you've created? Is one more helpful than the other? Why or why not?

Status of Plaintiff/ Content of Statement	Public Official or All Purpose Public Figure	Limited Purpose Public Figure + statement reasonably related to public controversy	Private Person + matter of public concern	Private Person + private matter
Prima Facie Case (**bold** type indicates requirement of clear and convincing burden of proof)	Defamatory statement Of and concerning plaintiff Published to third party **Falsity of statement** **Actual malice**	Defamatory statement Of and concerning plaintiff Published to third party **Falsity of statement** **Actual malice**	Defamatory statement Of and concerning plaintiff Published to third party **Falsity of statement** See damages	Defamatory statement Of and concerning plaintiff Published to third party
Recovery of presumed damages for libel and slander per se	Yes	Yes	Yes, if proof of **actual malice**	Yes
Recovery of actual damages	Yes	Yes	Yes, if proof of negligence	Yes, if proof of pecuniary loss

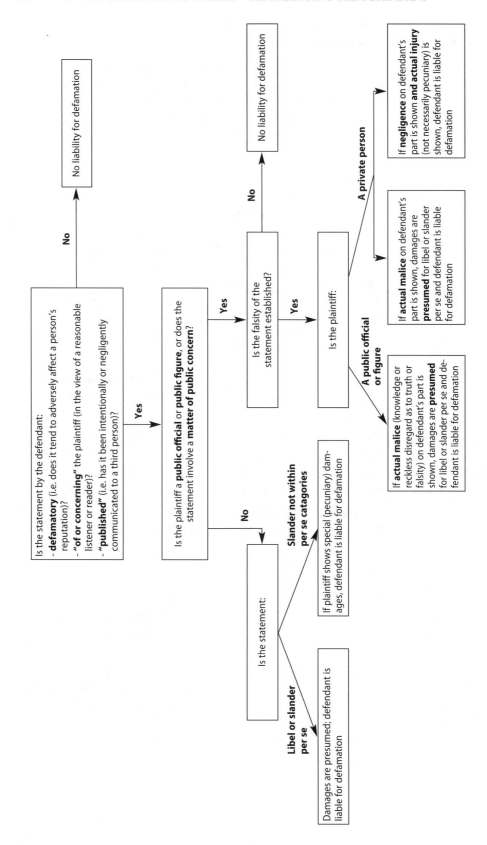

Exercise 5-10 Developing a Better Understanding of Constitutional Concerns

As you have seen in this chapter, application of the *New York Times* standard, requiring plaintiff to prove falsity and actual malice, by clear and convincing evidence, makes it extremely difficult for a plaintiff to prevail. For this reason, defendants will frequently attempt to categorize the plaintiff as a public official or public figure. Where that is not possible, categorizing the statements as relating to matters of public concern will at least require plaintiffs seeking presumed or punitive damages, to meet the same burden, although plaintiffs suffering actual injury need only prove falsity and that defendant did not act as a reasonable prudent person in attempting to confirm the accuracy of the information.

For this exercise, you may wish to review the material on constitutional defamation before you attempt to answer the following:

Will Fences is the very charismatic owner of FRUIT Computer Corp. He single-handedly revolutionized the computer industry with the creation of the iberry27, a personal electronic device that stores all of a person's data (including personal contacts, credit cards, health history, bank accounts and driving records) on a single device measuring 1/2 inch by 1/2 inch, and weighing less than 1 ounce. The device can be worn in a carrier resembling either a necklace or wrist watch. The consumer accesses data from the device by projecting an image onto any hard surface (like a wall or sheet of paper) much like a motion picture projector projects images onto a movie screen. The iberry27 was in high demand because of its' extreme portability and it sold out almost immediately. The iberry28, due out in a few months, sold out its' first production run through preorders and there is currently a wait list for the next run. Articles about Fences have appeared on the cover of several news magazines and he has been proclaimed the "Inventor of the Century."

Several months after the release of the iberry27 a substantial number of consumers began to experience severe headaches and vision problems as a result of reading the projections from the iberry27 "screen." As it turns out, the projections from the iberry27 produce a glare that is responsible for the symptoms. Only one alternative design currently exists, which would decrease portability of the device and delay production of the iberry28 by several months, most likely allowing the maker of a competing product (eMobile's drone) to gain a larger market share.

Recently, Will and his wife were having dinner on the outdoor patio of their secluded Malibu, California, home. Their housekeeper, who was paid substantial sums of money by FACES (a tabloid) to gain information about the iberry, placed a recording device in the fresh flower arrangement on the Fences' dinner table. She recorded a conversation in which Will sobbed to his wife that their dreams would all come crashing down if he could not maintain his consumer's brand loyalty for his beloved iberry.

The next day the conversation was broadcast on several national radio stations. The cover of FACES (the tabloid) carried a photo of the iberry28 prototype and the headline "CRYberry." FRUIT stock plummeted. Customers withdrew orders for the iberry28. Will was humiliated.

Assume this is a jurisdiction that allows corporations to file actions for defamation, and treats corporations as a "natural person" for purposes of defamation actions.

1.   Is FACES liable for Defamation:

    a.   To Will?

    b.   To FRUIT corp?

2.   Is there any additional research you should conduct before answering these questions?

Exercise 5-11 Law Practice

Find a practice guide for the state and area of law you plan to practice. How might this guide be useful to you when you are a lawyer?

Chapter Six

Putting It All Together—
Representing the Plaintiff

Objectives

Apply prior learning to a new context by:

Using the combined learning, study, and law practice skills developed in Chapters One through Five to represent a client

Using substantive knowledge developed in Chapters One through Five to represent a client

Introduction

In prior chapters, in addition to developing substantive legal knowledge, and a professional vocabulary, you have developed a number of important skills, including:

Expert legal reading skills

Reflective learning skills

The ability to:

Deconstruct rules

Apply and distinguish legal authority

Evaluate potential and existing claims and defenses

Evaluating legal documents and arguments drafted by other lawyers

Counsel a client

Find and utilize resources related to understanding non-legal concepts

Acquire and develop knowledge in areas other than the applicable law

Evaluate the facts of a case to determine:

Which facts are significant for purposes of proving or disproving liability

Whether additional factual information is needed

Evaluate expert opinions and testimony

Develop preliminary theories based on the facts and law

Identify the type of damages suffered by a plaintiff

Estimate the value of damages for purposes of engaging in settlement discussions

Develop an awareness of and empathy for client feelings and emotions

Acknowledge client emotions and feelings and understand how they impact a case

Evaluate whether a plaintiff's claim is barred or limited because of a defense

Determine the applicable statute of limitations period, when the limitations period begins to run, and whether the limitations period may be tolled

Determine what evidence is required to prove a cause of action

Obtain evidentiary support for a claim or defense

Use public policy to make an argument that a rule should be extended, modified or imposed

Evaluate policy arguments used by a court to justify the court's decision

Synthesize legal authority

Analyze a problem and make legal arguments using factors

Explain the reason(s) for the conclusion you want the court to adopt

Use a secondary source to:

> Obtain background information,
>
> Gain familiarity with an area of law
>
> Put primary sources in context
>
> Guide research
>
> Refine understanding of issues presented
>
> Organize information

Organize materials to reflect understanding of material and to help effectively evaluate a client's case

Use organized materials as a framework for understanding additional information

Use cases to enhance existing knowledge

Understand when further research may be necessary

Evaluate strengths and weakness in a client's case

Adapt learning to evaluate new cases

Understand a case sufficiently to prepare a client for deposition

Understand how the burden of proof impacts a client's case

"Teach" yourself a new or unfamiliar are of law

In this chapter you will have an opportunity to apply these critical skills in the context of representing the plaintiff in an action that has not yet been filed. You may (and should) use information you have learned from the previous five chapters — including study and learning skills, law practice skills and substantive knowledge. In other words, in addition to the material introducing new causes of action in this chapter (which will require you to employ learning, study and law practice skills to learn the material), you should think about what other causes of action and defenses might exist, based on your knowledge from previous chapters (which will require you to employ previously acquired substantive knowledge). You will need to organize what you learn, and apply it to effectively represent your client (which will require you to utilize the law practice skills you have acquired).

Because you represented the defendants in Chapter Five, you had some guidance in the form of the complaint—which narrowed the issues for you. This chapter adds a new dimension, in that there are no pleadings to guide you. Also, in order to simulate law practice, the title of the chapter and headings will not provide you with clues as to what potential causes of action you might allege. There will also not be step by step exercises you guide you. Instead, like law practice, you will have the opportunity to use your existing knowledge and skills to complete your task—directed by your own understanding. It may seem a little daunting at first, but if you've been doing the work up to this point, you have developed the necessary skills and this will be an opportunity for you to hone those skills, and become more "practice-ready."

Chapter Problem

The law firm where you are employed recently decided to represent residents of the city of Sunnyville, a small town of about 2,000 residents, located in upstate New York, not far from the Rolling River.

You have been given the task of determining what common law causes of action may exist. The partner assigned to the case is handling research relating to causes of action under federal environmental laws, including any preemption issues (meaning you do not have to determine whether the common law causes of action are preempted by the applicable federal laws).

Be aware that this assignment requires you to (1) identify potential causes of action; (2) determine whether you have sufficient facts to allege each cause of action; (3) determine whether you need additional information before you are able to decide whether to allege a cause of action (and if you need such information, where you might be able to find it and how you will go about getting it); (4) assess the strengths and weaknesses of such causes of action; (5) consider whether there are any areas where it will be difficult to obtain evidence or prove allegations at trial; and (6) determine what potential defenses might preclude recovery.

When you received your assignment you were told the following:

Sunnyville has about 900 occupied homes, all of which are located near an enormous oil refinery complex owned and operated by BIGOIL Company (the Refinery). The nearest homes are within approximately 500 feet of the Refinery's property line.

Benzene is a known component of crude oil, which BIGOIL refined and stored on its Refinery property, and transported by pipeline through Sunnyville to the Rolling River.

Since 1908, BIGOIL has owned and operated the Refinery—including manufacturing facilities in and near the east side of Sunnyville; associated storage tanks, sanitary and storm sewers; and pipeline and water supply lines running from the Refinery, under Sunnyville, to the Rolling River. There have been documented spills, leaks and other releases of benzene from these sources into the air, soil, and groundwater near Sunnyville.

The United States Environmental Protection Agency (EPA), the State Environmental Protection Agency, and the State Department of Public Health have determined that there is a Benzene Plume located underneath Sunnyville. Benzene and the other hydrocarbons that comprise the Benzene Plume are from leaks or discharges from the Refinery. There have been various volatile organic chemicals ("VOCs"), including benzene, found in the soil, in the air, and in various depths on the surface of the groundwater under Sunnyville.

Groundwater pumping from production wells at the Refinery has altered the natural flow of groundwater in the area, and has contributed to a lower water table beneath the Refinery, which has accelerated and exacerbated the spread of contaminants under Sunnyville. The contamination underlying Sunnyville is not stable, but instead continues to spread. In addition to the liquid portion of the Benzene Plume there is also a dissolved or vapor phase of the Plume, in which the benzene and other hydrocarbons are continuously dissolved and spread away from the liquid portion of the Plume.

In June 2011, the State Department of Public Health (SDPH) concluded that the contamination in Sunnyville poses a serious, long-term source of contamination to groundwater, and that there is good reason to expect that benzene vapors are entering homes in Sunnyville. The SDPH based its conclusion on its review of soil vapor testing results which have up to 20,000 times the level of contaminants as reports requiring action in a neighboring community that has suffered from the effects of a vast underground plume of hydrocarbons.

Residents of Sunnyville are concerned that they live in homes whose values are now severely diminished because of the Benzene Plume and that they will be unable to sell them because the Benzene Plume is poisoning the soil, surface water, and groundwater, as well as the air inside and outside—destroying the value of their property. Most of the residents of Sunnyville are working families, who live in one-story, wood frame construction homes. Many of the residents have lived in their homes for more than a generation, and the community is very close knit.

Many of the Sunnyville residents also have various health problems and conditions such as cancer, leukemia, respiratory difficulties and headaches, among others.

You were also given the following memo:

To: Associate

From: Law Clerk

Re: Sunnyville residents v. BIGOIL

You asked me to (1) review the documents provided by the client in yesterday's meeting and to determine what information BIGOIL may have had in its' possession (relating to the Benzene Plume); and (2) provide you with some background information about benzene, including known toxic effects.

(1) Information in BIGOIL's possession

BIGOIL first became aware of an excess rate of leukemia at its refineries in 1975 when one of its employees sued the company, alleging that benzene exposure had caused his leukemia. As a result of the suit, BIGOIL compiled a list of leukemia cases of its past employees. The Refinery in Sunnyville was the site of the largest number of leukemia deaths. In 1985, BIGOIL issued a letter to its employees stating that studies had been done on five refineries and that there were statistically significant cases of leukemia observed at the Sunnyville Refinery.

The letter went on to state that BIGOIL saw no reason to conclude that a leukemia risk currently existed at any of its refinery locations including the Sunnyville Refinery. The Director of the National Institute for Occupational Safety and Health criticized this letter by stating that studies show that even low levels of benzene exposure cause leukemia and that the letter to BIGOIL's employees was overly reassuring.

In 1985 BIGOIL performed studies to determine the dangers posed by benzene vapors entering homes. The studies confirmed that vapor contaminants can migrate up through the soil and eventually come into contact with the substructure of homes, exposing the occupants to known and probable cancer causing chemicals for extended periods of time.

In 1989 the Attorney General's office sued BIGOIL over repeated spills of gasoline and benzene, including a 290,000 gallon spill of unleaded gasoline from a ruptured pipeline.

In 1998 BIGOIL agreed to pay the U.S. Government $15 million for committing more than 100 environmental violations at the Refinery, including violations of the emissions standards for benzene.

In 2008 the state EPA sent BIGOIL a letter stating that the Benzene Plume was moving to the east, increasing the risk of vapor intrusion to Sunnyville homes, and that the concentration of contaminants present on the surface of the water table provided suitable conditions for vapor migration.

In late 2009, BIGOIL posted a memorandum on the Sunnyville Investigation page of its Website, for the citizens of Sunnyville to read, stating that "the Benzene Plume's soil vapors do not appear to pose a risk to the residents of Sunnyville." The State Department of Public Health sent a letter to the EPA in which they disputed the contents of the memorandum, and informed the EPA that "the elevated benzene concentrations at this site are of great concern when considering potential residential exposure" and that there was "good reason to expect benzene vapors may be entering homes in Sunnyville based on the levels detected in vapor monitoring points."

BIGOIL violated the State Environmental Protection Act thirty seven times by exceeding the standards for the release of benzene, ethylbenzene, toluene and xylene into the groundwater of Sunnyville, New York.

(2) BENZENE

The following is a summary of the information available from the U.S. Department of Health and Human Services, Environmental Protection Agency, Centers for Disease Control, Occupational Safety and Health Adminstration, and webMD.

Benzene is a volatile, colorless, and highly flammable liquid which dissolves easily in water and quickly evaporates in the air. Common synonyms for Benzene include Benzole, Cyclohexatriene, Phenyl-hydride, and coal tar naphtha. Benzene is detectable at elevated concentration levels due to its odor.

Benzene is made mostly from petroleum. It is used in industrial applications to make other chemicals for the production of plastics, resins, nylon and synthetic fibers. Its primary use is as an intermediate in the production of other chemicals, predominantly styrene (for Styrofoam and other plastics), cumene (for various resins), and cyclohexane (for nylon and other synthetic fibers). It is also used to make some types of rubbers, lubricants, dyes, detergents, drugs, pesticides, pharmaceuticals and agricultural chemicals. Historically Benzene has also been an important component of many industrial cleaning and degreasing formulations, although it has now been replaced by toluene, chlorinated solvents or mineral spirits.

Benzene is produced naturally, both volcanically and from forest fires, and is found in oil, gasoline, and cigarette smoke.

<u>Exposure</u>

Every day, most people are exposed to some amount of benzene, either outdoors, in the workplace, or at home. Exposure can occur through the ingestion of benzene-containing food or drinking water, as well as through the inhalation of fumes containing the chemical. Benzene occurs naturally in a wide variety of foods, with maximum concentrations in foods such as ground beef, uncooked bananas and carbonated colas.

While everyone is environmentally exposed to some level of benzene, the highest levels of exposure are suffered by those employed in industries that make or use benzene. Potentially high levels of exposure to benzene may be found in those using industrial solvents or using benzene to manufacture other chemicals in the workplace. However, the general public is susceptible to high benzene levels as well, through such common sources as gasoline fumes and cigarette smoke. In the United States, gasoline typically contains approximately 2% of Benzene by volume. Persons living around petroleum refining operations and petrochemical manufacturing sites may be exposed to higher levels of Benzene in the air.

Benzene is rapidly and extensively absorbed by inhalation and ingestion. In humans, approximately 50% of Benzene is absorbed after a four hour exposure to approximately 50 PPM in air. In addition to being inhaled, airborne Benzene is absorbed across intact skin.

Leaking from underground storage tanks, pipelines or other improper disposal of hazardous materials containing Benzene have resulted in Benzene contamination of groundwater used for drinking. In addition to being ingested, Benzene in water can also be absorbed through wet skin and inhaled as it volatilizes during showering, laundering or cooking.

Exposure to benzene found in soils is experienced through a number of possible exposure pathways, including dermal (skin) contact with soil, ingestion of soil, inhalation of soil particulates, and ingestion of contaminated groundwater.

<u>Toxicity and Effects</u>

Several agencies, including the U.S. Department of Health and Human Services, Environmental Protection Agency, and International Agency for Research on Cancer, classify Benzene as a confirmed human carcinogen.

After exposure, Benzene is found throughout the body, but it preferentially distributes into the bone marrow and tissues with either high perfusion rates or lipid content. Bone marrow is the main target organ of chronic Benzene toxicity.

The signs, symptoms, and subsequent adverse health effects of benzene exposure vary according to the intensity and route of exposure. If the skin comes in contact with benzene, it may become red and irritated, or it may result in scaly dermatitis, blisters and the development of secondary infections.

High concentrations of benzene can irritate the eyes, nose and respiratory tract, but if aspirated (into the lungs), it can cause immediate pulmonary edema and hemorrhaging. Ingestion may result in burning of the gastrointestinal tract as well as stomach pain, chest pain, nausea and vomiting.

Continued exposure can cause central nervous system ("CNS") depression resulting in decreased respirations, seizures, coma, and eventually may lead to death. Benzene concentrations of 20,000 parts per million ("PPM") are fatal to humans within five to ten minutes. Pathologic Findings in fatal cases have included respiratory tract inflammation, lung hemorrhages, kidney congestion and cerebral edema.

Chronic exposure, even at low levels, can result in a variety of symptoms and blood disorders. Complaints may include bleeding from the gums and nose, fatigue, nervousness, and loss of appetite. Blood tests may reveal the accelerated destruction of the three basic blood components—erythrocytes (red blood cells), leukocytes (white blood cells) and thrombocytes (platelets)—known as pancytopenia. Potentially fatal infections or hemorrhage can occur as a result. Research has shown that by removing the source of exposure, some disorders may be reversed.

It has been well documented that benzene can cause bone marrow suppression, which in turn results in the decreased production of blood cells, commonly called anemia. More specifically, benzene exposure is associated with a type of anemia known as aplastic anemia. People with benzene-induced aplastic anemia are further subjected to a significantly elevated risk of developing leukemia. Not all cases of benzene-induced leukemia, however, are preceded by aplastic anemia. Aplastic is defined as the inability of bone marrow to function properly, while anemia is the condition of having too few blood cells. About 3 out of every 1 million people in the United States get aplastic anemia each year. Anemia is commonly associated with a low red blood count, but in the case of aplastic anemia, all three cell types (red, white and platelets) are decreased.

Aplastic anemia frequently occurs without any known cause and benzene is only one of a number of associations. Others include drugs (gold, chemotherapy, antibiotic, seizure medication, non-steroidal anti-inflammatory), viruses (HIV, Epstein-Barr), radiation, pregnancy, other chemicals (solvents, insecticides), immune disorders (lupus, rheumatoid arthritis) and inherited disorders (Fanconi's anemia). For treatment, medication or hormones may be given to stimulate the bone marrow, blood transfusions are frequently needed, and immuno-suppression therapy may be instituted.

Leukemia is cancer of the blood where the normal life-cycle of a blood cell has been disrupted. Risk factors include some chemotherapy drugs, very high levels of radiation, certain chemicals such as benzene and formaldehyde, Down's Syndrome and various other genetic diseases. Symptoms of leukemia may include fever, night sweats, joint pain, headache, frequent infection, easy bruising and bleeding, in addition to weight loss.

Leukemia is distinguished by how quickly the symptoms develop and how rapidly the disease progresses. Chronic leukemia may be asymptomatic initially, but a gradual onset of vague symptoms may occur as the number of abnormal cells increase in the blood stream. Acute leukemia may quickly develop and is a rapidly progressive disease.

The two most common types of leukemia are lymphocytic (lymphoblastic) and myelogenous (myeloid) and these types can be either chronic or acute. Acute Myelogenous/Myeloid Leukemia ("AML") is the most common type of leukemia, affecting both children and adults, and is also the type of leukemia most commonly associated with benzene exposure. The typical latency period for benzene-induced leukemia is five to 15 years after first exposure to benzene, but in many cases the cause may not be known.

Advances in the treatment of leukemia have increased the rate of remissions. Sixty to seventy percent of adults with AML can be expected to go into complete remission and, of those, approximately 22% are expected to survive three or more years or be completely cured.

The latency period for Benzene induced leukemia is typically 5 to 15 years after first exposure.

The effects of benzene may be more pronounced in children and the elderly.

Regulation

OSHA has established permissible limits of benzene exposure in ambient air at one part of benzene per million parts of air (1 ppm) in the workplace, over an eight-hour day, with a short-term exposure limit of 5 ppm permitted for 15 minutes.

The federal government has also regulated the presence of benzene in drinking water. Under the 1974 Safe Drinking Water Act, the (EPA) has established a "maximum containment level" for benzene of 5 parts per billion (ppb). This level was determined to be the lowest level to which water systems can reasonably be required to remove benzene should it occur in drinking water; although the EPA has stated that the containment level goal should be zero ppb in order to completely avoid adverse health effects. There are no known safe levels of exposure to benzene, gasoline or other hydrocarbon vapors for residential exposure purposes in the United States.

Under the Resource Conservation and Recovery Act (RCRA) benzene became a regulated hazardous waste, making it illegal to treat, store or dispose of benzene-containing waste without a permit.

You might also be interested to know that in 1948 the American Petroleum Institute published a toxicological review on Benzene for its members stating it is generally considered that the only absolutely safe concentration for benzene is zero.

You were also handed this document, which is a map of the area, with notes written on it by the Partner supervising the handling of the case. The circled X's mark the location of the residences of the people who have contacted your firm.

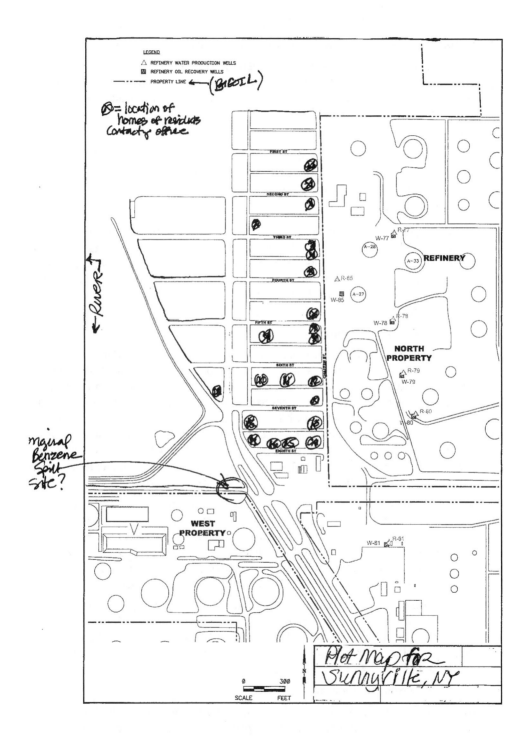

As you learned in Chapter Five, a practice guide is often a good place to begin, when you are unfamiliar with the specific area of law. Below is the *Practitioner's Guide to Toxic Tort and Environmental Litigation in New York*, Chapter VI:[1]

I. The role of the common law in environmental protection actions

In New York common-law claims supplement and enhance statutory environmental protection claims. Nuisance and other common-law claims, such as trespass, provide valuable remedies to parties attempting to abate air and water pollution, clean up contaminated sites and recover for damages.

A. Nuisance

This section address three types of common law nuisance actions : (1) public nuisance brought by public officials; (2) public nuisance brought by private persons; and (3) private nuisance brought by private persons.

1. Public Nuisance

Nuisance, specifically public nuisance, is the most likely of the common law causes of action available to challenge the operating conditions or the environmental conditions of the defendant's site. In New York, the release or threat of release of hazardous waste into the environment is a public nuisance as a matter of New York law. *State of New York v. Shore Realty Corp.*, 759 F.2d 1032, 1051 (2d Cir.1985); *Bologna v. Kerr-McGee Corp.*, 95 F. Supp. 2d 197, 205 (S.D.N.Y. 2000).

a. Public nuisance defined

A public nuisance is an interference with a public right; it is considered an offense against the state. New York courts have defined public nuisance as follows: "A public nuisance is conduct or omissions which offend, interfere with or cause damage to the public in the exercise of rights common to all, in a manner such as to offend public morals, interfere with use by the public of a public place or endanger or injure the property, health, safety or comfort of a considerable number of persons." *Copart Industries, Inc. v. Consolidated Edison Co. of New York, Inc.*, 41 N.Y.2d 564, 568, 394 N.Y.S.2d 169, 172, 362 N.E.2d 968, 971 (1977). A public nuisance is subject to an action for abatement or prosecution by the proper governmental agency.

> [I:101] Public nuisance claim used to compel restoration of land and natural resources contaminated by past releases of hazardous substances at Love Canal, an inactive hazardous waste dumpsite created by the former Hooker Chemicals & Plastics Corporation in Niagara Falls, New York. *U.S. v. Hooker Chemicals & Plastics Corp.*, 722 F.Supp. 960, 967–968 (W.D. N.Y. 1989); *U.S. v. Hooker Chemicals & Plastics Corp.*, 748 F.Supp. 67 (W.D. N.Y. 1990).

> [I:102] Court refused to dismiss public nuisance claims against a chemical company arising out of a contaminated dump site. *State v. Schenectady Chemicals, Inc.*, 117 Misc. 2d 960, 970–971, 459 N.Y.S.2d 971, 979, 13 Envtl. L. Rep. 20550 (Sup 1983), *order aff'd as modified*, 103 A.D.2d 33, 479 N.Y.S.2d 1010 (3d Dep't 1984).

b. Action by private persons

An action for public nuisance may be brought by a private individual or group of individuals. Such an action will typically emphasize protection of community rights

---

1. Again, no such guide exists; rather this guide is based on information from various practice guides, treatises and cases.

that are being infringed by the defendant's environmental abuses, but may also include recovery for plaintiffs personal damages. In order to bring such an action a private plaintiff must demonstrate injury different in kind, not merely degree, from injuries sustained by the community at large; a private plaintiff may not base an action for public nuisance on interference with her rights as a member of the community. *Hoover v. Durkee*, 212 A.D.2d 839, 840–841, 622 N.Y.S.2d 348, 349 (3d Dep't 1995).

[I:103] Plaintiffs did not allege loss that was "special and different in kind, not merely in degree," from those suffered by the public where plaintiffs alleged a diminution in property value, which others in the community also suffered. The court held that every person affected by the public nuisance was exposed to similar loss and that although the plaintiffs suffered it in a greater degree than others, it was not a different kind of harm, therefore the plaintiffs could not recover for the invasion of the public right. *Allen v. Gen. Elec. Co.*, 2003 WL 22433809 (N.Y. Sup. Ct. Sept. 29, 2003) aff'd, 16 A.D.3d 1095, 790 N.Y.S.2d 897 (2005).

[I:104] Where there is only one type of damage alleged and the entire affected community suffers it to one degree or another, the "particular harm" element of a public nuisance claim brought by a private person is not established. *532 Madison Ave. Gourmet Foods, Inc. v. Finlandia Center, Inc.*, 96 N.Y.2d 280, 727 N.Y.S.2d 49, 750 N.E.2d 1097 (2001).

[I:105] Public nuisance claim brought by private plaintiff alleging that defendant's operation of its quarry lowered the water table, causing plaintiffs' wells to run dry, was injury different in kind from general public since loss of the plaintiff's water supply was not suffered by everyone in the community. *Booth v. Hanson Aggregates New York, Inc.*, 16 A.D.3d 1137, 791 N.Y.S.2d 766 (App. Div. 4th Dep't 2005).

[I:106] Plaintiff's public nuisance claim was rejected where claim was based on allegation that golf balls were landing on a public road, making passage on the road dangerous to the public, and plaintiffs did not allege that they personally had been injured as a result of a golf ball landing on the road. Plaintiffs did not allege a special injury beyond that suffered by the community at large. *Gellman v. Seawane Golf & Country Club, Inc.*, 24 A.D.3d 415, 805 N.Y.S.2d 411 (2d Dep't 2005).

If private plaintiffs have suffered the requisite harm different from that suffered by the community at large, counsel should consider the benefits of alleging a public nuisance.

c. Benefits of alleging public nuisance

i. Strict liability

Liability to abate a public nuisance is strict and does not require proof of negligent or intentional acts. In other words, public nuisance cases do not require proof of fault on the part of the defendant.

[I:107] In an action brought by the state in the exercise of its police powers for either abatement or restitution, with respect to public nuisances and inherently dangerous activities, fault is not an issue. The inquiry is limited to whether the condition created, not the conduct creating it, is causing damage to the public. *U.S. v. Hooker Chemicals & Plastics Corp.*, 722 F.Supp. 960, 967–968 (W.D. N.Y. 1989), citing to 117 Misc.2d 960 at 970, 459 N.Y.S.2d 971 at 979 (Sup.Ct.,

Rensselaer County, 1983), aff'd as modified 103 A.D.2d 33, 479 N.Y.S.2d 1010 (3d Dep't 1984).

ii. Proof of actual harm not required

The toxic tort plaintiff need not prove actual harm from a public nuisance — just the threat of a release from the defendant's source is sufficient. *New York v. Shore Realty Corp*, 759 F2d 1032 (2d Cir 1985).

> [I:108] To state a claim for nuisance the plaintiff must provide a competent evidentiary showing of an actual or imminent threat of contamination or a reasonable probability and expectation of contamination in the future. *Plainview Water Dist. v. Exxon Mobil Corp. et al.*, No. 009975-01, slip op. at 16 (Sup.Ct. Nassau Co. Nov. 27, 2006).

iii. Balancing of interests not required

Another key distinction between private and public nuisance is that the balancing of interests of the parties that is required in private nuisance actions is inapplicable in public nuisance cases. *Hoover v. Durkee*, 212 A.D.2d 839, 842–843, 622 N.Y.S.2d 348 (3d Dept. 1995). This may be especially important in actions seeking injunction of an activity that has enormous societal value or importance.

See section I.2.b for discussion of balancing of interests in action based on private nuisance.

> [I:109] Economic consequences between the effect of the injunction and the effect of the nuisance may be appropriately considered in a private nuisance action, but they are not to be considered in a public nuisance action. In the context of a public nuisance lawsuit, the rule in New York is that the nuisance will be enjoined despite a marked disparity between the effect of the injunction and the effect of the nuisance. *Little Joseph Realty, Inc. v. Town of Babylon*, 41 N.Y.2d 738, 395 N.Y.S.2d 428, 363 N.E.2d 1163 (1977); *Hoover v. Durkee*, 212 A.D.2d 839, 842–843, 622 N.Y.S.2d 348 (3d Dept. 1995).

d. Unreasonable interference

"Unreasonable" is a key consideration by courts characterizing defendant's conduct as nuisance. Some factors counsel may want to consider when evaluating whether the interference is unreasonable include: (1) whether the actions were forbidden by law or regulation; (2) whether the conduct is of a continuing nature or has long-lasting effect; and (3) whether the defendant has reason to know its action has a significant effect on public health, safety, peace, or comfort.

> [I:110] Land uses in full compliance with zoning ordinances may be enjoined as a nuisance. *Little Joseph Realty, Inc. v. Town of Babylon*, 41 N.Y.2d 738, 395 N.Y.S.2d 428, 363 N.E.2d 1163 (1977).

> [I:111] "Coming to a nuisance" (i.e., an argument that the defendant's conduct pre-dated the plaintiff's arrival) is not a defense to an action for nuisance, but is merely one factor for the court to consider in determining whether conduct is unreasonable and amounts to nuisance. *Village of Euclid, Ohio v. Ambler Realty Co.*, 272 U.S. 365, 388, 47 S.Ct. 114, 118, 71 L.Ed. 303 (1926).

> [I:112] Each nuisance must be addressed on its own facts to determine whether under all the circumstances, such as location, surroundings, nature of the use, extent and frequency of the injury, and the effect on the enjoyment of life, health and property, the use of the property is unreasonable. *State v. Waterloo*

Stock Car Raceway, 96 Misc.2d 350, 355, 409 N.Y.S.2d 40, 43 (Sup.Ct., Seneca County, 1978).

[I:113] A nuisance may be merely a right thing in the wrong place. *Village of Euclid, Ohio v. Ambler Realty Co.*, 272 U.S. 365, 388, 47 S.Ct. 114, 118, 71 L.Ed. 303 (1926).

2. Private Nuisance

Private nuisance is a different cause of action from that for public nuisance. An action for private nuisance protects the private use and enjoyment of land, rather than a general community interest. When the pollution, release or spills by one land owner causes damage to the real property, or possessory rights in real property, of another private person, an action for private nuisance exists. Public and private nuisance are not mutually exclusive causes of action; when the nuisance, in addition to interfering with the public right, also interferes with the use and enjoyment of the plaintiff's land, it is a private nuisance as well as a public one.

Private nuisance is interference with the use and enjoyment of real property in which the plaintiff has a possessory interest. Thus, succeeding in a private nuisance action requires establishing (1) plaintiff had a property right and (2) defendant's chemicals interfered with that property right. "The elements of a cause of action for a private nuisance are: (1) an interference substantial in nature, (2) intentional in origin, (3) unreasonable in character, (4) with a person's property right to use and enjoy land, (5) caused by another's conduct in acting or failure to act." *Copart Indus. v. Consolidated Edison Co. of NY*, 41 N.Y.2d 564, 570, 394 N.Y.S.2d 169, 362 N.E.2d 968 (1977).

a. Requires fault

Private nuisance, unlike public nuisance, requires some showing of fault. The invasion of the interest in the private use and enjoyment of land must be intentional, negligent or reckless, although strict liability may be imposed where private nuisance results from abnormally dangerous activity, and so it should be considered as an alternative or supplement to nuisance in toxic tort cases. For a discussion of toxic tort claims based on abnormally dangerous activities, see section I.D. Also, the intentional and unreasonable standard is lower than it sounds, and is often met by establishing defendant had knowledge that the nuisance effects were "substantially certain to follow."

b. Interference must be substantial and unreasonable

Private nuisance is also limited to substantial and unreasonable interferences with the use or enjoyment of land. In reality this encompasses conduct that is not unreasonable at all but nonetheless provides the basis for liability for damage inflicted. Liability may exist where the harm caused is serious and the financial burden of compensating the injured party is feasible. This is a shift away from older cases where courts were reluctant to find nuisances even when damages were significant because they did not want to enjoin or abate useful enterprises. The so-called balance-of-utilities test required a finding that "the gravity of the harm outweighed the utility of the conduct" in order to find a nuisance existed. Today, this balancing is employed as a means for the court to determine whether an injunction is feasible, but it does not preclude an award of damages. In other words, a finding that the utility of the defendant's conduct outweighs the plaintiff's harm will not preclude a finding of nuisance and award of damages; likewise, a finding that the defendant's conduct is in fact a nuisance will not necessarily result in injunctive relief (abatement). *Boomer v. Atlantic Cement Co., Inc.*, 26 N.Y.2d 219, 309 N.Y.S.2d 312, 257 N.E.2d 870 (1970). Where plaintiff's goal is to stop the defendant's conduct, she must prove that the gravity of the harm caused by defendant's conduct outweighs the utility of the conduct. This balancing is not required in an action for public nuisance, which is why a plaintiff seeking injunctive relief should consider whether she meets the requirements for filing a claim based on public nuisance. For a discussion of these requirements see section I.A.1.

> [I:114] Where improper cleaning and demolition allowed hazardous waste to migrate onto plaintiffs' property, and the contamination interfered with use and enjoyment of land because of plaintiff's inconvenience in needing to have the hazardous waste removed from property, company was liable under a theory of private nuisance. *Scribner v. Summers*, 84 F.3d 554, 559 (2d Cir. 1996).

> [I:115] In action for private nuisance arising out of operations by a large cement plant which had recently been constructed in the vicinity, the Court of Appeals upheld determination that the comfortable use and enjoyment of the plaintiffs' property was impaired by the large quantities of dust, and excessive vibration from blasting. However, court did not award injunctive relief. *Boomer v. Atlantic Cement Co., Inc.*, 26 N.Y.2d 219, 309 N.Y.S.2d 312, 257 N.E.2d 870 (1970).

> [I:116] Persons living in organized communities must suffer some damage, annoyance and inconvenience from each other. To constitute a nuisance, the use must be such as to produce a tangible and appreciable injury to neighboring property, or such as to render its enjoyment specially uncomfortable or inconvenient. Reasonable use of property is dependent upon the circumstances of each case, including locale. *Campbell v. Seaman*, 63 N.Y. 568, 577 (1876).

B. Trespass

In toxic tort cases where it may be difficult, or even impossible, to prove that plaintiff's physical injuries were caused by defendant's pollution or hazardous chemicals, counsel may wish to rely on this common law cause of action because it enables the plaintiff to obtain a favorable jury verdict (and punitive damages) even if the plaintiff is unable to establish that the defendant's chemical caused damage to the plaintiff's health.

An action for trespass exists where there has been an intentional, physical invasion of property, which interferes with a plaintiff's exclusive possessory interest in land.

For purposes of a trespass action intent requires proof that the defendant intended the result or should have known the result was substantially likely to occur. To establish intent plaintiffs in toxic tort cases must establish that the action of the defendant (not the invasion itself) was an intentional act. In other words, plaintiff need only prove intent to do the act which resulted in the unlawful invasion; in practical terms, this means showing that the defendant acted in a way that resulted in contamination. For example, knowledge that chemicals that are being leaked, coupled with knowledge that when released the chemicals will move through groundwater onto an adjacent property, is enough to establish intent for purposes of trespass. Contamination may occur much later than the act and intent will still exist, so long as there is proof that defendant knew, or was substantially certain, that chemicals would eventually end up on plaintiff's property. Also, it is irrelevant whether defendant knows the entry is unauthorized (or believes that it isn't). Proving defendant knew or was substantially certain will often require circumstantial evidence; citations, letters or reports from government agencies may help establish this element.

[I:117] Court found trespass where defendants created situation where contaminants found in pesticide invaded plaintiff's property when applied to soil and contaminated the water in several of its public wells. *State v. Fermenta ASC Corp.*, 166 Misc. 2d 524, 630 N.Y.S.2d 884, 895 Sup.Ct., Suffolk County, 1995), aff'd in part, 238 A.D.2d 400, 656 N.Y.S.2d 342 (2d Dep't 1997).

[I:118] Plaintiffs' trespass claim survived summary judgment because there was an issue of fact as to whether the invasion of fumes from defendants' site onto plaintiffs' adjacent properties was an "immediate or inevitable consequence" of the burning of chemical wastes at the site by defendants. *Abbatiello v. Monsanto Co.*, 522 F. Supp. 2d 524 (S.D. N.Y. 2007).

[I:119] When polluting material has been deliberately put onto, or into, defendant's land, the defendant is liable for damage to his neighbor's land if the defendant "had good reason to know or expect that subterranean and other conditions were such that there would be passage from defendant's to plaintiff's land." Defendant must intend the act which amounts to or produces the unlawful invasion, and the intrusion must at least be the immediate or inevitable consequence of what he does. *Phillips v. Sun Oil Co.*, 307 N.Y. 328, 331, 121 N.E.2d 249, 251 (1954).

[I:120] Defendants' motion to dismiss trespass claims was denied. Court found allegations defendants intentionally created MTBE, intentionally added it to gasoline, and intentionally transported MTBE-containing gasoline through a distribution system they knew was susceptible to leaks and spills, knowing that MTBE had a higher propensity to contaminate groundwater than other gasoline additives, and that unintentional releases of gasoline frequently occurred, reasonably inferred that defendants willfully intruded upon plaintiffs' land. Defendants' intentional creation and distribution of MTBE-containing gasoline could be construed as the act which amounted to or produced the unlawful invasion of plaintiffs' property, and alleged awareness of the vulnerabilities in the gasoline distribution and storage system allowed inference it was substantially certain that MTBE would enter plaintiffs' property. *In re Methyl Tertiary Butyl Ether (MTBE) Products Liability Litigation*, 379 F. Supp. 2d 348, 426–428 (S.D. N.Y. 2005).

1. Benefits of alleging trespass

In some cases it may be easier to prove trespass than nuisance. For intentional trespass, there is liability without harm; for a private nuisance, liability requires significant harm. In trespass an intentional invasion of the plaintiff's possessory interest (i.e. a physical invasion of plaintiff's land) results in liability unless a defendant can show a privilege. In private nuisance actions an intentional interference with the plaintiff's use or enjoyment will not, by itself, result in liability; the plaintiff must prove unreasonableness of the interference in order to recover.

Although plaintiffs do not need to prove harm to property in order to establish trespass, absent proof of actual damages, plaintiffs may get only nominal damages. Counsel should also consider that injunctive relief against a continuation of the trespass may provide an equally or more valuable remedy to those plaintiffs most interested in stopping or remediating defendant's conduct. Additionally, in granting such an injunction, the court need not balance the reasonableness factors as would be required in a nuisance situation.

Trespasses may usually be enjoined for as long as they continue, however, as discussed below in section F of this chapter, the enactment of CPLR 214-c, changed the common law rule with respect to damages. Trespass actions to recover damages for injury to property "caused by the latent effects of exposure to any substance or combination of substances, in any form" must now be commenced within three years "from the date of discovery of the injury by the plaintiff or from the date when through the exercise of reasonable diligence such injury should have been discovered by the plaintiff, whichever is earlier." Note that CPLR 214-c was preempted by *Ruffing ex rel. Calton v. Union Carbide Corp.*, 193 Misc. 2d 350, 360, 746 N.Y.S.2d 798, 807 (Sup. Ct. 2002) aff'd sub nom. *Ruffing v. Union Carbide Corp.*, 1 A.D.3d 339, 766 N.Y.S.2d 439 (2003) to the extent that "Section 214-c(4) limits the benefit of the discovery of the cause accrual date to cases where the plaintiff discovers the cause of his injuries no later than five years after discovering his injury," since "Section 214-c(4) actually provides for an accrual date which is earlier than the FRCD for a claim of injury caused by the release of a hazardous substance, pollutant or contaminant into the environment from a facility." As of the writing of this edition, a proposed amendment remedying this issue was under consideration by the legislature. *See* 2011 NY A.B. 3714 (NS), 2011 New York Assembly Bill No. 3714, New York Two Hundred Thirty-Fourth Legislative Session, which provides that in toxic tort cases where the specific toxic etiological cause of injury is not known for up to ten years (instead of five years) after the injury itself is discovered a plaintiff shall have three years to file a claim from the time such specific cause is discovered.

C. Negligence

A negligence cause of action in a toxic tort scenario is indistinguishable from any other negligence action—a plaintiff must establish duty, breach, causation and damages. Toxic tort litigants frequently find negligence is harder to prove than other causes of action, with duty and causation typically presenting the greatest challenges. Information available to the manufacturer at the time of production may not have been sufficient to permit a reasonable manufacturer to foresee the dangers lurking for the consumer, thus creating no duty to injured persons. Often there could be a wide variety of other factors which may have caused the plaintiff's injury, and/or it may be difficult to clearly link a specific exposure which occurred many years ago with the plaintiff's injury, creating problems of proof of causation.

1. Duty

In a toxic tort case, the defendant's duty of care is measured by the conduct of a "reasonable person," situated as is the defendant. In many toxic tort cases, because the defendants are manufacturers, professional entities, or others with special expertise in the activities they conduct, they are expected to exercise a higher degree of care than the ordinary prudent person. The risk-utility balancing test developed by Judge Learned Hand, has also been applied in the toxic tort context to evaluate whether the defendant has breached the duty to use reasonable care. Industry practice, including expert testimony or industry standards may provide some evidence as to the reasonableness of the defendant's conduct, but it is not controlling. Reasonableness of the defendant's conduct is usually a jury question, and is evaluated based on the specific facts.

Duty is measured as of the time of the negligent act(s), not as of the time of trial. A plaintiff may not use safety standards adopted after the actual release to measure the duty owed.

Where the state or federal government has adopted a statute establishing a mandatory duty of care which the defendant has allegedly violated, and the plaintiff is in the class of persons intended to be protected by that law, the plaintiff may assert that breach of the duty is negligence per se. However, proof of compliance with a government requirement does not immunize the defendant from liability since compliance with existing laws is not a complete defense to a negligence allegation, and the common law negligence standard may be higher than the law's duties happen to be.

2. Causation

The leading New York decisions on the issue of causation are decisions from the New York Federal courts, and so the law of causation for toxic tort litigants is not entirely clear. A toxic tort plaintiff must prove that exposure to a toxic substance more probably than not caused the resulting injuries. According to the federal decisions, if the plaintiff relies solely on epidemiological evidence, the evidence must confirm that the cause and effect relationship between the plaintiff's exposure to the toxic substance and his resulting injury was more than 50% probable. If the plaintiff relies on both epidemiological and clinical evidence, and the evidence collectively satisfies the more probable than not standard, the plaintiff will survive summary judgment even if the epidemiological evidence, standing alone, would be insufficient to establish causation. On the other hand, the Appellate Division, First Department, applying the Court of Appeals' ruling in *Parker v. Mobil Oil Corp.*, 7 N.Y.3d 434, 824 N.Y.S.2d 584, 857 N.E.2d 1114 (2006), determined that a plaintiff can sustain a cause of action if he can establish causation based on accepted scientific principles—even if he cannot show the specific toxin to which he were exposed. According to the First Department, if a plaintiff can sufficiently demonstrate through epidemiological and toxicological data that his claimed illness is related to an exposure of some type of toxin, the causation element will be satisfied. *Nonnon v. City of New York*, 88 A.D.3d 384, 932 N.Y.S.2d 428 (1st Dep't 2011).

3. Injury

Actual physical injury is an essential element of any negligence claim and tort liability may not be premised on mere risk of potential future harm not yet suffered. See Section X, Damages, for further discussion.

D. Strict Liability Arising from Abnormally Dangerous Activities.

Toxic tort cases may seem like an extremely good fit for application of the doctrine of strict liability for abnormally dangerous activities because they so frequently involve hazardous substances. However, it is the activity, not the product, that must be abnormally dangerous in order to recover under this theory. New York has adopted the criteria from Restatement § 520 for determining whether an activity is abnormally dangerous. Those criteria are:

1) a high degree of risk of harm to the person, land or property of others;

2) likelihood that the harm that results will be great;

3) inability to eliminate the risk by the exercise of reasonable care;

4) the extent to which the activity is not a matter of common usage;

5) the inappropriateness of the activity to the place where it is carried on;

6) the extent to which its value to the community is outweighed by its dangerous attributes.

Application of these factors results in heightened scrutiny regarding whether the situation could have been easily avoided through the use of reasonable care. If so, New York courts are unlikely to impose strict liability. While it may not be easy to establish that a particular site or operator qualify as an abnormally dangerous activity, there are benefits that compensate for the difficulty. Toxic tort plaintiffs who are able to establish that strict liability applies have a tactical advantage against the defendant, since liability will essentially be a given.

E. Battery

Although not widely used, a common law action for battery may provide a basis for recovery. If a battery by toxic chemicals is pleaded, harmful contact must be shown, but the plaintiff need not prove immediate physical injury. However, the "mere exposure to toxic chemicals" released into the air does not rise to the level of an assault or battery. Absent intent to cause harmful or offensive contact, there is no battery.

> [I:121] Plaintiffs in action arising from death of worker allegedly caused by radiation exposure at nuclear power plant pleaded sufficient facts to state claim for battery under New York law, where they alleged defendants knew of the dangerous condition and nonetheless intentionally assigned decedent to work there with the intent that he become exposed to the radiation without his consent. *Corcoran v. New York Power Auth.*, 935 F. Supp. 376 (S.D.N.Y. 1996).

F. Statute of Limitations.

The toxic tort statute of limitations, N.Y. C.P.L.R. 214-c was enacted to overcome the effect of the line of decisions holding that toxic tort claims accrue upon "impact" or exposure. The goal of the statute was to provide relief to injured parties whose claims would otherwise be barred for untimeliness simply because they were unaware of latent injuries until after the limitations period had expired, such as where resulting illness did not manifest for a long time after exposure. The statute presupposes that at the time a plaintiff discovers injuries, she will know the cause of those injuries. In the event the plaintiff does not know the cause of injuries at the time of discovery of the injuries, the statute provides a grace period for filing suit, if plaintiff can prove technical or scientific knowledge was not available at the time plaintiff discovered her injuries and such knowledge would have enabled the plaintiff to discern the cause of the injuries. Section 214-c provides:

Certain actions to be commenced within three years of discovery

1. In this section: "exposure" means direct or indirect exposure by absorption, contact, ingestion, inhalation, implantation or injection.

2. Notwithstanding the provisions of section 214, the three year period within which an action to recover damages for personal injury or injury to property caused by the latent effects of exposure to any substance or combination of substances, in any form, upon or within the body or upon or within property must be commenced shall be computed from the date of discovery of the injury by the plaintiff or from the date when through the exercise of reasonable diligence such injury should have been discovered by the plaintiff, whichever is earlier.

3. For the purposes of sections fifty-e and fifty-i of the general municipal law, section thirty-eight hundred thirteen of the education law and the provisions of any general, special or local law or charter requiring as a condition precedent to commencement of an action or special proceeding that a notice of claim be filed or presented within a specified period of time after the claim or action

accrued, a claim or action for personal injury or injury to property caused by the latent effects of exposure to any substance or combination of substances, in any form, upon or within the body or upon or within property shall be deemed to have accrued on the date of discovery of the injury by the plaintiff or on the date when through the exercise of reasonable diligence the injury should have been discovered, whichever is earlier.

4. Notwithstanding the provisions of subdivisions two and three of this section, where the discovery of the cause of the injury is alleged to have occurred less than five years after discovery of the injury or when with reasonable diligence such injury should have been discovered, whichever is earlier, an action may be commenced or a claim filed within one year of such discovery of the cause of the injury; provided, however, if any such action is commenced or claim filed after the period in which it would otherwise have been authorized pursuant to subdivision two or three of this section the plaintiff or claimant shall be required to allege and prove that technical, scientific or medical knowledge and information sufficient to ascertain the cause of his injury had not been discovered, identified or determined prior to the expiration of the period within which the action or claim would have been authorized and that he has otherwise satisfied the requirements of subdivisions two and three of this section.

5. This section shall not be applicable to any action for medical or dental malpractice.

6. This section shall be applicable to acts, omissions or failures occurring prior to, on or after July first, nineteen hundred eighty-six, except that this section shall not be applicable to any act, omission or failure:

    a) which occurred prior to July first, nineteen hundred eighty-six, and

    b) which caused or contributed to an injury that either was discovered or through the exercise of reasonable diligence should have been discovered prior to such date, and

    c) an action which was or would have been barred because the applicable period of limitation had expired prior to such date.

Despite the apparent expansion of time for filing an action, failure to file within the statute of limitations remains a defense which defendants should not overlook. The defense will be particularly effective in suits where plaintiffs have been less than diligent in discovering their injuries; or where the plaintiff fails to discover the cause of the injury and is unable to demonstrate that "technical, scientific or medical knowledge and information sufficient to ascertain the cause" were unavailable at an earlier date.

In *Ruffing ex rel. Calton v. Union Carbide Corp.*, 193 Misc. 2d 350, 746 N.Y.S.2d 798 (Sup. 2002), the court held the Provision of Superfund Amendments and Reauthorization Act of 1986 (SARA) permitting state toxic tort claims to accrue upon discovery of the cause of the injury preempts the state toxic tort statute of limitations in a case which is based upon a claim of injury caused by release of a hazardous substance, pollutant, or contaminant into the environment from a facility.

1. Injury from date of discovery

Under current cases, the statute of limitations for a toxic tort begins to run from the date of discovery of the injury by the plaintiff, or from the date when through the exercise of reasonable diligence the injury should have been discovered by the plaintiff, whichever is earlier.

[I:122] Injury is "discovered" when some symptoms manifest even though the connection between the symptoms and the injured plaintiff's exposure to a toxic substance may not yet be recognized, and the underlying cause of the condition is unknown. The one exception is that if within five years of discovering the symptoms of a condition, the injured party discovers the cause, and "technical, scientific or medical knowledge sufficient to ascertain the cause" was unavailable at an earlier date. *Matter of New York County DES Litigation*, 89 N.Y.2d 506, 655 N.Y.S.2d 862, 678 N.E.2d 474 (1997).

[I:123] Technical, scientific or medical knowledge and information sufficient to ascertain the cause of injury is "discovered, identified or determined," when the existence of a causal relationship is generally accepted within the relevant technical, scientific or medical community. *Giordano v. Market America, Inc.*, 15 N.Y.3d 590, 915 N.Y.S.2d 884, 941 N.E.2d 727 (2010).

[I:124] The statute applies to toxic tort claims involving exposure which predates the effective date of the statute. Application of the discovery rule is inapplicable only if both exposure and discovery predate the statute's July 1, 1986, effective date. A plaintiff who discovers injury after July 1, 1986, will not be time-barred, even if the plaintiff's exposure to the injury-causing toxic substance occurred, in whole or in part, before that date. *Rothstein v. Tennessee Gas Pipeline Co.*, 87 N.Y.2d 90, 94, 637 N.Y.S.2d 674, 676, 661 N.E.2d 146, 148 (1995).

[I:125] Owners of property adjacent to the defendant's, who allegedly suffered pollution property damage as a result of the migration of waste generated by the defendants, were barred from bringing claim where owners had actual knowledge of both the injury to the site and its cause more than three years prior to commencement of the action. *Seneca Meadows, Inc. v. E.C.I. Liquidating, Inc.*, 983 F.Supp. 360 (W.D. N.Y. 1997).

[I:126] Accrual of a toxic tort cause of action is not tolled until the plaintiff determines the identity of each of the contaminants and each of the entities responsible for the relevant contamination. A cause of action for pollution property damage accrues under CPLR 214-c(2) when the plaintiff discovered or should have discovered some contamination on its property, even if the plaintiff was unaware of the identity of the specific contaminants and/or the entities responsible for the contamination. *Seneca Meadows, Inc. v. E.C.I. Liquidating, Inc.*, 983 F.Supp. 360 (W.D. N.Y. 1997).

[I:127] For purposes of determining that a party discovered, or in the exercise of reasonable diligence could have discovered, the primary condition on which their claim(s) are based, proof that the party manifested symptoms of the latent disease that the harmful substance produced or was diagnosed with a particular disease is sufficient. *Huggler v. City of New York*, 184 Misc. 2d 696, 709 N.Y.S.2d 380 (Sup 2000), rev'd on other grounds, 289 A.D.2d 240, 733 N.Y.S.2d 725 (2d Dep't 2001).

[I:128] Argument that defendant was equitably estopped from invoking the statute of limitations defense because it denied the existence of hazardous levels of chemicals was rejected where plaintiffs could not have relied on defendant's denial as a basis for foregoing their suit because the defendants made the denial after the 3-year limitation period of CPLR 214-c had already run. *Mancuso v. Consolidated Edison Co. of New York, Inc.*, 216 F.3d 1072, 1072 (2d Cir. 2000).

[I:129] Equitable estoppel can preserve the viability of a suit otherwise time-barred under CPLR 214-c; however, to successfully invoke the doctrine, a plaintiff must demonstrate the defendant provided less than full disclosure of information necessary to appreciate a potentially grave condition and that the plaintiff relied on that inadequate disclosure. *Mancuso v. Consolidated Edison Co. of New York, Inc.*, 216 F.3d 1072, 1072 (2d Cir. 2000).

[I:130] In a property damage action alleging soil vapor contamination resulting from chemicals released into the ground water, where the plaintiffs knew for two decades that the ground water was contaminated by the chemicals, but not that soil vapor contamination emanating from the ground water posed a potential problem, the statute of limitations began to run when the home-owners should have reasonably been aware of the presence of soil vapor contamination and the threat it presented to their properties, and not at the time when they knew the ground water was contaminated. *Aiken v. General Electric Company*, 869 N.Y.S.2d 263 (3rd Dep't 2008).

[I:131] The statute of limitations begins to run for actions brought to recover damages caused by a latent injury to a person or property as a result of exposure to harmful substances, when the plaintiff discovers the primary condition or particular substance on which the claim is based and has an objective level of awareness of the dangers and consequences. *Aiken v. General Electric Company*, 869 N.Y.S.2d 263 (3rd Dep't 2008).

[I:132] "Discovery" for purposes of the statute of limitations requirement that the statute begins to run "from the date of discovery of the injury by the plaintiff or from the date when through the exercise of reasonable diligence such injury should have been discovered by the plaintiff, whichever is earlier" is the discovery of the physical condition, not the discovery of "both the condition and the nonorganic etiology of that condition." *Scheidel v. AC and S, Inc.*, 685 N.Y.S. 2d 829 (N.Y. App. 1999), quoting *Matter of New York County DES Litig.*, 655 N.Y.S. 2d 862 (N.Y. 1997).

[I:133] The limitations period begins to run when the plaintiff discovered or should have discovered the "primary condition on which the claim is based"; the cause of the symptoms is not relevant. *Scheidel v. AC and S, Inc.*, 685 N.Y.S. 2d 829 (N.Y. App. 1999), quoting *Matter of New York County DES Litig.*, 655 N.Y.S. 2d 862 (N.Y. 1997).

2. Continuing injury

An allegation by plaintiffs that they are still being exposed to toxic emissions does not affect the accrual date of causes of action based on exposure to emissions under the toxic tort statute of limitations, since the date of discovery of the injury is the key time under the statute and there is no continuing-wrong exception under the statute. However, this limitation does not apply to an action for injunctive relief.

[I:134] The discovery rule applies only to actions for damages. The traditional common law rule applies to the extent that a plaintiff seeks injunctive relief. Under common law, a continuing injury to real property gives rise to successive causes of action for the duration of the injury, and the right of the property owner to invoke the equitable power of the court similarly continues, regardless of the lapse of time that might occur before the commencement of legal proceedings. A request for future remediation is consequently not barred by CPLR 214-c. *Town of Oyster Bay v. Occidental Chemical Corporation*, 987 F.Supp. 182 (E.D. N.Y. 1997).

3. Application to intentional torts

The discovery accrual rule has no application to an intentional tort such as battery because the rule carves out an exception to when the three year statute of limitations applicable to personal injury actions begins to run and intentional torts such as battery are governed by the one-year statute of limitations.

Index

A

Abnormally dangerous activities, 342–356, 513
Affidavits, 154, 156
Affirmative defenses, 90–91, 298–307
Answer, 438–440
Applying and distinguishing precedent
Generally, 77, 345
Lawyer's perspective, 87
Resolving disputes, 78
Supporting reasoning, 80
Assault, 54–55
Assumption of risk, 300–303
Implied, 300–302
Identifying risks, 302
Waiver, 300, 302

B

Battery, 16–30, 32–36, 39–46, 48–53, 514
Harmful or offensive contact, 46–47, 48
Intent, 17, 19–28, 29–34
State of mind required, 29–34
Transferred intent, 45–46
Burden of proof, 369, 379–382, 387–395, 456
Bystander recovery, 252–259,

C

Case briefing, 28–29
Case reading, 17–19
Causation, 260–298, 357–358, 425, 513
But for test, 260–261
Factual, 260–264, 311, 312, 322, 356, 359, 400, 401, 403
Marketshare liability, 262

Multiple causes, 262
Negligence, 260–298
Products liability, 425–426
Proving factual cause, 261
Proximate, 264–272
Selecting appropriate test, 263
Strict Liability, 357–358
Substantial factor test, 261–263
Circumstantial evidence, 29–30, 222–226, 381
Nature of, 29–30, 222–223
Res Ipsa Loquitor, 222–240
Civil system (chart), xxi
Comparative fault, 298–300
History, 298
Relationship to assumption of risk, 300
Relationship to contributory negligence, 298
Complaints, 36, 148, 432
McCoy v. Henry Ford Health Systems, 148
Strickland v. Wong, 432
Wynn v. MJ Harbor Hotel, 36
Consent, 50–54
Contributory negligence, 298–300

D

Damages, 241–260, 457–458, 517
Bystanders, 252–259
Calculating, 251
Caps, 251–252, 259–260
Comparative fault, 298–303
Emotional distress, 256–260, 458
Emotional injuries, 251–253, 259–260
Negligence, 251–260
Non-economic, 251–253, 259–260
Statutory limitations, 251–252

Defamation Practice Guide
   Absolute Privilege, 454
   Child Abuse, 457–458
   Common Law, 448
   Constitutional Constraints, 458
   Damages, 458
   Defamatory Statement, 448–449
   Defenses
      Privileged Communications, 452
      Qualified privilege, 453
      Truth, 455–456
   Employers, 457
   Identifying the Plaintiff, 449–450
   Immunity, 457
   Judicial proceedings, 454
   Legislative proceedings, 455
   Libel, 451, 452
   Limiting damages, 457
   Loss of privilege, 453
      Proof of actual malice, 453
      Proof of excessive publication, 454
   Notice, 456–457
   Prima facie case, 448
   Privileged Communications, 452
   Public concern, 462
   Public figures, 460
      General-purpose public figures, 460
      Limited-purpose public figures, 461
   Public officials, 459
   Publication, 450
   Qualified privilege, 453
   Republishing, 456
   Retraction, 457
   Slander per se, 451
   Slander, 451
   Substantial truth, 456
   Truth, 455–456
Defense of others, 90–115
Depositions, 164–178, 244–250, 272–297, 487–491
   Expert witness, 164–178, 244–250, 272–297
   Preparing client, 487–491
   Transcripts, 164–178, 244–250, 272–297
Develop a professional vocabulary, 17
Discovery, 419, 464, 487, 488–491
Dog bites, 318–319
Duty (*see* Negligence)

E

Emotional distress, 55–56, 251–260, 458
Environmental protection actions
   Abnormally Dangerous Activities, 513–514
   Battery, 514
   Benefits of alleging public nuisance, 507–508
      Balancing of interests not required, 508
      Proof of actual harm not required, 508
   Benefits of alleging trespass, 511–512
   Causation, 513
   Negligence, 512
      Duty, 512
      Injury, 513
   Nuisance, 506
      Fault, 509
      Private, 509
      Public, 506
   Private Nuisance, 509
   Public Nuisance, 506–509
      Action by private persons, 506–507
   Statute of Limitations, 514
      Accrual, 515–516
      Application to intentional torts, 518
      Continuing injury, 517–518
   Strict liability, 507, 513–514
   Trespass, 510
   Unreasonable interference, 508
Evaluating conflicting testimony, 163
Evaluating legal arguments, 34–36
Expert witness depositions, 164–178, 244–250, 292–297
Expert witnesses, 163, 272, 382–83, 387

F

Fact investigation and analysis, 47
Factual cause, 260–264
False imprisonment, 77–90
Foreseeability, 125, 132, 213, 264–272
   Duty (*see* Negligence)
   Proximate cause (*see* Causation)

I

Immunity, 8, 9, 12–15, 19, 20, 23, 24, 303, 373–375, 457